advantage

Dear Valued Customer,

We realize you're a busy professional with deadlines to hit. Whether your goal is to learn a new technology or solve a critical problem, we want to be there to lend you a hand. Our primary objective is to provide you with the insight and knowledge you need to stay atop the highly competitive and ever-changing technology industry.

Wiley Publishing, Inc., offers books on a wide variety of technical categories, including security, data warehousing, software development tools, and networking — everything you need to reach your peak. Regardless of your level of expertise, the Wiley family of books has you covered.

- For Dummies® – The *fun* and *easy* way® to learn
- The Weekend Crash Course® –The *fastest* way to learn a new tool or technology
- Visual™ – For those who prefer to learn a new topic *visually*
- The Bible – The *100% comprehensive* tutorial and reference
- The Wiley Professional list – *Practical* and *reliable* resources for IT professionals

The book you now hold, *More Java™ Pitfalls: 50 New Time-Saving Solutions and Workarounds*, shows experienced Java programmers how to avoid hidden pitfalls in the Java language and related J2EE™ technologies. The authors expose tricky problems even experienced Java developers encounter with EJBs, JSPs, servlets, and other core components of J2EE, and tackle more complex topics, including networking, XML and Java programming, and the Java Virtual Machine. This book is the result of thousands of hours of collective experience, both in Java programming and training. The result is a wealth of practical solutions to tough, real-world programming problems.

Our commitment to you does not end at the last page of this book. We'd want to open a dialog with you to see what other solutions we can provide. Please be sure to visit us at www.wiley.com/compbooks to review our complete title list and explore the other resources we offer. If you have a comment, suggestion, or any other inquiry, please locate the "contact us" link at www.wiley.com.

Finally, we encourage you to review the following page for a list of Wiley titles on related topics. Thank you for your support and we look forward to hearing from you and serving your needs again in the future.

Sincerely,

Richard K. Swadley

Richard K. Swadley
Vice President & Executive Group Publisher
Wiley Technology Publishing

15 HOUR WEEKEND CRASH COURSE

Visual™

Bible

DUMMIES®

WILEY
Wiley Publishing, Inc.

more information on related titles

More Java™ Pitfalls

50 New Time-Saving Solutions and Workarounds

More Java™ Pitfalls

50 New Time-Saving Solutions and Workarounds

Michael C. Daconta
Kevin T. Smith
Donald Avondolio
W. Clay Richardson

WILEY

Wiley Publishing, Inc.

Publisher: Joe Wikert
Executive Editor: Robert M. Elliott
Assistant Developmental Editor: Emilie Herman
Managing Editor: Micheline Frederick
New Media Editor: Angela Denny
Text Design & Composition: Wiley Composition Services

This book is printed on acid-free paper. ∞

Published by Wiley Publishing, Inc., Indianapolis, Indiana

Published simultaneously in Canada

For general information on our other products and services please contact our Customer Care Department within the United States at (800) 762-2974, outside the United States at (317) 572-3993 or fax (317) 572-4002.

Wiley also publishes its books in a variety of electronic formats. Some content that appears in print may not be available in electronic books.

Library of Congress Cataloging-in-Publication Data:

ISBN: 0-471-23751-5

Printed in the United States of America

10 9 8 7 6 5 4 3 2 1

This book is dedicated to the memory of Edsger W. Dijkstra who said,

"I mean, if 10 years from now, when you are doing something quick and dirty, you suddenly visualize that I am looking over your shoulders and say to yourself, 'Dijkstra would not have liked this', well that would be enough immortality for me."

We humbly disagree: 10 years of Dijkstra is just not long enough; may he happily haunt our consciousness for 10^{10} years. Such an increase is more befitting his stature.

Contents

Introduction

"Sometimes we discover unpleasant truths. Whenever we do so, we are in difficulties: suppressing them is scientifically dishonest, so we must tell them, but telling them, however, will fire back on us."
Edsger W. Dijkstra, "How do we tell truths that might hurt?"

Good programming is difficult. It is especially arduous for new programmers given the pace of change and the ever-expanding size of the software engineering body of knowledge (www.swebok.org) that they must master. The authors of this book have found that experience and in-depth understanding are key factors in both programmer productivity and reliable software. The bottom line is that experienced programmers don't stumble around in the dark. They know the lay of the land, they recognize patterns, and they avoid the hazardous areas. This book presents our experience and guidance on 50 discrete topics to assist you in avoiding some of those hazards.

What Is a Pitfall?

The formal definition, given in the first *Java Pitfalls* (Wiley, 2000) book, is as follows:

"A pitfall is code that compiles fine but when executed produces unintended and sometimes disastrous results."

This rather terse definition covers what we consider the "basic" pitfall. There are many variations on this theme. A broader definition could be any language feature, API, or system that causes a programmer to waste inordinate amounts of time struggling with the development tools instead of making progress on the resulting software.

The causes of pitfalls can be loosely divided into two groups: the fault of the platform designer or the fault of the inexperienced programmer. This is not to cast blame, but rather to determine the source of the pitfall in the construction of a pitfall taxonomy. For the same reason we create a formal definition of pitfalls, we present the pitfall taxonomy in Figure i.1 in order to attempt to better understand the things that trip us up.

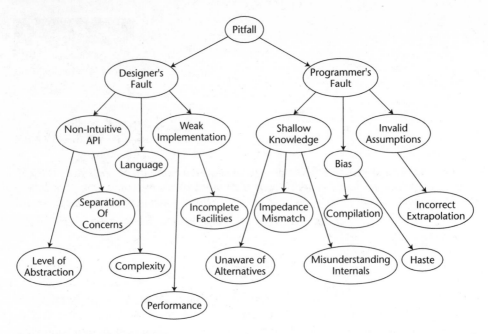

Figure i.1 A pitfall taxonomy.

The categories of pitfalls associated with the system designer are as follows:

Nonintuitive Application Programming Interfaces (APIs). The Java platform has thousands of classes and tens of thousands of methods. The sheer size of the platform has become a complexity pitfall. Some of these classes are well designed, like servlets, IO streams (excluding performance ramifications), and collections. Unfortunately, many APIs are nonintuitive for the following reasons:

- **Wrong level of abstraction.** Many APIs are layered over other software (like the operating system or native code) in order to simplify or aggregate functions. In layering, you must make a trade-off between simplicity and granularity of control. Thus, when setting the abstraction level, you must balance these appropriately for the particular context and target audience. Too high a level of abstraction (like URLConnection, Item 17) frustrates users with weak control mappings, while a too low level of abstraction reduces the average user's efficiency by over-cluttering the most common case.

- **Weak separation of concerns.** When an API tries to do too much, it often mixes metaphors and addresses its multiple concerns in a mediocre fashion. An example of this is the JAXR API that attempts to combine the diverse information models of UDDI and ebXML (Item 47).

- **Other deficiencies.** Too many method invocation sequences and dependencies will lead to incorrect ordering. Poor naming and weak parameters (object instead of a specific type) steer programmers toward dead ends.

Language Complexity. The Java language has many improvements over its predecessors yet also struggles with its own set of tradeoffs and idiosyncrasies. The cleanest language features are its strict object orientation, automatic memory management, and interfaces; while some overly complex areas are threading and synchronization, the tension between primitives and objects, and the effective use of exceptions.

Weak Implementation of Platform Areas. The most oft-cited example is poor performance. An example of this is the rewrite of the input/output facilities in the NIO package for performance reasons. Besides performance, there are thin APIs that ruin the Write Once, Run Anywhere (WORA) guarantee like the File.renameTo() (Item 20) method and the Runtime.exec() method (Item 1). There are also incomplete APIs where the programmer assumes complete functionality exists. These problems are fixable and often are resolved with each new release of the Java Development Kit (JDK).

The categories of pitfalls associated with the programmer are as follows:

Shallow Knowledge. Experience increases the depth of one's knowledge. It takes time to learn the underlying concepts, interactions, and nuances of a system. This is often manifest in choosing a weak implementation when a better alternative exists (like applets versus Web Start, Item 26), misunderstanding the internal workings of an API (like the consequence of instance variables in servlets, Item 31), and shock when implementations fail to meet your expectations of behavior (characterized as an impedance mismatch in Figure i-1). Such an impedance mismatch can occur with multiple concurrent result sets (Item 41).

Bias. Without many years of experience, a programmer can weigh previous experience too heavily to the point where it unfavorably biases him or her in a particular direction. Examples of this are to not take advantage of tools to automate the development process like Ant (Item 11) and JUnit (Item 12). Another example is to stick with legacy APIs over new ones for collections (Item 21) and regular expressions (Item 30). Lastly, one more effect of bias is to bring past habits into a new context like J2ME programming (Item 22).

Invalid Assumptions. A programmer can incorrectly base decisions on invalid assumptions—for example, assuming the most direct path to the solution is the best path. This often arises in designing larger systems with JSP (Item 24) and J2EE (Item 37).

Pitfalls can be extremely frustrating to programmers. We've experienced first hand this frustration. Our goal is to help you to avoid some situations we struggled through. So now that we understand pitfalls, let's see our method for exploring them.

Dissecting a Pitfall

There are three distinct parts of a pitfall:

The Symptom or Problem. The medium by which the pitfall manifests itself. We demonstrate this with a program entitled "BadXXX.java," where "XXX" refers to the type of pitfall in question.

The Root cause of the Problem. By far, this is the most important part of revealing the pitfall. Here, we go under the hood and explain the detailed internal workings, invalid assumptions, or API deficiencies that cause programmers to stumble into the trap. Usually this explanation is supported with a diagram.

The Solution or Workaround. The final part of the pitfall is to demonstrate a fix for the problem. This is done with a program entitled "GoodXXX.java" that is the reciprocal of the "BadXXX.java" program. The solution program will often be accompanied with a run of the results, or a table or graph, which proves the problem was indeed solved.

This method of dissecting a pitfall has proven an effective way to present these programming hazards.

How This Book Differs from *Java Pitfalls*

This book borrows all the good features from the first book and improves upon it in three ways:

Broader Coverage. The first book focused on the lang, util, io, and GUI packages, whereas this book covers the J2ME, J2SE, and J2EE platforms.

New Features. This book covers the majority of new features like regular expressions, NIO, assertions, JAXR, JAXM, JAX-RPC, and many more.

Better Coverage. The authors followed the "pitfall dissection" model more consistently and thoroughly, producing pitfalls with more detail and analysis.

In general, the authors strove to outdo the first book in every regard. We sincerely hope that we succeeded and encourage your feedback.

Organization of the Book

Like the first one, this book has 50 items. Unlike the first book, in this one they are divided into three parts corresponding to the three-tiered architecture:

Part One: The Client Tier. This part covers both J2ME and J2SE and explores pitfalls in developing both networked and standalone clients. Topics covered include preferences, application deployment, logging, IO performance, and many more. This part has 22 pitfalls.

Part Two: The Web Tier. This part examines pitfalls in components that run inside the Web container, like servlets and JavaServer Pages (JSPs). These applications generate dynamic Web pages or communicate with applets, JNLP, or standalone clients. This parts covers topics like JSP design, caching, servlet filters, database connections, form validation, and many others. This part includes 14 pitfalls.

Part Three: The Enterprise Tier. Here we look at components that are part of the J2EE platform or execute inside an Enterprise Java Beans (EJB) container, like session, entity, and message-driven beans. These components interact with other enterprise systems, legacy systems, the Web tier, or directly to clients. Because

Web services play a key role in the enterprise tier, pitfalls related to some of the Web services APIs (JAXR and JAX-RPC) are in this section. Some other topics in this part are J2EE design errors, session beans, Java Data Objects (JDO), security, transactions, and many more. This part includes 14 pitfalls.

How to Use the Book

This book can be used in three primary ways: as a reference manual on specific problems, as a tutorial on the topics exposed by the problems, or as a catalyst to your organization's technical mentoring program. Let's discuss each in detail:

As a Reference Manual. You can use the table of contents to examine a specific solution to a problem you are facing. The majority of readers use this book in this manner. Some readers reported using the first book as a corporate resource in the technical library.

As a Tutorial. You can read the book cover–to-cover to learn about the underlying cause of each pitfall. Another way to approach the book this way is to browse the contents or pages and then read the pitfalls that interest you. Lastly, another use is to treat each pitfall as a bite-sized tutorial to present at a "brown-bag lunch" internal training session or technical exchange meeting.

As Part of a Mentoring Program. You can use the book as a starting point for a technical mentoring program in your organization. This book is founded on the principle of peer mentoring. The dictionary definition of a mentor is a "wise and trusted counselor." This often miscasts a mentor as having great age or experience. I disagree with this definition because it leads to an extreme scarcity of good mentors. *At its essence, mentoring is one aspect in the search for truth.* Thus, the key quality for being a mentor is a deep understanding of at least one domain that you are willing to share with others. Anyone can participate in this process, and I encourage you to be involved in peer mentoring. Working together, I believe we can solve the software quality crisis.

What's on the Companion Web Site?

The companion Web site will contain four key elements:

Source Code.   The source code for all listings in the book will be available in a compressed archive.

Errata.   Any errors discovered by readers or the authors will be listed with the corresponding corrected text.

Examples.   Sample chapters, the table of contents and index will be posted for people who have not yet purchased the book to get a feel for its style and content.

Contact Addresses.   The email addresses of the authors will be available as well as answers to any frequently asked questions.

Comments Welcome

This book is written by programmers for programmers. All comments, suggestions, and questions from the entire computing community are greatly appreciated. It is feedback from our readers that both makes the writing worthwhile and improves the quality of our work. I'd like to thank all the readers who have taken time to contact us to report errors, provide constructive criticism, or express appreciation.

I can be reached via email at mike@daconta.net or via regular mail:

Michael C. Daconta
c/o Robert Elliott
Wiley Publishing, Inc.
111 River Street
Hoboken, NJ 07030

Best wishes,

Michael Daconta
Sierra Vista, Arizona

NOTE About the code: In many of the code listings you will find a wrap character at the far right of some lines of code. We have used this character, ⊃, to indicate turnovers where the space available did not allow for all the characters to set on the same line. The line of code directly below a ⊃ is a direct unbroken continuation of the line above it, where the ⊃ appears.

Acknowledgments

This book has been a difficult journey. It survived through three co-author changes, several delays, and a move to a new state. Along the way, the vision of the book never faded, and in some way it willed itself into existence. All the authors believe that uncovering pitfalls helps programmers produce better programs with less frustration. I would like to thank those people who helped me through this challenge: my family—Lynne, CJ, Greg, and Samantha; my editors at Wiley Publishing, Inc.—Bob Elliott and Emilie Herman; my co-authors—Kevin, Clay, and Donnie; Al Saganich for contributing two pitfalls; my supervisors, customer and coworkers on the Virtual Knowledge Base project—Ted Wiatrak, Danny Proko, Joe Broussard, Joe Rajkumar, Joe Vitale, Maurita Soltis, and Becky Smith; my editor at Javaworld—Jennifer Orr; my friends at Oberon—Jodi Johnson and Dave Young; and finally, I would like to thank our readers who share our goal of producing great programs. Thanks and best wishes!

Michael C. Daconta

First of all, I would like to thank my co-authors—Mike, Clay, and Don. Your hard work on this project, and our many brainstorming sessions together at Cracker Barrel, helped create a good book full of our Java experiences and lessons learned. Second, I would like to thank my other new friends at McDonald Bradley and our entire VKB team. What a team of incredible folks.

I would like to give special thanks to a few people who suggested pitfalls and ideas for this book—John Sublett from Tridium, Inc. in Richmond, Virginia, Kevin Moran from McDonald Bradley, and Jeff Walawender from Titan Systems. Lois G. Schermerhorn and Helen G. Smith once again served as readability editors for some of my material. Special thanks to Stan and Nicole Schermerhorn for allowing me to use their company's name, Lavender Fields Farm, in a fictional scenario in this book. Also, thanks to Al Alexander, who granted me permission to use DevDaily's DDConnectionBroker to demonstrate a solution to a common programming pitfall.

My experience on Java projects with many software engineers and architects over the years helped me in writing this book: Ralph Cook, Martin Batts, Jim Johns, John Vrankovich, Dave Musser, Ron Madagan, Phil Collins, Jeff Thomason, Ken Pratt, Adam Dean, Stuart Gaudet, Terry Bailey, JoAnn White, Joe Pecore, Dave Bishop, Kevin Walmsley, Ed Kennedy, George Burgin, Vaughn Bullard, Daniel Buckley, Stella Aquilina, Bill Flynn, Charlie Lambert, and Dave Cecil III. I would also like to thank Bill Lumbergh, and the TPS Report support team at Initech—Peter, Samir, and Michael.

I would like to express thanks to my dad, who jump-started my career in computer science by buying me a Commodore Vic-20 in 1981. Making the most of the 5 KB of memory on that box, I learned not to use memory-consuming spaces in my code—perhaps contributing to "readability" pitfalls when I started writing code in college. Thanks to my former teachers who helped me in my writing over the years—Audrey Guengerich-Baylor and Rebecca Wright-Reynolds.

Over the last year, I have been blessed with many new friends at New Hanover Presbyterian Church and neighbors in Ashcreek in Mechanicsville, Virginia. Special thanks to the guys in last year's Wednesday night Bible study—Rich Bralley, Billy Craig, Matt Davis, Dan Hulen, Chuck Patterson, Ben Roberson, Keith Scholten, Todd Tarkington, and Matt Van Wie. I would also like to thank folks who helped me take a break to focus on playing the trumpet this year—Ray Herbek, Jeff Sigmon, Rita Smith, and Kenny Stockman.

Finally, I would like to thank my wonderful wife Gwen. Without her love and support, this book would never have been possible!

Kevin T. Smith

All of my material for this book is drawn largely from an object-oriented class I teach and a lot of great developers I've worked with over the years. Specifically, I'd like to thank these people who inspired me with their probity and hard work: Peter Len, Joe Vitale, Scot Shrager, Mark "Mojo" Mitchell, Wendong Wang, Chiming Huang, Feng Peng, Henry Chang, Bin Li, Sanath Shetty, Henry, John and Andy Zhang, Swati Gupta, Chi Vuong, Prabakhar Ramakrishnan, and Yuanlin Shi.

Special thanks goes to my beloved wife Van and her support and assistance during the writing of this book and the three coauthors of this book who are really progressive thinkers and great guys to hang with.

Donald Avondolio

First, I would like to thank my wife Alicia for all of her patience and understanding while I wrote this book. You truly are the greatest and I love you more than you understand. To Jennifer, my baby doll, you are the greatest gift a father could ever receive. To Stephanie, I love you and I will never forget you. I would like to thank my parents, Bill and Kay, for being, well, my parents. Nothing I could write here could express the impact you have had on my life.

I would like to thank my fellow authors, Mike, Kevin, and Don, for being patient while I got up to speed. You guys are not only exceptional technical talents, but also exceptional people. To my team—Mark Mitchell (aka Mojo), Mauro Marcellino (Tre, who saw us here when we were riding ambulances together), Peter Len, Marshall Sayen, Scot Schrager, Julie Palermo/Hall/Bishop, and Joe Vitale, you guys are the greatest and it was a privilege to serve as your lead. Mojo, it has been enjoyable to watch you progress from apprentice to master. Vic Fraenckel and Mike Shea, you aren't on my team, but you are certainly on *the* team, in spite of being part of the Borg. To Becky Smith, my fellow warrior, we have been through a lot of battles (some with each other), but it has been a pleasure working with you and your team.

To all the guys who have served with me on Gainesville District VFD Duty Crew A (and particularly its leader, Captain Bob Nowlen)—Patrick Vaughn, Marshall Sayen, Gary Sprifke, Mike Nelson, Matt Zalewski, Doug Tognetti, Frank Comer; we have seen some crazy things together, and I have been happy to be the one to drive you there. Chief Richard Bird, I would like to thank you for your leadership of our department and service to our community, which has been ongoing since before I was born. To the guys at the Dumfries-Triangle VFD, now you know where I went (writing this book): Brian Thomason, Tim Trax, Brian Kortuem, Brian Lichty, Nick Nanna, Scott Morrison, Brian Martin, Jack Hoffman, Craig Johnson, and Randy Baum—I wish I could name all of you. Volunteer firefighters truly are the salt of the earth, and I am happy to be among you.

To those who have served as mentors of mine through the years (in no particular order): Tom Bachmann, Seth Goldrich, Don Avondolio, Danny Proko, Burr Datz, Kevin McPhilamy, Shawn Bohner, John Viega, Pat Wolfe, Alex Blakemore (nonpolitical matters), Sam Redwine, and many others that I will kick myself for forgetting later. To Ted Wiatrak and Major Todd Delong, I would like to thank you guys for believing in us and giving us a shot to help some very important people. In closing, I would like to thank two of my Brother Rats, Matt Tyrrell and Jeff Bradford, for being, well, like brothers to me.

W. Clay Richardson

The Client Tier

"Now, if we regard a programming language primarily as a means of feeding problems into a machine, the quality of a programming language becomes dependent on the degree in which it promotes 'good use of the machine.'"

Edsger W. Dijkstra,
"On the Design of Machine Independent Programming Languages"

There have been a number of high-profile failures with using Java for major client-side applications. Corel developed an office suite in Java but scrapped the project after an early beta release. Netscape embarked on a pure Java version of a Web browser (referred to as "Javagator"), but the project was canceled before any code was released. Although these were the early days of client-side Java, in the 1997 to 1998 time frame, it was enough to cast a pall over client-side Java, and the momentum shifted to server-side Java. Yet, even under that shadow of server-side Java, the client tier continued to improve. Richer user interfaces, faster virtual machines, a fine-grained security model, and easier network deployment came to the platform piecemeal with each new release. So, borrowing a play from the Microsoft playbook, client-side Java has continued to address its shortcomings and improve with each release. Today we have high-profile and successful commercial applications in Java like ThinkFree Office, Borland's JBuilder, TIBCO's Turbo XML editor, and TogetherSoft's Together Control Center UML modeling tool. So, it is possible to develop rich client applications in Java. This part will assist you in that endeavor.

This part explores pitfalls in three general areas of client-side development: performance, nonintuitive application programming interfaces (APIs), and better alternatives. Here are some highlights of pitfalls in each area.

Performance has long been the bane of client-side Java. The first book, *Java Pitfalls: Time-Saving Solutions and Workarounds to Improve Programs*, had numerous pitfalls on performance, and many other books and Web sites have come out on Java performance tuning. This part has two pitfalls on performance:

NIO Performance and Pitfalls (Item 2). This pitfall examines the IO performance improvements of the New IO package (NIO). The pitfall examines file channels, ByteBuffers, and non-blocking server IO.

J2ME Performance and Pitfalls (Item 22). This pitfall ports a Swing application to the J2ME platform and uncovers both API pitfalls and over 20 optimizations for these small footprint devices.

Nonintuitive APIs cause hours of frustration, and the majority of pitfalls in this part are in this area. We carefully dissect the APIs, examine the internal workings of the software, and offer workarounds to the problem. The workarounds sometimes involve a proper sequence of operations, the use of a different class, or the abandonment of the standard API for an open-source alternative.

When `Runtime.exec()` Won't (Item 1). This pitfall is a canonical example of a mismatch between user expectations and the capability of an incomplete API.

Avoiding Granularity Pitfalls in `java.util.logging` (Item 5). The new `java.util.logging` API has some hidden complexities and relationships that affect the level of reporting granularity. You must understand the relationship between loggers and handlers to effectively use this API.

The Wrong Way to Search a DOM (Item 8). With JDK 1.4, the Java platform provided native support for XML with the javax.xml package. Unfortunately, the most intuitive representation of a Document Object Model (DOM) is not the correct representation, and this pitfall goes under the hood to see why.

The Saving-a-DOM Dilemma (Item 9). While JAXP introduced standard ways to create and manipulate XML DOM trees, it provides weak capabilities for persisting them—forcing developers to use implementation-specific methods. This pitfall discusses those challenges.

The Failure to Execute (Item 13). Java Archives or JAR files are the primary binary distribution for Java components. Unfortunately, there is great confusion about how these files work and how to make them executable. This pitfall explores those problems and provides an explanation of the best practices in using JAR files.

When Posting to a URL Won't (Item 17). The URL and URLConnection classes in the `java.net` API were designed at a very high level of abstraction that can be confusing. This pitfall demonstrates several incorrect ways to use the API, the reasons behind the deficiencies, and both a solution and open-source alternative to the problem.

The existence of better alternatives is an ever-growing problem as the platform ages and poor alternatives are kept to maintain backward compatibility. In addition to new APIs in the platform, again, open-source alternatives are proving themselves to be the best solution for many services.

I Prefer Not to Use Properties (Item 3). This pitfall demonstrates some weaknesses of the Properties class and how java.util.prefs package offers a better solution.

When Information Hiding Hides Too Much (Item 4). A frequent problem with abstracting things from developers is that it can hide important information from developers. Exceptions are a classic example and this pitfall demonstrates how the new JDK 1.4 chained exception facility solves it.

When Implementations of Standard APIs Collide (Item 6). With XML becoming part of JDK 1.4, an immediate issue arose from the fact that the XML standards do not synchronize with JDK releases. This pitfalls address how JDK 1.4 supports upgrades to these endorsed standards.

My Assertions Are Not Gratuitous! (Item 7). There is often a lag between the introduction of a new feature and adoption of that feature by the majority of programmers. For key reliability enhancements like assertions, this adoption gap is a serious pitfall. This item walks you through this important facility.

Apache Ant and Lifecycle Management (Item 11). Though most pitfalls in this part occur at the language and API level, this pitfall takes a broader look at a better alternative for the software lifecycle. For team development, not using a build tool like Ant is a serious pitfall.

JUnit: Unit Testing Made Simple (Item 12). Much like the Ant build tool, JUnit is a critical tool in assuring the quality of code through unit tests. This pitfall demonstrates how to effectively use JUnit and why failing to use it is bad.

Use `Iteration` over `Enumeration` (Item 21). The `Collection` APIs have proven themselves both effective and popular. This pitfall uncovers a weakness in the `Enumeration` implementation, examines the internals to uncover the source of the problem, and reveals how `Iteration` solves the problem.

There are 22 pitfalls in this part of the book, covering a wide array of client-side traps to avoid. Using these workarounds and techniques will enable you to build robust client-side applications that make "good use of the machine." The remainder of the pitfalls in this section are:

Mouse Button Portability (Item 10). Java is an outstanding choice for cross development application development. Unfortunately, not all platforms are the same, especially when it comes to the most popular input device—the mouse. This pitfall shows the challenges involved in working with these different input devices.

What Do You Collect? (Item 14). The issue of over abstraction can be particularly acute when dealing with the `Collection` APIs. This pitfall shows examples of not knowing the type contained in a collection and discusses emerging strategies for solving this problem.

Avoid Singleton Pitfalls (Item 15). The Singleton pattern is a widely used pattern in Java development. Unfortunately, there are numerous mistakes that developers make in how they use a Singleton. This pitfall addresses these mistakes and suggests some remedies.

When `setSize()` Won't Work (Item 16). Frequently, developers, especially new developers, use methods without understanding the overall API associated with them. A perfect example is the use of `setSize()` which leads to unexpected results. This pitfall examines not only the mistaken use of `setSize()` but also the concepts of layout mangers.

Effective String Tokenizing (Item 18).   The operation of the `StringTokenizer` class is frequently misunderstood. Interesting problems occur with multiple character delimiting strings. This pitfall examines those problems, and explains how they can be avoided.

JLayered Pane Pitfalls (Item 19).   This pitfall examines issues with using Swing's `JLayered Pane`, particularly related to the use of layout mangers with it.

When `File.renameTo()` Won't (Item 20).   The interaction with files in Java can produce unexpected results, particularly in working across filesystems or platforms. This pitfall examines those unexpected results and offers solutions for resolving them.

Item 1: When Runtime.exec() Won't[1]

The class `java.lang.Runtime` has a static method called `getRuntime()` to retrieve the current Java runtime environment. This is the only way to get a reference to the `Runtime` object. With that reference you can run external programs by invoking the `exec()` method of the `Runtime` class. One popular reason to do this is to launch a browser to display some kind of help page in HTML. There are four overloaded versions of the `exec()` command. Those method prototypes are:

- `public Process exec(String command);`
- `public Process exec(String [] cmdArray);`
- `public Process exec(String command, String [] envp);`
- `public Process exec(String [] cmdArray, String [] envp);`

The general idea behind all of the methods is that a command (and possible a set of arguments) are passed to an operating system-specific function call to create an operating system-specific process (a running program) with a reference to a `Process` class returned to the Java Virtual Machine (VM). The `Process` class is an abstract class because there will be a specific subclass of `Process` for each operating system. There are three possible input parameters to these methods: a single `String` that represents both the program to execute and any arguments to that program, an array of `Strings` that separate the program from its arguments, and an array of environment variables. The environment variables are passed in the form *name=value*. It is important to note that if you use the version of `exec()` with a single `String` for both the program and its arguments, the `String` is parsed using whitespace as the delimiter via the `StringTokenizer` class.

The prevalent first test of an API is to code its most obvious methods. For example, to exec a process that is external to the JVM, we use the `exec()` method. To see the value that the external process returns, we use the `exitValue()` method on the `Process` class. In our first example, we will attempt to execute the Java compiler (javac.exe). Listing 1.1 is a program to do that.

---

[1] This pitfall was first printed by *JavaWorld* (www.javaworld.com) in "When Runtime.exec() won't", December 2000 (http://www.javaworld.com/javaworld/jw-12-2000/jw-1229-traps.html?) and is reprinted here with permission. The pitfall has been updated from reader feedback.

```
01: package org.javapitfalls.item1;
02:
03: import java.util.*;
04: import java.io.*;
05:
06: public class BadExecJavac
07: {
08:     public static void main(String args[])
09:     {
10:         try
11:         {
12:             Runtime rt = Runtime.getRuntime();
13:             Process proc = rt.exec("javac");
14:             int exitVal = proc.exitValue();
15:             System.out.println("Process exitValue: " + exitVal);
16:         } catch (Throwable t)
17:         {
18:             t.printStackTrace();
19:         }
20:     }
21: }
```

Listing 1.1   BadExecJavac.java

A run of BadExecJavac produces the following:

```
E:\classes\org\javapitfalls\item1 >java
org.javapitfalls.item1.BadExecJavac
java.lang.IllegalThreadStateException: process has not exited
        at java.lang.Win32Process.exitValue(Native Method)
        at BadExecJavac.main(BadExecJavac.java:13)
```

The program failed to work because the exitValue() method will throw an IllegalThreadStateException if the external process has not yet completed. While this is stated in the documentation, it is strange in that it begs the question: why not just make this method wait until it can give me a valid answer? A more thorough look at the methods available in the Process class reveals a waitFor() method that does precisely that. In fact, the waitFor() method returns the exit value, which means that you would not use both methods in conjunction. You choose one or the other. The only possible reason for you to use the exitValue() method over the waitFor() method is that you do not want to have your program block waiting on an external process that may never complete. Personally, I would prefer a boolean parameter called waitFor be passed into the exitValue() method to determine whether or not the current thread should wait. I think a boolean would be better because the name exitValue() is a better name for this method and it is unnecessary to have two methods perform the same function under different conditions. Such simple "condition" discrimination is the domain of an input parameter.

So, the first pitfall relating to `Runtime.exec()` is beware the `IllegalThread-StateException` and either catch it or wait for the process to complete. Now, let's fix the problem in the above program and wait for the process to complete. In Listing 1.2, the program again attempts to exec the program javac.exe and then waits for the external process to complete.

```
01: package org.javapitfalls.item1;
02:
03: import java.util.*;
04: import java.io.*;
05:
06: public class BadExecJavac2
07: {
08:     public static void main(String args[])
09:     {
10:         try
11:         {
12:             Runtime rt = Runtime.getRuntime();
13:             Process proc = rt.exec("javac");
14:             int exitVal = proc.waitFor();
15:             System.out.println("Process exitValue: " + exitVal);
16:         } catch (Throwable t)
17:         {
18:             t.printStackTrace();
19:         }
20:     }
21: }
```

Listing 1.2   BadExecJavac2.java

Unfortunately, a run of BadExecJavac2 produces no output. The program hangs and never completes! Why is the javac process never completing? The javadoc documentation provides the answer. It says, "Because some native platforms only provide limited buffer size for standard input and output streams, failure to promptly write the input stream or read the output stream of the subprocess may cause the subprocess to block, and even deadlock." So, is this just a case of programmers not following "RTFM" (read the f-ing manual)? The answer is partially yes. In this case, reading the manual would get you halfway there. It tells you that you need to handle the streams to your external process but does not tell you how. Besides RTFM, there is another variable at play here that cannot be ignored when you examine the large number of programmer questions and errors over this API in the newsgroups. The `Runtime.exec()` and `Process` APIs seem extremely simple, but that simplicity is deceiving, because the simple (translate to obvious) use of the API is prone to error.

The lesson here for the API designer is to reserve simple APIs for simple operations. Operations prone to complexities and platform-specific dependencies should reflect the domain accurately. It is possible for an abstraction to be carried too far. An example of a more complete API to handle these operations is the JConfig library (available at http://www.tolstoy.com/samizdat/jconfig.html). So, now let's follow the documentation and handle the output of the javac process. When you run javac without any arguments, it produces a set of usage statements that describe how to run the program and the meaning of all the available program options. Knowing that this is going to the stderr stream, it is easy to write a program to exhaust that stream before waiting on the process to exit. Listing 1.3 does just that. While that approach will work, it is not a good general solution. That is why the program in Listing 1.3 is named MediocreExecJavac; it is only a mediocre solution. A better solution would empty both the standard error stream and the standard output stream. And the best solution would empty these streams simultaneously (this is demonstrated later).

```
01: package org.javapitfalls.item1;
02:
03: import java.util.*;
04: import java.io.*;
05:
06: public class MediocreExecJavac
07: {
08:     public static void main(String args[])
09:     {
10:         try
11:         {
12:             Runtime rt = Runtime.getRuntime();
13:             Process proc = rt.exec("javac");
14:             InputStream stderr = proc.getErrorStream();
15:             InputStreamReader isr = new InputStreamReader(stderr);
16:             BufferedReader br = new BufferedReader(isr);
17:             String line = null;
18:             System.out.println("<ERROR>");
19:             while ( (line = br.readLine()) != null)
20:                 System.out.println(line);
21:             System.out.println("</ERROR>");
22:             int exitVal = proc.waitFor();
23:             System.out.println("Process exitValue: " + exitVal);
24:         } catch (Throwable t)
25:           {
26:             t.printStackTrace();
27:           }
28:     }
29: }
```

Listing 1.3   MediocreExecJavac.java

A run of MediocreExecJavac produces the following:

```
E:\classes\org\javapitfalls\item1>java
org.javapitfalls.item1.MediocreExecJavac
<ERROR>
Usage: javac <options> <source files>
where <options> includes
  -g                      Generate all debugging info
  -g:none                 Generate no debugging info
  -g:{lines,vars,source}  Generate only some debugging info
  -O                      Optimize; may hinder debugging or enlarge class
files
  -nowarn                 Generate no warnings
... some output removed for brevity ...
</ERROR>
Process exitValue: 2
```

So, MediocreExecJavac works and produces an exit value of 2. Normally, an exit value of 0 means success and nonzero means error. Unfortunately, the meaning of these exit values is operating system-specific. The Win32 error code for a value of 2 is the error for "file not found." This makes sense, since javac expects us to follow the program with the source code file to compile. So, the second pitfall to avoid with Runtime.exec() is ensuring you process the input and output streams if the program you are launching produces output or expects input.

Going back to windows, many new programmers stumble on Runtime.exec() when trying to use it for nonexecutable commands like dir and copy. So, we replace "javac" with "dir" as the argument to exec() like this:

```
Process proc = rt.exec("dir");
```

This line is replaced in the source file called BadExecWinDir, which when run produces the following:

```
E:\classes\org\javapitfalls\item1>java
org.javapitfalls.item1.BadExecWinDir
java.io.IOException: CreateProcess: dir error=2
        at java.lang.Win32Process.create(Native Method)
        at java.lang.Win32Process.<init>(Unknown Source)
        at java.lang.Runtime.execInternal(Native Method)
        at BadExecWinDir.main(BadExecWinDir.java:12)
```

As stated earlier, the error value of 2 means file not found—meaning that the executable named dir.exe could not be found. That is because the directory command is part of the window command interpreter and not a separate executable. To run the window command interpreter, you execute either command.com or cmd.exe depending on the windows operating system you are using. Listing 1.4 runs a copy of the Windows Command Interpreter and then executes the user-supplied command (like dir).

```
01: package org.javapitfalls.item1;
02:
03: import java.util.*;
04: import java.io.*;
05:
06: class StreamGobbler extends Thread
07: {
08:     InputStream is;
09:     String type;
10:
11:     StreamGobbler(InputStream is, String type)
12:     {
13:         this.is = is;
14:         this.type = type;
15:     }
16:
17:     public void run()
18:     {
19:         try
20:         {
21:             InputStreamReader isr = new InputStreamReader(is);
22:             BufferedReader br = new BufferedReader(isr);
23:             String line=null;
24:             while ( (line = br.readLine()) != null)
25:             {
26:                 System.out.println(type + ">" + line);
27:                 System.out.flush();
28:             }
29:         } catch (IOException ioe)
30:             {
31:                 ioe.printStackTrace();
32:             }
33:     }
34: }
35:
36: public class GoodWindowsExec
37: {
38:     public static void main(String args[])
39:     {
// ... command line check omitted for brevity ...
45:
46:         try
47:         {
48:             String osName = System.getProperty("os.name" );
49:             System.out.println("osName: " + osName);
50:             String[] cmd = new String[3];
```

Listing 1.4   GoodWindowsExec.java *(continued)*

```
51:
52:                if(osName.equals("Windows NT") ||
53:                    osName.equals("Windows 2000"))
54:                {
55:                    cmd[0] = "cmd.exe" ;
56:                    cmd[1] = "/C" ;
57:                    cmd[2] = args[0];
58:                }
59:                else if( osName.equals( "Windows 95" ) )
60:                {
61:                    cmd[0] = "command.com" ;
62:                    cmd[1] = "/C" ;
63:                    cmd[2] = args[0];
64:                }
65:
66:                Runtime rt = Runtime.getRuntime();
67:                System.out.println("Execing " + cmd[0] + " " + cmd[1]
68:                                    + "." + cmd[2]);
69:                Process proc = rt.exec(cmd);
70:                // any error message?
71:                StreamGobbler errorGobbler = new
72:                    StreamGobbler(proc.getErrorStream(), "ERROR");
73:
74:                // any output?
75:                StreamGobbler outputGobbler = new
76:                    StreamGobbler(proc.getInputStream(), "OUTPUT");
77:
78:                // kick them off
79:                errorGobbler.start();
80:                outputGobbler.start();
81:
82:                // any error???
83:                int exitVal = proc.waitFor();
84:                System.out.println("ExitValue: " + exitVal);
85:
86:            } catch (Throwable t)
87:            {
88:                t.printStackTrace();
89:            }
90:    }
91: }
```

Listing 1.4   *(continued)*

Running GoodWindowsExec with the `dir` command produces:

```
E:\classes\org\javapitfalls\item1>java
org.javapitfalls.item1.GoodWindowsExec "dir *.java"
Execing cmd.exe /C dir *.java
OUTPUT> Volume in drive E has no label.
OUTPUT> Volume Serial Number is 5C5F-0CC9
OUTPUT>
OUTPUT> Directory of E:\classes\com\javaworld\jpitfalls\article2
OUTPUT>
OUTPUT>10/23/00  09:01p                      805 BadExecBrowser.java
OUTPUT>10/22/00  09:35a                      770 BadExecBrowser1.java
... (some output omitted for brevity)
OUTPUT>10/09/00  05:47p                   23,543 TestStringReplace.java
OUTPUT>10/12/00  08:55p                      228 TopLevel.java
OUTPUT>               22 File(s)          46,661 bytes
OUTPUT>                          19,678,420,992 bytes free
ExitValue: 0
```

Running GoodWindowsExec with any associated document type will launch the application associated with that document type. For example, to launch Microsoft Word to display a Word document (a .doc extension), you type

```
>java org.javapitfalls.item1.GoodWindowsExec "yourdoc.doc"
```

Notice that GoodWindowsExec uses the `os.name` system property to determine which Windows operating system you are running in order to use the appropriate command interpreter. After execing the command interpreter, we handle the standard error and standard input streams with the `StreamGobbler` class. The `StreamGobbler` class empties any stream passed into it in a separate thread. The class uses a simple `String` type to denote which stream it is emptying when it prints the line just read to the console. So, the third pitfall to avoid is to know whether you are executing a standalone executable or an interpreted command. At the end of this section, I will demonstrate a simple command-line tool that will help you with that analysis.

It is important to note that the `Process` method used to get the output stream of the process is called `getInputStream()`. The thing to remember is that the perspective is from the Java program and not the external process. So, the output of the external program is the input to the Java program. And that logic carries over to the external programs input stream, which is an output stream to the Java program.

One final pitfall to cover with `Runtime.exec()` is not to assume that the `exec()` accepts any `String` that your command line (or shell) accepts. It is much more limited and not cross-platform. The primary cause of this pitfall is users attempting to use the `exec()` method that accepts a single `String` just like a command line. This confusion may be due to the parameter name for the `exec()` method being `command`. The programmer incorrectly associates the parameter command with anything he or she can type on a command line instead of associating it with a single program and its arguments, for example, a user trying to execute a program and redirect its output in one call to exec(). Listing 1.5 attempts to do just that.

```
01: package org.javapitfalls.item1;
02:
03: import java.util.*;
04: import java.io.*;
05:
// StreamGobbler removed for brevity
32:
33: public class BadWinRedirect
34: {
35:     public static void main(String args[])
36:     {
37:         try
38:         {
39:             Runtime rt = Runtime.getRuntime();
40:             Process proc = rt.exec(
                        "java jecho 'Hello World' > test.txt");
// remaining code same as GoodWindowsExec.java
63: }
```

Listing 1.5   BadWinRedirect.java

Running BadWinRedirect produces:

```
E:\classes\org\javapitfalls\Item1>java
org.javapitfalls.Item1.BadWinRedirect
OUTPUT>'Hello World' > test.txt
ExitValue: 0
```

The program BadWinRedirect attempted to redirect the output of a simple Java version of an echo program into the file test.txt. Unfortunately, when we check to see if the file test.txt is created, we find that it does not exist. The jecho program simply takes its command-line arguments and writes them to the standard output stream. The source for jecho is available on the Web site. The user assumed you could redirect standard output into a file just like you do on a DOS command line. Unfortunately, that is not the way you redirect the output. The incorrect assumption here is that the exec() method acts like a shell interpreter, and it does not. The exec() method executes a single executable (a program or script). If you want to process the stream to either redirect it or pipe it into another program, you must do that programmatically using the java.io package. Listing 1.6 properly redirects the standard output stream of the jecho process into a file.

```
01: package org.javapitfalls.item1;
02:
03: import java.util.*;
04: import java.io.*;
05:
06: class StreamGobbler extends Thread
07: {
08:     InputStream is;
09:     String type;
10:     OutputStream os;
11:
12:     StreamGobbler(InputStream is, String type)
13:     {
14:         this(is, type, null);
15:     }
16:
17:     StreamGobbler(InputStream is, String type, OutputStream
redirect)
18:     {
19:         this.is = is;
20:         this.type = type;
21:         this.os = redirect;
22:     }
23:
24:     public void run()
25:     {
26:         try
27:         {
28:             PrintWriter pw = null;
29:             if (os != null)
30:                 pw = new PrintWriter(os);
31:
32:             InputStreamReader isr = new InputStreamReader(is);
33:             BufferedReader br = new BufferedReader(isr);
34:             String line=null;
35:             while ( (line = br.readLine()) != null)
36:             {
37:                 if (pw != null)
38:                 {
39:                     pw.println(line);
40:                     pw.flush();
41:                 }
42:                 System.out.println(type + ">" + line);
43:             }
44:             if (pw != null)
45:                 pw.flush();
46:         } catch (IOException ioe)
```

Listing 1.6   GoodWinRedirect.java *(continued)*

```
47:                  {
48:                      ioe.printStackTrace();
49:                  }
50:      }
51: }
52:
53: public class GoodWinRedirect
54: {
55:      public static void main(String args[])
56:      {
// ... command argument check omitted for brevity ...
62:
63:          try
64:          {
65:              FileOutputStream fos = new FileOutputStream(args[0]);
66:              Runtime rt = Runtime.getRuntime();
67:              Process proc = rt.exec("java jecho 'Hello World'");
68:              // any error message?
69:              StreamGobbler errorGobbler = new
70:                  StreamGobbler(proc.getErrorStream(), "ERROR");
71:
72:              // any output?
73:              StreamGobbler outputGobbler = new
74:                  StreamGobbler(proc.getInputStream(), "OUTPUT", fos);
75:
76:              // kick them off
77:              errorGobbler.start();
78:              outputGobbler.start();
79:
80:              // any error???
81:              int exitVal = proc.waitFor();
82:              System.out.println("ExitValue: " + exitVal);
83:              fos.flush();
84:              fos.close();
85:          } catch (Throwable t)
86:            {
87:              t.printStackTrace();
88:            }
89:      }
90: }
```

Listing 1.6   *(continued)*

Running GoodWinRedirect produces

```
E:\classes\org\javapitfalls\item1>java
org.javapitfalls.item1.GoodWinRedirect test.txt
OUTPUT>'Hello World'
ExitValue: 0
```

After running GoodWinRedirect, we find that test.txt does exist. The solution to the pitfall was to simply handle the redirection by handling the standard output stream of the external process separate from the `Runtime.exec()` method. We create a separate `OutputStream`, read in the filename to redirect the output to, open the file, and write the output we receive from the standard output of the spawned process to the file. In Listing 1.7 this is accomplished by adding a new constructor to our `Stream-Gobbler` class. The new constructor takes three arguments: the input stream to gobble, the type `String`, which labels the stream we are gobbling, and lastly the output stream to redirect the input to. This new version of `StreamGobbler` does not break any of the previous code it was used in, since we have not changed the existing public API (just extended it). A reader of the *JavaWorld* article, George Neervoort, noted an important improvement to GoodWinRedirect is to ensure that the streams have completed reading input from the process. This is necessary because it is possible for the process to end before the threads have completed. Here is his solution to that problem (thanks George!):

```
int exitVal = proc.waitFor();
errorGobbler.join();
outputGobbler.join();
```

Since the argument to `Runtime.exec()` is operating system-dependent, the proper commands to use will vary from one operating system to another. So, before finalizing arguments to `Runtime.exec()`, it would be valuable to be able to quickly test the arguments before writing the code. Listing 1.7 is a simple command-line utility to allow you to do just that.

```
01: package org.javapitfalls.item1;
02:
03: import java.util.*;
04: import java.io.*;
05:
```

Listing 1.7 TestExec.java *(continued)*

```
// Class StreamGobbler omitted for brevity
32:
33: public class TestExec
34: {
35:     public static void main(String args[])
36:     {
// argument check omitted for brevity
42:
43:         try
44:         {
45:             String cmd = args[0];
46:             Runtime rt = Runtime.getRuntime();
47:             Process proc = rt.exec(cmd);
48:                                               // remaining code
Identical to GoodWindowsExec.java
68:         }
69: }
70:
```

Listing 1.7 *(continued)*

Running TestExec to launch the Netscape browser and load the Java help documentation produces:

```
E:\classes\org\javapitfalls\item1>java org.javapitfalls.item1.TestExec ⏎
"e:\java\docs\index.html"
java.io.IOException: CreateProcess: e:\java\docs\index.html error=193
        at java.lang.Win32Process.create(Native Method)
        at java.lang.Win32Process.<init>(Unknown Source)
        at java.lang.Runtime.execInternal(Native Method)
        at TestExec.main(TestExec.java:45)
```

So, our first test failed with an error of 193. The Win32 Error for value 193 is "not a valid Win32 application." This tells us that there is no path to an associated application (like Netscape) and the process cannot run an HTML file without an associated application. So, we can try the test again, this time giving it a full path to Netscape (or we could have added Netscape to our PATH environment variable). A second run of TestExec produces:

```
E:\classes\com\javaworld\jpitfalls\article2>java TestExec          ⏎
"e:\program files\netscape\program\netscape.exe e:\java\docs\index.html"
ExitValue: 0
```

This worked! The Netscape browser was launched, and it then loaded the Java help documentation.

One useful exercise would be to modify TestExec to redirect the standard input or standard output to a file. When you are executing the javac compiler on Windows 95 or Windows 98, this would solve the problem of error messages scrolling off the top of the limited command-line buffer. Here are the key lines of code to capture the standard output and standard error to a file:

```
FileOutputStream err = new FileOutputStream("stderror.txt");
FileOutputStream out = new FileOutputStream("stdout.txt");
Process proc = Runtime.getRuntime().exec(args);

// any error message?
StreamGobbler errorGobbler
  = new StreamGobbler(proc.getErrorStream(), "ERR", err);
// any output?
StreamGobbler outputGobbler
  = new StreamGobbler(proc.getInputStream(), "OUT", out);
```

One other improvement to TestExec would be a command-line switch to accept input from standard-in. This input would then be passed to the spawned external program using the `Process.getOutputStream()` method. This pitfall has explored several problems in using the `Runtime.exec()` method and supplied workarounds to assist you in executing external applications.

Item 2: NIO Performance and Pitfalls

The NIO packages represent a step forward for input/output (IO) performance and new features; however, these enhancements do not come without some cost in complexity and potential pitfalls. In this item, we examine some of the benefits and deficiencies in this new package. Before we examine specific features, let's get a high-level view of the package and its features. There are four major abstractions in the NIO packages:

Channels.   A channel represents a connection to entities capable of performing IO operations like files and sockets. Thus, channels are characterized by the thing they are connected to like `FileChannel` or `SocketChannel`. For fast IO, channels work in conjunction with buffers to read from the source or write to the sink. There are also interfaces for different roles a channel can play like `GatheringByteChannel` or `ScatteringByteChannel`, which can write or read from multiple sequences of buffers. Lastly, you can get a channel from the `FileInputStream`, `FileOutputStream`, `ServerSocket`, `Socket`, and `RandomAccessFile` classes. Unfortunately, adding these new IO metaphors to the existing crowded field (streams, pipes, readers, writers) is extremely confusing to most programmers. Also, the metaphors overlap and their APIs are intertwined. Overall, the complexity and overlapping functionality of the numerous IO classes is its biggest pitfall.

Buffers.   Buffers are generic data containers for random access manipulation of a single data type. These are integrated with the `Charsets` and `Channels` classes. Each buffer contains a mark, position, limit, and capacity value (and corresponding methods for manipulation). The position can be set to any point in the buffer. Buffers are set in a mode (reading or writing) and must be "flipped" to change the mode.

Charsets.   A charset is a named mapping between bytes and 16-bit Unicode characters. The names of these character sets are listed in the IANA charset registry (http://www.iana.org/assignments/character-sets).

Selectors.   A `Selector` is a class that multiplexes a `SelectableChannel`. A `SelectableChannel` has a single subclass called `AbstractSelectableChannel`. The `AbstractSelectableChannel` has four direct subclasses: `DatagramChannel`, `Pipe.SinkChannel`, `Pipe.SourceChannel`, `ServerSocketChannel`, and `SocketChannel`. In network communications, a multiplexer is a device that can send several signals over a single line. The `Selector` class manages a set of one or more "selectable" channels and provides a single point of access to input from any of them.

Table 2.1 lists all the key classes and interfaces in the NIO packages.

Table 2.1   Key NIO Classes and Interfaces

PACKAGE	CLASS/INTERFACE	DESCRIPTION
`java.nio`	`Buffer`	Random access data container for temporary data storage and manipulation.
`java.nio`	`ByteBuffer`, `CharBuffer`, `DoubleBuffer`, `FloatBuffer`, `IntBuffer`, `LongBuffer`, `ShortBuffer`	Buffer that stores the specific data type represented in its name.
`java.nio`	`MappedByteBuffer`	A `ByteBuffer` whose content is a memory-mapped region of a file. These are created via the `FileChannel.map()` method.
`java.nio`	`ByteOrder`	A typesafe enumeration of byte orders: `LITTLE_ENDIAN` or `BIG_ENDIAN`.
`java.nio.channels`	`Channel`	An interface that represents an open or closed connection to an IO device.
`java.nio.channels`	`Channels`	A class that contains utility methods for working with channels.

Table 2.1 *(Continued)*

PACKAGE	CLASS/INTERFACE	DESCRIPTION
java.nio.channels	FileChannel, Pipe, DatagramChannel, SocketChannel, ServerSocketChannel, SelectableChannel	Specific channel types to work with specific devices like files and sockets. A DatagramChannel is a channel for working with DatagramSockets (sockets that use User Datagram Protocol, or UDP). A pipe performs communication between threads.
java.nio.channels	FileLock	A class that represents a lock on a region of a file. An object of this type is created by calling either lock() or tryLock() on a FileChannel.
java.nio.channels	Selector, SelectionKey	As stated before, a Selector is a class that multiplexes one or more SelectableChannels. A SelectionKey is used to specify specific operations to listen for (or select) on a specific SelectableChannel.
java.nio.charset	Charset	An abstract class that provides a mapping between 16-bit Unicode characters and sequences of bytes. The standard character sets are US-ASCII (7-bit ASCII), ISO-8859-1 (ISO Latin), UTF-8, UTF-16BE (big endian order), UTF-16LE (little endian order), UTF-16 (uses a byte order mark).
java.nio.charset	CharsetEncoder, CharsetDecoder	A CharsetEncoder is an engine that encodes (or transforms) a set of 16-bit Unicode characters into a specific sequence of bytes specified by the specific character set. A CharsetDecoder performs the opposite operation.
java.nio.charset	CoderResult	A class that reports the state of an encoder or decoder. It reports any of five states: error, malformed, underflow, overflow, or unmappable.
java.nio.charset	CodingActionError	A class that is a typesafe enumeration that specifies how an encoder or decoder should handle errors. It can be set to IGNORE, REPLACE, or REPORT.

Unfortunately, we cannot demonstrate all of the functionality in the NIO package. Instead, we examine three examples: a canonical file copy, little endian byte operations, and non-blocking server IO.

Canonical File Copy

Our first example is a canonical file copy operation. The old way to implement the copy would be to loop while reading and writing from a fixed-size byte buffer until we had exhausted the bytes in the file. Listing 2.1 demonstrates that method.

```
01: package org.javapitfalls.item2;
02:
03: import java.io.*;
04: import java.nio.*;
05: import java.nio.channels.*;
06:
07: public class SlowFileCopy
08: {
09:     public static void main(String args[])
10:        {
// ...command line check omitted for brevity ...
16:
17:            try
18:            {
19:                long start = System.currentTimeMillis();
20:                // open files
21:                FileInputStream fis =
22:                       new FileInputStream(args[0]);
23:                FileOutputStream fos =
24:                       new FileOutputStream(args[1]);
25:
26:                int bufSize = 4096;
27:                byte [] buf = new byte[bufSize];
28:
29:                int cnt = 0;
30:                while ((cnt = fis.read(buf)) >= 0)
31:                    fos.write(buf, 0, (int) cnt);
32:
33:                fis.close();
34:                fos.close();
35:                long end = System.currentTimeMillis();
36:                System.out.println("Elapsed Time: "
+ (end - start) + " milliseconds.");
37:            } catch (Throwable t)
38:            {
39:                t.printStackTrace();
40:            }
41:     }
42: }
```

Listing 2.1   SlowFileCopy.java

In line 26 of Listing 2.1 we set the buffer size to be 4 KB. Obviously, given the simple space/time trade-off, we can increase the speed of this for large files by increasing the buffer size. A run of Listing 2.1 on a 27-MB file produces:

```
E:\classes\org\javapitfalls\item2>java
org.javapitfalls.item2.SlowFileCopy j2sdk-1_4_1-beta-windows-i586.exe ↩
j2sdk-copy1.exe


Elapsed Time: 13971 milliseconds.
```

Lines 30 and 31 of Listing 2.1 are the key workhorse loop of the program where bytes are transferred from the original file to the buffer and then are written from the buffer to a second file (the copy). The `FileChannel` class includes a method called `transferTo()` that takes advantage of low-level operating system calls specifically to speed up transfers between file channels. So, the loop in 26 to 31 can be replaced by the following code:

```
FileChannel fcin = fis.getChannel();
FileChannel fcout = fos.getChannel();
fcin.transferTo(0, fcin.size(), fcout);
```

The above snippet is from the program called FastFileCopy.java, which is identical to SlowFileCopy.java except for the lines above that replace the `while` loop. A run of FastFileCopy on the same large file produces:

```
E:\classes\org\javapitfalls\item2>java
org.javapitfalls.item2.FastFileCopy j2sdk-1_4_1-beta-windows-i586.exe ↩
j2sdk-copy2.exe

Elapsed Time: 2343 milliseconds.
```

The performance of FastFileCopy is very fast for all large files, but slightly slower for smaller files.

Little-Endian Byte Operations

A nice feature of the `NIO Buffer` class is the ability to perform reads and writes of the numeric data types using either Big Endian or Little Endian byte order. For those not familiar with the difference, for multibyte data types like short (2 bytes), integer and float (4 bytes), and long and double (8 bytes), Little Endian stores the bytes starting from the least significant byte ("littlest" number) toward the most significant. Of course, Big Endian stores bytes in the opposite direction. Processors from Motorola and Sun use Big Endian order, while Intel uses Little Endian. Prior to JDK 1.4, you would have to perform the byte-swapping yourself. I created a class called `LittleEndian-OutputStream` to do just that for a BMP Image encoder. Listing 2.2 demonstrates the byte swapping. This is necessary because the only order available for `DataOutput-Stream` is Big Endian.

```
008: class LittleEndianOutputStream extends OutputStream
009: {
010:     OutputStream os;
011:
012:     public LittleEndianOutputStream(OutputStream os)
013:     {
014:         this.os = os;
015:     }
016:
017:     public void write(int b) throws IOException
018:     {
019:         os.write(b);
020:     }
021:
022:     public void writeShort(short s) throws IOException
023:     {
024:         int is = (int) s; // promote
025:         int maskB1 = 0xff;
026:         int maskB2 = 0xff00;
027:
028:         byte [] b = new byte[2];
029:         b[0] = (byte)  (s & maskB1);
030:         b[1] = (byte) ((s & maskB2) >>> 8);
031:
032:         os.write(b);
033:     }
034:
035:     public void writeInt(int i) throws IOException
036:     {
037:         byte [] b = new byte[4];
038:         int maskB1 = 0xff;
039:         int maskB2 = 0xff00;
040:         int maskB3 = 0xff0000;
041:         int maskB4 = 0xff000000;
042:
043:         b[3] = (byte) ((i & maskB4) >>> 24);
044:         b[2] = (byte) ((i & maskB3) >>> 16);
045:         b[1] = (byte) ((i & maskB2) >>> 8);
046:         b[0] = (byte)  (i & maskB1);
047:
048:         os.write(b);
049:     }
050: }
```

Listing 2.2   LittleEndianOutputStream.java

The `LittleEndianOutputStream` was used in combination with a `DataOut-putStream` to write integers and shorts in a BMP encoder. Note how we manually swap the bytes when writing an integer to the underlying `OutputStream` in the `writeInt()` method. We swap the bytes by masking the byte in the original integer (Big Endian format), shifting it down to the lowest byte position and assigning it to its new byte position. LittleEndianOutputStream is now obsolete, as Listing 2.3 shows the encoder rewritten using NIO Buffers.

```
001: /** BmpWriter3.java */
002: package org.javapitfalls.item2;
003:
004: import java.awt.*;
005: import java.awt.image.*;
006: import java.io.*;
007: import java.nio.*;
008: import java.nio.channels.*;
009:
010: public class BmpWriter3
011: {
012:     // File Header - Actual contents (14 bytes):
013:     short fileType = 0x4d42;// always "BM"
014:     int fileSize;          // size of file in bytes
015:     short reserved1 = 0;    // always 0
016:     short reserved2 = 0;    // always 0
017:     int bitmapOffset = 54;  // starting byte position of image data
018:
019:     // BMP Image Header - Actual conents (40 bytes):
020:     int size = 40;          // size of this header in bytes
021:     int width;              // image width in pixels
022:     int height;   // image height in pixels (if < 0, "top-down")
023:     short planes = 1;       // no. of color planes: always 1
024:     short bitsPerPixel = 24;// number of bits per pixel: 1, 4, 8, ⤸
or 24 (no color map)
// Some data members omitted for brevity -- code available online.
037:
038:     public void storeImage(Image img, String sFilename) throws ⤸
IOException
039:     {
// ... getting Image width and height omitted for brevity ...
056:
057:         width = imgWidth;
058:         height = imgHeight;
059:
```

Listing 2.3   BmpWriter3.java *(continued)*

```
060:            imgPixels = new int[imgWidth * imgHeight];
061:            // pixels are stored in rows
062:            try
063:            {
064:                PixelGrabber pg = new
PixelGrabber(img,0,0,imgWidth,imgHeight,imgPixels,
065:                                                    0,imgWidth);
066:                pg.grabPixels();
067:            } catch (Exception e)
068:            {
069:                throw new IOException("Exception. Reason: "
+ e.toString());
070:            }
071:
072:            // now open the file
073:            FileOutputStream fos = new FileOutputStream(sFilename);
074:            FileChannel fc = fos.getChannel();
075:
076:            // write the "header"
077:            boolean padded=false;
078:            // first calculate the scanline size
079:            iScanLineSize = 3 * width;
080:            if (iScanLineSize % 2 != 0)
081:            {
082:                iScanLineSize++;
083:                padded = true;
084:            }
085:
086:            // now, calculate the file size
087:            fileSize = 14 + 40 + (iScanLineSize * imgHeight);
088:            sizeOfBitmap = iScanLineSize * imgHeight;
089:
090:            // create a ByteBuffer
091:            ByteBuffer bbuf = ByteBuffer.allocate(fileSize);
092:            bbuf.order(ByteOrder.LITTLE_ENDIAN);
093:            bbuf.clear();
094:
095:            // now put out file header
096:            bbuf.putShort(fileType);
097:            bbuf.putInt(fileSize);
098:            bbuf.putShort(reserved1);
099:            bbuf.putShort(reserved2);
100:            bbuf.putInt(bitmapOffset);
101:
// ... some output to buffer code omitted for brevity ...
```

Listing 2.3   *(continued)*

```
113:
114:          // put the pixels
115:          for (int i= (imgHeight - 1); i >= 0; i--)
116:          {
117:              byte pad = 0;
118:              for (int j=0; j < imgWidth; j++)
119:              {
120:                  int pixel = imgPixels[(i * width) + j];
121:                  byte alpha = (byte) ((pixel >> 24) & 0xff);
122:                  byte red   = (byte) ((pixel >> 16) & 0xff);
123:                  byte green = (byte) ((pixel >>  8) & 0xff);
124:                  byte blue  = (byte) ((pixel      ) & 0xff);
125:
126:                  // put them bgr
127:                  bbuf.put(blue);
128:                  bbuf.put(green);
129:                  bbuf.put(red);
130:              }
131:              if (padded)
132:                  bbuf.put(pad);
133:          }
134:
135:          bbuf.flip();
136:          fc.write(bbuf);
137:          fos.close();
138:      }
139:
140:      public static void main(String args[])
141:      {
// method omitted for brevity - available on Web site.
171:
172: }
173:
```

Listing 2.3   *(continued)*

The key lines of Listing 2.3 are as follows:

- At lines 64 and 65, we grab the image pixels (as integers) using the Pixel-Grabber class.

- At lines 73 and 74, we first create the FileOutputStream for the BMP output file and then get the FileChannel using the getChannel() method. This demonstrates the integration between the existing IO packages (FileOutput-Stream) and the new IO packages (FileChannel).

- At line 91, we create a ByteBuffer via the static allocate() method. It is important to note that there is also an allocateDirect() method, which allows you to create DirectBuffers. A DirectBuffer is a buffer allocated by the operating system to reduce the number of copies between the virtual machine and the operating system. How DirectBuffers are implemented differs for each operating system. Additionally, a direct buffer may be more expensive to create because of the interaction with the operating system, so they should be used for long-standing buffers.

- There are three values associated with all buffers: position, limit, and capacity. The position is the current location to read from or write to. The limit is the amount of data in the array. The capacity is the size of the underlying array.

- At line 92, we use the order() method to set the endian order to LITTLE_ENDIAN.

- At lines 96 and 97, we use putInt() and putShort() to write integers and shorts, respectively, in Little Endian order, to the byte buffer.

- At line 135, we flip the buffer from reading to writing using the flip() method. The flip() method sets the limit to the current position and the position back to 0.

- At line 136, we write the byte buffer to the underlying file.

Now we can finish our discussion of NIO by examining how the package implements non-blocking IO.

Non-Blocking Server IO

Before NIO, Java servers would create a thread to handle each incoming client connection. You would see a code snippet like this:

```
while (true)
{
    Socket s = serverSocket.accept();
    Thread handler = new Thread(new SocketHandler(s));
    handler.start();
}
```

More experienced programmers would reuse threads via a thread pool instead of instantiating a new thread each time. So, the first key new feature of NIO is the ability to manage multiple connections by way of a multiplexer class called a Selector. *Multiplexing* is a networking term associated with protocols like the User Datagram Protocol (UDP) that multiplexes communication packets to multiple processes. Figure 2.1 demonstrates multiplexing.

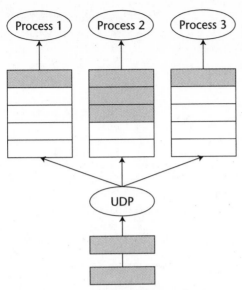

Figure 2.1   UDP multiplexing example.

So, after hearing about Selectable channels and deciding that they are a good thing, we set out to use them. We examine the JDK documentation and study the example programs like NBTimeServer.java. The "non-blocking time server" demonstrates non-blocking IO by creating a simple server to send the current time to connecting clients. For our demonstration program, we will write a server that is the start of a collaborative photo space. In that space we need to share images and annotations. Here we only scratch the surface of the application by creating a server to receive the images and annotations from clients. Listing 2.4 has the initial attempt at a non-blocking server:

```
001: /* ImageAnnotationServer1.java */
002: package org.javapitfalls.item2;
003:
004: import java.util.*;
005: import java.io.*;
006: import java.nio.*;
007: import java.net.*;
008: import java.nio.channels.*;
```

Listing 2.4   ImageAnnotationServer1.java *(continued)*

```
009:
010: public class ImageAnnotationServer1
011: {
012:      public static final int DEFAULT_IAS_PORT = 8999;
013:      boolean done;
014:
015:      public ImageAnnotationServer1() throws Exception
016:      {
017:           this(DEFAULT_IAS_PORT);
018:      }
019:
020:      public ImageAnnotationServer1(int port) throws Exception
021:      {
022:           acceptConnections(port);
023:      }
024:
025:      public void acceptConnections(int port) throws Exception
026:      {
027:           // get the ServerSocketChannel
028:           ServerSocketChannel ssc = ServerSocketChannel.open();
029:           System.out.println("Received a: " +
ssc.getClass().getName());
030:
031:           // get the ServerSocket on this channel
032:           ServerSocket ss = ssc.socket();
033:
034:           // bind to the port on the local host
035:           InetAddress address = InetAddress.getLocalHost();
036:           InetSocketAddress sockAddress = new
InetSocketAddress(address, port);
037:           ss.bind(sockAddress);
038:
039:           // set to non-blocking
040:           ssc.configureBlocking(false);
041:
042:           // create a Selector to multiplex channels on
043:           Selector theSelector = Selector.open();
044:
045:           // register this channel (for all events) with the
Selector
046:           // NOTE -- how do we know which events are OK????
047:           SelectionKey theKey = ssc.register(theSelector,
SelectionKey.OP_ACCEPT |
```

Listing 2.4   *(continued)*

```
048:                                          SelectionKey.OP_READ |
049:                                          SelectionKey.OP_CONNECT |
050:                                          SelectionKey.OP_WRITE);
051:
052:          while (theSelector.select() > 0)
053:          {
054:              // get the ready keys
055:              Set readyKeys = theSelector.selectedKeys();
056:              Iterator i = readyKeys.iterator();
057:
058:              // Walk through the ready keys collection and
process datarequests.
059:              while (i.hasNext())
060:              {
061:                  // get the key
062:                  SelectionKey sk = (SelectionKey)i.next();
063:
064:                  if (sk.isConnectable())
065:                  {
066:                      System.out.println("is Connectable.");
067:                  }
// ... other checks removed for brevity
083:                  }
084:          }
085:      }
086:
087:      public static void main(String [] args)
088:      {
// ... argument check removed for brevity
094:
095:          try
096:          {
097:              int p = Integer.parseInt(args[0]);
098:              ImageAnnotationServer1 ias1 = new
ImageAnnotationServer1(p);
099:          } catch (Throwable t)
100:          {
101:              t.printStackTrace();
102:          }
103:      }
104: }
105:
```

Listing 2.4   *(continued)*

Let's walk through the logic in this program one step at a time. These follow the bold lines in Listing 2.4. The steps are as follows:

1. At line 28, the program opens the `ServerSocketChannel`. You do not directly instantiate a `ServerSocketChannel`. Instead, you get an instance of one from the `Service Provider Interface` classes for this channel type.

2. At line 32, the program gets the `ServerSocket` from the `ServerSocketChannel`. The connection between the original `java.net` classes (`Socket` and `ServerSocket`) and their respective channels is more intertwined than the relationship between the original IO streams and their respective channels. In this case, a `ServerSocketChannel` is not a bound connection to a port; instead, you must retrieve the `ServerSocket` and bind it to the network address and port. Without you blindly copying the example code, it is unintuitive when you must switch from channels to their IO counterparts.

3. At line 37, the program binds the local host and port to the server socket.

4. At line 40, we configure the `ServerSocketChannel` to be non-blocking. This means that a call to read or write on a socket from this channel will return immediately whether there is data available or not. For example, in blocking mode, the program would wait until there was data available to be read before returning. It is important to understand that you can use these selectable channels on both clients and servers. This is the chief benefit of non-blocking IO— your program never waits on the IO but instead is notified when it occurs. This concept of the program reacting to multiplexed data instead of waiting until it occurs is an implementation of the Reactor pattern [Schmidt 96]. Figure 2.2 is a UML diagram of the Reactor pattern.

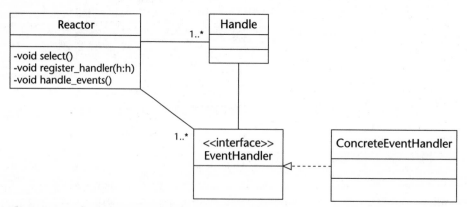

Figure 2.2 The Reactor pattern.

The Reactor pattern demultiplexes concurrent events to one or more event handlers. The key participants in the pattern are handles and a synchronous event demultiplexer. A handle represents the object of the event. In the NIO package implementation of this pattern, the handle is represented by the `SelectionKey` class. Thus, in relation to network servers, a handle represents a socket channel. The synchronous event demultiplexer blocks awaiting for events to occur on a set of handles. A common example of such a demultiplexer is the Unix `select()` system call. In the NIO package implementation of this pattern, the Selector class performs the synchronous event demultiplexing. Lastly, the Event Handler interface (and specific implementation) implements an object hook for a specific event handling. In the NIO implementation, the `SelectionKey` performs the object hook operation by allowing you to attach an object via the `attach()` method and retrieve the object via the `attachment()` method. Here is an example of attaching a `Callback` object to a key:

```
sk.attach(new Callback(sk.channel()));
```

1. At line 43, we create a `Selector` object (by calling the `Selector.open()` method) to multiplex all registered channels.

2. At line 47, we register the `SelectableChannel` with the `Selector` and specify which operations in the channel we want to be notified about. Here lies are first potential pitfall. If we do not register the correct operations for this channel object (which is provided by a Service Provider and not instantiated), an exception will be thrown. The operations that you can register for are `OP_ACCEPT`, `OP_CONNECT`, `OP_READ`, and `OP_WRITE`. In fact, in Listing 2.4, since we did not check which operations are valid on this channel with the `validOps()` method, an exception will be thrown.

3. At line 52, we call `select()` on the `Selector` to wait for operations on the registered channels.

4. At line 55, the `select()` method returns the number of `SelectionKeys` ready for processing. If the number is greater than 0, you can retrieve the set of selected `SelectionKeys`. A `SelectionKey` represents the registration and state of a `Channel` registered with a `Selector`. Once you have the `SelectionKey`, you can test its state and act accordingly.

Running Listing 2.4 produces:

```
E:\classes\org\javapitfalls\item2>java
org.javapitfalls.item2.ImageAnnotationServer1 5544
Received a: sun.nio.ch.ServerSocketChannelImpl

java.lang.IllegalArgumentException at
java.nio.channels.spi.AbstractSelectableChannel.register
(AbstractSelectableChannel.java:170)
```

The `IllegalArgumentException` is thrown because we attempted to register operations that were not valid on the `ServerSocketChannel`. The only operation we can register on that channel is `OP_ACCEPT`. Listing 2.5 registers the correct operation, accepts the channel, and receives a file from the client. Listing 2.5 presents the changes to the `acceptConnections()` method.

```
025: public void acceptConnections(int port) throws Exception
026: {
// ... omitted code Identical to Listing 2.4
053:    SelectionKey theKey = ssc.register(theSelector,
SelectionKey.OP_ACCEPT);
054:
055:    int readyKeyCnt = 0;
056:    while ( (readyKeyCnt = theSelector.select()) > 0)
057:    {
058:        System.out.println("Have " + readyKeyCnt + " ready keys...");
059:
060:        // get the ready keys
061:        Set readyKeys = theSelector.selectedKeys();
062:        Iterator i = readyKeys.iterator();
063:
064:        // Walk through the ready keys collection and process the
requests.
065:        while (i.hasNext())
066:        {
067:            // get the key
068:            SelectionKey sk = (SelectionKey)i.next();
069:            i.remove();
070:
071:            if (sk.isAcceptable())
072:            {
073:                System.out.println("is Acceptable.");
074:                // accept it
075:
076:                // get the channel
077:                ServerSocketChannel channel = (ServerSocketChannel)
sk.channel();
078:
079:                // using method in NBTimeServer JDK example
080:                System.out.println("Accepting the connection.");
081:                Socket s = channel.accept().socket();
082:
083:                DataInputStream dis = new
DataInputStream(s.getInputStream());
084:                DataOutputStream dos = new
DataOutputStream(s.getOutputStream());
085:
086:                // Code to read file from the client ...
112:                }
113:            }
114:    }
115:}
```

Listing 2.5   Changes to `acceptConnections()` method

After working our way through the simple incorrect event registration pitfall, we can create a non-blocking server that properly accepts a socket connection. Here are the key changes highlighted in Listing 2.5:

- At line 53, we register the single operation OP_ACCEPT on the server socket channel.

- At line 56, we call select() to wait on any events on the registered channel.

- At line 69, we remove the SelectionKey from the set of SelectionKeys returned from the select() method. This is a potential pitfall, because if you do not remove the key, you will reprocess it. So, it is the programmer's responsibility to remove it from the set. This is especially dangerous if you have multiple threads processing the selection keys.

- At line 71, we test if the key isAcceptable(),which is the only operation we registered for. However, it is important to understand that once accepted, you get a channel for each incoming connection (each a separate key), which can in turn be registered with the Selector for other operations (reads and writes).

- At line 77, we get the registered channel (in this case the ServerSocketChannel) from the SelectionKey via the channel() method.

- At line 81, we call the accept() method to accept the socket connection and get a SocketChannel object. Given this object we can either process the channel (which is the approach of our simple server) or register it with the Selector like this:

```
SocketChannel sockChannel = channel.accept();
sockChannel.configureBlocking( false );
SelectionKey readKey =
            sockChannel.register( theSelector,
            SelectionKey.OP_READ|SelectionKey.OP_WRITE  );
```

A run of Listing 2.5 (ImageAnnotationServer2) accepts a single connection, receives the file, and then exits. The problem is in line 56 where the while loop (which follows Sun's NBTimeServer example) only continues if there are greater than 0 events returned from select(); however, the documentation clearly states that 0 events may be returned. Therefore to fix this pitfall, it is necessary to loop forever in the server and not assume select() will block until at least one event is ready, like this:

```
int readyKeyCnt = 0;
// loop forever (even if select() returns 0 ready keys)
while (true)
        {
readyKeyCnt = theSelector.select();
// ...
}
```

With the above change made, ImageAnnotationServer3.java is ready to continually accept files from clients. This pitfall has introduced you to some of the major features of the NIO package. The package has some clear benefits at the cost of some additional complexity. Readers should be ready for more changes to Java's IO packages. The most glaring pitfall with this package is its separation from the IO package and the addition of brand-new metaphors. Having said that, most programmers will overlook that incongruity for the benefits of the new features. Overall, the performance improvements offered by NIO make up for the minor pitfalls mentioned here. All programmers should be encouraged to learn and use the NIO package.

Item 3: I Prefer Not to Use Properties

I have worked in a number of places where all development was done on an isolated network and a set of machines was used for office automation tasks like email, Web browsing, word processing, and time charging.

In this case, I really have two sets of properties that I need to handle. First, I have the set of properties that handle configuring the system in general. Examples of this would be the mail server that needs to be referenced, the network file server to point toward, and the timecard server. These are things that are clearly independent of any user and have more to do with the system than the individual user accessing the system.

Second, a multitude of user properties are required. It starts by being arranged by functional application, and then it is further organized by functional areas within the application.

Consider this properties file:

```
server=timecard.mcbrad.com
server=mail.mcbrad.com
server=ftp.mcbrad.com
```

This obviously wouldn't work, but it illustrates a simple problem in a properties file. You cannot give a common name to a particular property. Notice that naming a property "server" is remarkably appropriate in each of these cases. Furthermore, if you wanted to use a common piece of code to make a TCP/IP connection for all three apps listed, you couldn't do it without either writing custom code to parse out of three different files (a maintenance nightmare) or parsing the server subproperty.

This properties file shows a more typical example to avoid namespace collision:

```
timecard.server=timecard.mcbrad.com
mail.server=mail.mcbrad.com
ftp.server=ftp.mcbrad.com
```

Notice that these property names imply a sense of hierarchy. In fact, there is no hierarchy. There are only further qualified property names to make them more unique. However, our earlier example gave us the idea of being able to take the server subnode off of all of the primary nodes. There are no nodes since the properties file is not stored as a tree. This is where the Preferences API comes in handy. Listing 3.1 is an example of a preferences file.

```
01: <?xml version="1.0" encoding="UTF-8"?>
02: <!DOCTYPE preferences SYSTEM
'http://java.sun.com/dtd/preferences.dtd'>
03:
04: <preferences EXTERNAL_XML_VERSION="1.0">
05:
06:   <root type="user">
07:     <map />
08:     <node name="com">
09:       <map>
10:         <entry key="addr" value="8200 Greensboro Dr." />
11:         <entry key="pi" value="3.1416" />
12:         <entry key="number" value="23" />
13:       </map>
14:       <node name="mcbrad">
15:         <map />
16:         <node name="prefs">
17:           <map>
18:             <entry key="mail" value="mail" />
19:             <entry key="ftp" value="shortbus" />
20:             <entry key="timecard" value="spectator" />
21:           </map>
22:         </node>
23:       </node>
24:     </node>
25:
26:   </root>
27: </preferences>
28:
```

Listing 3.1 A preferences file

This preferences file shows the hierarchical organization of its XML format. It is very helpful when organizing multiple preferences under a particular user's settings.

Hang on, though. This just jumped from a discussion of system properties to user properties. Being able to do that in a single file is probably the best example of how we benefit from a hierarchical format. Now that we have a tree structure, not only can we separate nodes between different parts of the system, but we can also make a separation between the system and the user. Once that separation can be defined, we can make a distinction between users. This makes it easier to maintain a large number of users, all separated on the tree.

Using properties, you must store user properties within the context of the user's home directory, and then you almost always need to store those values in a file that is hard-coded into the system. This adds an additional problem with trying to ensure consistent access to these hard-coded locations. Listing 3.2 is an example of how a developer might use properties.

```
01: package org.pitfalls.prefs;
02:
03: import java.util.Properties;
04: import java.io.*;
05:
06: public class PropertiesTest {
07:
08:   private String mailServer;
09:   private String timecardServer;
10:   private String userName;
11:   private String ftpServer;
12:
13:
14:   public PropertiesTest() {
15:   }
16:
17:   [ GETTER AND SETTER METHODS FOR MEMBER VARIABLES... ]
18:
19:   public void storeProperties() {
20:
21:     Properties props = new Properties();
22:
23:     props.put("TIMECARD", getTimecardServer());
24:     props.put("MAIL", getMailServer());
25:     props.put("FTP", getFtpServer());
26:     props.put("USER", getTimecardServer());
27:
28:     try {
29:
30:       props.store(new FileOutputStream("myProps.properties"),
"Properties");
31:
32:     } catch (IOException ex) {
33:
34:       ex.printStackTrace();
35:
36:     }
37:
38:   }
39:
```

Listing 3.2 Storing user properties

Here is the example of the properties file that is produced:

```
#Properties
#Sun Feb 24 23:16:09 EST 2002
TIMECARD=time.mcbrad.com
FTP=ftp.mcbrad.com
USER=time.mcbrad.com
MAIL=mail.mcbrad.com
```

Instead, Listing 3.3 shows the same example with preferences:

```
package org.pitfalls.prefs;

import java.util.prefs.Preferences;

public class PreferencesTest {

  private String mailServer;
  private String timecardServer;
  private String userName;
  private String ftpServer;

  public PreferencesTest() {

  }

  [ GETTER AND SETTER METHODS FOR MEMBER VARIABLES... ]

  public void storePreferences() {
    Preferences prefs = Preferences.userRoot();
    prefs.put("timecard", getTimecardServer());
    prefs.put("MAIL", getMailServer());
    prefs.put("FTP", getFtpServer());
    prefs.put("user", getTimecardServer());

  }

  public static void main(String[] args) {

    PreferencesTest myPFTest = new PreferencesTest();
    myPFTest.setFtpServer("ftp.mcbrad.com");
    myPFTest.setMailServer("mail.mcbrad.com");
    myPFTest.setTimecardServer("time.mcbrad.com");
    myPFTest.setUserName("Jennifer Richardson");

    myPFTest.storePreferences();

  }
```

Listing 3.3   Storing user preferences

Figure 3.1 shows the preferences stored, in this case, in the Windows Registry. Notice the slashes prior to each of the capital letters? This is due to the implementation on the Windows Registry, which does not support case-sensitive keys. The slashes signify a capital letter.

Figure 3.1   Preferences stored in the Windows Registry.

So is the hierarchical nature of preferences the reason to use them instead of properties? While that is certainly a great reason, it is not the only reason. Properties files have no standardized way of placing configuration information within the filesystem. This means that you need a configuration file to find your configuration file! Furthermore, you must have a filesystem available, so a lot of devices cannot use the `Properties` API.

What about using JNDI? JNDI is a hierarchical structure. JNDI is a solid choice for maintaining information about users, applications, and distributed objects. Two things run against JNDI, however:

- It doesn't give any indication of how the hierarchy is structured. Just because you can access the naming or directory service through JNDI doesn't give the information necessary to find the root of your specific context.

- It can seem like driving a tack with a sledgehammer. JNDI requires a directory server to be available. Often the directory server is maintained by a separate organization, which may not see value in maintaining the fact that a guy named Marshall likes to have his email messages display their text in hot pink. No matter what your application, there is likely to be something that should be maintained in a more simple fashion.

Why not have a solution that handles properties in a hierarchical fashion and is independent of the back end storage mechanism? This is what the `Preferences` API gives you.

Item 4: When Information Hiding Hides Too Much

When you are developing a framework that will be used by a large project, it is sometimes helpful to abstract the details of another API from the developers using your framework. For example, in an access control system, it may not be necessary to tell the users of your API that you are using database access control, directory server access control, or your own homegrown method of access control. Instead, you may simply hide the fact of what mechanism you are using and provide a public class (or interface) called `AccessControl`. When you write the implementation class, you will handle the mechanism of access control.

Many times, when API developers abstract the implementation of these classes, sometimes *too much* is abstracted where implementation-specific exceptions are involved. As an example, see Listing 4.1, which is an implementation of an access control mechanism with a Lightweight Directory Access Protocol (LDAP)-based directory server.

```
01: package org.javapitfals.item4;
02: import netscape.ldap.*;
03: public class AccessControl
04: {
05:     private String m_host       = null;
06:     private int    m_port       = 389;
07:     private int    m_ldapversion = 3;
08:     private LDAPConnection m_ld  = null;
09:
10:
// 1 and 2 argument constructors removed for brevity...
20:     public AccessControl(String hostname, int portnumber,
                            int ldapversion)
21:     {
22:         m_host = hostname;
23:         m_port = portnumber;
24:         m_ldapversion = ldapversion;
25:     }
26:     private void createConnection() throws LDAPException
27:     {
28:         m_ld = new LDAPConnection();
29:         m_ld.connect(m_host, m_port);
30:     }
31:     /**
32:      *  The purpose of this function is to authenticate to
33:      *  the Directory Server with credentials.
34:      *
35:      *  @param uname the user name
36:      *  @param pw the password
37:      *  @return successful authentication
38:      */
```

Listing 4.1 A bad example of abstracting details *(continued)*

```
39:      public boolean authenticate(String uname, String pw)
40:      {
41:          boolean result = false;
42:          String dn = "uid=" + uname + ",ou=People,dc=pitfalls.org";
43:          try
44:          {
45:              createConnection();
46:              m_ld.authenticate( m_ldapversion, dn, pw );
47:              result = true;
48:          }
49:          catch ( LDAPException e )
50:          {
51:              //here, result is originally set to false, so do nothing
52:          }
53:          return (result);
54:      }
55:  }
```

Listing 4.1   *(continued)*

In lines 39 through 54 of Listing 4.1, there exists a method called `authenticate()` that returns a boolean value, denoting a successful login to the access control mechanism. In line 42, the username is turned into a LDAP distinguished name, and in lines 45 and 46, the method creates a connection and attempts to authenticate the user. If an `LDAPException` is thrown, the method simply returns false.

This is a good example of how ignoring exceptions for the purpose of hiding detail can cause hours and hours of pain for developers using this code. Of course, this class compiles fine. If the infrastructure is in place for this example (network connectivity, a directory server, the correct username and password), the method will return a boolean true value, and everything will work correctly. However, if there is another problem, such as a directory server problem or network connectivity problems, it will return false. How does the implementer using this API handle the problem or know what the problem is? The original API used by this class throws an `LDAPException`, but the authenticate method in listing 4.1 simply ignores it and returns false.

What is the API developer of this class to do? First of all, a simple design change to use an interface that has the `authenticate()` method could be used along with a creational design pattern. This way, multiple implementation classes could be written (`LDAPAccessControl`, `DatabaseAccessControl`, etc.) that can realize this interface, depending on which mechanism we are using. The developer using the API would still not need to know the internals but would have to handle an exception thrown by that method, as shown in the code segment below.

```
public interface iAccessControl
{
  public boolean authenticate(String user, String passwd) throws
      AccessException;
}
```

The inclusion of a new exception brings up another possible pitfall, however. We have created a new AccessException class because we do not want the API user to have to handle exceptions such as LDAPException that are dependent on our hidden implementation. In the past, developers have handled this in a way shown in Listing 4.2.

```
01:    public boolean authenticate(String uname, String pw)
       throws AccessException
02:    {
03:        boolean result = false;
04:        String dn = "uid=" + uname + ",ou=People,dc=pitfalls.org";
05:        try
06:        {
07:            createConnection();
08:            m_ld.authenticate( m_ldapversion, dn, pw );
09:            result = true;
10:        }
11:        catch ( LDAPException e )
12:        {
13:            throw new AccessException(e.getMessage());
14:        }
15:        return (result);
16:    }
17: }
```

Listing 4.2 Losing information with a new exception

On line 13 of Listing 4.2, we throw a new AccessException class to hide the LDAP-specific exception from the API user. Unfortunately, sometimes this complicates debugging because we lose a lot of information about the original cause of the exception, which was contained in our original LDAPException. For example, perhaps there was an actual bug in the LDAP API we are using. We lose a vast majority of debugging information by discarding the "causative exception," which was LDAPException in our example.

Prior to JDK 1.4, situations like these presented quite a few problems for debugging. Thankfully, JDK 1.4 released much-needed enhancements to allow "chained exceptions." Changes to the java.lang.Throwable class can be seen in Table 4.1, and the implementation of Throwable.printStackTrace() was also changed to show the entire "causal" chain for debugging purposes. As you can see by looking at Table 4.1, Throwable classes can now be associated as the "cause" for other Throwable classes.

Table 4.1   New Chained Exception Capabilities Added to Throwable in JDK 1.4

METHOD	DESCRIPTION
`public Throwable getCause()`	Returns the cause of this throwable or null if the cause is nonexistent or unknown. (The cause is the throwable that caused this throwable to get thrown.)
`public Throwable initCause(Throwable c)`	Initializes the cause of this throwable to the specified value. (The cause is the throwable that caused this throwable to get thrown.)
`public Throwable(Throwable cause)`	Constructs a new throwable with the specified cause.
`public Throwable(String message, Throwable cause)`	Constructs a new throwable with the specified detail message and cause.

Of course, `java.lang.Exception` and `java.lang.Error` are subclasses of `Throwable`, so now we can make minor adjustments to our code, passing in the cause of the exception to our new `AccessException` class. This is seen in Listing 4.3.

```
01:    public boolean authenticate(String uname, String pw)
       throws AccessException
02:    {
03:      boolean result = false;
04:      String dn = "uid=" + uname + ",ou=People,dc=pitfalls.org";
05:        try
06:        {
07:            createConnection();
08:            m_ld.authenticate( m_ldapversion, dn, pw );
09:            result = true;
10:        }
11:        catch ( LDAPException e )
12:        {
13:            throw new AccessException(e);
14:        }
15:        return (result);
16:    }
17:  }
```

Listing 4.3   Modifying `authenticate()`, passing causality

Listing 4.3 shows a simple way to handle our exception without losing information. Finally, Listing 4.4 shows the resulting class that replaces the listing in 4.1. As you can see in line 3 of Listing 4.4, we create a class that implements our `iAccessControl` interface, and we have modified our `authenticate()` method to throw an `AccessException`, passing the causal exception to the constructor in lines 39 to 55.

```
01: package org.javapitfals.item4;
02: import netscape.ldap.*;
03: public class LDAPAccessControl implements iAccessControl
04: {
05:     private String m_host       = null;
06:     private int    m_port       = 389;
07:     private int    m_ldapversion = 3;
08:     private LDAPConnection m_ld  = null;
09:
10:
11:     public LDAPAccessControl(String hostname)
12:     {
13:         this(hostname, 389, 3);
14:     }
15:
16:     public LDAPAccessControl(String hostname, int portnumber)
17:     {
18:         this(hostname, portnumber, 3);
19:     }
20:     public LDAPAccessControl(String hostname, int portnumber,
                                 int ldapversion)
21:     {
22:         m_host = hostname;
23:         m_port = portnumber;
24:         m_ldapversion = ldapversion;
25:     }
26:     private void createConnection() throws LDAPException
27:     {
28:         m_ld = new LDAPConnection();
29:         m_ld.connect(m_host, m_port);
30:     }
31:     /**
32:      *  The purpose of this function is to authenticate to
33:      *  the Directory Server with credentials.
34:      *
35:      *  @param uname the user name
36:      *  @param pw the password
37:      *  @return successful authentication
```

Listing 4.4 The better implementation *(continued)*

```
38:      */
39:      public boolean authenticate(String uname, String pw)
40:      throws AccessException
41:      {
42:          boolean result = false;
43:          String dn = "uid=" + uname + ",ou=People,dc=pitfalls.org";
44:          try
45:          {
46:              createConnection();
47:              m_ld.authenticate( m_ldapversion, dn, pw );
48:              result = true;
49:          }
50:          catch ( LDAPException e )
51:          {
52:              throw new AccessException(e);
53:          }
54:          return (result);
55:      }
56:  }
```

Listing 4.4   *(continued)*

This pitfall showed the traps that can present themselves when you try to hide the implementation details when creating an API for use by other developers. The key points that you should keep in mind are as follows:

- Take advantage of interfaces when hiding your implementation details.

- Be wary of not handling exceptions properly. Instead of returning a value from a method (such as false or null), think about the cause of your returning these values. If there could be multiple causes, throw an exception.

- Instead of taking some information from one exception and placing it a new exception, take advantage of the new JDK 1.4 changes to Throwable and add the original exception to your new exception.

Item 5: Avoiding Granularity Pitfalls in java.util.logging

The release of J2SDK 1.4 brought us a new logging API—java.util.logging. For those of us who have been frustrated by our own implementations of logging over the years, this can be a powerful package that comes out of the box with the J2SE. An application can create a logger to log information, and several handlers (or objects that "log" the data) can send logging information to the outside world (over a network, to a file, to a console, etc.) Loggers and handlers can filter out information, and handlers can use Formatter objects to format the resulting output of the Handler object.

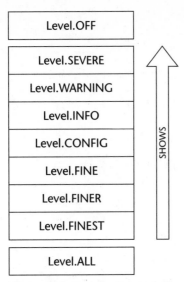

Figure 5.1 Levels of granularity.

At first glance, adding a logging solution into your application looks incredibly easy and quite intuitive. When you start changing the granularity of logging, however, there are some potential pitfalls that lie in your path. Figure 5.1 shows the levels of granularity from the class `java.util.logging.Level`, with the lowest level of granularity being `Level.FINEST`. The key point to know is that when a logger is set to show messages at a level of granularity, it will show messages labeled at that level and above. For example, a logger set to the `FINEST` level of granularity will show all messages labeled `Level.FINEST` and above in Figure 5.1. When a logger is set to show messages at `Level.INFO`, it will show messages labeled `Label.INFO`, `Label.WARNING`, and `Label.SEVERE`. Of course, as Figure 5.1 shows, the `Level` class also includes "ALL" for logging all messages and "OFF" for logging no messages.

A first attempt at using this log package, experimenting with levels of granularity, can be shown in Listing 5.1.

```
01: package org.javapitfalls.item5;
02:
03: import java.io.*;
04: import java.util.logging.*;
05:
06:  public class BadLoggerExample1
07:  {
08:     private Logger m_log = null;
09:
10:     public BadLoggerExample1(Level l)
```

Listing 5.1 BadLoggerExample 1 *(continued)*

```
11:     {
12:
13:
14:       //This creates the logger!
15:       m_log =
Logger.getLogger("org.pitfalls.BadLoggerExample1.logger");
16:
17:         m_log.setLevel(1);
18:     }
19:     /*
20:      * This tests the levels of granularity!
21:      */
22:     public void test()
23:     {
24:         System.out.println("The level for the log is: "
25:                             + m_log.getLevel());
26:         m_log.finest("This is a test for finest");
27:         m_log.finer("This is a test for finer");
28:         m_log.fine("This is a test for fine");
29:         m_log.info("This is a test for info");
30:         m_log.warning("This is a warning test");
31:         m_log.severe("This is a severe test");
32:     }
33:
34:     /*
35:      * A very simple example, where we will optionally
36:      * pass in the level of granularity to our application
37:      */
38:     public static void main(String[] args)
39:     {
40:         Level loglevel = Level.INFO;
41:
42:         if ( args.length !=0 )
43:         {
44:             if ( args[0].equals("ALL") )
45:             {
46:                 loglevel = Level.ALL;
47:             }
48:             else if ( args[0].equals("FINE") )
49:             {
50:                 loglevel = Level.FINE;
51:             }
52:             else if ( args[0].equals("FINEST") )
53:             {
54:                 loglevel = Level.FINEST;
55:             }
56:             else if ( args[0].equals("WARNING") )
57:             {
58:                 loglevel = Level.WARNING;
```

Listing 5.1   *(continued)*

```
59:            }
60:            else if ( args[0].equals("SEVERE") )
61:            {
62:                loglevel = Level.SEVERE;
63:            }
64:
65:        }
66:        BadLoggerExample1 logex = new BadLoggerExample1(loglevel);
67:        logex.test();
68:    }
69:}
```

Listing 5.1   *(continued)*

In Listing 5.1, you can see that we create a simple logger and call a test function that tests the levels of granularity. In the `main()` method of this class, we pass it an argument pertaining to the level of granularity (`ALL`, `FINE`, `FINEST`, `WARNING`, `SEVERE`), or if there is no argument, the loglevel defaults to `INFO`. If you run this program without an argument, you will see the following printed to standard error, which is correct output:

```
The level for the log is: INFO
Feb 16, 2002 3:42:08 PM org.pitfalls.logging.BadLoggerExample1 test
INFO: This is a test for info
Feb 16, 2002 3:42:08 PM org.pitfalls.logging.BadLoggerExample1 test
WARNING: This is a warning test
Feb 16, 2002 3:42:08 PM org.pitfalls.logging.BadLoggerExample1 test
SEVERE: This is a severe test
```

Additionally, if you pass SEVERE as an argument, you will see the following correct output:

```
The level for the log is: SEVERE
Feb 16, 2002 3:42:09 PM org.pitfalls.logging.BadLoggerExample1 test
SEVERE: This is a severe test
```

However, if you run this program with the argument `FINE`, you will see the following:

```
The level for the log is: FINE
Feb 16, 2002 3:42:10 PM org.pitfalls.logging.BadLoggerExample1 test
INFO: This is a test for info
Feb 16, 2002 3:42:10 PM org.pitfalls.logging.BadLoggerExample1 test
WARNING: This is a warning test
Feb 16, 2002 3:42:10 PM org.pitfalls.logging.BadLoggerExample1 test
SEVERE: This is a severe test
```

What happened? Where are the "fine" messages? Is something wrong with the Logger? We set the level of granularity to FINE, but it still acts as if its level is INFO. We know that is wrong, because we printed out the level with the Logger's getLevel() method. Let us add a FileHandler to our example, so that it will write the log to a file, and see if we see the same output. Listing 5.2 shows the BadLoggerExample2, where we add a FileHandler to test this. On lines 20 and 21 of Listing 5.2, we create a new FileHandler to write to the log file log.xml, and we add that handler to our Logger object.

```
01: package org.javapitfalls.item5;
02:
03: import java.io.*;
04: import java.util.logging.*;
05:
06: public class BadLoggerExample2
07: {
08:     private Logger m_log = null;
09:
10:     public BadLoggerExample2(Level l)
11:     {
12:        FileHandler fh = null;
13:
14:       //This creates the logger!
15:        m_log =
Logger.getLogger("org.pitfalls.BadLoggerExample2.logger");
16:
17:       //Try to create a FileHandler that writes it to file!
18:        try
19:        {
20:            fh = new FileHandler("log.xml");
21:            m_log.addHandler(fh);
22:        }
23:        catch ( IOException ioexc )
24:        {
25:            ioexc.printStackTrace();
26:        }
27:
28:        m_log.setLevel(l);
29:     }
30:     /*
31:      * This tests the levels of granularity!
32:      */
33:     public void test()
34:     {
35:         System.out.println("The level for the log is: "
```

Listing 5.2   BadLoggerExample2.java *(continued)*

```
36:                           + m_log.getLevel());
37:         m_log.finest("This is a test for finest");
38:         m_log.finer("This is a test for finer");
39:         m_log.fine("This is a test for fine");
40:         m_log.info("This is a test for info");
41:         m_log.warning("This is a warning test");
42:         m_log.severe("This is a severe test");
43:     }
44:
45:     /*
46:      * A very simple example, where we will optionally
47:      * pass in the level of granularity to our application
48:      */
49:     public static void main(String[] args)
50:     {
51:         Level loglevel = Level.INFO;
52:
53:         if ( args.length !=0 )
54:         {
55:             if ( args[0].equals("ALL") )
56:             {
57:                 loglevel = Level.ALL;
58:             }
59:             else if ( args[0].equals("FINE") )
60:             {
61:                 loglevel = Level.FINE;
62:             }
63:             else if ( args[0].equals("FINEST") )
64:             {
65:                 loglevel = Level.FINEST;
66:             }
67:             else if ( args[0].equals("WARNING") )
68:             {
69:                 loglevel = Level.WARNING;
70:             }
71:             else if ( args[0].equals("SEVERE") )
72:             {
73:                 loglevel = Level.SEVERE;
74:             }
75:
76:         }
77:         BadLoggerExample2 logex = new BadLoggerExample2(loglevel);
78:         logex.test();
79:     }
80: }
```

Listing 5.2   *(continued)*

This time, we see the same output as before when we pass in the FINE argument, but a log file is generated, showing the XML output, shown in Listing 5.3! Now, standard error prints out the same seemingly incorrect thing as before, not showing the FINE test, and the FileHandler seems to write the correct output. What is going on? Why does the file output not match the output written to standard error?

```xml
<?xml version="1.0" encoding="windows-1252" standalone="no"?>
<!DOCTYPE log SYSTEM "logger.dtd">
<log>
<record>
  <date>2002-02-16T15:51:00</date>
  <millis>1013892660502</millis>
  <sequence>0</sequence>
  <logger>org.pitfalls.BadLoggerExample2.logger</logger>
  <level>FINE</level>
  <class>org.pitfalls.logging.BadLoggerExample2</class>
  <method>test</method>
  <thread>10</thread>
  <message>This is a test for fine</message>
</record>
<record>
  <date>2002-02-16T15:51:00</date>
  <millis>1013892660522</millis>
  <sequence>1</sequence>
  <level>INFO</level>
... <logger> <class>, <method> and <thread> elements same as above ...
  <message>This is a test for info</message>
</record>
<record>
  <date>2002-02-16T15:51:00</date>
  <millis>1013892660612</millis>
  <sequence>2</sequence>
  <level>WARNING</level>
  <message>This is a warning test</message>
</record>
<record>
  <date>2002-02-16T15:51:00</date>
  <millis>1013892660622</millis>
  <sequence>3</sequence>
  <level>SEVERE</level>
  <message>This is a severe test</message>
</record>
</log>
```

Listing 5.3 XML-formatted output from FileHandler

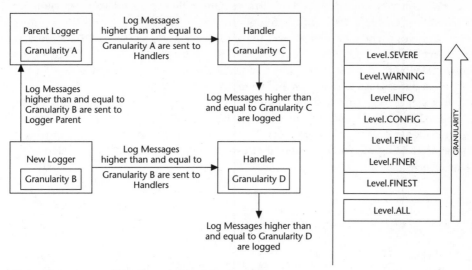

Figure 5.2   Logger/handler relationship diagram.

This behavior is quite strange. What happened? There are actually three things that we need to understand in order to understand this strange behavior:

Default Configurations of Loggers and Handlers.   Loggers and handlers have default configurations, read from a preference file in your JRE's lib directory. A key thing to understand is that granularities may be set for each, using the `setLevel()` method.

Inheritance of Loggers.   Another key thing to understand about the logging API is that each logger has a parent, and all data sent to a logger will go to its parent as well. The top parent is always the Root Logger, and you can create an inheritance tree descending from the Root Logger. In our initial example in Listing 5.1, we did not set a handler, but we still had output. Why? The reason is the Root Logger had a `ConsoleHandler`, whose default content level is `Level.INFO`. You can disable sending log messages to your parent's handler by calling the `setUseParentHandlers(false)` on the `Logger` class.

The Relationship between Handlers and Loggers.   As we mentioned before, there are default levels of handlers. By default, all `ConsoleHandlers` log at the `Level.INFO` level, and all `FileHandlers` log at the `Level.ALL` level. The logger itself can set its level, and you can also set the level of the handlers. The key is that the level of the handler can never show a lower level of granularity than the logger itself. For example, if the logger's level is set to `Level.INFO`, the attached handlers will only see `Level.INFO` levels and above (from our diagram in Figure 5.1). In our example in Listing 5.2, we set our logger level to `Level.FINE`, and because the `FileHandler`'s level was the default level (`Level.ALL`), it only saw what the logger was able to pass through (`FINE` and below).

Confusing? We have presented this graphically in Figure 5.2 for your convenience. In our earlier example tests with BadLoggerExample1.java in Listing 5.1, everything seemed to work when we set the level to `Level.INFO` and `Level.SEVERE`, because those levels were higher than `Level.INFO`, the default level for the parent logger. However, when we set the level to `Level.FINE`, the parent's logger's handler was only passed messages higher than and equal to `Level.INFO`.

Luckily, it is very simple to set the levels for your handlers and loggers with the `setLevel()` method, and it is possible to not send messages to your logger's parent with the logger's `setUseParentsHandlers(false)` method. Listing 5.4 shows our changes to Listing 5.2, where we modify the constructor to set all of the handlers at the same level.

```
10:     public GoodLoggerExample(Level 1)
11:     {
12:         FileHandler fh = null;
13:         ConsoleHandler ch = new ConsoleHandler();
14:
15:        //This creates the logger!
16:         m_log =
Logger.getLogger("org.pitfalls.GoodLoggerExample.logger");
17:         m_log.addHandler(ch);
18:        //Try to create a FileHandler that writes it to file!
19:        try
20:        {
21:            fh = new FileHandler("log.xml");
22:            m_log.addHandler(fh);
23:        }
24:        catch ( IOException ioexc )
25:        {
26:            ioexc.printStackTrace();
27:        }
28:
29:        /* This will set everything to the same level! */
30:        m_log.setLevel(1);
31:        m_log.setUseParentHandlers(false);
32:        fh.setLevel(1);
33:        ch.setLevel(1);
34:     }
```

Listing 5.4   Better constructor—GoodLoggerExample.java

In Listing 5.4, we want to create our own `ConsoleHandler` to log user-friendly messages to standard error, and we will continue to have our own `FileHandler` to write XML messages to file. On line 13, we instantiate a new `ConsoleHandler`, and on line 17, we add it to our logger. Finally, lines 29 to 33 fix the rest: we set the level of the logger (and every handler) to the same level, and we set our logger to not send messages to our parent's handler. The result of this program is the expected output.

Understanding the relationships of loggers and handlers and levels of granularity, shown in Figure 5.2, is very important. Our examples in this pitfall were created to give you an understanding of these relationships, and often, you will not want the same levels of granularity for every handler. Most of the time, logs to the console will be "user-friendly" warning messages, and log files may be debugging information for programmers and system administrators. The fact that you can create your own handlers, and set your logging levels at runtime, is very powerful. Studying this pitfall should lead to a better understanding of the `java.util.logging` package.

Item 6: When Implementations of Standard APIs Collide

Over the past three years, a plethora of XML processing software packages were released. First there were proprietary APIs, and then as the SAX and DOM standards evolved, vendors developed Java toolkits for developers to use. Developers began writing programs with these APIs, and as the standards evolved, you changed your code. As different toolkits used different levels of DOM compliancy, and as you integrated more software into your baseline, you had to go through your entire codebase, trying to determine which DOM API was needed for which application, and trying to determine if two modules using different levels of DOM compliancy could run together in the same application, since both used the `org.w3c.dom.*` classes, but some were based on different underlying implementations and different levels of DOM compliancy. If you started using one implementation of the DOM and later switched to another implementation of the DOM, sometimes your code needed to be tweaked. If you were one of the early adopters of processing XML in Java, you know our pain.

The release of JDK 1.4 brought a little complexity to the issue, because classes such as `org.w3c.dom.*` and `org.xml.sax.*` are now in the standard runtime environment, and thus read before your classpath which is chock full of your favorite XML JAR files. Because of this, if you use a later implementation of SAX or DOM than the classes in the JDK, or if you use a method that is implementation-specific, you may run into problems. A good example can be seen in Listing 6.1, ScheduleSwitcher.java. Here we simply parse an XML "schedule file," with an example schedule shown in Listing 6.2.

```
001: package org.javapitfalls.item6;
002: import org.w3c.dom.*;
003: import javax.xml.parsers.*;
004: :
005: /**
006:  * A simple class that demonstrates different functionality
007: * between DOM implementations
008: */
009: public class ScheduleSwitcher
010: {
011:   /* The DOM document loaded in memory */
```

Listing 6.1 ScheduleSwitcher.java *(continued)*

```
012:    Document m_doc = null;
013:    public ScheduleSwitcher(String filename)
014:    {
015:      /* Parse a file */
016:      try
017:      {
018:        DocumentBuilderFactory factory =
019:        DocumentBuilderFactory.newInstance();
020:        DocumentBuilder builder = factory.newDocumentBuilder();
021:        m_doc = builder.parse(filename);
022:      }
023:      catch ( Exception e )
024:      {
025:        System.err.println("Error processing " +
026:                              filename + "." +
027:                              "Stack trace follows:");
028:        e.printStackTrace();
029:      }
030:    }
031:
032:    /*
033:     * A very simple method that switches values of
034:     * days in an XML document and prints it out.
035:     *
036:     * @param a the value for one day
037:     * @param b the value for another day
038:     * @param keep a boolean value, designating if you
039:     *        want to keep this version of the DOM tree.
040:     */
041:    public void showSwitchedDays(String a , String b,
042:                                    boolean keep)
043:    {
044:      Document newdoc = null;
045:
046:      if ( m_doc == null )
047:      {
048:        System.out.println("Error - no document.. ");
049:        return;
050:      }
051:
052:      /**
053:       * If the keep variable was set, do the manipulation
054:       * to the instance variable m_doc.. Otherwise, just
055:       * do the manipulation of the copy of the tree.
056:       *
057:       */
058:      if ( !keep )
059:        newdoc = (Document)m_doc.cloneNode(true);
060:      else
```

Listing 6.1   *(continued)*

```
061:        newdoc = m_doc;
062:
063:      /* Use the DOM API to switch days */
064:      NodeList nl = newdoc.getElementsByTagName("day");
065:      int len = nl.getLength();
066:      for ( int i = 0; i < len; i++ )
067:      {
068:
069:        Element e = (Element)nl.item(i);
070:
071:        if ( e.getAttribute("name").equals(a) )
072:        {
073:          e.setAttribute("name",b);
074:        } else if ( e.getAttribute("name").equals(b) )
075:        {
076:          e.setAttribute("name", a);
077:        }
078:      }
079:
080:      System.out.println(
081:        newdoc.getDocumentElement().toString()
082:        );
083:
084:    }
085:
086:    /* Print out the DOM Tree */
087:    public void showDays()
088:    {
089:      System.out.println(
090:        m_doc.getDocumentElement().toString()
091:        );
092:    }
093:
094:    public static void main(String[] args)
095:    {
096:      if ( args.length < 1 )
097:      {
098:        System.err.println("Usage: Argument must be the " +
099:                           "filename of an XML file");
100:        System.exit(-1);
101:      }
102:      String filename = args[0];
103:
104:      ScheduleSwitcher switcher = new ScheduleSwitcher(filename);
105:
106:      System.out.println("\nIf you switched " +
107:                         " the Wed & Thurs meetings ");
108:      System.out.println("this is what it would " +
109:                         "look like:\n*******");
```

Listing 6.1   *(continued)*

```
110:
111:     switcher.showSwitchedDays("wednesday", "thursday", false);
112:
113:     System.out.println("\nHere is the current " +
114:                         " schedule:\n********");
115:     switcher.showDays();
116:
117:   }
118: }
```

Listing 6.1   *(continued)*

In our simple example, we have written a method, `showSwitchedDays()`, on line 41 of Listing 6.1, that switches the name attribute on the `<day/>` tag of an XML file by manipulating the DOM and prints the resulting XML file to standard out. If the boolean value `keep` is true, then the DOM manipulation affects the DOM tree instance variable. If the Boolean value `keep` is false, then the method simply prints out a copy of the switched schedule but keeps the original DOM in memory. On lines 106-109 of Listing 6.1, we tell the class to print the meetings as if Wednesdays and Thursdays were switched, but to not permanently alter the schedule. Listing 6.3 shows the output of this program using the XML file in Listing 6.2, when we ran this with JDK 1.3.1, and implementations of the DOM in the crimson.jar file.

```xml
<?xml version="1.0"?>
<meetings>
 <day name="wednesday">
  <meeting desc="romans">
    <member name="ben"/><member name="billy"/><member name="chuck"/>
    <member name="dan"/><member name="keith"/><member name="kevin"/>
    <member name="matt d."/><member name="matt v."/><member
name="rich"/>
    <member name="todd"/>
  </meeting>
 </day>
 <day name="thursday">
  <meeting desc="all">
    <member name="avery"/><member name="catherine"/><member
name="dawn"/>
    <member name="doverly"/><member name="gwen"/><member name="heidi"/>
    <member name="holly"/><member name="jenny"/><member name="patrice"/>
    <member name="sandy b."/><member name="sandy c."/><member
name="sarah"/>
    <member name="shelly"/><member name="suzanne"/>
  </meeting>
 </day>
</meetings>
```

Listing 6.2   XML schedule file (schedule.xml)

```
C:\pitfalls\week5>c:\jdk1.3.1\bin\java -classpath .;crimson.jar;jaxp.jar
ScheduleSwitcher schedule.xml

If you switched the Wed & Thurs meetings,
this is what it would look like:
*******
<meetings>
 <day name="thursday">
  <meeting desc="romans">
   <member name="ben" /><member name="billy" /><member name="chuck" />
   <member name="dan" /><member name="keith" /><member name="kevin" />
   <member name="matt d." /><member name="matt v."
/><member name="rich" />
   <member name="todd" />
  </meeting>
 </day>
 <day name="wednesday">
  <meeting desc="all">
   <member name="avery"/><member name="catherine"
/><member name="dawn" />
   <member name="doverly"/><member name="gwen" /><member name="heidi" />
   <member name="holly"/><member name="jenny"/><member name="patrice"/>
   <member name="sandy b."/><member name="sandy c."/><member
name="sarah" />
   <member name="shelly" /><member name="suzanne" />
  </meeting>
 </day>
</meetings>

Here is the current schedule:
********
<meetings>
 <day name="wednesday">
  <meeting desc="romans">
    <member name="ben" /><member name="billy" /><member name="chuck" />
    <member name="dan" /><member name="keith" /><member name="kevin" />
    <member name="matt d." /><member name="matt v." /><member
name="rich" />
    <member name="todd" />
  </meeting>
 </day>
 <day name="thursday">
  <meeting desc="all">
   <member name="avery" /><member name="catherine"
/><member name="dawn" />
   <member name="doverly" /><member name="gwen"
/><member name="heidi" />
   <member name="holly" /><member name="jenny"
/><member name="patrice" />
```

Listing 6.3   Output with JDK 1.3 and DOM implementation *(continued)*

```
   <member name="sandy b."/><member name="sandy c."/><member
name="sarah" />
   <member name="shelly" /><member name="suzanne" />
  </meeting>
 </day>
</meetings>
```

Listing 6.3   *(continued)*

Listing 6.3 has the expected output, and it ran correctly. As you can see, the "Wednesday" and "Thursday" meetings were switched, but when the final schedule was printed, the original DOM tree was printed out. However, when we upgraded our application to JDK 1.4, we ran into problems. The result of running this in JDK 1.4 is shown in Listing 6.4. As you can see, what ran fine in an earlier version of the JDK now throws an exception. When we call `cloneNode()` on `org.w3c.dom.Document` on line 27, we get a "HIERARCHY_REQUEST_ERR:" message! Looking into the documentation on the `cloneNode()` method, it is inherited from `org.w3c.dom.Node`, and the documentation says that cloning `Document`, `DocumentType`, `Entity`, and `Notation` nodes is implementation dependent.

```
C:\pitfalls\week5>java -classpath . ScheduleSwitcher schedule.xml


If you switched the Wed & Thurs meetings,
this is what it would look like:
*******
org.apache.crimson.tree.DomEx: HIERARCHY_REQUEST_ERR: This node isn't
allowed there. at
org.apache.crimson.tree.XmlDocument.changeNodeOwner(XmlDocument.java:115
6)
at
org.apache.crimson.tree.XmlDocument.changeNodeOwner(XmlDocument.java:117
7)
at org.apache.crimson.tree.XmlDocument.cloneNode(XmlDocument.java:1101)
        at ScheduleSwitcher.showSwitchedDays(ScheduleSwitcher.java:27)
                at ScheduleSwitcher.main(ScheduleSwitcher.java:68)
Exception in thread "main"
```

Listing 6.4   Output with JDK 1.4, with built-in DOM

So what should we do in a situation like this? Since there are many implementations of DOM and SAX APIs, we are bound to run into these problems. Added to this dilemma is the fact that standards and new implementations evolve quickly, and we may want to use newer implementations of these standards before they are integrated into the JDK. Luckily, with the release of JDK 1.4, there is the Endorsed Standards Override Mechanism (ESOM), which is used to replace implementations of these standard classes. Following is the complete list of the packages that can be overriden:

```
javax.rmi.CORBA
org.omg.CORBA, org.omg.CORBA.DynAnyPackage, org.omg.CORBA.ORBPackage,
org.omg.CORBA.portable, org.omg.CORBA.TypeCodePackage, org.omg.CORBA_2_3,
org.omg.CORBA_2_3.portable, org.omg.CosNaming,
org.omg.CosNaming.NamingContextExtPackage,
org.omg.CosNaming.NamingContextPackage, org.omg.Dynamic,
org.omg.DynamicAny, org.omg.DynamicAny.DynAnyFactoryPackage,
org.omg.DynamicAny.DynAnyPackage, org.omg.IOP ,
org.omg.IOP.CodecFactoryPackage, org.omg.IOP.CodecPackage,
org.omg.Messaging,
org.omg.PortableInterceptor,
org.omg.PortableInterceptor.ORBInitInfoPackage, org.omg.PortableServer,
org.omg.PortableServer.CurrentPackage,
org.omg.PortableServer.POAManagerPackage,
org.omg.PortableServer.POAPackage, org.omg.PortableServer.portable,
org.omg.PortableServer.ServantLocatorPackage, org.omg.SendingContext,
org.omg.stub.java.rmi, org.w3c.dom, org.xml.sax, org.xml.sax.ext,
org.xml.sax.helpers
```

As you can see, these include standard classes from the Object Management Group (OMG) as well as the W3C. To take advantage of the ESOM, follow these steps:

1. Create a directory called endorsed in the jre/lib directory.

2. Copy your JAR file implementations of your APIs into that directory.

3. Run your application.

In our simple example, we followed these steps, and the application worked perfectly. It is sometimes difficult to stay away from methods that are implementation-specific—as `Document.cloneNode()` was in this example. Remembering how to override the standards with the use of the ESOM will make your life a lot easier!

Item 7: My Assertions Are Not Gratuitous!

In *Java Pitfalls*, we finished the book by discussing the emerging JSR concerning a Java Assertion Facility. At the time, we suggested a mechanism that would allow an assertion-like facility. As of JDK 1.4, the language now includes an assertion facility.

Many developers do not understand why or how to use assertions, and this has caused them to go widely unused. Some developers use them improperly, causing them to be ineffective or counterproductive to the development effort.

How to Use Assertions

When writing code, we make assumptions all of the time. Assertions are meant to capture those assumptions in the code. By capturing those assumptions, you move closer to implementing a significant concept in quality software: design by contract.

Design by Contract holds there are three concepts embodied in any piece of code: preconditions, postconditions, and invariants. Preconditions involve the assumptions about the state prior to the execution of code. Postconditions involve the assumptions about the state after the execution of the code. Invariants capture the underlying assumptions upon which the execution occurs.

Consider the following method signature:

```
public String lookupPlayer (int number)
```

In this method, I provide a service to look up a player by his number. In explaining this signature, I have already specified a set of assumptions. The first assumption is players do not have numbers greater than 99 (they don't fit on a jersey well, and most teams don't have more than 100 players on their roster). Also, players do not have negative numbers either. Therefore, the preconditions are that we have a number provided that is less than or equal to zero and less than or equal to 99. An invariant is to assume that the list of players and numbers actually exists—that is, it has been initialized and is properly available (note that this action is subject to its own set of assumptions). The assumption on the postcondition is that there will be an actual `String` value returned from the method (and not a null).

How many times have you seen a problem with the code being debugged by a set of `System.out.println()` statements? This is because, essentially, the developer is going back in and creating visibility to check against assumptions that are made in writing the code. This can be relatively painless and easy for the developer who wrote the code—at the time he or she wrote the code. However, this becomes quite painful for others who may not understand what is going on inside the code.

Assertions can be thought of as automatic code checks. By writing assertions, you capture your assumptions, so that an error will be thrown at the incorrect assumption when the code is running. Even if a bug occurs that does not throw an `Assertion-Error`, they still enable the developer to eliminate many possible assumptions as causes of error.

There are really four conditions you should meet in order to determine that you do not need to use assertions:

- You wrote and maintain all of the code in question.
- You will always maintain every piece of that code.
- You have analyzed to perfection all of the different scenarios that your code may experience through some method like a formal code proof.
- You like and can afford to operate without a net.

With the exception of the last condition, if you have done all of these, you have already realized that you need some assertionlike capability. You probably have already littered your code with `System.out.println()` or `log()` statements trying to give yourself places to start like that demonstrated in Listing 7.1.

```
01: package org.javapitfalls.item7;
02:
03: public class AssertionExample {
04:
05: public AssertionExample() { }
06:
07: private void printLeague (String abbreviation) {
09:   if (abbreviation.equals("AL")) {
10:
11:         System.out.println("I am in the American League!");
12:
13:   } else if (abbreviation.equals("NL")) {
14:
15:         System.out.println("I am in the National League!");
16:
17:   } else {
19:         // I should never get here...
20:         assert false;
22:   }
23: }
24:
25: public static void main (String [] args) {
27:   String al = "AL";
28:   String nl = "NL";
29:   String il = "IL";
31:   AssertionExample myExample = new AssertionExample();
33:   myExample.printLeague(al);
34:   myExample.printLeague(il);
35:   myExample.printLeague(nl);
37: }
39: }
```

Listing 7.1   AssertionExample.java

So, we compile this code and the following happens:

```
C:\pitfallsBook\#7>javac AssertionExample.java
AssertionExample.java:20: warning: as of release 1.4, assert is a
keyword, and may not be used as an identifier
              assert false ;
              ^
AssertionExample.java:20: not a statement
              assert false ;
```

```
                      ^
AssertionExample.java:20: ';' expected
                assert false ;
2 errors
1 warning
```

What happened? I thought assertions were supported in JDK 1.4! I am using JDK 1.4. Well, as it turns out, for backward compatibility purposes, you have to specify a flag in order to compile source with assertions in it.

So, you would want to compile it like this instead:

```
javac -source 1.4 AssertionExample.java
```

Now that I have successfully compiled my example, here is what I do to run it:

```
C:\pitfallsBook\#7>java -cp . org.javapitfalls.item7.AssertionExample
I am in the American League!
I am in the National League!
```

Notice that it didn't throw an `AssertionError` when I passed in the "IL" abbreviation. This is because I didn't enable assertions. The requirement to enable assertions is so that your code will not have any performance defect by having the assertions within the code when you choose not to use them. When assertions are not switched on, they are effectively the same as empty statements.

```
C:\pitfallsBook\#7>java -ea -cp .
org.javapitfalls.item7.AssertionExample
I am in the American League!
Exception in thread "main" java.lang.AssertionError
        at org.javapitfalls.item7.AssertionExample.printLeague(Unknown
Source)
        at org.javapitfalls.item7.AssertionExample.main(Unknown Source)
```

Now the assertion is thrown, but it is not very descriptive as to which assertion was the cause of the problem. In this simple example, this is not a problem; it is still very easy to tell which assertion caused the problem. However, with many assertions (as is good practice), we need to better distinguish between assertions. So if we change line 20 to read

```
assert false : "What baseball league are you playing in?";
```

this will give us a more descriptive response:

```
C:\pitfallsBook\#7>java -ea -cp .
org.javapitfalls.item7.AssertionExample
I am in the American League!
```

```
Exception in thread "main" java.lang.AssertionError: What baseball
league are you playing in?
        at org.javapitfalls.item7.AssertionExample.printLeague(Unknown
Source)
        at org.javapitfalls.item7.AssertionExample.main(Unknown Source)
```

An important thing to note is that printLeague() is declared private. While the example was meant to show assertions to mark unreachable conditions, it was declared private in order to avoid confusion about an important point: *You should never use assertions to do precondition checks for public methods.* When assertions are turned off, you will not receive the benefit of any precondition checking. Furthermore, the AssertionError is a relatively simple methodology for returning errors, and more sophisticated mechanisms like typed exceptions would serve the cause better.

In Listing 7.2, we show how to use assertions to check postconditions.

```
01: package org.javapitfalls.item7;
02:
03: public class AnotherAssertionExample {
05: private double taxRate;
06:
07: public AnotherAssertionExample(double tax) {
09:   taxRate = tax;
11: }
12:
13: private double returnMoney (double salary) {
15:   double originalSalary = salary;
17:   if (salary > 10000) salary = salary * (1 - taxRate);
19:   if (salary > 25000) salary = salary * (1 - taxRate);
21:   if (salary > 50000) salary = salary * (1 - taxRate);
23:   assert salary > 0 : "They can't take more than you have?";
25:   assert salary <= originalSalary : "You can't come out ahead!";
27:   return salary;
29: }
30:
31: public static void main (String [] args) {
33:   AnotherAssertionExample myExample = new
AnotherAssertionExample(.3);
34:   System.out.println("Tax Rate of 30%\n");
35:   System.out.println("Salary of 5000:"+myExample.returnMoney(5000));
36:   System.out.println("Salary of
24000:"+myExample.returnMoney(24000));
37:   System.out.println("Salary of
35000:"+myExample.returnMoney(35000));
38:   System.out.println("Salary of
75000:"+myExample.returnMoney(75000));
39: //      System.out.println("Salary of
75000:"+myExample.returnMoney(-75000));
40:
```

Listing 7.2 AnotherAssertionExample.java *(continued)*

```
41:   myExample = new AnotherAssertionExample(-.3);
42:   System.out.println("\n\nTax Rate of -30%\n");
43:   System.out.println("Salary of 5000:"+myExample.returnMoney(5000));
44:   System.out.println("Salary of                                    ↩
24000:"+myExample.returnMoney(24000));
45:   System.out.println("Salary of                                    ↩
35000:"+myExample.returnMoney(35000));
47: }
49: }
```

Listing 7.2 *(continued)*

This shows how to check postconditions with an assertion. Here is the output from this example:

```
C:\pitfallsBook\#7>java -ea -cp .
org.javapitfalls.item7.AnotherAssertionExample

Tax Rate of 30%
Salary of 5000:5000.0
Salary of 24000:16800.0
Salary of 35000:24500.0
Salary of 75000:36750.0

Tax Rate of -30%

Salary of 5000:5000.0
Exception in thread "main" java.lang.AssertionError: You can't come out
ahead!
        at
org.javapitfalls.item7.AnotherAssertionExample.returnMoney(Unknown Source)
        at org.javapitfalls.item7.AnotherAssertionExample.main(Unknown
Source)
```

You can see that there are two assertions about the postconditions. First, we assert that you cannot return with less than zero money, and then we assert that you cannot return with more money than you started. There are examples of how to break both assertions: a negative salary (commented out) and a negative tax rate. The first example is commented out, because execution stops after the assertion error, and we wanted to demonstrate that the second assertion would also work.

Now that we have covered the assertion basics, we will go over some other interesting things about assertions. First, you can enable and disable assertions as desired by specifying them in the switches to the JVM. Here are some more examples:

■ Enable all assertions:

```
java -ea org.javapitfalls.item7.MyClass
```

■ Enable system assertions only:

```
java -esa org.javapitfalls.item7.MyClass
```

- Enable all assertions in the `org.javapitfalls` package and its sub-packages:

  `java -ea:org.javapitfalls org.javapitfalls.item7.MyClass`

- Enable all assertions in the `org.javapitfalls` package and its sub-packages, but disable the ones in `AnotherAssertionExample`:

  `java -ea:org.javapitfalls -da:`
  `org.javapitfalls.item7.AnotherAssertionExample`
  `org.javapitfalls.item7.MyClass`

Also, there are situations where you want to require that assertions be enabled in your class. An example would be if you had some safety-sensitive class that should operate only if the assertions are true (in addition to normal control checking). Listing 7.3 shows our previous example with assertions always on.

```
01: package org.javapitfalls.item7;
02:
03: public class AnotherAssertionExample {
04:
05: static {
06:   boolean assertions = false;
07:   assert assertions = true;
08:
09:   if (assertions==false)
10:         throw new RuntimeException("You must enable assertions
to use this class.");
11: }
12:
13: private double taxRate;
14: // [...] remaining code Identical to listing 7.2
```

Listing 7.3   AnotherAssertionExample.java (modified)

So, if you run this example without assertions enabled, you receive the following message:

```
C:\pitfallsBook\#7>java -cp .
org.javapitfalls.item7.AnotherAssertionExample
Exception in thread "main" java.lang.ExceptionInInitializerError
Caused by: java.lang.RuntimeException: You must enable assertions to use
this class.
  at org.javapitfalls.item7.AnotherAssertionExample.<clinit>(Unknown
Source)
```

In closing, there are a few rules to follow in dealing with assertions:

- DO use assertions to test postconditions on methods.
- DO use assertions to test places where you believe control flow should not execute.
- DO NOT use assertions to test preconditions on public methods.
- DO use assertions to test preconditions on helper methods.
- DO NOT use assertions that affect the normal operation of the code.

Item 8: The Wrong Way to Search a DOM[2]

All well-formed XML files have a tree structure. For example, Listing 8.1 can be represented by a tree with two ADDRESS nodes:

```
01: <?xml version="1.0"?>
02: <!DOCTYPE ADDRESS_BOOK SYSTEM "abml.dtd">
03: <ADDRESS_BOOK>
04:   <ADDRESS>
05:         <NAME>Joe Jones </NAME>
06:         <STREET>4332 Sunny Hill Road </STREET>
07:         <CITY>Fairfax</CITY>
08:         <STATE>VA</STATE>
09:         <ZIP>21220</ZIP>
10:   </ADDRESS>
11:   <ADDRESS>
12:         <NAME>Sterling Software </NAME>
13:         <STREET> 7900 Sudley Road</STREET>
14:         <STREET> Suite 500</STREET>
15:         <CITY>Manassas</CITY>
16:         <STATE>VA </STATE>
17:         <ZIP>20109 </ZIP>
18:   </ADDRESS>
19: </ADDRESS_BOOK>
```

Listing 8.1   myaddresses.xml

The pitfall is assuming the DOM tree will look exactly like your mental picture of the XML document. Let's say we have a task to find the first NAME element of the first ADDRESS. By looking at Listing 8.1, you may say that the third node in the DOM (line 05) is the one we want. Listing 8.2 attempts to find the node in that way.

[2] This pitfall was first printed by *JavaWorld* (www.javaworld.com) in the article, "An API's looks can be deceiving", June 2001, (http://www.javaworld.com/javaworld/jw-06-2001/jw-0622-traps.html?) and is reprinted here with permission. The pitfall has been updated from reader feedback.

```
01: package org.javapitfalls.item8;
02:
03: import javax.xml.parsers.*;
04: import java.io.*;
05: import org.w3c.dom.*;
06:
07: public class BadDomLookup
08: {
09:     public static void main(String args[])
10:     {
11:         try
12:         {
13:             if (args.length < 1)
14:             {
15:                 System.out.println("USAGE: " +
16:              "org.javapitfalls.item8.BadDomLookup xmlfile");
17:                 System.exit(1);
18:             }
19:
20:             DocumentBuilderFactory dbf =
21:                     DocumentBuilderFactory.newInstance();
22:             DocumentBuilder db = dbf.newDocumentBuilder();
23:             Document doc = db.parse(new File(args[0]));
24:
25:             // get first Name of first Address
26:             NodeList nl = doc.getElementsByTagName("ADDRESS");
27:             int count = nl.getLength();
28:             System.out.println("# of \"ADDRESS\" elements: " + count);
29:
30:             if (count > 0)
31:             {
32:                 Node n = nl.item(0);
33:                 System.out.println("This node name is: " +
n.getNodeName());
34:                 // get the NAME node of this ADDRESS node
35:                 Node nameNode = n.getFirstChild();
36:                 System.out.println("This node name is: "
37:                                     + nameNode.getNodeName());
38:             }
39:         } catch (Throwable t)
40:         {
41:             t.printStackTrace();
42:         }
43:     }
44: }
45:
```

Listing 8.2   BadDomLookup.java

The simple program, BadDomLookup, uses the Java API for XML Processing (JAXP) to parse the DOM (this example was tested with both Xerces and Sun's default JAXP parser). After we get the W3C Document object, we retrieve a `NodeList` of `ADDRESS` elements (line 26) and then look to get the first `NAME` element by accessing the first child under `ADDRESS` (line 35).

Upon executing Listing 8.2, we get

```
e:\classes\org\javapitfalls\>java org.javapitfalls ... BadDomLookup  ⤸
myaddresses.xml
# of "ADDRESS" elements: 2
This node name is: ADDRESS
This node name is: #text
```

The result clearly shows that the program fails to accomplish its task. Instead of an `ADDRESS` node, we get a text node. What happened? Unfortunately, the complexity of the DOM implementation is different from our simple conceptual model. The primary difference is that the DOM tree includes text nodes for what is called "ignorable whitespace," which is the whitespace (like a return) between tags. In our example, there is a text node between the `ADDRESS` and the first `NAME` element. The W3C XML specification states, "An XML processor must always pass all characters in a document that are not markup through to the application. A validating XML processor must also inform the application which of these characters constitute white space appearing in element content."[3] To visualize these whitespace nodes, Figure 8.1 displays all the DOM nodes in myaddresses.xml in a JTree.

There are three solutions to this problem, and our rewrite of the program demonstrates two of them. Listing 8.3, GoodDomLookup.java, fixes the problem demonstrated above in two ways.

Figure 8.1   Display of all DOM nodes in myaddresses.xml.

---

[3] *Extensible Markup Language (XML) 1.0* (Second Edition). W3C recommendation; October 6, 2000; http://www.w3.org/TR/REC-xml.

```
001: package org.javapitfalls.item8;
002:
003: import javax.xml.parsers.*;
004: import java.io.*;
005: import org.w3c.dom.*;
006:
007: class DomUtil
008: {
009:     public static boolean isBlank(String buf)
010:     {
011:         if (buf == null)
012:             return false;
013:
014:         int len = buf.length();
015:         for (int i=0; i < len; i++)
016:         {
017:             char c = buf.charAt(i);
018:             if (!Character.isWhitespace(c))
019:                 return false;
020:         }
021:
022:         return true;
023:     }
024:
025:     public static void normalizeDocument(Node n)
026:     {
027:         if (!n.hasChildNodes())
028:             return;
029:
030:         NodeList nl = n.getChildNodes();
031:         for (int i = 0; i < nl.getLength(); i++)
032:         {
033:             Node cn = nl.item(i);
034:             if (cn.getNodeType() == Node.TEXT_NODE &&
035:                 isBlank(cn.getNodeValue()))
036:             {
037:                 n.removeChild(cn);
038:                 i--;
039:             }
040:             else
041:                 normalizeDocument(cn);
042:         }
043:     }
044:
045:     public static Element getFirstChildElement(Element elem)
046:     {
047:         if (!elem.hasChildNodes())
048:             return null;
```

Listing 8.3   GoodDomLookup.java *(continued)*

```
049:
050:        for (Node cn = elem.getFirstChild(); cn != null;
051:            cn = cn.getNextSibling())
052:        {
053:            if (cn.getNodeType() == Node.ELEMENT_NODE)
054:                return (Element) cn;
055:        }
056:
057:        return null;
058:    }
059: }
060:
061: public class GoodDomLookup
062: {
063:    public static void main(String args[])
064:    {
065:        try
066:        {
// ... command line check omitted for brevity ...
073:
074:            DocumentBuilderFactory dbf =
075:                    DocumentBuilderFactory.newInstance();
076:            DocumentBuilder db = dbf.newDocumentBuilder();
077:            Document doc = db.parse(new File(args[0]));
078:
079:            // get first Name of first Address
080:            System.out.println("Method #1: Skip Ignorable White ⮌
space...");
081:            NodeList nl = doc.getElementsByTagName("ADDRESS");
082:            int count = nl.getLength();
083:            System.out.println("# of \"ADDRESS\" elements: " + count);
084:
085:            if (count > 0)
086:            {
087:                Node n = nl.item(0);
088:                System.out.println("This node name is: " + ⮌
n.getNodeName());
089:                // get the NAME node of this ADDRESS node
090:                Node nameNode = ⮌
DomUtil.getFirstChildElement((Element)n);
091:                System.out.println("This node name is: " +
092:                                    nameNode.getNodeName());
093:            }
094:
095:            // get first Name of first Address
096:            System.out.println("Method #2: Normalize document...");
097:            DomUtil.normalizeDocument(doc.getDocumentElement());
098:            // Below is exact code in BadDomLookup
```

Listing 8.3   *(continued)*

```
099:                nl = doc.getElementsByTagName("ADDRESS");
100:                count = nl.getLength();
101:                System.out.println("# of \"ADDRESS\" elements: " +
count);
102:
103:                if (count > 0)
104:                {
105:                    Node n = nl.item(0);
106:                    System.out.println("This node name is: " +
107:                                            n.getNodeName());
108:                    // get the NAME node of this ADDRESS node
109:                    Node nameNode = n.getFirstChild();
110:                    System.out.println("This node name is: " +
111:                                            nameNode.getNodeName());
112:                }
113:
114:          } catch (Throwable t)
115:            {
116:                t.printStackTrace();
117:            }
118:        }
119: }
120:
```

Listing 8.3   *(continued)*

The key class in GoodDomLookup is the DomUtil class that has three methods.
Those three methods solve the DOM lookup problem in two ways. The first method is
to retrieve the first child element (and not the first node) when performing a lookup.
The implementation of the getFirstChildElement() method will skip any intermediate nodes that are not of type ELEMENT_NODE. The second approach to the problem is to eliminate all "blank" text nodes from the document. While both solutions will
work, the second approach may remove some whitespace not considered ignorable.

A run of GoodDomLookup.java gives us the following:

```
e:\classes\org\javapitfalls >java org.javapitfalls.item8.GoodDomLookup
myaddresses.xml
Method #1: Skip Ignorable White space...
# of "ADDRESS" elements: 2
This node name is: ADDRESS
This node name is: NAME
Method #2: Normalize document...
# of "ADDRESS" elements: 2
This node name is: ADDRESS
This node name is: NAME
```

A better way to access nodes in a DOM tree is to use an XPath expression. XPath is a W3C standard for accessing nodes in a DOM tree. Standard API methods for evaluating XPath expressions are part of DOM Level 3. Currently, JAXP supports only DOM Level 2. To demonstrate how easy accessing nodes is via XPath, Listing 8.4 uses the DOM4J open source library (which includes XPath support) to perform the same task as GoodDomLookup.java.

```
01: package org.javapitfalls.item8;
02:
03: import javax.xml.parsers.*;
04: import java.io.*;
05: import org.w3c.dom.*;
06: import org.dom4j.*;
07: import org.dom4j.io.*;
08:
09: public class XpathLookup
10: {
11:     public static void main(String args[])
12:     {
13:         try
14:         {
15:             if (args.length < 1)
16:             {
17:                 System.out.println("USAGE: " +
18:                 "org.javapitfalls.item8.BadDomLookup xmlfile");
19:                 System.exit(1);
20:             }
21:
22:             DocumentBuilderFactory dbf =
23:                     DocumentBuilderFactory.newInstance();
24:             DocumentBuilder db = dbf.newDocumentBuilder();
25:             org.w3c.dom.Document doc = db.parse(new File(args[0]));
26:
27:             DOMReader dr = new DOMReader();
28:             org.dom4j.Document xpDoc = dr.read(doc);
29:             org.dom4j.Node node = xpDoc.selectSingleNode(
30:                                     "/ADDRESS_BOOK/ADDRESS[1]/NAME");
31:             System.out.println("Node name : " + node.getName());
32:             System.out.println("Node value: " + node.getText());
33:         } catch (Exception e)
34:         {
35:             e.printStackTrace();
36:         }
37:     }
38: }
39:
```

Listing 8.4   XpathLookup.java

A run of XpathLookup.java on myaddresses.xml produces the following output:

```
E:\classes\org\javapitfalls>javaorg.javapitfalls.item8.XpathLookup
myaddresses.xml

Node name : NAME
Node value: Joe Jones
```

The XpathLookup.java program uses the `selectSingleNode()`method in the DOM4J API with an XPath expression as its argument. The XPath recommendation can be viewed at http://www.w3.org/TR/xpath. It is important to understand that evaluation of XPath expressions will be part of the org.w3c.dom API when DOM Level 3 is implemented by JAXP. In conclusion, when searching a DOM, remember to handle whitespace nodes, or better, use XPath to search the DOM, since its robust expression syntax allows very fine-grained access to one or more nodes.

Item 9: The Saving-a-DOM Dilemma

One of the motivations for JAXP was to standardize the creation of a DOM. A DOM can be created via parsing an existing file or instantiating and inserting the nodes individually. JAXP abstracts the parsing operation via a set of interfaces so that different XML parsers can be easily used. Figure 9.1 shows a simple lifecycle of a DOM.

Figure 9.1 focuses on three states of a DOM: New, Modified, and Persisted. The New state can be reached either by instantiating a DOM object via the new keyword or by loading an XML file from disk. This "loading" operation action invokes a parser to parse the XML file. An edit, insert, or delete action moves the DOM to the modified

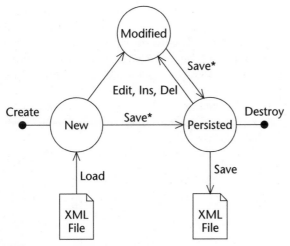

Figure 9.1 DOM lifecycle.

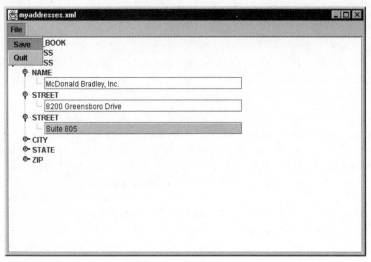

Figure 9.2 DomEditor saving a DOM.

state. The Save action transitions the DOM to the Persisted state. The asterisk by the save operation indicates that Save is implemented by saving the DOM to an XML file (the "save" operation without the asterisk). An enhancement to the DomViewer program demonstrated in Item 8 is to allow editing of the DOM nodes and then save the modified DOM out to a file (persist it). Figure 9.2 is a screen shot of the DomEditor program that implements that functionality.

When implementing the save operation in the DomEditor, we run into a dilemma on how to implement saving the DOM. Unfortunately, we have too many ways to save a DOM, and each one is different. The current situation is that saving a DOM depends on which DOM implementation you choose. The dilemma is picking an implementation that will not become obsolete with the next version of the parser. In this item, we will demonstrate three approaches to saving a DOM. Each listing will perform the same functionality: load a document from a file and save the DOM to the specified output file. The toughest part of this dilemma is the nonstandard and nonintuitive way prescribed by Sun Microsystems and implemented in JAXP to perform the save. The JAXP method for saving a DOM is to use a default XSLT transform that copies all the nodes of the source DOM (called a DOMSource) into an output stream (called a StreamResult). Listing 9.1 demonstrates saving an XML document via JAXP.

```
01: package org.javapitfalls.item9;
02:
03: import javax.xml.parsers.*;
```

Listing 9.1 JaxpSave.java

```
04: import javax.xml.transform.*;
05: import javax.xml.transform.dom.*;
06: import javax.xml.transform.stream.*;
07: import java.io.*;
08: import org.w3c.dom.*;
09:
10: class JaxpSave
11: {
12:     public static void main(String args[])
13:     {
14:         try
15:         {
// ... command-line check omitted for brevity ...
22:
23:             // load the document
24:             DocumentBuilderFactory dbf =
25:                         DocumentBuilderFactory.newInstance();
26:             DocumentBuilder db = dbf.newDocumentBuilder();
27:             Document doc = db.parse(new File(args[0]));
28:             String systemValue = doc.getDoctype().getSystemId();
29:
30:             // save to output file
31:             File f = new File(args[1]);
32:             FileWriter fw = new FileWriter(f);
33:
34:             /* write method USED To be in Sun's XmlDocument class.
35:                 The XmlDocument class preceded JAXP. */
36:
37:             // Currently only way to do this is via a transform
38:             TransformerFactory tff =
TransformerFactory.newInstance();
39:             // Default transform is a copy
40:             Transformer tf = tff.newTransformer();
41:             tf.setOutputProperty(OutputKeys.DOCTYPE_SYSTEM,
systemValue);
42:             DOMSource ds = new DOMSource(doc.getDocumentElement());
43:             StreamResult sr = new StreamResult(fw);
44:             tf.transform(ds, sr);
45:             fw.close();
46:         } catch (Throwable t)
47:         {
48:             t.printStackTrace();
49:         }
50:     }
51: }
```

Listing 9.1   *(continued)*

While JAXP is the "official" API distributed with Sun's JDK, using a transform to save a DOM is not recommended. It is nonintuitive and not close to the proposed W3C DOM Level 3 standard discussed next. The method to perform the save via JAXP uses the XSLT classes in JAXP. Specifically, a TransformerFactory is created, which in turn is used to create a transformer. A transform requires a source and a result. There are various different types of sources and results. Line 40 of Listing 9.1 is the key to understanding the source, since it creates the default transformer. This line is key because normally an XSLT transform is performed via an XSLT script; however, since we are only interested in a node-for-node copy, we don't need a script, which is provided by the no-argument `newTransformer()` method. This way the "default" transformer provides the copy functionality. There is another `newTransformer(Source s)` that accepts an XSLT source script. To sum up, once we have a transformer, a source, and a result, the transform operation will perform the copy and thus serialize the DOM. One extra step is necessary if we want to preserve the Document Type declaration from the source document. Line 41 sets an output property on the transformer to add a Document Type declaration to the result document, which we set to be the same value as the source document.

Why has JAXP not defined the standard for saving a DOM? Simply because the DOM itself is not a Java standard but a W3C standard. JAXP currently implements DOM Level 2. The W3C is developing an extension to the DOM called DOM Level 3 to enhance and standardize the use of the DOM in multiple areas. Table 9.1 details the various parts of the DOM Level 3 specification.

Table 9.1   DOM Level 3 Specifications

DOM LEVEL 3 SPECIFICATIONS	DESCRIPTION
DOM Level 3 Core	Base set of interfaces describing the document object model. Enhanced in this third version.
DOM Level 3 XPath Specification	A set of interfaces and methods to access a DOM via XPATH expressions.
DOM Level 3 Abstract Schemas and Load and Save Specification	This specification defines two sub-specificatons: the Abstract Schemas specification and the Load and Save specification. The Abstract Schemas specification represents abstract schemas (DTDs and schemas) in memory. The Load and Save specification specifies the parsing and saving of DOMs.
DOM Level 3 Events Specification	This specification defines an event generation, propagation, and handling model for DOM events. It builds on the DOM Level 2 event model.
DOM Level 3 Views and Formatting	This specification defines interfaces to represent a calculated view (presentation) of a DOM. It builds on the DOM Level 2 View model.

Table 9.2   DOM Level 3 Load and Save Interfaces

W3C DOM LEVEL 3 LS INTERFACES	DESCRIPTION
DOMImplementationLS	A DOMImplementation interface that provides factory methods for creating the DOMWriter, DOMBuilder, and DOMInputSource objects.
DOMBuilder	A parser interface.
DOMInputSource	An interface that encapsulates information about the document to be loaded.
DOMEntityResolver	An interface to provide a method for applications to redirect references to external entities.
DOMBuilderFilter	An interface to allow element nodes to be modified or removed as they are encountered during parsing.
DOMWriter	An interface for serializing DOM Documents.
DocumentLS	An extended document interface with built-in load and save methods.
ParseErrorEvent	Event fired if there is an error in parsing.

The part of the DOM specification that solves our dilemma is the specification to Load and Save a DOM. Table 9.2 details the interfaces defined in the specification. It is important to note that JAXP will even change its method for bootstrapping parsers, since its current method is slightly different than the DOM Level 3 load interfaces (specifically, DOMBuilder versus DocumentBuilder).

The Xerces parser implements the DOM Level 3 specification. Listing 9.2 uses the Xerces parser to demonstrate both the loading and saving of a DOM via the DOM Level 3 standard.

```
01: package org.javapitfalls.item9;
02:
03: import org.apache.xerces.jaxp.*;
04: import org.apache.xerces.dom3.ls.*;
05: import org.apache.xerces.dom.DOMImplementationImpl;
06: import org.apache.xerces.dom3.ls.DOMImplementationLS;
```

Listing 9.2   XercesSave.java *(continued)*

```
07:
08: import javax.xml.parsers.*;
09: import java.io.*;
10: import org.w3c.dom.*;
11:
12: class XercesSave
13: {
14:     public static void main(String args[])
15:     {
16:         try
17:         {
// ... command line check omitted for brevity ...
24:
25:             // Xerces 2 implements DOM Level 3
26:             // get DOM implementation
27:             DOMImplementationLS domImpl =
28:              (DOMImplementationLS)
DOMImplementationImpl.getDOMImplementation();
29:
30:             // Create a DOM Level 3 - DOMBuilder
31:             DOMBuilder db =
32:                 domImpl.createDOMBuilder(
DOMImplementationLS.MODE_SYNCHRONOUS);
33:             DOMInputSource dis = domImpl.createDOMInputSource();
34:             dis.setByteStream(new FileInputStream(args[0]));
35:             Document doc = db.parse(dis);
36:
37:             // save to output file
38:             FileOutputStream fos = new FileOutputStream(args[1]);
39:
40:             // create a DOM Writer
41:             DOMWriter writer = domImpl.createDOMWriter();
42:             writer.writeNode(fos, doc);
43:
44:             fos.close();
45:         } catch (Throwable t)
46:         {
47:             t.printStackTrace();
48:         }
49:     }
50: }
51:
```

Listing 9.2   *(continued)*

XercesSave.java uses the "LS" (which stands for Load and Save) version of the
DOMImplemenation to create the DOMBuilder (line 31) and DOMWriter (line 41)

objects. Once created, the DOMBuilder creates the DOM via the `parse()` method, and the DOMWriter saves the DOM via the `writeNode()` method. The `writeNode()` method can write either all or part of a DOM.

One final implementation worth mentioning is the load and save operations in the Java Document Object Model (JDOM). JDOM is a reimplementation of DOM for Java and is optimized for seamless integration into the Java platform. JDOM stresses ease of use for Java developers, whereas the W3C DOM is designed to be language-neutral (specified in CORBA IDL) and then provides bindings to specific languages. Of all the examples in this item, the JDOM implementation is the simplest; however, its functionality often lags behind the W3C DOM; its `Document` class is not a subclass of the `W3C Document` class and is thus incompatible with third-party software that expects a W3C DOM as an argument (although conversion is provided). Listing 9.3 demonstrates the load and save operations in JDOM.

```
01: package org.javapitfalls.item9;
02:
03: import org.jdom.*;
04: import org.jdom.input.*;
05: import org.jdom.output.*;
06: import java.io.*;
07:
08: class JdomSave
09: {
10:     public static void main(String args[])
11:     {
12:         try
13:         {
// ... command line check omitted for brevity ...
20:
21:             // load the document
22:             DOMBuilder db = new DOMBuilder();
23:             Document doc = db.build(new File(args[0]));
24:
25:             // save to output file
26:             FileOutputStream fos = new FileOutputStream(args[1]);
27:             XMLOutputter xout = new XMLOutputter();
28:             xout.output(doc, fos);
29:             fos.close();
30:         } catch (Throwable t)
31:         {
32:             t.printStackTrace();
33:         }
34:     }
35: }
36:
```

Listing 9.3   JdomSave.java

Like the W3C Load and Save specification, JDOM also uses a DOMBuilder class (but bootstraps it differently) and then builds an org.jdom.Document (line 23). It is important to note that a JDOM Document is NOT a W3C Document. To save the JDOM Document, an XMLOutputter class is instantiated that can output() (line 28) a document.

All three implementations of the program (JaxpSave, XercesSave, and JdomSave) produce nearly identical outputs, and thus it is not necessary to list them here. In conclusion, at this time of rapid evolution of the DOM, the safest bet is to align your code to the W3C standards and implementations that follow them. Thus, to save a DOM, the Xerces implementation is currently the best choice.

Item 10: Mouse Button Portability

Unfortunately for cross-platform computing, all computer mice are not created equal. There are one-button mice, two-button mice, three-button mice, and two-button-with-mouse-wheel mice. Like the AWT, to cover all of these options, Java initially took a least common denominator (LCD) approach that supported receiving a single mouse event and using modifiers and modifier keys to differentiate between the different types. A second problem Java programmers encounter regarding the mouse is that the Java platform evolves its mouse support with each major release, adding support for new features (like mouse wheels) and new convenience methods. Table 10.1 lists the interfaces and methods for capturing mouse events.

Table 10.1   Mouse Event Interfaces

INTERFACE	METHOD	DESCRIPTION
MouseListener	mouseClicked	Invoked when a mouse is clicked on a component
	mousePressed	Invoked when a mouse is pressed
	mouseReleased	Invoked when a mouse is released
	mouseEntered	Invoked when a mouse enters a component's bounds
	mouseExited	Invoked when a mouse exits a component's bounds
MouseMotionListener	mouseDragged	Invoked when a mouse button is pressed on a component and then dragged
	mouseMoved	Invoked when a mouse is moved around a component
MouseWheelListener	mouseWheelMoved	Invoked when the mouse wheel is rotated

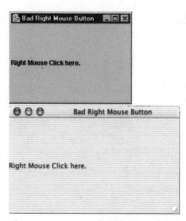

Figure 10.1 BadRightMouseButton on Windows (top) and Mac OS X (bottom).

A common problem is an application that needs to process clicks from a right mouse button across platforms. For example, say we had an application that captured right mouse clicks to both display a context-sensitive popup menu and change the mode of a tool from select, on the left mouse click, to select and execute for a right mouse click. Figure 10.1 displays the user interface of a simple application to capture these two activities of a right mouse click. Figure 10.1 shows the application run on both Windows NT and Mac OSX, since our Java application supports both operating systems.

Listing 10.1 displays the source code for BadRightMouseButton.java.

```
01: /* BadRightMouseButton.java */
02: import java.awt.event.*;
03: import java.awt.*;
04: import javax.swing.*;
05:
06: public class BadRightMouseButton extends JFrame implements
MouseListener
07: {
08:     public BadRightMouseButton()
09:     {
10:         super("Bad Right Mouse Button");
11:
12:         JLabel l = new JLabel("Right Mouse Click here.");
13:         getContentPane().add("Center", l);
14:
15:         addMouseListener(this);
16:
17:         setSize(400,200);
18:         setLocation(100,100);
19:         setVisible(true);
20:         addWindowListener(new WindowAdapter()
21:                         {
22:                             public void windowClosing(WindowEvent evt)
```

Listing 10.1 BadRightMouseButton.java *(continued)*

```
23:                              {
24:                                  System.exit(1);
25:                              }
26:                          });
27:
28:      }
29:
30:   public static void main(String [] args)
31:   {
32:       try
33:       {
34:          BadRightMouseButton win = new BadRightMouseButton();
35:
36:       } catch (Throwable t)
37:       {
38:              t.printStackTrace();
39:       }
40:   }
41:
42:     public void mouseClicked(MouseEvent e)
43:     {
44:         int modifiers = e.getModifiers();
45:         if ((modifiers & InputEvent.BUTTON1_MASK) ==                    ⏎
InputEvent.BUTTON1_MASK)
46:             System.out.println("Button 1 clicked.");
47:
48:         if ((modifiers & InputEvent.BUTTON2_MASK) ==                    ⏎
InputEvent.BUTTON2_MASK)
49:             System.out.println("Button 2 clicked.");
50:
51:         if ((modifiers & InputEvent.BUTTON3_MASK) == )                  ⏎
InputEvent.BUTTON3_MASK) )
52:             System.out.println("Button 3 clicked.");
53:
54:         // modifier keys
55:         System.out.println("isControlDown? " + e.isControlDown());
56:         System.out.println("isMetaDown? " + e.isMetaDown());
57:         System.out.println("isAltDown? " + e.isAltDown());
58:         System.out.println("isShiftDown? " + e.isShiftDown());
59:         System.out.println("isAltGraphDown? " + e.isAltGraphDown());
60:
61:         /* 1.4 methods
62:         int buttonNumber = e.getButton();
63:         System.out.println("Button # is : " + buttonNumber);
64:
65:         int mods = e.getModifiersEx();
66:         System.out.println("Modifiers: " +                             ⏎
InputEvent.getModifiersExText(mods));
67:         */
```

Listing 10.1 *(continued)*

```
68:
69:          // is this a Popup Trigger?
70:          System.out.println("In mouseClicked(), isPopupTrigger? " + ⤸
e.isPopupTrigger());
71:      }
72:
73:      public void mousePressed(MouseEvent e)
74:      { }
75:      public void mouseReleased(MouseEvent e)
76:      { }
77:      public void mouseEntered(MouseEvent e)
78:      { }
79:      public void mouseExited(MouseEvent e)
80:      { }
81: }
```

Listing 10.1   *(continued)*

JDK 1.4 has added some new methods as demonstrated (but commented out) in lines 62 and 65. These are additional convenience methods that enable you to eliminate the need for ANDing the modifier integer with the constant flags (lines 45, 48, and 51).

Here is a run of BadRightMouseButton on Windows with a two-button mouse with a mouse wheel. When the program was executed, the right mouse button was clicked, followed by the left mouse button and then the mouse wheel. This produced the following `println` statements:

```
>>>java BadRightMouseButton  (on Windows NT with 2 button mouse with
mousewheel)
Button 3 clicked.
isControlDown? false
isMetaDown? true
isAltDown? false
isShiftDown? false
isAltGraphDown? false
In mouseClicked(), isPopupTrigger? false

Button 1 clicked.
isControlDown? false
isMetaDown? false
isAltDown? false
isShiftDown? false
isAltGraphDown? false
In mouseClicked(), isPopupTrigger? false

Button 2 clicked.
isControlDown? false
isMetaDown? false
isAltDown? true
```

```
isShiftDown? false
isAltGraphDown? false
In mouseClicked(), isPopupTrigger? false
```

Here is a run of BadRightMouseButton.java on Mac OSX with a single-button mouse. When the program was executed, the single mouse button was clicked (which maps to button 1), then the Ctrl key was held and the mouse button clicked, then the special "apple" key was held and the mouse button clicked.

```
>>>java BadRightMouseButton   (on MacOSX with a single mouse button)
Button 1 clicked.
isControlDown? false
isMetaDown? false
isAltDown? false
isShiftDown? false
isAltGraphDown? false
In mouseClicked(), isPopupTrigger? false

Button 2 clicked.
isControlDown? true
isMetaDown? false
isAltDown? true
isShiftDown? false
isAltGraphDown? false
In mouseClicked(), isPopupTrigger? false

Button 3 clicked.
isControlDown? false
isMetaDown? true
isAltDown? false
isShiftDown? false
isAltGraphDown? false
In mouseClicked(), isPopupTrigger? false
```

There are two problems you should notice when examining the results from both operating systems besides the fact that they are not consistent. First, there is no clear indication of a right mouse button click even though we know that the Windows mouse clearly has a right and left mouse button. Instead of "sides" of the mouse, we have the ability in the InputEvent class (which is the parent class of MouseEvent) to check which button was clicked: button 1, 2, or 3. Unfortunately, there is no way to correlate a button with a side for a cross-platform application. The second problem is that the call to isPopupTrigger() has always returned false when we know that a right-button mouse click is the trigger on Windows for a popup and the Ctrl-mouse click combination is the trigger on the Mac. Listing 10.2, GoodRightMouseButton.java, solves both of these problems.

```
01: /* GoodRightMouseButton.java */
02: import java.awt.event.*;
03: import java.awt.*;
04: import javax.swing.*;
05:
06: public class GoodRightMouseButton extends JFrame implements  ⤳
MouseListener
07: {
08:     public GoodRightMouseButton()
09:     {
            // ... constructor identical to Listing #10.1
28:     }
29:
30:   public static void main(String [] args)
31:   {
32:         try
33:         {
34:             GoodRightMouseButton win = new GoodRightMouseButton();
35:
36:         } catch (Throwable t)
37:           {
38:                 t.printStackTrace();
39:           }
40:   }
41:
42:     public void mouseClicked(MouseEvent e)
43:     {
// ... getModifiers() code Identical to listing 10.1 ...
68:
69:         // is this a Popup Trigger?
70:         System.out.println("In mouseClicked(), isPopupTrigger? " + ⤳
e.isPopupTrigger());
71:
72:         // Use SwingUtilities to disambiguate
73:         boolean lb = SwingUtilities.isLeftMouseButton(e);
74:         boolean mb = SwingUtilities.isMiddleMouseButton(e);
75:         boolean rb = SwingUtilities.isRightMouseButton(e);
76:
77:         System.out.println("Left button? " + lb);
78:         System.out.println("Middle button? " + mb);
79:         System.out.println("Right button? " + rb);
80:     }
81:
82:     public void mousePressed(MouseEvent e)
```

Listing 10.2   GoodRightMouseButton.java *(continued)*

```
83:     {
84:          // is this a Popup Trigger?
85:          System.out.println("In mousePressed(), isPopupTrigger? " + ⤶
e.isPopupTrigger());
86:     }
87:     public void mouseReleased(MouseEvent e)
88:     {
89:          // is this a Popup Trigger?
90:          System.out.println("In mouseReleased(), isPopupTrigger? " + ⤶
e.isPopupTrigger());
91:     }
92:
93:     public void mouseEntered(MouseEvent e)
94:     { }
95:     public void mouseExited(MouseEvent e)
96:     { }
97: }
98:
```

Listing 10.2   *(continued)*

Here is a run of GoodRightMouseButton on Windows. When executing the program, the right mouse button was clicked, followed by the left mouse button and then the mouse wheel. This produced the following `println` statements:

```
>>>java GoodRightMouseButton  (on Windows NT with 2 button mouse with
mousewheel)
In mousePressed(), isPopupTrigger? false
In mouseReleased(), isPopupTrigger? true
Button 3 clicked.
isControlDown? false
isMetaDown? true
isAltDown? false
isShiftDown? false
isAltGraphDown? false
In mouseClicked(), isPopupTrigger? false
Left button? false
Middle button? false
Right button? true

In mousePressed(), isPopupTrigger? false
In mouseReleased(), isPopupTrigger? false
Button 1 clicked.
isControlDown? false
isMetaDown? false
isAltDown? false
isShiftDown? false
isAltGraphDown? false
```

```
In mouseClicked(), isPopupTrigger? false
Left button? true
Middle button? false
Right button? false


In mousePressed(), isPopupTrigger? false
In mouseReleased(), isPopupTrigger? false
```
Button 2 clicked.
```
isControlDown? false
isMetaDown? false
isAltDown? true
isShiftDown? false
isAltGraphDown? false
In mouseClicked(), isPopupTrigger? false
Left button? false
Middle button? true
Right button? false
```

Here is a run of GoodRightMouseButton.java on Mac OSX. When the program was executed, the single mouse button was clicked, then the Ctrl key was held and the mouse button clicked, then the special "apple" key was held and the mouse button clicked.

```
>>>java GoodRightMouseButton  (on MacOSX with a single mouse button)
In mousePressed(), isPopupTrigger? false
In mouseReleased(), isPopupTrigger? false
```
Button 1 clicked.
```
isControlDown? false
isMetaDown? false
isAltDown? false
isShiftDown? false
isAltGraphDown? false
In mouseClicked(), isPopupTrigger? false
Left button? true
Middle button? false
Right button? false


In mousePressed(), isPopupTrigger? true
In mouseReleased(), isPopupTrigger? false
```
Button 2 clicked.
```
isControlDown? true
isMetaDown? false
isAltDown? true
isShiftDown? false
isAltGraphDown? false
In mouseClicked(), isPopupTrigger? false
Left button? false
Middle button? true
Right button? false


In mousePressed(), isPopupTrigger? false
In mouseReleased(), isPopupTrigger? false
```

```
Button 3 clicked.
isControlDown? false
isMetaDown? true
isAltDown? false
isShiftDown? false
isAltGraphDown? false
In mouseClicked(), isPopupTrigger? false
Left button? false
Middle button? false
Right button? true
```

The new results show that we can determine which mouse button (left, right, or middle) was clicked and whether that click is the popup trigger event. The solution has two parts: first, the SwingUtilities class contains a set of methods that allow you to test a mouse event to determine which side of the mouse was clicked. It is slightly nonintuitive to have these separated from the other test methods in InputEvent or MouseEvent; however, that could change in a future release. Second, you should notice how you have to test for the popupTrigger in the mousePressed() and mouseReleased() to accurately determine the trigger event. It is interesting to note that the Ctrl-mouse combination on the Macintosh is considered the middle mouse button and not the right mouse button. It would be better if the popup trigger was consistent on Windows and the Mac (both being considered a "right click").

In conclusion, using the SwingUtilities class and understanding when to call isPopupTrigger() allows us to better process mouse events in cross-platform applications.

Item 11: Apache Ant and Lifecycle Management

The software lifecycle process describes the life of a software product from its conception to its implementation and deployment. An important aspect of this process is the need to impose consistency and structure on all lifecycle activities that can guide actions through development to deployment. This practice is often compared to a cookbook, where knowledge is captured and then transferred to others so that they can emulate similar actions. Unfortunately, most projects incorporate inconsistent practices where developers create and deploy on disparate platforms and apply their individual techniques for building and testing code, which becomes problematic during integration when disparities between scripts make them difficult to understand and implement.

An important solution to this problem is a utility available through the Apache Software Foundation called Ant ("Another Neat Tool"). Ant's main purpose is to facilitate application builds and deployments. This is achieved by combining Java programming language applications and XML build files, which can be run on multiple platforms and offer open-architecture flexibility. By maintaining applications and program builds with Ant, consistency levels can be achieved by disparate groups of developers, and the best practices can be propagated throughout a project.

With Ant, targets are generated in project files for compilation, testing, and deployment tasks. The aim of the Ant build file which follows is to highlight some useful target generation tasks that can facilitate software lifecycle activities so that manual development processes can be automated, which will free up developers' time for greater creativity in their own applications rather than being tied down with mundane build and deployment activities.

Most Ant scripts start with the initialization of application properties demonstrated in lines 11 to 23. These same properties could also be established from the command line and delivered to the Ant build script in the same manner as Java programs with the -D parameter during the Ant build invocation. One important thing to consider about properties that are set in an Ant script is that these are immutable constants that cannot be changed once declared. Line 31 shows the depends tag that signals that the target "compile" depends on the "init" target being run prior to its execution. Most scripts will use the depends tag to execute sequential build processes.

```
001: <?xml version="1.0"?>
002: <project name="lifecycle management">
003:
004:        <!--
005:        ********************************************************
006:        ** Initialize global properties.
007:        ********************************************************-->
008: <target name="init" description="initialize lifecycle properties.">
009:
010: <tstamp/>
011: <property name="testdir" value="." />
012: <property name="rootdir" value="."/>
013: <property name="builddir" value="build"/>
014: <property name="driver" value="org.gjt.mm.mysql.Driver" />
015: <property name="url" value="jdbc:mysql://localhost/States" />
016: <property name="userid" value="" />
017: <property name="password" value="" />
018: <property name="destdir" value="bugrat" />
019: <property name="zip.bugrat" value="bugrat.zip" />
020: <property name="destdir.bugrat" value="${destdir}/test" />
021: <property name="catalina.home" value="c:\apache\tomcat403"/>
022:    <property name="cvs.repository"
value=":pserver:<username>@<hostname>:c:\cvsrep"/>
023:    <property name="cvs.package" value="tests"/>
024:
025: </target>
026:
027: <!--
028:        ********************************************************
029:        ** Java compilation
030:        ********************************************************-->
031: <target name="compile" depends="init">
032:        <javac srcdir="." destdir="." classpath="junit.jar" />
033: </target>
034:
```

Listing 11.1   lifecycle_build.xml *(continued)*

Lines 39 to 57 illustrate how Ant can be used to run JUnit tests on your Java applications. JUnit is an open-source testing framework that allows developers to build test suites so that unit testing can be performed on Java components. Personally, we like to use them to create unit tests on JavaBean applications to ensure that developers on our team do not corrupt these files during development activities. If a developer is experiencing a problem with some code, we run some tests that were crafted during development to verify that no bugs have been introduced into an application.

```
035:  <!--
036:        ***************************************************
037:        ** JUnit tests
038:        ***************************************************-->
039:  <target name="test" depends="compile">
040:
041:        <echo message="Running JUnit tests." />
042:        <junit printsummary="true">
043:        <!-- <formatter type="plain" usefile="false" /> -->
044:        <formatter type="xml" />
045:              <test name="AllTests2" />
046:              <classpath>
047:                    <pathelement location="." />
048:              </classpath>
049:        </junit>
050:        <junitreport todir=".">
051:              <fileset dir=".">
052:                    <include name="TEST-*.xml" />
053:              </fileset>
054:              <report format="frames" todir="." />
055:        </junitreport>
056:
057:  </target>
058:
```

Listing 11.1   *(continued)*

Obviously, the setting of appropriate classpath properties is paramount when running Ant and compiling individual Java code. This is accomplished by setting the paths and their components on lines 63 to 69.

```
059:        <!--
060:        ***************************************************
061:        ** Classpath properties.
062:        ***************************************************-->
063:        <path id="classpath.path">
064:              <pathelement location="${builddir}"/>
065:              <fileset dir="cache/lib">
066:              <include name="*.jar"/>
067:              </fileset>
068:              <pathelement location="cache/lib/servlet.jar"/>
069:        </path>
070:
```

Listing 11.1   *(continued)*

Additionally, directory creation scripts on lines 75 to 104 are needed to move source code to proper deployment areas so that they are accessible to other Ant targets.

```
071:        <!--
072:        ************************************************************
073:        ** Create the output directory structure.
074:        ************************************************************-->.
075:        <target name="prepare">
076:
077:        <mkdir dir="${builddir}"/>
078:        <mkdir dir="${builddir}/tests"/>
079:        <mkdir dir="${builddir}/WEB-INF/lib"/>
080:        <mkdir dir="${builddir}/WEB-INF/classes/cache"/>
081:
082:        <copy todir="${builddir}/WEB-INF/classes/cache">
083:                <fileset dir="cache/beans"/>
084:        </copy>
085:        <copy todir="${builddir}">
086:                <fileset dir="cache/src"/>
087:        </copy>
<!-- some copy elements deleted for brevity ... -->
104: </target>
105:
```

Listing 11.1   *(continued)*

All Ant scripts should provide Help targets to assist end users in their build operations as verified on lines 110 to 115. Cleanup targets should be created to remove unwanted files and directories, and to ensure that legacy code that is no longer pertinent does not get added to production builds, which is demonstrated on lines 121 to 125.

```
106:        <!--
107:        ************************************************************
108:        ** Help
109:        ************************************************************-->
110:        <target name="help" description="Lifecycle Help">.
111:
112:        <echo message="Lifecycle Help"/>
113:        <echo message="Type 'ant -projecthelp' for more        ⮐
assistance..."/>
114:
115: </target>
116:
117:        <!--
118:        ************************************************************
119:        ** Remove the (build/release) directories
120:        ************************************************************-->
121:        <target name="clean">.
122:
123:        <delete dir="${builddir}"/>
124:
125: </target>
126:
```

Listing 11.1   *(continued)*

On many development efforts, code repositories and versioning systems are deployed to share code among programmers and to save modifications for redistribution. Often, an open-source application called Concurrent Versioning System (CVS) is used to perform these tracking and coordination activities. With CVS, check-in and checkout procedures allow users to access source code repositories to ensure that proper builds are deployed and archived. Source code control is an absolute necessity during multiple developer projects because it prevents inconsistencies in program updates and automates coordination among developers. A very simple glimpse of a CVS update operation embedded in Ant is shown on lines 131 to 139.

The combination of these three open-source applications, CVS/JUnit/Bugrat, can be an effective configuration management toolset that developers can integrate with Ant to facilitate their development activities. Configuration management systems are important in that they minimize risk and promote traceability through source control, test coordination, bug tracking, and resolution. Normal CVS operations and JUnit test scripts can be embedded in Ant scripts. The BugRat tracking tool can be built or deployed by using an Ant script to place the zipped Web Archive BugRat file in your J2EE Web container. Lines 146 to 179 show how to initialize, deploy, and clean up a BugRat installation.

```
127: <!--
128:    ********************************************************
129:    ** CVS
130:    ********************************************************-->
131:    <target name="cvs" description="Check out CVS files...">
132:
133:    <echo message="Check out CVS files..."/>
134:    <cvs cvsRoot=":pserver:anoncvs@cvs.apache.org:/home/cvspublic"
135:            package="jakarta-ant"
136:            dest="c:\Java_Pitfalls\Antidote\jakarta-ant-antidote" />
137:        <cvs command="update -A -d"/>
138:
139: </target>
140:
141: <!--
142:    ********************************************************
143:    ** Bugrat - Bug Tracking Tool
144:    ********************************************************-->
145:
146: <target name="initBugrat">
147:
148:    <!-- Create the time stamp -->
149:    <tstamp/>
150:    <!-- Create the build directory structure used by compile -->
151:    <available property="haveBugrat" type="dir"
file="${destdir.bugrat}"/>
152:
153: </target>
154:
```

Listing 11.1   (continued)

```
155: <target name="prepareBugrat" depends="initBugrat">
156:
157:     <mkdir dir="${destdir}"/>
158:
159: </target>
160:
161: <target name="installBugrat" depends="prepareBugrat"
unless="haveBugrat">
162: <unzip src="${zip.bugrat}" dest="${destdir}"/>
163: </target>
164:
165: <target name="deployBugrat" depends="installBugrat"
description="Install Bugrat">
166:
167:     <pathconvert targetos="windows" property="bugrat_home">
168:          <path location="${destdir.bugrat}"/>
169:     </pathconvert>
170:
171: </target>
172:
173: <target name="cleanBugrat">
174:
175:     <!-- Delete the ${build} and ${dist} directory trees -->
176:     <delete dir="${destdir}" />
177:     <!-- For the sake of brevity, I've omitted the SQL scripts that
need to be run to build the Bugrat repository. These files include:
defconfig.sql, defproperties.sql, examplecats.sql, and mysqlschema.sql -->
178:
179: </target>
```

Listing 11.1   *(continued)*

As in life, with software, increasing complexity leads to the natural occurrence of more problems. During software development, source code needs to be consistently reviewed to determine where code can be refactored, or rewritten, to improve efficiencies. Refactoring increases quality through design improvements and the reduction of defects. Two open-source Java utilities, JDepend and JavaNCSS, can be used within an Ant script to provide metrics so that program behaviors can be observed and improvements can be tested.

The JDepend application reads Java class and source file directories to generate metric measurements that can be used to determine software quality. Designs are more extensible when they are independent of implementation details, which allows them to adapt to new modifications without breaking the entire system. JDepend isolates program couplings to determine where dependencies lie and where migrations can occur among lower levels of software hierarchies to higher levels so that redundancies can be decreased. JavaNCSS provides noncommented source code measurements so that large, cumbersome programs can be discovered and possibly be rewritten to improve readability or performance.

Certainly, measurements from both JDepend and JavaNCSS should be used only to gauge software quality and not be deemed absolute predictors as to what needs to be performed in order to make code more efficient.

```
181: <!--
182:        *********************************************************
183:        ** JDepend
184:        *******************************************************-->
185: <target name="jdepend">
200:        <jdepend outputfile="docs/jdepend-report.txt">
201:        <sourcespath>
202:            <pathelement location="./ant/src" />
203:        </sourcespath>
204:        <classpath location="." />
206:        </jdepend>
208: </target>
209:
210: <!--
211:        *********************************************************
212:        ** JavaNCSS
213:        *******************************************************-->
214: <target name="javancss">
223: <taskdef name="javancss" classname="javancss.JavancssAntTask"
classpath="${CLASSPATH}"/>
231: <javancss srcdir="./ant/src"
232:            generateReport="true"
233:                    outputfile="javancss_metrics.xml"
234:            format="xml"/>
236: </target>
```

Listing 11.1   *(continued)*

Developers can include a splash screen target to signal that something is actually occurring during an Ant command-line build operation by adding lines 242 to 248.

```
238: <!--
239:        *********************************************************
240:        ** Splash screen
241:        *******************************************************-->
242: <target name="splash" description="Display splash screen...">
243:
244:        <echo message="Display splash screen..."/>
245:        <splash imageurl="./ant/images/ant_logo_large.gif"
246:            showduration="5000" />
248: </target>
```

Listing 11.1   *(continued)*

Checkstyle is a Java development tool that helps programmers write Java code that adheres to a recognized coding standard. It automates the process of visually checking through Java code to ensure that previously established coding rules are incorporated into individual source code components.

Some of the useful standards that Checkstyle looks for are unused or duplicate import statements, that Javadoc tags for a method match the actual code, the incorporation of specified headers, that @author tags exist for class and interface Javadoc comments, that periods (.) are not surrounded by whitespace, that brackets ({}) are used for if/while/for/do constructs, that lines do not contain tabs, and that files are not longer than a specified number of lines. To implement Checkstyle, a user would need to use lines 254 to 263.

```
250: <!--
251:        *****************************************************
252:        ** Checkstyle
253:        *****************************************************-->
254: <target name="checkStyle" description="Coding standard met?...">
256:        <taskdef name="checkstyle"
257:
classname="com.puppycrawl.tools.checkstyle.CheckStyleTask"/>
258:        <echo message="Coding standard met?..."/>
259:        <checkstyle allowTabs="yes">
260:                <fileset dir="./ant/src" includes="**/*.java"/>
261:                </checkstyle>
263: </target>
```

Listing 11.1 *(continued)*

Document preparation is an important but often overlooked activity during software implementation. Users often need to understand what APIs are being used to propagate data across systems. Javadoc provides hyperlinked documents for Web browser viewing, which allows users to share copies and facilitates distribution. Javadocs are easily updateable, which helps maintain consistency.

```
266: <!--
267:        *****************************************************
268:        ** Javadoc
269:        *****************************************************-->
270:        <target name="javadoc" description="Generate Javadoc
artifacts">
272:        <echo message="Generating Javadoc artifacts..."/>
273:        <javadoc packagenames="*"
274:                sourcepath="./ant/src"
275:                 sourcefiles="./ant/src/**"
276:                excludepackagenames="com.dummy.test.doc-files.*"
277:                defaultexcludes="yes"
278:                destdir="docs/api"
279:                author="true"
280:                version="true"
281:                use="true"
282:                windowtitle="Test API">
283:        <doctitle><![CDATA[<h1>Test</h1>]]></doctitle>
284:        <bottom><![CDATA[<i>Copyright &#169; 2002 Java
Pitfalls II All Rights Reserved.</i>]]></bottom>
285:        </javadoc>
286:
287: </target>
```

Listing 11.1 *(continued)*

In the Servlet/JavaServer Page model, Web ARchive (WAR) files are portable components that can be deployed across a wide range of J2EE Web containers. The code below shows how Java source is compiled and packaged for deployment.

```
288:
289:        <!--
290:        ***********************************************************
291:        ** Build WAR file
292:        ***********************************************************-->
293:        <target name="distribute" depends="prepare">
294:
295:        <echo message="Compiling source..."/>
296:
297:        <javac srcdir="cache/beans" destdir="${builddir}/WEB-
INF/classes/">
298:              <classpath><path
refid="classpath.path"/></classpath>
299:        </javac>
300:
301:        <echo message="Creating WAR file [cache.war]..."/>
302:        <war warfile="${builddir}/cache.war"
webxml="cache/deployment/web.xml">
303:              <fileset dir="${builddir}">
304:
        <patternset id="_source">
305:                      <include name="*.jsp"/>
306:                </patternset>
307:                <patternset id="_stylesheet">
308:                      <include name="*.css"/>
309:        </patternset>
310:        </fileset>
311:        <webinf dir="${builddir}/WEB-INF">
312:                <patternset id="_tld">
313:                      <include name="*.tld"/>
314:                </patternset>
315:        </webinf>
316:        <classes dir="${builddir}/WEB-INF/classes" >
317:                <patternset id="_classes">
318:                      <include name="**"/>
319:                </patternset>
320:        </classes>
321:        <lib dir="${builddir}/WEB-INF/lib"  />
322:        </war>
324:    </target>
```

Listing 11.1 *(continued)*

Database creation, population, and destruction can also be accomplished with Ant scripts. Prior to discovering this capability, our development team was experiencing great difficulties in performing these operations on both Intel and Unix platforms. Different scripts needed to be maintained in order to run the SQL commands, which proved quite cumbersome. By employing Ant, we were able to use the same script on both platforms, which allowed us to facilitate operations.

```
326:        <!--
327:        **********************************************************
328:        ** SQL - table creation, population and deletion
329:        **********************************************************-->
330:
331: <target name="createMySQLCacheTables">
333: <sql driver="${driver}" url="${url}" userid="${userid}"
password="${password}">
334:        <classpath>
335:        <fileset dir=".">
336:              <include name="mm.mysql-2.0.4-bin.jar" />
337:        </fileset>
338:        </classpath>
339:
340:        <!--
341:        NOTE: Could logon to MySQL thru URL mysql
(default database) and create the States dB instance
342:        or do this manually through this step: create database
States;
343:        -->
345:        CREATE TABLE GeneralInfo (
346:              State VARCHAR(40) NOT NULL,
347:              Flower VARCHAR(50),
348:              Bird VARCHAR(50),
349:                    Capital VARCHAR(40),
350:              PRIMARY KEY(State)
351:        );
352:
353:              CREATE TABLE Topics (
354:              State VARCHAR(40) NOT NULL,
355:              AutomobileDealers VARCHAR(40),
356:              BikeTrails VARCHAR(50),
357:              Gyms VARCHAR(50),
358:                    Hospitals VARCHAR(50),
359:                    Laundromats VARCHAR(50),
360:                    Parks VARCHAR(50),
361:                    Physicians VARCHAR(50),
362:                    PetStores VARCHAR(50),
363:                    Restaurants VARCHAR(50),
364:                    RestAreas VARCHAR(50),
365:                    Supermarkets VARCHAR(50),
366:              PRIMARY KEY(State)
367:        );
369: </sql>
371: </target>
372:
373: <target name="dropMySQLCacheTables">
375: <sql driver="${driver}" url="${url}" userid="${userid}"
password="${password}">
376:        <classpath>
377:        <fileset dir=".">
378:              <include name="mm.mysql-2.0.4-bin.jar" />
379:        </fileset>
```

Listing 11.1   *(continued)*

```
380:            </classpath>
382:                  DROP TABLE GeneralInfo;
383:                  DROP TABLE Topics;
385: </sql>
386: </target>
387:
388: <target name="populateMySQLCacheTables">
390: <sql driver="${driver}" url="${url}" userid="${userid}"
password="${password}">
391:        <classpath>
392:              <fileset dir=".">
393:                    <include name="mm.mysql-2.0.4-bin.jar" />
394:              </fileset>
395:        </classpath>
396:
397:        INSERT INTO GeneralInfo VALUES ('Alabama', 'Camellia',  ⤵
'Yellowhammer', 'Montgomery');
399:        INSERT INTO Topics VALUES ('Alabama', 'KIA', 'Bama Path',
'Mr. Muscles', 'St. Lukes', 'Mr. Clean', 'Tuscaloosa', 'Dr. Nick', 'Mr.
Pickles', 'Joes Pizzaria', 'Selma', 'Mr. Goodshoes');
401: </sql>
402: </target>
```

Listing 11.1 *(continued)*

The key to having efficient operations during development is predicated on the automation of tedious operations, especially testing. An open-source offering called CruiseControl can be embedded in Ant scripts to allow developers to check out source code from CVS so that release builds can be made and modules can be tested. This is an important component of all software operations. Batch scripts can be used to create nightly builds with CruiseControl so that daily software modifications can be tested for defects overnight and addressed by developers before they are forgotten and remain undetected on a system.

```
404: <!--
405:        ********************************************************
406:        ** Cruise control
407:        ********************************************************-->
408:    <target name="all" depends="clean, compile, javadoc,      ⤵
distribute, junit" description="prepare application for CruiseControl"/>
410: <target name="cruise" description="Start the automated build  ⤵
process with CruiseControl">
412:        <copy todir="${catalina.home}/webapps/"               ⤵
file="Cruisecontrol/cruisecontrol/buildservlet.war" />
414:        <java classname="net.sourceforge.cruisecontrol.MasterBuild" ⤵
fork="yes" >
415:              <arg line="-properties cruisecontrol.properties -  ⤵
lastbuild 20020901010101 -label test 1"/>
416:              <classpath>
```

Listing 11.1 *(continued)*

```
417:                         <pathelement
location="Cruisecontrol\cruisecontrol\cruisecontrol.jar"/>
418:                         <pathelement path="${java.class.path}"/>
419:                         <pathelement path="${compile.classpath}"/>
420:                         <pathelement location="."/>
421:                 </classpath>
422:             </java>
424:       </target>
425:
426:       <target name="checkout" description="Update package from CVS">
427:           <cvs cvsroot="${cvs.repository}" package="${cvs.package}"
dest="." passfile="etc\.passwd" />
428:       </target>
429:
430:       <target name="modificationcheck" depends="prepare"
description="Check modifications since last build">
431:
432:           <taskdef name="modificationset"
classname="net.sourceforge.cruisecontrol.ModificationSet"/>
433:           <echo message="Checking for modifications..."/>
434:           <modificationset lastbuild="${lastGoodBuildTime}"
quietperiod="30" dateformat="yyyy-MMM-dd HH:mm:ss">
435:               <cvselement cvsroot="${cvs.repository}"
localworkingcopy="." />
436:           </modificationset>
437:       </target>
438:
439:       <target name="masterbuild"
depends="modificationcheck,checkout,all"  description="Cruise Control
master build"/>
440:       <target name="cleanbuild" depends="clean,masterbuild"
description="Cruise Control clean build"/>
442: </project>
```

Listing 11.1   *(continued)*

Let's face it, the Internet has made it difficult for all software companies to keep up with platform and tool evolutions. Many integrated development environments (IDEs), both proprietary and open-source, have implemented Ant in their applications, but disparities in Ant versions and proprietary tag extensions in these applications have made these tools less desirable for application builds and deployments. These inconsistencies make Ant a much more powerful tool when run from the command line and not from an IDE application that could introduce incompatibility problems.

NOTE The lifecycle build script shown above highlights Ant's ability to ease the construction and deployment of Java projects by automating source code packaging, integration, script execution, and production system deployment. Hopefully, users can use these Ant build techniques to make their lifecycle activities more efficient.

Item 12: JUnit: Unit Testing Made Simple

My wife is a good cook, a really good cook, but she drives me crazy sometimes with experiments on existing recipes that I like and expect to taste a certain way. Sometimes she does this because she's run out of some ingredient or she just feels like trying something new. Me, I don't like to try new things and prefer consistency in what I eat. My wife has made several suggestions on what I should do about this problem, the cleanest version being that I cook for myself. Rather than taking a chance that I might actually learn how to cook, I've graciously learned to accept her unpredictable ways.

Software testing exhibits these same qualities and inconsistencies. Many times developers don't write proper tests because they feel that they don't have the time to do so, and when they do, they often introduce their own programming biases in their manual tests, making them irrelevant. Software testers often don't understand what they are testing because developers don't communicate very well what exactly needs to be tested. Growing code repositories and deadline pressures complicate this matter, as well as the attrition of developers on many projects.

To address this problem, development teams need to enforce some order into their systems to prevent the chaos that habitually occurs, and that can be accomplished by implementing the JUnit framework to test logic boundaries and to ensure that the overall logic of your software components is correct.

JUnit is an open-source unit-testing framework written in Java that allows users to create individual test cases that are aggregated in test suites for deployment. Lines 16 and 17 illustrate this. The test case for my unit test is called OneTestCase.class, and my test suite is "test". If a test class does not define a suite method, then the TestRunner application will extract a suite and fill it with all methods that start with "test" using the Java reflection mechanism.

```
01:
02: import junit.framework.*;
03: import junit.runner.BaseTestRunner;
04:
05: /**
06:  * TestSuite that runs all the sample tests
07:  *
08:  */
09: public class AllTests {
10:
11:    public static void main(String[] args) {
12:            junit.textui.TestRunner.run(suite());
13:    }
14:
15:    public static Test suite() {
16:            testsuite suite= new testsuite("Framework Tests");
17:            suite.addTestSuite(OneTestCase.class);
18:            return suite;
19:    }
20: }
```

Listing 12.1   AllTests.java

Since we develop Web applications on many of our projects, our unit tests focus primarily on JavaBean components to ensure that our program logic is sound and consistent. In the code below, an employee form validates user inputs from a Web page. Lines 59 to 71 demonstrate how to add JUnit test code to our JavaBean applications for unit testing.

```
01:
02: import java.util.*;
03: import junit.framework.*;
04: import junit.runner.BaseTestRunner;
05:
06: public class employeeFormBean {
07:   private String firstName;
08:   private String lastName;
09:   private String phone;
10:   private Hashtable errors;
11:
12:   public boolean validate() {
13:         boolean allOk=true;
14:
15:         if (firstName.equals("")) {
16:             errors.put("firstName","Please enter your first name");
17:             firstName="";
18:             allOk=false;
19:         }
20:         if (lastName.equals("")) {
21:             errors.put("lastName","Please enter your last name");
22:             lastName="";
23:             allOk=false;
24:         }
25:         return allOk;
26:   }
27:
28:   public String getErrorMsg(String s) {
29:         String errorMsg =(String)errors.get(s.trim());
30:      return (errorMsg == null) ? "":errorMsg;
31:   }
32:
33:   public employeeFormBean() {
34:         firstName="";
35:         lastName="";
36:         // errors
37:         errors = new Hashtable();
38:   }
39:
40:   // GET methods ------------------------------------------------
41:   public String getFirstName() {
42:         return firstName;
43:   }
```

Listing 12.2 employeeFormBean.java *(continued)*

```
44:
45:    public String getLastName() {
46:            return lastName;
47:    }
48:
49:    // SET methods --------------------------------------------------
50:    public void setFirstName(String fname) {
51:            firstName =fname;
52:    }
53:
54:    public void setLastName(String lname) {
55:            lastName =lname;
56:    }
57:
58:    /* main */
59:    public static void main(String[] args) {
60:            junit.textui.TestRunner.run(suite());
61:    }
62:
63:    /**
64:     * TestSuite that runs all the sample tests
65:     *
66:     */
67:    public static Test suite() {
68:            TestSuite suite= new TestSuite("Employee Form Unit Tests");
69:            suite.addTestSuite(employeeFormBeanTestCase.class);
70:            return suite;
71:    }
73: }
```

Listing 12.2   *(continued)*

Listing 12.3 illustrates how a test case should be written to test the JavaBean that was created. Notice the assert statements that check the getter/setter methods in the employeeFormBean component. These asserts ensure that expected behavior is maintained in our code and that bugs that might be introduced to this application are captured and resolved easily. One thing to be aware of when you do create unit tests with JUnit is that if you insert System.out.println() statements in your test cases, it does not print the text output to the console when you run your test from the command line.

```
01: import junit.framework.TestCase;
02:
03: public class employeeFormBeanTestCase extends TestCase {
04:   public employeeFormBeanTestCase(String name) {
```

Listing 12.3   employeeFormBeanTestCase.java

```
05:            super(name);
06:    }
07:    public void noTestCase() {
08:    }
09:    public void testCase1() {
10:            employeeFormBean eForm = new employeeFormBean();
11:            assertTrue(eForm != null);
12:    }
13:    public void testCase2() {
14:            employeeFormBean eForm = new employeeFormBean();
15:            assertTrue(eForm != null);
16:
17:            eForm.setFirstName("Steven");
18:            assertTrue("Steven" == eForm.getFirstName());
19:    }
20:    public void testCase3() {
21:            employeeFormBean eForm = new employeeFormBean();
22:            assertTrue(eForm != null);
23:
24:            eForm.setLastName("Fitzgerald");
25:            assertTrue("Fitzgerald" == eForm.getLastName());
26:    }
27:    public void testCase4() {
28:            employeeFormBean eForm = new employeeFormBean();
29:            assertTrue(eForm != null);
30:
31:            eForm.setFirstName("John");
32:            eForm.setLastName("Walsh");
33:            assertTrue(eForm.validate());
34:    }
35:    public void testCase5() {
36:            employeeFormBean eForm = new employeeFormBean();
37:            assertTrue(eForm != null);
38:
39:            String s = eForm.getErrorMsg("firstName");
40:            assertTrue(!s.equals("Please enter your first name"));
41:    }
42:    public void testCase6() {
43:            employeeFormBean eForm = new employeeFormBean();
44:            assertTrue(eForm != null);
45:
46:            String s = eForm.getErrorMsg("lastName");
47:            assertTrue(!s.equals("Please enter your last name"));
48:    }
49:    public void testCase(int arg) {
50:    }
51: }
```

Listing 12.3   *(continued)*

Additionally, unit tests can be created to ensure that data in a database remains consistent and has not been corrupted during testing and integration operations. This is accomplished by creating unit tests that validate JDBC connections and user queries on database data.

```
01:
02: import java.sql.*;
03: import java.util.*;
04: import junit.framework.*;
05: import junit.runner.BaseTestRunner;
06:
07: public class dbQueryBean {
08:
09:    private static final String DRIVER_NAME="org.gjt.mm.mysql.Driver";
10:    private static final String DB_URL="jdbc:mysql://localhost/States";
11:    private static final String USERNAME="";
12:    private static final String PASSWORD="";
13:    private static final String QUERY="Select * from Topics";
14:
15:    Connection conn = null;
16:    Statement stmt = null;
17:    ResultSet rslt = null;
18:
19:    public dbQueryBean() {
20:
21:        try {
22:                // get driver
23:                Class.forName(DRIVER_NAME);
24:                // connect to the MySQL db
25:                Connection conn =
DriverManager.getConnection(DB_URL, USERNAME, PASSWORD);
26:                Statement stmt = conn.createStatement();
27:                ResultSet rslt = stmt.executeQuery(QUERY);
28:        }
29:        catch(Exception e) {
30:        }
31:    }
32:
33:    public void closeDb()
34:    {
35:        try {
36:                // get driver
37:                this.conn.close();
38:        }
39:        catch(Exception e) {
40:        }
41:    }
42:
```

Listing 12.4   dbQueryBean.java

```
43:  public ResultSet getResultSet() {
44:          return this.rslt;
45:  }
46:
47:  public Connection getConnection() {
48:          return this.conn;
49:  }
50:
51:  public Statement getStatement() {
52:          return this.stmt;
53:  }
54:
55:  /* main */
56:  public static void main(String[] args) {
57:          junit.textui.TestRunner.run(suite());
58:  }
59:
60:  /**
61:   * TestSuite that runs all the sample tests
62:   *
63:   */
64:  public static Test suite() {
65:          TestSuite suite= new TestSuite("DB Query Unit Tests");
66:          suite.addTestSuite(dbQueryBeanTestCase.class);
67:          return suite;
68:  }
70: }
```

Listing 12.4   *(continued)*

The dbQueryBeanTestCase in Listing 12.5 demonstrates how to assess database connections and result sets that are returned from database queries. In most cases, a simple instantiation of your bean followed by an assert after the invocation of your bean's methods is the way to unit test your code. In this example, static database information is tested; on many enterprise systems the data is dynamic and tests like this would not be proper.

```
01: import java.sql.*;
02: import junit.framework.TestCase;
03:
04: public class dbQueryBeanTestCase extends TestCase {
05:   public dbQueryBeanTestCase(String name) {
06:          super(name);
07:   }
```

Listing 12.5   dbQueryBeanTestCase.java *(continued)*

```
08:   public void noTestCase() {
09:   }
10:   public void testCase1() {
11:         employeeFormBean eForm = new employeeFormBean();
12:         assertTrue(eForm != null);
13:   }
14:   public void testCase2() {
15:
16:         try {
17:
18:                 dbQueryBean db = new dbQueryBean();
19:                 assertTrue(db != null);
20:
21:                 // Get the resultset meta-data
22:                 ResultSet rslt = db.getResultSet();
23:                 ResultSetMetaData rmeta = rslt.getMetaData();
24:
25:                 // Use meta-data to determine column #'s in each row
26:                 int numColumns = rmeta.getColumnCount();
27:                 String[] s = new String[numColumns];
28:
29:                 for (int i=1; i < numColumns; i++) {
30:                         s[i] = rmeta.getColumnName(i);
31:                 }
32:
33:                 // check to see if db columns are correct
34:                 assertTrue(s[1].equals("State"));
35:                 assertTrue(s[2].equals("AutomobileDealers"));
36:                 assertTrue(s[3].equals("BikeTrails"));
37:                 assertTrue(s[4].equals("Gyms"));
38:                 assertTrue(s[5].equals("Hospitals"));
39:                 assertTrue(s[6].equals("Laundromats"));
40:                 assertTrue(s[7].equals("Parks"));
41:                 assertTrue(s[8].equals("Physicians"));
42:                 assertTrue(s[9].equals("PetStores"));
43:                 assertTrue(s[10].equals("Restaurants"));
44:                 assertTrue(s[11].equals("RestAreas"));
45:         }
46:         catch(Exception e) {}
47:   }
48:   public void testCase3() {
49:
50:         try {
51:
52:                 dbQueryBean db = new dbQueryBean();
53:                 assertTrue(db != null);
54:
55:                 // Get the resultset meta-data
```

Listing 12.5   *(continued)*

```
56:                ResultSet rslt = db.getResultSet();
57:                ResultSetMetaData rmeta = rslt.getMetaData();
58:
59:                // Use meta-data to determine column #'s in each row
60:                int numColumns = rmeta.getColumnCount();
61:                String[] s = new String[numColumns];
62:
63:                for (int i=1; i < numColumns; i++) {
64:                        s[i] = rmeta.getColumnName(i);
65:                }
66:
67:                while (rslt.next()) {
68:                 for (int i=1; i < numColumns; ++i) {
69:                  if (rslt.getString(i).trim().equals("Alabama")) {
70:                        assertEquals(rslt.getString(i).trim(),      ⮌
"Alabama");
71:                        assertEquals(rslt.getString(i+1).trim(),    ⮌
"KIA");
72:                        assertEquals(rslt.getString(i+2).trim(),    ⮌
"Bama Path");
73:                        assertEquals(rslt.getString(i+3).trim(),    ⮌
"Mr. Muscles");
74:                        assertEquals(rslt.getString(i+4).trim(),    ⮌
"St. Lukes");
75:                        assertEquals(rslt.getString(i+5).trim(),    ⮌
"Mr. Clean");
76:                        assertEquals(rslt.getString(i+6).trim(),    ⮌
"Tuscaloosa");
77:                        assertEquals(rslt.getString(i+7).trim(),    ⮌
 "Dr. Nick");
78:                        assertEquals(rslt.getString(i+8).trim(),    ⮌
"Mr. Pickles");
79:                        assertEquals(rslt.getString(i+9).trim(),    ⮌
"Joes Pizzaria");
80:                        assertEquals(rslt.getString(i+10).trim(),   ⮌
"Selma");
81:                        assertEquals(rslt.getString(i+11).trim(),   ⮌
"Mr. Goodshoes");
82:                                        break;
83:                        }
84:                   }
85:                }
87:           }
88:          catch(Exception e) {}
89:  }
90:  public void testCase(int arg) {
91:  }
92: }
```

Listing 12.5   *(continued)*

JUnit allows developers and testers to assess module interfaces to ensure that information flows properly in their applications. Local data structures can be examined to verify that data stored temporarily maintains its integrity, boundaries can be checked for logic constraints, and error handling tests can be developed to ensure that potential errors are captured. All developers should implement the JUnit framework to test their software components and to make certain that development teams don't accept inconsistencies in their programs.

Item 13: The Failure to Execute

Executable JAR files, CLASSPATHs, and JAR conflicts challenge developers as they deploy their Java applications. Frequently, developers run into problems because of inadequate understanding of the Java extension mechanism. This pitfall costs a developer time and effort, and it can lead to substantial configuration control issues. I have seen numerous developers have problems with executable JAR files. They build desktop applications and deploy them via executable JAR files. However, for some reason, sometimes the JAR file will not execute.

When executed using the conventional `java classname` command, the code runs fine. The developer adds all of the classes to a JAR file and sets the main class attribute. Executing the `java -jar jarname` command, the following error returns:

```
Exception in thread "main" java.lang.NoClassDefFoundError:
com/borland/jbcl/layout/XYLayout
        at execution.application.ExecFrame.<init>(ExecFrame.java:23)
        at execution.application.ExecApp.<init>(ExecApp.java:11)
        at execution.application.ExecApp.main(ExecApp.java:40)
```

This is one example of this familiar error for these developers. It is unable to find a particular class, in this case, `com.borland.jbcl.layout.XYLayout`. In this case, the developer did not select the proper JAR packaging for the JBuilder IDE. This is not unique to JBuilder, though, nor IDEs. This is part of a bigger issue in regard to tracking the classpath of applications.

Another classic example of this issue, prior to JDK 1.4, was the use of XML libraries like Xerces. This instance is not a problem in JDK 1.4, because XML is now part of the JVM, but developers cannot wait for every additional JAR to be bundled into the JDK.

So since these developers still haven't learned the underlying problem, they try something else. They try to ensure that the JAR was made correctly, the CLASSPATH is correct, and the JAR is uncompressed and executed in the conventional manner. Everything works right. Recompress it and it no longer works.

```
Manifest-Version: 1.0
Main-Class: Example
Created-By: 1.3.1
```

Why doesn't this work? First, it is important to recognize that the command-line ("java Example") invocation of the JVM uses the same CLASSPATH as the compiler. So, obviously, if it compiled then, it will run.

However, double-clicking on a JAR file, or executing `java -jar` (except in the JDK HOME\bin directory), attempts to use the JRE, which has its own `CLASSPATH`. So, the additional necessary JARs can be placed in the JRE HOME\lib\ext directory. Note that it is not the lib directory itself, unlike the JDK.

However, unless you want to install the classes into that directory, you should add them into your JAR file and reference them in the JAR's manifest file.

```
Manifest-Version: 1.0
Main-Class: Example
Class-Path: jaxp.jar xalan.jar xerces.jar
Created-By: 1.3.1
```

Deploying Java Applications

A tremendous number of problems in installing, configuring, and running Java applications has to do with the misunderstanding of how to specify how the JVM should find classes to load. The first method used looks like the one found in Listing 13.1.

```
01: APPDATA=C:\Documents and Settings\crichardson\Application Data
02: CLASSPATH=D:\soap-2_2;C:\Program Files\Apache Tomcat
4.0\webapps\soap\WEB-INF\classes;D:\soap-2_2\lib\mail.jar;D:\soap-
2_2\lib\activation.jar;D:\soap-2_2\lib\mailapi.jar
03: CommonProgramFiles=C:\Program Files\Common Files
04: COMPUTERNAME=CLAYSVAIO
05: ComSpec=C:\WINNT\system32\cmd.exe
06: HOMEDRIVE=C:
07: HOMEPATH=\
08: OS=Windows_NT
09: [...]
```

Listing 13.1   Environment variables

This shows the classic and traditional way of handling the Java `CLASSPATH`. Set an environment variable, or rather, add to the already existing environment variable. A number of other environment variables were left in this example to highlight how broad the spectrum of things stored in the environment is and the number of applications that must make use of it.

Furthermore, we have one `CLASSPATH` that all applications use. This provides a major issue for deploying applications, because there are possible conflicts that can occur among executable JAR files. This is just the Java version of the "DLL hell" phenomenon—not only for the presence or absence of JAR files, but also the difference in versions of JAR files.

Another mechanism that is used for assembling a `CLASSPATH` is the `-cp` switch in executing the Java Virtual Machine execution.

```
C:\j2sdk1.4.0\jre\bin\javaw -cp
"D:\pkoDev\beans\classes;C:\dom4j\lib\dom4j.jar;D:\java_xml_pack-winter-
01-dev\jaxp-1.2-ea1\xalan.jar;D:\java_xml_pack-winter-01-dev\jaxp-1.2-
ea1\xerces.jar;D:\java_xml_pack-winter-01-dev\jaxm-1.0.1-
ea1\lib\activation.jar;D:\java_xml_pack-winter-01-dev\jaxm-1.0.1-
ea1\lib\dom4j.jar;D:\java_xml_pack-winter-01-dev\jaxm-1.0.1-
ea1\lib\jaxm.jar;D:\java_xml_pack-winter-01-dev\jaxm-1.0.1-
ea1\lib\log4j.jar;D:\java_xml_pack-winter-01-dev\jaxm-1.0.1-
ea1\lib\mail.jar;D:\jaxpack\java_xml_pack-fall01\jaxm-
1.0\jaxm\client.jar"  org.javapitfalls.jar.Example
```

While this option allows for a more explicit and direct way to control the CLASSPATH for your application, it still is neither very user-friendly nor very configuration-friendly. In effect, this is what happens with a lot of applications; everyone packages their own JAR files and references them using the CLASSPATH JVM option in order to control what is available in their applications.

However, this can lead to a great deal of redundancy. For example, I searched for "xerces*.jar" on my development machine. This would capture all of the versions of the popular Apache XML parsing API Xerces. Granted, a development box is not exactly the most representative example of a deployment machine, but I got 73 instances of Xerces. Basically, every Java application running on my machine that uses XML, some of which are not development tools or APIs, has a copy of Xerces to process XML. Those 73 instances take up 108 MB of disk space, to do essentially the same thing.

What if there is a bug fix out for Xerces that needs to be integrated into my applications, or even bigger, a performance improvement. I have to copy it to 73 different places in my application. Furthermore, with the introduction of XML into JDK 1.4, there is a potential for class conflicts. This is because the Java platform has evolved to the point where it provides new features, and XML processing is part of it.

So, why not be able to extend the platform? Earlier, we discussed an example of what people do wrong in creating an executable JAR file. Those mistakes are due to poor understanding of the Java extension mechanism.

The Java Extension Mechanism

The Java Extension Mechanism is how developers can extend the Java platform without having to worry about the issues concerning the CLASSPATH. The most obvious way to create an extension is to copy a JAR file into the JRE HOME/lib/ext directory. Furthermore, Java Plug-in and Java Web Start provide facilities for installing extensions on demand and automatically.

Figure 13.1 shows the architecture of the Java Extension Mechanism. There are sets of classes that make up the core system classes, and developers can provide the ability to add their own classes into the Java Runtime Environment. These are called "optional packages" (formerly known as "standard extensions").

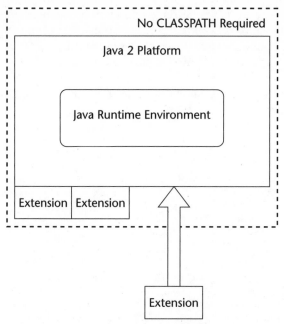

Figure 13.1   Java Extension Mechanism.

We should note that in our previous example, there were references to three optional packages: jaxp.jar, xerces.jar, and xalan.jar. When the executable JAR file shown in that example is executed, the Java Runtime Environment knows to look in those JAR files for classes needed to execute the application. It should be noted that it checks those only if they are not already available in the system class loader; therefore, redundant references to JAR files are not a problem. Class loading from the JAR files is lazy, or as needed.

Sealed Packages

Developers can choose to seal their optional packages. The purpose of sealing a package is to ensure consistency among versions of a particular JAR file. When a package is sealed, it means that every class defined in this JAR must originate from this JAR. Therefore, a sealed Xerces package would assume precedence over other xerces.jar files. This can cut both ways, and it requires that developers are cognizant of which of the optional packages may be controlling the loading of classes.

A perfect example of this is when it becomes necessary to change the order in which JAR files are placed in the CLASSPATH. If a sealed package is loaded first, and then a newer version is loaded later in the sequence, the newer version will not be used; in fact, `ClassNotFoundExceptions` and `ClassCastExceptions` are common symptoms. Tomcat 3.x versions are known to have this problem in regard to XML. It should be noted that this is addressed in another pitfall regarding the endorsed standards override mechanism.

Listing 13.2 gives an example of the Java Versioning Specification combined with the optional package sealing mechanism.

```
01: Name: org/javapitfalls/
02: Sealed: true
03: Extension-List: ThisClass ThatClass
04: ThisClass-Extension-Name: org.javapitfalls.ThisClass
05: ThisClass-Specification-Version: 1.2
06: ThisClass-Implementation-Version: 1.2
07: ThisClass-Implementation-Vendor-Id: org.javapitfalls
08: ThisClass-Implementation-URL: http://javapitfalls.org/ThisClass.jar
09: ThatClass-Extension-Name: org.javapitfalls.ThatClass
10: ThatClass-Specification-Version: 1.2
11: ThatClass-Implementation-Version: 1.2
12: ThatClass-Implementation-Vendor-Id: org.javapitfalls
13: ThatClass-Implementation-URL: http://javapitfalls.org/ThatClass.jar
14:
```

Listing 13.2   Versioning and sealing an optional package

This shows that any files in the `org.javapitfalls` package will be sealed—that is, they must all come from this JAR file. The rest shows the appropriate information to allow `ClassLoaders` to understand the versioning of extensions. The Plug-in is an example of an application that will use this to determine the need to download this version of the package.

Security

These installed optional packages are restricted to the sandbox unless they are from a trusted source. This requires a signing of the JAR file and appropriate permissions being handled in the Java security policy for the application that uses the extension.

Executable JAR files, `CLASSPATHs`, JAR conflicts—these are all things that challenge developers as they deploy their Java applications. Frequently, developers run into problems because of inadequate understanding of the Java extension mechanism. This pitfall costs a developer time and effort and can lead to substantial configuration control issues.

Item 14: What Do You Collect?

We are building a system that provides a "virtual file cabinet" to browse articles available all over the World Wide Web. The Web site provides a hierarchical format that organizes knowledge for visibility. The topics can be nested inside each other to go as deeply as the content organizer desires. Each topic maps over to one or more categories. Furthermore, a category can appear in multiple topics. This scenario might seem a bit confused, but it is based on a real system. Essentially, the topics refer to how the Web site wants to organize content, and the categories refer to how content syndicates tag their documents.

As the folders are opened, subfolders are displayed below it on the tree, and the appropriate documents for the categories are displayed in the right pane. Users can browse down the hierarchy to view the data that they want.

This whole logic is based on an XML file that maintains the nesting of topics and mappings to categories. Listing 14.1 shows an excerpt of the XML document that the Web site uses.

```
01: <?xml version = "1.0" encoding = "UTF-8"?>
02: <navigation>
03:  <taxonomy text = "Donnie's Subscription Service" value = "default">
04:        <topic value = "1" text = "Computer Technology News">
05:              <topic value = "3" text = "Software Technology">
06:                 <topic value = "4" text = "J2SE">
07:                        <category>2611</category>
08:              </topic>
09:                 <topic value = "5" text = "J2EE">
10:                        <category>2612</category>
11:              </topic>
12:                 <topic value = "6" text = "J2ME">
13:                        <category>2613</category>
14:              </topic>
<!-- ... some topics omitted for brevity ... -->
32:              </topic>
33:              <topic value = "13" text = "Network Technology">
34:                   <category>2612</category>
35:                   <category>2700</category>
46:              </topic>
47:              <topic value = "22" text = "Hardware">
48:                 <topic value = "23" text = "Server Technology">
49:                        <category>1511</category>
50:              </topic>
51:                 <topic value = "24" text = "Desktop Technology">
52:                        <category>1512</category>
53:              </topic>
54:                 <topic value = "25" text = "Wireless Technology">
55:                        <category>1513</category>
56:              </topic>
57:        <...>
58:  </taxonomy>
59: </navigation>
```

Listing 14.1 Navigation.xml

Listing 14.2 demonstrates the code that is used to process the Navigation.xml file for supporting the Web site. It has been stripped down to show the necessary methods and the one of interest (listCategories).

```
001: package org.javapitfalls;
002:
003: import java.io.*;
004: import java.net.*;
005: import java.util.*;
006: import org.dom4j.Document;
// ... some dom4j Imports removed for brevity ... Code available on Web
site
014:
015: public class BadNavigationUtils {
017:    private Document document;
018:
019:    public BadNavigationUtils () {
020:        try {
021:            setFile(getClass().getResource("/Navigation.xml"));
022:            setDates();
023:            } catch (Exception e) { e.printStackTrace();  }
024:    }
025:
026:    public void setFile ( String path ) throws DocumentException {
027:        SAXReader reader = new SAXReader();
028:        document = reader.read(path);
029:    }
030:
031:    public void setFile ( URL path ) throws DocumentException {
032:        SAXReader reader = new SAXReader();
033:        document = reader.read(path);
034:    }
035:
036:
037:    public void writeFile (String path) {
039:       try {
040:
041:        // write to a file
042:        XMLWriter writer = new XMLWriter(
043:            new FileWriter( path ),
OutputFormat.createPrettyPrint() );
044:        writer.write( document );
045:        writer.close();
046:
047:       } catch (IOException ioe )  {
048:
049:        ioe.printStackTrace();
051:       }
```

Listing 14.2   BadNavigationUtils.java

```
052:    }
053:
054:
055:    public List listCategories (String[] topics) {
057:         HashSet mySet = new HashSet();
060:         for (int i=0; i < topics.length - 1; i++) {
062:         List list = document.selectNodes( "//topic[@value='" + ⤶
topics[i] + "']/category" );
064:             mySet.addAll(list);
066:         }
067:
068:         ArrayList theList = new ArrayList();
070:         theList.addAll(mySet);
073:         return theList;
074:
075:    }
076:
077:    public static void main(String[] args) {
079:        try {
080:
081:     String [] topics = new String[3];
083:            topics[0] = "4";
084:     topics[1] = "5";
085:         topics[2] = "13";
086:
087:         BadNavigationUtils topicCategory = new BadNavigationUtils ⤶
();
089:         topicCategory.setFile("Navigation.xml");
091:         List categories = topicCategory.listCategories(topics);
092:         for ( int i = 0; i < categories.size(); i++ ) {
093:             Element myElement = (Element) categories.get(i);
094:             System.out.println(myElement.getText());
096:         }
099:     } catch (Exception e) { e.printStackTrace();}
101:  }
102: }
103:
```

Listing 14.2 BadNavigationUtils.java *(continued)*

BadNavigationUtils.java uses DOM4J to parse an XML file into a DOM tree, and then uses an XPath expression to pull back a List of category nodes (in the `listCat-egories` method). This is the result of executing this code:

```
01: 2611
02: 2612
03: 2612
```

```
04: 2700
05: 2710
06: 2711
07: 2712
08: 2713
09: 2714
10: 2715
11: 2720
12: 2730
13: 2740
14: 2750
```

The idea was to filter out the duplicates in the list, but it is clear that this didn't work. The category "2612" is shown twice. Why didn't this work? After all, HashSet is supposed to not allow duplicates in the collection.

As it turns out, this method returns a list of nodes to the user. Those nodes represent the location of that particular element on the tree. Therefore, there is a distinction between the 2612 in the topic with id of 5 and the 2612 in the topic with id of 13. When we print out the text of each of the nodes, we find that there are duplicate values.

So, if we want to make sure we have a true Set, we need to pay more careful attention to the type of object being stored in the collection. To handle this problem, we modify the code to actually store the text value of the nodes. Listing 14.3 shows how we do that.

```
01:    public List listCategories (String[] topics) {
03:        TreeSet mySet = new TreeSet();
06:        for (int i=0; i < topics.length - 1; i++) {
08:            List list = document.selectNodes( "//topic[@value='" +
topics[i] + "']/descendant-or-self::*/category" );
09:
10:            for ( Iterator it = list.listIterator(); it.hasNext(); )
{
11:                mySet.add( ((Element) it.next()).getText() );
12:            }
14:        }
15:
16:        ArrayList theList = new ArrayList();
18:        theList.addAll(mySet);
20:        return theList;
22:    }
```

Listing 14.3   GoodNavigationUtils.java (listCategories)

Notice in this example we are calling the getText() method on the Element returned in the Iterator. The returned String is then added to the HashSet.

An interesting development has evolved in the Java Community Process program (JCP). JSR 14, "Add Generic Types to the Java Programming Language," offers a mechanism for providing parameterized classes (JSR stands for "Java Specification Request"). In this case, we have a `List` being returned to us, which we were unable to determine what type was in the list without closely consulting the API documentation. Of course, since all code is well documented in excruciating detail, we always know the types that are returned to us. In reality, the only documentation on which you can ever truly count (and frequently the only documentation that is read) is the method signature. Of course, if you were up on XML libraries, you would understand that a method called `selectNodes` is going to return `Node` objects.

This gets to the essence of the problem: The Collection classes are a very popular feature in the Java platform. Their power, efficiency, and flexibility are highly valued. However, as this example has shown, it is very difficult to know precisely how collections are handled. This requires that numerous casts and type checks are needed in order to handle something generically.

That is what JSR 14 hopes to accomplish. Now, you would be able to pass a type to the `List` class. For example, you could declare a vector like this:

```
Vector<String> x = new Vector<String>();
```

Generics are a feature to be added to the Java 2 Standard Edition 1.5, code-named "Tiger." Until then, developers will have to be aware of what types are being held in their collections.

Item 15: Avoiding Singleton Pitfalls

As programmers, we love design patterns! They allow us to use repeatable solutions to problems, and they offer us an easy way to communicate in software engineering projects. Used wisely, these patterns offer us the capability to quickly build elegant, flexible designs. Using them without fully understanding their purpose and impact could lead to a brittle software architecture. More importantly, creating an incorrect implementation of existing patterns could lead to disastrous results.

The Singleton design pattern, presented by Gamma, Helm, Johnson, and Vlissides in *Design Patterns: Elements of Reusable Software*, is a creational pattern that ensures that a class has one instance and provides a global point of access to it.[4] In the Java programming language, a correct implementation of a Singleton ensures that there will be one instance of a class per JVM. There are many Singleton classes throughout the Java API itself, with a few examples being *java.util.Calendar* and *java.util.DateFormat*. The Singleton is useful in cases where you want a single point of access to a resource. In Item 32, we created a Singleton class that was a single point of access to a database. Listings 15.1 and 15.2 show two common ways of implementing a Singleton class. The constructors in both classes are private, so that only the static `getInstance()` method can instantiate the class. In Listing 15.1, the Singleton's constructor is called when the class is first loaded, on line 4. When a class calls the `getInstance()` method shown in lines 16 to 18, the static `m_instance` variable is returned.

---

[4] Gamma, Helm, Johnson, Vlissides, *Design Patterns: Elements of Reusable Software*, Addison-Wesley, Reading, Massachusetts, 1984.

```
01: public class ClassLoadSingleton
02: {
03:     //called at class-load time
04:     private static ClassLoadSingleton
05:                     m_instance = new ClassLoadSingleton();
06:
07:     private ClassLoadSingleton()
08:     {
09:         //implementation details go here
10:     }
11:
12:     /**
13:      * point of entry to this class
14:      */
15:     public static ClassLoadSingleton getInstance()
16:     {
17:         return m_instance;
18:     }
20: }
```

Listing 15.1   Singleton instantiated at class loading time

Listing 15.2 shows a different approach. Instead of calling the constructor at class load time, the class uses *lazy instantiation*—that is, the constructor is not called until getInstance() is called the first time. Lines 14 to 20 of Listing 15.2 show the logic of returning the FirstCallSingleton class from the getInstance() method.

```
01: public class FirstCallSingleton
02: {
03:
04:     private static FirstCallSingleton m_instance = null;
05:
06:     private FirstCallSingleton()
07:     {
08:         //implementation details go here
09:     }
10:
11:     /**
12:      * point of entry to this class
13:      */
14:     public static synchronized FirstCallSingleton getInstance()
15:     {
16:         if (m_instance == null)
17:             m_instance = new FirstCallSingleton();
```

Listing 15.2   Singleton instantiated at first call

```
18:
19:        return m_instance;
20:    }
21: }
```

Listing 15.2 *(continued)*

Now that we've provided a review of the Singleton design pattern, let's discuss what could go wrong. The following sections discuss bad practices that we have commonly seen and provide suggestions on resolving the resulting dilemmas that occur.

When Multiple Singletons in Your VM Happen

Right now, you're thinking, "What? Isn't this contrary to the definition of a Singleton?" Yes, you're absolutely correct. However, if a Singleton class is not written correctly in a one-VM multithreaded system, problems can arise.

Consider a Singleton designed to use lazy instantiation, as implemented in Listing 15.2. If the getInstance() method is not synchronized, the following could happen: Two threads could call getInstance() simultaneously, and two different versions of FirstCall could be returned. Figure 15.1 shows a pictorial representation of how this could occur in one virtual machine. At time t=30, two threads in one virtual machine call FirstCall.getInstance(), and two different objects are returned. This could be extremely dangerous if, for example, the Singleton is supposed to guarantee a single point of access to an external resource. If the Singleton class is writing data to a file, for example, several problems could arise, ranging from corrupted data to unintended mutual exclusion problems.

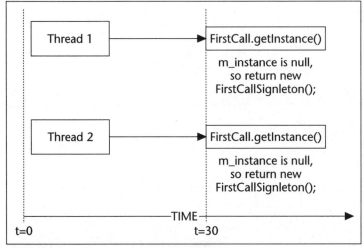

Figure 15.1 The synchronization problem.

Like most concurrency issues, this is a difficult problem to debug. *The key point here is to make certain that your* getInstance() *method is synchronized when you are using the lazy instantiation Singleton strategy shown in Listing 15.2.*

When Singletons are Used as Global Variables, or Become Non-Singletons

Sometimes the Singleton class is abused. One example that we've unfortunately seen quite a bit is when a Singleton class is used as a "global variable" to eliminate parameter passing. Using a Singleton in this manner is poor practice, and it may affect the flexibility of your project's software architecture. One example that we have seen is where a code author placed his main application's GUI object in a Singleton with synchronized setGUI() and getGUI() methods, to avoid passing the user interface component to other objects in the system. The strategy worked well, until the software customer requested multiple applications per VM. Because some of the classes got a handle to the application's user interface with the getGUI() method in the Singleton, this had to be rewritten.

We shudder to even show this next example, but an extreme case is shown in Listing 15.3.

```
01: public class GlobalVarSingleton
02: {
03:
04:     private static GlobalVarSingleton
05:                 m_instance = new GlobalVarSingleton();
06:
07:     //The use of this class is NOT recommended!
08:     public int x = 0;
09:     public int y = 1;
10:     public int z = 2;
11:
12:     private void GlobalVarSingleton()
13:     {
14:     }
15:
16:     /**
17:      * point of entry to this class
18:      */
19:     public static synchronized GlobalVarSingleton getInstance()
20:     {
21:         return m_instance;
22:     }
23:
24:     public static void main(String[] args)
25:     {
26:         //Bad usage example:
27:
```

Listing 15.3   Singleton as global variable

```
28:          GlobalVarSingleton globals =
29:                  GlobalVarSingleton.getInstance();
30:          globals.x = 333;
31:          globals.y = 40803;
32:          globals.z = 21;
33:
34:      /**
35:          At this point, the offender calls other classes
36:          who call GlobalVarSingleton.getInstance() to get
37:          (and change) values of x, y, and z.
38:        **/
39:
40:      }
41: }
```

Listing 15.3   *(continued)*

Listing 15.3 shows the poor choice of using a Singleton to hold variables. In lines 8, 9, and 10, there are public instance variables x, y, and z. The main() method of Listing 15.3 shows an example usage of this, where a class in the VM gets the Singleton, alters the variables, and calls another class, which gets the values of those variables and changes them. It goes without saying that there will be synchronization issues in this example, and it also goes without saying that this is poor design. Of course, many Singletons are not as blatant as this; some are designed correctly, but somewhere along the road, an unenlightened programmer could add things to it to accomplish ends like this. Please be aware that this is poor practice, and keep an eye on your existing Singleton classes.

Over time, a code base evolves. Software engineers modify classes, and every once in a while, we have seen times where Singletons, accidentally or intentionally, stop being Singletons. One of the most common events that we have seen is when a novice programmer changes the private constructor to a public one, leading to havoc throughout the baseline. Watch your baseline!

In conclusion, when you are deciding whether to create a Singleton class, first ask yourself the following questions:

- Does there need to be one global entry point to this class?
- Should there be only one instance to this class in the VM?

If your answer is yes, then use a Singleton. If no, don't use this design pattern.

If you do use the Singleton design pattern, be sure to implement your Singleton classes correctly—use a private constructor, and synchronize methods that need to be synchronized, looking at the code skeletons in Listing 15.1 and 15.2. Finally, again, watch your baseline! Poor practices, such as using Singletons as global variables, as well as the evolution of your Singletons into non-Singletons, can cause problems that will keep you up too late at night.

Item 16: When setSize() Won't Work[5]

Most developers stumble upon pitfalls sequentially, based on their experience level with Java. The `setSize()` pitfall usually presents itself shortly after Java developers begin serious GUI development, specifically when they try to set the size of their first newly created custom components. `BadSetSize`, as follows, creates a simple custom button that we want to size to 100 by 100 pixels. Here is the code to create our custom button:

```
class CustomButton extends Button
{
    public CustomButton(String title)
    {
        super(title);
        setSize(100,100);
    }
}
```

In the constructor, developers often mistakenly assume that they can use `set-Size()(width, height)` in the same way they do when sizing a frame. The problem arises when the developer hasn't yet gained the knowledge of the Abstract Windowing Toolkit's (AWT) inner workings to understand that this code will only work under certain situations. He or she has no idea that `setSize()` will fail to correctly size the component. For example, when we place our custom button in the frame with other components using a simple grid layout, we get the results in Figure 16.1. Our button is 66 by 23, not 100 by 100! What happened to our call to `setSize()`? The method was executed, of course. However, it did not give the final word on the size of our component.

Listing 16.1 shows the source code for BadSetSize.java.

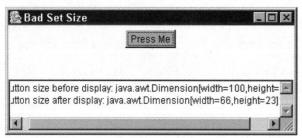

Figure 16.1   Run of BadSetSize.class.

[5] This pitfall was first published by *JavaWorld* (www.javaworld.com) in the article "Steer clear of Java Pitfalls", September 2000 (http://www.javaworld.com/javaworld/jw-09-2000 /jw-0922-javatraps.html?) and is reprinted here with permission. The pitfall has been updated from reader feedback.

```
01: package org.javapitfalls.item16;
02:
03: import java.awt.*;
04: import java.awt.event.*;
05:
06: class CustomButton extends Button
07: {
08:     public CustomButton(String title)
09:     {
10:         super(title);
11:         setSize(100,100);
12:     }
13: }
14:
15: public class BadSetSize extends Frame
16: {
17:     TextArea status;
18:
19:     public BadSetSize()
20:     {
21:         super("Bad Set Size");
22:
23:         setLayout(new GridLayout(2,0,2,2));
24:         Panel p = new Panel();
25:         CustomButton button = new CustomButton("Press Me");
26:         p.add(button);
27:         add(p);
28:         status = new TextArea(3, 50);
29:         status.append("Button size before display: " +
button.getSize() + "\n");
30:         add(status);
31:         addWindowListener(new WindowAdapter()
32:                     {
33:                         public void windowClosing(WindowEvent we)
34:                         { System.exit(1); }
35:                     });
36:         setLocation(100,100);
37:         pack();
38:         setVisible(true);
39:         status.append("Button size after display: " +
button.getSize());
40:     }
41:
42:     public static void main(String args [])
43:     {
44:         new BadSetSize();
45:     }
46: }
```

Listing 16.1   BadSetSize.java

Let's examine the correct approach to sizing a component. The key to understanding why our code failed is to recognize that after we create the component, the layout manager—called `GridLayout`—reshapes the component in accordance with its own rules. This presents us with several solutions. We could eliminate the layout manager by calling `setLayout(null)`, but as the layout manager provides numerous benefits to our code, this is a poor remedy. If the user resizes the window, we still want to be able to automatically resize our user interface, which is the layout manager's chief benefit. Another alternative would be to call `setSize()` after the layout manager has completed its work. This only provides us with a quick fix: By calling `repaint()`, the size would change, yet again when the browser is resized. That leaves us with only one real option: Work with the layout manager only to resize the component. Below we rewrite our custom component:

```
class CustomButton2 extends Button
{
    public CustomButton2(String title)
    {
        super(title);
        // setSize(100,100); - unnecessary
    }

    public Dimension getMinimumSize()
    { return new Dimension(100,100); }

    public Dimension getPreferredSize()
    { return getMinimumSize(); }
}
```

Our custom component overrides the `getMinimumSize()` and `getPreferred-Size()` methods of the `Component` class to set the component size. The layout manager invokes these methods to determine how to size an individual component. Some layout managers will disregard these hints if their pattern calls for that. For example, if this button was placed in the center of a `BorderLayout`, the button would not be 100 by 100, but instead would stretch to fit the available center space. `GridLayout` will abide by these sizes and anchor the component in the center. The `GoodSetSize` class below uses the `CustomButton2` class.

```
01: package org.javapitfalls.item16;
02:
03: import java.awt.*;
04: import java.awt.event.*;
05:
06: class CustomButton2 extends Button
07: {
```

Listing 16.2   GoodSetSize.java

```
08:     public CustomButton2(String title)
09:     {
10:         super(title);
11:         System.out.println("Size of button is : " + this.getSize());
12:     }
13:
14:     public Dimension getMinimumSize()
15:     { return new Dimension(100,100); }
16:
17:     public Dimension getPreferredSize()
18:     { return getMinimumSize(); }
19: }
20:
21: public class GoodSetSize extends Frame
22: {
23:     TextArea status;
24:
25:     public GoodSetSize()
26:     {
27:         super("Good Set Size");
28:
29:         setLayout(new GridLayout(2,0));
30:         Panel p = new Panel();
31:         CustomButton2 button = new CustomButton2("Press Me");
32:         p.add(button);
33:         add(p);
34:         status = new TextArea(3,50);
35:         status.append("Button size before display: " +
button.getSize() + "\n");
36:         add(status);
37:         addWindowListener(new WindowAdapter()
38:                     {
39:                         public void windowClosing(WindowEvent we)
40:                         { System.exit(1); }
41:                     });
42:         setLocation(100,100);
43:         pack();
44:         setVisible(true);
45:         status.append("Button size after display: " +
button.getSize());
46:     }
47:
48:     public static void main(String args [])
49:     {
50:         new GoodSetSize();
51:     }
52: }
```

Listing 16.2   *(continued)*

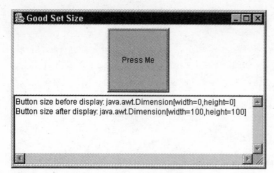

Figure 16.2   Run of GoodSetSize.class.

Running GoodSetSize.java results in Figure 16.2.

It is interesting to note that our solution to setting the size of a component involved not using the `setSize()` method. This pitfall is caused by the design complexity of a cross-platform user interface and a developer's unfamiliarity with the chain of events necessary to display and resize an interface. Unfortunately, the supplied documentation of `setSize()` fails to suggest these prerequisites.

This solution also highlights the importance of properly naming methods and parameters. Should you use `setSize()` when you only need to set some internal values that may or may not be used by your display mechanisms? A better choice would be `setInternalValues()`, which at least clearly warns a developer of the limited guarantee this method offers.

Item 17: When Posting to a URL Won't[6]

Now that the Simple Object Access Protocol (SOAP) and other variants of XML Remote Procedure Calls (RPC) are becoming popular, posting to a Uniform Resource Locator (URL) will be a more common and more important operation. While implementing a standalone SOAP server, I stumbled across multiple pitfalls associated with posting to a URL; starting with the nonintuitive design of the URL-related classes and ending with specific usability pitfalls in the `URLConnection` class.

Connecting via HTTP with the java.net Classes

To perform a Hypertext Transfer Protocol (HTTP) post operation on a URL, you would hope to find a simple `HttpClient` class to do the work, but after scanning the java.net package, you would come up empty. There are several open-source HTTP clients available, and we examine one of them after examining the built-in classes. As an aside, it is interesting to note that there is an `HttpClient` in the sun.net.www.http package that is shipped with the JDK (and used by `HttpURLConnection`) but not part of the

[6] This pitfall was first published by *JavaWorld* (www.javaworld.com) in the article, "Dodge the traps hiding in the URLConnection Class", March 2001 (http://www.javaworld.com /javaworld/jw-03-2001/jw-0323-traps.html?)and is reprinted here with permission. The pitfall has been updated from reader feedback.

public API. Instead, the java.net URL classes were designed to be extremely generic and take advantage of dynamic class loading of both protocols and content handlers. Before we jump into the specific problems with posting, let's examine the overall structure of the classes we will be using (either directly or indirectly). Figure 17.1 is a UML diagram (created with ArgoUML downloadable from www.argouml.org) of the URL-related classes in the java.net package and their relationships to each other. For brevity, the diagram only shows key methods and does not show any data members.

The main class this pitfall centers around is the `URLConnection` class; however, you cannot instantiate that class directly (it is abstract) but only get a reference to a specific subclass of URLConnection via the URL class. If you think that Figure 17.1 is complex, I would agree. The general sequence of events works like this: A static URL commonly specifies the location of some content and the protocol needed to access it. The first time the URL class is used, a URLStreamHandlerFactory Singleton is created. This factory will generate the appropriate `URLStreamHandler` that understands the access protocol specified in the URL. The `URLStreamHandler` will instantiate the appropriate `URLConnection` class that will then open a connection to the URL and instantiate the appropriate `ContentHandler` to handle the content at the URL. So, now that we know the general model, what is the problem? The chief problem is that these classes lack a clear conceptual model by trying to be overly generic. Donald Norman's book *The Design of Everyday Things* states that one of the primary principles of good design is a good conceptual model that allows us to "predict the effects of our actions."[7] Here are some problems with the conceptual model of these classes:

- The URL class is conceptually overloaded. A URL is merely an abstraction for an address or an endpoint. In fact, it would be better to have URL subclasses to differentiate static resources from dynamic services. What is missing conceptually is a `URLClient` class that uses the URL as the endpoint to read from or write to.

- The URL class is biased toward retrieving data from a URL. There are three methods you can use to retrieve content from a URL and only one way to write data to a URL. This disparity would be better served with a URL subclass for static resources that only has a read operation. The URL subclass for dynamic services would have both read and write methods. That would provide a clean conceptual model for use.

- The naming of the protocol handlers "stream" handlers is confusing because their primary purpose is to generate (or build) a connection. A better model to follow would be the one used in the Java API for XML Parsing (JAXP) where a `DocumentBuilderFactory` produces a `DocumentBuilder` that produces a `Document`. Applying that model to the URL classes would yield a `URLConnectorFactory` that produces a `URLConnector` that produces a `URLConnection`.

Now that we have the general picture, we are ready to tackle the `URLConnection` class and attempt to post to a URL. Our goal is to create a simple Java program that posts some text to a Common Gateway Interface (CGI) program. To test our programs, I created a simple CGI program in C that echoes (in an HTML wrapper) whatever is passed in to it. Listing 17.1 is the source code for that CGI program called echocgi.c.

---

[7] Norman, Donald A., *The Design of Everyday Things*, Doubleday, 1988, page 13.

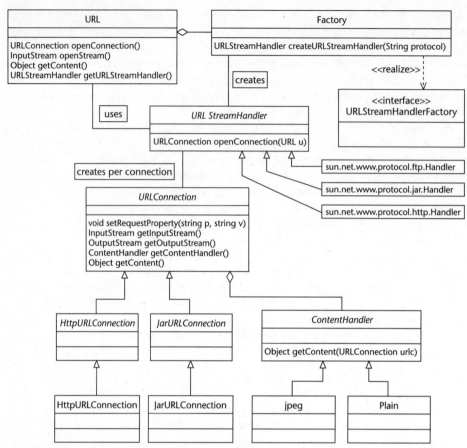

Figure 17.1   URL Classes in the java.net package.

```
01: #include <stdio.h>
02: #include <stdlib.h>
03: #include <string.h>
04:
05: void main(int argc, char **argv)
06: {
07:   char *request_method = NULL;
08:   char *content_length = NULL;
09:   char *content_type = NULL;
10:   int length=0;
11:   char *content = NULL;
12:   int read = 0;
13:
```

Listing 17.1   echocgi.c

```
14:   /* get the key environment variables. */
15:   request_method = getenv("REQUEST_METHOD");
16:   if (!request_method)
17:   {
18:           printf("Not being run as a CGI program.\n");
19:           exit(1);
20:   }
21:
22:   // set outgoing content type
23:   printf("Content-type: text/html\n\n");
24:
25:   if (strcmp(request_method, "POST") == 0)
26:   {
27:           content_length = getenv("CONTENT_LENGTH");
28:           content_type = getenv("CONTENT_TYPE");
29:
30:           length = atoi(content_length);
31:           if (length > 0)
32:           {
33:                   content = (char *) malloc(length + 1);
34:                   read = fread(content, 1, length, stdin);
35:                   content[length] = '\0'; /* NUL terminate */
36:           }
37:
38:           printf("<HEAD>\n");
39:           printf("<TITLE> Echo CGI program </TITLE>\n");
40:           printf("</HEAD>\n");
41:           printf("<BODY BGCOLOR='#ebebeb'>");
42:           printf("<CENTER>\n");
43:           printf("<H2> Echo </H2>\n");
44:           printf("</CENTER>\n");
45:           if (length > 0)
46:           {
47:                   printf("Length of content: %d\n", length);
48:                   printf("Content: %s\n", content);
49:           }
50:           else
51:                   printf("No content! ERROR!\n");
52:           printf("</BODY>\n");
53:           printf("</HTML>\n");
54:   }
55:   else
56:   {
57:           // print out HTML error
58:           printf("<HTML> <HEAD> <TITLE> Configuration Error ⤶
</TITLE></HEAD>\n");
59:           printf("<BODY> Unable to run the Echo CGI Program. <BR>\n");
60:           printf("Reason: This program only tests a POST method. ⤶
<BR>\n");
```

Listing 17.1   *(continued)*

```
61:            printf("Report this to your System Administrator. </BR>\n");
62:            printf("</BODY> </HTML>\n");
63:            exit(1);
64:    }
66: }
```

Listing 17.1   *(continued)*

Testing the CGI program requires two things: a Web server and a browser or program to post information to the program. For the Web server, I downloaded and installed the Apache Web server from www.apache.org. Figure 17.2 displays the simple HTML form used to post information (two fields) to the CGI program. When the "Submit your vote" button is clicked in the HTML form, the two values are posted to the CGI program (on the localhost) and the response page is generated as is shown in Figure 17.3.

Now that we have a simple CGI program to echo data posted to it, we are ready to write our Java program to post data. To send data to a URL, we would expect it to be as easy as writing data to a socket. Fortunately, by examining the `URLConnection` class we see that it has `getOutputStream()` and `getInputStream()` methods, just like the `Socket` class. Armed with that information and an understanding of the HTTP protocol, we write the program in Listing 17.2, BadURLPost.java.

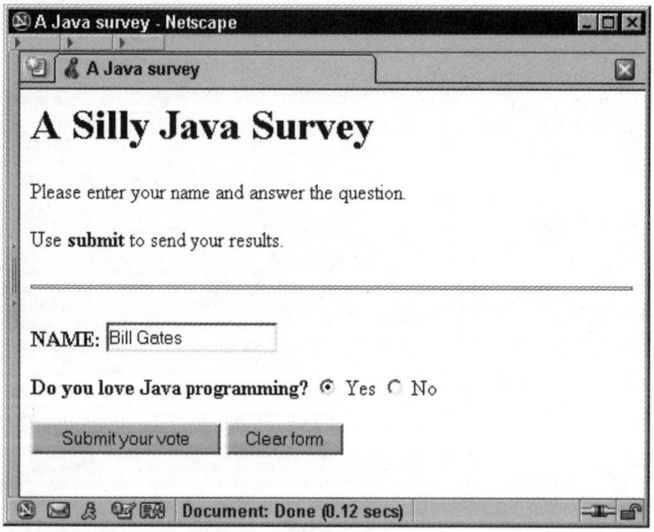

Figure 17.2   HTML Form to test echocgi.exe.

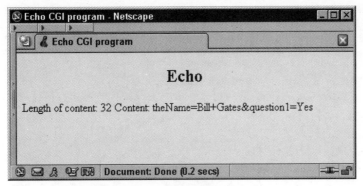

Figure 17.3   HTML response from echocgi.exe.

```
01: /** BadURLPost.java */
02: package org.javapitfalls.item17;
03:
04: import java.net.*;
05: import java.io.*;
06:
07: public class BadURLPost
08: {
09:     public static void main(String args[])
10:     {
11:         // get an HTTP connection to POST to
12:         if (args.length < 1)
13:         {
14:             System.out.println("USAGE: java
GOV.dia.mditds.util.BadURLPost url");
15:             System.exit(1);
16:         }
17:
18:         try
19:         {
20:             // get the url as a string
21:             String surl = args[0];
22:             URL url = new URL(surl);
23:
24:             URLConnection con = url.openConnection();
25:             System.out.println("Received a : " +
con.getClass().getName());
26:
```

Listing 17.2   BadURLPost.java *(continued)*

```
27:            con.setDoInput(true);
28:            con.setDoOutput(true);
29:            con.setUseCaches(false);
30:
31:            String msg = "Hi HTTP SERVER! Just a quick hello!";
32:            con.setRequestProperty("CONTENT_LENGTH", "5"); // Not ⤵
checked
33:            con.setRequestProperty("Stupid", "Nonsense");
34:
35:            System.out.println("Getting an input stream...");
36:            InputStream is = con.getInputStream();
37:
38:            System.out.println("Getting an output stream...");
39:            OutputStream os = con.getOutputStream();
40:
41:            /*
42:            con.setRequestProperty("CONTENT_LENGTH", "" + ⤵
msg.length());
43:            Illegal access error - can't reset method.
44:            */
45:
46:            OutputStreamWriter osw = new OutputStreamWriter(os);
47:            osw.write(msg);
48:            /** REMEMBER THIS osw.flush(); **/
49:            osw.flush();
50:            osw.close();
51:
52:            System.out.println("After flushing output stream. ");
53:
54:            // any response?
55:            InputStreamReader isr = new InputStreamReader(is);
56:            BufferedReader br = new BufferedReader(isr);
57:            String line = null;
58:
59:            while ( (line = br.readLine()) != null)
60:            {
61:                System.out.println("line: " + line);
62:            }
63:        } catch (Throwable t)
64:        {
65:            t.printStackTrace();
66:        }
67:    }
68: }
```

Listing 17.2   *(continued)*

A run of Listing 17.2 produces the following:

```
E:\classes\org\javapitfalls\Item17>java
org.javapitfalls.item17.BadURLPost http://localhost/cgi-bin/echocgi.exe ⤵
Received a : sun.net.www.protocol.http.HttpURLConnection
Getting an input stream...
Getting an output stream...
java.net.ProtocolException: Cannot write output after reading input.
        at
sun.net.www.protocol.http.HttpURLConnection.getOutputStream(HttpURLCo
nnection.java:507)
        at
com.javaworld.jpitfalls.article3.BadURLPost.main(BadURLPost.java:39)
```

When trying to get the output stream of the `HttpURLConnection` class, the program informed me that I cannot write output after reading input. The strange thing about this error message is that we have not tried to read any data yet. Of course, that assumes the `getInputStream()` method behaves in the same manner as in other IO classes. Specifically, there are three problems with the above code:

- The `setRequestProperty()` method parameters are not checked. This is demonstrated by setting a property called "`stupid`" with a value of "nonsense." Since these properties actually go into the HTTP request and they are not validated by the method (as they should be), you must be extra careful to ensure the parameter names and values are correct.

- The `getOutputStream()` method causes the program to throw a `ProtocolException` with the error message "Can't write output after reading input." By examining the JDK source code, we find that this is due to the `getInputStream()` method having the side effect of sending the request (whose default request method is "`GET`") to the Web server. As an aside, this is similar to a side effect in the `ObjectInputStream` and `ObjectOutput-Stream` constructors that are detailed in my first pitfalls book. So, the pitfall is the assumption that the `getInputStream()` and `getOutputStream()` methods behave just like they do for a `Socket` connection. Since the underlying mechanism for communicating to the Web server actually is a socket, this is not an unreasonable assumption. A better implementation of `HttpURLConnection` would be to postpone the side effects until the initial read or write to the respective input or output stream. This could be done by creating an `HttpInputStream` and `HttpOutputStream`. That would keep the socket metaphor intact. One could argue that HTTP is a request/response stateless protocol and the socket metaphor does not fit. The answer to that is that the API should fit the conceptual model. If the current model is identical to a socket connection, it should behave as such. If it does not, you have stretched the bounds of abstraction too far.

- Although it is commented out, it is also illegal to attempt to set a request property after getting an input or output stream. The documentation for URLConnection does state the sequence to set up a connection, although it does not state this is a mandatory sequence.

If we did not have the luxury of examining the source code (which definitely should not be a requirement to use an API), we would be reduced to trial and error (the absolute worst way to program). Neither the documentation nor the API of the HttpURLConnection class afford us any understanding of how the protocol is implemented, so we feebly attempt to reverse the order of calls to getInputStream() and getOutputStream(). Listing 17.3, BadURLPost1.java, is an abbreviated version of that program.

```
01: package org.javapitfalls.item17;
02:
03: import java.net.*;
04: import java.io.*;
05:
06: public class BadURLPost1
07: {
08:     public static void main(String args[])
09:     {
// removed for brevity
35:             System.out.println("Getting an output stream...");
36:             OutputStream os = con.getOutputStream();
37:
38:             System.out.println("Getting an input stream...");
39:             InputStream is = con.getInputStream();
// removed for brevity
67:     }
68: }
```

Listing 17.3   BadURLPost1.java

A run of Listing 17.3 produces the following:

```
E:\classes\org\javapitfalls\Item17>java org.javapitfalls.
item17.BadURLPost1 http://localhost/cgi-bin/echocgi.exe
Received a : sun.net.www.protocol.http.HttpURLConnection
Getting an output stream...
Getting an input stream...
After flushing output stream.
line: <HEAD>
line: <TITLE> Echo CGI program </TITLE>
line: </HEAD>
line: <BODY BGCOLOR='#ebebeb'><CENTER>
```

```
line: <H2> Echo </H2>
line: </CENTER>
line: No content! ERROR!
line: </BODY>
line: </HTML>
```

Although the program compiles and runs, the CGI program reports that no data was sent! Why? Again we were bitten by the side effects of getInputStream(), which caused the POST request to be sent before anything was put in the post's output buffer, thus sending an empty post request.

Now, after having failed twice, we understand that the getInputStream()is the key method that actually writes the requests to the server. Therefore, we must perform the operations serially (open output, write, open input, read) as we do in Listing 17.4, GoodURLPost.java.

```
01: package org.javapitfalls.item17;
02:
03: import java.net.*;
04: import java.io.*;
05:
06: public class GoodURLPost
07: {
08:     public static void main(String args[])
09:     {
10:         // get an HTTP connection to POST to
11:         if (args.length < 1)
12:         {
13:             System.out.println("USAGE: java
GOV.dia.mditds.util.GoodURLPost url");
14:             System.exit(1);
15:         }
16:
17:         try
18:         {
19:             // get the url as a string
20:             String surl = args[0];
21:             URL url = new URL(surl);
22:
23:             URLConnection con = url.openConnection();
24:             System.out.println("Received a : " +
con.getClass().getName());
25:
26:             con.setDoInput(true);
27:             con.setDoOutput(true);
28:             con.setUseCaches(false);
29:
30:             String msg = "Hi HTTP SERVER! Just a quick hello!";
```

Listing 17.4   GoodURLPost.java *(continued)*

```
31:            con.setRequestProperty("CONTENT_LENGTH", "" +
msg.length()); // Not checked
32:            System.out.println("Msg Length: " + msg.length());
33:
34:            System.out.println("Getting an output stream...");
35:            OutputStream os = con.getOutputStream();
36:
37:            OutputStreamWriter osw = new OutputStreamWriter(os);
38:            osw.write(msg);
39:            /** REMEMBER THIS osw.flush(); **/
40:            osw.flush();
41:            osw.close();
42:
43:            System.out.println("After flushing output stream. ");
44:
45:            System.out.println("Getting an input stream...");
46:            InputStream is = con.getInputStream();
47:
48:            // any response?
49:            InputStreamReader isr = new InputStreamReader(is);
50:            BufferedReader br = new BufferedReader(isr);
51:            String line = null;
52:
53:            while ( (line = br.readLine()) != null)
54:            {
55:                System.out.println("line: " + line);
56:            }
57:        } catch (Throwable t)
58:        {
59:            t.printStackTrace();
60:        }
61:    }
62: }
```

Listing 17.4   *(continued)*

A run of Listing 17.4 produces the following:

```
E:\classes\
org\javapitfalls\Item17>javaorg.javapitfalls.item17.GoodURLPost
http://localhost/cgi-bin/echocgi.exe
Received a : sun.net.www.protocol.http.HttpURLConnection
Msg Length: 35
Getting an output stream...
After flushing output stream.
Getting an input stream...
line: <HEAD>
line: <TITLE> Echo CGI program </TITLE>
```

```
line: </HEAD>
line: <BODY BGCOLOR='#ebebeb'><CENTER>
line: <H2> Echo </H2>
line: </CENTER>
line: Length of content: 35
line: Content: Hi HTTP SERVER! Just a quick hello!
line: </BODY>
line: </HTML>
```

Finally, success! We now can post data to a CGI program running on a Web server. To summarize, to avoid the HTTP post pitfall, do not assume the methods behave as they do for a socket. Instead, the `getInputStream()` method has the side effect of writing the requests to the Web server. Therefore, the proper sequence must be observed.

One final note on this class is to understand the complexity of writing characters to the Web server. In the above programs, I use the default encoding when writing the `String` to the underlying socket. You could explicitly write bytes instead of characters by first retrieving the bytes via `getBytes()` of the `String` class. Additionally, you could explicitly set the encoding of the characters using the `OutputStreamWriter` class.

An Alternative Open Source HTTP Client

A more intuitive open source package called `HTTPClient` can be downloaded from http://www.innovation.ch/java/HTTPClient. We will use two classes in this package, `HTTPConnection` and `HTTPResponse`, to accomplish the same functionality in GoodURLPost.java. Listing 17.5 demonstrates posting raw data using this package.

```
01: package org.javapitfalls.item17;
02:
03: import HTTPClient.*;
04:
05: import java.net.*;
06: import java.io.*;
07:
08: public class HTTPClientPost
09: {
10:     public static void main(String args[])
11:     {
12:         // get an HTTP connection to POST to
13:         if (args.length < 2)
14:         {
15:             System.out.println("USAGE: java
org.javapitfalls.net.mcd.il.HTTPClientPost host cgi-program");
16:             System.exit(1);
17:         }
```

Listing 17.5 HTTPClientPost.java *(continued)*

```
18:
19:         try
20:         {
21:             // get the url as a string
22:             String sHost = args[0];
23:             String sfile = args[1];
24:
25:             HTTPConnection con = new HTTPConnection(sHost);
26:
27:             String msg = "Hi HTTP SERVER! Just a quick hello!";
28:
29:             HTTPResponse resp = con.Post(sfile, msg);
30:             InputStream is = resp.getInputStream();
31:
32:             // any response?
33:             InputStreamReader isr = new InputStreamReader(is);
34:             BufferedReader br = new BufferedReader(isr);
35:             String line = null;
36:
37:             while ( (line = br.readLine()) != null)
38:                 System.out.println("line: " + line);
39:         } catch (Throwable t)
40:             {
41:                 t.printStackTrace();
42:             }
43:     }
44: }
```

Listing 17.5   *(continued)*

A run of the HttpClientPost program produces:

```
E:\classes\org\javapitfalls>java org.javapitfalls.Item17.HTTPClientPost
localhost /cgi-bin/echocgi.exe
line: <HEAD>
line: <TITLE> Echo CGI program </TITLE>
line: </HEAD>
line: <BODY BGCOLOR='#ebebeb'><CENTER>
line: <H2> Echo </H2>
line: </CENTER>
line: Length of content: 35
line: Content: Hi HTTP SERVER! Just a quick hello!
line: </BODY>
line: </HTML>
```

As you can see, the results are the same as with GoodURLPost. Instead of raw data, you may want to send form input. Listing 17.6 is an example that sends the same form input as demonstrated in Figure 17.1.

```
01: package org.javapitfalls.item17;
02:
03: import HTTPClient.*;
04:
05: import java.net.*;
06: import java.io.*;
07:
08: public class HTTPClientPost2
09: {
10:     public static void main(String args[])
11:     {
12:         // get an HTTP connection to POST to
13:         if (args.length < 2)
14:         {
15:             System.out.println("USAGE: java
org.javapitfalls.net.mcd.i1.HTTPClientPost2 host cgi-program");
16:             System.exit(1);
17:         }
18:
19:         try
20:         {
21:             // get the url as a string
22:             String sHost = args[0];
23:             String sfile = args[1];
24:
25:             HTTPConnection con = new HTTPConnection(sHost);
26:
27:             NVPair form_data[] = new NVPair[2];
28:             form_data[0] = new NVPair("theName", "Bill Gates");
29:             form_data[1] = new NVPair("question1", "No");
30:
31:             HTTPResponse resp = con.Post(sfile, form_data);
32:             InputStream is = resp.getInputStream();
33:
34:             // any response?
35:             InputStreamReader isr = new InputStreamReader(is);
36:             BufferedReader br = new BufferedReader(isr);
37:             String line = null;
38:
39:             while ( (line = br.readLine()) != null)
40:                 System.out.println("line: " + line);
41:         } catch (Throwable t)
42:         {
43:             t.printStackTrace();
44:         }
45:     }
46: }
```

Listing 17.6   HTTPClientPost2.java

A run of the program HTTPClientPost2 produces the following:

```
E:\classes\org\javapitfalls\net\mcd\i1>java org.javapitfalls.net
.mcd.i1.HTTPClientPost2 localhost /cgi-bin/echocgi.exe
line: <HEAD>
line: <TITLE> Echo CGI program </TITLE>
line: </HEAD>
line: <BODY BGCOLOR='#ebebeb'><CENTER>
line: <H2> Echo </H2>
line: </CENTER>
line: Length of content: 31
line: Content: theName=Bill+Gates&question1=No
line: </BODY>
line: </HTML>
```

The results of HTTPClientPost2 are identical to the results in Figure 17.3. In conclusion, while you can use URLConnection to post data to Web servers, you will find it more intuitive to use an open-source alternative.

Item 18: Effective String Tokenizing[8]

This pitfall revealed itself when a junior developer needed to parse a text file that used a three-character delimiter (###) between tokens. His first attempt used the StringTokenizer class to parse the input text. He sought my advice after he discovered what he considered to be strange behavior. The run of the program below demonstrates code similar to his:

```
>java org.javapitfalls.util.mcd.i1.BadStringTokenizer
input: 123###4#5###678###hello###wo#rld###9
delim: ###
If '###' treated as a group delimiter expecting 6 tokens...
tok[0]: 123
tok[1]: 4
tok[2]: 5
tok[3]: 678
tok[4]: hello
tok[5]: wo
tok[6]: rld
tok[7]: 9
# of tokens: 8
```

As is demonstrated in the above listing, the developer expected six tokens, but if a single "#" character was present in any token, he received more. The junior developer wanted the delimiter to be the group of three pound characters, not a single pound

---

[8] This pitfall was first published by *JavaWorld* (www.javaworld.com) in the article, "Steer clear of Java Pitfalls", September 2000 (http://www.javaworld.com/javaworld/jw-09-2000 /jw-0922-javatraps-p2.html) and is reprinted here with permission. The pitfall has been updated from reader feedback.

character. BadStringTokenizer.java in Listing 18.1 is the incorrect way to parse with a delimiter of "###".

```
01: package org.javapitfalls.item18;
02:
03: import java.util.*;
04:
05: public class BadStringTokenizer
06: {
07:     public static String [] tokenize(String input, String delimiter)
08:     {
09:         Vector v = new Vector();
10:         StringTokenizer t = new StringTokenizer(input, delimiter);
11:         String cmd[] = null;
12:
13:         while (t.hasMoreTokens())
14:             v.addElement(t.nextToken());
15:
16:         int cnt = v.size();
17:         if (cnt > 0)
18:         {
19:             cmd = new String[cnt];
20:             v.copyInto(cmd);
21:         }
22:
23:         return cmd;
24:     }
25:
26:     public static void main(String args[])
27:     {
28:         try
29:         {
30:             String delim = "###";
31:             String input = "123###4#5###678###hello###wo#rld###9";
32:             System.out.println("input: " + input);
33:             System.out.println("delim: " + delim);
34:             System.out.println("If '###' treated as a group
delimiter expecting 6 tokens...");
35:             String [] toks = tokenize(input, delim);
36:             for (int i=0; i < toks.length; i++)
37:                 System.out.println("tok[" + i + "]: " + toks[i]);
38:             System.out.println("# of tokens: " + toks.length);
39:         } catch (Throwable t)
40:         {
41:             t.printStackTrace();
42:         }
43:     }
44: }
```

Listing 18.1   BadStringTokenizer.java

The tokenize() method is simply a wrapper for the StringTokenizer class. The StringTokenizer constructor takes two String arguments: one for the input and one for the delimiter. The junior developer incorrectly inferred that the delimiter parameter would be treated as a group of characters instead of a set of single characters. Is that such a poor assumption? I don't think so. With thousands of classes in the Java APIs, the burden of design simplicity rests on the designer's shoulders and not on the application developer's. It is not unreasonable to assume that a String would be treated as a single group. After all, that is its most common use: a String represents a related grouping of characters.

A correct StringTokenizer constructor would require the developer to provide an array of characters, which would better signify that the delimiters for the current implementation of StringTokenizer are only single characters—though you can specify more than one. This incompletion is an example of API laziness. The API designer was more concerned with rapidly developing the API implementation than the intuitiveness of the implementation. We have all been guilty of this, but it is something we should be vigilant against.

To fix the problem, we create two new static tokenize() methods: one that takes an array of characters as delimiters, the other that accepts a Boolean flag to signify whether the String delimiter should be regarded as a single group. The code for those two methods (and one additional utility method) is in the class GoodStringTokenizer:

```
01: package org.javapitfalls.item18;
02:
03: import java.util.*;
04:
05: public class GoodStringTokenizer
06: {
07:     // String tokenizer with current behavior
08:     public static String [] tokenize(String input, char []
delimiters)
09:     {
10:         return tokenize(input, new String(delimiters), false);
11:     }
12:
13:     public static String [] tokenize(String input, String
delimiters, boolean delimiterAsGroup)
14:     {
15:         String [] result = null;
16:         List l = toksToCollection(input, delimiters,
delimiterAsGroup);
17:         if (l.size() > 0)
18:         {
19:             result = new String[l.size()];
20:             l.toArray(result);
21:         }
```

Listing 18.2   GoodStringTokenizer.java

```
22:          return result;
23:      }
24:
25:      public static List toksToCollection(String input, String      ⟳
delimiters, boolean delimiterAsGroup)
26:      {
27:          ArrayList l = new ArrayList();
28:
29:          String cmd[] = null;
30:
31:          if (!delimiterAsGroup)
32:          {
33:              StringTokenizer t = new StringTokenizer(input, delimiters);
34:              while (t.hasMoreTokens())
35:                  l.add(t.nextToken());
36:          }
37:          else
38:          {
39:              int start = 0;
40:              int end = input.length();
41:
42:              while (start < end)
43:              {
44:                      int delimIdx = input.indexOf(delimiters,start);
45:                      if (delimIdx < 0)
46:                      {
47:                              String tok = input.substring(start);
48:                              l.add(tok);
49:                              start = end;
50:                      }
51:                      else
52:                      {
53:                              String tok = input.substring(start,      ⟳
delimIdx);
54:                              l.add(tok);
55:                              start = delimIdx + delimiters.length();
56:                      }
57:              }
58:          }
59:
60:          return l;
61:      }
62:
63:      public static void main(String args[])
64:      {
65:          try
66:          {
```

Listing 18.2   *(continued)*

```
67:                     String delim = "###";
68:                     String input = "123###4#5###678###hello###wo#rld###9";
69:                     // expecting     1     2     3     4     5     6  ⤶
tokens
70:                     System.out.println("input: " + input);
71:                     System.out.println("delim: " + delim);
72:                     System.out.println("If '###' treated as a group  ⤶
delimiter expecting 6 tokens...");
73:                     String [] toks = tokenize(input, delim, true);
74:                     for (int i=0; i < toks.length; i++)
75:                         System.out.println("tok[" + i + "]: " + toks[i]);
76:                     System.out.println("# of tokens: " + toks.length);
77:               } catch (Throwable t)
78:                 {
79:                     t.printStackTrace();
80:                 }
81:         }
82: }
83:
```

Listing 18.2   *(continued)*

Following is run of `GoodStringTokenizer` that demonstrates the new static method, `tokenize()`, that treats the token `String` "###" as a single delimiter:

```
>java org.javapitfalls.util.mcd.i1.GoodStringTokenizer
input: 123###4#5###678###hello###wo#rld###9
delim: ###
If '###' treated as a group delimiter expecting 6 tokens...
tok[0]: 123
tok[1]: 4#5
tok[2]: 678
tok[3]: hello
tok[4]: wo#rld
tok[5]: 9
# of tokens: 6
```

Beyond solving the "delimiter as a group" problem, GoodStringTokenizer adds a utility method to convert the set of tokens into a java `Collection`. This is important, as `StringTokenizer` is a pre-`Collection` class that has no built-in support for collections. By returning a collection, we can take advantage of the utility methods, specifically, those for sorting and searching, in the `Collections` class. The class below, `TokenCollectionTester.java`, demonstrates the benefits of a `Collection` of tokens.

```
01: package org.javapitfalls.item18;
02:
03: import java.util.*;
04:
05: public class TokenCollectionTester
06: {
07:     public static void main(String args[])
08:     {
09:         try
10:         {
11:             String input = "zuchinni, apple, beans, hotdog, ↵
hamburger," +
12:                             "wine, coke, drink, rice, fries, chicken";
13:             String delim = ", ";
14:             List l = GoodStringTokenizer.toksToCollection(input,
15:                                         delim, false);
16:             String top = (String) Collections.max(l);
17:             System.out.println("Top token is: " + top);
18:             Collections.sort(l);
19:             System.out.println("Sorted list: ");
20:             Iterator i = l.iterator();
21:             while (i.hasNext())
22:                 System.out.println(i.next());
23:
24:         } catch (Throwable t)
25:         {
26:             t.printStackTrace();
27:         }
28:     }
29: }
```

Listing 18.3   TokenCollectionTester.java

Running TokenCollectionTester produces the following output:

```
>java org.javapitfalls.util.mcd.i1.TokenCollectionTester
Top token is: zuchinni
Sorted list:
apple
beans
chicken
coke
drink
fries
hamburger
```

```
wine
hotdog
rice
zuchinni
```

In this item, we have carefully examined the workings of the StringTokenizer class, highlighted some shortcomings, and created some utility methods to improve the class.

Item 19: JLayered Pane Pitfalls[9]

While working on the jXUL project (an open-source effort to integrate XUL, or Extensible User-Interface Language, with Java) for the book *Essential XUL Programming*, I ported a Pacman arcade game clone called Pagman to a Java-based XulRunner platform. XulRunner is a Java class that executes XUL applications; it's similar to the JDK's AppletRunner. Figure 19.1 provides a screen shot of Pagman port's current version, which successfully allows the ghost sprites to move on a JLayeredPane's top layer. The sprites move over the background images, which exist in a layer beneath. (Many thanks to my coauthor Kevin Smith, who worked through these pitfalls with me to bring Pagman to fruition.)

Instead of examining this pitfall in the XulRunner code, which is rather large, we will examine a simpler example that demonstrates the problem. Those interested in the Pagman code can download it from the jXUL Web site (http://www.sourceforge .net/jxul).

Our simple BadLayeredPane example in Listing 19.1 attempts to create a frame that has a colored panel in a background layer and a button in a foreground layer with a JLayeredPane:

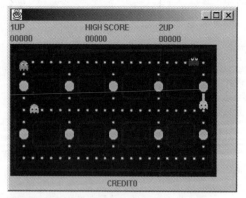

Figure 19.1   Pagman using a JlayeredPane.

Graphics © Dan Addix, Brian King, and David Boswell.

---

[9] This pitfall was first published by *JavaWorld* (www.javaworld.com) in the article, "Practice makes perfect" November 2001 (http://www.javaworld.com/javaworld/jw-11-2001/jw-1116-traps .html?) and is reprinted here with permission. The pitfall has been updated from reader feedback.

```
01: package org.javapitfalls.item19;
02:
03: import java.awt.*;
04: import javax.swing.*;
05: import java.awt.event.*;
06:
07: public class BadLayeredPane extends JFrame
08: {
09:     public BadLayeredPane()
10:     {
11:         // Error 1: using the Root layered pane
12:         JLayeredPane lp = getLayeredPane();
13:
14:         // set the size of this pane
15:         lp.setPreferredSize(new Dimension(100,100));
16:
17:         // add a Colored Panel
18:         JPanel jpnl = new JPanel();
19:         jpnl.setSize(100,100);
20:         jpnl.setOpaque(true);
21:         jpnl.setBackground(Color.red);
22:
23:         // Error 2: these MUST be of type Integer.
24:         lp.add(jpnl, 2);
25:
26:         // put a Button on top
27:         Button b = new Button("Hi!");
28:         // Error 3: adding button wrong
29:         lp.add(b, 1);
30:     }
31:
32:     public static void main(String [] args)
33:     {
34:         JFrame frame = new BadLayeredPane();
35:
36:         frame.addWindowListener(
37:         new WindowAdapter()
38:         {
39:             public void windowClosing(WindowEvent e)
40:             {
41:                 System.exit(0);
42:             }
43:         });
44:
45:         frame.pack();
46:         frame.setVisible(true);
47:     }
48: }
49:
```

Listing 19.1   BadLayeredPane.java

Figure 19.2   Run of BadLayeredPane.

When Listing 19.1 runs, it produces the screen in Figure 19.2.

Not only is our JLayeredPane not working properly, it has no size! We must first work through the size problem before we can approach the heart of our pitfall. Listing 19.1 features three errors (called out in the comments); I'll tackle the first two now and address the third later. First, the JLayeredPane that is part of the JFrame's JRootPane causes our size problem. When you examine the source code for JRootPane, you see that the JRootPane's RootLayout does not use the JLayeredPane to calculate its size; JLayeredPane only calculates the size of the content pane and the menu bar. Second, when adding components to our JLayeredPane, we use integers instead of Integer objects.

With this knowledge, let's examine our second attempt at displaying our two simple layers. Listing 19.2 fixes two of our problems.

```
01: package org.javapitfalls.item19;
02:
03: import java.awt.*;
04: import javax.swing.*;
05: import java.awt.event.*;
06:
07: public class BadLayeredPane2 extends JFrame
08: {
09:     public BadLayeredPane2()
10:     {
11:         // Fix 1: Create a JLayeredPane
12:         JLayeredPane lp = new JLayeredPane();
13:
14:         // set the size of this pane
15:         lp.setPreferredSize(new Dimension(100,100));
16:
17:         // add a Colored Panel
18:         JPanel jpn1 = new JPanel();
19:         jpn1.setSize(100,100);
20:         jpn1.setOpaque(true);
21:         jpn1.setBackground(Color.red);
22:
23:         // Fix 2: using Integer objects
24:         lp.add(jpn1, new Integer(2));
```

Listing 19.2   BadLayeredPane2.java

```
25:
26:            // put a Button on top
27:            Button b = new Button("Hi!");
28:            lp.add(b, new Integer(1));
29:
30:            // Part of Fix 1
31:            getContentPane().add(lp);
32:      }
33:
// main method() Identical to BadLayeredPane.java
50: }
```

Listing 19.2   *(continued)*

We'll first study the fixes applied and then the results. There are two fixes in Listing 19.2 (called out in the comments):

- First, we create a new `JLayeredPane`, which we add to the `ContentPane`. The `RootLayout` manager uses the `ContentPane` to calculate the frame's size, so now the `JFrame` is packed properly.

- Second, we correctly add components to the `JLayeredPane` using an `Integer` object to specify the layer.

Figure 19.3 shows the result of these fixes.

Figure 19.3 clearly demonstrates that we have not yet accomplished our goal. Though the colored panel displays, the button fails to appear on the layer above the panel. Why? Because we assume we add components to a `JLayeredPane` the same way we add components to `Frames` and `Panels`. This assumption is our third error and the `JLayeredPane` pitfall. Contrary to `Frame` and `Panel`, the `JLayeredPane` lacks a default `LayoutManager`; thus, the components have no sizes or positions provided for them by default. Instead, a component's size and position must be explicitly set before adding them to the `JLayeredPane`, which Fix 1 achieves in Listing 19.3.

Figure 19.3   Run of BadLayeredPane2.

```
01: package org.javapitfalls.item19;
02:
03: import java.awt.*;
04: import javax.swing.*;
05: import java.awt.event.*;
06:
07: public class GoodLayeredPane extends JFrame
08: {
09:     public GoodLayeredPane()
10:     {
11:         JLayeredPane lp = new JLayeredPane();
12:
13:         // set the size of this pane
14:         lp.setPreferredSize(new Dimension(100,100));
15:
16:         // add a Colored Panel
17:         JPanel jpnl = new JPanel();
18:         jpnl.setSize(100,100);
19:         jpnl.setOpaque(true);
20:         jpnl.setBackground(Color.red);
21:
22:         lp.add(jpnl, new Integer(1));
23:
24:         // put a Button on top
25:         Button b = new Button("Hi!");
26:         // Fix 1: set the size and position
27:         b.setBounds(10,10, 80, 40);
28:         lp.add(b, new Integer(2));
29:
30:         getContentPane().add(lp);
31:     }
32:
// main() method Identical to BadLayeredPane.java
49: }
```

Listing 19.3   GoodLayeredPane.java

When run, Listing 19.3 produces the correct result, shown in Figure 19.4.

Figure 19.4   Run of GoodLayeredPane.

In summary, the key pitfall in our JLayeredPane example is wrongly assuming that the JLayeredPane has a default LayoutManager like JFrame and JPanel. Experience tells us to eliminate that assumption and position and size the components for each layer. Once we do so, the JLayeredPane works fine.

Item 20: When File.renameTo() Won't[10]

The File class and specifically the File.renameTo() method suffers from pitfalls in both design and implementation. Many pitfalls stem from confusion regarding the expected behavior of classes in the Java libraries. Unfortunately, the input/output (IO) classes in Java have been prone to significant revision as the Java platform has evolved. An early overhaul added readers and writers to the input and output streams to distinguish between character-based IO and byte-based IO. With JDK 1.4, another overhaul has taken place, adding a lower layer of high-performance access via Channel classes. Figure 20.1 displays the major file-related classes in the java.io and java.nio packages.

Unfortunately, just the fact that there are five classes and two interfaces all pertaining to different facets of a file increases the complexity of using these classes properly. That is especially true if the distinction between classes is small or if the role of the class is ill defined. Let's examine each class and its purpose:

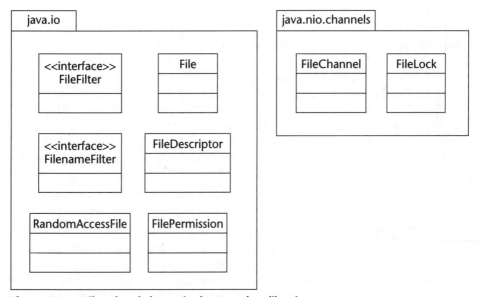

Figure 20.1   File-related classes in the Java class libraries.

[10] This pitfall was first published by *JavaWorld* (www.javaworld.com) in the article, "Practice makes perfect" November 2001 (http://www.javaworld.com/javaworld/jw-11-2001/jw-1116-traps-p2.html) and is reprinted here with permission. The pitfall has been updated from reader feedback.

File. Present since JDK 1.0, a class that represents a file or directory pathname. This class contains a wide array of methods to test characteristics of a file, delete a file, create directories, and, of course, rename a file. Unfortunately, this class suffers from a vague scope in that it incorporates behaviors of a directory entry, like `isFile()`, `isDirectory()`, and `lastModified()`, and behaviors of a physical file like `createNewFile()`, `delete()`, and `renameTo()`. We will discuss this more later.

FilenameFilter. Present since JDK 1.0, an interface to test the occurrence of a list of `File` objects via the `File.list()` method and `FileDialog.setFilename-Filter()` method. The confusion over scope stated above is evident in the contradiction between this interface and the next one (`FileFilter`) in terms of their names. This interface has a single method called `accept()` that receives a `File` object representing a directory and a `String` representing the name of the file to filter on.

FileFilter. Added in JDK 1.2, an interface to filter in the same manner as `File-nameFilter` except that the `accept()` method receives only a single `File` object. Unfortunately, this interface is a prime example of a superfluous convenience interface that does more harm than good because of the new name. It would have been far better to follow the precedent of the awt package where `LayoutManager2` extends `LayoutManager` to add methods. The difference between the two design strategies is that the `LayoutManager` interfaces are clearly semantically congruent, whereas `FilenameFilter` and `FileFilter` are not.

FileDescriptor. A class to provide an opaque handle to the operating system-specific File data structure. As its name implies, this class is a very thin abstraction over an operating system structure. The class only has two methods. As a general design rule, it would be preferable to combine our abstractions of a physical file into a single class. Unfortunately, the requirements of backward compatibility cause future developers to suffer with multiple abstractions. Since the New IO package (NIO), split IO operations at the package level (which also spoils the platform's cohesiveness), there is an opportunity to start from scratch with new classes in the NIO package.

FilePermission. A class to represent access to a file directory. This was part of the 1.2 fine-grained security mechanisms—again, a nice candidate for conceptual consolidation.

RandomAccessFile. Present since JDK 1.0, a class that represents the characteristics and behaviors (taken from the C standard library) of a binary file. This allows low-level reading and writing of bytes to a file from any random file position. This class stands on its own and does not fit in to the IO stream metaphor and does not interact with those classes. It is interesting to note that the word "File" in this class name actually refers to a physical file and not just its name. Unfortunately, this package lacks such consistency.

FileChannel. Added to JDK 1.4, a class to provide a high-performance pathway for reading, writing, mapping, and manipulating a file. You get a `FileChannel` from a `FileInputStream`, `FileOutputStream`, or `RandomAccessFile` class. A key benefit of this class is the ability to map a file to memory. Item 2 examined the NIO performance improvements. Lastly, a region of the file (or the whole file) may be locked to prevent access or modification by other programs via methods that return a `FileLock` object.

FileLock. Added to JDK 1.4, a class to represent a lock on a region of a file. A lock can be either exclusive or shared. These objects are safe for use by multiple threads but only apply to a single virtual machine.

Now let's narrow our focus to the `File` class. Listing 20.1 demonstrates some `File` class behaviors and pitfalls.

```
01: package org.javapitfalls.item20;
02:
03: import java.io.*;
04:
05: public class BadFileRename
06: {
07:     public static void main(String args[])
08:     {
09:         try
10:         {
11:             // check if test file in current dir
12:             File f = new File("dummy.txt");
13:             String name = f.getName();
14:             if (f.exists())
15:                 System.out.println(f.getName() + " exists.");
16:             else
17:                 System.out.println(f.getName() +
" does not exist.");
18:
19:             // Attempt to rename to an existing file
20:             File f2 = new File("dummy.bin");
21:             // Issue 1: boolean status return instead of Exceptions
22:             if (f.renameTo(f2))
23:                 System.out.println(
24:                     "Rename to existing File Successful.");
25:             else
26:                 System.out.println(
27:                     "Rename to existing File Failed.");
28:
29:             // Attempt to rename with a different extension
30:             int dotIdx = name.indexOf('.');
31:             if (dotIdx >= 0)
32:                 name = name.substring(0, dotIdx);
33:             name = name + ".tst";
34:             String path = f.getAbsolutePath();
35:             int lastSep = path.lastIndexOf(File.separator);
36:             if (lastSep > 0)
```

Listing 20.1   BadFileRename.java *(continued)*

```
37:                    path = path.substring(0,lastSep);
38:                System.out.println("path: " + path);
39:                File f3 = new File(path + File.separator + name);
40:                System.out.println("new name: " + f3.getPath());
41:                if (f.renameTo(f3))
42:                    System.out.println(
43:                        "Rename to new extension Successful.");
44:                else
45:                    System.out.println(
46:                        "Rename to new extension failed.");
47:
48:                // delete the file
49:                // Issue 2: Is the File class a file?
50:                if (f.delete())
51:                    System.out.println("Delete Successful.");
52:                else
53:                    System.out.println("Delete Failed.");
54:
55:                // assumes program not run from c drive
56:                // Issue 3: Behavior across operating systems?
57:                File f4 = new File("c:\\" + f3.getName());
58:                if (f3.renameTo(f4))
59:                    System.out.println(
"Rename to new Drive Successful.");
60:                else
61:                    System.out.println("Rename to new Drive failed.");
62:            } catch (Throwable t)
63:            {
64:                t.printStackTrace();
65:            }
66:        }
67: }
68:
```

Listing 20.1   *(continued)*

When this code is run from a drive other than C, and with the file dummy.txt in the current directory, it produces the following output:

```
E:\classes\org\javapitfalls\Item20>java
org.javapitfalls.item20.BadFileRename
dummy.txt exists.
Rename to existing File Failed.
path: E:\classes\org\javapitfalls\Item20
new name: E:\classes\org\javapitfalls\Item20\dummy.tst
Rename to new extension Successful.
Delete Failed.
Rename to new Drive Successful.
```

Listing 20.1 raises three specific issues, which are called out in the code comments. At least one is accurately characterized as a pitfall, and the others fall under poor design:

- First, returning a Boolean error result does not provide enough information about the failure's cause. That proves inconsistent with exception use in other classes and should be considered poor design. For example, the failure above could have been caused by either attempting to `renameTo()` a file that already exists or attempting to `renameTo()` an invalid filename. Currently, we have no way of knowing.

- The second issue is the pitfall: attempting to use the initial `File` object after a successful rename. What struck me as odd in this API is the use of a `File` object in the `renameTo()` method. At first glance, you assume you only want to change the filename. So why not just pass in a `String`? In that intuition lies the source of the pitfall. The pitfall is the assumption that a `File` object represents a physical file and not a file's name. In the least, that should be considered poor class naming. For example, if the object merely represents a filename, then it should be called `Filename` instead of `File`. Thus, poor naming directly causes this pitfall, which we stumble over when trying to use the initial `File` object in a `delete()` operation after a successful rename.

- The third issue is `File.renameTo()`'s different behavior between operating systems. The `renameTo()` works on Windows even across filesystems (as shown here) and fails on Solaris (reported in Sun's Bug Parade and not shown here). The debate revolves around the meaning of "Write Once, Run Anywhere" (WORA). Sun programmers verifying reported bugs contend that WORA simply means a consistent API. That is a cop-out. A consistent API does not deliver WORA; there are numerous examples in existing APIs where Sun went beyond a consistent API to deliver consistent behavior. The best-known example of this is Sun's movement beyond the Abstract Windowing Toolkit's consistent API to Swing's consistent behavior. If you claim to have a platform above the operating system, then a thin veneer of an API over existing OS functionality will not suffice. A WORA platform requires consistent behavior; otherwise, "run anywhere" means "maybe run anywhere." To avoid this pitfall, you check the "os.name" System property and code `renameTo()` differently for each platform.

Out of these three issues, we can currently only fix the proper way to delete a file after a successful rename, as Listing 20.2 demonstrates. Because the other two issues result from Java's design, only the Java Community Process (JCP) can initiate these fixes.

```
01: package org.javapitfalls.item20;
02:
03: import java.io.*;
04:
05: public class GoodFileRename
06: {
```

Listing 20.2   GoodFileRename.java *(continued)*

```
07:     public static void main(String args[])
08:     {
09:         try
10:         {
11:             // check if test file in current dir
12:             File f = new File("dummy2.txt");
13:             String name = f.getName();
14:             if (f.exists())
15:                 System.out.println(f.getName() + " exists.");
16:             else
17:                 System.out.println(f.getName() +
" does not exist.");
18:
19:             // Attempt to rename with a different extension
20:             int dotIdx = name.indexOf('.');
21:             if (dotIdx >= 0)
22:                 name = name.substring(0, dotIdx);
23:             name = name + ".tst";
24:             String path = f.getAbsolutePath();
25:             int lastSep = path.lastIndexOf(File.separator);
26:             if (lastSep > 0)
27:                 path = path.substring(0,lastSep);
28:             System.out.println("path: " + path);
29:             File f3 = new File(path + File.separator + name);
30:             System.out.println("new name: " + f3.getPath());
31:             if (f.renameTo(f3))
32:                 System.out.println(
33:                     "Rename to new extension Successful.");
34:             else
35:                 System.out.println(
36:                     "Rename to new extension failed.");
37:
38:             // delete the file
39:             // Fix 1: delete via the "Filename" not File
40:             if (f3.delete())
41:                 System.out.println("Delete Successful.");
42:             else
43:                 System.out.println("Delete Failed.");
44:         } catch (Throwable t)
45:         {
46:             t.printStackTrace();
47:         }
48:     }
49: }
50:
```

Listing 20.2   *(continued)*

A run of Listing 20.2 produces the following output:

```
E:\classes\org\javapitfalls\Item20> java org.javapitfalls.item20
.GoodFileRename
dummy2.txt exists.
path: E:\classes\org\javapitfalls\Item20
new name: E:\classes\org\javapitfalls\Item20\dummy2.tst
Rename to new extension Successful.
Delete Successful.
```

Thus, don't use the `File` class as if it represents a file instead of the filename. With that in mind, once the file is renamed, operations such as `delete()` only work on the new filename.

Item 21: Use Iteration over Enumeration[11]

`Enumeration` is the original interface, available since JDK 1.0, to iterate over (step through) all the elements in a collection. In terms of semantics, it would have been better to call the interface "Enumerator," as it expresses the role a class is "putting on" by implementing the interface, instead of "Enumeration," which specifies an occurrence of the activity. This is in line with all the more recent interfaces in the `java.util` package like `Observer`, `Comparator`, and `Iterator`. Table 21.1 compares the `Enumeration` interface to the `Iterator` interface.

Table 21.1   Enumeration versus Iterator

ENUMERATION METHODS	DESCRIPTION	ITERATOR METHODS	DESCRIPTION
`boolean hasMoreElements();`	Checks if this enumeration has more elements.	`boolean hasNext()`	Checks if this iterator has more elements.
`Object nextElement();`	Returns the next element in the enumeration if there is at least 1 more.	`Object next()`	Returns the next element in the iterator if there is at least one more.
		`void remove()`	Removes from the underlying collection the last element returned. (optional)

[11] This pitfall was first published by *JavaWorld* (www.javaworld.com) in the article, "Practice makes perfect" November 2001, (http://www.javaworld.com/javaworld/jw-11-2001/jw-1116-traps-p2 .html) and is reprinted here with permission. The pitfall has been updated from reader feedback.

The idiom for using both an Enumeration and Iterator is the same:

```
while (i.hasNext())
{
    Object o = i.next();
    // do something with o
}
```

As is evident in Table 21.1, both Iterator and Enumeration are functionally identical except for two differences:

- Iterators allow you to safely remove an element from the underlying collection in a well-defined way.
- The iterator method names have been simplified.

There is a removal of elements pitfall in the Enumeration implementation class of Vector where its behavior differs from Iteration. Listing 21.1 demonstrates the behavior in question.

```
01: package org.javapitfalls.item21;
02:
03: import java.util.*;
04:
05: public class BadVisitor
06: {
07:     public static void main(String args[])
08:     {
09:         Vector v = new Vector();
10:         v.add("one"); v.add("two"); v.add("three"); v.add("four");
11:
12:         Enumeration enum = v.elements();
13:         while (enum.hasMoreElements())
14:         {
15:             String s = (String) enum.nextElement();
16:             if (s.equals("two"))
17:                 v.remove("two");
18:             else
19:             {
20:                 // Visit
21:                 System.out.println(s);
22:             }
23:         }
24:
25:         // see what's left
```

Listing 21.1   BadVisitor.java

```
26:        System.out.println("What's really there...");
27:        enum = v.elements();
28:        while (enum.hasMoreElements())
29:        {
30:            String s = (String) enum.nextElement();
31:            System.out.println(s);
32:        }
33:    }
34: }
```

Listing 21.1   *(continued)*

When run, Listing 21.1 produces the following:

```
E:\classes>java org.javapitfalls.item21.BadVisitor
one
four
What's really there...
one
three
four
```

You would expect to have visited elements "one", "three", and "four", but instead only visited elements "one" and "four". The problem is that we are assuming that the Enumeration implementation and the Vector class work in sync, which is not the case. What has happened is the index integer (called count) is not modified when the Vector.remove() method is called. This is demonstrated in Figure 21.1. Listing 21.2 demonstrates how an iterator handles this situation.

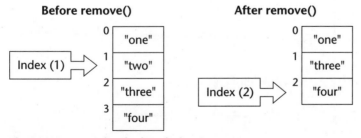

Figure 21.1   Under the hood of a Vector.

```
01: package org.javapitfalls.item21;
02:
03: import java.util.*;
04:
05: public class BadVisitor2
06: {
07:     public static void main(String args[])
08:     {
09:         Vector v = new Vector();
10:         v.add("one"); v.add("two"); v.add("three"); v.add("four");
11:
12:         Iterator iter = v.iterator();
13:         while (iter.hasNext())
14:         {
15:             String s = (String) iter.next();
16:             if (s.equals("two"))
17:                 v.remove("two");
18:             else
19:             {
20:                 // Visit
21:                 System.out.println(s);
22:             }
23:         }
24:
25:         // see what's left
26:         System.out.println("What's really there...");
27:         iter = v.iterator();
28:         while (iter.hasNext())
29:         {
30:             String s = (String) iter.next();
31:             System.out.println(s);
32:         }
33:     }
34: }
```

Listing 21.2   BadVisitor2.java

When run, Listing 21.2 produces the following:

```
E:\classes>java org.javapitfalls.item21.BadVisitor2
one
Exception in thread "main" java.util.ConcurrentModificationException
    at
java.util.AbstractList$Itr.checkForComodification(AbstractList.java:445)
    at java.util.AbstractList$Itr.next(AbstractList.java:418)
    at
com.javaworld.jpitfalls.article5.BadVisitor2.main(BadVisitor2.java:15)
```

As the output shows, the class implementing the `Iterator` interface specifically checks for this type of concurrent modification (modification outside of the iteration implemenation class while we are iterating) and throws an exception. It would be nice if the `Enumeration` implementation class was upgraded with this same behavior. Now let's examine the correct way to do this. Listing 21.3 demonstrates both visiting and modifying with an `Iterator`.

```
01: package org.javapitfalls.item21;
02:
03: import java.util.*;
04:
05: public class GoodVisitor
06: {
07:     public static void main(String args[])
08:     {
09:         Vector v = new Vector();
10:         v.add("one"); v.add("two"); v.add("three"); v.add("four");
11:
12:         Iterator iter = v.iterator();
13:         while (iter.hasNext())
14:         {
15:             String s = (String) iter.next();
16:             if (s.equals("two"))
17:                 iter.remove();
18:             else
19:             {
20:                 // Visit
21:                 System.out.println(s);
22:             }
23:         }
24:
25:         // see what's left
26:         System.out.println("What's really there...");
27:         iter = v.iterator();
28:         while (iter.hasNext())
29:         {
30:             String s = (String) iter.next();
31:             System.out.println(s);
32:         }
33:     }
34: }
```

Listing 21.3   GoodVisitor.java

When Listing 21.3 is run, it produces the following:

```
E:\classes>java org.javapitfalls.item21.GoodVisitor
one
```

```
three
four
What's really there...
one
three
four
```

Notice that the remove method is performed via the Iterator class and not using the Vector class. So, in general, for classes that support it, use an Iterator over Enumeration. All classes that implement the Collection interface support iteration through the following method:

```
public Iterator iterator();
```

The classes that implement the Collection interface are AbstractCollection, AbstractList, AbstractSet, ArrayList, BeanContextServicesSupport, BeanContextSupport, HashSet, LinkedHashSet, LinkedList, TreeSet, and Vector. Some classes like Hashtable and HashMap (all the classes that implement the Map interface) indirectly support iteration by returning a Collection via the values() method. There are still some classes that only implement Enumeration like StringTokenizer, java.security.Permissions, and classes in Swing and JNDI.

Item 22: J2ME Performance and Pitfalls

The Java 2 Micro Edition (J2ME) is a subset of the Java platform created for developing applications on small footprint devices, like personal digital assistants (PDAs) and cell phones. These devices are significantly constrained in terms of processor speed, memory, and storage space. While the amounts vary between devices, you can easily expect several orders of magnitude difference between your desktop PC and these devices. There are three main classes of pitfalls associated with the J2ME platform: memory consumption pitfalls, performance pitfalls, and API differences. Both memory consumption and performance pitfalls have more to do with programming habit than the J2ME platform. The fact is our habits have developed around creating reusable, modular, and readable J2SE/J2EE programs where memory and processing speed are abundant. Unfortunately, those very habits deemed "good style" for J2SE/J2EE lead to either nonperforming or poor-performing J2ME applications. The API pitfalls relate to different method calls for classes implemented in both J2SE and J2ME.

My approach to exploring these J2ME pitfalls is to port a J2SE application to the J2ME platform. First, we take the most direct approach and then optimize our approach. Unfortunately, to demonstrate a nontrivial application (which we do) requires significant amounts of code. To reduce the size of the code listings, I have deleted simple, similar, and redundant code. Additionally, to avoid long runs of uninterrupted code, I have interspersed the code descriptions and explanations for all major methods instead of putting it all after the code.

The J2SE application we will port is called SwinginAmazonSearch. The main frame of the application is displayed in Figure 22.1.

The purpose of the application is to enable you to query Amazon.com's database using a Representational State Transfer (REST) approach. REST is an architectural style that describes how the World Wide Web (WWW) works. The term was coined by Roy Fielding in his Ph.D. thesis (available at http:// www.ics.uci.edu/~fielding/pubs /dissertation/top.htm). The Web uses Uniform Resource Identifiers (URIs) to retrieve representation and to change state by transferring to other representations. Amazon implemented this by encoding all query parameters in the URI and returning an XML document as the resulting representation.

The layout of the main interface in Figure 22.1 is divided into two halves: the top half to select and enter search terms and the bottom half to display the results after clicking "Search."After the results are displayed, you can examine more detail on a single entry by clicking "Details" or receive an additional "page" of results by clicking "Next Results."Amazon.com limits all queries to a single "page" of 10 hits and requires all queries to include a page number. Table 22.1 lists and defines the key parameters in an Amazon.com query.

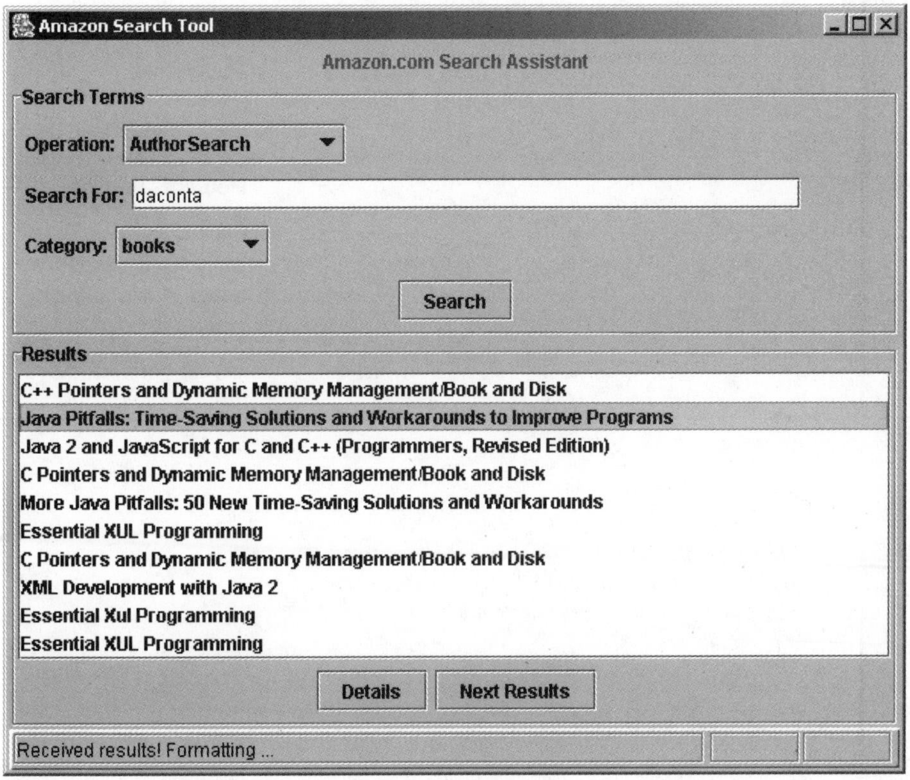

Figure 22.1   A Swing-based Amazon search application.

Table 22.1   Amazon.com Query parameters

FIELD TYPE	FIELD NAME	FIELD VALUES	DEFINITION
Operation	KeywordSearch, BrowseNodeSearch, AsinSearch, UpcSearch, AuthorSearch, ArtistSearch, ActorSearch, DirectorSearch, ManufacturerSearch, ListManiaSearch, SimilaritySearch	Free text with keywords, authors, etc. corresponding to the search type.	The type of search to perform.
Mode	mode	baby, books, classical, dvd, electronics, garden, kitchen, magazines, music, pc-hardware, photo, software, toys, universal, vhs, videogames	A taxonomy of areas to search. Would be better to have been called category.
Return Type	type	lite, heavy	The DTD of the returned XML where the heavy version contains many more elements than the lite version.
Page #	page	An integer	The page of 10 hits to return (if available).
Format	f	xml or URI to an XSLT stylesheet	A return in XML or any format generated by the XSLT stylesheet.

Now let's examine the source code in Listing 22.1 that implements the application.

```
001: /* SwinginAmazonSearch.java */
002: package org.javapitfalls.item22;
003:
// - removed Import statements
015:
016: class SwinginAmazonSearch extends JFrame implements ActionListener
017: {
018:     public static final boolean debug;
019:
// - removed static block to set debug variable
```

Listing 22.1   SwinginAmazonSearch.java

```
035:
036:     public static final String CMD_SEARCH = "Search";
// - removed CMD_DETAILS, CMD_NEXT_TEN, and ELEMENT_PRODUCT_NAME Strings
040:
041:     JButton searchButton = new JButton(CMD_SEARCH);
042:     JButton detailsButton = new JButton(CMD_DETAILS);
043:     JButton nextResultsButton = new JButton(CMD_NEXT_TEN);
044:     JList results = new JList();
045:     JComboBox opsCombo = new JComboBox(AmazonHttpGet.legalOps);
046:     JComboBox modeCombo = new JComboBox(AmazonHttpGet.legalModes);
047:     JTextField targetTF = new JTextField(40);
048:     StatusPanel status = new StatusPanel();
049:     AmazonHttpGet getter = new AmazonHttpGet();
050:     int page = 1;
051:
052:     DocumentBuilderFactory dbf;
053:     DocumentBuilder db;
054:     Document doc;
055:     NodeList productNodes;
056:
```

Listing 22.1   *(continued)*

The class SwinginAmazonSearch extends a Swing JFrame and implements the
Action Listener interface to receive events from the buttons on the main window. Lines
16-56 of the code contain the class declaration and class data members. The data members consist of some static constants, GUI components (JButton, JList, JComboBox),
a reference to a class performing the HTTP networking functions called Amazon-
HttpGet, and references to XML parsing and the W3C Document class to manipulate
the returned XML. It is important to note the use of static constants for all fixed
Strings (like in line 36 and those deleted) in case the protocol changes at a later date.
This then makes it easy to modify the protocol by only changing the string in one location instead of hunting down the occurrence of each String where it is used. Such
"future proofing" is a good habit for J2SE/J2EE development, but one that wastes precious heap space in J2ME. We will see workarounds for this later. The constructor
(below) creates and displays the main frame.

```
057:     public SwinginAmazonSearch() throws ParserConfigurationException
058:     {
059:         super("Amazon Search Tool");
060:
061:         dbf = DocumentBuilderFactory.newInstance();
062:         db = dbf.newDocumentBuilder();
063:
064:         // USE a vertical box for north Panel
065:         Box northWithTitle = new Box(BoxLayout.Y_AXIS);
066:         this.getContentPane().add("North", northWithTitle);
```

Listing 22.1   *(continued)*

```
067:
068:        // add label first
069:        // add label up north
070:        JPanel title = new JPanel(new FlowLayout(FlowLayout.CENTER));
071:        JLabel titleLabel = new JLabel("Amazon.com Search
Assistant");
072:        titleLabel.setForeground(Color.green.darker());
073:        title.add(titleLabel);
074:        northWithTitle.add(title);
075:
076:        Box northPanel = new Box(BoxLayout.Y_AXIS);
077:        northWithTitle.add(northPanel);
078:        northPanel.setBorder(new TitledBorder(new EtchedBorder(),
"Search Terms"));
079:
080:        // add operation drop down
081:        JPanel panel1 = new JPanel(new FlowLayout(FlowLayout.LEFT));
082:        northPanel.add(panel1);
083:        panel1.add(new JLabel("Operation:"));
084:        opsCombo.setEditable(false);
085:        panel1.add(opsCombo);
086:
// - removed adding most of the GUI components for brevity
// - removed adding status panel and WindowListener
132:
133:        this.setSize(600,400);
134:        this.setLocation(100,100);
135:        this.setVisible(true);
136:
137:    }
```

Listing 22.1   *(continued)*

The constructor (lines 57 to 137) instantiates the components, groups them in
`JPanels`, adds them to `LayoutManagers`, and then sizes and shows the window.
Unfortunately, the GUI components in the J2ME platform are different from (but similar to) those used in Swing:

```
139:    public void actionPerformed(ActionEvent aevt)
140:    {
141:        String command = aevt.getActionCommand();
142:        if (command.equals(CMD_SEARCH))
143:        {
144:            // check we have the valid parameters\
145:            String targets = targetTF.getText();
146:            if (targets.length() == 0)
147:            {
148:                status.setText("'Search For' text field cannot be
empty.");
149:            }
```

Listing 22.1   *(continued)*

```
150:            else
151:            {
152:               try
153:               {
154:                  page = 1; // reset
155:                  doAmazonSearch(page, targets);
156:               } catch (MalformedURLException mue)
// - removed exception handling, simply displayed an error message
164:               }
165:            }
166:         else if (command.equals(CMD_DETAILS))
167:         {
168:            // popup a new window with the details for this product
169:            String selectedProductName = (String)
results.getSelectedValue();
170:
171:            // get the parent ELEMENT node of the node with a
ProductName with this Value
172:            if (productNodes != null)
173:            {
174:               Node n =
findNodeWithContent(productNodes,selectedProductName);
175:
176:               // get the Details element parent
177:               Node parent = n.getParentNode();
178:
179:               if (debug) System.out.println("parent: " +
parent.getNodeName());
180:               if (parent != null)
181:               {
182:                  // display a Details Window
183:                  new DetailsDialog(this, parent,
selectedProductName);
184:               }
185:            }
186:            else
187:            {
188:               status.setText("Internal error.  Try another search.");
189:            }
190:         }
// - removed handling NEXT_TEN for brevity
207:      }
```

Listing 22.1   *(continued)*

The Action event handler responds to the various button clicks generated by the GUI. Notice that I use the String.equals() method to determine which button was pressed. This will need to be changed, as string comparisons are slow. The two key events to respond to are the search request (line 142) and a details request (line 166). To respond to either event, some parameters are gathered (like the search term, line 145, or the XML node to report details on, line 174), and then doAmazonSearch() is invoked (line 155) or a new DetailsDialog window instantiated (line 183). Notice the `DetailsDialog` is instantiated as an anonymous reference and not saved in a variable for reuse. Such an assumption of abundant memory and trust in the efficiency of the garbage collector is a pitfall for J2ME programming:

```
209:     private void doAmazonSearch(int page, String targets) throws ⊃
Exception
210:     {
211:         getter.newBaseURL(); // reset
212:
213:         // get the operation
214:         String op = (String) opsCombo.getSelectedItem();
215:
216:         // get the mode
217:         String mode = (String) modeCombo.getSelectedItem();
218:
219:         status.setText("Contacting Amazon.com...");
220:
221:         getter.addOperation(op, targets);
222:         getter.addMode(mode);
223:         getter.addType("lite");
224:         getter.addPage("" + page);
225:         getter.addFormat();
226:
227:         // GET it
228:         String response = getter.httpGet();
229:         if (response != null && response.length() > 0)
230:             status.setText("Received results! Formatting ...");
231:
232:         if (debug) System.out.println("response: " + response);
233:
234:         // parse the XML, extract ProductNames
235:         String [] productNames = null;
236:         ByteArrayInputStream bais = new                             ⊃
ByteArrayInputStream(response.getBytes());
237:         doc = db.parse(bais);
238:         if (doc != null)
239:             removeBlankNodes(doc.getDocumentElement());
240:
241:         productNodes =                                              ⊃
doc.getElementsByTagName(ELEMENT_PRODUCT_NAME);
242:         if (productNodes != null)
243:         {
244:             int len = productNodes.getLength();
245:             productNames = new String[len];
246:             for (int i=0; i < len; i++)
247:             {
248:                 Node n = productNodes.item(i);
249:                 Node t = n.getFirstChild();
250:                 if (t.getNodeType() == Node.TEXT_NODE)
251:                     productNames[i] = t.getNodeValue();
252:             }
253:         }
```

Listing 22.1   *(continued)*

```
254:
255:        if (productNames != null && productNames.length > 0)
256:        {
257:            // populate the list
258:            results.setListData(productNames);
259:        }
// - removed else error condition handling for brevity
267:     }
// - removed utility method isBlank()
// - removed utility method removeBlankNodes()
// - removed utility method findNodeWithContent()
// - removed main() which merely Instantiates SwinginAmazonSearch
333: }
```

Listing 22.1   *(continued)*

The method doAmazonSearch() (lines 209 to 267) has four key functions:

- Format a URL.

- Send an HTTP GET request to xml.amazon.com.

- Parse the resulting XML to extract the product names.

- Populate the JList with the product names.

Both formatting the URL and "getting" it are performed in conjunction with the AmazonHttpGet class discussed later. It is important to note the modularity of the formatting operation for the URL displayed in lines 221 to 225. The formatting of a URL is broken into separate functions to assemble the URL in any order or length you want. Such modularity and the building of "generic code" will have to be sacrificed in our J2ME implementation for speed. At line 228, the httpGet() method is invoked which returns a String containing an XML document. Here is a portion of a sample return document:

```
<Details url="http://www.amazon.com/exec/obidos/redirect?tag=webservices-
20%26creative=D3AG4L7PI53LPH%26camp=2025%26link_code=xm2%26path=ASIN/047
1237515">
    <Asin>0471237515</Asin>
    <ProductName>More Java Pitfalls: 50 New Time-Saving Solutions and  ⤴
Workarounds</ProductName>
    <Catalog>Book</Catalog>
    <Authors>
        <Author>Michael C. Daconta</Author>
        <Author>Kevin T. Smith</Author>
        <Author>Donald Avondolio </Author>
        <Author>W. Clay Richardson</Author>
    </Authors>
    <ReleaseDate>03 February, 2003</ReleaseDate>
    <Manufacturer>John Wiley &amp; Sons</Manufacturer>
    <ListPrice>$40.00</ListPrice>
    <OurPrice>$40.00</OurPrice>
</Details>
```

The XML response is then fed into the standard JDK XML Parser, and a Document Object Model (DOM) is constructed (the `org.w3c.Document` class) at line 237. All the elements with a tag of "ProductName" are retrieved (line 241) and their text content extracted. Since the XML document is guaranteed to be only 10 products at a time, this Swing application can comfortably construct a DOM even though it requires more memory than a SAX Parser or Pull Parser approach; however, this approach proves to use too much memory in our J2ME port. Several utility methods were created to search and manipulate the DOM, like `removeBlankNodes()` and `findNodeWithContent()`, but were deleted since they do not pertain to J2ME pitfalls:

```
335: class DetailsDialog extends JDialog
336: {
337:     JTextArea textArea = new JTextArea(5,60);
338:     public DetailsDialog(Frame f, Node detailsNode, String
productName)
339:     {
340:         super(f, "Details for " + productName, false);
341:
342:         getContentPane().setLayout(new BorderLayout(2,2));
343:         JScrollPane scroller = new JScrollPane(textArea);
344:         getContentPane().add("Center", scroller);
345:
346:         // initialize the text Area
347:         textArea.setEditable(false);
348:         textArea.setBackground(Color.lightGray);
349:
350:         NodeList children = detailsNode.getChildNodes();
351:         int len = children.getLength();
352:         for (int i=0; i < len; i++)
353:         {
354:             // display element children with a text node
355:             Node child = children.item(i);
356:             if (child.getNodeType() == Node.ELEMENT_NODE)
357:             {
358:                 Node txt = child.getFirstChild();
359:                 if (txt != null && txt.getNodeType() == Node.TEXT_NODE)
360:                 {
361:                     String label = child.getNodeName();
362:                     String value = txt.getNodeValue();
363:
364:                     if (value.length() > 0)
365:                         textArea.append("" + label + ": " + value +
"\n");
366:                 }
367:             }
368:         }
369:
// - removed setting window size and location
372:         this.setVisible(true);
373:     }
374: }
```

Listing 22.1   *(continued)*

```
 375:
// - removed StatusPanel Class for brevity
 439:
```

Listing 22.1   *(continued)*

The `DetailsDialog` presents a frame with a single `JTextArea` where each tag name becomes the label (line 361) and each node value of the XML element is presented as the labels value separated by a colon (line 365). This approach relies on detailed knowledge of the XML format.

Now let's examine Listing 22.2 that presents the utility class, `AmazonHttpGet`, that performs the networking operations of the application.

```
001: package org.javapitfalls.item22;
002:
003: import java.net.*;
004: import java.io.*;
005:
006: class AmazonHttpGet
007: {
008:     public static final boolean debug;
009:
// - removed static block that sets debug variable
025:
026:     public static final String DEVTAG = "YOUR-DEV-TAG-HERE";
027:     public static final String [] legalOps = { "KeywordSearch",
// - removed other keywords listed In Table 22.1
"SimilaritySearch", };
031:
032:     public static final String OP_KEYWORD_SEARCH = "KeywordSearch";
033:     public static final String OP_BROWSE_NODE_SEARCH =
"BrowseNodeSearch";
// - removed remaining "operation" constants
043:
044:     public static final String [] legalModes = { "baby", "books",
// - removed other keywords listed In Table 22.1
047:                            "videogames", };
048:
049:     public static final String MODE_BABY = "baby";
050:     public static final String MODE_BOOKS = "Books";
// - removed remaining "mode" constants
065:
066:     public static final String KEYWORD_MODE = "mode";
// - removed other KEYWORD constants
069:
070:     public static final String TYPE_LIGHT = "lite";
071:     public static final String TYPE_HEAVY = "heavy";
072:
// - removed stringExists() utility method
092:
093:     private StringBuffer urlBuf;
```

Listing 22.2   AmazonHttpGet.java *(continued)*

This class was designed with modularity and reusability in mind. The class data members consist mostly of static constants (though many have been removed for brevity). The key data members are the DEVTAG provided when you register at Amazon.com and the urlBuf StringBuffer. In fact, this class does not go far enough in terms of composability of the various queries and additional checking of parameter combinations. Unfortunately, as you will see, most of this flexibility will be eliminated in the J2ME port to reduce the number of method invocations. Throughout this pitfall, you should notice the recurring theme of a mind set shift required to program for small devices. The StringBuffer contains a string representation of the URL we will GET:

```
// - removed urlBuf accessor method
097:
098:    public AmazonHttpGet()
099:    {
100:       newBaseURL();
101:    }
102:
103:    public void newBaseURL()
104:    {
105:       urlBuf = new StringBuffer("http://xml.amazon.com/
onca/xml?v=1.0&t=webservices-20&dev-t=" + DEVTAG);
106:    }
107:
108:    public boolean validOp(String op)
109:    {
110:       if (stringExists(op, legalOps, false))
111:          return true;
112:       else
113:          return false;
114:    }
115:
// - removed validMode() as it is similar to validOp()
// - removed validType() as it is similar to validOp()
// - removed validPage() as it is similar to validOp()
145:
146:    public void addOperation(String operation, String target)
throws MalformedURLException
147:    {
148:       // validate the operation
149:       if (validOp(operation))
150:       {
151:          urlBuf.append('&');
152:          urlBuf.append(operation);
153:          urlBuf.append('=');
154:          if (target != null)
155:          {
156:             target.trim();
157:             target = replaceString(target, " ", "%20", 0);
158:
159:             urlBuf.append(target);
```

Listing 22.2   *(continued)*

```
160:            }
161:         else
162:             throw new MalformedURLException("Invalid target");
163:         }
164:      else
165:         throw new MalformedURLException("Invalid operation.");
166:   }
167:
// - removed addMode() as it is similar to addOperation()
// - removed addType() as it is similar to addOperation()
// - removed addPage() as it is similar to addOperation()
206:
207:    public void addFormat()
208:    {
209:        urlBuf.append("&f=xml"); // TBD: allow XSLT stylesheet
210:    }
211:
// - removed replaceString() utility method
```

Listing 22.2 *(continued)*

The formatting of the URL involves validating and then appending name/value pairs to the urlBuf StringBuffer. The addOperation() (line 146), addMode(), and addType() methods add the parameters discussed in Table 22.1 to the StringBuffer. Two utility methods were removed for brevity: stringExists() checked for the existence of a String in an array of Strings and replaceString() replaces a portion of a String with supplied replacement text:

```
233:    public String httpGet() throws IOException
234:    {
235:        if (debug) System.out.println("URL: " + urlBuf.toString());
236:
237:        // Create a URL object
238:        URL url = new URL(urlBuf.toString());
239:        // get the connection object
240:        URLConnection con = url.openConnection();
241:
242:        con.setDoOutput(true);
243:        con.setUseCaches(false);
244:
245:        InputStream in = con.getInputStream();
246:        BufferedReader br = new BufferedReader(new
InputStreamReader(in));
247:
248:        // read response
249:        String line = null;
250:        StringWriter sw2 = new StringWriter();
251:        PrintWriter pw2 = new PrintWriter(sw2);
252:        while ( (line = br.readLine()) != null)
```

Listing 22.2 *(continued)*

```
253:        {
254:            pw2.println(line);
255:        }
256:
257:        String response = sw2.toString();
258:        return response;
259:    }
260:
// - removed main() method (used for testing)
323: }
```

Listing 22.2   *(continued)*

The `httpGet()` method instantiates a URL object from the `urlBuf` `StringBuffer` (line 238), opens a connection to the URL (line 240) and then reads lines of text from the Web server (line 252) and prints them to a `PrintWriter/StringWriter` buffer. Lastly, the contents of the `StringWriter` are retrieved as a single `String` (line 257).

To examine the API differences between J2SE and J2ME, we attempt a straightforward port of the code to J2ME, changing as little code as necessary. Listing 22.3 is our direct port of SwinginAmazonSearch.java to J2ME. We will examine specific API differences as we cover each section of code.

```
001: package org.javapitfalls.item22;
002:
003: import java.io.*;
004: import java.util.*;
005: import javax.microedition.midlet.*;
006: import javax.microedition.lcdui.*;
007: import org.kxml.*;
008: import org.kxml.kdom.*;
009: import org.kxml.parser.*;
010:
011: public class BadMicroAmazonSearch extends MIDlet implements
CommandListener
012: {
013:     public static final String CMD_SEARCH = "Search";
014:     public static final String CMD_DETAILS = "Details";
015:     public static final String CMD_NEXT_TEN = "More";
// - removed other static constant Strings
019:
020:     // commands
021:     private Command searchCommand;
022:     private Command detailsCommand;
// - removed other Command references for brevity
026:
027:     // display
028:     private Display display;
029:
030:     // screens
```

Listing 22.3   BadMicroAmazonSearch.java

```
031:       private Form searchScreen;
032:       private List resultsScreen;
033:       private TextBox detailsScreen;
034:
035:       // screen components
036:       ChoiceGroup opsChoice;
037:       ChoiceGroup modeChoice;
038:       TextField targetTF;
039:       BadMicroAmazonHttpGet getter = new BadMicroAmazonHttpGet();
040:       int page = 1;
041:
042:       Vector productNodes;
043:
044:       boolean debug = true;
045:       Timer ticker = new Timer();
046:
```

Listing 22.3   *(continued)*

The class `BadMicroAmazonSearch` extends `MIDlet` and implements `CommandListener` (instead of implementing `ActionListener`). A MIDlet is a Mobile Information Device Profile (MIDP) application. The `MIDlet` is an abstract class with three abstract methods that must be overridden by the subclass: `startApp()`, `pauseApp()`, and `destroyApp()`. In this sense, a MIDlet is similar to an applet in that it has a lifecycle controlled by an external Management application.

Before we examine the details of the class, notice the import statements: two packages are the same as J2SE packages (`java.io` and `java.util`), although they are limited in scope, and the two javax packages are new (`javax.midlet`, which has the `MIDlet` class, and `javax.lcdui`, which has the GUI classes). The `kxml` package is an open-source package available at http://kxml.enhydra.org/. We will discuss the `kxml` package in more detail later. Now let's examine the GUI differences apparent in the `BadMicroAmazonSearch` class definition. Since we are dealing with such a small screen size, as shown in Figure 22.2, I divided the single Swing Frame into three "displayable" screens (`Screen` objects).

Figure 22.2   MIDP screen size on a Motorola phone.
Motorola and the Motorola logo are trademarks of Motorola, Inc.

A major difference between Swing and J2ME GUIs is that there are no Frames in J2ME. In essence, there is only a single Display (line 28) and you can switch the Display to any subclass of Screen. Our Screen subclasses are a Form for the search screen, a List for the results screen, and a TextBox for the details screen. One other important difference is that there are no JButton or Button classes in J2ME; instead, there is a Command class. You add your commands to the appropriate screen. You will also notice that we shortened the "Next Results" label to "More" (line 15) to take into account the smaller screen size. The last difference is that ComboBox has been replaced by ChoiceGroup (lines 36 and 37).

```
047:    public BadMicroAmazonSearch()
048:    {
049:        // Create GUI components here...
050:        display = Display.getDisplay(this);
051:
052:        // commands
053:        searchCommand = new Command(CMD_SEARCH, Command.SCREEN, 1);
054:        detailsCommand = new Command(CMD_DETAILS, Command.SCREEN, 1);
// - removed the Instantiation of other Commands
058:
059:        // Create 3 screens: 1. Search, 2. Results, 3. Details
060:        // search form
061:        searchScreen = new Form("Search Terms");
062:        opsChoice = new ChoiceGroup("Operation:", Choice.EXCLUSIVE, ⤵
BadMicroAmazonHttpGet.legalOps, null);
063:        searchScreen.append(opsChoice);
064:        targetTF = new TextField("Search For:", "", 20, ⤵
TextField.ANY);
065:        searchScreen.append(targetTF);
066:        modeChoice = new ChoiceGroup("Category:", Choice.EXCLUSIVE, ⤵
BadMicroAmazonHttpGet.legalModes, null);
067:        modeChoice.setSelectedIndex(1, true);
068:        searchScreen.append(modeChoice);
069:        searchScreen.addCommand(searchCommand);
070:        searchScreen.addCommand(exitCommand);
071:        searchScreen.setCommandListener(this);
072:
073:        // results list
074:        resultsScreen = new List("Results", List.EXCLUSIVE);
075:        resultsScreen.addCommand(detailsCommand);
// - removed adding other commands to resultsScreen
080:
081:        // details text box
082:        detailsScreen = new TextBox("Details", "", 1024, ⤵
TextField.ANY);
// - removed adding commands to detailsScreen
086:    }
```

Listing 22.3   *(continued)*

The constructor for BadMicroAmazonSearch performs three key functions:

■ Gets the Display object via Display.getdisplay() (line 50)

■ Instantiates the `Commands` (lines 53 to 57) and `Screens` (lines 61, 74, and 82)

■ Adds the `Commands` and subcomponents (for the `Form`) to the screens

There are many minor differences in a MIDP GUI compared to a J2SE GUI, such as not adding the screens to the `Display` (as we would to a `JFrame`); instead, we call `Display.setCurrent()` to a `Display` object (as we will in the `startApp()` method below):

```
088:      public void startApp()
089:      {
090:          display.setCurrent(searchScreen);
091:      }
092:
// - removed pauseApp() and destroyApp() as they did nothing
102:
103:      public void commandAction(Command c, Displayable s)
104:      {
105:          String cmd = c.getLabel();
106:          if (cmd.equals(CMD_EXIT))
107:          {
108:             destroyApp(false);
109:             notifyDestroyed();
110:          }
111:          else if (cmd.equals(CMD_SEARCH))
112:          {
113:              // check we have the valid parameters\
114:              String targets = targetTF.getString();
115:              if (targets.length() == 0)
116:              {
117:                 display.setCurrent(new Alert("Search Error", "'Search
For' text field cannot be empty.", null, AlertType.ERROR));
118:              }
119:              else
120:              {
121:                  try
122:                  {
123:                      page = 1; // reset
124:                      doAmazonSearch(page, targets);
125:                  } catch (Exception e)
126:                  {
127:                       e.printStackTrace();
128:                       display.setCurrent(new Alert("SearchError",
"ERROR: reason: " + e.toString(),null, AlertType.ERROR));
129:                  }
130:              }
131:          }
// - removed handling CMD_DETAILS for brevity
136:      }
```

Listing 22.3 *(continued)*

The `commandAction()` method is analogous to the `actionPerformed()` method in J2SE. Note that instead of the `getActionCmd()`, we call `getLabel()` to retrieve the text label of the Command. Although this is similar to the method used in the Swing application, it is a classic pitfall, since it is much slower than comparing the Command references passed in with the references of our predefined Command objects (like searchCommand). We make this optimization in the next version of the program. The rest of the method is nearly identical to the actionPerformed() method, except the error reporting requires the creation of an Alert screen. Although here in this "bad" version we create temporary objects (lines 117 and 128), hopefully, you noticed this waste and the opportunity for optimization:

```
138:     private void doAmazonSearch(int page, String targets) throws ⤵
Exception, IOException
139:     {
140:         ticker.reset("Started Timer in doAmazonSearch()");
141:         getter.newBaseURL(); // reset
142:
143:         // get the operation
144:         int idx = opsChoice.getSelectedIndex();
145:         String op = (String) opsChoice.getString(idx);
146:
// - removed getting the mode as it is similar to getting the op
150:
// - removed getter.addXXX methods -- no change.
156:
157:         // GET it
158:         byte [] response = getter.httpGet();
159:         System.out.println("Have response. Size is: " +
response.length);
160:
161:         // parse the XML, extract ProductNames
162:         // Kxml required ~ 200k for a full parse.
163:         String [] productNames = null;
164:         ByteArrayInputStream bais = new
ByteArrayInputStream(response);                                          ⤵
165:         InputStreamReader isr = new InputStreamReader(bais);
166:         XmlParser parser = new XmlParser(isr);
167:         Document doc = new Document();
168:         doc.parse(parser);
169:
170:         productNodes = new Vector();
171:         getProductNames(doc.getRootElement(), productNodes);
172:         if (productNodes != null)
173:         {
174:             int len = productNodes.size();
```

Listing 22.3   *(continued)*

```
175:            System.out.println("# of products found: " + len);
176:            productNames = new String[len];
177:            for (int i=0; i < len; i++)
178:            {
179:                Node n = (Node) productNodes.elementAt(i);
180:                productNames[i] = n.getText();
181:            }
182:        }
183:
184:        if (productNames != null && productNodes.size() > 0)
185:        {
186:            // populate the list
187:            for (int i=0; i < productNames.length; i++)
188:                resultsScreen.append(productNames[i], null);
189:
190:            // set the display to the results
191:            display.setCurrent(resultsScreen);
192:        }
// - removed the else block for brevity
200:        ticker.printStats("Method doAmazonSearch()");
201:    }
202:
203:    public void getProductNames(Node root, Vector v)
204:    {
205:        int cnt = root.getChildCount();
206:        for (int i=0; i < cnt; i++)
207:        {
208:            Object o = root.getChild(i);
209:            if (o instanceof Node)
210:            {
211:                Node n = (Node) o;
212:                String name = n.getName();
213:                if (name.equals(ELEMENT_PRODUCT_NAME))
214:                {
215:                    v.addElement(n);
216:                }
217:
218:                // element?
219:                if (n.getChildCount() > 0)
220:                    getProductNames(n, v);
221:            }
222:        }
223:    }
224: }
```

Listing 22.3   *(continued)*

The doAmazonSearch()method is similar to its Swing counterpart with a few exceptions. For example, you cannot directly get a selected item (like with the getSelectedItem()method) from a ChoiceGroup or List; instead, you must get the index (line 144) and then call getString() (line 144). Such minor API changes can be frustrating, though in this case the purpose is to eliminate the need for casting (in this direct port it was accidentally left in but is corrected in the next version). On line 158 notice that the httpGet() method returns a byte array (which is required by the kxml parser). Lines 164 to 167 represent the parsing of the XML document using the kxml package. At line 171, we call the utility method, getProductNames(), to recursively traverse the document tree and extract the product Nodes. Unfortunately, this was necessary because the kdom package does not have a getElementsByTagName() method.

Like the minor API changes in the javax.microedition packages, the kdom package has a slightly different API than the w3c DOM package. Such API changes only cause a serious pitfall when such a change eliminates any implicit guarantee of the former abstraction. For the DOM, a tree of Nodes represents the "flattened view" where every object is of type Node. This uniformity makes traversal easy and consistent. Unfortunately, kxml breaks the metaphor by mixing Nodes and other objects (like Strings). This nonuniformity led to runtime ClassCastExceptions (due to the assumption of uniformity—a classic pitfall) and required explicit testing (line 209). Additionally, the kxml changed the method names from getNodeName() to getName()and from getNodeValue() to getText().

Figure 22.3 displays the Network Monitor application, which is part of Sun Microsystems J2ME Wireless Toolkit. This toolkit allows you to emulate J2ME on a personal computer or workstation and enabled the writing and testing of this pitfall. Sun Microsystems did a real service to developers in delivering such a high-quality emulation environment for Java programmers. You can download the kit from http://java.sun.com/products/j2mewtoolkit/.

The Network Monitor application captures all communication between your MIDlet and the Web server. The left pane shows a tree with all HTTP requests and responses. Clicking on a request or response displays the details of the communication in the right pane in both hexadecimal and ASCII. Now we can examine the port of AmazonHttpGet to the J2ME platform in Listing 22.4.

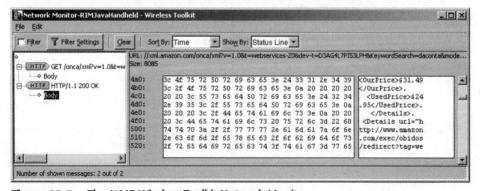

Figure 22.3   The J2ME Wireless Toolkit Network Monitor.

```
001: /* BadMicroAmazonHttpGet.java */
002: package org.javapitfalls.item22;
003:
004: import javax.microedition.io.*;
005: import java.io.*;
006: import java.util.*;
007:
008: public class BadMicroAmazonHttpGet
009: {
// - deleted static constants -- No change
056:
057:     static Timer ticker = new Timer();
058:
// - deleted stringExists() method -- No change
076:
077:     private StringBuffer urlBuf;
078:
079:     public StringBuffer getUrlBuf()
080:     { return urlBuf; }
081:
082:     public BadMicroAmazonHttpGet()
083:     {
084:         newBaseURL();
085:     }
086:
// - deleted method newBaseURL() -- No change
// - deleted all validation methods -- No change
// - deleted all addXXX methods -- No change
// - deleted replaceString() -- No change
216:
217:     public byte [] httpGet() throws IOException
218:     {
219:         ticker.reset("Started Timer in httpGet()");
220:         // get the connection object
221:         String surl = urlBuf.toString();
222:         surl.trim();
223:         System.out.println("url: " + surl);
224:
225:         HttpConnection con = (HttpConnection) Connector.open(surl);
226:         int respCode = con.getResponseCode();
227:         System.out.println("Response code: " + respCode);
228:
229:         InputStream in = con.openInputStream();
230:         ByteArrayOutputStream baos = new ByteArrayOutputStream();
231:
232:         // read response
233:         int b = 0;
234:         while ( (b = in.read()) != -1)
235:         {
```

Listing 22.4   BadMicroAmazonHttpGet.java *(continued)*

```
236:          baos.write(b);
237:      }
238:
239:      ticker.printStats("Method httpGet()");
240:      return baos.toByteArray();
241:   }
// - deleted main() method -- No change.
```

Listing 22.4   *(continued)*

In the `BadMicroAmazonHttpGet` class, all of the URL formatting methods remained unchanged (and thus were removed for brevity); however, the `httpGet()` method underwent significant changes. The porting changes are as follows:

- There is no `java.net` package; instead, the networking classes are in `javax.microedition.io` (line 4). Not only does this confuse it with the J2ME version of `java.io`, this limits future differentiation between IO and networking support in the platform. This is a prime example of change for the sake of change that slows productivity by forcing a context switch without good reason.

- There is no `MalformedURLException` or URL class; instead, the `HttpConnection` class accepts a `String` (line 225).

- There is no `URLConnection` class; instead, you use an `HttpConnection` (line 225).

- There is no `getInputStream()` method for the connection; instead, you use `openInputStream()`. Another example of useless incompatibility.

- There was no `BufferedReader` class, so instead we read in bytes (instead of Strings) and wrote into a `ByteArrayOutputStream` (line 236). This then led to returing a byte array (line 240).

With the memory limit set at 128 KB, a run of BadMicroAmazonSearch produces:

```
Started Timer in doAmazonSearch(). Free Memory: 73076
Started Timer in httpGet(). Free Memory: 71628
url: http://xml.amazon.com/onca/xml?v=1.0&t=webservices-20&dev-
t=D3AG4L7PI53LPH&KeywordSearch=daconta&mode=books&type=lite&page=1&f=xml
Response code: 200
Method httpGet(): 5678. Free Memory: 63924
Have response. Size is: 8085
java.lang.OutOfMemoryError at
javax.microedition.lcdui.Display$DisplayAccessor.commandAction(+165)
        at com.sun.kvem.midp.lcdui.EmulEventHandler$EventLoop.run(+459)
```

When I increased the memory to 200 KB the program was able to run and produced the following:

```
Started Timer in doAmazonSearch(). Free Memory: 141096
Started Timer in httpGet(). Free Memory: 139648
url: http://xml.amazon.com/onca/xml?v=1.0&t=webservices-20&dev-
t=D3AG4L7PI53LPH&KeywordSearch=daconta&mode=books&type=lite&page=1&f=xml
Response code: 200
Method httpGet(): 5718. Free Memory: 139152
Have response. Size is: 8085
# of products found: 8
Method doAmazonSearch(): 36082. Free Memory: 46240
Started Timer in doAmazonSearch(). Free Memory: 65044
```

Even though the BadMicroAmazonSearch ran within 200 KB, you should also notice the poor performance of the method (a noticeably long pause after selecting the Search command). The output of the run shows that the method took 36,082 milliseconds to run. The Wireless Toolkit also provides a Memory Monitor application, as shown in Figure 22.4. As you can see, the large peak in the memory graph occurs when the kxml package is parsing the XML document.

Unfortunately, we could not afford to allow the application to run within 200 KB in order to run it in the Palm emulator. At the time of this writing, the Palm emulator only allowed a Java application to have 64 KB of memory. Figure 22.5 shows our goal with the final code running under the Palm emulator.

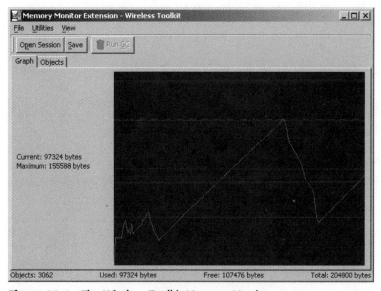

Figure 22.4   The Wireless Toolkit Memory Monitor.

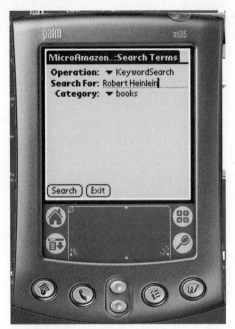

Figure 22.5 MicroAmazonSearch running in a Palm emulator.

Now we are ready to optimize our J2ME application to get it to have both adequate performance and memory consumption. Listing 22.5 is the optimized code for MicroAmazonSearch.java. We will not discuss the functionality of MicroAmazonSearch, since that has been covered in the preceding pages; instead, we will focus only on the optimizations.

```
001: /* MicroAmazonSearch.java */
002: package org.javapitfalls.item22;
003:
004: import java.io.*;
005: import java.util.*;
006: import javax.microedition.midlet.*;
007: import javax.microedition.lcdui.*;
008:
009: public class MicroAmazonSearch extends MIDlet implements
CommandListener
010: {
011:     public static final int MAX_RECORDS = 10;
012:
```

Listing 22.5 MicroAmazonSearch.java

```
013:      // commands
014:      private Command searchCommand;
015:      private Command detailsCommand;
// - removed additional Command references for brevity
019:
020:      // Alerts
021:      Alert searchAlert;
022:      Alert detailAlert;
// - removed other Alert references for brevity
025:
026:      // display
027:      private Display display;
028:
029:      // screens
030:      private Form searchScreen;
031:      private List resultsScreen;
032:      private TextBox detailsScreen;
033:
034:      // screen components
035:      ChoiceGroup opsChoice;
036:      ChoiceGroup modeChoice;
037:      TextField targetTF;
038:      int page = 1;
039:
040:      Vector products;
041:      String xmlBuf;
042:      int [] detailIndexes;
043:      boolean updateIndexes;
044:
045:      boolean debug = true;
046:      Timer ticker = new Timer();
```

Listing 22.5   *(continued)*

Here are the optimizations in the class definition:

Guess the Size of Vectors. Resizing Vectors is expensive. This is demonstrated by using the constant in line 11.

Use Local Variables. Local variables are accessed faster than class members. You will notice that we have eliminated all of the public static Strings. This optimization could be used further in this code.

Avoid String Comparisons. Notice in lines 14 to 18 that the Command references are declared as class members, and these will be compared against in the event handler instead of comparing Strings.

Avoid Temporary Objects. In lines 21 to 24 we use class data members for the Alert references and thus reuse the objects after instantiating them lazily.

```
048:     public MicroAmazonSearch()
049:     {
050:         final String [] legalOps = { "KeywordSearch",      ⤶
"BrowseNodeSearch", "AsinSearch",
051:                         "UpcSearch", "AuthorSearch",        ⤶
"ArtistSearch",
052:                         /* reduce to work in 64k ...
053:                         "ActorSearch", "DirectorSearch",    ⤶
"ManufacturerSearch",
054:                         "ListManiaSearch", "SimilaritySearch",
055:                         */
056:                         };
057:
058:         final String [] legalModes = { "baby", "books",     ⤶
"classical", "dvd", "electronics",
059:                         /* reduce to conserve memory (< 64k)....
060:                         "garden", "kitchen", "magazines",   ⤶
"music", "pc-hardware",
061:                         "photo", "software", "toys",        ⤶
"universal", "vhs",
062:                         "videogames",
063:                         */
064:                         };
065:         final String CMD_SEARCH = "Search";
// - removed remaining final Strings for brevity
070:
071:         // Create GUI components here...
072:         display = Display.getDisplay(this);
073:
074:         // commands
075:         searchCommand = new Command(CMD_SEARCH, Command.SCREEN, 1);
076:         detailsCommand = new Command(CMD_DETAILS, Command.SCREEN,
1);
077:         nextResultsCommand = new Command(CMD_NEXT_TEN,
Command.SCREEN, 1);
078:         backCommand = new Command(CMD_BACK, Command.SCREEN, 2);
079:         exitCommand = new Command(CMD_EXIT, Command.SCREEN, 2);
080:
081:         // Create 3 screens: 1. Search, 2. Results, 3. Details
082:         // search form
083:         searchScreen = new Form("Search Terms");
// removed the construction of the searchScreen — no change.
094:
095:         // other screens, lazy instantiated
096:     }
```

Listing 22.5 *(continued)*

The MicroAmazonSearch constructor has three optimizations:

Use Local Variables. The arrays for operations (lines 50 to 63) and modes were
  moved to become local variables so the memory is reclaimed at method return.

Declare Variables and MethodsFinal. Final references are accessed faster and declaring both final and static is the fastest. Both the arrays and line 65 demonstrate this.

UseLazy Instantiation. Line 95 no longer contains the other screens, as we wait until they are needed by the user to create them.

```
098:    public void startApp()
099:    {
100:        display.setCurrent(searchScreen);
101:        // clean up as User decides what to do
102:        System.gc();
103:    }
104:
// - removed pauseApp() and destroyApp as they do nothing
114:
115:    public void commandAction(Command c, Displayable s)
116:    {
117:        String targets = null;
118:        try
119:        {
120:            if (c == exitCommand)
121:            {
122:                destroyApp(false);
123:                notifyDestroyed();
124:            }
125:            else if (c == searchCommand)
126:            {
127:                // check we have the valid parameters\
128:                targets = targetTF.getString();
129:                if (targets.length() == 0)
130:                {
131:                    // lazy instantiation!
132:                    if (searchAlert == null)
133:                        searchAlert = new Alert("Search Error",
"'Search For' text field cannot be empty.", null, AlertType.ERROR);
134:                        display.setCurrent(searchAlert);
135:                }
136:                else
137:                {
138:                    page = 1; // reset
139:                    xmlBuf = null;
140:                    updateIndexes = true;
141:                    // memory intensive, so get as much as we can
142:                    System.gc();
143:                    doAmazonSearch(page, targets);
144:                    System.gc();
145:                }
146:            }
147:            else if (c == detailsCommand)
148:            {
149:                // get item selected in list
```

Listing 22.5   *(continued)*

```
150:            int selected = resultsScreen.getSelectedIndex();
151:            if (selected >= 0)
152:            {
153:                String product =
resultsScreen.getString(selected);
154:                showDetails(product, xmlBuf);
155:            }
156:            else
157:            {
158:                if (detailAlert == null)
159:                    detailAlert = new Alert("Error", "Must
select a product to see details.", null, AlertType.ERROR);
160:                display.setCurrent(detailAlert);
161:            }
162:          }
// - removed handling of backCommand and nextResultsCommand for brevity
182:        } catch (Throwable t)
183:        {
184:            if (debug) t.printStackTrace();
185:            if (genericAlert == null)
186:                genericAlert = new Alert("Error", "ERROR: reason:
" + t.toString(),null, AlertType.ERROR);
187:            else
188:                genericAlert.setString("ERROR: reason: " +
t.toString());
189:            display.setCurrent(genericAlert);
190:            if (t instanceof OutOfMemoryError)
191:            {
192:                Runtime r = Runtime.getRuntime();
193:                long free = 0, freed = 0;
194:                int trys = 0;
195:                while ( (freed += (r.freeMemory() - free)) > 0 &&
trys < 20)
196:                {
197:                    free = r.freeMemory();
198:                    System.gc();
199:                    trys++;
200:                }
201:                if (debug) System.out.println("Freed " + freed +
" bytes.");
202:
203:            }
204:        }
205:    }
```

Listing 22.5 *(continued)*

The event handler demonstrates three optimizations:

Reduce `String` Comparisons. Lines 120 and 125 demonstrate comparing against
a reference instead of using **String** comparison.

Lines 132 and 185 again demonstrate using lazy instantiation.

Handle OutOfMemoryError. This error is much more common in small footprint devices and must be handled explicitly, like in lines 190 to 200.

```
207:    private final void showDetails(String product, String xmlBuf)
208:    {
209:        final String ELEMENT_DETAILS = "Details";
210:        final String ELEMENT_AUTHORS = "Authors";
211:
212:        // lazy instantiation
213:        if (detailsScreen == null)
214:        {
215:            // details text box
216:            detailsScreen = new TextBox("Details", "", 1024,
TextField.ANY);
// - removed adding the Commands to detailsScreen — no change.
220:        }
221:
222:        ticker.reset("Started Timer in showDetails()");
223:
224:        // clear the text box
225:        detailsScreen.delete(0, detailsScreen.size());
226:
227:        // display tagName : value
228:        // first, find the product
229:        int prodIdx = xmlBuf.indexOf(product);
230:        if (prodIdx >= 0)
231:        {
232:            int productCount = products.size();
233:            if (updateIndexes)
234:            {
235:                if (detailIndexes == null)
236:                    detailIndexes = new int[MAX_RECORDS];
237:                int tmpIdx = 0;
238:                // this loops needs to count up
239:                for (int i=0;i < productCount; i++)
240:                {
241:                    String tgt = "<" + ELEMENT_DETAILS;
242:                    detailIndexes[i] = xmlBuf.indexOf(tgt, tmpIdx);
243:                    tmpIdx = detailIndexes[i] + 1;
244:                }
245:            }
246:
247:            updateIndexes = false;
248:            int detailIdx = -1;
249:            for (int i=productCount-1; i >= 0; i—)
250:            {
251:                if (detailIndexes[i] < prodIdx)
252:                {
253:                    detailIdx = i;
254:                    break;
255:                }
256:            }
```

Listing 22.5   *(continued)*

```
257:
258:          int startIdx = detailIndexes[detailIdx];
259:          int endIdx = ( (detailIdx + 1) < detailIndexes.length ⤵
)? detailIndexes[detailIdx + 1] : xmlBuf.length();
260:
261:          int traverseIdx = startIdx + 1;
262:          while (traverseIdx < endIdx)
263:          {
264:              // find a tag
265:              int tagStartIdx = xmlBuf.indexOf('<', traverseIdx);
266:              int tagEndIdx = xmlBuf.indexOf('>', tagStartIdx);
267:              String tag = xmlBuf.substring(tagStartIdx+1, ⤵
tagEndIdx);
268:              if (tag.equals("/" + ELEMENT_DETAILS))
269:                  break;
270:
271:
272:              // now get the tag contents
273:              int endTagStartIdx = xmlBuf.indexOf("</" + tag, ⤵
tagEndIdx);
274:              String contents = xmlBuf.substring(tagEndIdx + 1, ⤵
endTagStartIdx);
275:
276:              if (!tag.equals(ELEMENT_AUTHORS))
277:              {
278:                  detailsScreen.insert(tag + ":", ⤵
detailsScreen.size());
279:                  detailsScreen.insert(contents + "\n", ⤵
detailsScreen.size());
280:              }
281:
282:              traverseIdx = endTagStartIdx+1;
283:          }
284:
285:      // set the display to the results
286:      display.setCurrent(detailsScreen);
287:      }
288:      ticker.printStats("Method showDetails()");
289:  }
```

Listing 22.5 *(continued)*

The method showDetails() contains five optimizations:

Line 207 demonstrates declaring methods as final for faster access.

Line 213 again demonstrates lazy instantiation.

Use ArraysInstead of Objects. Line 236 uses an integer array instead of a Vector to store indexes, and it also guesses the maximum size so as to not have to resize the array. These optimizations could be used further in the code to gain additional speed and memory conservation.

Iterate Loops Down to Zero. Comparing against zero is the fastest, so coding loops to count down instead of up is more efficient. Lines 249 and 259 demonstrate this.

Only Code the Necessary Functionality. We have abandoned the kxml DOM implementation for performing the minimal number of string comparisons and substrings that we need. You will see this again used in doAmazonSearch().

```
291:       private final void doAmazonSearch(int page, String targets) ⤷
throws Exception, IOException
292:       {
293:           final String ELEMENT_PRODUCT_NAME = "ProductName";
294:           final String LITE_FORMAT = "lite";
295:
296:           ticker.reset("Started Timer in doAmazonSearch()");
297:
298:           // get the operation
299:           int idx = opsChoice.getSelectedIndex();
300:           String op = opsChoice.getString(idx);
301:
302:           // get the mode
303:           idx = modeChoice.getSelectedIndex();
304:           String mode = modeChoice.getString(idx);
305:           // static method is fastest
306:           String sURL = MicroAmazonHttpGet.createURL(op, targets, ⤷
mode, LITE_FORMAT, "" + page);
307:
308:           // GET it via static method
309:           xmlBuf = MicroAmazonHttpGet.httpGet(sURL);
310:
311:           // very lazy instantiation
312:           if (resultsScreen == null)
313:           {
314:               // results list
315:               resultsScreen = new List("Results", List.EXCLUSIVE);
// removed adding Commands to resultsScreen — no change.
321:           }
322:
323:           String [] productNames = null;
324:           if (products == null)
325:           {
326:               products = new Vector(10); // Amazon returns 10 entries
327:           }
328:           else
329:           {
330:               products.setSize(0);
331:               int rcnt = resultsScreen.size();
332:               if (rcnt > 0)
333:               {
334:                   // clear it
335:                   for (int i=rcnt - 1; i >= 0; i—)
336:                       resultsScreen.delete(i);
337:               }
338:           }
339:
340:           int index = 0;
```

Listing 22.5   *(continued)*

```
341:        String productName = null;
342:        while ( (index = xmlBuf.indexOf(ELEMENT_PRODUCT_NAME, ⤶
index)) > 0)
343:        {
344:            int endIdx = xmlBuf.indexOf(ELEMENT_PRODUCT_NAME, ⤶
index + 1);
345:            if (endIdx > index)
346:            {
347:                productName = xmlBuf.substring(index + ⤶
ELEMENT_PRODUCT_NAME.length() + 1, endIdx - 2);
348:                products.addElement(productName);
349:            }
350:            index = endIdx + 1;
351:        }
352:        productName = null;
353:
354:        int productCount = products.size();
355:        if (products != null && productCount > 0)
356:        {
357:            // populate the list
358:            for (int i=productCount - 1; i >= 0; i—)
359:                resultsScreen.append((String)products.elementAt(i), ⤶
null);
360:
361:            // set the display to the results
362:            display.setCurrent(resultsScreen);
363:        }
// - removed the else block for brevity
370:        ticker.printStats("Method doAmazonSearch()");
371:    }
372: }
```

Listing 22.5   *(continued)*

The method doAmazonSearch() contains five optimizations:

Line 291 declares the method final for faster access.

Lines 293 and 294 use local variables.

Line 326 sets the size of the Vector.

Line 330 avoids instantiating a new Vector by reusing it.

Set References to Null. This will assist the garbage collector in more efficiently reclaiming unused memory. Line 352 makes the productName String available for reclamation.

Listing 22.6 presents the optimized version of BadMicroAmazonHttpGet. This version has changed drastically to increase performance and conserve memory. There are even further improvements available, like ensuring that the data returned from the Web server can be stored in memory (or pared down to do so).

```
001: /* MicroAmazonHttpGet.java */
002: package org.javapitfalls.item22;
003:
// - removed Import statements -- no change.
007:
008: public class MicroAmazonHttpGet
009: {
010:    public static final String DEVTAG = "D3AG4L7PI53LPH";
011:    static Timer ticker = new Timer();
012:
013:    // Memory saving but not thread safe
014:    private static StringBuffer urlBuf;
015:    private static ByteArrayOutputStream baos;
016:    private static byte [] buf;
017:
```

Listing 22.6   MicroAmazonHttpGet.java

The Class definition of MicroAmazonHttpGet has two optimizations. First, most of the static Strings have been eliminated to conserve memory. Second, all of the data members have been declared as class data members (to eliminate instantiation) but declared as static for fast access. This means that the class is no longer thread safe, but this is okay because only a single thread uses it. In fact, another improvement may be to just eliminate the class and roll the methods into MicroAmazonSearch:

```
018:    public static final String createURL(String operation, String ⤸
target, String mode, String type,
019:                           String page) throws Exception
020:    {
021:        final String KEYWORD_MODE = "mode";
022:        final String KEYWORD_TYPE = "type";
023:        final String KEYWORD_PAGE = "page";
024:
025:        if (urlBuf == null)
026:        {
027:            urlBuf = new
StringBuffer("http://xml.amazon.com/onca/xml?v=1.0&t=webservices-20& ⤸
dev-t=");
028:                urlBuf.append(DEVTAG);
029:        }
030:        else
031:        {
032:            urlBuf.setLength(0);
033:
urlBuf.append("http://xml.amazon.com/onca/xml?v=1.0&t=webservices- ⤸
20&dev-t=");
034:            urlBuf.append(DEVTAG);
```

Listing 22.6   *(continued)*

```
035:        }
036:
037:        urlBuf.append('&');
038:        urlBuf.append(operation);
039:        urlBuf.append('=');
040:        if (target != null)
041:        {
042:            target.trim();
043:            target = replaceString(target, " ", "%20", 0);
044:
045:            urlBuf.append(target);
046:        }
047:        else
048:            throw new Exception("Invalid target");
049:
050:        // add Mode
051:        urlBuf.append('&');
052:        urlBuf.append(KEYWORD_MODE);
053:        urlBuf.append('=');
054:        urlBuf.append(mode);
055:
// removed code for adding Type and Page -- no change, just Inlined
069:        }
```

Listing 22.6 *(continued)*

The createURL method is a brand-new method that replaced all of the addXXX methods in the previous class. This class demonstrates six optimizations:

Line 18 demonstrates declaring a method both final and static for the fastest access.

Lines 21 to 23 demonstrate using local variables.

Lines 25 to 29 demonstrate lazy instantiation.

Manually Inline Methods. Lines 51 to 54 were previously in the addMode() method, and instead we inlined the method within the createURL method.

Minimize Method Calls. Inlining all of the addXXX methods demonstrates minimizing method calls. This should especially be followed for any method calls inside of loops (like a call to check length() or size()).

```
// - deleted replaceString() — No Change.
091:
092:    public static final String httpGet(String sURL) throws
IOException
093:    {
094:        ticker.reset("Started Timer in httpGet()");
095:        // get the connection object
```

Listing 22.6 *(continued)*

```
096:        System.out.println("url: " + sURL);
097:
098:        HttpConnection con = (HttpConnection) Connector.open(sURL);
099:        int respCode = con.getResponseCode();
100:        System.out.println("Response code: " + respCode);
101:        InputStream in = con.openInputStream();
102:
103:        // lazy instantiate!
104:        if (baos == null)
105:            baos = new ByteArrayOutputStream(1024);
106:        else
107:            baos.reset();
108:        if (buf == null)
109:            buf = new byte[1024];
110:        String response = null;
111:        int cnt=0;
112:        while ( (cnt = in.read(buf)) != -1)
113:        {
114:            baos.write(buf,0,cnt);
115:        }
116:        response = baos.toString();
117:        ticker.printStats("Method httpGet()");
118:        return response;
119:    }
120: }
```

Listing 22.6   *(continued)*

The `httpGet()` method demonstrates three optimizations:

Line 92 declares the method final and static.

Lines 104 and 108 demonstrate lazy instantiation. Also, lines 105 and 109 guess the size of objects to avoid resizing—though `ByteArrayOutputStream` could be better sized with better sampling of average query sizes.

Read More than 1 Byte from a Stream at a Time. All network connections will buffer more than a single byte so reading larger chunks of data is more efficient.

Here are some additional optimization tips:

Avoid `String` Concatenation. `String` concatenation has been proven extremely slow, so use `StringBuffers` or streams to avoid this. This can be better taken advantage of in this application.

Avoid Synchronization. Synchronization is slow because of the overhead of implementation the thread controls.

If adding by 1, int++ is the fastest operation. This is faster than expressions like "I = I + 1;".

Improve Perceived Performance. Use progress meters to inform the user that the computer is active.

Only Include Necessary Classes. To conserve memory required to store your application, only include necessary classes in the deployment archive.

Use Shift Operator to Multiply by 2. The shift operator is faster than the multiplication operator.

Avoid Casting. Casting is expensive, so have methods return only one type.

Use `int` as Much as Possible. Other types like `byte`, `short`, and `character` are promoted to an `int`. So eliminate the promotion by using `int`s directly.

Avoid Using Exceptions. Exceptions require additional checking by the VM, so your code will be faster using more traditional procedural programming (with status returns).

The new, optimized code runs extremely well within 128 KB. Here is a run of the code demonstrating that by performing three queries and multiple showing of details:

```
Started Timer in doAmazonSearch(). Free Memory: 108760
Started Timer in httpGet(). Free Memory: 102160
url: http://xml.amazon.com/onca/xml?v=1.0&t=webservices-20&dev-
t=D3AG4L7PI53LPH&KeywordSearch=daconta&mode=books&type=lite&page=1&f=xml
Response code: 200
Method httpGet(): 8572. Free Memory: 35372
Method doAmazonSearch(): 8773. Free Memory: 32792
Started Timer in showDetails(). Free Memory: 75040
Method showDetails(): 20. Free Memory: 68768
// - removed second query for brevity
Started Timer in doAmazonSearch(). Free Memory: 63284
Started Timer in httpGet(). Free Memory: 60692
url: http://xml.amazon.com/onca/xml?v=1.0&t=webservices-20&dev-
t=D3AG4L7PI53LPH&AuthorSearch=Robert%20Heinlein&mode=books&type=lite&pag
e=1&f=xml
Response code: 200
Method httpGet(): 8502. Free Memory: 23512
Method doAmazonSearch(): 9143. Free Memory: 21244
Started Timer in showDetails(). Free Memory: 63736
Method showDetails(): 1082. Free Memory: 57560
Execution completed successfully
1578454 bytecodes executed
750 thread switches
324 classes in the system (including system classes)
2491 dynamic objects allocated (344132 bytes)
600 garbage collections (283784 bytes collected)
Total heap size 131072 bytes (currently 56276 bytes free)
```

Figure 22.6 displays MicroAmazonSearch being emulated on a BlackBerry device.

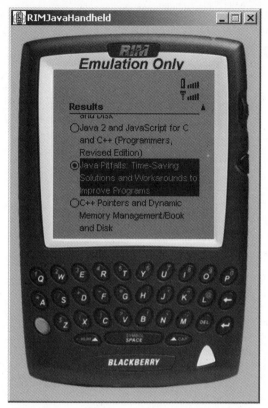

Figure 22.6   MicroAmazonSearch emulated on a BlackBerry.

Copyright © 2002 Research In Motion Limited.

In conclusion, this pitfall has ported a Swing application to the J2ME platform in order to reveal two categories of pitfalls: a bias to programming for the J2SE platform and pitfalls caused by API differences. Lastly we covered and demonstrated over 20 techniques for optimizing J2ME code.

PART

Two

The Web Tier

"The original impulse for modularity came from a desire for flexibility, in particular how to subdivide a sizeable program text into 'modules' . . . But the emphasis has shifted from such mere replaceability to the question of how to break down the whole task most effectively: the demands are such that elegance is no longer a dispensable luxury, but decides between success and failure."

Edsger W. Dijkstra, "On a Cultural Gap"

It is difficult to overstate the transforming nature of Java on the server side. While the adoption of Enterprise JavaBeans and other parts of the J2EE platform has been successful, there is no mistaking how transforming Java has been in the Web tier space.

The accessibility of Java has provided many developers and would-be developers with the opportunity to jump right in to building Web applications with the Java platform. The strong technological advantages contained in servlets, filters, JSPs, and tag libraries have caused many developers to become early adopters.

The early adoption and ease of use of the Java technologies is at the root of many of the Web tier pitfalls. Many developers have found things that work for them and have not understood the underlying implementation concerns. Furthermore, the nature of Web applications having multiple concurrent users is not readily apparent to many developers. Some notable pitfalls in this section:

Cache, It's Money (Item 23). One of the overriding principles of Web applications is the latency of the data being served by these applications. Many Web apps are built to query a database on every request despite the fact that the data has not changed.

JSP Design Errors (Item 24). JavaServer Pages are very powerful—combining the flexibility of scripting and the power of compilation. However, this can have unseen impact in the areas of readability, maintenance, and reuse.

When Servlet HTTPSessions Collide (Item 25). The nature of the Web is such that users jump from site to site with impunity. This can cause issues with systems that rely on the integrity of variables in the HTTPSession class. Collisions between these can cause interesting issues in Web applications.

When Applets Go Bad (Item 26). Any developer that has developed and deployed applet-based Web applications is well aware of the nightmares involved. Java Web Start has proven to be a terrific redesign for all of the problems of applets.

Transactional LDAP—Don't Make That Commitment (Item 27). The delivery of personalized Web content to authenticated users is a complicated process that involves tough questions about proper profile data storage operations needed to perform this activity. This pitfall addresses the decision to store profile attributes in a Relational Database Management System (RDBMS), an LDAP directory, or a combination of both.

Problems with Filters (Item 28). The Servlet 2.3 specification introduced a new Web component called the filter. This pitfall addresses problems encountered in the use of this new component.

Some Direction about JSP Reuse and Content Delivery (Item 29). JavaServer Pages are important visualization components because of their ability to be reused in Web applications. An important aspect of this reusability is their ability to swap in dynamic content from both default application contexts as well as remote contexts. This pitfall will show you how to do both.

Form Validation Using Regular Expressions (Item 30). A new feature of the JDK 1.4 is support for regular expressions. This new support greatly extends the capabilities of Web applications to perform validation of entered data.

Item 23: Cache, It's Money

Every developer's nightmare is developing code on a local development environment and migrating to a different enterprise deployment platform, only to discover substandard latency times during back-end document queries. This problem often occurs because of disparities between development and deployment systems, and because software developers and database administrators tend to work separately from one another. Unfortunately, this "Big Bang" theory, where all forces are expected to come together during integration and work as expected, is a common delusion for most projects.

A recent development effort we were part of exemplified this when we were confronted with latency issues on our front-end portal application that performed SOAP requests and XSLT translations on data received from a back-end database that was managed by a different contractor. Our customer's concerns about protracted query results forced us to take a fresh look at the problem. We knew that the database had documents that were updated roughly every month and had been relatively stable, and the user community was estimated to be between 1,000 and 5,000 concurrent users.

Our analysis led us to the conclusion that our document queries had to be cached, which would alleviate the strains that a relatively large user community might place on our database. This was possible because of the nature of our data that remained stable until the end of every month. The downside of this solution was our understanding that the relevance of the document data could be diminished if older, less significant data was cached and rendered on user queries. Our final solution involved the implementation of two innovative open-source applications: the OSCache tag library from OpenSymphony and the JMeter application from the Apache Software Foundation. OSCache tags were used to cache database queries, and JMeter was used to emulate user requests.

Our aim was to cache the sections of our code where database queries were performed so that repeat trips back to the database could be avoided, thereby increasing performance. During normal operations, any new documents that were added to the database repository would be cached upon insertion. The caching process would be facilitated by implementing JMeter scripts with URL parameters that emulated all the different combinations of user responses. We determined that our entire site could be cached in 45 minutes every month.

To demonstrate this process, some example JavaServer Pages (JSPs) and JMeter XML `ThreadGroup` scripts were developed to cache query data from a simple MySQL database. The Web page shown in Figure 23.1 demonstrates two portlet-like tables with information items: Bike Trails, Gyms, and so on, and the 50 different U.S. states where these information items can be found, which would total 550 different link combinations. The caching process could have been performed manually by hitting each page with the OSCache tags, but this would take too much time and effort. We felt that a more efficient process would involve the creation of a test generation application and the implementation of JMeter to run those tests.

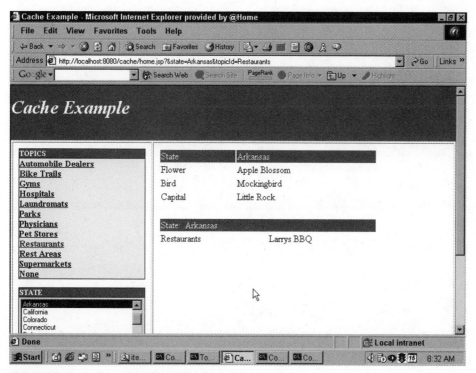

Figure 23.1 Cache example application.

The main focus of our implementation (see Listing 23.1) is a JSP named home.jsp because it renders dynamic query information to the user display and uses the OSCache tag library to cache that data. In the home.jsp code below, the tag library OSCache is specified on line 07. The URI for this class is specified in the deployment descriptor (web.xml). Please note that the <cache:cache></cache:cache> tags on lines 31 to 40 surround the content.jsp page include, which actually performs the database query. On line 31, we set the cache duration using the ISO-8601 format (YYYY-MM-DD). We could have also set the caching duration using the time attribute, whose default value is 3600 seconds, which is 1 hour.

```
01: <%@page import="java.util.*" %>
02: <%@page import="java.io.*" %>
03: <%@page import="java.sql.*" %>
04:
05: <jsp:useBean id="cacheHelper"
06:   class="org.javapitfalls.item23.cacheHelper" scope="request"/>
07: <%@ taglib uri="OSCache" prefix="cache" %>
08:
09: <%
10: String topicId = request.getParameter("topicId");
11: String state = request.getParameter("state");
12: if (topicId == null) topicId = "";
13: if (state == null) state = "";
14: %>
15:
16: <title>
17: Cache Example
18: </title>
19:
20: <jsp:include page="header.jsp" >
21:   <jsp:param name="topicId" value="<%= topicId %>" />
22:   <jsp:param name="state" value="<%= state %>" />
23: </jsp:include>
24:
25: <table border="1" width="100%">
26: <tr valign="top">
27:   <td width="25%" valign="top">
28:         <jsp:include page="leftNav.jsp" />
29:   </td>
30:   <td width="75%" valign="top">
31:   <cache:cache scope="session" duration="2002-01-31">
32:         <% try { %>
33:                 <jsp:include page="content.jsp"/>
34:                 <jsp:param name="topicId" value="<%= topicId %>" />
35:                 <jsp:param name="state" value="<%= state %>" />
36:                 </jsp:include>
37:         <% } catch (Exception e) { %>
```

Listing 23.1 home.jsp

```
38:                    <cache:usecached />
39:          <%,} %>
40:   </cache:cache>
41:   </td>
42: </tr>
43: </table>
44:
45:
46: <jsp:include page="footer.jsp" />
47:
48:
```

Listing 23.1 *(continued)*

The OSCache tag library implementation includes a properties file that is installed in the /WEB-INF/classes directory, which allows the user to set attributes for operational preferences. We've included only the properties that are pertinent to our implementation in Listing 23.2. The cache.path property points to the location where we want to place our cache files. The cache.debug property specifies that we want to see debugging messages, and the cache.unlimited property ensures that the cache disk space is unlimited.

```
# CACHE DIRECTORY
01:#
02:# This is the directory on disk where caches will be stored.
03:# it will be created if it doesn't already exist, but OSCache
04:# must be able to write to here.
05:#
06: cache.path=c:\\cachetagscache
07:
08:# DEBUGGING
09:#
10:# set this to true if you want to see log4j debugging messages
11:#
12:cache.debug=false
13:
14:
15:# CACHE UNLIMITED DISK
16:# Use unlimited disk cache or not
17:cache.unlimited_disk=false
```

Listing 23.2 oscache.properties

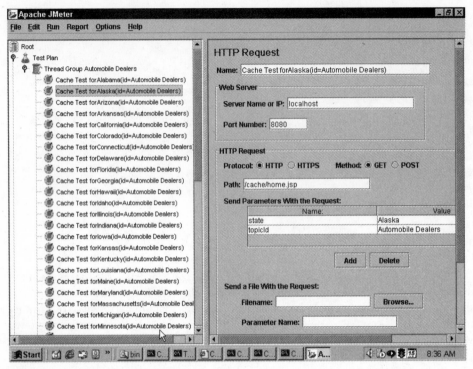

Figure 23.2   Run of Apache JMeter.

After properly inserting the cache tag library tags in the source code, we generated JMeter `ThreadGroup` scripts to replicate a user hitting each page with the `state` and `topicId` parameters.

The JMeter application, as shown in Figure 23.2, is a Java desktop tool that performs automated load testing and user activity measurements, and it comes with visualization tools that provide test feedback and performance metrics. Our application uses this tool to hit all possible user selections so that these pages could be cached. By caching these pages, user queries do not have to go to the back end to draw back data.

Users can generate these `ThreadGroup` tests manually using the JMeter GUI, but we felt that a more efficient option was to write a program called generateTests.java to build these tests automatically. Listing 23.3 hard-codes the `state` and `topicId` data, but an optimal solution would use a file or a database to store these values so that the data would not be tightly coupled with the application and changes could be accommodated more easily. In the generateTests.java program, lines 81 to 85 show a constant timer tag that will kick off a test every second or 1,000 milliseconds. Once these tests are generated, users can use the JMeter GUI to execute these tests, or they can run them manually from the command line using the nongui script:

```
prompt> nongui -o my_test.jmx -h <servername> -p <port #>
```

```
01: import java.io.*;
02: import java.util.*;
03:
04: class generateTests
05: {
06:  public static void main(String[] args) throws IOException
07:  {
08:   if (args.length != 0) {
09:    System.out.println("USAGE: java generateTests");
10:   } else {
11:    String[] states = { "Alabama", "Alaska", "Arizona", "Arkansas",
12:         "California", "Colorado", "Connecticut", "Delaware",
13:         "Florida", "Georgia", "Hawaii", "Idaho", "Illinois",
14:         "Indiana", "Iowa", "Kansas", "Kentucky", "Louisiana",
15:         "Maine", "Maryland", "Massachusetts", "Michigan",
16:         "Minnesota", "Mississippi", "Missouri", "Montana",
17:         "Nebraska", "Nevada", "New Hampshire", "New Jersey",
18:         "New Mexico", "New York", "North Carolina", "North Dakota",
19:         "Ohio", "Oklahoma", "Oregon", "Pennsylvania",
20:         "Rhode Island", "South Carolina", "South Dakota",
21:         "Tennessee", "Texas", "Utah", "Vermont", "Virginia",
22:         "Washington", "West Virginia", "Wisconsin", "Wyoming" };
23:
24:    String[] topicIds = { "Automobile Dealers", "Bike Trails",
25:          "Gyms", "Hospitals", "Laundromats", "Parks",
26:          "Physicians", "Pet Stores", "Restaurants",
27:          "Rest Areas", "Supermarkets" };
28:
29:    for (int x=0; x < topicIds.length; x++) {
30:
31:     PrintWriter pw = new PrintWriter(new
32:         FileOutputStream("Cache_Test_" + topicIds[x] + ".jmx"));
33:     pw.write("<?xml version=\"1.0\"?>\n");
34:     pw.write("<TestPlan>\n");
35:     pw.write("<threadgroups>\n");
36:     pw.write("<ThreadGroup name=\"Thread Group " + topicIds[x] + "\"
37:         numThreads=\"1\" rampUp=\"0\">");
38:     pw.write("<controllers>\n");
39:     pw.write("<LoopController
40:          type=\"org.apache.jmeter.control.LoopController\"
41:          name=\"Loop Controller\" iterations=\"1\">");
42:     pw.write("<configElements>\n");
43:     pw.write("</configElements>\n");
44:     pw.write("<controllers>\n");
45:
46:     for (int y=0; y < states.length; y++) {
```

Listing 23.3   generateTests.java *(continued)*

```
47:        pw.write("<HttpTestSample
48:        type=\"org.apache.jmeter.protocol.http.control.HttpTestSample\"
49:        name=\"Cache Test for" + states[y] +
50:        "(id=" + topicIds[x] + ")" + "\" getImages=\"false\">\n");
51:        pw.write("<defaultUrl>\n");
52:        pw.write("<ConfigElement  type=\"
53:        org.apache.jmeter.protocol.http.config.MultipartUrlConfig\">
54:        \n");
55:        pw.write("<property name=\"port\">8080</property>\n");
56:        pw.write("<property name=\"PROTOCOL\">http</property>\n");
57:        pw.write("<property name=\"domain\">localhost</property>\n");
58:        pw.write("<property name=\"arguments\">\n");
59:        pw.write("<Arguments>\n");
60:        pw.write("<argument name=\"state\"> " + states[y] +
61:              "</argument>\n");
62:        pw.write("<argument name=\"topicId\">" + topicIds[x] +
63:              "</argument>\n");
64:        pw.write("</Arguments>\n");
65:        pw.write("</property>\n");
66:        pw.write("<property name=\"path\">
67:              /cachePage/home.jsp</property>\n");
68:        pw.write("<property name=\"method\">GET</property>\n");
69:        pw.write("</ConfigElement></defaultUrl>\n");
70:        pw.write("<configElements>\n");
71:        pw.write("</configElements>\n");
72:        pw.write("<controllers>\n");
73:        pw.write("</controllers>\n");
74:        pw.write("</HttpTestSample>\n");
75:        }
76:
77:    pw.write("</controllers>\n");
78:    pw.write("</LoopController>\n");
79:    pw.write("</controllers>\n");
80:    pw.write("<timers>\n");
81:    pw.write("<Timer type=\"org.apache.jmeter.timers.ConstantTimer\"
82:              name=\"Constant Timer\">\n");
83:    pw.write("<delay>1000</delay>\n");
84:    pw.write("<range>0.0</range>\n");
85:    pw.write("</Timer>\n");
86:    pw.write("</timers>\n");
87:    pw.write("<listeners>\n");
88:    pw.write("</listeners>\n");
89:    pw.write("</ThreadGroup>\n");
90:    pw.write("</threadgroups>\n");
91:    pw.write("<configElements>\n");
92:    pw.write("</configElements>\n");
```

Listing 23.3 *(continued)*

```
93:      pw.write("</TestPlan>\n");
94:      pw.close();
95:      System.out.println("Finished writing: " + topicIds[x]);
96:    }
97:   }
98:  }
99: }
```

Listing 23.3 *(continued)*

Figure 23.3 demonstrates what occurs in our Web application when we use the JMeter test scripts to cache our database queries. These scripts ping the database with the query operations indicated by the number 1 in the figure and cache the pages to the cache repository so that future database queries hit the cached scripts as indicated by the number 2.

In the end, our scripts allowed us to cache our entire site and reduce query result times, which pleased our customer. Additionally, the knowledge we acquired from our JMeter implementation allowed us to engage our test personnel earlier in our next program, which facilitated our integration efforts between our front-end and database developers.

In all Web development efforts, it is paramount that developers pay some consideration to the implementation of a caching strategy so that pertinent data can be delivered in a timely fashion and database server overloads can be avoided. If your site serves up document artifacts that don't change regularly, it will serve you well. Consider that at the JavaOne 2002 Conference there was significant discussion of the JCACHE specification (JSR 107), whose purpose is to standardize caching of Java objects. Feature enhancements with existing tag libraries like OSCache, along with new implementations like JCACHE, will continue to produce faster Web page response times and make Web content queries a much more pleasant experience.

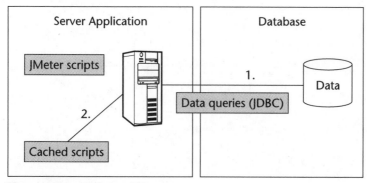

Figure 23.3 Cache architecture.

Item 24: JSP Design Errors

The evolution of Web applications followed two different paths: scripts and compiled executables. Servlets provided a strong improvement on the compiled code examples but suffered their own limitations in terms of presentation. The arrival of JSP caused many people to use them as self-compiling scripts. They saw the flexibility of script programming combined with the power of compiled code. Unfortunately, this can cause significant problems in maintenance, reuse, and flexibility.

My development team was assigned a task of building a Web-based workflow system that persisted information to a conventional relational database. Having built systems like this with a few different technologies, including most recently a servlet implementation of a similar system, we were eager to try JSP to eliminate our endless `println` statements, as well as eliminate the fundamental maintenance nightmare of trying to maintain HTML code inside our servlets.

JSP turned out to be a set of challenges in its own right. Before discussing the blow by blow, let's quickly review the basics of Web application development.

Request/Response Paradigm

Web applications, independent of technological implementation, come down to a few fundamental concepts. Having built quite a few of these systems with a number of technological solutions, we've found that it boils down to a simple process:

- Parse parameters from request.

- Apply business logic (query/update the database in our case).

- Present results to the user in the response.

Listing 24.1 is an example of what this looks like in a servlet implementation.

```
01: public void doPost(HttpServletRequest request, HttpServletResponse
02:                     response) throws ServletException, IOException {
03:
04:     // Parse parameters from the request
05:     String salary = request.getParameter("salary");
07:
08:     // Execute Business Logic (query a DB in this case)
09:     try {
11:     statement.setFloat(1, Float.parseFloat(salary));
12:
13:     // statement is a PreparedStatement initialized in the init()
method
14:     ResultSet results =
15:         statement.executeQuery();
```

Listing 24.1   doPost() from SalaryServlet

```
16:
17:
18:     //  Present the results to the user in the response
19:     response.setContentType("text/html");
20:
21:     PrintWriter out = response.getWriter();
22:     out.println("<html>");
23:     out.println("<head><title>SalaryServlet</title></head>");
24:     out.println("<body>");
25:     out.println("<table>");
26:     out.println("<tr>");
27:     out.println("<td><b>Employee</b></td></tr>");
28:
29:     while (results.next()) {
30:       out.println("<tr>");
31:       out.println("<td>");
32:       out.println(results.getString(1));
33:       out.println("</td>");
34:       out.println("</tr>");
35:     }
36:
37:     out.println("</table>");
38:     out.println("</body></html>");
40:     } catch ( SQLException sqle ) {
41:
42:       sqle.printStackTrace();
44:     }
45:
46:   }
```

Listing 24.1 *(continued)*

Maintaining State

The other issue that comes up in building Web applications is that HTTP is a stateless protocol—that is, one request is independent of the next. Therefore, some method must be chosen to determine how to maintain information about what was done prior to and after this request. A classic example of maintaining state is the user login. A user should not need to provide a login credential with each request. Therefore, there must be some way of keeping track of whether or not this user has been authenticated. There are a few options for how to do this:

Passing parameters. Obviously, the Web application can pass the parameters with each request and embed "hidden" form elements in the response, so that the user doesn't need to re-enter these parameters. The obvious problem is that this can become quite burdensome, involving continuously passing information that is essentially passed through and not really relevant to this particular screen.

Cookies. Cookies provide the ability to store pieces of information on the remote machine; therefore, the application can check to determine if it has previously set information on that machine. However, obviously, major concerns arise out of whether the user will allow such information to be set on his or her machine and how long such information can be counted on being available.

Session variables. HTTP actually provides the ability to put variables in the HTTP session; this was the mechanism that HTTP uses for its basic authentication scheme. Session variables can be helpful but can be problematic—especially with regard to maintaining the session and avoiding other variables with the same name.

JSP the Old Way

Let's take a second to discuss the evolution of Web applications. Originally, Web applications came in two forms: compiled executables (usually written in C or C++) and server scripts (usually written in Perl). They both used the Common Gateway Interface (CGI) to execute requests. To make Web applications easier to build, other scripting languages evolved like server-side JavaScript, JScript, and VBScript. The choice seemed to boil down to power (compiled code was always faster) versus ease of use.

The servlet implementation of my Web application brings me a number of advantages. It is compiled, so I get a performance increase. It operates in a shared process, the servlet engine, so it scales particularly well. Also, the shared process allows for the creation of shared resources like database connections. This is a particular advantage over previously compiled options, which would create new processes (and resources) to handle each request. This caused problems with scalability and with security (the command executed in its own space, without any managing thread to contain malignant or runaway code).

The problem with compiled code is that it is just that, compiled. Notice that I have embedded a great deal of HTML code into my servlet. That means any changes to the presentation require a recompile of the code. Furthermore, anyone who has created these `out.println()` commands of HTML understands the pain of escape sequences.

Along comes JSP, which allows the developer to invert his or her servlet and embed the logic into the presentation code. This proves very helpful to script writers who suffer from limited-capability scripting languages and convoluted programming structures (like conditional loops and iterators). Furthermore, a JSP is compiled into a servlet, so you receive the benefits of compiled code in a script-driven programming environment.

Listing 24.2 is an example JSP implementation of the previous salary servlet.

```
01: <%@ page import="java.util.*"%>
02: <%@ page import="java.sql.*"%>
03: <HTML>
04: <HEAD>
05: <TITLE>
06: Salary Jsp
```

Listing 24.2   BadSalaryJsp.jsp

```
07: </TITLE>
08: </HEAD>
09: <BODY>
10: <H1>
11: Here are the people who make over $<%=
request.getParameter("salary") %>:
12: <%
13:     // Database config information
14:     String driver = "oracle.jdbc.driver.OracleDriver";
15:     String url = "jdbc:oracle:thin:@joemama:1521:ORACLE";
16:     String username = "scott";
17:     String password = "tiger";
18:
19:     String salary = request.getParameter("salary");
20:
21:     // Establish connection to database
22:     try {
23:       Class.forName(driver);
24:       Connection connection =
25:         DriverManager.getConnection(url, username, password);
26:
27:         PreparedStatement statement
28:             = connection.prepareStatement("SELECT ename FROM emp
WHERE sal > ?");
29:
30:         statement.setFloat(1, Float.parseFloat(salary));
31:
32:         ResultSet results =
33:             statement.executeQuery();
34: %>
35: </H1>
36: <table>
37: <tr>
38: <td><b>Employee</b></td>
39: </tr>
40:
41: <%    while (results.next()) {   %>
42: <tr>
43: <td>
44: <%=   results.getString(1) %>
45: </td>
46: </tr>
47: </table>
48: <%    }
49:
50:     } catch(ClassNotFoundException cnfe) {
51:       System.err.println("Error loading driver: " + cnfe);
52:
53:     } catch(SQLException sqle) {
```

Listing 24.2   *(continued)*

```
54:              sqle.printStackTrace();
55:      }
56:
57: %>
58: </BODY>
59: </HTML>
60:
```

Listing 24.2   *(continued)*

This approach looks a lot like the servlet pulled inside out. In fact, to demonstrate how close this is to reality, Listing 24.3 shows a snippet of the source generated by Apache Tomcat to compile the JSP.

```
01:              // HTML // begin
[file="/BadSalaryJsp.jsp";from=(0,31);to=(1,0)]
02:                  out.write("\r\n");
03:
04:              // end
05:              // HTML // begin
[file="/BadSalaryJsp.jsp";from=(1,30);to=(10,35)]
06:                  out.write("\r\n<HTML>\r\n<HEAD>\r\n<TITLE>\r\nSalary
Jsp\r\n</TITLE>\r\n</HEAD>\r\n<BODY>\r\n<H1>\r\nHere are the people who
make over $");
07:
08:              // end
09:              // begin
[file="/BadSalaryJsp.jsp";from=(10,38);to=(10,70)]
10:              out.print( request.getParameter("salary") );
11:          // end
12:              // HTML // begin
[file="/BadSalaryJsp.jsp";from=(10,72);to=(11,0)]
13:                  out.write(":\r\n");
14:
15:          // end
16:          // begin
[file="/BadSalaryJsp.jsp";from=(11,2);to=(33,0)]
17:
18:                  // Database config information
19:                  String driver =
"oracle.jdbc.driver.OracleDriver";
20:                  String url =
"jdbc:oracle:thin:@joemama:1521:ORACLE";
21:                  String username = "scott";
22:                  String password = "tiger";
```

Listing 24.3   Apache Tomcat-generated BadSalaryJsp.jsp

```
23:
24:                      String salary = request.getParameter("salary");
25:
26:                      // Establish connection to database
27:                      try {
28:                        Class.forName(driver);
29:                        Connection connection =
30:                          DriverManager.getConnection(url, username, ⟳
password);
31:
32:                        PreparedStatement statement
33:                          = connection.prepareStatement("SELECT ⟳
ename FROM emp WHERE sal > ?");
34:
35:                        statement.setFloat(1,                      ⟳
Float.parseFloat(salary));
36:
37:                        ResultSet results =
38:                          statement.executeQuery();
39:            // end
40:            // HTML // begin                                       ⟳
[file="/BadSalaryJsp.jsp";from=(33,2);to=(40,0)]
41:
out.write("\r\n</H1>\r\n<table>\r\n<tr>\r\n<td><b>Employee</b></td>\r\n</⟳
tr>\r\n\r\n");
42:
43:            // end
44:            // begin                                               ⟳
[file="/BadSalaryJsp.jsp";from=(40,2);to=(40,32)]
45:                        while (results.next()) {
46:            // end
```

Listing 24.3   *(continued)*

So what is wrong with that? The user gets the ease of scripting combined with the power of compilation. This seems like the best of both worlds. However, the example JSP shows the most obvious problem. Why do I want to put database configuration information in each of my pages? This is a maintenance nightmare. A fundamental of good software development, particularly object-oriented development, is the separation of concerns. The database is a common piece that should be accessible to numerous JSP pages.

While it is possible to do some of this by creating an independent JSP, this kind of issue—accessing an enterprise resource—screams for a programmatic implementation. The solution to this came almost immediately with the JSP specification: Use JavaBeans—now known as the Model 1 Architecture—to encapsulate your business logic.

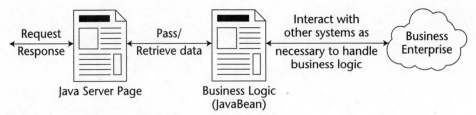

Figure 24.1   Model 1 Architecture.

JSP Development with Beans (Model 1 Architecture)

Figure 24.1 shows the JSP Model 1 Architecture.

The architecture features the following:

- Beans provide encapsulated data structure and logic.

- External resources (databases, Web services, etc.) are abstracted from presentation layer.

Although this is an improvement, the following drawbacks still exist:

- Control logic is still tied to presentation.

- Maintenance is better but still poor—too closely coupled to presentation logic.

Listing 24.4 shows the logic from the previous JSP in a bean.

```
01: public class SalaryServletBean {
02:    private String salary = "30000";
03:    private LinkedList nameList;
04:    private Connection connection;
05:    private PreparedStatement statement;
06:
07:    public SalaryServletBean() {
08:
09:      // Database config information
10:      String driver = "oracle.jdbc.driver.OracleDriver";
11:      String url = "jdbc:oracle:thin:@joemama:1521:ORACLE";
12:      String username = "scott";
13:      String password = "tiger";
14:
15:      // Establish connection to database
16:      try {
17:        Class.forName(driver);
18:        connection =
19:          DriverManager.getConnection(url, username, password);
20:
21:        PreparedStatement statement
```

Listing 24.4   SalaryServletBean.java

```
22:               = connection.prepareStatement("SELECT ename FROM emp ⤶
WHERE sal > ?");
23:
24:    } catch(ClassNotFoundException cnfe) {
25:       System.err.println("Error loading driver: " + cnfe);
26:
27:    } catch(SQLException sqle) {
28:          sqle.printStackTrace();
30:    }
31: }
32:
33:   /**Retrieve the List of Names*/
34:   public LinkedList getNameList() {
36:     return nameList;
37:   }
38:
39:   /**Specify the salary level for getting the list of names*/
40:   public void setSalary(String newValue) {
41:     if (newValue!=null) {
42:        salary = newValue;
43:     }
44:
45:     statement.setFloat(1, Float.parseFloat(salary));
46:
47:     ResultSet results =
48:         statement.executeQuery();
49:
50:     nameList.clear();
51:
52:     while (results.next()) {
53:        nameList.add(results.getString(1));
54:     }
56:   }
57: }
58:
```

Listing 24.4   (continued)

Listing 24.5 shows the accompanying JSP that uses the bean.

```
01: <%@ page import="java.util.*"%>
02: <HTML>
03: <HEAD>
04: <jsp:useBean id="mySalaryServletBean" scope="session" ⤶
class="SalaryServletBean" />
```

Listing 24.5   SalaryJsp.jsp (continued)

```
05: <jsp:setProperty name="mySalaryServletBean" property="*" />
06: <TITLE>
07: Salary Servlet Jsp
08: </TITLE>
09: </HEAD>
10: <BODY>
11: <H1>
12: Salary Jsp
13: </H1>
14: <table>
15: <tr>
16: <td><b>Employee</b></td>
17: </tr>
18:
19: <%
20:        LinkedList myList = mySalaryServletBean.getNameList();
21:        ListIterator li = myList.listIterator();
22:        while (li.hasNext()) {
25: %>
26: <tr>
27: <td>
28: <%=       (String)li.next() %>
29: </td>
30: </tr>
31: <% } %>
32: </table>
33:
34: </BODY>
35: </HTML>
36:
```

Listing 24.5   *(continued)*

Another way to abstract business logic out of the JSP code is through the use of JSP custom tag libraries. This approach allows for component reuse of particular code and also allows content developers to have access to complex Java code programming logic in a form that is familiar to them: HTML-like tags.

Listing 24.6 is an example of our salary business logic in a custom tag library. Notice this tag library has not been designed for the purpose of reuse, but rather to show the same logic expressed in a different manner.

```
01: package mypackage;
02: import javax.servlet.jsp.tagext.TagSupport;
03: import javax.servlet.jsp.tagext.BodyContent;
```

Listing 24.6   SalaryTag.java

```
04: import javax.servlet.jsp.JspException;
05: import javax.servlet.jsp.JspTagException;
06: import javax.servlet.jsp.JspWriter;
07: import javax.servlet.jsp.PageContext;
08: import javax.servlet.ServletRequest;
09: import java.io.PrintWriter;
10:
11: public class salarytag extends TagSupport
12: {
13:    /*
14:    tag attribute: salary
15:    */
16:
17:    private String salary = "30000";
18:
19:    /**
20:     * Method called at start of tag.
21:     * @return SKIP_BODY
22:     */
23:    public int doStartTag() throws JspException
24:    {
25:      try
26:      {
27:        JspWriter out = pageContext.getOut();
28:        SalaryServletBean mySalaryBean = new SalaryServletBean();
29:        mySalaryBean.setSalary(salary);
30:        LinkedList myList = mySalaryBean.getNameList();
31:        ListIterator li = myList.listIterator();
32:        while (li.hasNext()) {
33:
34:          out.println("<tr><td>");
35:          out.println((String)li.next());
36:          out.println("</td></tr>");
37:        }
38:
39:      }
40:      catch(Exception e)
41:      {
42:        e.printStackTrace();
43:      }
44:
45:      return SKIP_BODY;
46:    }
47:
49:    /**
50:     * Method called at end of tag.
51:     * @return SKIP_PAGE
52:     */
53:    public int doEndTag()
```

Listing 24.6   (continued)

```
54:    {
55:      return SKIP_PAGE;
56:    }
57:
58:    public void setSalary(String value)
59:    {
60:      salary = value;
61:    }
62:
63:    public String getSalary()
64:    {
65:      return salary;
66:    }
67:
68: }
69:
```

Listing 24.6   *(continued)*

To deploy this tag library, you need to define it using a tag library descriptor (see Listing 24.7).

```
01: <?xml version = '1.0' encoding = 'windows-1252'?>
02: <!DOCTYPE taglib PUBLIC "~//Sun Microsystems, Inc.//DTD JSP Tag
Library 1.1//EN" "http://java.sun.com/j2ee/dtds/web-
jsptaglibrary_1_1.dtd">
03: <taglib>
04:    <tlibversion>1.0</tlibversion>
05:    <jspversion>1.1</jspversion>
06:    <shortname>salary</shortname>
07:    <uri>javapitfalls </uri>
08:    <info>Shows how to encapsulate the salary business logic in a
taglib.</info>
09:    <tag>
10:      <name>salarytag</name>
11:      <tagclass>mypackage.SalaryTag</tagclass>
12:      <bodycontent>empty</bodycontent>
13:      <attribute>
14:        <name>salary</name>
15:        <required>true</required>
16:        <rtexprvalue>true</rtexprvalue>
17:      </attribute>
18:    </tag>
19: </taglib>
20:
```

Listing 24.7   Salary.tld

However, neither of these shows the tag library in action. All of the complexity is gone, so your developer has an easy task. Listing 24.8 is an example of a JSP using our tag library.

```
01: <%@ page contentType="text/html;charset=windows-1252"%>
02: <%@ page import="java.util.*"%>
03: <%@ taglib uri="javapitfalls" prefix="jp" %>
04: <HTML>
05: <HEAD>
06: <TITLE>
07: Salary Servlet Jsp
08: </TITLE>
09: <META HTTP-EQUIV="Content-Type" CONTENT="text/html; charset=windows-
1252">
10: </HEAD>
11: <BODY>
12: <H1>
13: Salary Jsp
14: </H1>
15: <table>
16: <tr>
17: <td><b>Employee</b></td>
18: </tr>
19:
20: <!-- Down to this simple line -->
21:
22: <jp:salary salary="<%= request.getParameter("salary") %>" />
23:
24: </table>
25:
26: </BODY>
27: </HTML>
28:
```

Listing 24.8 SalaryTag.jsp

All of this modularization has not addressed the fundamental problem we found in our workflow system. While we successfully separated logic from presentation, we had not separated out the flow control of the application. This is critical in most Web systems, but particularly in our workflow system.

The solution to this problem is the Model 2 Architecture.

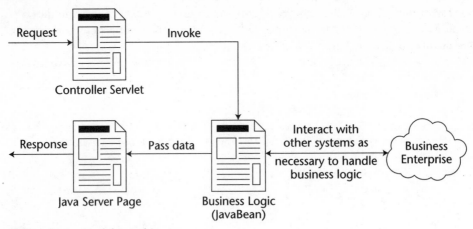

Figure 24.2   Model 2 Architecture.

JSP Development in the Model 2 Architecture

Figure 24.2 shows the Model 2 Architecture. This architecture is a JSP/servlet implementation of the popular and powerful Model-View-Controller pattern. Included is the controller, which is a servlet that responds to a request and dispatches it to the appropriate business logic component. The JavaBean wraps the business logic that needs to be executed to handle the request. From there, the bean hands off to a JavaServer Page, which controls the presentation returned in the response.

It seems like a great idea, but is it realistic to expect Web applications to build this entire infrastructure, especially considering the history of ad hoc Web development? The good thing is that you don't have to build this infrastructure. The Apache Software Foundation's Jakarta project has a rather sophisticated implementation of the Model 2 Architecture, called the Struts framework (http://jakarta.apache.org/struts).

Item 25: When Servlet HttpSessions Collide

Picture this scenario. A user is on the Internet, shopping at Stockman's Online Hardware Store, where there is an electronic commerce user interface with "shopping cart" functionality. As he browses the Web site, he decides to put a belt sander, a drill press, and an air compressor in his shopping cart. Instead of checking out what he has put in his shopping cart, he decides that he'd better buy something for his wife to ease the pain when she discovers his hardware purchases. He quickly goes to "Lace Lingerie Online," where they also have an e-commerce interface. There, he builds a shopping cart consisting of "Sensual Bubble Bath," the "Romantic Lunch Box Package for Two," and the "Lace Gift Certificate." He checks out of the lingerie store, enters his credit card information, and leaves the Web site. Now that his conscience is cleared, the user goes back to the hardware store Web site. He clicks on the "Check out" button, but, to his surprise, his shopping cart at the Stockman Hardware store is filled with "Sensual Bubble Bath," the "Romantic Lunch Box Package for Two," and the "Lace Gift Certificate." The user is confused. Frankly, the folks processing orders at the hardware store are baffled and are calling the programmers who designed the Web site. What could have happened?

Believe it or not, that could be a feasible user scenario when this pitfall relating to the HttpSession class is introduced into Java servlets. HttpSession is a wonderful class for persisting state on the server. It is an interface that is implemented by services to provide an association (session) between a browser and the Web server's servlet engine over a period of time. Using the HttpSession class, you can store a great deal of information without the use of browser client-side cookies and hidden fields. In fact, you can store very complex data structures of information with the API of the HttpSession, which is shown in Table 25.1.

Table 25.1   HttpSession Interface

METHOD	DESCRIPTION
long getCreationTime()	Returns the time at which this session was created.
String getId()	Returns the unique identifier assigned to this session.
long getLastAccessedTime()	Returns the last time the current client requested the session.
int getMaxInactiveInterval()	Returns the maximum interval between requests that the session will be kept by the server.
Object getValue(String)	Returns a data object stored in the session represented by the parameter String. See putValue().
String[] getValueNames()	Returns an array of all names of data objects stored in this session.
void invalidate()	Causes this session to be invalidated and removed.
boolean isNew()	Returns true if the session has been created by the server but the client hasn't acknowledged joining the session; otherwise, it returns false.
void putValue(String, Object)	Assigns (binds) a data object to correspond with a String name. Used for storing session data.

(continues)

Table 25.1 HttpSession Interface *(Continued)*

METHOD	DESCRIPTION
void removeValue(String)	Removes the data object bound by the String-represented name created with the putValue() method.
void setMaxInactiveInterval()	Sets the maximum interval between requests that the session will be kept by the server.

The API of the interface is quite simple. The most-used methods are getValue() and putValue(), where it is possible to save any Java object to the session. This is very helpful if you are developing an application that needs to save state information on the server between requests. In discussing this pitfall, we will discuss the use of this class in depth.

How does a servlet get access to the HttpSession object? The servlet's request object (HttpRequest) that is passed into the servlet's doGet() and doPost() methods contains a method called getSession() that returns a class that implements HttpSession. Listing 25.1 shows a good example of the doGet() method in a servlet using the HttpSession class. This block of code originates from our hardware store scenario discussed at the beginning of this pitfall. Notice that in line 6 of the listing, the servlet calls getSession() with the boolean parameter true. This creates an HttpSession if it doesn't already exist. On line 13, the user checks to see if the session is a new one (or if the client has never interacted with the session) by calling the isNew() method on HttpSession.

```
01:  public void doGet(HttpServletRequest request,
02:    HttpServletResponse response)
03:  throws ServletException, IOException
04:  {
05:    PrintWriter out;
06:    HttpSession session = request.getSession(true);
07:    Vector shoppingcart = null;
08:
09:    response.setContentType("text/html");
10:    out = response.getWriter();
11:    out.println("<HTML><TITLE>Welcome!</TITLE>");
12:    out.println("<BODY BGCOLOR='WHITE'>");
13:    if (session.isNew())
14:    {
15:      out.println("<H1>Welcome to Stockman Hardware!</H1>");
16:      out.println("Since you're new.. we'll show you how ");
17:      out.println(" to use the site!");
```

Listing 25.1 Block of servlet code using HttpSession

```
18:   //...
19:   }
20:   else
21:   {
22:     String name = (String)session.getValue("name");
23:     shoppingcart = (Vector)session.getValue("shoppingcart");
24:     if (name != null && shoppingcart != null)
25:     {
26:       out.println("<H1>Welcome back, " + name + "!</H1>");
27:       out.println("You have " + shoppingcart.size() + " left "
28:                  + " in your shopping cart!");
29:     //...
30:     }
31:   }
32:   //more code would follow here..
32: }
```

Listing 25.1 *(continued)*

On line 23, we see that the getValue() method is called on HttpSession to retrieve a String representing the name of the user and also a vector representing the user's shopping cart. This means that at one time in the session, there was a scenario that added those items to the session with session.putValue(), similar to the following block of code:

```
String myname="Scott Henry";

Vector cart = new Vector();
cart.add("Belt sander ID#21982");
cart.add("Drill press ID#02093");
cart.add("Air compressor ID#98983");

session.putValue("name", myname);
session.putValue("shoppingcart", cart);
```

In fact, the preceding block of code was made to follow the scenario we discussed at the beginning of this pitfall. Everything seems to follow the way the documentation describes the HttpSession API in Table 25.1. What could go wrong?

As we discussed earlier, an HttpSession exists between a browser and a servlet engine that persists for a period of time. If the values name and shoppingcart are placed to represent data objects in the HttpSession, then this session will exist *for every servlet-based application* on the server. What could this mean? If there are multiple servlet applications running on your server, they may use values such as name and shoppingcart to store persistent data objects with HttpSession. If, during the same session, the user of that session visits another servlet application on that server that uses the same values in HttpSession, bad things will happen! In the fictional scenario where we discussed the "switched shopping carts," where lingerie items appeared in the hardware store shopping cart, it just so happened that both e-commerce sites resided on the same server and the visits happened during the same HTTP session.

"Isn't this probability slim?" you may ask. We don't think so. In the present Internet environment, it is not uncommon for e-commerce sites to exist on the same server without the end user knowing about it. In fact, it is not uncommon for an Internet hosting company to host more than one e-commerce site on the same server without the developers of the applications knowing about it!

What does this mean for you as a programmer? When using the HttpSession class, try to make certain that you will not collide with another application. *Avoid using common names storing types in* HttpSession *with the* putValue() *method.* Instead of name and shoppingcart, it may be useful to put your organization, followed by the name of the application, followed by the description of the item you are storing. For example, if you are ACME.COM, and you are developing the e-commerce application for the Stockman Hardware example, perhaps com.acme.StockmanHardware. shoppingcart would be a better choice for storing your data.

Keeping the idea of collisions in mind, look at Listing 25.2, which is used for a shopping cart "checkout" to finalize a transaction on the "Lace Lingerie" e-commerce site. Can you find anything that could cause unexpected behavior to happen? As you can see in the code listing in line 16, the programmer is using a better naming convention for the shopping cart. However, in a new scenario, when the user finishes his purchase at Lace Lingerie and returns to Stockman Hardware, his shopping cart is empty. How could this happen?

```
01:  public void checkout(PrintWriter out, HttpSession session)
02:  {
03:  /*
04:  * Call the chargeToCreditCard() method, passing the session
05:  * which has the user's credit card information, as well as the
06:  * shopping cart full of what he bought.
07:  */
08:  chargeToCreditCard(session);
09:
10:  out.println("<H2>");
11:  out.println("Thank you for shopping at Lace Lingerie Online!")
12:  out.println("</H2>");
13:  out.println("<B>The following items have been charged to ");
14:  out.println("your credit card:</B><BR>");
15:  Vector cart =
16:        session.getValue("com.acme.lacelingerie.shoppingcart");
17:
18:  Iterator it = cart.iterator();
19:
20:  while (it.hasNext())
21:  {
22:    out.println("<LI>" + it.next());
```

Listing 25.2 A checkout()portion of a Web site

```
23:  }
24:
25:  out.println("<H2>Have a nice day!</H2>");
26:
27:  session.invalidate();
28:}
```

Listing 25.2   *(continued)*

The problem lies in line 27 in Listing 25.2. As we showed in Table 25.1, calling the `invalidate()` method of the `HttpSession` interface eliminates the session and all of the objects stored in the session. Unfortunately, this will affect the *user's session for every application on the server*. In our e-commerce shopping scenario, if the user returns to another online store on the server that keeps any information in an `HttpSession`, that data will be lost.

What is the solution? Avoid the `invalidate()` method in `HttpSession`. If you are worried about leaving sensitive data in the `HttpSession` object, a better solution is shown in Listing 25.3.

```
01:  public void checkout(PrintWriter out, HttpSession session)
02:  {
03:  /*
04:  * Call the chargeToCreditCard() method, passing the session
05:  * which has the user's credit card information, as well as the
06:  * shopping cart full of what he bought.
07:  */
08:  chargeToCreditCard(session);
09:
10:  out.println("<H2>");
11:  out.println("Thank you for shopping at Lace Lingerie Online!")
12:  out.println("</H2>");
13:  out.println("<B>The following items have been charged to ");
14:  out.println("your credit card:</B><BR>");
15:
16:  Vector cart =
17:        session.getValue("com.acme.lacelingerie.shoppingcart");
18:
19:  Iterator it = cart.iterator();
20:
21:  while (it.hasNext())
22:  {
23:    out.println("<LI>" + it.next());
24:  }
25:
```

Listing 25.3   Better alternative for checkout( ) *(continued)*

```
26:    out.println("<H2>Have a nice day!</H2>");
27:
28:    /*
29:     * Delete all Information related to this transaction,
30:     * because It Is confidential and/or sensitive!
31:     */
32:    session.removeValue("com.acme.lacelingerie.customername");
33:    session.removeValue("com.acme.lacelingerie.shoppingcart");
34:    session.removeValue("com.acme.lacelingerie.creditcard");
35:    session.removeValue("com.acme.lacelingerie.bodydimensions");
36:
37: }
```

Listing 25.3   *(continued)*

In lines 32 to 35 of Listing 25.3, the programmer deleted all of the objects specific to his application from the HttpSession. This can be a better alternative to the invalidate() method.

What other collision pitfalls could you encounter with this class? If you look back at the code in Listing 25.1, note the else clause in lines 20 to 31. The code assumed that since the isNew() method returned false on line 13, the user had previously visited that site. Now we know better. When isNew() returns false, it means that there exists a session between the browser and the server that has persisted over a matter of time. It does not mean that the user has established a session with the current servlet. The better way to write the block of code in Listing 25.1 is shown in Listing 25.4.

Listing 25.4 sends the user to the showNewbieTheSite() method if the isNew() method of HttpSession returns true on line 13. Also, it tests to see if the customer's name is in the HttpSession on lines 19 to 21. If the getValue() method returns null, then we know that although the session is not new, the user has not set up an account with the current e-commerce application.

```
01:    public void doGet(HttpServletRequest request,
02:     HttpServletResponse response)
03:    throws ServletException, IOException
04:    {
05:     PrintWriter out;
06:     HttpSession session = request.getSession(true);
07:     Vector shoppingcart = null;
08:
09:     response.setContentType("text/html");
10:     out = response.getWriter();
11:     out.println("<HTML><TITLE>Welcome!</TITLE>");
12:     out.println("<BODY BGCOLOR='WHITE'>");
13:     if (session.isNew())
```

Listing 25.4   A smarter way for assuming past usage

```
14:    {
15:          showNewbieTheSite(out);
16:    }
17:    else
18:    {
19:       String name =(String)session.getValue(
20:                       "com.acme.stockmanhardware.customername"
21:                       );
22:       if (name == null)
23:       {
24:           /* Here, the person might have an existing session,
25:            * but not with us!
26:            */
27:           showNewbieTheSite(out);
28:           return;
29:       }
30:       else
31:       {
32:           /* NOW we can assume that they've visited the site! */
33:           out.println("<H1>Welcome back, " + name + "!</H1>");
34:           shoppingcart = (Vector)session.getValue("shoppingcart");
35:           if (shoppingcart != null)
36:           {
37:           out.println("You have " + shoppingcart.size() +
38:                       " left in your shopping cart!");
39:           //...
40:       }
41:    }
42:    //more code would follow here..
43: }
```

Listing 25.4   *(continued)*

Finally, lines 32 to 40 can assume that the user has used the e-commerce application before!

In conclusion, be careful about your use of HttpSession in servlets. Be aware of the collision pitfalls that could await you in regard to naming data objects with put-Value(), terminating the session with invalidate(), and testing for first-time use of the session with the isNew() method.

Item 26: When Applets Go Bad

In the pitfall "J2EE Architecture Considerations" (Item 37) in Part Three, we discuss a software project where we had proposed a solution that can be viewed like Figure 26.1. In that pitfall, we discuss the several scenarios for the client-side behaviors.

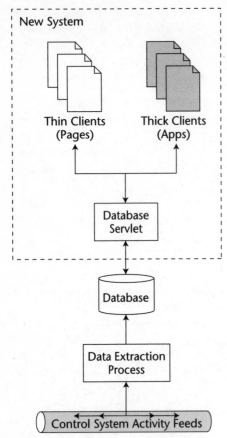

Figure 26.1 The proposed system.

Analyzing the requirements, we found there were really two types of users envisioned for this system. There were analyst personnel who needed a rich toolset by which they could pour through this voluminous set of data. Also, management personnel needed an executive-level summary of system performance. Therefore, there were truly two different clients that needed to be Web-enabled.

The analyst client needed functionality that included mapping, time lines, and spreadsheets. This was going to be the primary tool used for these personnel to perform their job and was expected to perform like the rest of the applications on their desktop machine. They wanted to be able to print reports, save their work, and most other things that users have come to expect from their PCs.

The manager client was meant to show some commonly generated displays and reports. Essentially, this would be similar to portfolio summary and headlines views. They didn't want anything more involved than pointing their Web browser at a Web site and knowing the latest information.

It was critical that the application needed to be centrally managed. Since the analysts were a widely distributed group, there could not be any expectation of doing desktop support or ensuring that the proper version or update was installed.

So we built an applet for the analyst's toolkit. Immediately, we noticed a number of problems with the applet:

It was approximately 3 MB in size. No matter what we looked at, the time line, graphing, and mapping components were simply too large to allow us to reduce the size any more. We tried a phased loading approach, but that didn't really help much; since this was a visualization suite, we couldn't really background-load anything.

The JVM versions were problematic. Moving to the Java plug-in was better, but we still had small subtleties that bothered us. Applets run within the context of the browser; even with the plug-in, they are still at the mercy of the browser's handling.

The security model was buggy and convoluted. Trying to assign permissions inside something that runs within the context of another application is fraught with issues. We had problems with saving and printing from the applet. The biggest showstopper was the fact that our Web server ran on a separate host than the database server. So if we couldn't get the permissions problem to work out, we would not be able to attach to the DB server at all. We intended to use a database access servlet, but we didn't want our hand forced this way over something that should work.

The application ran into responsiveness problems. It had buggy behavior about being unable to find a class that was not repeatable. However, it seemed these problems went away when it was run from an application.

Most of the problems regarding the security model and browser versioning were nuisances that could be worked around. However, we could not get past the long download time of the application. Since the users were widely dispersed and had varying degrees of network communications, this could be an unbearable wait.

The solution to this problem is Java Web Start. Java Web Start is Sun's implementation of the Java Network Launching Protocol (JNLP) and is packaged with JDK 1.4. Java Web Start essentially consists of a specialized configuration file (with the "jnlp" extension) associated with a special MIME type, combined with the Java class loader to allow deployment of Java class files over HTTP. Since the class loading and Java Runtime Environment are configured in accordance with the JNLP, the class files can be cached and downloaded as needed. This provides a solution for centrally managing Java applications and allowing clients to cache Java classes locally. When a patch or change is released, it is propagated automatically out to the clients without your having to download all of the classes again.

Furthermore, Java Web Start provides the ability to update the Java Runtime Environment versions as necessary to suit the applications being deployed. Also, the Java Security model is consistent and built into Java Web Start. The "sandbox" is in effect by default, and the user must grant permissions as appropriate. An interesting thing to note is that you get the security sandbox in a full application context (i.e., a main method) without having to use the indirection execution of an applet.

Examining the JNLP file format provides a great deal of insight into the capabilities of Java Web Start. Listing 26.1 is an example file.

```
01: <?xml version="1.0" encoding="utf-8"?>
02: <!-- JNLP File for Analyst's Toolkit Demo Application -->
03: <jnlp
04:   spec="1.0+"
05:   codebase="http://www.javapitfalls.org/apps"
06:   href="toolkit.jnlp">
07:   <information>
08:     <title>Analyst's Toolkit</title>
09:     <vendor>McDonald-Bradley, Inc.</vendor>
10:     <homepage href="docs/help.html"/>
11:     <description>Analyst's Toolkit Application</description>
12:     <description kind="tooltip">The Analyst's Toolkit</description>
13:     <icon href="http://www.javapitfalls.org/images/toolkit.jpg"/>
14:     <offline-allowed/>
15:   </information>
16:   <security>
17:       <all-permissions/>
18:   </security>
19:   <resources>
20:     <j2se version="1.4"/>
21:     <j2se version="1.3"/>
22:     <jar href="lib/toolkit.jar"/>
23:   </resources>
24:   <application-desc main-class="Toolkit"/>
25: </jnlp>
26:
```

Listing 26.1   toolkit.jnlp

This file shows the configuration of the Java Web Start software. There are four different subsections in the JNLP file: information, security, resources, and application.

The information element provides the display information for the user to view the application before having to run it. It provides descriptions, icons, vendor, and title. However, there is one more interesting tag in the information element: `<offline-allowed/>`. This means that the Web Start application can be run without being connected to the network! This is another advantage over applets.

The security element defines the permissions needed to run this application. If the `<all permissions>` tag is not used, then the application runs within the sandbox by default (as it would if the user chose not to grant permissions). Note that if the `<all-permissions>` tag is used, then all JAR files must be signed.

The resources element specifies how the system should download resources like JAR files and native libraries. Also, it specifies the version of the JRE that is required to run the application, as well as the preference order by which compatible ones should be used. For instance, in the example above, both the JRE 1.4 and 1.3 are allowed as compatible JREs, and JRE 1.2 is not. It prefers JRE 1.4 but will settle for JRE 1.3. The native libraries can be specified in terms of the operating systems with which they are compatible. Also, all resources can be specified as to whether they should be downloaded in an eager or lazy mode—that is, whether they should be downloaded immediately or as allowable.

Figure 26.2 is an example of what happens when a client requests a Java Web Start application.

The question becomes how to check on whether or not JNLP is installed. The way to handle this is to use a client-side script to ask the browser whether it can handle the `application/x-java-jnlp-file` MIME type. Listing 26.2 is the example provided by Sun in the Java Web Start developer's kit (http://java.sun.com/products /javawebstart/docs/developersguide.html):

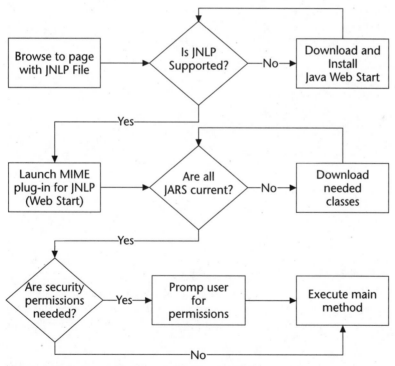

Figure 26.2 Java Web Start application invocation.

```
01:    <SCRIPT LANGUAGE="Javascript">
02:       var javawsInstalled = 0;
03:       isIE = "false";
04:
05:       if (navigator.mimeTypes && navigator.mimeTypes.length) {
06:           x = navigator.mimeTypes['application/x-java-jnlp-file'];
07:           if (x) javawsInstalled = 1;
08:       } else {
09:           isIE = "true";
10:       }
11:
12:       function insertLink(url, name) {
13:        if (javawsInstalled) {
14:             document.write("<a href=" + url + ">"  + name + "</a>");
15:           } else {
16:             document.write("Need to install Java Web Start");
17:           }
18:       }
19:    </SCRIPT>
20:
21:    <SCRIPT LANGUAGE="VBScript">
22:       on error resume next
23:       If isIE = "true" Then
24:         If Not(IsObject(CreateObject("JavaWebStart.IsInstalled"))) ⤵
Then
25:             javawsInstalled = 0
26:         Else
27:             javawsInstalled = 1
28:         End If
29:       End If
30:    </SCRIPT>
31:
```

Listing 26.2   Script to check for Java Web Start

Figure 26.3 is an example of how the deployment of a Java Web Start application is handled.

So, Java Web Start is really cool and makes great sense as a mechanism for centrally managing cross-platform applications, but there is also a full set of APIs that allow the application developer to control the Java Web Start functionality in his or her application.

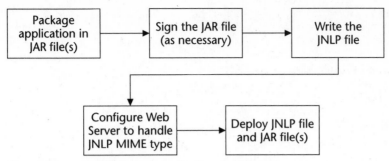

Figure 26.3 Java Web Start application deployment.

Here are some examples of the services in the `javax.jnlp` package:

BasicService. This service provides functionality like `AppletContext`, which allows the user to do things like kicking off the environments default browser to display a URL.

ClipboardService. This service provides access to the system's clipboard. If the user is operating inside the sandbox, he will be warned about the security risk.

DownloadService. This service manages the downloading and caching of Web Start JAR files.

FileOpenService. Browsers have the functionality in Web pages to allow the user to browse for a file to open. You most often see this in file upload forms. This service does a similar thing even from inside the sandbox.

FileSaveService. This replicates the "Save as" functionality of Web browsers, even within the sandbox.

PersistenceService. This can be thought of like a cookie, which allows certain information to be stored even within the browser security model.

PrintService. This allows the user to print files from the Web Start application, after accepting the Print Service prompt.

Looking at the JNLP API, we note all of these services are defined as interfaces. Listing 26.3, from Sun's documentation (http://java.sun.com/products/javawebstart /1.2/docs/developersguide.html), shows how you can get an object that implements these interfaces and also demonstrates using it for controlling the `DownloadService`.

```
01: import javax.jnlp.*;
02:     ...
03:
04:     DownloadService ds;
05:
06:     try {
07:         ds =
(DownloadService)ServiceManager.lookup("javax.jnlp.DownloadService");
08:     } catch (UnavailableServiceException e) {
09:         ds = null;
10:     }
11:
12:     if (ds != null) {
13:
14:         try {
15:             // determine if a particular resource is cached
16:             URL url =
17:                 new
URL("http://java.sun.com/products/javawebstart/lib/draw.jar");
18:             boolean cached = ds.isResourceCached(url, "1.0");
19:             // remove the resource from the cache
20:             if (cached) {
21:                 ds.removeResource(url, "1.0");
22:             }
23:             // reload the resource into the cache
24:             DownloadServiceListener dsl =
ds.getDefaultProgressWindow();
25:             ds.loadResource(url, "1.0", dsl);
26:         } catch (Exception e) {
27:             e.printStackTrace();
28:         }
29:     }
30:
```

Listing 26.3 Example using DownloadService

Looking at these services, we see that it begins to look like Java Web Start is a pseudo Web browser. Consider the evolution of applets. Many saw them as the answer to centrally managed applications deployed over HTTP in a Web browser. However, this model of running within the context of a browser became very inconsistent and buggy. Therefore, the answer was to reengineer the entire solution, looking at the disadvantages and determining how to effectively handle this problem. Java Web Start and the Java Native Launching Protocol is the answer to this problem.

Item 27: Transactional LDAP—Don't Make that Commitment

The advent of distributed Web applications has created new channels for people to perform business transactions and to communicate with one another. These online dealings spawned the need for authentication mechanisms to ensure end users were properly recognized so that they would be privy to proprietary content. Eventually, this led to the creation of profile files that captured user roles inside and outside of an organization so that Web site content could be targeted properly during operations.

The practice of role assignments and efforts to define user communities evolved into a process called *personalization*. Personalization was predicated on an understanding of a user's preferences and role information. Back-end matching algorithms were developed so that pertinent data could be rendered to users based on their preferences and roles.

Profile data often constituted generic data about users (name, address, phone number), and role information often indicated his or her position inside and outside a corporation. When users did not belong to an organization, they were afforded the status of guest.

These authentication and personalization activities raised many questions about data exposure and integrity, along with proper delivery and storage mechanisms for that information. Some, specifically, database vendors, suggested that role and preference information should be stored in a database. Others suggested that this information should be collected in an LDAP directory server. For enterprise system deployments, both can be implemented, but the proper manner to store and retrieve profile and personalization information would be a combination of both. An LDAP directory should be used to house fairly static information—namely, items that don't change all that often—and user role information. Databases should be used for dynamic data, which means data that changes often.

From an architectural perspective, Relational Database Management Systems (RDBMSs) are flat tables with no mechanisms that reflect their organizational structure, while LDAP directories render data in treelike structures that allow users to retrieve organized data and view their spatial relationships. LDAP directories were designed for high-speed read operations and high availability through replication. Migration of dynamic data to an LDAP directory server would be a bad idea because that would be forcing the protocol to perform operations that it was not designed to do.

Two differences between LDAP directories and database systems are how they retain data and perform security activities. RDBMSs typically use table-oriented read/write operations, while LDAP directories concentrate on attribute-oriented security. LDAP directories are constructed to work with multivalue attributes, while traditional relational databases would have to perform SQL join operations to achieve the same functionality. This join-ing of tables in database operations generally hampers performance.

Since LDAP directories were designed for low-throughput and high-speed operations as well as high availability through replication, they've been known to produce incorrect answers from their repositories because of transactional consistencies during write and replication activities. Aberrations like these can be tolerated for storage and retrieval of simple queries, but not with mission-critical data, and that is why data transactions in LDAP directories should be avoided.

RDBMS support for ACID transactions (i.e., transactions that support atomicity, consistency, isolation, and durability) make databases the preferred choice for handling important data. Their implementation ensures predictability and reliability of data transactions. The hierarchical nature of LDAP directories often models real-world data better than flat files in relational databases. It just makes sense to store dynamic data in RDBMSs because they are more flexible and reliable in handling transactions, especially commit and rollback operations.

Personalization is generally considered a dynamic and personalized content delivery system that promotes self-service activities, which in turn strengthens user relationships. The objective of personalization is to deliver pertinent and targeted content to users so that user retention can be maintained and strengthened. When users talk about personalization, they often confuse it with customization. Customization should be considered a subset of personalization, because personalization dictates what content the user has access to and customization allows users to whittle down and modify the presentation of that data. On many applications, specifically, portals, users can customize visualization preferences (what portlets do I want to view? where I want to view them on the page?). More often than not, personalization is based on predetermined role information or previous clickstream detections. In some instances, personalization is based on information explicitly provided by users who are confident in their application's security to provide personal information like salary information or buying preferences. With personalized data, applications can create user communities and matching agents can target content to users based on that information.

To demonstrate how an LDAP directory and an RDBMS can be used in tandem to deliver personalized content, a sample application was developed that retrieves relatively stable profile data in an LDAP directory and stores more dynamic data in a relational data store. The authentication and personalization process is illustrated in Figure 27.1.

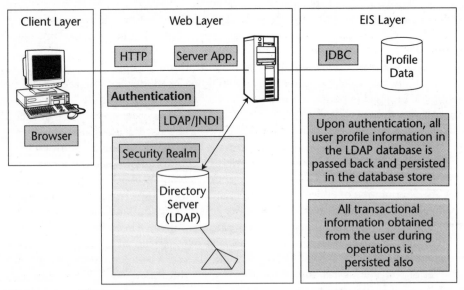

Figure 27.1   LDAP authentication.

The `ControllerServlet` class in Listing 27.1 implements the Front Controller pattern to control all requests through a single servlet application and dispatches requests based upon user role information derived from an LDAP directory server. If a user is recognized as a valid entry in the LDAP directory, that user will be forwarded to the Web page that reflects his or her role.

```
001: package org.javapitfalls.item27;
002:
003: import java.io.*;
004: import java.util.*;
005: import javax.servlet.*;
006: import javax.servlet.http.*;
007: import org.javapitfalls.item27.*;
008:
009: public class ControllerServlet extends HttpServlet {
010:
011:     String direction;
012:     String pageNumber;
013:     String username;
014:     String password;
015:     boolean loggedIn = false;
016:     ldapAuthenticate la;
017:     authenticateHelper helper;
018:
019:     public void service(HttpServletRequest req,
020:                         HttpServletResponse res)
021:                         throws ServletException, java.io.IOException {
022:
023:       direction = req.getParameter("direction");
024:       pageNumber = req.getParameter("page");
025:       username = req.getParameter("username");
026:       password = req.getParameter("password");
027:       if (loggedIn) {
028:
029:         if ( (username != la.getUsername()) ||
030:              (password != la.getPassword()) ) {
031:           loggedIn = false;
032:         }
033:       }
034:       if (!loggedIn) {
035:         if ((username != null) && (password != null) &&
036:             (!username.equals("")) && (!password.equals(""))) {
037:
```

Listing 27.1 ControllerServlet.java *(continued)*

On line 38, an instance of the authentication application named ldapAuthenticate is passed the username and password entered by the user from the login.jsp file dispatched on line 83. When valid entries have been made by the user, the profile data collected from the LDAP authentication and query will be passed along to the database through the helper class authenticateHelper.java. This process is shown in Figure 27.1.

```
038:            la = new ldapAuthenticate(username, password);
039:
040:            if ( (la.validUser()) && (la.getSearchCount() > 0) ) {
041:
042:               loggedIn = true;
043:               helper.setDB(la.getEmail());
044:
045:            } else {
046:
047:               System.out.println("ERROR: Invalid user.");
048:               getServletConfig().getServletContext().
049:                 getNamedDispatcher("InvalidUser").forward(req, res);
050:            }
051:          }
052:
053:        }
054:
055:    if (loggedIn) {
056:
057:        if (pageNumber == null) {
058:
059:          pageNumber = "Page1";
060:
061:        } else {
062:
```

Listing 27.1   *(continued)*

The isUserInRole method checks for authenticated users in the application so that proper navigation can take place. This role information is passed from the LDAP directory and the JNDI realm that was implemented to expose those roles. If a user is determined to possess an admin role, that user will be forwarded to the Page4.jsp.

```
063:            if (req.isUserInRole("admin")) {
064:
065:               pageNumber = "Page4";
066:
067:            } else if (req.isUserInRole("manager")) {
068:
069:               pageNumber = "Page3";
```

Listing 27.1   *(continued)*

```
070:
071:            } else if (req.isUserInRole("tester")) {
072:
073:              pageNumber = "Page2";
074:
075:            } else {
076:
077:              pageNumber = "Page1";
078:
079:          }
080:
081:        }
082:
083:        getServletConfig().getServletContext().
084:          getNamedDispatcher(pageNumber).forward(req, res);
085:
086:    } else {
087:
088:        System.out.println("Login error...");
089:        getServletConfig().getServletContext().
090:          getNamedDispatcher("Login").forward(req, res);
091
092:    }
093:
094:  }
095:
```

Listing 27.1   *(continued)*

The Front Controller pattern was employed in this application indicated by the `Servlet` controller, the dispatcher process shown on Lines 48, 83, and 89. Also part of that pattern implementation is a helper routine shown in the `init()` method on lines 97 and 98. This one-time call determines the database properties and performs connection and query update operations on profile data that needs to be pushed to the backend data store and predetermined and user-defined personalization preferences.

```
095:    public void init() throws ServletException {
096:
097:      helper = new authenticateHelper();
098:      helper.getDBProperties();
099:
100:    }
101:
102: }
103:
```

Listing 27.2   authenticateHelper.java

The `authenticateHelper` class shown in Listing 27.3 loads the database.properties file. It then extracts the key properties and stores them in instance variables:

```
01: package org.javapitfalls.item27;
02:
03: import java.io.*;
04: import java.net.*;
05: import java.util.*;
06: import javax.servlet.*;
07: import javax.servlet.http.*;
08:
09: public class authenticateHelper extends HttpServlet {
10:
11:   String driver;
12:   String dbname;
13:   String username;
14:   String password;
15:
16:   authenticateHelper() {}
17:
18:   public void getDBProperties() {
19:
20:     URL url = null;
21:     Properties props = new Properties();
22:
23:     try {
24:       url = this.getClass().getClassLoader().
25:                         getResource("database.properties");
26:       props.load( new FileInputStream(url.getFile()) );
27:       // Get properties
28:       driver = props.getProperty("driver");
29:       dbname = props.getProperty("dbname");
30:       username = props.getProperty("username");
31:       password = props.getProperty("password");
32:     }
33:     catch(Exception e) {
34:       System.out.println("ERROR:" + e.toString());
35:     }
36:
37:   }
38:
39:   public void setDB(String s) {
40:
41:     System.out.println("INSIDE setDB()...email= " + s);
42:     // UPDATE entry in database with email address.
43:   }
44: }
```

Listing 27.3 authenticateHelper

The ldapAuthenticate routine in Listing 27.4 receives the username and password from the login.jsp and searches the LDAP directory to determine if the user is a valid user that should be authenticated.

```
001: package org.javapitfalls.item27;
002:
003: import java.io.*;
004: import java.net.*;
005: import java.util.*;
006: import java.text.*;
007: import java.util.Date;
008: import javax.naming.*;
009: import javax.naming.directory.*;
010:
011: public class ldapAuthenticate {
012:
013:   String username;
014:   String password;
015:   String firstname;
016:   String lastname;
017:   String email;
018:   int searchCount;
019:
020:     public ldapAuthenticate(String u, String p)
021:     {
022:       username = u;
023:       password = p;
024:       setUsername(u);
025:       setPassword(p);
026:     }
027:
028:     public boolean validUser() {
029:
030:       try {
031:         search();
032:       }
033:       catch(Exception e) {
034:         System.out.println("ERROR: " + e.toString());
035:         return false;
036:       }
037:       return true;
038:     }
039:
040:     public boolean search() {
041:
```

Listing 27.4   ldapAuthenticate.java *(continued)*

The `DirContext` class allows our application to search the directory for the username specified in the login script. This operation is followed by the `Attribute` operation on the `DirContext` object, which is used for the username lookup.

```
042:    try {
043:        DirContext ctx =  getDirContext();
044:        Attributes matchAttrs = new BasicAttributes(true);
045:        matchAttrs.put(new BasicAttribute("uid", username));
046:
047:        NamingEnumeration result = ctx.search("dc=avey",
048:                                              matchAttrs);
049:        int count = 0;
050:        while (result.hasMore()) {
051:          SearchResult sr = (SearchResult)result.next();
052:          System.out.println("RESULT:" + sr.getName());
053:          printAttributes(sr.getAttributes());
054:          count++;
055:        }
056:        System.out.println("Search returned "+ count+ " results");
057:        setSearchCount(count);
058:        ctx.close();
059:    }
060:    catch(NamingException ne) {
061:      System.out.println("ERROR: " + ne.toString());
062:      return false;
063:    }
064:    catch(Exception e) {
065:      System.out.println("ERROR: " + e.toString());
066:      return false;
067:    }
068:    return true;
069:  }
070:
071:    public void printAttributes(Attributes attrs)throws Exception {
072:
073:      if (attrs == null) {
074:        System.out.println("This result has no attributes");
075:      } else {
076:
077:      try {
078:
079:        for (NamingEnumeration enum = attrs.getAll();
080:                                              enum.hasMore();) {
081:          Attribute attrib = (Attribute)enum.next();
082:
083:          for(NamingEnumeration e = attrib.getAll();e.hasMore();) {
084:            String s = e.next().toString();
085:            System.out.println("attrib = " + s + "\n");
086:
```

Listing 27.4 *(continued)*

```
087:                        if (attrib.getID().equals("mail")) {
088:                          setEmail(s);
089:                        } else if (attrib.getID().equals("givenName")) {
090:                          setFirstname(s);
091:                        } else if (attrib.getID().equals("surName")) {
092:                          setLastname(s);
093:                      }
094:                  }
095:              }
096:
097:      } catch (NamingException ne) {
098:          System.out.println("ERROR: " + ne.toString());
099:      }
100:
101:   }
102:
103:  }
104:
105:  public DirContext getDirContext() throws Exception {
106:
```

Listing 27.4   *(continued)*

The `InitialDirContext` class is the starting context for performing directory operations. The `Hashtable` items are the environment properties that allow the application to construct a directory context to be searched.

```
107:      Hashtable env = new Hashtable(11);
108:      env.put(Context.INITIAL_CONTEXT_FACTORY,
109"              "com.sun.jndi.ldap.LdapCtxFactory");
110:      env.put(Context.PROVIDER_URL, "ldap://localhost:389");
111:      env.put(Context.SECURITY_PRINCIPAL, username);
112:      env.put(Context.SECURITY_CREDENTIALS, password);
113:      DirContext ctx = new InitialDirContext(env);
114:      return ctx;
115:
116:  }
166:  }
167:
```

Listing 27.4   *(continued)*

Customarily, the personalization process is incorporated after several iterations of a program, because it is a difficult process to capture. Personalization preferences and matching algorithms often vacillate, which hampers their implementation. That is why role information, which is relatively stable, should be stored in a directory server and personalization preferences should be part of a database that can handle transactions in a more efficient manner.

Consider the following. An LDAP directory is a lightweight database that acts as a central repository for object management and is searched far more often than it should be written to. Its real strength lies in its ability to replicate data across networks, which comes at the expense of transactional protections. Because of this, an RDBMS should be deployed to manage dynamic data, like personalization preferences, which often change regularly.

When you are building distributed business systems, keep in mind that transactional data should be handled with a database, and role information and static user profile information should be managed by an LDAP directory. LDAP directories serve as a complementary technology to database systems, because they can be used to organize and search for relatively static user information in an efficient manner, while database systems can accommodate frequent fluctuations in data.

Item 28: Problems with Filters

Most Web developers want to craft applications that handle user requests, accommodate modifications, and render pertinent content in an efficient manner. Often this means migration to a controller that processes requests and renders different views based on user selections. More often than not, the Model-View-Controller (MVC) pattern is used because it allows components to be separated from application interdependencies, which enables modifications to be made in an easy fashion.

The three elements of the MVC pattern are as follows:

- A *model* that represents the application data and business logic that dictates the availability and changes of the application data.

- A *view* that renders the model data and forwards user input to the controller.

- A *controller* that determines presentation views and dispatches user requests.

Applications that adhere to the MVC design pattern decouple application dependencies, which means that component behavior can be separated and modifications to one layer, say the model tier, can be made and will not affect the view and controller tiers. This improves application flexibility and reusability because changes don't reverberate through the entire system. The MVC paradigm also reduces code duplication and makes applications easier to maintain. It also makes handling data easier, whether you are adding new data sources or changing data presentation, because business logic is kept separate from data.

The MVC solution seems simple enough, but the implementation of simple solutions can often be a different matter. Application controller implementations can assume many forms. Sometimes they involve having several applications pass requests among each other with hard-coded navigation context paths. In many JavaServer Page solutions, a left navigation page is incorporated into a home page that includes header, footer, and content pages, and requests propagate between all of these pages. Problems arise when modifications need to be made to those pages that share a link, perhaps a header and a footer page, because corrections need to be made to both pages. Additionally, the management of parameters between applications becomes cumbersome, and changes don't always propagate properly.

Depending on your situation, the JSP solution described above could be right for your deployment, but for enterprise deployments, the appropriate solution is a single servlet or JavaServer controller page that serves as a common entry point for all application requests. When a single servlet controller is implemented, it makes examining and monitoring all process requests easy.

In addition to servlet controller implementations in MVC applications, filters are needed to enhance request processing because of their ability to transform requests and forward responses. Filters also allow applications to log, audit, and perform security role administration operations prior to request forwarding, which previously had to be performed by additional code and requests.

Filters are generally used to modify request headers and data. More importantly, filters allow requests to be processed in a chainlike fashion. Filter chain implementations locate chain items sequentially through the `doFilter` method and pass along request and response objects through the chain. When the last filter in the filter chain has been processed, the target servlet is summoned.

Figure 28.1 visually demonstrates how a Web controller implementation should be developed. All configuration data should be aggregated in the deployment descriptor (web.xml), including servlet, filter, and JSP mappings. With this architecture, all requests are "filtered" prior to being passed on to the servlet controller that passes control to the JSP visualization applications. The persistence layer on the outer perimeter interacts with both the servlet and JSP applications.

The J2EE specification defines a deployment descriptor as an XML file that describes components between the application assembler and the deployer. In Listing 28.1 all JSP and servlet mappings are migrated to the web.xml file. All controller management emanates from the web.xml file, which simplifies the application's deployment and facilitates modifications.

As part of the deployment described below, the Front Controller pattern is applied to the controller implementation in the ControllerServlet.java program. With this pattern, a controller component manages the user requests, and a dispatcher component manages navigation and user views.

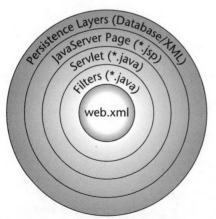

Figure 28.1 Web controller architecture.

```
01: package org.javapitfalls.item28
02: import java.io.*;
03: import java.util.*;
04: import javax.servlet.*;
05: import javax.servlet.http.*;
06:
07: public class ControllerServlet extends HttpServlet {
08:
09:   public void service(HttpServletRequest req,
10:                       HttpServletResponse res)
11:                          throws ServletException, java.io.IOException {
12:
13:       String direction = req.getParameter("direction");
14:       String pageNumber = req.getParameter("page");
15:       if (pageNumber == null)
16:         pageNumber = "Page1";
17:       else {
18:         if (direction.equals("next")) {
```

Listing 28.1 ControllerServlet.java

Line 19 in Listing 28.1 illustrates how J2SDK 1.4 regular expressions can be used to parse string variables. The code parses the first four characters of the page request variable with \\w{4} and extracts the fifth character and, depending on the direction parameter, increases or decreases that value and resets the page mapping request parameter with the new value.

```
19:         int iPage =
Integer.parseInt(pageNumber.replaceAll("^(\\w{4})(\\d{1})", "$2")) + 1;
20:         if (pageNumber.equals("Page4"))
21:           pageNumber = "Page1";
22:         else
23:           pageNumber = "Page" + String.valueOf(iPage);
24:       }
25:       else {
26:         int iPage =
Integer.parseInt(pageNumber.replaceAll("^(\\w{4})(\\d{1})", "$2")) - 1;
27:         if (pageNumber.equals("Page1"))
28:           pageNumber = "Page4";
29:         else
30:           pageNumber = "Page" + String.valueOf(iPage);
31:       }
32:     }
33:     // forward page request: Page1, Page2, Page3, Page4
34:     // works too
35:     // RequestDispatcher rd =
36:     //      req.getRequestDispatcher("/test2/jsp/second.jsp");
37:     // rd.forward(req, res);
```

Listing 28.1 (continued)

```
38:      // works too
39:      // String contextPath = req.getContextPath();
40:      // res.sendRedirect( contextPath + "/test2/jsp/second.jsp" );
41:      getServletConfig().getServletContext().
42:                  getNamedDispatcher(pageNumber).forward(req, res);
43:   }
44:
45: }
46:
```

Listing 28.1 *(continued)*

On line 35 of Listing 28.1 the getRequestDispatcher method gets a Request-Dispatcher instance from its request object so that it can dispatch the JSP component to the given URI path "/test2/jsp/second.jsp". In other words, this method takes a user-specified path that is relative to the servlet's root context and wraps it with a RequestDispatcher object to forward a user request. The relative pathname cannot extend outside the current servlet context, so if the path begins with a "/", it is interpreted as relative to the current context root. The forward method of the RequestDispatcher interface emulates the JSP directive <jsp:forward>, which will throw the IllegalStateException if the application's response buffer has data that has not been committed to the user requests. The forward operation delegates all processing of the request to the target application. With filters, applications can now perform preprocessing prior to the forward operation, which includes logging, security, and request header modifications.

The migration of JSP, filter, and servlet configuration mappings to the deployment descriptor allows the getNamedDispatcher method on line 41 to map the appropriate JSP page in the pageNumber variable so that the request can be forwarded properly. The web.xml file in Listing 28.6 specifies all the JSP pages (Page1, Page2, Page3, Page4) that are available for invocation.

An important result of moving the business logic into the servlet controller is that scriptlet code is reduced in the JSP user interface components and maintenance is facilitated.

```
01:
02: <form method="post">
03:
04:    [ content goes here. ]
05:
06:    <input type="hidden" name="page" value="Page1">
07:    <input type="submit" name="direction" value="prev">
08:    <input type="submit" name="direction" value="next">
09:
10:
11:    </form>
```

Listing 28.2 This is a sample test page test1.jsp

The FileServlet application in Listing 28.3 is invoked after the filter applications are processed. In our sample application the FileServlet application processes the file-name parameter in the URL and displays the content data in HTML and XML format based on that XSL stylesheet filename and the XML filename affiliated with that request. Figure 28.2 shows the HTML presentation based on the filename htmlStates.xsl being applied to the states.xml file. The filename (states.xml) that has the user-specified XSL stylesheet applied to it is specified in line 31 of the web.xml file, which is a lot easier to maintain and modify than the property file (controller.properties) shown on lines 19 to 22.

```
01: package org.javapitfalls.item28;
02:
03: import java.net.URL;
04: import java.io.*;
05: import java.util.*;
06: import javax.servlet.*;
07: import javax.servlet.http.*;
08:
09: public class FileServlet extends HttpServlet {
10:
11: private String filename = "";
12:
13: public void doGet (HttpServletRequest req,
14:                    HttpServletResponse res)
15:                    throws ServletException, IOException {
16:    PrintWriter out = res.getWriter();
17:    try {
18:      /*
19:      Properties resource = new Properties();
20:      URL url = this.getClass().getClassLoader().
21:                   getResource("controller.properties");
22:      resource.load( new FileInputStream(url.getFile()) );
23:      */
24:      // use filename from init() method
25:      // File file = new File(getServletContext().
26:      //          getRealPath(resource.getProperty("filename")));
27:      File file = new
28:            File(getServletContext().getRealPath(filename));
29:      BufferedReader reader =
30:            new BufferedReader(new FileReader(file));
31:      while(reader.ready()) out.println(reader.readLine());
32:    } catch (Exception e){
33:       out.println("ERROR: " + e.toString());
```

Listing 28.3   FileServlet.java

```
34:   }
35:   out.close();
36: }
37:
38: public void init() throws ServletException {
39:    filename = getInitParameter("filename");
40: }
41:
42: }
43:
```

Listing 28.3   *(continued)*

The Web display in Figure 28.2 is the result of the XSL stylesheet displayed in List-ing 28.7 called htmlStates.xsl being applied to the xml.states file. A different view would be rendered if the alternative sample stylesheet xmlState.xsl was specified.

The XSLTransformFilter application in Listing 28.4 performs a transformation on the states.xml file with the user-specified XSL stylesheet in the `filename` parameter in the URL request.

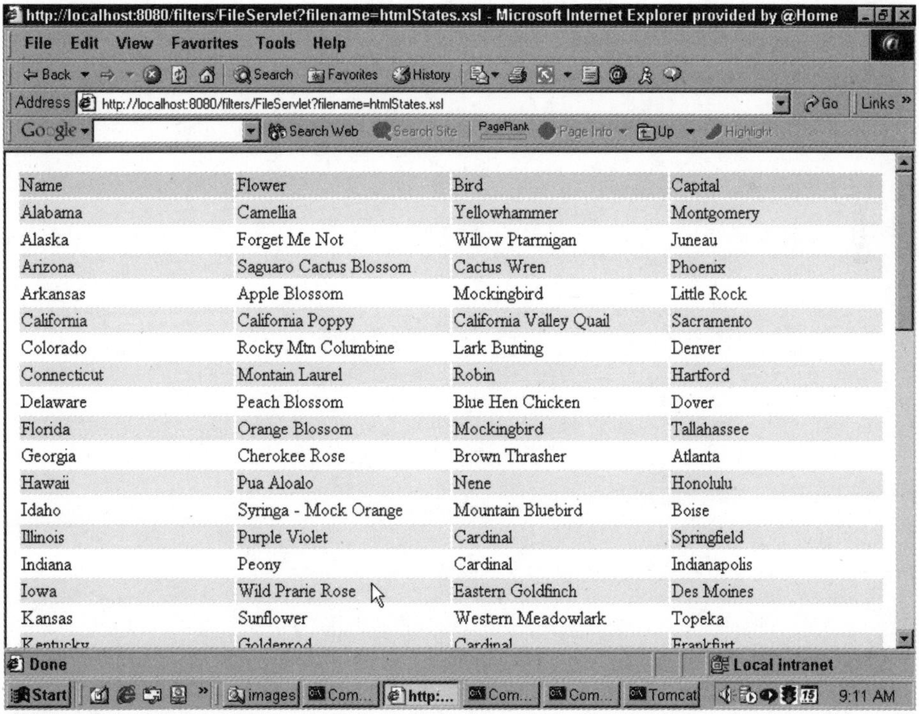

Figure 28.2   XSLT output.

```
01: package org.javapitfalls.item28;
02:
03: import java.io.*;
04: //import java.util.logging.*;
05: import javax.servlet.*;
06: import javax.servlet.http.*;
07: import javax.xml.transform.*;
08: import javax.xml.transform.stream.*;
09:
10: public class XSLTransformFilter implements Filter {
11:
12:    private FilterConfig filterConfig = null;
13:    // Reference below renders a compile-time error [reference to
14:    // Filter is ambiguous] because javax.servlet.Filter and
15:    // java.util.logging.Filter conflict
16:    // private static java.util.logging.Logger logger =
17:    // java.util.logging.Logger.getLogger(XSLTFilter.class.getName());
18:
19:    public void doFilter(ServletRequest request,
20:                         ServletResponse response, FilterChain chain)
21:                         throws IOException, ServletException {
22:
23:      // commented out because of Filter conflict
24:      // logger.setLevel(Level.ALL);
25:      // logger.info("[XSLTFilter]");
26:
27:      String filename = request.getParameter("filename");
28:      String contentType = "text/html";
29:      String styleSheet = "/data/" + filename;
30:      if (filename.startsWith("xml"))
31:          contentType = "text/plain";
32:
33:      response.setContentType(contentType);
34:      String stylePath = filterConfig.getServletContext().
35:                                        getRealPath(styleSheet);
36:      Source styleSource = new StreamSource(stylePath);
37:      PrintWriter out = response.getWriter();
38:      Wrapper wrapper = new Wrapper((HttpServletResponse)response);
39:
40:      chain.doFilter(request, wrapper);
41:
42:      StringReader sr = new StringReader(wrapper.toString());
43:
44:      StreamSource xmlSource = new StreamSource(
filterConfig.getServletContext().getRealPath("/data/states.xml") );
45:
46:      try {
47:        TransformerFactory transformerFactory =
                TransformerFactory.newInstance();
```

Listing 28.4 XSL TransformFilter.java

```
48:        Transformer transformer =
49:            transformerFactory.newTransformer(styleSource);
50:        ByteArrayOutputStream baos = new ByteArrayOutputStream();
51:        StreamResult result  = new StreamResult(baos);
52:        transformer.transform(xmlSource, result);
53:        response.setContentLength(baos.toString().length());
54:        out.write(baos.toString());
55:
56:      } catch(Exception ex) {
57:        out.println(ex.toString());
58:        out.write(wrapper.toString());
59:      }
60:    }
61:    public void init(FilterConfig filterConfig) {
62:     this.filterConfig = filterConfig;
63:    }
64:    public void destroy(){
65:     this.filterConfig = null;
66:    }
67: }
68:
```

Listing 28.4 *(continued)*

The filter's `FilterConfig` object on line 61 has access to the `ServletContext` of the Web application, so the container can pass information to the application and state information can be stored.

In Listing 28.4, lines 04 and 17 attempt to use the `Logger` class that is part of the J2SDK 1.4 implementation but renders a compile-time error (reference to Filter is ambiguous) because the `javax.servlet.Filter` class conflicts with the `java.util.logging.Filter` class.

```
01: package org.javapitfalls.item28;
02:
03: import java.io.*;
04: import java.util.*;
05: import javax.servlet.*;
06: import javax.servlet.http.*;
07:
08: public final class ControllerFilter extends HttpServlet
09:                                           implements Filter {
10:
11:    private ServletContext ctx;
12:
```

Listing 28.5 ControllerFilter.java *(continued)*

```
13:    public void doFilter(ServletRequest req,
14:                         ServletResponse res,
15:                         FilterChain chain)
16:                         throws IOException, ServletException {
17:
18:        PrintWriter out = res.getWriter();
19:        Wrapper wrapper = new Wrapper((HttpServletResponse)res);
20:        chain.doFilter(req, wrapper);
21:        String filename = req.getParameter("filename");
22:        String wts = wrapper.toString();
23:
24:        if (filename != null && filename.startsWith("html")) {
25:          StringBuffer sb = new StringBuffer();
26:          sb.append("<html><body>");
27:          sb.append(wts);
28:          sb.append("</body></html>");
29:          res.setContentLength(sb.toString().length());
30:          out.write(sb.toString());
31:        } else {
32:          out.write(wrapper.toString());
33:        }
34:        out.close();
35:    }
36:
37:    public void destroy() {}
38:    public void init(FilterConfig config) throws ServletException {
39:        ctx = config.getServletContext();
40:    }
41: }
42:
```

Listing 28.5   *(continued)*

Because the filters' applications are run sequentially prior to the invocation of the requested servlet, the doFilter() method of XSLTFilter will be run prior to the same method in the ControllerFilter application. The invocation sequence can be seen in Listing 28.6 on lines 7 and 13.

```
01: <?xml version="1.0" encoding="ISO-8859-1"?>
02: <!DOCTYPE web-app
03:     PUBLIC "-//Sun Microsystems, Inc.//DTD Web Application 2.3//EN"
04:     "http://java.sun.com/dtd/web-app_2_3.dtd">
05: <web-app>
06:   <filter>
07:     <filter-name>XSLTranformFilter</filter-name>
```

Listing 28.6   Web.xml

```
08:      <filter-class>
09:       org.javapitfalls.item28.XSLTransformFilter
10:      </filter-class>
11:    </filter>
12:    <filter>
13:     <filter-name>ControllerFilter</filter-name>
14:     <filter-class>
15:       org.javapitfalls.item28.ControllerFilter
16:     </filter-class>
17:    </filter>
18:    <filter-mapping>
19:       <filter-name>XSLTranformFilter</filter-name>
20:       <servlet-name>FilteredFileServlet</servlet-name>
21:    </filter-mapping>
22:    <filter-mapping>
23:       <filter-name>ControllerFilter</filter-name>
24:       <url-pattern>/ControllerFilter</url-pattern>
25:    </filter-mapping>
26:    <servlet>
27:     <servlet-name>FilteredFileServlet</servlet-name>
28:     <servlet-class>
29:       org.javapitfalls.item28.FileServlet
30:     </servlet-class>
31:     <init-param>
32:       <param-name>filename</param-name>
33:       <param-value>/data/states.xml</param-value>
34:     </init-param>
35:    </servlet>
36:    <servlet>
37:        <servlet-name>Page1</servlet-name>
38:        <jsp-file>/test1/jsp/first.jsp</jsp-file>
39:    </servlet>
40:
41:    <!--- second.jsp, third.jsp, fourth.jsp excluded -- >
42:
56:    <servlet-mapping>
57:       <servlet-name>FilteredFileServlet</servlet-name>
58:       <url-pattern>/FileServlet</url-pattern>
59:    </servlet-mapping>
60:
61: </web-app>
62:
```

Listing 28.6 *(continued)*

With respect to the Filter environment, initialization parameters can be associated with a filter using the init-params element in the deployment descriptor (web.xml). The names and values of those parameters are available to the filter at runtime using the getInitParameter and getInitParameterNames methods.

```
01: <?xml version="1.0" ?>
02: <xsl:stylesheet version="1.0"
03:  xmlns:xsl="http://www.w3.org/1999/XSL/Transform">
04:
05: <xsl:output method="html"/>
06: <xsl:template match="/">
07: <xsl:choose>
08: <xsl:when test="//state">
09:
10: <table border="0" width="100%">
11:
12:  <tr>
13:  <td bgcolor="#dcdcff" width="25%">Name</td>
14:  <td bgcolor="#dcdcff" width="25%">Flower</td>
15:  <td bgcolor="#dcdcff" width="25%">Bird</td>
16:  <td bgcolor="#dcdcff" width="25%">Capital</td>
17:  </tr>
18:
19: <xsl:for-each select="//state">
20:  <xsl:if test="position() mod 2 != 0">
21:  <tr>
22:  <td bgcolor="#eeeeee" width="25%">
23:    <xsl:value-of select="name"/></td>
24:  <td bgcolor="#eeeeee" width="25%">
25:    <xsl:value-of select="flower"/></td>
26:  <td bgcolor="#eeeeee" width="25%">
27:    <xsl:value-of select="bird"/></td>
28:  <td bgcolor="#eeeeee" width="25%">
29:    <xsl:value-of select="capital"/></td>
30:  </tr>
31:  </xsl:if>
32:  <xsl:if test="position() mod 2 = 0">
33:  <tr>
34:  <td width="25%"><xsl:value-of select="name"/></td>
35:  <td width="25%"><xsl:value-of select="flower"/></td>
36:  <td width="25%"><xsl:value-of select="bird"/></td>
37:  <td width="25%"><xsl:value-of select="capital"/></td>
38:  </tr>
39:  </xsl:if>
40: </xsl:for-each>
41:
42: </table>
43:
44: </xsl:when>
45: </xsl:choose>
46: </xsl:template>
47: </xsl:stylesheet>
48:
```

Listing 28.7   htmlstates.xsl

Design patterns serve as building blocks for propagating best practices in software development. In our sample application, the MVC and Front Controller patterns demonstrate how to avoid programming pitfalls that inevitably reveal themselves in superfluous code that is hard to maintain and deploy. The migration of our configuration mappings to our deployment descriptor helped our application management, and the `getNamedDispatcher` method helped avoid the hard-coding of context paths in our application. The dispatcher component manages the application navigation and display views. Applications and program paths change during normal development lifecycles, and when business logic is spread across your application, they become very difficult to maintain and modify.

Additionally, when control logic is moved into a controller class, processing is facilitated because all requests are coordinated and an application's business logic is centralized. A controller servlet application is also employed by a popular Apache Software Foundation offering called the Struts framework, mentioned in Item 24, which is a much more sophisticated application than the one demonstrated in our example and has been well received by the development community. Servlet controllers and XML transform filters can be a powerful combination when processing user requests, specifically SOAP requests. One shortcoming that needs mention is that a single servlet controller can become unmanageable when too much business logic is transferred into the application, which would warrant additional controllers.

Lastly, filter applications are important architectural considerations that need to be included in all enterprise development design decisions. Essentially, they are building blocks that allow applications to layer logic and transform user requests, which allow developers to promote reuse.

Item 29: Some Direction about JSP Reuse and Content Delivery

Your boss just asked you to storyboard his latest and greatest business plan so that it could be shown to local and remote management teams at next week's status meeting. Your previous development experience involved crafting Java Swing components for the accounting department and building some static HTML pages for your office lottery selections.

You've determined that in order to satisfy your requirement to serve both local and remote users, your application should run in a browser, and that JavaServer Pages would be a perfect vehicle to serve up dynamic content. When you asked your boss about the content needed for the presentation, his reply was that it was still being worked on, and it was possible that it could be published by one of those remote management teams that will participate in next week's meeting. His response has led you to believe that a simple content management application might be needed to accommodate the inclusion of dynamic content from this remote source.

Your task appears to be a lot of work to deliver in one week's time, but with a better understanding of JSP page fragmentation and dynamic content inclusion, you should have a pretty good chance of making yourself and your boss look good. JSP page fragmentation will allow the application to be reusable and fairly maintainable, which means that additional functionality can be added without having to rewrite the entire application. The most difficult aspect of this task will be obtaining content from a different context than the application being executed, but we'll look into that later.

Certainly, every development effort should start with a simple storyboard to envision what the application might look like. Figure 29.1 is a start.

Not only will your storyboard show spatial relationships and interface behaviors, it will also allow you to organize your files into subdirectories to make them easier to identify and maintain. In our case, we'll need two file structures, one for the default application, and another for the remote location to drop in content.

Now that your look and feel has been determined, we'll add our page fragments in a file called home.jsp, displayed in Listing 29.1. The JSP include directive on line 06 reads, translates, and pastes the specified file (header.jsp) into your JSP page one time only. If any modifications are made to your header.jsp code, your Web container will need to retranslate the code to reflect these changes. The JSP include action on line 74 includes the footer.jsp page during request time. The include action is more robust than the directive because it performs an automatic update dynamically.

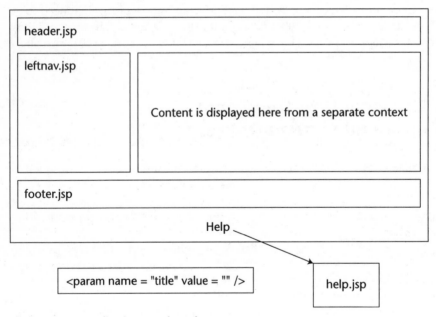

Figure 29.1 Application storyboard.

```
01: <%@ taglib uri="http://java.sun.com/jstl/ea/core" prefix="c" %>
02: <%@page import="java.net.*" %>
03:
04: <title>Fruit Stand</title>
05:
06: <jsp:include page="header.jsp" flush="true" />
07:
08: <table border="0" width="100%">
09: <tr valign="top">
10: <td width="25%" align="center" valign="top">
11: <jsp:include page="leftnav.jsp" flush="true" />
12: </td>
13: <td width=75%" align="center" valign="top">
14:    <%
15:      String sMode = request.getParameter("mode");
16:      String sTopicID = request.getParameter("topic");
17:    %>
18:
19:    <table width="100%" border="0" cellspacing="0" cellpadding="0"
20:                                                    valign="top">
21:    <tr>
22:    <td bgcolor="#ffffff" align="center" class="portletBoxTitle">
23:      <b><font face="Verdana" size="2" color="#FFFFFF">
INFORMATION</font></b>
24:    </td>
25:    </tr>
26:    <tr>
27:    <td bgcolor="#ffffff" align="center" class="portletBoxBody">
28:    <font face="Verdana" size="2"><br>
29:    <%
30:    StringBuffer strbuf = new StringBuffer();
31:    strbuf.append("/default/" + sTopicID);
32:    strbuf.append("/index.html");
33:
34:    String s = strbuf.toString();
35:
36:    // Obtain the custom view context
37:    ServletContext scTemp = getServletConfig().getServletContext();
38:    ServletContext scHome =  getServletConfig().getServletContext();
39:    ServletContext scRemote = scTemp.getContext("/newstuff");
40:
```

Listing 29.1   home.jsp *(continued)*

```
41:     // Create the absolute url for c:import tag to use
42:     String sURL = request.getScheme() + "://" +
43:         request.getServerName() + ":" + request.getServerPort() +
44:         "/newstuff/" + s;
45:     URL urlRsrcFile = null;
46:
47:     try {
48:        // Try to obtain resource from remote context
49:        urlRsrcFile = scRemote.getResource((String)s);
50:     } catch (Exception e) {
51:        scTemp.log("\n\nError: home.jsp - error occured when trying
to obtain a resource from the 'REMOTE' context. Please verify that
the server is configured to allow cross-context access.\n\n", e);
52:     }
53:
54:     if (urlRsrcFile != null) {
55:     %>
56:        <c:import url="<%= sURL %>" />
57:     <%--
58:      This does not work.
59:      <jsp:include page="<%= sURL %>" />
60:      --%>
61:     <%
62:     }
63:     %>
64:
65:     </font>
66:     </td>
67:     </tr>
68:   </table>
69:
70:   </td>
71: </tr>
72: </table>
73:
74: <jsp:include page="footer.jsp" />
```

Listing 29.1 *(continued)*

All appears to be okay until you attempt to add the content using the `include` directive as shown on line 59 from the [newstuff] context. Why? Apparently, JSP `include` operations add resources that are relative to their context, and since the application is being run from the [customviews] context, it looks there for the resource inclusion. To rectify this problem, we'll need to use the Java Standard Template Library (JSTL) implementation of the `import` tag because it allows for the retrieval of absolute URLs, which we'll need to obtain data from the [newstuff] context. Additionally, an entry has to be made to set the context path for your remote inclusion. With Tomcat, this means a context path inclusion in the server.xml file:

```
<Context    path="/newstuff"    docBase="newstuff"    debug="0"
crossContext="true"/>
```

which will allow the customviews application to access the newstuff pages.

In the home.jsp script, the `import` tag library is used on line 56 to import a resource from a directory that lies outside the context of the current application [customviews]. With the `import` tag, a simple drop-off mechanism like a WebDAV client can be used to drop content into the [newstuff] location outside of your deployment area in [customviews]. This simple content management process will enable you to work uninterrupted, and without concern that someone outside of your office will corrupt your development platform.

Lastly, we'll look at the `forward` tag and its implementation in our application. In Listing 29.2, the forward action `<jsp:forward...>` on line 12 passes the request to the help.jsp page. Normally, if a response has already been partially sent to the browser, the forwarding operation will throw an `IllegalStateException` error. This could occur if a user specifies a page buffer equal to `"none"`, as shown on line 02. A buffer size is generally set to `"none"` on Web pages that are slow and to which the developer wants to feed the content as it comes in, rather than waiting for it to reach its buffer maximum or for the page to load to render data. This error can be captured by inserting a try/catch exception handler like the one shown in lines 10 to 17 below. When the page buffer directive is omitted, a default value of 8 KB is allocated and the request will be forwarded properly.

```
01: <%--
02: <%@ page buffer="none" %>    // bad idea. throws an
IllegalStateException error.
03: --%>
04:
05: <%
06: String mode = request.getParameter("mode");
07: if (mode==null) mode="";
08:
09: if (mode.equals("forward")) {
10:  try {
11: %>
12:  <jsp:forward page="help.jsp" >
13:  <jsp:param name="title" value="Help Screen Topic passed from
[footer.jsp]" />
14:  </jsp:forward>
15: <%
16:  }
17:  catch (IllegalStateException e) { System.out.println("ERROR: " +
e.toString()); }
18: }
19: %>
20:
```

Listing 29.2 footer.jsp *(continued)*

```
21: <table width="100%" border="0" cellspacing="0" cellpadding="0">
22:    <tr bgcolor="#FFFFFF">
23:       <td height="4"></td>
24:    </tr>
25:    <tr bgcolor="#3399CC">
26:       <td height="2"></td>
27:    </tr>
28:    <tr class="largetext">
29:       <td height="19">
30:  
31:       </td>
32:    </tr>
33:    <tr bgcolor="#CCCC99">
34:       <td height="2"></td>
35:    </tr>
36:    <tr>
37:       <td height="2"> </td>
38:    </tr>
39:    <tr>
40:       <td>
41:          <div align="center"><font color="#3399CC">
42:             <b><font size="2" face="Arial, Helvetica, sans-serif"><a ⤵
href="footer.jsp?mode=forward">Help</a></font></b>
43:          </div>
44:       </td>
45:    </tr>
46: </table>
```

Listing 29.2   *(continued)*

A finished prototype of your design could look like that shown in Figure 29.2.

When developing JSP Web pages, you need to understand when to use `include` *directives*, which are included during the JSP-to-servlet translation phase, and when to use `include` *actions*, which are included during request time. In addition, keep in mind that `forward` operations should always test for `IllegalStateException` errors. Lastly, it is imperative that you implement the `c:import` tag to retrieve remote URLs in your JSP Web pages, rather than attempting to use JSP `include` directives/actions for pages that differ in context from the application being run.

Hopefully, our simple example has shown you proper JSP development strategies that will prevent you from realizing these pitfalls and will allow you to deliver robust JSP applications and dynamic storyboards in a timely manner. It is important to consider that the architecture you have chosen adheres to the Model 1 design, which is considered "page-centric" because application flow is controlled by the JSP page logic. Understand that this could present maintenance problems because of the tight coupling of the flow and the logic, but it seems preferable to those with little experience in Web development, and your tight delivery schedule. A better solution would incorporate a Model 2 architecture that implements a mediating application that decouples hard-coded Web page references.

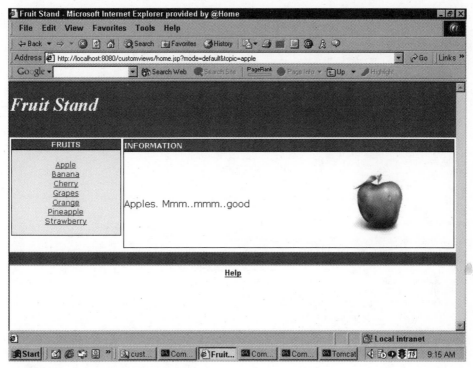

Figure 29.2 Completed prototype.

Item 30: Form Validation Using Regular Expressions

The latest Merlin release (Java SDK 1.4) introduced regular expressions so that developers can manipulate character text in an easier fashion than previously released string handling methods. This enhancement has strengthened the maturing language and facilitated error checking and text manipulation, which is so important to Web application components.

Search and search-and-replace activities are among the more common uses of regular expressions, but they can also be used to perform Boolean tests on text patterns and data streams. Anyone familiar with Unix should recognize regular expressions and their powerful capabilities because of their prevalence in Unix tools and commands. I like to use regular expressions to parse form text and perform validation and replacement activities in my JavaBean components. In Figure 30.1, a Web form demonstrates user validation on input fields and error text that is rendered to the user display when improper data is submitted by the end user. The code that follows will make obvious how important regular expressions can be for Web developers and how the Java language is the "programming language that keeps on giving."

The form above takes user inputs and validates the data prior to passing the application on to the next application in the workflow. The validation bean in Listing 30.1 reads and remembers the user input using the Memento pattern and checks to see if valid entries have been submitted. Improper entries are tagged and sent back to the user display to indicate what the proper input format should be.

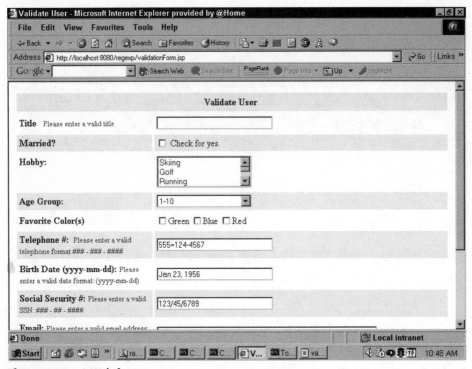

Figure 30.1   A Web form.

Telephone numbers are typically character strings separated by delimiters for readability, so our regular expression should capture digits only ranging from 0 to 9 and be linked by dash characters. The telephone number pattern shown on line 36 ensures that a 10-digit value is input by the user and that an optional dash delimiter can be used for input. Several string manipulations would be needed to perform the same operation that is performed in just one line. Note the double backslash notation in the regular expression `"\\d"`, which differs from the single backslash notation used in Perl, because it differentiates escape character values from regular expressions. The brace notation "{}" indicates the number of decimals values that should be found in the string literal being examined.

```
001: package org.javapitfalls.item30;
002:
003: import java.util.*;
004: import java.text.*;
005: import java.util.Date;
006: import java.util.regex.*;
007:
008: public class validateBean {
009: private String title;
010: private String marriedFlag;
```

Listing 30.1   validateBean.java

```
011: private String hobbies[];
012: private String colors[];
013: private String ageGroup;
014: private String telephoneNumber;
015: private String birthDate;
016: private String ssn;
017: private String email;
018: private String comments;
019: private SimpleDateFormat dateFormat;
020:     private String DATE_FORMAT_PATTERN;
021:
022: private Hashtable errors;
023:
024: public boolean validate() {
025:     boolean errorsFound=false;
026:     if (title.equals("")) {
027:         errors.put("title","Please enter a valid title");
028:         errorsFound=true;
029:     }
030:
031:     if (telephoneNumber.equals("")) {
032:     errors.put("telephoneNumber","Please enter a valid telephone ⤸
#");
033:         errorsFound=true;
034:     }
035:     else {
036:         if (!(telephoneNumber.matches("\\+?([0-9]+-)+([0-9]+- ⤸
)+[0-9]+"))) {
037:             errors.put("telephoneNumber","Please enter a valid ⤸
telephone format ### - ### - ####");
038:             errorsFound=true;
039:         }
040:  }
041:
```

Listing 30.1 *(continued)*

Social security numbers are typically nine-digit strings separated by dash delimiters, so our regular expression needs to capture the digit value and size constraints in a similar fashion as the telephone number pattern.

```
042:     if (ssn.equals("")) {
043:     errors.put("ssn","Please enter a valid Social Security #");
044:     errorsFound=true;
045:     }
046:     else {
047:     if (!(ssn.matches("(\\d{3}\\-?)+(\\d{2}\\-?)+\\d{4}+"))) {
```

Listing 30.1 *(continued)*

```
048:          errors.put("ssn","Please enter a valid SSN: ### - ## - ####");
049:          errorsFound=true;
050:      }
051: }
052:
```

Listing 30.1   *(continued)*

Date of birth formats come in many different varieties, but our application will validate user input on entries that adhere to the "YYYY-MM-DD" format. The commented text shown in lines 63 to 77 was implemented previously for DOB validation. Again, the ability to do more with less is evident in this code segment.

```
053:      if (birthDate.equals("")) {
054:          errors.put("birthDate","Please enter a valid date");
055:          errorsFound=true;
056:      }
057:      else {
058:
059:      if (!(birthDate.matches("(\\d{4}\\-?)+(\\d{2}\\-?)+\\d{2}+"))) {
060:          errors.put("birthDate","Please enter a valid date format: ⤶
(yyyy-mm-dd)");
061:          errorsFound=true;
062:      }
063:      /*
064:      Date date=null;
065:      try
066:      {
067:         dateFormat.applyPattern(DATE_FORMAT_PATTERN);
068:          // dateFormat.setLenient(false);
069:          date = dateFormat.parse(birthDate);
070:      }
071:      catch(ParseException parseexception) { }
072:      if (date==null) {
073:          errors.put("birthDate","Please enter a valid date format: ⤶
(yyyy-mm-dd)");
074:          birthDate="";
075:          errorsFound=true;
076:        }
077: */
078: }
```

Listing 30.1   *(continued)*

Email account validation is achieved with the pattern described on line 85. The pattern text checks for alphanumeric text, with underlines and periods, that is separated by the "at sign"(@) and terminated with a 3-byte extension.

```
080:        if (email.equals("")) {
081:           errors.put("email","Please enter a valid email address");
082:           errorsFound=true;
083:        }
084:        else {
085:           if (!(email.matches("[-A-Za-z0-9_.]+@[-A-Za-z0-9_.]+\\.[-A-Za-⤸
z]{2,}"))) {
086:              errors.put("email","Please enter a valid email address: ex. ⤸
name@company.org");
087:              errorsFound=true;
088:        }
089: }
```

Listing 30.1   *(continued)*

A pet peeve of mine is being forced to fill out an inordinate amount of information about myself in order to gain access to something I'm interested in. This annoyance typically leads to puerile inputs, which become more vulgar the longer I have to keep typing. I know that I'm not the only one doing this because most sites have some kind of dirty word checking to ensure that improper language is not propagated to their database.

The code shown between lines 94 and 96 checks user input to ensure that inappropriate language is captured and replaced with more mild, less offensive text. The regular expression (darn | shoot ....) is run against the comment text input by the user, and if a match is found, replaced by the replaceAll(text) method of the Matcher class.

```
090:     if (comments.equals("")) {
091:        errors.put("comments","Please enter a comment");
092:            errorsFound=true;
093:     } else {
094:          Pattern pattern =                                          ⤸
Pattern.compile("(darn|shoot|damn|jerk|stupid|dummy)");
095:            Matcher match = pattern.matcher(comments);
096: if (match.find()) { comments = match.replaceAll("#%&@"); }
097:          }
098: return errorsFound;
099: }
```

Listing 30.1   *(continued)*

The following code illustrates how to use parenthesized subexpressions to replace text and return a new string value. In the example below, my intention is to cut off all of the digits after the decimal point with the exception of the first two. This can be accomplished by matching the first two digits after the decimal point with the "\\.\\d\\d" pattern. If the code segment below is run, then testAnswer will print out 111.63.

```
String test = "111.63642343422";
String testAnswer = test.replaceAll("(\\.\\d\\d?)\\d+", "$1"); // 111.63
System.out.println("testAnswer=" + testAnswer);
```

Another simple example that performs grouping operations is a code snippet that performs pig Latin string manipulation shown below. In pig Latin, all strings that start with a nonvowel character move the first character to the end of the string and add the "ay" characters to the end of the string. Since *Eagles* starts with E, the string operation will be skipped. All of the other strings will be replaced with their Pig latin string manipulation.

```
String testAnswer="";
String[] s = { "PigLatin", "Eagles", "Redskins", "Giants" };
for (int i=0; i < s.length; i++) {
   testAnswer = s[i].replaceAll("^([^aeiouAEIOU])(.+)", "$2$1ay");
   System.out.println("testAnswer=" + testAnswer);
}
```

A big problem for developers with regular expressions on Unix systems is inconsistent behavior with its tools, specifically ed, ex, vi, sed, awk, grep, and egrep. Different conventions often lead to unpredictable behavior that requires lots of patience and work to better understand the pattern syntax of their regular expression libraries. Users often have problems when describing patterns and recognizing the context in which they appear. These same problems exist in Java applications that use third-party regular expression libraries. Hopefully, the implementation of regular expressions in the latest Java SDK will address this and provide pattern consistency across applications and different platforms.

The regular expression libraries that shipped with the Merlin release were a long-awaited addition to an already powerful enterprise programming language. Pattern matching and replacement should unleash a great deal of flexibility in Java development efforts and will facilitate Web development in the future. With regular expressions, metacharacter implementations in patterns will improve text range matching and make text processing a much more pleasant experience.

According to the published Java 2 Standard Edition APIs, the Java Regular Expressions API does not support the following operations that are supported by the Perl 5 scripting language:

- *Conditional constructs.* (?{X}).
- *Embedded code constructs.* (?{code}).
- *Embedded comment syntax.* To parse comments from a string, the ?#comment is used.
- *Preprocessing operations.* This includes the implementation of the "\l \L \u \U" constructs. To perform lowercase and uppercase operations on an entire string, the \L and \U are used. To perform lowercase and uppercase on the next character in a string, the \l and \u constructs need to be used.

Also, the constructs that are supported by the Java Regular Expressions class that are not supported by the Perl 5 scripting language are as follows:

Possessive quantifiers. The inability to backtrack to another operation when a condition has been met. This results in a greedy match operation.

Character class operator precedence. Literal escape, Grouping, Range, Union, Intersection.

The validation code shown above is okay for parsing user input, but there are cases where you might want to parse text within a Web page. The code below is used to strip meta data from all HTML pages that are spidered. On line 166, the `Pattern` class is used to set up the string pattern to parse on the page. There are two tag elements that are part of the pattern, `meta name` and `content`. The `Matcher` class is given the Web page content in the `pageOutput` string, and all of the items are stripped out using the new `split` method of the `String` class.

```
163:    // strip out metadata -----------------------------------------↩
----------------------
164:     StringBuffer metadata = new StringBuffer();
165:
166:     Pattern p = Pattern.compile("<meta name=\"XX.data1\"          ↩
(CONTENT|content)=\"(.*)");
167:     Matcher m = p.matcher(pageOutput);
168:     int z;
169:     if (m.find()) {
170:         String[] sw1 = m.group(0).split("[\"]");
171:         String[] data1 = sw1[3].split("[,]");
172:         for (z=0; z < data1.length; z++)
173:             metadata.append("<data1>" + data1[z] + "</data1>");
174:     }
175:
176:     p = Pattern.compile("<meta name=\"XX.data2\"                   ↩
(CONTENT|content)=\"(.*)");
177:     m = p.matcher(pageOutput);
178:     if (m.find()) {
179:         String[] sw2 = m.group(0).split("[\"]");
180:         String[] data2 = sw2[3].split("[,]");
181:         for (z=0; z < data2.length; z++)
182:             metadata.append("<data2>" + data2[z] + "</data2>");
183:     }
184:
185:     p = Pattern.compile("<meta name=\"XX.data3\"                   ↩
(CONTENT|content)=\"(.*)");
186:     m = p.matcher(pageOutput);
187:     if (m.find()) {
188:         String[] sw3 = m.group(0).split("[\"]");
189:         String[] data3 = sw3[3].split("[,]");
190:         for (z=0; z < data3.length; z++)
191:             metadata.append("<data2>" + data3[z] + "</data2>");
192:     }
193:
194:     System.out.println("metadata= " + metadata.toString());
```

Listing 30.1 *(continued)*

A new regular expression pattern is used to strip out additional links in the HTML pages to spider on subsequent levels. The <a href></a> pattern is the target expression to be parsed from the text. The (a|A) groupings are used so that both lowercase and uppercase expressions are matched.

```
Pattern pattern = Pattern.compile("<(a|A) href+[^<]*</(a|A)>");
 Matcher match = pattern.matcher(pageOutput);
 %>
 <tr bgcolor="#eeeeee">
 <td align="center"> Links for next Level: <%= filename %></td>
 </tr>
 <%
  // display all the references found in the URI
  while (match.find()) {

  // split words
  String[] sw = match.group(0).split("[\"]");
  if ((sw.length > 1) && (sw[1].startsWith("http://")) &&
(sw[1].endsWith("html"))) {
  %>
  <tr><td>
  <%
  out.println("webpage=" + sw[1]);
  vRef.addElement(sw[1]);
  %>
  </td></tr>
  <%
  }
  }
```

The Web page displayed in Figure 30.2 is the result of the spidering action of the code snippet above, which resides in the regexpTest.jsp application. The results shown below the Submit button are the links parsed from the Web page requested in the URI field.

Java Regular Expressions are a powerful new language construct that strengthens string manipulation activities for developers. With Java Regular Expressions, Java developers can realize in their text processing activities what Perl programmers have been lauding about for years.

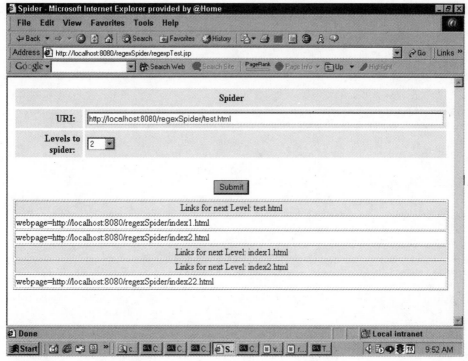

Figure 30.2   Spider results.

Item 31: Instance Variables in Servlets

A common trap that new servlet developers find themselves in revolves around the use of instance variables. Unfortunately, the symptoms of this problem are not easy to diagnose until the last minute. The developer writes the servlet, and it goes through standalone testing just fine. When it is load-tested (or when it goes into production with many concurrent users), however, strange things start to occur on an ad hoc basis: garbled strings of nonsense begin appearing in Web browsers, users of the enterprise Web system begin receiving other users' information, and seemingly "random" errors appear in the application. What went wrong?

A simple example of this situation can be seen in Listing 31.1, where we have an example application that serves as a library of technical resources. Our fictional "Online Technobabble Library" is a document repository where multiple users can check out, check in, and read multiple documents with a lot of technobabble. The servlet takes a parameter, `userid`, which tells the servlet where to get the user's information.

```
001: package org.javapitfalls.item31;
002: import java.io.*;
003: import java.text.*;
004: import java.util.*;
005: import javax.servlet.*;
006: import javax.servlet.http.*;
007: /**
008: * This example demonstrates using instance variables
009: * in a servlet.. The example features a fictional
010: * "TechnoBabble Library", where users can check out
011: * and check in technical documentation.
012: */
013: public class BadTechnobabbleLibraryServlet
014: extends HttpServlet
015: {
016:
017:    PrintWriter      m_out      = null;
018:    String           m_useridparam  = null;
019:
020:
021:    /**
022:     * doGet() method for a HTTP GET
023:     *
024:     * @param  request   the HttpServletRequest object
025:     * @param  response  the HttpServletResponse object
026:     */
027:    public void doGet(HttpServletRequest request,
028:                      HttpServletResponse response)
029:    throws ServletException, IOException
030:    {
031:      String title = "Online Technobabble Library";
032:      response.setContentType("text/html");
033:      m_out = response.getWriter();
034:      m_useridparam = request.getParameter("userid");
035:
036:      m_out.println("<HTML>");
037:      m_out.println("<TITLE>" + title + "</TITLE>");
038:      m_out.println("<BODY BGCOLOR='WHITE'>");
039:      m_out.println("<CENTER><H1>" + title +
040:                    "</H1></CENTER>");
041:      m_out.println("<HR>");
042:
043:      //This will put the user's personal page in..
044:      putInUserData();
045:      m_out.println("<HR>");
046:      m_out.println("</BODY></HTML>");
047:    }
048:
049:
```

Listing 31.1   A bad example!

```
050:    /**
051:     * doPost() method for a HTTP PUT
052:     *
053:     * @param  request   the HttpServletRequest Object
054:     * @param  response  the HttpServletResponse Object
055:     */
056:    public void doPost(HttpServletRequest request,
057:                       HttpServletResponse response)
058:    throws ServletException, IOException
059:    {
060:      doGet(request, response);
061:    }
062:
063:
064:    /**
065:     * This method reads the user's data from the filesystem
066:     * and writes the data to the browser screen.
067:     */
068:    private void putInUserData() throws IOException
069:    {
070:
071:      BufferedReader br = null;
072:      String fn = m_useridparam + ".html";
073:      String htmlfile =
074:      getServletContext().getRealPath(fn);
075:
076:      System.out.println("debug: Trying to open "
077:                         + htmlfile);
078:
079:      File htmlSnippetFile = new File(htmlfile);
080:      try
081:      {
082:        String  line;
083:
084:        //Check to see if it exists first
085:        if (!htmlSnippetFile.exists())
086:        {
087:          m_out.println("File " + fn + "not found!");
088:          return;
089:        }
090:
091:        br = new BufferedReader(new FileReader(htmlfile));
092:
093:        /*
094:         * Now, let's read it..
095:         * Since finding the bad behavior in this pitfall
096:         * revolves around timing, we will only read 2
097:         * characters at a time so that the bad behavior
098:         * can be easily seen.
```

Listing 31.1   *(continued)*

```
099:       */
100:
101:       char[] buffer = new char[2];
102:       int count = 0;
103:       do
104:       {
105:         m_out.write(buffer, 0, count);
106:         m_out.flush();
107:         count = br.read(buffer, 0, buffer.length);
108:       }
109:       while (count != -1);
110:     }
111:     catch (Exception e)
112:     {
113:       m_out.println(
114:                 "Error in reading file!!"
115:                 );
116:       e.printStackTrace(System.err);
117:     }
118:     finally
119:     {
120:       if (br != null)
121:         br.close();
122:     }
123:
124:   }
125: }
126:
127:
```

Listing 31.1 *(continued)*

Looking at the code in lines 17 and 18 of Listing 31.1, we have two instance variables. The `PrintWriter m_out` and the `String m_useridparam` are assigned in the `doGet()` method on lines 33 and 34. After the `doGet()` method initializes these variables, the `putInUserData()` method is called to read the user-specific HTML files and print these out to the browser screen. Tested alone, a screen capture of the browser window looks fine, as shown in Figure 31.1.

However, during load testing, multiple users log in and many see the screen shown in Figure 31.2. The result seems like a combination of many screens and looks like nonsense. What happened?

Because instance variables are set in the `doGet()` method in Listing 31.1 and are used later in the servlet in the `putInUserData()` method, the servlet is not thread-safe. Because many users access the servlet at the same time, and because the instance variables are written to and referenced by multiple areas of the servlet, the values of the `m_out` variable and the `m_useridparams` variables have the potential to be clobbered!

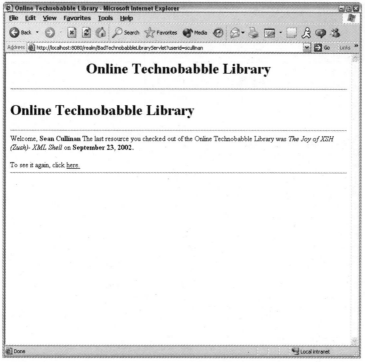

Figure 31.1   Our example with one concurrent user.

For example, when one user runs his servlet, the servlet could be setting the m_out variable for his session while another user's session is writing with the m_out variable.

Figure 31.3 shows us a time line of how this strange behavior occurred in our example from Listing 31.1. In the time line, we have two fictitious users of the system, Alice and Bob. At time t0, the servlet engine first instantiates the servlet, where the instance variables are declared in lines 17 and 18 of Listing 31.1. At time t1, the servlet engine calls the servlet's init() method. At time t2, Alice loads the servlet, which calls the servlet's doGet() method. At time t3, the instance variables m_out and m_useridparam are set just for Alice. At the same time, Bob loads the servlet, which calls the servlet's doGet() method. At time t4, Alice's servlet gets to the point where the putInUserData() method is called, which loads her information and begins printing to the PrintWriter variable, m_out. At the same time, Bob's servlet is in the execution of doGet(), where the instance variables m_out and m_useridparam are set.

Time t5 in Figure 31.3 is where everything seems to go nuts. Since Bob reset the servlet's instance variable m_out, Alice continues to print her information, but it goes to Bob's browser! When Bob also begins printing to m_out, he sees a combination of his information and Alice's information. The result is something like the screen shot that we showed in Figure 31.2.

Figure 31.2   Chaos: Our example with concurrent users.

In fact, we chose the example so that this strange behavior could be shown easily. Each servlet client (or user Web browser) will need its own `PrintWriter`, and because each servlet is a thread in the server's virtual machine, `m_out` can be trampled on whenever a new user loads the servlet, producing scary output. In practice, these types of errors can be difficult to detect until load testing, because errors occur with timing when multiple clients hit the server at once. In fact, we couldn't see any tangible ramifications of assigning the variable `m_useridparam`, because the timing has to be right to actually see the effects. We have seen one situation where a customer's requirements were to provide sensitive and confidential data to its users. The software developers used instance variables in their servlets for printing information gathered from each user's database connection. When the developers were testing it alone, the system seemed to work fine. When the system went in for load testing with several different users, the testers saw the other users' confidential data.

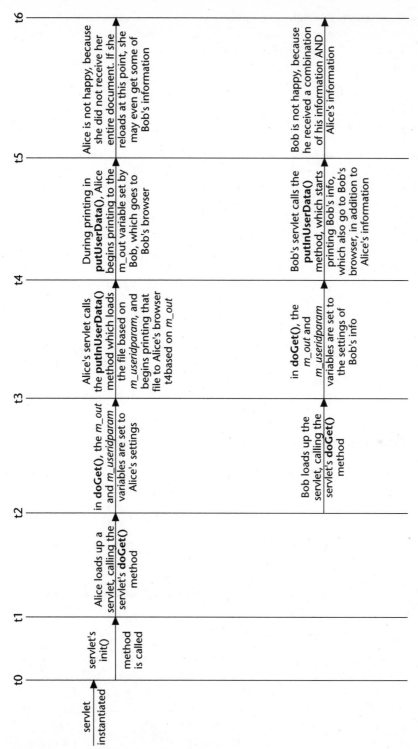

Figure 31.3 Time line of data corruption.

What if you use instance variables but only set them at instantiation? In this case, you may not run into any concurrency issues. However, this could lead to other pitfalls if you do not keep the lifecycle of the servlet in mind. Here is a bad example that we saw recently:

```
//Here Is an Instance variable that we will be using later

ServletContext m_sc = getServletContext();
```

The programmer who wrote that snippet of code assumed that since the variable was set at instantiation and never set again, no concurrency issues would arise. That is true. Unfortunately, because the init() method sets the servlet's ServletContext object after instantiation, the servlet ran into a big problem: The value of the instance variable m_sc was null, resulting in a NullPointerException later on in the servlet. Because the instance variable was set at instantiation of the servlet, and not after the init() method was called, the servlet had big problems.

So what is the best solution to this pitfall? Be very hesitant in using instance variables in servlets. Certainly, you could continue to use instance variables and synchronize them whenever you need to access or set the instance variable, but that could create code that is very complex-looking, inflexible, and ugly. Instead, try to pass the variables and objects that you will need to your other methods. If it gets to the point where you believe that you have too many variables to pass around, create a class that serves as a container for these variables. Instantiate the class with the variables you need, and pass the object around.

Listing 31.2 shows a better approach to our earlier "Online Technobabble Library" example. Instead of having instance variables, we create the variables that we need in the doGet() method in lines 32 and 33, and we pass them to the putInUserData() method. The result is code that is thread-safe.

```
001: package org.javapitfalls.item31;
002: import java.io.*;
003: import java.text.*;
004: import java.util.*;
005: import javax.servlet.*;
006: import javax.servlet.http.*;
007: /**
008: * This example demonstrates using instance variables
009: * in a servlet.. The example features a fictional
010: * "TechnoBabble Library", where users can check out
011: * and check in technical documentation.
012: */
013: public class GoodTechnobabbleLibraryServlet extends
014: HttpServlet
015: {
016:
017:    /**
018:     * doGet() method for a HTTP GET
```

Listing 31.2   A better application solution

```
019:    *
020:    * @param  request   the HttpServletRequest object
021:    * @param  response  the HttpServletResponse object
022:    */
023:   public void doGet(HttpServletRequest request,
024:                     HttpServletResponse response)
025:   throws ServletException, IOException
026:   {
027:     PrintWriter out;
028:     String userid;
029:     String title = "Online Technobabble Library";
030:
031:     response.setContentType("text/html");
032:     out = response.getWriter();
033:     userid = request.getParameter("userid");
034:
035:     out.println("<HTML>");
036:     out.println("<TITLE>" + title + "</TITLE>");
037:     out.println("<BODY BGCOLOR='WHITE'>");
038:     out.println("<CENTER><H1>" + title +
039:                 "</H1></CENTER>");
040:     out.println("<HR>");
041:
042:     //This will put the user's personal page in..
043:     putInUserData(out, userid);
044:     out.println("<HR>");
045:     out.println("</BODY></HTML>");
046:   }
047:
048:
049:   /**
050:    * doPost() method for a HTTP PUT
051:    *
052:    * @param  request   the HttpServletRequest Object
053:    * @param  response  the HttpServletResponse Object
054:    */
055:   public void doPost(HttpServletRequest request,
056:                      HttpServletResponse response)
057:   throws ServletException, IOException
058:   {
059:     doGet(request, response);
060:   }
061:
062:
063:   /**
064:    * This method reads the user's data from the filesystem
065:    * and writes the data to the browser screen.
066:    *
067:    * @param out  the printwriter we are using
```

Listing 31.2   *(continued)*

```
068:    * @param userid   the userid of the accessing user
069:    */
070:   private void putInUserData(PrintWriter out,
071:                              String userid)
072:   throws IOException
073:   {
074:     BufferedReader br = null;
075:     String fn = userid + ".html";
076:     String htmlfile =
077:       getServletContext().getRealPath(fn);
078:
079:     System.out.println("debug: Trying to open "
080:                        + htmlfile);
081:
082:     File htmlSnippetFile = new File(htmlfile);
083:     try
084:     {
085:       String  line;
086:
087:       //Check to see if it exists first
088:       if (!htmlSnippetFile.exists())
089:       {
090:         out.println("File " + fn + "not found!");
091:         return;
092:       }
093:
094:       br = new BufferedReader(new FileReader(htmlfile));
095:
096:       /*
097:        * Now, let's read it..
098:        * Since finding the bad behavior in this pitfall
099:        * revolves around timing, we will only read 2
100:        * characters at a time so that the bad behavior
101:        * can be more easily seen.
102:        */
103:
104:       char[] buffer = new char[2];
105:       int count = 0;
106:       do
107:       {
108:         out.write(buffer, 0, count);
109:         out.flush();
110:         count = br.read(buffer, 0, buffer.length);
111:       }
112:       while (count != -1);
113:     }
114:     catch (Exception e)
115:     {
116:       out.println(
```

Listing 31.2   *(continued)*

```
117:                    "Error in reading file!!"
118:                    );
119:         e.printStackTrace(System.err);
120:     }
121:     finally
122:     {
123:        if (br != null)
124:          br.close();
125:     }
126:
127:   }
128: }
129:
130:
```

Listing 31.2   *(continued)*

Now that we have eliminated instance variables in Listing 31.2, we have fixed our problems with thread safety! Be hesitant in using instance variables in servlets. If there is a better way, do it.

Item 32: Design Flaws with Creating Database Connections within Servlets

Connecting to a database is a convenient way for generating Web content. That being said, there can be many performance issues with creating database connections in servlets. It is imperative that a Web-enabled application be able to scale to the demand of its users. For that reason, preparation for a large amount of users is a necessity.

We will present a sample scenario where we are developing a Java Servlet-based system for a local shop, "Lavender Fields Farm." The decision makers on the project have decided that we will need to use a database for the online purchases and transactions. At the same time, we will need to use that database to keep track of inventory. This example will focus on the development of that "inventory servlet."

Listing 32.1 shows a servlet that queries the database to show inventory. In lines 52 to 75, in the servlet's `doPost()` method, we establish a connection to the database, and we create an HTML table showing the name of each item available, the description, and the amount that the shop has in stock. Figure 32.1 shows a screen capture of the result. In testing, everything with this example works wonderfully. When many users begin to use the system, the database becomes a bottleneck. Finally, after intense usage of the Web application, the database begins refusing new connections. What happened?

```
01: package org.javapitfalls.item32;
02: import java.io.*;
03: import java.sql.*;
04: import java.text.*;
05: import java.util.*;
06: import javax.servlet.*;
07: import javax.servlet.http.*;
08: public class BadQueryServlet extends HttpServlet
09: {
10:    /**
11:     *  simply forwards all to doPost()
12:     */
13:    public void doGet(HttpServletRequest request,
14:                      HttpServletResponse response)
15:    throws IOException, ServletException
16:    {
17:        doPost(request,response);
18:    }
19:
20:    /**
21:     * The main form!
22:     */
23:    public void doPost(HttpServletRequest request,
24:                      HttpServletResponse response)
25:    throws IOException, ServletException
26:    {
27:        PrintWriter out = response.getWriter();
28:        out.println("<TITLE>Internal Inventory Check</TITLE>");
29:        out.println("<BODY BGCOLOR='white'>");
30:        out.println("<H1>Lavender Fields Farm Internal Inventory</H1>");
31:
32:        //show the date.
33:        SimpleDateFormat sdf =
34:            new SimpleDateFormat ("EEE, MMM d, yyyy h:mm a");
35:        java.util.Date newdate = new
36:        java.util.Date(Calendar.getInstance().getTime().getTime());
37:        String datestring = sdf.format(newdate);
38:
39:        out.println("<H3>Inventory as of: " + datestring + "</H3>");
40:
41:        out.println("<TABLE BORDER=1>");
42:        out.println("<TR><TD BGCOLOR='yellow'><B><CENTER>Name</CENTER>"+
43:                "</B></TD><TD BGCOLOR='yellow'><B><CENTER>" +
44:                "Description</CENTER></B></TD><TD BGCOLOR='yellow'>" +
45:                "<B><CENTER>Inventory Amount</CENTER></B></TD></TR>");
46:
47:        //Load the inventory from the database.
48:
49:        try
50:        {
```

Listing 32.1 Specifying connection in a servlet

```
51:
52:            Class.forName("sun.jdbc.odbc.JdbcOdbcDriver");
53:            String connect = "jdbc:odbc:Lavender";
54:
55:            Connection con = DriverManager.getConnection(connect);
56:
57:            Statement stmt = con.createStatement();
58:            ResultSet rs = stmt.executeQuery("select * from Inventory");
59:
60:            while (rs.next())
61:            {
62:                String amtString = "";
63:                int amt = rs.getInt("Amount");
64:                if (amt < 50)
65:                    amtString ="<TD><CENTER><FONT COLOR='RED'>" + amt +
66:                            "</FONT></CENTER></TD>";
67:                else
68:                    amtString ="<TD><CENTER>" + amt + "</CENTER></TD>";
69:
70:                out.println("<TR><TD><CENTER>" + rs.getString("Name") +
71:                        "</CENTER></TD><TD><CENTER>" +
72:                        rs.getString("Description") + "</CENTER>" +
73:                        "</TD>" + amtString + "</TR>");
74:            }
75:            rs.close();
76:            out.println("</TABLE><HR>Items in <FONT COLOR='red'>RED" +
77:                    "</FONT> denote low inventory levels. Click " +
78:                    "Here to Contact <A HREF='mailto:mgmt@localhost'>" +
79:                    "MANAGEMENT</A> to order more supplies.");
80:        }
81:    catch (Exception e)
82:        {
83:          out.println("There were errors connecting to the database." +
84:                    " See your systems administrator for details.");
85:          e.printStackTrace();
86:        }
87:
88:
89:    }
90:
91:
92:}
```

Listing 32.1   *(continued)*

The problem is twofold: opening a new connection to the database is a computationally expensive operation, and there is a finite number of open connections that a database can have. In line 55 in Listing 32.1, we open a new connection on line 55 every time a user loads the Web page. On line 75, we close the result set, resulting in the eventual termination of the connection. When there are hundreds (or thousands) of users connecting to that online store, that strategy will simply not suffice.

What is a better solution? This is where the specifics of your application impact your decision. If this servlet were the only one connecting to the database, you could design it so that the servlet shares connections with itself. That is, a set of connections could be shared, reused, recycled, and managed by this servlet. If, however, the entire Web server shared connections between servlets, you should design it so that all the servlets share the management of connections with each other.

This is where *connection pooling* comes into play. Connection pooling involves allocating database connections in advance, along with the reuse and management of the connections. You could write your own connection pool package that your servlet could use, but many are available on the Internet. For our next example, we used an open-source connection broker called `DDConnectionBroker`, from http://opensource .devdaily.com/. This package offers the basics that any connection pooling class should—including the pre-allocation, reuse, and management of database connections.

In Listing 32.2, we use the connection broker within the servlet. In our `init()` method, we instantiate the connection broker, specifying the details of our database connection and setting our broker to be the instance variable in line 13. Since the `init()` method is only called once (right after instantiation), our connection pool is initialized once. We specify that the connection pool will have a maximum number (10) of database connections. This number is dependent on the configuration of your database. After setting up the connection broker in the `init()` method, the only further change to the servlet is that instead of creating the connection in the `doPost()` method, we call the method `m_broker` `.getConnection()` in line 95 and call the method `m_broker.freeConnection()` in line 119. The result is that every thread going through this servlet (every user loading the Web page) will use a connection pool in getting to the database.

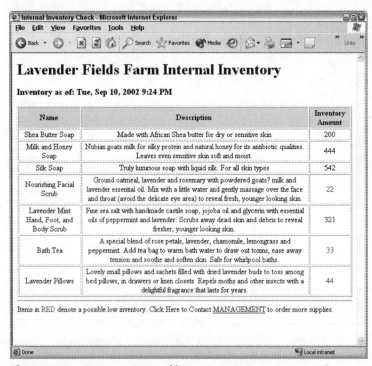

Figure 32.1 Screen capture of inventory page.

```
000: package org.javapitfalls.item32;
001: import com.devdaily.opensource.database.DDConnectionBroker;
002: import java.io.*;
003: import java.sql.*;
004: import java.text.*;
005: import java.util.*;
006: import javax.servlet.*;
007: import javax.servlet.http.*;
008:
009:  public class BetterQueryServlet extends HttpServlet
010: {
011:     //only set in the init() method, so concurrency
012:     //issues should be fine.
013:     private DDConnectionBroker m_broker = null;
014:
015:     public void init()
016:     {
017:         String driver        = "sun.jdbc.odbc.JdbcOdbcDriver";
018:         String url           = "jdbc:odbc:Lavender";
019:         String uname = "";
020:         String passwd = "";
021:
022:         int minConnections = 1;
023:         int maxConnections = 10;
024:         long timeout      = 100;
025:         long leaseTime    = 60000;
026:         String logFile      = "c:/tmp/ConnectionPool.log";
027:
028:         try
029:         {
030:             m_broker = new DDConnectionBroker(driver,
031:                                               url, uname, passwd,
032:                                               minConnections,
033:                                               maxConnections,
034:                                               timeout,
035:                                               leaseTime,
036:                                               logFile);
037:         }
038:         catch (SQLException se)
039:         {
040:             System.err.println( se.getMessage() );
041:         }
042:
043:
044:     }
045:     /**
046:      *  simply forwards all to doPost()
047:      */
048:     public void doGet(HttpServletRequest request,
```

Listing 32.2 Sharing a connection within a servlet *(continued)*

```
049:                         HttpServletResponse response)
050:     throws IOException, ServletException
051:     {
052:         doPost(request,response);
053:     }
054:
055:     /**
056:      * The main form!
057:      */
058:     public void doPost(HttpServletRequest request,
059:                         HttpServletResponse response)
060:     throws IOException, ServletException
061:     {
062:         PrintWriter out = response.getWriter();
063:
064:         if (m_broker == null)
065:         {
066:             out.println("<B>There are currently database problems. " +
067:                     "Please see your administrator for details.</B>");
068:             return;
069:         }
070:       out.println("<TITLE>Internal Inventory Check</TITLE>");
071:       out.println("<BODY BGCOLOR='white'>");
072:       out.println("<H1>Lavender Fields Farm Internal Inventory</H1>");
073:
074:       //show the date.
075:       SimpleDateFormat sdf =
076:          new SimpleDateFormat ("EEE, MMM d, yyyy h:mm a");
077:       java.util.Date newdate =
078:      new java.util.Date(Calendar.getInstance().getTime().getTime());
079:       String datestring = sdf.format(newdate);
080:
081:       out.println("<H3>Inventory as of: " + datestring + "</H3>");
082:
083:       out.println("<TABLE BORDER=1>");
084:       out.println("<TR><TD BGCOLOR='yellow'>" +
085:     "<B><CENTER>Name</CENTER></B></TD>" +
086:     "<TD BGCOLOR='yellow'><B><CENTER>Description</CENTER></B></TD>" +
087:     "<TD BGCOLOR='yellow'><B><CENTER>Inventory Amount</CENTER></B>" +
088:        "</TD></TR>");
089:
090:       //Load the inventory from the database.
091:
092:       try
093:       {
094:
095:           Connection con = m_broker.getConnection();
096:
097:           Statement stmt = con.createStatement();
```

Listing 32.2 *(continued)*

```
098:            ResultSet rs = stmt.executeQuery("select * from Inventory");
099:
100:            while (rs.next())
101:            {
102:                String amtString = "";
103:                int amt = rs.getInt("Amount");
104:              if (amt < 50)
105:                amtString ="<TD><CENTER><FONT COLOR='RED'>" + amt +
                        "</FONT></CENTER></TD>";
106:              else
107:                amtString ="<TD><CENTER>" + amt + "</CENTER></TD>";
108:              out.println("<TR><TD><CENTER>" + rs.getString("Name") +
109:                        "</CENTER></TD><TD><CENTER>"        +
                            rs.getString("Description") + "</CENTER>" +
110:                        "</TD>" + amtString + "</TR>");
111:            }
112:          rs.close();
113:          out.println("</TABLE><HR>Items in
                        <FONTCOLOR='red'>RED</FONT>"
114:                    +" denote a possible low inventory. Click Here to
115:                    " Contact <A HREF='mailto:mgmt@localhost'>" +
116:                    "MANAGEMENT</A> to order more supplies.");
117:
118:          //Free the connection!
119:          m_broker.freeConnection( con );
120:
121:        }
122:        catch (Exception e)
123:        {
124:            out.println("There were errors connecting to the database.
125:                    "See your systems administrator for details.");
126:            e.printStackTrace();
127:        }
128:
129:    }
130:
131:
132:}
```

Listing 32.2   *(continued)*

The effect of Listing 32.2 is that every user that runs the servlet BetterQueryServlet will share the connection broker object, so that connections will be shared and reused. Even better, our DDConnectionBroker object is instantiated in the init() method, where it pre-allocates connections before they are requested. This will make performance of this servlet better, and it is a good method of database connection management when that servlet is the only application talking to your database.

In our scenario, however, we said that customers at our online store will be connecting to the database as well. This means that it will be wise to share the database connections across all servlets. How could we do this? One of the best ways to do this is to use the Gang of Four's Singleton design pattern.[1] A very convenient design pattern, a Singleton is used when there should be only one instance of a class in a virtual machine. In our scenario, it would be great to get an instance of a connection broker from any servlet and be able to use one of the connections. Listing 32.3 shows a simple Singleton that also acts as an adapter to a few methods of the connection broker. This class, LavenderDBSingleton, will be our single point of entry to the database for our "Lavender Fields Farm" example. In our private constructor in lines 17 to 50, we instantiate our connection pool. In our getInstance() method in lines 55 to 63, you can see that this class will only be instantiated once. Finally, freeConnection() and getConnection() are simply wrappers to the methods in the DDConnection-Broker class.

```
01:  package org.javapitfalls.item32;
02:
03:  import com.devdaily.opensource.database.DDConnectionBroker;
04:  import java.io.*;
05:  import java.sql.*;
06:
07:    /**
08:    /* This is our class that will be shared across all of the
09:     * servlets for the 'Lavender' database. It is a singleton,
10:     * and also works as an adapter to the connection broker
11:     * class that we are using.
12:    */
13:    public class LavenderDBSingleton
14:    {
15:
16:       private DDConnectionBroker m_broker;
17:       private static LavenderDBSingleton m_singleton = null;
18:
19:       private LavenderDBSingleton()
20:       {
21:          /*
22:           * We will put all of our database-specific information
23:           * here. Please note that we could have read this
24:           * information from a properties file.
25:           */
26:
27:          String driver          = "sun.jdbc.odbc.JdbcOdbcDriver";
28:          String url             = "jdbc:odbc:Lavender";
29:          String uname = "";
30:          String passwd = "";
```

Listing 32.3 Singleton class for sharing a connection pool

[1]Gamma, Helm, Johnson, Vlissides. *Design Patterns: Elements of Reusable Object-Oriented Software*. 1995. Reading, Mass.: Addison-Wesley.

```
31:
32:            int minConnections   = 1;
33:            int maxConnections   = 10;
34:            long timeout         = 100;
35:            long leaseTime       = 60000;
36:            String logFile        = "c:/tmp/ConnectionPool.log";
37:
38:            try
39:            {
40:                m_broker = new DDConnectionBroker(driver,
41:                                                   url, uname, passwd,
42:                                                   minConnections,
43:                                                   maxConnections,
44:                                                   timeout,
45:                                                   leaseTime,
46:                                                   logFile);
47:            }
48:            catch (SQLException se)
49:            {
50:                System.err.println( se.getMessage() );
51:            }
52:        }
53:    /**
54:     *  getInstance() returns the class, instantiating it
55:     *  if there is not yet an instance in the VM.
56:     */
57:    public synchronized static LavenderDBSingleton getInstance()
58:    {
59:        if (m_singleton == null)
60:        {
61:            m_singleton = new LavenderDBSingleton();
62:        }
63:
64:        return (m_singleton);
65:    }
66:
67:    /*
68:     * calls getConnection() on the broker class
69:     */
70:    public synchronized Connection getConnection() throws Exception
71:    {
72:        if (m_broker == null)
73:        {
74:            throw new Exception("Can't get Connection broker!");
75:        }
76:        return (m_broker.getConnection());
77:    }
78:
79:    /*
```

Listing 32.3   *(continued)*

```
80:        * frees the connection from the broker class
81:        */
82:        public synchronized void freeConnection(Connection con)
83:         throws Exception
84:         {
85:            if (m_broker == null )
86:            {
87:                throw new Exception("Can't get Connection broker!");
88:            }
89:            m_broker.freeConnection(con);
90:        }
91:    }
92:
93:
```

Listing 32.3   *(continued)*

Listing 32.4 shows the final version of our servlet with our Singleton class in
action. In the init() method, we get the instance of our Singleton class on line 23.
On line 72, we call the getConnection() method of our Singleton, and finally, on line
107, we free the connection. If the other servlets in our example use the Singleton that
does connection pooling and database connection management, we will maximize the
efficiency of our servlet, reducing the overhead of creating connections for every client.

```
001: package org.javapitfalls.item32;
002:
003: import java.io.*;
004: import java.sql.*;
005: import java.text.*;
006: import java.util.*;
007: import javax.servlet.*;
008: import javax.servlet.http.*;
009:
010: public class BestQueryServlet extends HttpServlet
011: {
012:    //only set in the init() method, so concurrency
013:    //issues should be fine.
014:    private LavenderDBSingleton m_dbsingleton = null;
015:
016:    public void init()
017:    {
018:      /*
019:       * This will instantiate it within the Servlet's
020:       * virtual machine if it hasn't already. If it
021:       * has, we have the instance of it.
022:       */
023:        m_dbsingleton = LavenderDBSingleton.getInstance();
```

Listing 32.4   Servlet Sharing Connection Pool Across Server

```
024:   }
025:   /**
026:    *  simply forwards all to doPost()
027:    */
028:   public void doGet(HttpServletRequest request,
029:                     HttpServletResponse response)
030:   throws IOException, ServletException
031:   {
032:     doPost(request,response);
033:   }
034:
035:   /**
036:    * The main form!
037:    */
038:   public void doPost(HttpServletRequest request,
039:                      HttpServletResponse response)
040:   throws IOException, ServletException
041:   {
042:     PrintWriter out = response.getWriter();
043:
044:     out.println("<TITLE>Internal Inventory Check</TITLE>");
045:     out.println("<BODY BGCOLOR='white'>");
046:     out.println("<H1>Lavender Fields Farm Internal Inventory</H1>");
047:
048:     //show the date.
049:     SimpleDateFormat sdf =
050:     new SimpleDateFormat ("EEE, MMM d, yyyy h:mm a");
051:     java.util.Date newdate =
052:     new java.util.Date(
053:       Calendar.getInstance().getTime().getTime()
054:       );
055:     String datestring = sdf.format(newdate);
056:
057:     out.println("<H3>Inventory as of: " + datestring + "</H3>");
058:
059:     out.println("<TABLE BORDER=1>");
060:     out.println("<TR><TD BGCOLOR='yellow'>" +
061:                 "<B><CENTER>Name</CENTER></B></TD>" +
062:                 "<TD BGCOLOR='yellow'><B>" +
063:                 "<CENTER>Description</CENTER></B></TD>" +
064:                 "<TD BGCOLOR='yellow'><B>" +
065:                 "<CENTER>Inventory Amount</CENTER></B></TD></TR>");
066:
067:     //Load the inventory from the database.
068:
069:     try
070:     {
071:
072:       Connection con = m_dbsingleton.getConnection();
073:       if (con == null)
```

Listing 32.4 *(continued)*

```
074:        {
075:            out.println("<B>There are currently database problems. " +
076:                        "Please see your administrator for details.</B>");
077:            return;
078:        }
079:
080:
081:        Statement stmt = con.createStatement();
082:        ResultSet rs = stmt.executeQuery("select * from Inventory");
083:
084:        while (rs.next())
085:        {
086:          String amtString = "";
087:          int amt = rs.getInt("Amount");
088:          if (amt < 50)
089:            amtString ="<TD><CENTER><FONT COLOR='RED'>" +
090:                        amt + "</FONT></CENTER></TD>";
091:          else
092:            amtString ="<TD><CENTER>" +
093:                        amt + "</CENTER></TD>";
094:
095:            out.println("<TR><TD><CENTER>" + rs.getString("Name") +
096:                        "</CENTER></TD><TD><CENTER>" +
097:                        rs.getString("Description") +
098:                        "</CENTER></TD>" + amtString + "</TR>");
099:        }
100:        rs.close();
101:        out.println("</TABLE><HR>Items in <FONT COLOR='red'>RED</FONT>"
102:                    + " denote a possible low inventory. Click Here to " +
103:                    " contact <A HREF='mailto:mgmt@localhost'>" +
104:                    "MANAGEMENT</A> to order more supplies.");
105:
106:        //Free the connection!
107:        m_dbsingleton.freeConnection( con );
108:
109:    }
110:    catch (Exception e)
111:    {
112:      out.println("There were errors connecting to the database." +
113:              " Please see your systems administrator for details.");
114:      e.printStackTrace();
115:    }
116:
117:  }
118:
119:
120: }
121:
122:
```

Listing 32.4   *(continued)*

Using this `Singleton` class, you would simply need to do the following in your servlet:

```
LavenderDBSingleton singleton = LavenderDBSingleton.getInstance();
Connection con = singleton.getConnection();
try
{
  Statement stmt = con.createStatement();
  ResultSet rs = stmt.executeQuery("select * from Inventory");
  //do the rest...
  singleton.freeConnection(con);
}
catch (Exception e)
{
  //...
}
```

If the other servlets on our Web server VM use the Singleton in this manner, we will maximize the efficiency of our servlet, reducing the overhead of creating connections for every client (and for every thread!). The initial performance overhead may be the initial instantiation of the Singleton. For that purpose, it may be wise to instantiate it in the servlet's `init()` method. For the purposes of brevity, we have not included a full program example of this in the book. The Web site, however, will have a code listing that you can use.

In this pitfall, we discussed a few of the performance pitfalls that can arise when servlets communicate directly to a database. We presented two methods of connection pooling with servlets—one where a servlet shares a connection pool with its clients and one where all servlets share a connection pool by calling a `Singleton` class that will reside in memory in the virtual machine.

It should be noted, however, that there are ways of abstracting the database connection away from the user interface (servlet) model. Using servlets as the front end in a J2EE architecture where Enterprise JavaBeans (EJBs) worry about database connections is a good way for accomplishing this abstraction. While this pitfall was meant for developers who build applications where servlets connect to the database, there will be other pitfalls in this book that will discuss the use of EJBs.

For more information about other methods of connection pooling, see Item 45 in Part Three, "The Enterprise Tier."

Item 33: Attempting to Use Both Output Mechanisms in Servlets

If you've done a lot of servlet programming, you probably recognize this pitfall. The Servlet API provides two mechanisms for printing out a response: `PrintWriter` and `ServletOutputstream`. This pitfall discusses problems that may occur in using these two objects and will demonstrate an example.

In Listing 33.1, we have created a simple servlet that takes a quick voting poll on the Internet. We use this servlet along with a helper object called `VoterApp`, which has methods that tally votes, create an HTML-formatted "Poll of the Day," and create a graphical image representing the current tally of today's votes. Our servlet either shows the HTML Poll and creates a form for the user to vote or it shows the user a graph of the current tally. If the `vote` parameter in our servlet is `null`, it will create the poll, as shown in Listing 33.1 on line 29. In lines 33 to 40 of our servlet's `doGet()` method, we create an HTML form, with most of the contents returned from the `getPollOfTheDay()` method on the `VoterApp` object.

```
01: package org.javapitfalls.item33;
02: import java.io.*;
03: import java.text.*;
04: import java.util.*;
05: import javax.servlet.*;
06: import javax.servlet.http.*;
07: /* Bad Voter Servlet Example */
08: public class BadVoterServlet extends HttpServlet
09: {
10:
11:     public void doGet(HttpServletRequest request,
12:                          HttpServletResponse response)
13:     throws IOException, ServletException
14:     {
15:         doPost(request,response);
16:     }
17:
18:
19:     public void doPost(HttpServletRequest request,
20:                          HttpServletResponse response)
21:     throws IOException, ServletException
22:     {
23:         String vote = request.getParameter("vote");
24:
25:         PrintWriter out = response.getWriter();
26:
27:         VoterApp voter = VoterApp.getInstance();
28:
29:         if ( vote == null )
30:         {
31:             //Let's print out the Poll of the Day!
32:             response.setContentType("text/html");
33:             out.println("<TITLE>Poll of the Day!</TITLE>");
34:             out.println("<FORM METHOD='POST' ACTION='" +
35:                        request.getRequestURI() + "'>");
36:
37:             out.println(voter.getPollOfTheDay());
38:
39:             out.println("<INPUT TYPE='SUBMIT' VALUE='Vote Now!'>");
40:             out.println("</FORM>");
41:         }
```

Listing 33.1   BadVoterServlet.java

```
42:         else
43:         {
44:             //Have our voter object tally up the results
45:             voter.addToPollResults(vote);
46:
47:             //Get the generated poll results graph
48:             byte[] generatedGraph = voter.generateImageBytes();
49:             if ( generatedGraph == null )
50:             {
51:                 response.setContentType("text/html");
52:                 out.println("<B>Technical difficulties.. Please see" +
53:                             " your administrator for details.</B>");
54:                 return;
55:             }
56:             else
57:             {
58:                 //We need to get the outputstream to write binary data
59:
60:                 ServletOutputStream os = response.getOutputStream();
61:                 response.setContentType("image/gif");
62:
63:                 os.write(generatedGraph, 0, generatedGraph.length);
64:                 os.flush();
65:             }
66:         }
67:     }
68:
69: }
70:
```

Listing 33.1 *(continued)*

The first time we run this servlet (with no parameters), the browser shows the poll of the day, as seen in Figure 33.1. Once we vote, however, we see an error message that appears on our browser:

```
java.lang.IllegalStateException: Writer is already being used for this
request at
org.apache.tomcat.facade.HttpServletResponseFacade.getOutputStream(HttpS
ervletResponseFacade.java:156)
    at BadVoterServlet.doPost(BadVoterServlet.java:63)
```

What went wrong? The problem is that we requested the PrintWriter on line 25 of our servlet, and then we requested the ServletOutputStream object on line 60 of our servlet in Listing 33.1. Servlet documentation tells us that we should use ServletOutputStream for printing binary data and use PrintWriter for printing out character text. But our servlet writes both binary data *and* character text. What should we do?

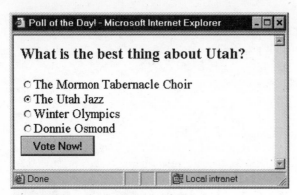

Figure 33.1   The first part works!

We can either use one or the other. `ServletOutputStream` is an abstract class that extends `java.io.OutputStream`, and `PrintWriter` is a class that extends `java.io.Writer`. The difference is that `PrintWriter` is character-based and `ServletOutputStream`, like `java.io.OutputStream`, is byte-based. To make life easier, `ServletOutputStream` adds `print()` and `println()` methods for primitive types and `Strings`, as shown in Table 33.1.

Table 33.1   javax.servlet.ServletOutputStream Methods

METHOD
void print(boolean b);
void println(boolean b);
void print(char c);
void println(char c);
void print(double d);
void println(double d);
void print(float f);
void println(float f);
void print(int i);
void println(int i);
void print(long l);
void println(long l);
void print(String s);
void println(String s);
void println();

Because ServletOutputStream contains print() and println() methods, it is easy to see that you may print character-based data with the print() and println() methods, and binary data with the write() methods inherited from java.io.OutputStream. To mix binary and text data in a multipart response, you may use a ServletOutputStream and manage the character sections with the methods in Table 33.1. Still, the rule of thumb is that if you are only sending character data, use the PrintWriter object returned by getWriter().

If your servlet is used for both binary and character data, you may be wise to use ServletOutputStream, rather than getting one or the other in an if-then clause or a try-catch clause. We have seen instances where code asks for the ServletOutput-Stream right before printing binary data, but asks for the PrintWriter if an error occurs in processing. This is a bad idea and can introduce conditional complexity to your servlet code, making the lifetime of your servlet difficult to manage. Listing 33.2 shows a segment of servlet code that will compile but could introduce complexity and bugs as time goes on. In that listing, the developer gets the ServletOutputStream in the try{} segment, and if an error occurs, it asks for the PrintWriter in the catch() segment.

```
01: //This is a very bad idea!
02: PrintWriter pw;
03: ServletOutputStream out;
04: try
05: {
06:    //get binary data
07:    out = response.getOutputStream();
08:    //now write the binary data with out
09: }
10: catch (Exception e)
11: {
12:    pw = response.getWriter();
13:    pw.println("There was an error: " + e.getMessage())
14:}
```

Listing 33.2   Using control flow to determine output

Listing 33.2 is simple enough, but if the servlet is changed to include more and more conditionals, code management could be a nightmare as time goes on. What if more processing goes on after that segment of code? You would have to keep track of which one is used, and that is a bad idea. It is a lot easier to simply use the ServletOutput-Stream object alone, if there is a case where you are printing binary data.

The important thing to remember is that if you are sending different types of data to the client, make sure to set the content type with the HttpServletResponse object, as shown in Listing 33.1 on lines 51 and 61. Since our "Poll of the Day" servlet example

prints either binary or character-based data, we should simply ask for the
ServletOutputStream. Listing 33.3 shows the good example.

```
01: import java.io.*;
02: import java.text.*;
03: import java.util.*;
04: import javax.servlet.*;
05: import javax.servlet.http.*;
06:
07: /* Good Voter Servlet Example */
08: public class GoodVoterServlet extends HttpServlet
09: {
10:
11:     public void doGet(HttpServletRequest request,
12:                       HttpServletResponse response)
13:     throws IOException, ServletException
14:     {
15:         doPost(request,response);
16:     }
17:
18:
19:     public void doPost(HttpServletRequest request,
20:                        HttpServletResponse response)
21:     throws IOException, ServletException
22:     {
23:         String vote = request.getParameter("vote");
24:
25:         ServletOutputStream out = response.getOutputStream();
26:
27:         VoterApp voter = VoterApp.getInstance();
28:
29:         if ( vote == null )
30:         {
31:             //Let's print out the Poll of the Day!
32:             response.setContentType("text/html");
33:             out.println("<TITLE>Poll of the Day!</TITLE>");
34:             out.println("<FORM METHOD='POST' ACTION='" +
35:                             request.getRequestURI() + "'>");
36:
37:             out.println(voter.getPollOfTheDay());
38:
39:             out.println("<INPUT TYPE='SUBMIT' VALUE='Vote Now!'>");
40:             out.println("</FORM>");
41:         }
42:         else
43:         {
44:             //Have our voter object tally up the results
45:             voter.addToPollResults(vote);
46:
```

Listing 33.3   GoodVoterServlet.java

```
47:                    //Get the generated poll results graph
48:                    byte[] generatedGraph = voter.generateImageBytes();
49:                    if ( generatedGraph == null )
50:                    {
51:                        response.setContentType("text/html");
52:                        out.println("<B>Technical difficulties.. Please see " +
53:                                    "your administrator for details.</B>");
54:                        return;
55:                    }
56:                    else
57:                    {
58:
59:                        response.setContentType("image/gif");
60:
61:                        out.write(generatedGraph, 0, generatedGraph.length);
62:                        out.flush();
63:                    }
64:                }
65:            }
66:
67: }
68:
```

Listing 33.3 *(continued)*

As you can see in Listing 33.3, we get the `ServletOutputStream` on line 25. We use the `println()` methods for character-based data in lines 32 to 40 after setting the content-type to "`text/html`" on line 32. When there is an error in getting the binary image, we use the same mechanism for printing binary data on lines 49 to 55. Finally, when we have binary data to produce, we set the content-type to "`image/gif`", and write the binary data (or the graphed poll results in this example) to the user's browser with the methods inherited from `java.io.OutputStream` on lines 59 to 62.

This item showed the possible pitfalls that may lurk in your code when you try to use `PrintWriter` and `ServletOutputStream` together in a servlet. We showed you how to determine which object to use and showed how to eliminate this problem from your code.

Item 34: The Mysterious File Protocol

Many developers have built applications that read files from both the Internet and the local filesystem. Invariably, as developers get more seasoned, they discover that they are able to use the "file protocol" to reference local files as URLs. Because of this, a growing number of tools and APIs are beginning to simply accept URLs as references for files.

A lot of Java classes are overloaded to handle both the conventional local file syntax and also the URL syntax for files. Figure 34.1 shows an example of a simple Web browser, built with one of those classes, `JEditorPane`. Observe that it is a simple `JFrame` with a `JTextField` and a `JScrollPane` containing the `JEditorPane`. A URL is typed into the `JTextField`, which is then browsed by calling the `set-Page(String url)` method on the `JEditorPane`.

With the exception of the HTML rendering being more primitive than the average Web browser user expects, it works quite well as a basic Web browser. However, when the user tries to take advantage of the "file protocol" to browse the local filesystem, he or she needs to be careful. If the user simply substitutes the file protocol for the HTTP protocol, thus creating a URL that starts with "file://" instead of the usual "http://", then the user will be surprised to find the error shown in Figure 34.2 popping up.

The developer feverishly checks to determine if the slashes must go the other way, if the colon after the drive letter must come out, if a pipe character needs to substitute for the colon—anything to make the exception shown in Listing 34.1 go away.

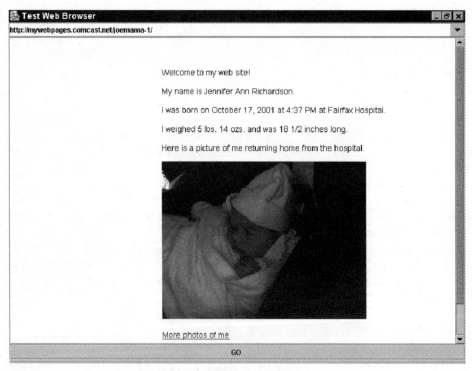

Figure 34.1   JEditorPane loading normally.

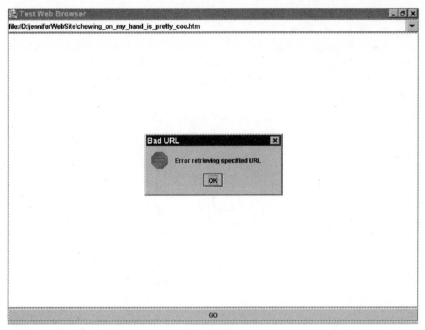

Figure 34.2   Loading with file protocol misapplied.

```
01: java.net.UnknownHostException: D
02:    at java.net.InetAddress.getAllByName0(InetAddress.java:571)
03:    at java.net.InetAddress.getAllByName0(InetAddress.java:540)
04:    at java.net.InetAddress.getByName(InetAddress.java:449)
05:    at java.net.Socket.<init>(Socket.java:100)
06:    at sun.net.NetworkClient.doConnect(NetworkClient.java:50)
07:    at sun.net.NetworkClient.openServer(NetworkClient.java:38)
08:    at sun.net.ftp.FtpClient.openServer(FtpClient.java:267)
09:    at sun.net.ftp.FtpClient.<init>(FtpClient.java:381)

20:    at [...]
21:
```

Listing 34.1   UnknownHostException

The developer starts thinking: "UnknownHostException! That cannot be right. Shouldn't it be a MalformedURLException?" Desperate for a workaround, other measures are thrown around, "What if I test for the 'file://' and then strip the rest out and load it as a local file? That won't work . . . now I need to find another method to set the page, because setPage deals with URLs."

The developer takes another look at the URL class and sees this gem:

Class URL represents a Uniform Resource Locator, a pointer to a "resource" on the World Wide Web. A resource can be something as simple as a file or a directory, or it can be a reference to a more complicated object, such as a query to a database or to a search engine. More information on the types of URLs and their formats can be found at http://archive.ncsa.uiuc.edu/SDG/Software/Mosaic/Demo/url-primer.html.

The developer quickly browses over to confirm his understanding of the proper format of the file protocol, and this is what he finds:

File URLs
Suppose there is a document called "foobar.txt"; it sits on an anonymous ftp server called "ftp.yoyodyne.com" in directory "/pub/files". The URL for this file is then:
   file://ftp.yoyodyne.com/pub/files/foobar.txt
The toplevel directory of this FTP server is simply:
   file://ftp.yoyodyne.com/
The "pub" directory of this FTP server is then:
   file://ftp.yoyodyne.com/pub
That's all there is to it.[2]

"That's all there is to it!" If that isn't adding insult to injury! The information posted reminds the developer of two things: his understanding of the file protocol is correct and he is still at square one.

Desperate to make some sort of progress, the developer starts considering other options and inspecting the File class. In the File class there is a method called toURL(), which claims to convert the path and filename into a URL specifying the file protocol. The developer decides to add a JFileChooser into the mix and use the resulting selected file to create the URL:

```
try {

textField.setText(chooser.getSelectedFile().toURL().toString());

} catch (MalformedURLException malE) { malE.printStackTrace(); }
```

Figure 34.3 shows how that looks in the application.

After the developer gets this code up and running, the JFileChooser is now handling the URL specification for the application. This approach turns out to be a successful one, as shown in Figure 34.4.

---

[2]http://archive.ncsa.uiuc.edu/SDG/Software/Mosaic/Demo/url-primer.html

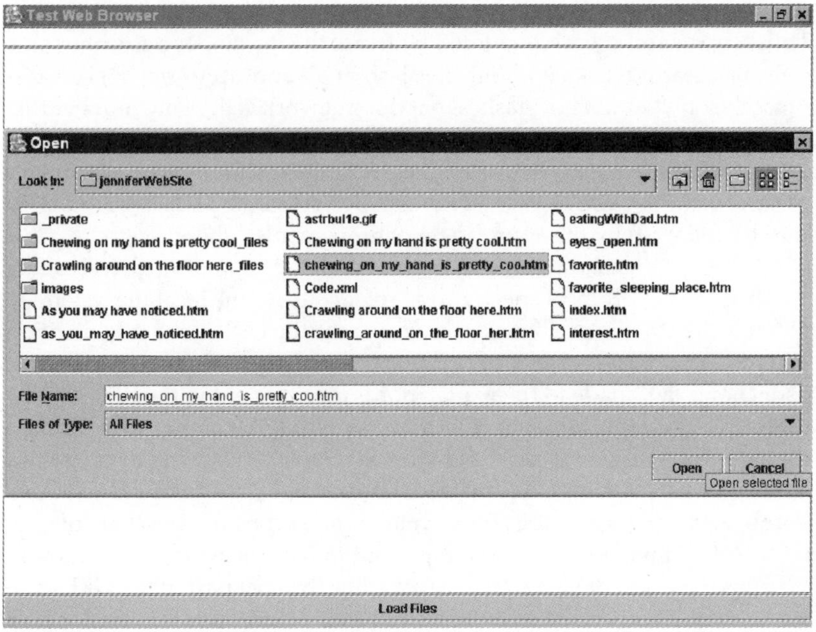

Figure 34.3   The JFileChooser strategy in action.

Figure 34.4   Properly loaded local file.

Wanting to determine why the representation in the JTextField has only one slash and whether that would work if entered by hand, the developer performs some tests. He determines that it works without the slash at all and up to seven slashes—then realizes that the only number of slashes that doesn't work is the only number that should: two.

Why does this problem occur? Well, reviewing RFC2396 (URLs) more closely, we note a distinction is made between local and remote files. Absolute paths are annotated with single slashes, followed by the appropriate path segments, whereas remote paths are indicated by the double slashes. This is a common misunderstanding, driven out of the assumption that the file protocol specification refers only to the local filesystem. In fact, looking more closely at the previous example, we see the URL is actually pointing at a remote file server, an FTP server, and hence the two slashes. Note, however, that this subtle distinction is not made to the reader, nor is it prominent in the RFC.

Now that it has been established that the URL was wrong all along, why didn't a MalformedURLException get thrown when the developer was trying to create this URL? After all, this is an incorrect URL. Instead, unexpectedly an UnknownHostException is thrown. To understand this, the developer must consider the challenges of implementing such functionality. First, it is important to recognize that an Unknown-HostException is the result of being unable to resolve the host part of the URL to an IP address. As such, variability must be built in to allow for both hosts that do not exist and hosts that are simply unavailable. After all, how can it be determined that "vol1" is incorrectly referring to a local volume, as opposed to a file server on the network known as "vol1"? This requires the inconvenient problem of receiving an Unknown-HostException rather than a MalformedURLException.

However, this still does not explain why seven slashes works—in fact, any multiple of slashes other than two works. It appears that this is merely because the code checks for two slashes to be a remote host and resolves any number of slashes other than that to a path. This clearly does not strictly adhere to RFC2396, but this is not something developers frequently know or even care about until running across this problem.

Item 35: Reading Files from Servlets

When developers begin to write servlet code, they quickly come across one major reality: They are writing code that runs within the context of another application (a servlet engine). Since they are within the context of another application, they are forced to live within that context, or at least they should be. Unfortunately, this is not always the case. One major advantage of servlets is their access to the entire Java programming language, but it means that servlets can be written to do a number of ill-advised things within the servlet engine. This includes reading files from the local filesystem.

Listing 35.1 is an example of the problem. For the sake of simplicity, ignore the practice of hard-coding "header.html" into the example.

```
01: public class ReallyBadReadingServlet extends HttpServlet {
02:    private static final String CONTENT_TYPE = "text/html";
03:    private StringBuffer strBuf;
04:    private String header;
05:
06:    /**Initialize global variables*/
07: public void init(ServletConfig config) throws ServletException {
08:       super.init(config);
09:
10:       strBuf = new StringBuffer();
11:       try {
12:
13: BufferedReader bufRead = new BufferedReader(new
FileReader("header.html"));
14:
15:         while (bufRead.read() != -1){
16:            strBuf.append(bufRead.readLine());
17:         }
18:
19:         bufRead.close();
20:
21:       } catch (IOException ioe) {
22:          ioe.printStackTrace();
23:       };
24:
25:       header = strBuf.toString();
27:    }
28:
```

Listing 35.1 ReallyBadReadingServlet.java

The example shows a conventional BufferedReader buffering a FileReader. The servlet is reading a header file to include with output. This is a simplified example of reading and processing a file.

The major problem with this code is that the working directory, where it will seek the "header.html" file, cannot be reliably determined between servlet engine implementations. As an example, some vendors run their servlet engine in the same process as their HTTP daemon (to improve performance). In an effort to keep the implementation simple, a frustrating search for where to place the file begins, which ends up costing the developer a lot more time over a small subtlety in the servlet specification. It bites the developer again if he or she deploys the servlet into another servlet engine.

The servlet specification does have a couple of methods that can help avoid this problem. First, every servlet has a `ServletContext` object, which has a `getReal-Path(String virtualPath)` method. This means that it will give the local filesystem path for the specified virtual path. Notice in the example in Listing 35.2 that `localPath` is prepended to the "header.html" filename.

```
01: public class StillBadReadingServlet extends HttpServlet {
02:    private static final String CONTENT_TYPE = "text/html";
03:    private StringBuffer strBuf;
04:    private String header;
05:
06:    /**Initialize*/
07:    public void init(ServletConfig config) throws ServletException {
08:       super.init(config);
09:
10:       ServletContext context = config.getServletContext();
11:
12:       String localPath = context.getRealPath("/myapp");
13:
14:       strBuf = new StringBuffer();
15:       try {
16:
17: BufferedReader bufRead = new BufferedReader(new FileReader(localPath ⤶
+ "header.html"));
18:
19:        while (bufRead.read() != -1){
20:           strBuf.append(bufRead.readLine());
21:        }
22:
23:        bufRead.close();
24:
25:     } catch (IOException ioe) {
26:        ioe.printStackTrace();
27:     };
28:
29:        header = strBuf.toString();
30:
31:    }
32:
```

Listing 35.2   StillBadReadingServlet.java

The problem with using `getRealPath()` occurs when the path you are attempting to get is within a Web Application Archive, also known as a WAR. The `getRealPath()` method will return `null` as its result. A WAR can be thought of as the Web equivalent of a JAR file. It provides a deployable component to plug into a Web server, which contains all of the servlets, filters, JSPs, tag libraries, HTML pages, and images.

In the situation shown in Listing 35.3, the developer specifies an explicit path for the file in the local filesystem (e.g., `C:\pitfallsbook\code\header.html`). This definition is specified within parameters passed to the `ServletConfig` object, but the concept can be implemented in a number of ways. No longer using an implicit path definition, the developer decides to place the burden of the deployer to specify a path that is valid (and accessible). So, while this solves the first problem of not definitively knowing where files should be stored, it still doesn't help if we are using the WAR (as is a good practice).

```
01: public class OKReadingServlet extends HttpServlet {
02:    private static final String CONTENT_TYPE = "text/html";
03:    private StringBuffer strBuf;
04:    private String header;
05:
06:    /**Initialize global variables*/
07:    public void init(ServletConfig config) throws ServletException {
08:      super.init(config);
09:
10:      ServletContext context = config.getServletContext();
11:
12:      //Explicit specification of the path via file property
13:      String configFile = config.getInitParameter("Config-File");
14:
15:      strBuf = new StringBuffer();
16:      try {
17:
18:        BufferedReader bufRead = new BufferedReader(new
FileReader(configFile));
19:
20:        while (bufRead.read() != -1){
21:          strBuf.append(bufRead.readLine());
22:        }
23:
24:        bufRead.close();
25:
26:      } catch (IOException ioe) {
27:        ioe.printStackTrace();
28:      };
29:
30:      header = strBuf.toString();
33:    }
```

Listing 35.3 OKReadingServlet.java

To alleviate this issue, the servlet specification adopted the paradigm first introduced in the Applet. As shown in Listing 35.4, the solution is to call getResource(String path), which returns a URL object of the file at the path—a relative URL to the file. This methodology coincides with the way applets retrieve resources from a JAR file.

```
01: public class GoodReadingServlet extends HttpServlet {
02:    private static final String CONTENT_TYPE = "text/html";
03:    private StringBuffer strBuf;
04:    private String header;
05:
06:    /**Initialize global variables*/
07:    public void init(ServletConfig config) throws ServletException {
08:       super.init(config);
09:
10:       ServletContext context = config.getServletContext();
11:
12:       strBuf = new StringBuffer();
13:       try {
14:          //  Using an init parameter
15:          URL headerURL = context.getResource(config
.getInitParameter("header"));
16:          //  Getting the Content directly
17:          strBuf.append(headerURL.getContent());
18:
19:       } catch (IOException ioe) {
20:          ioe.printStackTrace();
21:       };
22:
23:       header = strBuf.toString();
24:
25:    }
```

Listing 35.4   GoodReadingServlet.java

Notice how this allows the user to avoid having to create a reader and iterate through the reader to populate the header string. When the purpose is merely to read the file into a variable, the getResource() method provides the most direct way.

However, often the developer wants to process the file, not just load its content into a variable. To perform this function, the developer has a better way: call getResourceAsStream(). This method, shown in Listing 35.5, returns an Input-Stream, which can be enclosed in whatever reader the developer needs to handle the processing.

```
01: public class AnotherGoodReadingServlet extends HttpServlet {
02:   private static final String CONTENT_TYPE = "text/html";
03:   private StringBuffer strBuf;
04:   private String header;
05:
06:   /**Initialize global variables*/
07:   public void init(ServletConfig config) throws ServletException {
08:     super.init(config);
09:
10:     ServletContext context = config.getServletContext();
11:
12:     strBuf = new StringBuffer();
13:     try {
14:         //  Using an init parameter
15:         BufferedReader bufRead = new BufferedReader(
16:          new InputStreamReader(
17:            context.getResourceAsStream(
config.getInitParameter("header"))));
18:
19:         //line by line reading allows for any additional processing
to occur
20:         while (bufRead.read() != -1){
21:           strBuf.append(bufRead.readLine());
22:         }
23:
24:         bufRead.close();
28:     } catch (IOException ioe) {
29:       ioe.printStackTrace();
30:     };
31:
32:     header = strBuf.toString();
34:   }
```

Listing 35.5   AnotherGoodReadingServlet.java

Good software development practice demands avoiding the use of hard-coded configuration information. Because of this, strong consideration should be given to placing the information in the servlet engine's Web Application Deployment Descriptor.

This pitfall has introduced the concept of the Web Application Archive and briefly mentioned the Web Application Deployment Descriptor. Now we will discuss the Web Application Deployment Descriptor in greater detail.

Web Application Deployment Descriptors

A primary part of a Web application is its Web Application Deployment Descriptor. This is euphemistically known as the "web.xml", as it is stored in a file by that name. Also, the file is stored in the *mywebapp*/WEB-INF directory.

Listing 35.6 is an annotated version of a Web Application Deployment Descriptor for a common Web application. See the comments in Listing 35.6 for an explanation of each part.

```
001: <?xml version="1.0"?>
002: <!DOCTYPE web-app PUBLIC "-//Sun Microsystems, Inc.//DTD Web
Application 2.3//EN" "http://java.sun.com/j2ee/dtds/web-app_2_3.dtd">
003: <web-app>
004:
005: <!--
006: Basic Web Application Description information.  Mostly used for
Tools to display the web app in a more user friendly manner.
007: -->
008:
009:     <display-name>example</display-name>
010:     <description>My example web application</description>
011:
012: <!--
013: Filters are new to the Servlet 2.3 Specification.
014:
015: This declares the clickstreamFilter, which is an instance of the
com.opensymphone.clickstream.ClickstreamFilter class.
016: This class should be located in the CLASSPATH, but the most common
place to put it is in the WEB-INF/classes or WEB-INF/lib
017: directories.
018:
019: Clickstream tracks all accesses to the site.  See
http://opensymphony.com for more details.
021: -->
022:
023:     <filter>
024:         <filter-name>clickstreamFilter</filter-name>
025:         <filter-
class>com.opensymphony.clickstream.ClickstreamFilter</filter-class>
026:     </filter>
027:
028: <!--
030: The filter-mapping applies the filter to all requests that match
the url-pattern.
032: -->
033:
034:     <filter-mapping>
035:         <filter-name>clickstreamFilter</filter-name>
036:         <url-pattern>*.jsp</url-pattern>
```

Listing 35.6   Web Application Deployment Descriptor (web.xml)

```
037:      </filter-mapping>
038:
039:      <filter-mapping>
040:          <filter-name>clickstreamFilter</filter-name>
041:          <url-pattern>*.html</url-pattern>
042:      </filter-mapping>
043:
044: <!--
046: The servlet listener is new to Servlet 2.3 also.  It also is up ⤸
to the developer to define a listener to monitor lifecycle events.
047:
048: In this case, the ClickstreamListener waits for an HTTPSession to ⤸
terminate, and then logs the HTTP Session information.
050: -->
051:
052:      <listener>
053:          <listener-                                              ⤸
class>com.opensymphony.clickstream.ClickstreamListener</listener-class>
054:      </listener>
055:
056:
057: <!--
059: This declares the XYZServlet, which is in a class by the same name.⤸
By convention, it usually is in the WEB-INF/classes
060: directory or in a jar in the WEB-INF/lib directory
062: -->
063:
064:
065:      <servlet>
066:          <servlet-name>XYZServlet</servlet-name>
067:          <servlet-class>XYZServlet</servlet-class>
068:      </servlet>
069:
070:
071: <!--
073: This servlet mapping dictates that all urls that end in *.xyz will ⤸
be handled by the XYZServlet.
075: -->
076:
077:      <servlet-mapping>
078:          <servlet-name>
079:              XYZServlet
080:          </servlet-name>
081:          <url-pattern>
082:              /*.xyz
083:          </url-pattern>
084:      </servlet-mapping>
085:
086: <!--
```

Listing 35.6   *(continued)*

```
088: These files are the files that are loaded (in the listed order) if ⤵
they exist when the webapp is
089: called without a file specified (e.g. /examples/ )
091: -->
092:
093:    <welcome-file-list>
094:          <welcome-file>home.jsp</welcome-file>
095:          <welcome-file>index.jsp</welcome-file>
096:          <welcome-file>index.html</welcome-file>
097:    </welcome-file-list>
098:
099: <!--
101: These are the tag library definitions.  The taglib-uri gives a ⤵
unique identifier.
102: The taglib-location gives the location of the taglib's tag library ⤵
definition.
103:
104: These taglibs are the Jakarta IO, XTags, and DBTags all very good ⤵
libraries from
105: http://jakarta.apache.org/taglibs.
106:
107: The last one is from opensymphony.com, the oscache tag library, ⤵
which is an outstanding
108: tag library for caching web documents.
110: -->
111:
112:
113:    <taglib>
114:          <taglib-uri>http://jakarta.apache.org/taglibs/io- ⤵
1.0</taglib-uri>
115:          <taglib-location>/WEB-INF/taglibdefs/io.tld</taglib-location>
116:    </taglib>
117:
118:    <taglib>
119:          <taglib-uri>http://jakarta.apache.org/taglibs/xtags- ⤵
1.0</taglib-uri>
120:          <taglib-location>/WEB-INF/lib/xtags.tld</taglib-location>
121:    </taglib>
122:
123:    <taglib>
124:          <taglib- ⤵
uri>http://jakarta.apache.org/taglibs/dbtags</taglib-uri>
125:          <taglib-location>/WEB-INF/lib/dbtags.tld</taglib-location>
126:          </taglib>
127:
128:    <taglib>
129:          <taglib-uri>oscache</taglib-uri>
130:             <taglib-location>/WEB-INF/lib/oscache.tld</taglib- ⤵
location>
```

Listing 35.6 *(continued)*

```
131:     </taglib>
132:
133: <!--
135: This defines a resource reference that is available to the web ⤸
application.
136:
137: It should be noted that it doesn't make the resource, just ⤸
declares the reference.
138:
139: In Tomcat, you would still need to declare the resource factory in ⤸
the server.xml.
141: -->
142:
143: <resource-ref>
144:
145:    <description>
147:       Resource reference to a javax.sql.DataSource
149:    </description>
151:    <res-ref-name>
153:       jdbc/myDB
155:    </res-ref-name>
157:    <res-type>
159:       javax.sql.DataSource
161:    </res-type>
163:    <res-auth>
165:       Container
167:    </res-auth>
169: </resource-ref>
172: <!--
174: This declares a security constraint on the web application.  First ⤸
there is definition of the collection,
175: in this case the JSP that flushes the cache, and the auth- ⤸
constraint defines the user and/or roles that
176: this constraint applies to.  In this case, the role "hero" is able ⤸
to access this source.
177:
178: This facility is available programmatically through the ⤸
request.isUserInRole(roleName) method.
180: -->
181:
182:
183:    <!-- Protect certain pages with a password -->
184:    <security-constraint>
185:      <web-resource-collection>
186:        <web-resource-name>Flush Cache</web-resource-name>
187:        <url-pattern>/flush.jsp</url-pattern>
188:      </web-resource-collection>
189:      <auth-constraint>
190:        <role-name>hero</role-name>
```

Listing 35.6   *(continued)*

```
191:      </auth-constraint>
192:    </security-constraint>
193:
194:    <!--
196:    This defines the way that user logs into the web application. ⏎
In this case, it uses a FORM, with the
197:    login page and error page defined.
199:      -->
200:
201:    <login-config>
202:      <auth-method>FORM</auth-method>
203:      <realm-name>Example Authentication</realm-name>
204:       <form-login-config>
205:          <form-login-page>/login.jsp</form-login-page>
206:          <form-error-page>/error.jsp</form-error-page>
207:       </form-login-config>
208:    </login-config>
209:
210:    <!--
212:    This is the place where environment entries can be made for the ⏎
web application.  This is quite preferable to a
213:    properties file in that this is part of the configuration.  To ⏎
read this environment entry you could use these
214:    lines of code:
215:
216: String configDirectory = "";
217: Context initCtx = new InitialContext();
218:    Context ctx = (Context) initCtx.lookup("java:comp/env");
219:    configDirectory = (String) ctx.lookup("configDirectory");
220:
221:    -->
224:        <env-entry>
225:        <env-entry-name>configDirectory</env-entry-name>
226:        <env-entry-value>C:/pitfallsBook</env-entry-value>
227:        <env-entry-type>java.lang.String</env-entry-type>
228: </env-entry>
230: </web-app>
```

Listing 35.6   *(continued)*

Item 36: Too Many Submits

The primary purpose of the Web site today is to display dynamic content. Of course, that means at some point the user sends input to a Web application, the input is processed, and the result is returned. Typically, operations on the back end run fast enough that under normal circumstances little can go wrong. However, occasionally, more time-consuming processing must take place—processing that takes more than a second or two. The problem of handling operations that run for long periods of time isn't a new one. Java provides a robust threading mechanism for supporting creating background tasks. Additionally, with the arrival of the EJB 2.0 specification, message-based EJBs can be used to perform background operations. The problem with both of these mechanisms is that they are designed to primarily handle asynchronous operations. You start a thread or background process, and then at some point, you are notified or you check for a result.

The too-many-submits problem occurs when an application is synchronous in nature but still somewhat long-running. Imagine the scenario where a concertgoer logs on to her favorite Web site to order tickets for a show that's just gone on sale. Under normal circumstances, the site performs fine, and our would-be concertgoer purchases her tickets and is on her way. However, when a heavy load occurs, the server slows down, and the buyer gets frustrated waiting for the site and thinks her request to purchase tickets failed. So she hits the Submit button again and again. Unfortunately, earlier requests didn't fail, they were just slow, and so each press of the Submit button ends up ordering *another* set of tickets.

There are many ways to handle the multiple-submit problem. Two of the most obvious is to prevent the user from submitting the same request over and over. The second is to somehow track that a user has previously submitted a request and revert to the previously submitted action. Figure 36.1 shows the output from a simple servlet that processes the input as it arrives and assigns a ticket number to each request.

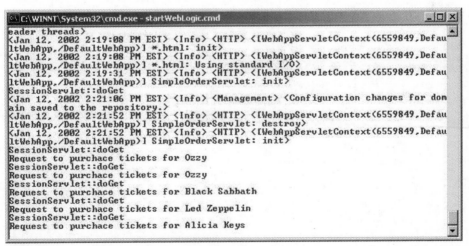

Figure 36.1 Processing simple submissions.

Preventing Multiple Submits

The first and most effective way to handle the multiple-submit problem is to not allow it to happen in the first place. Listing 36.1 shows the underlying HTML for a simple form that captures the name of a concert and submits it to a servlet to order tickets. The form works perfectly fine when the Web site performs adequately speedwise. However, if the Web site bogs down and the submit is not processed quickly enough, the user gets frustrated and processing such as that shown in Figure 36.2 results; the submit happens over and over.

```
01: <HTML>
02: <HEAD><TITLE>Online Concert Tickets</TITLE></HEAD>
03:
04: <CENTER><H1>Order Tickets</H1></CENTER>
05:
06: <FORM NAME="Order" ACTION="./SimpleOrder" METHOD="GET">
07:    <TABLE BORDER="2" WIDTH="50%" ALIGN="CENTER" BGCOLOR="CCCCCC">
08:      <TR><TD ALIGN="RIGHT" WIDTH="40%">Concert: </TD>
09:          <TD WIDTH="60%"><INPUT TYPE="TEXT" NAME="Concert"
VALUE=""></TD></TR>
10:
11:      <TR><TD COLSPAN="2" ALIGN="CENTER">
12:      <INPUT TYPE="submit" NAME="btnSubmit"
13:             VALUE="Do Submit"></TD></TR>
14:    </TABLE>
15: </FORM>
16: </BODY>
17: </HTML>
```

Listing 36.1   ConcertTickets.html form

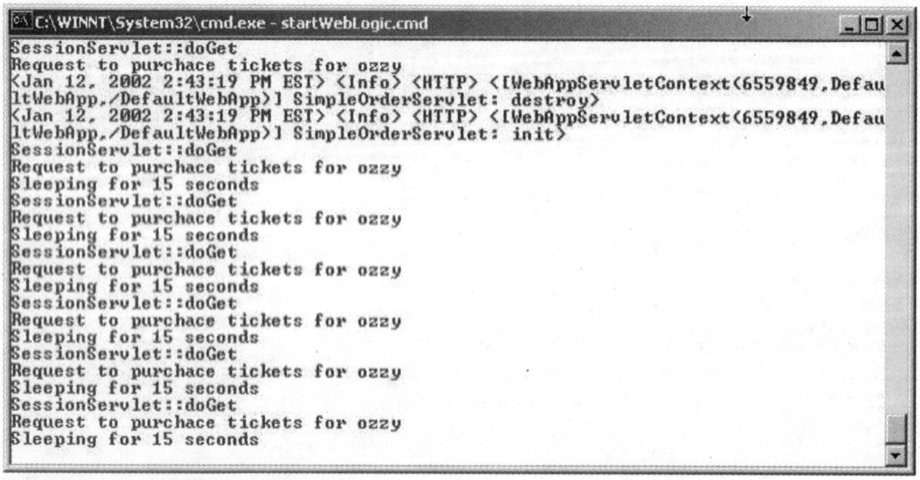

Figure 36.2   Repeated submissions.

As we said, the simplest way to handle the multiple-submit problem is to stop it from happening. Listing 36.2 shows a subtly different version of our concert order form—one that has a small amount of embedded Java script. The embedded Java script "remembers" if the Submit button was previously pressed, and if so, an alert pops up and the submit isn't processed. We short-circuit the normal submit processing by adding an `onClick` attribute to the Submit button. Every time the button is pressed, the code described in the `onClick` is processed. In our case this results in the JavaScript `checksubmitcount()` method being called. However, just calling a function doesn't really help. If we did no more then add the `onClick`, we'd get our popup alert box every time the Submit button was pressed, and then immediately the submit would happen. The user would be alerted that he or she made a mistake, and the request would be sent anyway. This is an improvement over our prior problem, but only from the user's perspective; the end result was the same: multiple submits.

We can solve the problem by going one step further and subtly changing the way our page works. Sharp readers might have noticed the one additional change. The type of our button, line 12, was originally "submit," but now it is replaced by "button." The look and feel of the page is identical. However, the default action associated with the form, shown on line 6 of Listing 36.1, to invoke the servlet, is no longer automatic. We can now programmatically choose to submit the form to our server, and our problem is solved. Or is it?

```
01: <HTML>
. . .<!-- repeated code removed //-->
12:     <INPUT TYPE="button" NAME="btnSubmit"
13:            VALUE="Do Submit"
14:            onClick="checksubmitcount();"></TD></TR>
15:   </TABLE>
16: </FORM>
17:
18: <SCRIPT LANGUAGE="JAVASCRIPT">
19: <!--
20:     var submitcount = 0;
21:     function checksubmitcount()
22:     {
23:         submitcount++;
24:         if (1 == submitcount )
25:         {
26:             document.Order.submit();
27:         }
28:         else
29:         {
30:          if ( 2 == submitcount)
31:                 alert("You have already submitted this form");
32:          else
33:                 alert("You have submitted this form "
34:                       + submitcount.toString()
35:                       + " times already");
```

Listing 36.2 Concert2.html form *(continued)*

```
36:              }
37:        }
38: //-->
39: </SCRIPT>
40: </BODY>
41: </HTML>
```

Listing 36.2   *(continued)*

Handling Multiple Submits

Listing 36.2 was certainly an improvement, but we've still got a ways to go. A number of issues still could go wrong. For example, what if the user pushes the back button and starts over? What if his or her browser has JavaScript disabled, or for some other reason, handling the processing in the browser cannot be used? We can still solve the problem, but now instead of preventing multiple submits, we need to handle them on the back end, via the servlet that processes the form.

To understand how to solve the multiple-submit problem, we must first understand how servlets work with respect to *sessions*. As everyone knows, HTTP is inherently a stateless protocol. To handle state, we need some way for the browser to communicate to the back end that the current request is part of a larger block of requests. Additionally, the server needs a way to manage the data for a given set of requests. The servlet *session* provides us a solution to this problem. The HttpServlet methods doGet() and doPost() are provided with two specific parameters: HttpServletRequest and HttpServletResponse. The servlet request parameter allows us to access what is commonly referred to as the *servlet session*. Servlet sessions have mechanisms for accessing and storing state information. But what exactly is a servlet session?

A servlet session is a number of things. It is:

- A set of states managed by the Web server and represented by a specific identifier
- Shared by all requests for a given client
- A place to store state data
- Defined, at least for HttpServlets, via the HttpSession interface

Before we look at how we can solve our problem with multiple submits with a server-side solution, we need to understand the servlet session lifecycle. As with EJBs and other server-side entities, servlet sessions go through a defined set of states during their lifetime. Figure 36.3 shows pictorially the lifecycle of a servlet session.

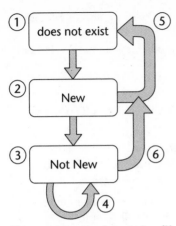

Figure 36.3 Servlet session lifecyle.

Examining how a session moves through its various states during its lifecycle will help us understand how we can solve the multiple-submit problem with a session. Servlets move through three distinct states: *does not exist*, *new*, and *not new* or *in-use*.

1. Initially, a servlet session *does not exist*. A session starts here or returns to this state for a number of reasons. The most likely are that the user has never accessed the state before or the session was invalidated because the user left the site (timed out) or explicitly left (logged out).

2. Sessions move from *does not exist* to *new* when the session is first created. The distinction between *new* and *not new* is important because the HTTP is stateless. Sessions cannot move to not new from being a prospective session to an actual session according to the servlet specification, until the client returns the session back to the server. Thus, sessions are new because the client does not yet know about the session or the client decides not to join the session.

3. When the session is returned back to the server from the client via a cookie or URL rewriting (more on URL rewriting in a moment), then the session becomes in-use or not new.

4. Continued use of the session, via its various get and set methods, results in the session remaining in use.

5. Transitions 5 and 6 happen when a session times out because inactivity of a session causes it to be explicated invalidated. Application servers handle time-outs in a variety of ways. BEA WebLogic Server handles timeouts by allowing the application deployer the ability to set the session timeout via a special deployment descriptor (weblogic.xml) packaged with the Web application.

Now that we understand the lifecycle of a session, how do we go about obtaining a session and using it to our advantage?

The HttpServletRequest interface offers two methods for obtaining a session:

- public HttpSession getSession(). Always returns either a new session or an existing session.

  - getSession() returns an existing session if a valid session ID was provided via a cookie or in some other fashion.

  - getSession() returns a new session if it is the client's first session (no ID), the supplied session has timed out, the client provided an invalid session, or the provided session has been explicitly invalidated.

- public HttpSession getSession(boolean). May return a new session or an existing session or null depending on how the Boolean is set.

  - getSession(true) returns an existing session if possible; otherwise, it creates a new session

  - getSession(false) returns an existing session if possible; otherwise, it returns null.

> **NOTE** At first glance, it appears that we should always use
> getSession(true). **However, you should be careful in that an out-of-memory style of attack can be performed on your site by always creating new sessions on demand. An unscrupulous hacker could discover your site was creating sessions and keep pumping requests, each of which would result in a new session. By using** getSession(false) **and then redirecting to a login page when a session is not detected, you can protect against such attacks.**

There are a number of interesting methods on HttpSession objects such as isNew(), getAttribute(), setAttribute(), and so on. For an exhaustive review, see the Servlet specification or any of the excellent John Wiley & Sons publications.

Getting back to our problem at hand, we have still only solved half of our problem. We'd like to be able to use our sessions to somehow skip over the *session new* state and move to the *session in-use* stage automatically. We can achieve this final step by redirecting the browser back to the handling servlet automatically. Listing 36.3 combines servlet session logic with the ability to redirect, with a valid session, the client back to the handling servlet.

```
01: package org.javapitfalls.item36;
02:
03: import java.io.*;
04: import java.util.Date;
05: import javax.servlet.*;
06: import javax.servlet.http.*;
```

Listing 36.3   RedirectServlet.java

```
07:
08: public class RedirectServlet extends HttpServlet {
09:
10:   static int count = 2;
11:
12:   public void doGet(HttpServletRequest req, HttpServletResponse res)
throws ServletException, IOException {
13:
14:     HttpSession session = req.getSession(false);
15:     System.out.println("");
16:     System.out.println("----------------------------------------");
17:     System.out.println("SessionServlet::doGet");
18:     System.out.println("Session requested ID in request: " +
req.getRequestedSessionId());
19:
20:     if ( null == req.getRequestedSessionId() ) {
21:       System.out.println("No session ID, first call, creating new
session and forwarding");
22:       session = req.getSession(true);
23:       System.out.println("Generated session ID in Request: " +
session.getId());
24:       String encodedURL = res.encodeURL("/resubmit/TestServlet");
25:       System.out.println("res.encodeURL(\"/TestServlet\";=" + encodedURL);
26:       res.sendRedirect(encodedURL);
27:       //
28:       // RequestDispatcher rd = getServletContext()
.getRequestDispatcher(encodedURL);
29:       // rd.forward(req, res);
30:       //
31:       return;
32:     }
33:     else {
34:       System.out.println("Session id = " + req.getRequestedSessionId() );
35:       System.out.println("------------------------------------------------");
36:     }
37:
38:     HandleRequest(req, res);
39:     System.out.println("SessionServlet::doGet returning");
40:     System.out.println("-------------------------------");
41:     return;
42:   }
43:
44:   void HandleRequest(HttpServletRequest req, HttpServletResponse
res) throws IOException {
45:
46:     System.out.println("SessionServlet::HandleRequest called");
47:     res.setContentType("text/html");
48:     PrintWriter out = res.getWriter();
```

Listing 36.3 *(continued)*

```
49:    Date date = new Date();
50:    out.println("<html>");
51:    out.println("<head><title>Ticket Confirmation</title></head>");
52:    // javascript
53:    out.println("<script language=\"javascript\">");
54:    out.println("<!--");
55:    out.println("var submitcount = " + count + ";");
56:    out.println("function checksubmitcount()");
57:    out.println("{");
58:    out.println(" if ( 2 == submitcount )");
59:    out.println("    alert(\"You have already submitted this form.\");");
60:    out.println("   else");
61:    out.println("      alert(\"You have submitted this form " + count +
" times already.\");");
62:    out.println(" document.Order.submit();");
63:    out.println("}");
64:    out.println("//-->");
65:    out.println("</script>");
66:    // body
67:    out.println("<body>");
68:    out.println("<center>");
69:    out.println("<form name=\"Order\" action=\"./RedirectServlet\"
method=\"GET\">");
70:    out.println("<table border=\"2\" width=\"50%\" align=\"center\"
bgcolor=\"#cccccc\">");
71:    out.println("<tr>");
72:    out.println("<td align\"right\" width=\"40%\">Concert:</td>");
73:    out.println("<td width=\"60%\"><input type=\"text\"
name=\"Concert\" value=\"\"></td>");
74:    out.println("</tr>");
75:    out.println("<tr>");
76:    out.println("<td colspan=\"2\" align=\"center\">");
77:    out.println("<input type=\"button\" name=\"btnSubmit\" value=\"Do
Submit\" onClick=\"checksubmitcount();\">");
78:    out.println("</td>");
79:    out.println("</tr>");
80:    out.println("</form>");
81:    // message
82:    out.println("<br>");
83:    out.println("<h1>The Current Date and Time Is:</h1><br>");
84:    out.println("<h3>You have submitted this page before</h3><br>");
85:    out.println("<h3>" + date.toString() + "</h3>");
86:    out.println("</body>");
87:    out.println("</html>");
88:
89:    count++;
90:
```

Listing 36.3 *(continued)*

```
91:    System.out.println("SessionServlet::HandleRequest returning.");
92:    return;
93:  }
94:
95: }
```

Listing 36.3 *(continued)*

Just how does Listing 36.3 solve our problem? If we examine the code closely, we see that on line 14 we try to obtain a handle to a session. On line 20 we identify that an active session exists by comparing the session to `null` or by checking for a valid session ID. Either method suffices. Lines 20 to 31 are executed if no session exists, and to handle our problem, we:

1. Create a session, as shown on line 22.

2. Use URL encoding to add the new session ID to our URL, as shown on line 24.

3. Redirect our servlet to the newly encoded URL, as shown on line 26.

Those readers unfamiliar with URL rewriting are directed to lines 18 and 25. The request parameter to an `HttpServlet` can do what is known as *URL rewriting*. URL rewriting is the process whereby a session ID is automatically inserted into a URL. The underlying application server can then use the encoded URL to provide an existing session automatically to a servlet or JSP. Note that depending on the application server, you may need to enable URL rewriting for the above example to work.

WARNING Lines 28 and 29, while commented out, are shown as an example of something *not to do*. On first glance, `forward` seems to be a better solution to our problem because it does not cause a round-trip to the browser and back. However, `forward` comes at a price: The new session ID *is not* attached to the URL. Using `forward` in Listing 36.3 would cause the servlet to be called over and over in a loop and ultimately kill the application server.

The JavaScript/servlet implementation described above is okay for many situations, but I've been on several programs that wanted to limit the amount of JavaScript used on their deployments, so I thought it would beneficial to include an example that satisfies that requirement. In the example below, a controller servlet will be used to prohibit multiple user form requests using the Front Controller pattern.

```
01: package org.javapitfalls.item36;
02:
03: import java.io.*;
```

Listing 36.4 ControllerServlet.java *(continued)*

```
04: import java.util.*;
05: import javax.servlet.*;
06: import javax.servlet.http.*;
07: import org.javapitfalls.item36.*;
08:
09: public class ControllerServlet extends HttpServlet {
10:
11: private static String SESSION_ID;
12:
13:   public void destroy() {}
```

Listing 36.4   *(continued)*

Our application reads an `id` tag and its initial value from the deployment descriptor embedded in the `param-name` and `param-value` tags in Listing 36.5 on lines 29 and 30. This read operation takes place in the `init()` method on line 17 of the controller servlet in Listing 36.4 and will be used to identify the user session. The controller application uses three parameters: `numTickets`, `stadiumTier`, and `ticketPrice`, as data items to process from the ticketForm application shown in Listing 36.4. The `getNamedDispatcher` forwards all requests by the name mappings specified in the deployment descriptor. The form request associates the `ticketForm.jsp` with the "form" label on line 44 of the web.xml in Listing 36.5. This method is preferred over dispatching requests by application path descriptions because this exposes the path information to the client, which could present a safety concern. Additionally, it is a good practice to migrate applications and their dependencies to the deployment descriptor so that modifications can be made more easily.

```
14:
15: public void init() throws ServletException {
16:
17:     SESSION_ID = getInitParameter("id");
18:
19: }
20:
21: protected void doGet(HttpServletRequest req, HttpServletResponse
res) throws ServletException, IOException {
22:
23:   process(req, res);
24:
25: }
26:
27: protected void process(HttpServletRequest req,
28:                        HttpServletResponse res)
29:                        throws ServletException, IOException {
30:
```

Listing 36.4   *(continued)*

```
31:     HttpSession session = req.getSession(false);
32:     String numTickets = req.getParameter("numTickets");
33:     String stadiumTier = req.getParameter("stadiumTier");
34:     String ticketPrice = req.getParameter("ticketPrice");
35:     if(session == null) {
36:       if( (numTickets == null) || (stadiumTier == null) ||
37:                                   (ticketPrice == null) ) {
38:
39:         getServletConfig().getServletContext().
40:             getNamedDispatcher("form").forward(req, res);
41:
42:       } else {
43:         throw new ServletException("[form] Page Not Found");
44:       }
45:
46:     } else {
47:
48:       if ( (!numTickets.equals("Please enter a Ticket #")) &&
49:            (!stadiumTier.equals("Please enter a Stadium Tier")) &&
50:            (!ticketPrice.equals("Please enter a Ticket Price")) ) {
51:
```

Listing 36.4   *(continued)*

The `session.getAttribute` operation on line 52 reads the ID name captured in the `init` method on line 17 during the initialization of the controller servlet. This ID, `SESSION_ID`, will serve as the session identifier for the submit page. If the user has entered all the proper form information on the ticketForm page, and the session ID is not null, then the controller will remove the ID and forward the application to the successful completion page. When the form has been properly completed and the session ID is equal to null, then the user will be forwarded to the error page that indicates that the `ticketForm` has already been completed satisfactorily and cannot be resubmitted.

```
52:         String sessionValidatorID =
53:             (String)session.getAttribute(SESSION_ID);
54:         if(sessionValidatorID != null ) {
55:
56:           session.removeAttribute(SESSION_ID);
57:           getServletConfig().getServletContext().
58:             getNamedDispatcher("success").forward(req, res);
59:
60:         } else {
61:           getServletConfig().getServletContext().
62:             getNamedDispatcher("resubmit").forward(req, res);
63:         }
64:
```

Listing 36.4   *(continued)*

```
65:         } else {
66:
67:             getServletConfig().getServletContext().
68:                     getNamedDispatcher("form").forward(req, res);
69:         }
70:
71:     }
72:   }
73:
74: }
75:
```

Listing 36.4   *(continued)*

Lastly, the deployment descriptor exhibits the application's mappings that allow requests to be forwarded and processed by the controller. As mentioned earlier, the session ID token is read from the parameter tags on lines 25 and 26 of Listing 35.5. The JavaServer Pages that are used for presentation are shown on lines 42 to 55. When the controller uses the getNamedDispatcher method, a label is passed that is associated with a JSP script. When a user attempts to resubmit the ticketForm page, the resubmit label is passed through controller, which forwards control to the resubmit error page (resubmitError.jsp).

```
01: <?xml version="1.0"?>
02: <!DOCTYPE web-app PUBLIC "-//Sun Microsystems, Inc.//DTD Web
Application 2.3//EN" "http://java.sun.com/j2ee/dtds/web-app_2_3.dtd">
03: <web-app>
04:
05:   <servlet>
06:     <servlet-name>RedirectServlet</servlet-name>
07:     <display-name>RedirectServlet</display-name>
08:     <description>RedirectServlet</description>
09:     <servlet-class>
10:        org.javapitfalls.item36.RedirectServlet
11:     </servlet-class>
12:   </servlet>
13:   <servlet>
14:     <servlet-name>SimpleOrder</servlet-name>
15:     <display-name>SimpleOrder</display-name>
16:     <description>SimpleOrder</description>
17:     <servlet-class>
18:        org.javapitfalls.item36.SimpleOrder
19:     </servlet-class>
20:   </servlet>
21:   <servlet>
22:     <servlet-name>ControllerServlet</servlet-name>
23:     <display-name>ControllerServlet</display-name>
```

Listing 36.5   web.xml

```
24:        <description>ControllerServlet</description>
25:        <servlet-class>
26:          org.javapitfalls.item36.ControllerServlet
27:        </servlet-class>
28:        <init-param>
29:        <param-name>id</param-name>
30:        <param-value>id</param-value>
31:        </init-param>
32:      </servlet>
33:
34:      <servlet>
35:        <servlet-name>TestServlet</servlet-name>
36:        <display-name>TestServlet</display-name>
37:        <description>TestServlet</description>
38:        <servlet-class>
39:          org.javapitfalls.item36.TestServlet
40:        </servlet-class>
41:      </servlet>
42:      <servlet>
43:          <servlet-name>form</servlet-name>
44:          <jsp-file>/ticketForm.jsp</jsp-file>
45:      </servlet>
46:
47:      <servlet>
48:          <servlet-name>success</servlet-name>
49:          <jsp-file>/success.jsp</jsp-file>
50:      </servlet>
51:
52:      <servlet>
53:          <servlet-name>resubmit</servlet-name>
54:          <jsp-file>/resubmitError.jsp</jsp-file>
55:      </servlet>
56:
57:      <servlet-mapping>
58:        <servlet-name>RedirectServlet</servlet-name>
59:        <url-pattern>/RedirectServlet</url-pattern>
60:      </servlet-mapping>
61:
62:      <servlet-mapping>
63:        <servlet-name>SimpleOrder</servlet-name>
64:        <url-pattern>/SimpleOrder</url-pattern>
65:      </servlet-mapping>
66:
67:      <servlet-mapping>
68:        <servlet-name>ControllerServlet</servlet-name>
69:        <url-pattern>/ControllerServlet</url-pattern>
70:      </servlet-mapping>
71:
72:      <servlet-mapping>
```

Listing 36.5 *(continued)*

```
73:        <servlet-name>TestServlet</servlet-name>
74:        <url-pattern>/TestServlet</url-pattern>
75:    </servlet-mapping>
76:
77: </web-app>
78:
```

Listing 36.5 *(continued)*

In this pitfall we discussed a number of solutions to the multiple-submit problem. Each solution, as with almost every solution, had its positive and negative aspects. When solving problems, we must clearly understand the various pros and cons of a solution so we can assess the value of each trade-off. Our final JavaScript example had the benefit of solving the problem at hand, but had the trade-off that we needed to make an extra round-trip to the client in order to make it work. The first JavaScript solution was perhaps the most elegant, but required that the client enables JavaScript for it to work. The final application would serve those well that opted to forego the use of JavaScript to avoid browser incompatibilities with the scripting language. As with any problem, there is often a world of solutions, each one with its own trade-offs. By understanding the trade-offs of a given solution, we can make the most informed choice for a given problem.

The Enterprise Tier

"Machine capacities give us room galore for making a mess of it. Opportunities unlimited for fouling things up! Developing the austere intellectual discipline of keeping things sufficiently simple is in this environment a formidable challenge, both technically and educationally."

**Edsger W. Dijkstra,
from "The Threats to Computing Science," EWD Manuscript #898**

In that paper, which he wrote in 1984, Dijkstra suggests that in a world of incredibly fast computers and increasingly complex programming environments, simplicity is the key. "We know perfectly well what we have to do," he writes, "but the burning question is, whether the world we are a part of will allow us to do it."[1] I would contend that the frameworks present in Java, and specifically on the server side today, provide the beginnings of such a world—not that this will completely keep us from fouling things up! As this book shows you, there are always opportunities for that. However, when we do not have to worry about the management of services such as memory, threads, connection pooling, transactions, security, and persistence, things get simpler. When we allow the container to handle the details of these services for us, we can focus where Dijkstra thought we should focus: on the logic of our application itself.

The J2EE environment provides the atmosphere for Java programmers to focus on application logic. Because application servers focus on the "hard stuff," we can focus on the business logic of our applications. However, since programming in this environment represents a change in mind-set, new enterprise developers stumble into

---

[1] Dijkstra, Edsger. "The Threats to Computing Science." EWD manuscript #898. Available at http://www.cs.utexas.edu/users/EWD/ewd08xx/EWD898.PDF.

quite a few traps. Because the Java language is so flexible, there is the ability for programmers to add unneeded complexity (thread management, etc.) even when the container provides this support. Because of misunderstandings of the J2EE environment, design errors pop up. The use of database connections and different types of databases present other challenges, and the use of new Java Web services APIs, such as Java API for XML-based Remote Procedure Calls (JAX-RPC) and the Java API for XML Registries (JAXR), provides more opportunities for misunderstandings and traps to occur.

In this section of the book, we have tried to focus on areas of the enterprise tier where we have seen and experienced problems and confusion. Although some of the pitfalls could possibly be tied to the other tiers (JDBC pitfalls, for example), we placed them in this section because developers make use of them in the enterprise tier. Many of the pitfalls in this section revolve around Enterprise JavaBeans, some focus on APIs related to Web services, and some focus on design pitfalls. In this section, many pitfalls focus on "the big picture" in a multi-tier environment.

Here are highlights of pitfalls in this section:

J2EE Architecture Considerations (Item 37). J2EE has become a major player in enterprise IT solutions. Developers are often confused about how to apply this architecture to their solution. This pitfall discusses how those mistakes occur and considerations for avoiding them.

Design Strategies for Eliminating Network Bottleneck Pitfalls (Item 38). This pitfall focuses on pitfalls where network calls and bandwidth are a major factor and shows performance-tuning design strategies to use between tiers.

I'll Take the Local (Item 39). EJB 2.0 introduced the local interface as a mechanism for referencing EJBs within the same process. This pitfall discusses the why and how of local interfaces over the traditional remote interface.

Image Obsession (Item 40). Frequently, Enterprise Java applications are developed on one platform and deployed on another. This can cause some cross platform issues. This pitfall examines one of those issues regarding server generated images.

The Problem with Multiple Concurrent Result Sets (Item 41). When you have to interface with many different types of databases, your connections may be handled in different ways. This pitfall addresses a problem that can arise when you use multiple `ResultSet` objects concurrently.

Generating Primary Keys for EJB (Item 42). There are many ways to create unique primary keys for entity beans. Some of these techniques are wrong, some suffer performance problems, and some tie your implementation to the container. This pitfall discusses the techniques and offers solutions.

The Stateful Stateless Session Bean (Item 43). Developers frequently confuse the stateless nature of the stateless session bean. This pitfall provides an example of where this confusion can cause problems and clarifies just how stateful the stateless bean is.

The Unprepared PreparedStatement (Item 44). The `PreparedStatement` is a powerful capability in server side applications that interface with a database. This pitfall explores a common mistake made in the use of the `PreparedStatement`.

Take a Dip in the Resource Pool (Item 45). Container resource pools are frequently overlooked by developers, who instead rely on several techniques that predate this capability. This pitfall explores techniques currently used and how a container resource pool is the superior choice.

JDO and Data Persistence (Item 46). Data persistence is an important component for all enterprise systems. This pitfall introduces Java Data Objects as a new persistence mechanism that uses both Java and SQL constructs for data transactions.

Where's the WSDL? Pitfalls of Using JAXR with UDDI (Item 47). This item addresses pitfalls with using JAXR with UDDI. The advent of Web services brought us a new API—the Java API for XML Registries. Problems can occur when you are querying UDDI registries with JAXR. This pitfall discusses the problems in depth.

Performance Pitfalls in JAX-RPC Application Clients (Item 48). As JAX-RPC is adopted into the J2EE environment, it is important to know the gory details of how slow or fast your connections could be when using some of JAX-RPC's features on the client side. This pitfall demonstrates an example and shows speed statistics.

Get Your Beans Off My Filesystem! (Item 49) The EJB specification lists certain programming restrictions for EJB developers. This pitfall shows an example of how one of these restrictions is often violated and provides an alternative solution.

When Transactions Go Awry , or Consistent State in Stateful Session EJBs (Item 50). Data transactions are an important part of all distributed system applications. This pitfall shows how the `SessionSynchronization` interface and the Memento pattern can be employed as vehicles in enterprise applications to save and restore data.

Item 37: J2EE Architecture Considerations

I was assigned to be the software lead of a project to Web-enable a legacy XWindows database visualization application. This application consisted of a large database and a data-handling interface that captured data coming from various control systems, correlated it, and loaded it. The data from the control systems was immense, and the interface to them was customized and optimized for its purpose. It worked well, and the goal was merely trying to make this data interface available to a wider audience. How better than to make it a Web application? While database-driven Web applications had been around for a while, including relatively stable versions of servlets and JSPs, commercial J2EE containers were beginning to proliferate. Figure 37.1 shows the architecture of the "as is" system.

Analyzing the requirements, we found there were really two types of users envisioned for this system:

- Analyst personnel, who needed a rich toolset by which they could pour through this voluminous set of data

- Management personnel, who needed an executive-level summary of system performance

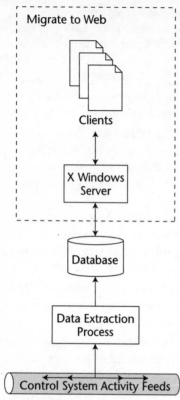

Figure 37.1 The current system.

Therefore, there were truly two different clients that needed to be Web-enabled.

The analyst client needed functionality that included mapping, time lines, and spreadsheets. This was going to be the primary tool used for these personnel to perform their job, and they had expectations that it would perform like the rest of the applications on their desktop machine. They wanted to be able to print reports, save their work, and perform most other tasks that users have come to expect from their PCs.

The manager client was meant to show some commonly generated displays and reports. Essentially, this would be similar to portfolio summary and headlines view. They didn't want anything more involved than essentially to point their Web browser at a Web site and view the latest information.

We proposed to solve the problem of two clients by building a servlet/JSP Web site for the managers with a restricted area that included a Java Web Start deployed application for the analysts (for further explanation of the Java Web Start versus applet decision, see Item 26, "When Applets Go Bad"). There would be a query servlet interface to the database, which would be reused by both clients, using XML as the wire data transmission format. (It should be noted that there were also restrictions on the network enforced by firewalls.) Figure 37.2 outlines the proposed solution.

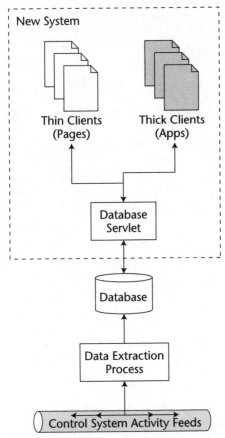

Figure 37.2 The proposed solution.

The customer accepted this as a sound approach and approved the project. Then senior management attended a demonstration on J2EE from an application server vendor, who gave an inspiring presentation. They used the very impressive-looking J2EE Blueprint picture, which is shown in Figure 37.3 (no longer in use by Sun). I pointed out to them that principles were entirely consistent with our design. However, they seemed stuck on the fact that the yellow tier was not present in our design. More specifically, they didn't understand how we could in good conscience not use EJB.

This is a textbook case of what Allen Holub calls "bandwagon-oriented programming" in his interesting article, "Is There Anything to JavaBeans but Gas?"[2] The central point of the article was that problems should not be solved in a "follow the herd" mentality. While I agree with this statement, Mr. Holub forgets that the inverse of that is also problematic. Just because an approach is popular does not mean that it is without merit.

---

[2] Holub, Allen. "Is There Anything to JavaBeans but Gas?" *C/C++ Users Journal*. Available at http://www.cuj.com/java/forum.htm?topic=java.

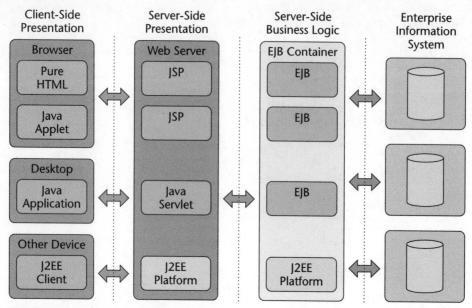

Figure 37.3 J2EE Blueprint diagram (old).

Enterprise JavaBeans, and the J2EE in general, are based on sound engineering principles and fill a major void in the enterprise application market (a platform-neutral standard for enterprise applications and services). So although we've now seen an example where J2EE is "bad," this doesn't necessarily mean that it can't be good.

Let's clarify. Both solutions deal with J2EE. I took issue with the use of EJB, and here is why. EJB is not an object-relational mapping (ORM) tool. The purpose of entity beans is to provide fault-tolerant persistent business objects. Corrupt data, particularly transactions like orders, bills, and payments, cost businesses money—*big* money. Such persistence costs resources and time. This application was a data visualization suite for lots of data, which would amount to having to handle negotiating "locks" from the database vernacular over a tremendous number of records. This would slow performance to incredibly slow levels.

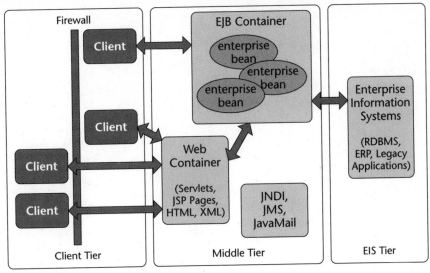

Figure 37.4   J2EE tiers (new).

But the original solution was a J2EE solution, what became known as the "Web tier" by Sun. Figure 37.4 is a diagram representing the new vision that Sun has for different containers for the tier of solution needed.

As to whether the original specification intended to have the flexibility of providing simply Web tier solutions, it was not readily apparent from the initial blueprints. This is why Sun separated them—to clarify that all solutions did not need to center on EJB. This caused a lot of frustration on my team's part (and I know that we were not alone judging from the backlash against EJB I have read).

Figure 37.5 illustrates the various containers that the Java platform envisions. The handheld clients are not shown but are not really relevant relative to the server-side technologies. Note the distinction between the Web container and the EJB container. Also note how the Web container can serve as a façade for the EJB container.

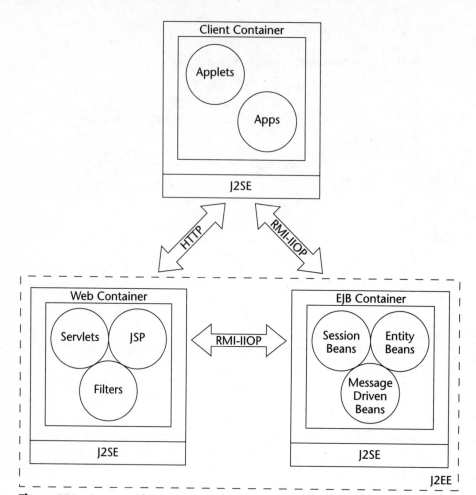

Figure 37.5   Java containers.

So how do we tell if the EJB tier (container) is necessary in our application? This boils down to looking at what EJB provides:

Scalability. Everyone wants scalability, but how scalable? Essentially, we want all of our apps to scale immensely and forever, because something in our system design mentality says, "It can handle anything." However, bigger is not always better, and benchmarks from 2000 show servlets having peak performance on the order of 400 requests per second. Now, you would want to look into your own benchmarking studies, especially concerning the specific vendor solutions you want, but it is not safe to assume that if you want a highly scalable system, you must use EJB.

Transactions. Transactions are a strong capability of EJB containers. This is probably a major selling point when you are dealing with distributed or complex transaction scenarios (multiple systems, phased transactions). However, a great number of developers use transactions to ensure that a series of SQL statements execute together in the same RDBMS. If this is the level of complexity required, then the JDBC transaction capability is probably more than sufficient.

Security. If you have complex, role-based security or complicated access control lists, this is probably a good place for the EJB container. While the filtering mechanisms in the new servlet specification are very helpful for building good user authentication, it is pretty transparent in EJB.

Reliability. A lot of people define reliability as whether their system ever crashes. In fact, there are a number of semantic debates over reliability versus fault tolerance versus redundancy, but what we are talking about is how well the system responds to something going wrong. As previously mentioned, entity beans were designed around the old data processing nightmare, so if this is a major concern to you, then EJB is probably a good idea.

Componentization. J2EE revolves around the idea of being able to build and reuse components, allowing for the classic build versus buy engineering equation to be introduced into enterprise applications. It is easy to assume that the market for EJB container components is more vibrant than Web container components, but it is quite the opposite. There are tremendous numbers of Web container components available, including some very good open-source ones. A classic example is the Jakarta Taglibs or Struts framework (http://jakarta.apache.org/).

Clustering, Load Balancing, Failover. These are classic examples of the need for the EJB tier. When your applications need to be spread over several containers in a transparent way to support things like clustering (multiple cooperating instances to improve performance), load balancing (assigning requests to different instances to level the load among all instances), and failover (when one instance fails, another is able to pick up on it quickly).

Because it was the first cross-platform enterprise component architecture, J2EE has gained a tremendous amount of attention. While the attention caused a great amount of hype as well, it is wrong to assume J2EE is a technology without merit. J2EE is a collection of technologies, so it is almost always inappropriate to suggest it is a bad solution for any enterprise scenario, despite the care that must be taken in determining whether EJB is a helpful technology to your enterprise solution.

Item 38: Design Strategies for Eliminating Network Bottleneck Pitfalls

In a distributed world where, as Sun Microsystems says, "the network is the computer," the network is also where a lot of performance bottlenecks can be found. If your software communicates over the network, your design must be flexible enough to tune your performance so that waiting for network traffic does not become the weakest link in your system. Whether you are programming with Sockets, Remote Method Invocation (RMI), CORBA, Enterprise JavaBeans, or using SOAP messaging for Web services using JAXM or JAX-RPC, it is important that you concentrate on your design so that network latency is not a factor. At the same time, you want to design your system with a flexible architecture.

Although some Java programmers experience problems when designing parallel processing algorithms in network computing, most of the pitfalls we've experienced relate to call granularity in remote messages or method calls. That is, the more messages and calls sent over a network, the more network traffic may impact the performance of your application. In network programming, many developers design their systems where clients send multiple small messages over the network, giving the client more details in the specifics of the transaction but increasing the amount of network connections in an application session. Most of the time, systems that are designed without performance in mind fall into this "granular messaging" trap. In this pitfall, we provide a scenario where we discuss design patterns and strategies for general network programming, and we discuss examples for systems developed with Enterprise JavaBeans.

A Scenario

To demonstrate these challenges, let's look at a scenario for a network application for an automobile service center. An enterprise application for this auto shop supports troubleshooting for its vehicle service. When customers arrive at the auto shop, they tell the employees their customer number and the make and model of their automobile, and they describe their problem. This online application allows the employees and mechanics to look up information about their automobile, find troubleshooting solutions, and provide real-time assistance in fixing the problem. The use cases for the auto shop workflow are shown in Figure 38.1. As you can see from the figure, the auto shop employee enters the car trouble information (probably with the customer's information), gets the owner information from the database, gets the vehicle history from the database, gets possible solutions to the problem, and finally, gets part numbers related to those solutions that are provided.

Looking past the use case and into how data is stored, we see that the application needs to talk to *four databases:* the owner database with information about the owner's automobile and his or her service history, the "car trouble" database with common problems and solutions, the automobile database about makes and models of cars, and the parts database that keeps part numbers for different makes and models of cars.

General Design Considerations

Before we even look at the pitfalls that occur in each API, the following should be made abundantly clear: Although there are four databases full of information, it would be a bad decision to design your client in such a way as to query the databases directly, as shown in Figure 38.2. Such a design would put too much implementation detail in the client, and a very possible bottleneck will be in the management of the JDBC connections, as well as the amount of network calls happening. In Figure 38.2, for each network transaction, there is significant overhead in the establishment and setup of each connection, leading to performance problems. In addition, such a solution is an example of a very brittle software architecture: If the internal structure of one of these databases changes, or if two databases are combined, a client application designed as shown in Figure 38.2 will have to be rewritten. This causes a software maintenance nightmare.

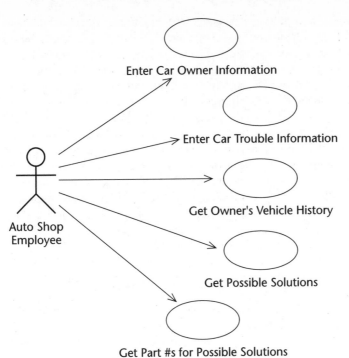

Figure 38.1   Use cases of auto shop scenario.

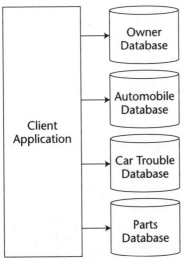

Figure 38.2   Bad client design: calling databases directly.

Figure 38.3 shows an approach that abstracts the implementation details about the four databases from the clients. Instead of the client communicating directly with the four databases, the client communicates with four Java objects. This is good because implementation-specific details in each database are abstracted from the client. The abstraction objects hide these details from the client, but the workflow logic still exists in the client. Added to that is that there is still a potential performance bottleneck: The solution still requires many network calls from the client. For example, if there were eight possible solutions to a car trouble problem, the solution in Figure 38.3 would require 11 network connections (one connection each to the owner, automobile, and car trouble abstractions, and eight connections asking for parts for possible solutions). If this system were live, the performance of this would be unacceptable.

Figure 38.4, on the other hand, seems to eliminate all of the problems that we previously discussed. In Figure 38.4, the client application sends one big message to a gigantic "object that talks to everything." This object talks to all four databases, encapsulates all the business logic, and returns the results back to the client application. On the surface, the application design shown in Figure 38.4 seems perfect—but is it? We have definitely eliminated the bottleneck of too many network connections, and we have eliminated the tight coupling between the client and the databases, but we have now a monstrous object that is tightly coupled to the databases! This design is still inflexible, similar to the design in Figure 38.1, but we have simply added another layer.

Finally, the diagram in Figure 38.5 shows a better solution. We have a client making one network call to an object, which then calls the abstractions to the databases. The database abstractions do the database-specific logic, and the object does the workflow for our use cases. The client application passes in the customer information and symptoms of car trouble to an object, which then delegates that work to abstractions to talk to the database. Finally, when the possible problems and their respective solution part numbers are returned to the object, this information is passed back to the client in one connection. Because only one network connection happens, this creates a positive impact on performance.

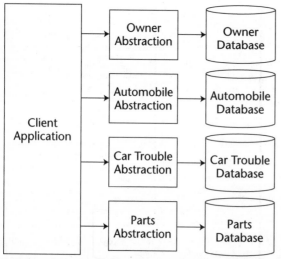

Figure 38.3   Bottleneck: too many network calls from client.

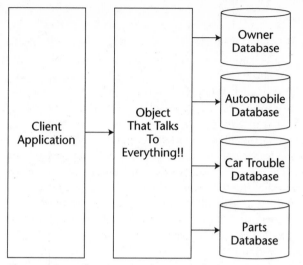

Figure 38.4 The extreme: better performance, but inflexible.

Looking at this scenario, we see that there could be many solutions to designing this system. Before we go into the pitfalls that could occur in each API, let's mention that the key goal for designing this system for this scenario is network performance.

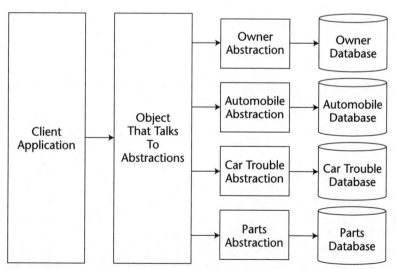

Figure 38.5 A more flexible solution.

EJB Design Considerations

Because we have discussed the potential design pitfalls in this scenario in depth, these pitfalls easily translate to design pitfalls using Enterprise JavaBeans. One problem similar to the poorly thought out designs shown in Figures 38.2 and 38.3 is the design solution where clients directly call entity beans. When this happens, clients become too tightly coupled to the logic of entity beans, putting unneeded logic and workflow in the client, creating multiple network transactions, and creating an architecture that is very unflexible. If the entity bean changes, the client has to change.

Luckily, session beans were made to handle transactional logic between your client and your entity beans. Instead of having your clients call your entity beans directly, have them talk to session beans that handle the transactional logic for your use case. This cuts down on the network traffic and executes the logic of a use case in one network call. This is an EJB design pattern called the Session Façade pattern and is one of the most popular patterns used in J2EE.[3] In our very simple use case for our example, we could have a stateless session bean handle the workflow logic, talking to our session beans, as shown in Figure 38.6.

Of course, you could also use the EJB Command pattern to accomplish the abstraction and to package your network commands into one network call. For more information about these design patterns and for similar patterns in Enterprise JavaBeans, read *EJB Design Patterns* by Floyd Marinescu. It's a great book. (In fact, I had to throw away several pitfall ideas because they were described so well in that book!)

In this pitfall, we discussed network programming design that can relate to any area of Java programming—RMI, Sockets, CORBA, Web Services, or J2EE programming. As you can see by our discussions related to EJB, the basic concepts of design and programming for network performance do not change. With J2EE, we discussed the Session Façade and the Command patterns, which were similar to the solutions we discussed in Figure 38.5. In fact, the J2EE architecture itself helps the flexibility and stability of our architecture.

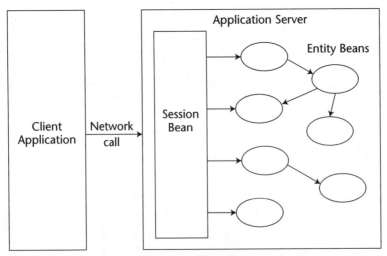

Figure 38.6   Using the session façade pattern.

[3]Marinescu. *EJB Design Patterns*. John Wiley & Sons, 2002.

In conclusion, use the following pieces of advice when designing network applications:

- Abstract details from the client.
- Abstract things in a multi-tiered solution.
- When the network has the potential to be a bottleneck, use the "plan and execute" strategy—it is often better to send one large message with lots of information than to send smaller messages over the network.

Item 39: I'll Take the Local

I have worked with a team that is providing EJBs available via the Web services protocols (SOAP over HTTP). They use a servlet to receive SOAP messages over HTTP. Based on the SOAP message, the appropriate EJB is referenced and called.

For the sake of clarity and simplicity, we will use a more stripped-down version to demonstrate the same concept (see Figure 39.1).

This is the source of the handler, which extends `JAXMServlet` and implements the `ReqRespListener` (a JAXM convention for handling requests that return a synchronous response).

This servlet:

1. Receives the SOAP message.
2. Parses a parameter from the SOAP message.
3. Looks up the `EJBHome` interface object.
4. Narrows the object into a `SOAPHome` object.
5. Calls `create()` on the `SOAPHome` object to create a `SOAPHandler` object.
6. Calls the `convert()` method on the `SOAPHandler` object.
7. Builds a response SOAP message.

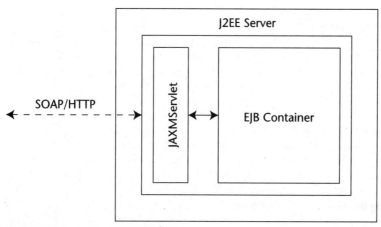

Figure 39.1   Architecture overview.

Listing 39.1 demonstrates this servlet.

```
001: /*
002:  * RemoteEJBServlet.java
003:  *
004:  */
005:
006: import javax.servlet.*;
007: import javax.servlet.http.*;
008: import javax.xml.messaging.*;
009: import javax.xml.soap.SOAPMessage;
010: import javax.xml.soap.SOAPPart;
011: import javax.xml.soap.SOAPEnvelope;
012: import javax.xml.soap.SOAPHeader;
013: import javax.xml.soap.SOAPElement;
014: import javax.xml.soap.Name;
015: import javax.xml.soap.SOAPException;
016:
017: import org.xml.sax.*;
018: import org.xml.sax.helpers.*;
019: import javax.xml.parsers.*;
020:
021: import org.w3c.dom.*;
022: import javax.xml.transform.*;
023: import javax.xml.transform.dom.*;
024: import javax.xml.transform.stream.*;
025:
026: import java.net.URL;
027:
028: import javax.naming.*;
029:
030: import javax.rmi.PortableRemoteObject;
031:
032: public class RemoteEJBServlet extends JAXMServlet implements ⤶
ReqRespListener {
033:
034:     /** Initializes the servlet.
035:      */
036:     public void init(ServletConfig config) throws ServletException {
037:         super.init(config);
038:
039:     }
040:
041:     /** Destroys the servlet.
042:      */
043:     public void destroy() {
044:
045:     }
046:
```

Listing 39.1   RemoteEJBServlet

```
047:
048:     /** Returns a short description of the servlet.
049:      */
050:     public String getServletInfo() {
051:         return "Example of a servlet accessing an EJB through the ⤵
remote interface.";
052:     }
053:
054:     /** This method receives the message via SOAP, gets a Local ⤵
EJB Home interface,
055:      *  creates the EJB, invokes the appropriate method on the ⤵
EJB, and sends
056:      *  the response in a SOAP message.
057:      */
058:     public SOAPMessage onMessage(SOAPMessage message) {
059:
060:         SOAPMessage respMessage = null;
061:
062:         try {
063:             //retrieve the number element from the message
064:             SOAPBody sentSB = message.getSOAPPart()    ⤵
.getEnvelope().getBody();
065:             Iterator it = sentSB.getChildElements();
066:             SOAPBodyElement sentSBE = (SOAPBodyElement)it.next();
067:             Iterator beIt = sentSBE.getChildElements();
068:             SOAPElement sentSE = (SOAPElement) beIt.next();
069:
070:             //get the text for the number element to put in response
071:             String value = sentSE.getValue();
072:
073:             Context ctx = new InitialContext();
074:
075:             Object obj = ctx.lookup("mySOAPHome");
076:
077:             SOAPHome obj = (SOAPHome) PortableRemoteObject.narrow ⤵
(obj, SOAPHome.class);
078:
079:             SOAPHandler soapHandler = soapHm.create();
080:
081:             String responseData = soapHandler.convert(value);
082:
083:              //create the response message
084:             respMessage = fac.createMessage();
085:             SOAPPart sp = respMessage.getSOAPPart();
086:             SOAPEnvelope env = sp.getEnvelope();
087:             SOAPBody sb = env.getBody();
088:             Name newBodyName = env.createName("response",
089:                     "return", "http://www.javapitfalls.org");
090:             SOAPBodyElement response =
```

Listing 39.1   *(continued)*

```
091:                  sb.addBodyElement(newBodyName);
092:
093:            //create the orderID element for confirmation
094:            Name thingName = env.createName("thing");
095:            SOAPElement newThing =
096:                    response.addChildElement(thingName);
097:            newThing.addTextNode(responseData);
098:
099:            respMessage.saveChanges();
100:
101:        } catch (SOAPException soapE) {
102:            // log this problem
103:            soapE.printStackTrace();
104:        }
105:
106:        return respMessage;
107:    }
108:
109: }
110:
```

Listing 39.1   *(continued)*

What is wrong with this approach? Actually, there is nothing explicitly wrong. Countless systems have been built that use this servlet-to-EJB paradigm. However, in this case, both the Web container and the EJB container are running in the same process (in this case the JBoss Application Server). Therefore, this is what happens:

1. The client calls a local stub.

2. That stub performs the necessary translations (marshalling) to make the Java objects suitable for network transport.

3. The skeleton receives the stub's transmission and converts everything back to Java objects.

4. The actual EJBObject is called, and it does all of its necessary magic (why you built it).

5. The response is transformed back into a network neutral format.

6. The skeleton returns the response.

7. The stub converts back into Java stuff.

This is typical RMI stuff, right? So what is the big deal? Well, in this case we are operating in the same process. No one would ever make RMI calls to interact with their local objects, so why would you do it in EJB? It used to be that you had to do it; the EJB 1.x specifications gave you no other option. This was based on a basic principle in distributed objects: Design things to be independent of their location.

Furthermore, let's not forget that the Web server and EJB server running in different processes is not that uncommon. As a matter of fact, it is very common to see Web containers running on entirely different machines. However, in this case, we have provided a SOAP interface to our EJBs. That it communicates like a Web server, in other words, over HTTP, is not really the point. We are essentially writing a protocol wrapper to our business objects. It makes little sense to write a protocol wrapper that communicates in an entirely different protocol when it doesn't have to do so.

NOTE All signs point to J2EE 1.4 containing the Web services protocols as an inherent part of J2EE. However, this shows that it is not required in order to use SOAP right now.

So how do you solve this problem? EJB 2.0 offers a solution: local interfaces. When you use a local interface, you can interact directly with the object. This avoids all the network-related issues. This is a remarkable timesaver when you consider just how much is dependent on the size and complexity of the objects.

Listing 39.2 shows the code that changes to use the local interface.

```
1:          //get the text for the number element to put in response
2:          String value = sentSE.getValue();
3:          Context ctx = new InitialContext();
4:          SOAPHome obj = (SOAPHome)ctx.lookup("mySOAPHome");
5:          SOAPHandler soapHandler = soapHm.create();
6:          String responseData = soapHandler.convert(value);
7:
```

Listing 39.2   LocalEJBServlet

That doesn't look much different than our previous example—because it isn't. In this case, I have only removed the narrowing of the Home object. I left the names of the other interfaces the same. Why? Because the real difference is in the back end. Listing 39.3 is an example of a remote home interface.

```
01: package org.javapitfalls;
02:
03: /**
04:  * This is an example of SOAPHome as a remote interface.
07:  */
08:
09: public interface SOAPHome extends javax.ejb.EJBHome
10: {
```

Listing 39.3   SOAPHome (remote) *(continued)*

```
11:
12:  /**
13:   * This method creates the SOAPHandler Object
16:   */
17:
18:  SOAPHandler create() throws java.rmi.RemoteException,
javax.ejb.CreateException;
19:
20: }
21:
```

Listing 39.3 *(continued)*

Listing 39.4 is the exact same thing as a local interface.

```
01: package org.javapitfalls;
02:
03: /**
04:  * This is an example of SOAPHome as a local interface.
07:  */
08:
09: public interface SOAPHome extends javax.ejb.EJBLocalHome
10: {
12:  /**
13:   * This method creates the SOAPHandler Object
16:   */
17:
18:  SOAPHandler create() throws javax.ejb.CreateException;
20: }
21:
```

Listing 39.4 SOAPHome (local)

Notice that this extends `EJBLocalHome` instead of `EJBHome` as in the remote case. Furthermore, notice how the methods in the local version do not throw `RemoteException`. This is because it is local. It won't have problems with remote access, because it won't be dealing with things that are remote.

But this isn't all. Let's examine the actual business interface and notice its differences. Listing 39.5 is an example of a remote `SOAPHandler` object.

```
01: package org.javapitfalls;
02:
03: /**
04:  * This is an example of SOAPHandler remote interface.
07:  */
08:
09: public interface SOAPHandler extends javax.ejb.EJBObject
10: {
11:
12:   /**
13:    * This method converts the parameter into the response
16:    */
17:
18:   String convert(String param) throws javax.rmi.RemoteException;
20: }
```

Listing 39.5 SOAPHandler (remote)

Listing 39.6 is the exact same thing as a local SOAPHandler object.

```
01: package org.javapitfalls;
02:
03: /**
04:  * This is an example of SOAPHandler local interface.
07:  */
08:
09: public interface SOAPHandler extends javax.ejb.EJBLocalObject
10: {
12:   /**
13:    * This method converts the parameter into the response
16:    */
17:
18:   String convert(String param);
20: }
```

Listing 39.6 SOAPHandler (local)

There is something important to understand about this configuration. Since the servlet and EJBs need to be run in the process space, they need to be able to have each other in the same context. To accomplish this, you should place any Web components that use the local interfaces in the same EAR (Enterprise ARchive) as the classes that implement them.

So, should you always use local interfaces? Not necessarily. There is really one major thing to consider: Are your Web container and EJB container running in the same process, or should they be? This all depends on your individual architecture, but here are some thoughts to consider:

- Do you need separate processes for the Web container and the EJB container? Most people believe that in order to load-balance the Web servers, they must be kept separate from the EJB servers. This is untrue; in fact, it is likely that clustering multiple "combined" application servers will provide just as good, if not better, results.

- Is the EJB container going to be a resource burden on the Web container, since they are running in the same process? If your architecture is light on EJBs and heavy on Web components, perhaps they should be refactored out of the equation. A Web tier solution may be best.

This example is done to illustrate a point about using local interfaces for Enterprise JavaBeans. The example itself is quite helpful, but it is sure to become moot with the release of J2EE 1.4. In this release, JAX-RPC will become another communication protocol for interacting with EJB containers, like RMI is right now. Also, JAXM will become another protocol for interacting with the Java Message Service. These enhancements will make the Web services protocols just another transparent mechanism for communicating with the Java 2 Enterprise Edition.

Item 40: Image Obsession

Java has been enormously successful on the server side, largely tracking with the rise of the Internet and distributed computing. This has given rise to many, many thin clients. One of the biggest issues in thin clients is trying to deliver more expressive user interfaces. This was the idea behind XWindows—a big, powerful machine generates user interface components for thin clients.

A classic example in Web interfaces is to dynamically generate images. We built a graphical reporting tool that generated images using the open-source JFreeChart package (http://www.object-refinery.com/jfreechart/) and the open-source Cewolf custom tag library (http://cewolf.sourceforge.net/).

Our application generates a pie chart showing the percentages of Web browser usage on this particular site. We developed this application on our Windows development boxes. Listing 40.1 is what it looks like both in code (simplified, see the Cewolf docs for more information) and on the screen.

```
01: <%@page import="java.util.*" %>
02: <%@page import="de.laures.cewolf.*" %>
03: <%@page import="com.jrefinery.data.*" %>
04:
```

Listing 40.1 Example code

```
05: <%@ taglib uri="http://cewolf.sourceforge.net/taglib/cewolf.tld" ⤴
prefix="cewolf" %>
06:
07: <%
08: class DatasetProducerImpl implements DatasetProducer {
09:     private Object obj;
10:
11:     public DatasetProducerImpl(Object obj) {
12:         this.obj = obj;
13:     }
14:
15:     public Object produceDataset(HashMap params) throws        ⤴
DatasetProduceException {
16:             return obj;
17:     }
18: }
19: %>
20:
21: <html>
22:     <head>
23:         <title>Browser Graph</title>
24:     </head>
25:
26: <body>
27: <%
28: try {
29:
30:     DefaultPieDataset pieData = new DefaultPieDataset();
31:     pieData.setValue("Internet Explorer", new Integer(23405));
32:     pieData.setValue("Netscape", new Integer(12313));
33:     pieData.setValue("Mozilla", new Integer(11202));
34:   pieData.setValue("Opera", new Integer(1333));
35:
36:     DatasetProducer pieProducer = new DatasetProducerImpl(pieData);
37:     pageContext.setAttribute("browserPie", pieProducer,           ⤴
PageContext.APPLICATION_SCOPE);
38:
39: %>
40:
41: <center>
42: <h1>Usage of Site by Browser</h1>
43: </center>
44: <p> 
45: <table border="0" cellpadding="2" align="center">
46: <tr>
47:     <td colspan="2">
48: <cewolf:chart
49:     id="browserPieChart"
50:     title="Browser Usage"
```

Listing 40.1 *(continued)*

```
51:        renderer="servlet/chart"
52:        width="400" height="300"
53:        type="pie"
54:        antialias="true">
55:        <cewolf:data>
56:            <cewolf:producer id="browserPie" />
57:        </cewolf:data>
58: </cewolf:chart>
59:        </td>
60: </tr>
61: </table>
62: <p>
63: <%
64:
65: } catch (Exception e) {
66:     e.printStackTrace();
67: }
68:
69: %>
70:
71: </body>
72: </html>
```

Listing 40.1   *(continued)*

Figure 40.1 shows our beautiful graph, easy to build and deploy. At this point, we start thinking that it cannot be this easy, so then we deploy our Web application on our production Solaris machine.

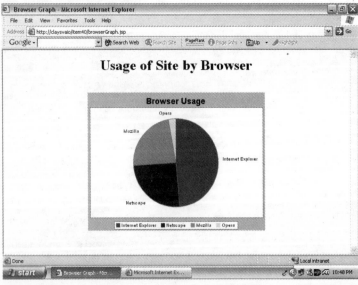

Figure 40.1   Rendered chart example (Windows).

Figure 40.2   Example (Solaris 8).

After bragging about our new graph tool and showing it off on our development boxes, our stomach turned when we saw what showed up on our deployment systems. Figure 40.2 shows the source of our nightmare.

What happened to the image? We ran the exact same code with the same configuration. When we examine the stack trace, we see the problem, shown in Listing 40.2 (abridged).

```
01: 2002-08-15 17:53:43 StandardWrapperValve[chart]: Servlet.service()
for servlet chart threw exception
02: javax.servlet.ServletException: Servlet execution threw an exception
03:   at org.apache.catalina.core.ApplicationFilterChain
.internalDoFilter(ApplicationFilterChain.java:269)
04:   at org.apache.catalina.core.ApplicationFilterChain.doFilter
(ApplicationFilterChain.java:193)
05:   at org.apache.catalina.core.StandardWrapperValve.invoke
(StandardWrapperValve.java:243)
06:   at org.apache.catalina.core.StandardPipeline.invokeNext
(StandardPipeline.java:566)
07: {...}
08:   at org.apache.catalina.connector.http.HttpProcessor.run
(HttpProcessor.java:1107)
09:   at java.lang.Thread.run(Thread.java:536)
10: ----- Root Cause -----
11: java.lang.NoClassDefFoundError: com.jrefinery.chart.AxisConstants
12:   at com.jrefinery.chart.ChartFactory.createPieChart(Unknown Source)
```

Listing 40.2   Stack trace *(continued)*

```
13:   at de.laures.cewolf.DefaultChartRenderer.getChartInstance        ⤵
(DefaultChartRenderer.java:61)
14:   at de.laures.cewolf.AbstractChartRenderer.renderChart            ⤵
(AbstractChartRenderer.java:99)
15:   at de.laures.cewolf.CewolfRenderer.renderChart(CewolfRenderer    ⤵
.java:85)
16:   at de.laures.cewolf.CewolfRenderer.doGet(CewolfRenderer.java:71)
17:   at javax.servlet.http.HttpServlet.service(HttpServlet.java:740)
18:   at javax.servlet.http.HttpServlet.service(HttpServlet.java:853)
19: {...}
20:
```

Listing 40.2   *(continued)*

We get a `NoClassDefFoundError`. We look to see if the class is not within the `CLASSPATH`. Searching through the JFreeChart JAR file, we find the named class, `AxisConstants`, is there. So we check to see if the jar is somehow not getting loaded. Searching through the Tomcat logs, we find the line that shows it mounts the jar just like the rest of the (working) JARs.

`NoClassDefFoundError` clearly doesn't make sense. After all, it means that the JVM cannot find the definition of a particular class, when, in fact, it can. Rather than continue to try to chase this inexplicable phenomenon, we follow the stack trace a bit further. It comes from rendering a pie chart in the `CewolfRenderer`. This causes us to think about it a little closer.

What has changed? The operating system has, but that isn't supposed to matter in Java! As it turns out, we have a small anomaly in how Windows and Unix handle their windowing environments. Windows, as the name implies, is tied to its windowing environment. However, Unix does not require a windowing environment and uses an X server to generate its user interface.

Actually, the heart of the problem has to do with the way the Abstract Windowing Toolkit (AWT) is implemented. The implementation expects to find an X server running when it is created, despite the fact that no user interface components are going to be used. This is relevant to our problem because certain classes out of the Java image classes use the AWT (e.g., `BufferedImage`).

So, there are a couple of solutions to this problem. First, attach a monitor and run the server as a logged-in user. (You should ignore any random images that pop up on the screen as you are working.) However, this is not a very elegant or useful solution.

The real solution depends on which version of the JDK you are using. If you are running on JDK 1.3 or earlier, you should download an X emulator. One you can download is called xvfb, which is at http://www.x.org.

However, JDK 1.4 comes with what is known as the "headless AWT." This allows the J2SE components to be run on the server side without an X server. To use this, you need to specify the following JVM option:

```
-Djava.awt.headless=true
```

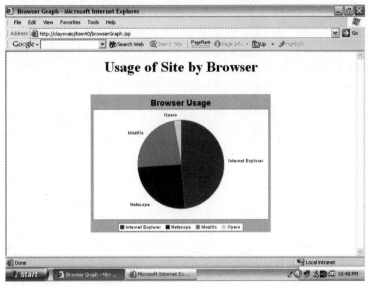

Figure 40.3 Working version.

Sun recommends if you are running a server-side application without any graphical user interface that you specify this option.

Figure 40.3 is the outcome of making this 24-character addition to our JVM invocation.

Item 41: The Problem with Multiple Concurrent Result Sets

Over the years, we've run into many situations where we have needed to write Java applications that have the capability of connecting to "any database." If there is a JDBC driver available for that database, this shouldn't be a problem. In those situations, we typically design our application, write the code, and initially test our application against one type of database. Requirements for the development of many applications beg the need for *query builders*—graphical user interfaces that allow users to click on a selection of tables and columns from the database, allowing them to create advanced queries. Of course, if you have created an application like this, you know that the `java.sql.DatabaseMetaData` class allows you to get column and table information from the database.

Before you build this query builder application, you need to write a simple method that will print this database information to the screen. Later, you will probably change this method to return a structure with all of the tables and columns of the database. Listing 41.1 shows a portion of your code, where you get the table information from the database and print out each table and column of the database.

```
01:    /**
02:     * this goes through the database and lists all the
03:     * tables and columns of the database.
04:     *
05:     * @throws exception
06:     */
07:   public void printMetaDataStuff(Connection conn) throws Exception
08:   {
09:       String[] tabletypes = {"TABLE"};
10:
11:       if (conn == null)
12:       {
13:           throw new Exception("Could not establish a connection!");
14:       }
15:
16:       DatabaseMetaData dmd  = conn.getMetaData();
17:
18:       ResultSet rs   = dmd.getTables(null,null,null,tabletypes);
19:
20:       if (rs == null)
21:       {
22:           throw new Exception("No metadata!");
23:       }
24:       while (rs.next())
25:        {
26:           String table = rs.getString("TABLE_NAME");
27:
28:           System.out.println("ResultSet 1: Got table " + table);
29:           ResultSet rs2  = dmd.getColumns(null,null,table,null);
30:
31:            if (rs2 == null)
32:            {
33:                throw new Exception ("No Metadata!");
34:            }
35:            while (rs2.next())
36:            {
37:                String col = rs2.getString("COLUMN_NAME");
38:                System.out.println("ResultSet2: Table " + table +
39:                                   " has column " + col);
40:            }
41:        }
42:   }
```

Listing 41.1   printMetaDataStuff( ) from BadResultSet.java

Initially, you test your code with one database, and it works fine. Many developers stop there and continue to build their application. However, just to be on the safe side, you decide to test this class against several databases running on different operating systems, including Microsoft Access, Microsoft SQL Server, MySQL, Sybase, and Oracle. Your class takes a database URL and driver class as an argument, builds a connection, and passes it to your `printMetaDataStuff()` function in Listing 41.1. You write a script that passes the JDBC URL and the driver class to the application, shown in Listing 41.2.

```
echo testing Access

java BadResultSet jdbc:odbc:TestAccessDB sun.jdbc.odbc.JdbcOdbcDriver

echo testing SQL Server
java BadResultSet jdbc:odbc:TestSQLServer sun.jdbc.odbc.JdbcOdbcDriver
testuser testpass

echo testing MySQL

java BadResultSet jdbc:mysql://testmachine:3306/metadotdb
org.gjt.mm.mysql.Driver testuser testpass

echo testing Sybase

java BadResultSet jdbc:sybase:Tds:testmachine:3000/TestDB
com.sybase.jdbc2.jdbc.SybDriver testuser testpass

echo testing ORACLE

java BadResultSet jdbc:oracle:thin:@testmachine:1521:dppo
oracle.jdbc.driver.OracleDriver testuser testpass
```

Listing 41.2 Script for testing

As you can see in Listing 41.2, you are testing this application against different databases using different drivers. The output is shown in Listing 41.3. As you can see, many of these databases (MS Access, MySQL, and Sybase) were able to run `printMetaDataStuff()` from Listing 41.1 with no problems. However, the SQL Server driver throws a `java.lang.SQLException`, saying that the "Connection is busy with the results of another hstmt." The Oracle database throws an ORA-1000 error, saying that you have exceeded your maximum open cursors. What happened?

```
testing Access

ResultSet 1: Got table EQP
ResultSet2: Table EQP has column ACQUIRED_CC
ResultSet2: Table EQP has column ACQUIRED_DATE
ResultSet2: Table EQP has column ACTIVITY
ResultSet 1: Got table EQP_AFLD
ResultSet2: Table EQP_AFLD has column ARRESTING_BARRIER
ResultSet2: Table EQP_AFLD has column ARRESTING_CABLE
ResultSet2: Table EQP_AFLD has column BAYS_QTY
...

testing SQL Server

ResultSet 1: Got table AuthorizedUsers
java.sql.SQLException: [Microsoft][ODBC SQL Server Driver]Connection is
busy with results for another hstmt
       at sun.jdbc.odbc.JdbcOdbc.createSQLException(JdbcOdbc.java:6031)
       at sun.jdbc.odbc.JdbcOdbc.standardError(JdbcOdbc.java:6188)
       at sun.jdbc.odbc.JdbcOdbc.SQLColumns(JdbcOdbc.java:2174)
       at sun.jdbc.odbc.JdbcOdbcDatabaseMetaData.getColumns
(JdbcOdbcDatabaseMetaData.java:2576)
       at BadResultSet.printMetaDataStuff(BadResultSet.java:92)
       at BadResultSet.main(BadResultSet.java:127)

testing MySQL

ResultSet 1: Got table addressbook
ResultSet2: Table addressbook has column ciid
ResultSet2: Table addressbook has column fname
ResultSet2: Table addressbook has column mname
ResultSet2: Table addressbook has column lname
ResultSet2: Table addressbook has column nname
ResultSet 1: Got table channel
ResultSet2: Table channel has column cid
ResultSet2: Table channel has column isa
ResultSet2: Table channel has column name
ResultSet2: Table channel has column description
--

testing Sybase

ResultSet 1: Got table PERSONNEL
ResultSet2: Table PERSONNEL has column PERSONNEL_ID
ResultSet2: Table PERSONNEL has column SOURCE_ID
ResultSet2: Table PERSONNEL has column PERSONNEL_NUMBER
```

Listing 41.3   Output of script

```
ResultSet 1: Got table UNIT_STATUS
ResultSet2: Table UNIT_STATUS has column UNIT_ID
ResultSet2: Table UNIT_STATUS has column STATUS_TIME
ResultSet2: Table UNIT_STATUS has column SOURCE_ID
...


testing ORACLE

ResultSet 1: Got table DR$CLASS
ResultSet2: Table DR$CLASS has column CLA_ID
ResultSet2: Table DR$CLASS has column CLA_NAME
ResultSet2: Table DR$CLASS has column CLA_DESC
ResultSet2: Table DR$CLASS has column CLA_SYSTEM
ResultSet 1: Got table DR$DELETE
ResultSet2: Table DR$DELETE has column DEL_IDX_ID
ResultSet2: Table DR$DELETE has column DEL_DOCID
ResultSet 1: Got table DR$INDEX
ResultSet2: Table DR$INDEX has column IDX_ID
ResultSet2: Table DR$INDEX has column IDX_OWNER#
ResultSet2: Table DR$INDEX has column IDX_NAME
java.sql.SQLException: ORA-01000: maximum open cursors exceeded
      at oracle.jdbc.dbaccess.DBError.throwSqlException(DBError.java:168)
      at oracle.jdbc.ttc7.TTIoer.processError(TTIoer.java:208)
      at oracle.jdbc.ttc7.Oopen.receive(Oopen.java:118)
      at oracle.jdbc.ttc7.TTC7Protocol.open(TTC7Protocol.java:466)
      at oracle.jdbc.driver.OracleStatement.<init>(OracleStatement.java:413)
      at oracle.jdbc.driver.OracleStatement.<init>(OracleStatement.java:432)
      at oracle.jdbc.driver.OraclePreparedStatement
.<init>(OraclePreparedStatement.java:182)
      at oracle.jdbc.driver.OraclePreparedStatement
.<init>(OraclePreparedStatement.java:165)
      at oracle.jdbc.driver.OracleConnection.privatePrepareStatement
(OracleConnection.java:604)
      at oracle.jdbc.driver.OracleConnection.prepareStatement
(OracleConnection.java:485)
      at oracle.jdbc.OracleDatabaseMetaData.getColumns
(OracleDatabaseMetaData.java:2533)
        at BadResultSet.printMetaDataStuff(BadResultSet.java:92)
        at BadResultSet.main(BadResultSet.java:127)
```

Listing 41.3   *(continued)*

Why did some of the databases run through your code without any problems? Why did your queries to the other databases throw exceptions? It revolves around the use of multiple concurrent result sets. Some databases, depending on their configurations, can handle having more than one result set open at once. From your output in Listing 41.3, you can see that while SQL Server driver threw an exception immediately when the getColumns() method was called on the DatabaseMetaData object, the Oracle database itself continued to run for a while until its maximum cursors threshold was exceeded.

To write code that is portable across databases, you unfortunately shouldn't make assumptions about what databases can handle having multiple ResultSet objects open at a time. Lucky for you, you went through this testing process by writing the script in Listing 41.2 before you wrote your main query builder application. Other developers could have tested it against one database and deployed the application, only to discover that the application couldn't be ported to a few databases.

How can we solve this problem? A simple change in our design will work. Listing 41.4 shows our new printMetaDataStuff() method that uses an initial ResultSet object to get the table names of the database in line 13 and puts each database table in a LinkedList object in lines 21 to 23. Finally, the initial result set is closed in line 26. In lines 30 to 45, we loop through the linked list of table names that we created, opening up one ResultSet object at a time and printing out the column names for each table.

```
01:    public void printMetaDataStuff() throws Exception
02:    {
03:        LinkedList ll = new LinkedList();
04:        String[] tabletypes = {"TABLE"};
05:
06:        if (conn == null)
07:        {
08:            throw new Exception("Could not establish a connection!");
09:        }
10:
11:        DatabaseMetaData dmd  = conn.getMetaData();
12:
13:        ResultSet rs   = dmd.getTables(null,null,null,tabletypes);
14:
15:        if (rs == null)
16:        {
17:            throw new Exception("No metadata!");
18:        }
19:        while (rs.next())
20:        {
21:            String table = rs.getString("TABLE_NAME");
22:            ll.add(table);
23:            System.out.println("ResultSet 1: Got table " + table);
24:
25:        }
26:        rs.close();
27:
28:        ListIterator li = ll.listIterator(0);
29:
```

Listing 41.4 A better printMetaDataStuff() method

```
30:          while (li.hasNext())
31:          {
32:              String table = li.next().toString();
33:              ResultSet rs2  = dmd.getColumns(null,null,table,null);
34:
35:              if (rs2 == null)
36:              {
37:                  throw new Exception ("No Metadata!");
38:              }
39:              while (rs2.next())
40:              {
41:                  String col = rs2.getString("COLUMN_NAME");
42:                  System.out.println("ResultSet2: Table " + table +
43:                                     " has column " + col);
44:              }
45:              rs2.close();
46:          }
47:      }
```

Listing 41.4　*(continued)*

After you replace your `printMetaDataStuff()` method, you run the same script shown in Listing 41.2. Now your connection to each database prints out all tables and columns without any errors, and you are ready to create your query builder application.

This pitfall showed how important it is to be aware of the problem of using more than one `ResultSet` at once. While many JDBC drivers will support the use of multiple concurrent `ResultSet` objects, many will not. Many databases will exceed the number of maximum open cursors. To achieve maximum portability, rethink your designs so that you will only have one open at a time.

Item 42: Generating Primary Keys for EJB

In a distributed environment, it is imperative to be able to distinguish different instances of objects. With the distributed model of Enterprise JavaBeans, it is important to be able to distinguish instances of entity beans from each other. A common trap that many EJB developers fall into relates to the methods of generating primary keys for entity beans. This item provides an example scenario, gives several examples of how an EJB developer could fall into such a trap, and provides solutions to the problem.

A Simple Scenario

A large video store chain wants to provide national access to accounts throughout the United States. When a customer brings her identity card to the store, the store would like to look up account information and allow the customer to check out videos—no matter where the customer started the account. It was decided early on that the J2EE model would provide a flexible solution for this video chain. In a high-level design phase, they decided that their JSP would eventually talk to a session bean called `SignOnVideoBean`, which would create an entity bean called `VideoUser`, as shown in Figure 42.1. The question is this: How should the primary key for `VideoUser` be created? We will look at many approaches and discuss pitfalls that lie in each solution.

A "Client Control" Approach

In many small systems, it is commonplace to have the client application (or sometimes the user) generate a unique identifier that represents a new user. An example of this could be an application where a user chooses a user identifier (userid) for access into a portal. In these types of applications, a servlet or JSP from the Web tier initiates a transaction that eventually triggers the creation of an entity bean, which uses the passed-in user identifier as its primary key. This is a valid practice, and depending on the back-end database constraints for primary keys, strings that are guaranteed to be unique (such as email addresses) can be used as the unique identifiers. If there is a collision, the EJB will throw a `javax.ejb.CreateException`. The difficulty is finding a recipe for the creation of these primary keys—throwing and passing exceptions over a network can be bandwidth costly and pretty annoying.

To prevent primary key collisions, they chose a recipe for creating a primary key in such a way that the date, time, store number, clerk ID, and customer name compose the primary key. For example, if "Matt Van Wie" were to start an account at the second Mechanicsville, Virginia, branch of the video store on March 1, 2003, at 5:30 P.M., and the clerk was "Todd Tarkington," the primary key would be "MattVanWie-03-01-2003-530pm-MechanicsvilleVA2-ToddTarkington". This approach is shown in Figure 42.2.

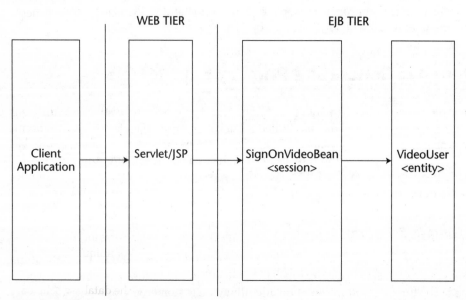

Figure 42.1   Creating video user accounts.

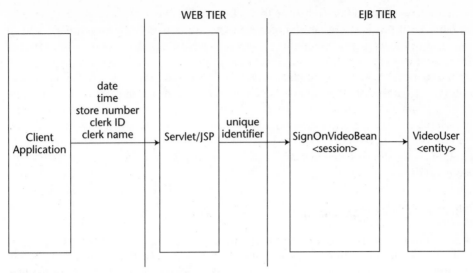

Figure 42.2   Client control solution.

In Figure 42.2, the client application passes the system date, time, store number, clerk identifier, clerk ID, and client name to the servlet/jsp, which creates the unique identifier and creates a reference to `SignOnVideoBean`, which is the session bean that is used to access customer information and create users. `SignOnVideoBean` creates a `VideoUser` entity bean, which is the entity bean that represents the video store customer. This particular approach has many problems that could lead to collisions and chaos:

- For owner names and clerk names that are commonplace, such as "Steve Jones" and "Kevin Smith," there is potential for primary key collisions.

- The solution assumes that a clerk will be only be logged in to the system at one location. If, in the scenario, Todd is the manager and logs in to all of the client workstations at the beginning of the day, this could increase the possibility of name collisions.

- This solution assumes that all client workstations have a way to synchronize date and time. A company policy must be written to specify how time synchronization must work on each store basis. Even if the Web container in this solution generated the system date and time, it is possible that many Web containers at remote locations may be communicating with the EJB tier, and time there must be synchronized.

- The solution assumes that each branch of the video store has a unique name. This requires the assignment of unique store names at a central location, and when new stores are added and removed, just the control of unique store names causes much management overhead.

- The format of the primary key identifier is dependent on the database schema, making one more constraint between the client/Web tier and the EJB tier.

This scenario should demonstrate that allowing the client application to choose the primary key from a certain "recipe" can cause an administrative nightmare. For one, it puts more of a burden on the logic of the client and end users. Second, the burden for creating and enforcing policy that fits into the primary "recipe" will put a huge burden on the manager of the system. Finally, each J2EE system may have a large number of entity beans, and even if you have a great recipe for generating primary keys for one entity bean, you will probably run out of ideas. This is something that may work great for username account generation on a Web site, but you will eventually find that you will need a solution on the server side.

ASSESSMENT: This approach can become unmanageable and burdensome, and it is not recommended.

The Singleton Approach

After the software designers for the video store applications decided that the "Client Control" solution was too unmanageable, they decided that the use of the Singleton design pattern (discussed in Item 15) could be helpful. They decided to create a Singleton that implements a counter, so that it would be the central place to generate primary keys. The team made a simple Singleton called `UIDSingleton`, with a synchronized `getNextKey()` method to generate the key, shown in Figure 42.3.

Satisfied that this would solve the EJB primary key problem, the solution was deployed. Unfortunately, what they didn't understand is that the use of "pure Singletons" in J2EE is not recommended. A Singleton ensures that there is one instance of a class per virtual machine. With most J2EE servers, there are multiple VMs involved. As a result, the result is primary key chaos, resulting in primary key collisions—and one very flawed system.

ASSESSMENT: Don't do it.

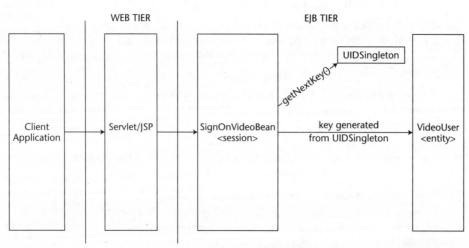

Figure 42.3 Attempting to use a Singleton for PK generation.

The Networked Singleton Approach

Convinced that they were on the right track with the Singleton approach, the team decides to ensure that there is one Singleton for the J2EE system by giving it a network identifier. In this approach, the software developers decided to create a Singleton that is callable via RMI and found by using JNDI. This Singleton implements a synchronized counter and ensures that there are no primary key collisions.

Satisfied that this solution was better than the earlier solution, the software team quickly implemented it. This was easy because each entity bean calls it via RMI and calls `getNextKey()`. In functionality testing, the system worked wonderfully. When it was load-tested with thousands of users, however, the system slowed to a crawl. What happened?

The solution here—and the problem—revolves around the nature of a Singleton. Because a unique network identifier ensures that there is a single object that generates primary keys, this is also a single point of failure. Every entity bean in the system must make a JNDI lookup and then must call the Singleton over the network. While this may work in small-scale solutions, this approach will not scale.

ASSESSMENT: It works, but performance will not scale on large projects.

An Application Server-Specific Approach

At this point, the developers writing the video store application notice that their J2EE application server provides an easy solution to the entity bean/primary key problem. It is a proprietary solution, but it seems to work great. The team develops the entire application, and it works beautifully. However, when it is mandated that they need to change application servers, the team is in trouble. Their entire video store application is now tied to their app server vendor, and it will take a long time to rewrite everything.

In many cases, application servers provide a simple solution to create primary keys for your entity beans. A danger here is nonportability. When you tie your solution to a particular application server with features like these, your solution will undoubtedly work great. Unfortunately, porting your J2EE application to other application servers will be a real headache. Keep in mind that when you go down this route, you may be stuck with the app server you use.

ASSESSMENT: May work great, but at what cost?

Database Autogeneration Approaches

As the designers of the video store solution research new approaches, they decide to use the autogeneration facilities that their chosen database vendor provides. The database vendor supports a counter for the primary key that is incremented every time a new record is created. This is powerful because it provides a centralized mechanism for generating primary keys, guaranteeing uniqueness. In the solution, the `VideoUser` entity bean manages its own persistence. A potential problem here is the nonportability of this solution. If there is a need to switch to another database vendor that does not support autogeneration, the application will be in trouble. Luckily, many database vendors do support autogeneration, so developers may consider this to be a minor concern.

Of the approaches we've discussed so far, this seems to have the most merit. In the past, it has been difficult to make SQL calls to get autogenerated IDs in a nonproprietary way. It was also a challenge to get the autogenerated key right after the insert, because there was not a way to retrieve the generated key from the resulting `Result-Set`. Luckily, with the release of JDK 1.4, an inserted row can return the generated key using the `getGeneratedKeys()` method in `java.sql.Statement`, as can be seen in the code segment below.

```
int primkey = 0;
Statement s = conn.prepareStatement();

s.execute("INSERT INTO VIDEOUSERS" +
   "(name,phone,address,creditcard)" +
   "VALUES ('Matt Van Wie', '555-9509', '91 Habib Ave',
     '208220902033XXXX')",
    Statement.RETURN_GENERATED_KEYS);
ResultSet rs = s.getGeneratedKeys();
if (rs.next())
{
  primkey = rs.getInt(1);
}
```

Many developers using an earlier version of the JDK (or JDBC 2.0 or earlier drivers) that cannot take advantage of this feature use stored procedures in SQL that can be called from Java with the `CallableStatement` interface. The "Stored Procedures for Autogenerated Keys" EJB Design Pattern from Floyd Marinescu's book, *EJB Design Patterns*, provides such a solution that does an insert and returns the autogenerated key.[4]

ASSESSMENT: This is a good solution. With the release of JDK 1.4 and the ability to get generated keys returned from the `java.sql.Statement` *interface, this provides a sound mechanism for solving the EJB primary key problem.*

Other Approaches

It is important to note that *EJB Design Patterns* (Marinescu, 2002), discussed in the previous section, provides a few design patterns to solve this problem. One worth mentioning is a Universally Unique Identifier (UUID) pattern for EJB, which is a database-independent server-side algorithm for generating primary keys. Another pattern, called Sequence Blocks, creates primary keys with fewer database accesses, using a combination of an entity bean that serves as a counter and a stateless session bean that caches many primary keys from the entity bean at a time.

[4] Marinescu, Floyd. *EJB Design Patterns*. John Wiley & Sons, 2002.

ASSESSMENT: *These are good design patterns for solving the problem and are described in detail in the book. You can also check out discussions on this topic at* http://www.theserverside .com/.

There are many traps that a J2EE architect can fall into when attempting to generate unique identifiers for primary keys. There are also many approaches to solving this problem. This pitfall showed several approaches and provided assessments for each. By avoiding some of the traps discussed in this pitfall item, you will save yourself time and headaches.

Item 43: The Stateful Stateless Session Bean

A developer approached me the other day with an interesting problem. He had an existing API that he wanted to use (in a bean) that builds an index once and then provides search access to it. It seems a pretty simple idea in objected-oriented parlance. There is an object with a member variable, the index, which is built at initialization, and then methods that provide access to it (in this case, search). Figure 43.1 is a simplified example of what the class would look like.

There was concern about how to build this. This developer had some experience with EJB and understood the basic concepts. There are three types of Enterprise Java Beans: session beans, entity beans, and message-driven beans. In addition, there are two flavors of session beans: stateful and stateless. The idea is that stateful session beans maintain their state across invocations, and stateless session beans do not. Entity beans provide real-time persistence of business objects.

The developer had developed EJBs prior to this, but his work had been confined to new development—that is, from whole cloth—and dealt with basic problems. This was the first time where he was trying to use something else in the EJB paradigm.

To examine this dilemma, we reviewed the different options.

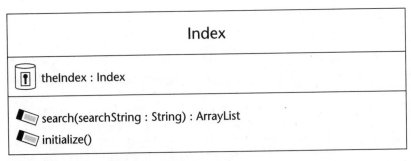

Figure 43.1   The index class diagram.

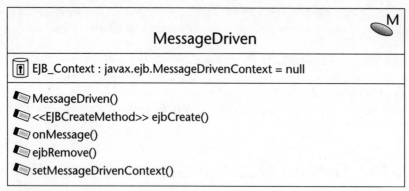

Figure 43.2   The MessageDriven EJB class diagram.

Message-Driven Beans

The container creates message-driven beans to handle the receipt of an asynchronous message. Figure 43.2 shows a message-driven EJB called MessageDriven. Notice that there are no interfaces from which client applications can directly invoke the bean. This means that the only access to this bean would be to send a message to the queue that this message-driven bean would handle. When that happens, the container calls the onMessage() method. All of the business logic would be contained within that onMessage() method.

This is clearly problematic for two reasons. First, reinitializing the index on every invocation is completely inconsistent with our purposes (a shared instance). Second, the means of communicating with our EJB is not supposed to be asynchronous. So, clearly this option was not seriously considered, but for the sake of completeness, we had to look at it.

Entity Bean

Next, we considered using an entity bean. Thinking about it, we realized that the index could be considered a persistent business object. Figure 43.3 shows the Entity EJB class diagram.

Notice that the EntityHome interface contains the pertinent create() and findByPrimaryKey() methods. The remote interface, Entity, has the search() method within it. Notice that all of the clients would have to try the findByPrimaryKey() method to see if the index was created, and if not, create it. Once the reference has been grabbed, the client could call the search() method.

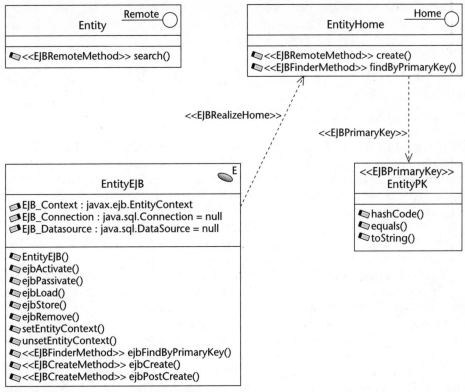

Figure 43.3   The Entity EJB class diagram.

Seems to be a good idea, right? Well, this ignores the fact that entity beans are notoriously slow and it is considered bad practice to interact with them directly, instead of referencing them through session beans (known commonly as the Session Façade pattern). Of course, even if using the Session Façade, this is a classic example of using a sledgehammer to drive a tack—that is, overkill. It could be counterproductive in terms of the additional processing time required to maintain the index in persistence and it could cost more time than re-creating the index on each invocation. After all, the purpose of the entity bean is to ensure that the object survives system failure. Also, if the system fails, then the index can be re-created upon reinitialization of the system. Since we are now persisting this object, we will need to have a methodology to propagate changes to the index so that it does not become a permanently configured instance. This requires additional functionality to handle a case that is not really a requirement for this problem (persistence).

Furthermore, writing the persistence code for something that does not map very congruently with a database (an object) can be a really big pain. Even if the effort is not as bad as it appears, it is still more than is necessary.

Therefore, we saw some real drawbacks in using the entity bean solution. So we decided to review further ideas, which brought us to session beans.

Stateful Session Bean

The stateful session bean provides an interesting alternative. The stateful session bean maintains state across client invocations but does not have the performance overhead of attempting to maintain persistence to survive system crashes. If the system crashes, then the state is lost and must be reestablished.

Figure 43.4 is the class diagram for the stateful session bean, called Stateful. The diagram shows the remote and home interfaces for the stateful session bean. Notice the `create()` method and the requisite index object `theIndex`. Also, the remote interface contains the `search()` method for searching the index.

However, the purpose of the stateful session bean is to maintain the conversation state between the client and server across invocation, essentially tracking the interaction. As such, this means that there is a separate context for each client conversation. This in turn means that every client would create its own index object at the beginning of interaction. Then the client would invoke the search method, and the interaction would end. This is not a shared instance, as the performance hit from initialization comes with each client.

So, this method would not work for us. This left us with one option left for an EJB solution. The stateless session bean seemed like the least likely solution, because the name implies that it lacks state. Or does it?

Stateless Session Bean

By process of elimination, we were left with the stateless session bean approach. The stateless session bean does not track any context between requests. The practical use is to allow the EJB container to provide a highly scalable solution to handling client requests. The container creates a pool of beans to handle the number of requests being received by the container.

The key concept is that the container can assign a stateless session bean to handle any client request, without guaranteeing that the next request by the same client will get the same bean. This allows for much more efficient resource allocation.

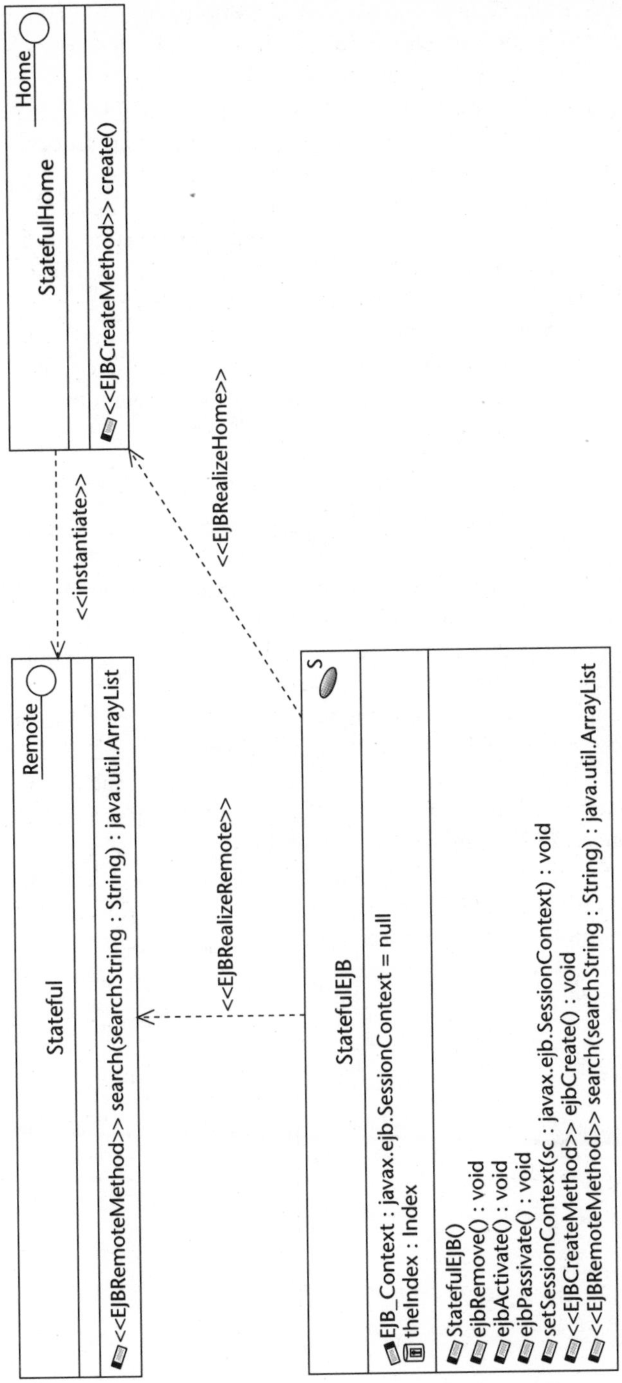

Figure 43.4 The Stateful EJB class diagram.

Frequently overlooked in this scenario is that a stateless session bean can contain member variables that are independent of the client request. Figure 43.5 is a class diagram of a stateless session diagram, called Stateless.

This shows the member variable called `theIndex`, which is populated at initialization when the `create()` method is called on the home interface. After that, requests can be executed by calling the `search()` method on the remote interface.

But the obvious question arises. Isn't every client calling the `create()` method? If so, doesn't this give us the same problem? Actually, this is a common misconception. Because EJB relies on indirection through the container, frequently there is confusion with regard to what a given method on the EJB home and remote interfaces actually does before it gets to the EJB implementation. In fact, the call to `create()` doesn't necessarily mean that the EJB container will create a new stateless session bean. It probably will not, unless this request actually causes the container implementation to determine that it is necessary to create another bean.

This raises an interesting point, though. There is no way to predict or determine how many stateless session beans will be created. Any bean using the member variables needs to take this into account in its design. This becomes even more critical when the container uses clustering.

This means that if we are trying to create a Singleton, or any pattern that demands a resource exists once and only once, this method cannot be used safely.

However, the Singleton pattern and other resource pooling patterns are generally used to ensure the number of instances do not grow out of control. That design goal is achieved implicitly by the design of stateless session beans. They use resource-pooling algorithms to determine the number of session beans that should exist.

Note that this example is not a database connection member variable. In fact, there are certain connection pools that are specified in the EJB 2.0 specification. Actually, it is a called a *resource manager connection factory*, and it entails more than just pooling (deployment, authentication). However, bean developers are required to use the standard ones for JDBC, JMS, JavaMail, and HTTP connections. The container developers are required to provide implementations of these factories.

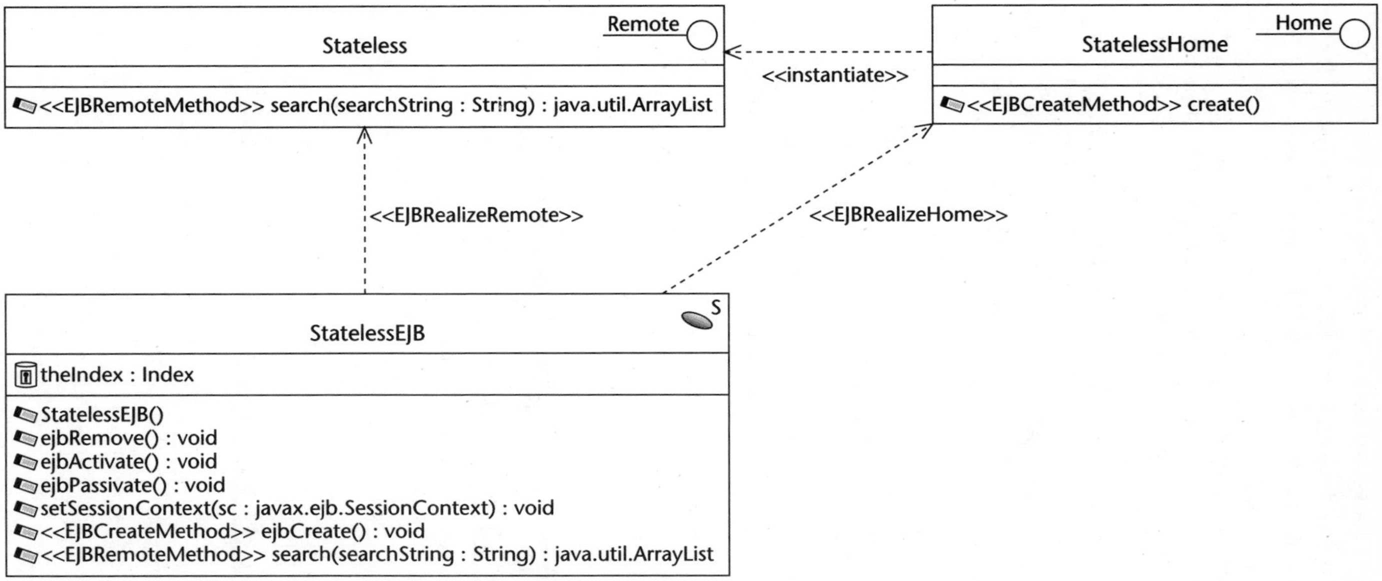

StatelessHome

<u>Home</u> ○

🖋 <<EJBCreateMethod>> create()

<<instantiate>>

<<EJBRealizeHome>>

Stateless

<u>Remote</u> ○

🖋 <<EJBRemoteMethod>> search(searchString : String) : java.util.ArrayList

<<EJBRealizeRemote>>

StatelessEJB

S

🔲 theIndex : Index

🖋 StatelessEJB()
🖋 ejbRemove() : void
🖋 ejbActivate() : void
🖋 ejbPassivate() : void
🖋 setSessionContext(sc : javax.ejb.SessionContext) : void
🖋 <<EJBCreateMethod>> ejbCreate() : void
🖋 <<EJBRemoteMethod>> search(searchString : String) : java.util.ArrayList

Figure 43.5   The Stateless EJB class diagram.

> **NOTE** These resource manager connection factory objects are part of the
> movement to the J2EE Connector Architecture, thus fulfilling the third piece of the
> J2EE paradigm (connectors, along with the current containers and components).

A subtlety in the EJB session bean specification is often overlooked. A large number of developers believe that stateless session beans can maintain no state information at all. This causes confusion on how to maintain instance information that is neutral to any particular request.

This pitfall explored how this misunderstanding can lead the developer into a real bind. By looking at how to solve this particular issue, the developer can gain insight on how each of the beans work behind the scenes and can gain a better appreciation of what is really happening in the container, since it serves as the intermediary in all EJB development.

Item 44: The Unprepared PreparedStatement

JDBC is one of the most popular APIs in the Java platform. Its power and ease of use combined with its easy integration in the Java Web application APIs has caused a proliferation of database-driven Web applications. The most popular of these Web applications is the classic HTML form driving a SQL query to present the data back to the user in HTML. Figure 44.1 is an example of one such Web application. Figure 44.2 shows the response.

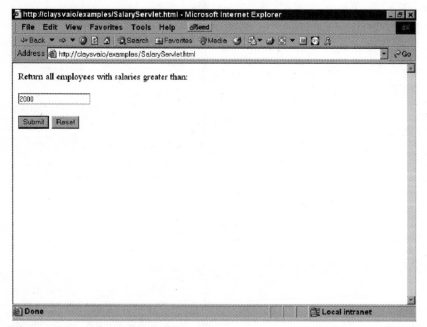

Figure 44.1   Salary HTML form.

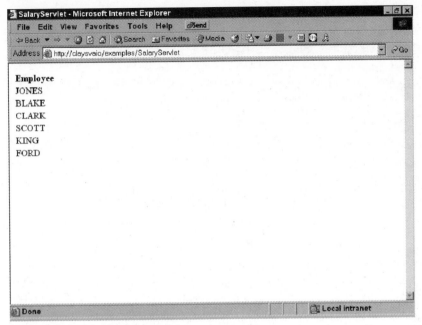

Figure 44.2   HTML form results.

As we look at the code for this example, there are a few things to note. First, it is a very simplified example meant to show all the pieces together in one class. Second, this is an example of a servlet running in the Tomcat servlet container, connecting to an Oracle database. Listing 44.1 shows the code of the class.

```
01: import javax.servlet.*;
02: import javax.servlet.http.*;
03: import java.io.*;
04: import java.util.*;
05: import java.sql.*;
06:
07: public class SalaryServlet extends HttpServlet {
08:
09: Connection connection;
11:
12:   private static final String CONTENT_TYPE = "text/html";
13:
14:   public void init(ServletConfig config) throws ServletException {
15:     super.init(config);
16:
17:     // Database config information
```

Listing 44.1   SalaryServlet *(continued)*

```
18:      String driver = "oracle.jdbc.driver.OracleDriver";
19:      String url = "jdbc:oracle:thin:@joemama:1521:ORACLE";
20:      String username = "scott";
21:      String password = "tiger";
22:
23:      // Establish connection to database
24:      try {
25:        Class.forName(driver);
26:        connection =
27:          DriverManager.getConnection(url, username, password);
28:
29:      } catch(ClassNotFoundException cnfe) {
30:        System.err.println("Error loading driver: " + cnfe);
31:
32:      } catch(SQLException sqle) {
33:          sqle.printStackTrace();
34:
35:      }
36:    }
37:    /**Process the HTTP Post request*/
38:    public void doPost(HttpServletRequest request,
HttpServletResponse response) throws ServletException, IOException {
39:      response.setContentType(CONTENT_TYPE);
40:
41:      String salary = request.getParameter("salary");
42:
43:      String queryFormat =
44:        "SELECT ename FROM emp WHERE sal > ";
45:
46:      try {
47:
48:      Statement statement = connection.createStatement();
49:
50:      ResultSet results =
51:          statement.executeQuery(queryFormat + salary);
52:
53:      PrintWriter out = response.getWriter();
54:      out.println("<html>");
55:      out.println("<head><title>SalaryServlet</title></head>");
56:      out.println("<body>");
57:      out.println("<table>");
58:      out.println("<tr>");
59:      out.println("<td><b>Employee</b></td></tr>");
60:
61:      while (results.next()) {
62:        out.println("<tr>");
63:        out.println("<td>");
64:        out.println(results.getString(1));
```

Listing 44.1   *(continued)*

```
65:        out.println("</td>");
66:        out.println("</tr>");
67:      }
68:
69:    out.println("</table>");
70:    out.println("</body></html>");
72:    } catch ( SQLException sqle ) {
74:      sqle.printStackTrace();
76:    }
77:
78:  }
79:  /**Clean up resources*/
80:  public void destroy() {
82:    connection.close();
84:  }
85: }
86:
```

Listing 44.1 *(continued)*

Notice that the init() method handles all of the database connection issues. Keep in mind that if this were going to be a production servlet, the connection handling and pooling would be delegated to another class (possibly another servlet). The doPost() method handles the building and execution of a JDBC statement from the connection, as well as the parsing of the resulting result set into HTML. Once again, best practice would cause this handling and presentation to be delegated elsewhere (usually a JSP), rather than building all of these out.println() statements to render the HTML.

This method is the most simplistic, but it clearly lacks efficiency. Essentially, a new String is constructed each time the user makes a request with the parameter appended to that String. What about precompiling the query so that only the parameter must be passed into the query? JDBC provides a method to do this, called the PreparedStatement. Listing 44.2 gives an example of the doPost() method rewritten to use a PreparedStatement.

```
01: public void doPost
02: (HttpServletRequest request, HttpServletResponse response)
03: throws ServletException, IOException {
04:     response.setContentType(CONTENT_TYPE);
05:
06:     String salary = request.getParameter("salary");
07:
08:     try {
09:
10:     PreparedStatement statement
```

Listing 44.2 Using prepared statements *(continued)*

```
11:        = connection.prepareStatement("SELECT ename FROM emp WHERE
sal > ?");
12:
13:      statement.setFloat(1, Float.parseFloat(salary));
14:
15:      ResultSet results =
16:          statement.executeQuery();
17:
// ... remaining code Identical to Listing 44.1 ...
```

Listing 44.2   *(continued)*

This example shows precompiling the statement and accepting parameters instead of any string. This is helpful for controlling data types and escape sequences. For example, calling `setDate()` or `setString()` handles the appropriate escape characters for the specific database being used, and it also prevents mismatching types—like specifying a `String` for a long field.

However, while this is a common practice among many developers, the `Prepared-Statement` is not reused. This means that the statement is recompiled each time; thus, no advantage is seen in the precompiling, aside from data typing. So, the `Prepared-Statement` should persist between invocations to receive the most effective and efficient results. Listing 44.3 is an example of the servlet rewritten to reuse the `PreparedStatement`.

```
01: import javax.servlet.*;
02: import javax.servlet.http.*;
03: import java.io.*;
04: import java.util.*;
05: import java.sql.*;
06:
07: public class SalaryServlet extends HttpServlet {
08:
09:   Connection connection; // Shouldn't be member variable under
normal conditions.
10:   PreparedStatement statement;
11:
12:   private static final String CONTENT_TYPE = "text/html";
13:
14:   public void init(ServletConfig config) throws ServletException {
15:     super.init(config);
16:
17:     // Database config information
18:     String driver = "oracle.jdbc.driver.OracleDriver";
19:     String url = "jdbc:oracle:thin:@joemama:1521:ORACLE";
```

Listing 44.3   Best use of prepared statements

```
20:     String username = "scott";
21:     String password = "tiger";
22:
23:     // Establish connection to database
24:     try {
25:       Class.forName(driver);
26:       connection =
27:         DriverManager.getConnection(url, username, password);
28:
29:       PreparedStatement statement
30:         = connection.prepareStatement("SELECT ename FROM emp ↵
WHERE sal > ?");
31:
32:     } catch(ClassNotFoundException cnfe) {
33:       System.err.println("Error loading driver: " + cnfe);
34:
35:     } catch(SQLException sqle) {
36:         sqle.printStackTrace();
37:
38:     }
39:   }
40:   /**Process the HTTP Post request*/
41:   public void doPost(HttpServletRequest request,                  ↵
HttpServletResponse response) throws ServletException, IOException {
42:     response.setContentType(CONTENT_TYPE);
43:
44:     String salary = request.getParameter("salary");
45:
46:     try {
47:
48:     statement.setFloat(1, Float.parseFloat(salary));
49:
50:     ResultSet results =
51:         statement.executeQuery();
52:
// ... remaining code Identical to listing 44.1 ...
85: }
86:
```

Listing 44.3   *(continued)*

Notice in this example that the parameter is set and the PreparedStatement is executed. This allows the reuse of the PreparedStatement between requests to the servlet. This improves the responsiveness, since it does not require the repetitive and time-consuming step of recompiling the statement on every invocation of the servlet.

It seems logical that there would be a performance improvement in reusing rather than recompiling statements. Testing was conducted to determine how much better the reuse option was. The three previously mentioned scenarios were tested. All used an Oracle database over a local area network. A test class was built to connect to the database and sequentially call a method representing each scenario, using the same connection for each. The same query was executed 100 times using each methodology. Here is the output of the tester class:

```
Executing prepared statement 100 times took 0.791 seconds.
Executing raw query 100 times took 1.472 seconds.
Executing repeated prepared statements 100 times took 1.622 seconds.
```

This class was executed several times with very similar results. Notice two things: First, the reused prepared statement was approximately 40 to 50 percent faster than the raw query statement, and second, the repeated compiling of prepared statements actually gave about a 10 percent performance hit.

This example shows a classic pitfall in the use of JDBC. When building desktop applications or when in the development phase of Web and enterprise applications, many developers fail to notice the performance hit that comes from not effectively using the PreparedStatement. A 50 percent hit in response time can get very significant in Web applications when loads can go up tremendously without much notice.

Item 45: Take a Dip in the Resource Pool

Most of the time, an "interactive Web site" is really a controlled chaos of Web applications that gradually evolve into a common purpose. Most organizations come up with an idea that "we can put these applications on the Web," and they usually do. Depending on the skill level of the development organization, various technologies are used to "Web-enable" their application.

This phenomenon is not limited to the spread of Web application platforms available—PHP, Cold Fusion, ASP, and so on. This occurs within Java also. The power of servlets, the ease of JSP, and the reuse of JSP tag libraries have caused a lot of developers to use a wide variety of techniques to Web-enable applications in Java.

Here are a few common ways that Web developers handle database connections. The first is to create a simple class to abstract the DB from the rest of the code, as Listing 45.1 demonstrates.

```
01: package org.javapitfalls;
02:
03: import java.io.*;
04: import java.net.*;
05: import java.sql.*;
06: import java.util.*;
07:
08: public class DbAbstract implements java.io.Serializable {
09:
10:    private Connection connection;
```

Listing 45.1   DBAbstract.java

```
11:    private Statement statement;
12:
13:    public DbAbstract ()
14:        throws ClassNotFoundException, SQLException
15:    {
16:
17:      String driverName = "";
18:      String className = "";
19:      String user = "";
20:      String pass = "";
21:
22:    Properties resource = new Properties();
23:    // Obtain a resource bundle that will allow use to get the
24:    // appropriate configurations for the server.
25:    try
26:    {
27:      URL url =
this.getClass().getClassLoader().getResource("db.properties");
28:        resource.load( new FileInputStream(url.getFile()) );
29:        // Get properties
30:        driverName = resource.getProperty("driverName");
31:        className = resource.getProperty("className");
32:        user = resource.getProperty("user");
33:        pass = resource.getProperty("pass");
34:        System.out.println("Using parameters from the db.properties
file for Database.");
35:        } catch (Exception e) {
36:          System.out.println("ERROR: Couldn't load db.properties."
+ e.toString());
37:        }
38:
39:        Class.forName(className);
40:        connection = DriverManager.getConnection(driverName,user, pass);
41:
42:        connection.setAutoCommit(false);
43:
44:        statement = connection.createStatement();
45:    }
46:
47:    public void executeUpdate(String sqlCommand)
48:      throws SQLException
49:    {
50:      statement.executeUpdate(sqlCommand);
51:    }
52:
53:    public ResultSet executeQuery(String sqlCommand)
54:      throws SQLException
55:    {
56:      return statement.executeQuery(sqlCommand);
```

Listing 45.1   *(continued)*

```
57:    }
58:
59:    public void commit() throws SQLException
60:    {
61:      connection.commit();
62:    }
63:
64:    public void rollback() throws SQLException
65:    {
66:      connection.rollback();
67:    }
68:
69:    protected void finalize() throws SQLException
70:    {
71:      statement.close();
72:      connection.close();
73:    }
74: }
75:
```

Listing 45.1 *(continued)*

This example works very well. Taking it one step further, we find the development of servlets to pool database connections or broker database connections. I have seen a number of innovative approaches to creating these types of servlets, including HTTP interfaces to get state information, manipulate the interface, or control lifecycle events. Because I don't want to take anything away from these approaches or distract from my main point, I've just provided a simple example of one of these in Listing 45.2.

```
01: package org.java.pitfalls;
02:
03: import javax.servlet.*;
04: import javax.servlet.http.*;
05: import java.io.*;
06: import java.util.*;
07: import java.sql.*;
08: import java.text.*;
09: import com.javaexchange.dbConnectionBroker.*;
10:
11: public class CPoolServlet extends HttpServlet
12:                                 implements SingleThreadModel {
13:
14:
15:     ServletContext      context = null;
16:     DbConnectionBroker  broker = null;
```

Listing 45.2 CPoolServlet.java

```
17:     String            logDir = "";
18:
19:     public void init(ServletConfig config) {
20:
21:       try {
22:
23:         startBroker();
24:
25:           // Set it up so that other servlets can get a handle to ⟳
it.
26:           context = config.getServletContext();
27:           context.setAttribute("pooler", broker);
28:
29:       }catch (IOException e) {
30:           System.out.println(
31:             "CPoolServlet: Problems with database connection: " + ⟳
e);
32:
33:       }catch (Exception e) {
34:           System.out.println(
35:             "CPoolServlet: General pooler error: " + e);
36:       }
37:     }
38:
39:     public void doPost(HttpServletRequest request,            ⟳
HttpServletResponse response)
40:               throws IOException {
41:       doGet(request, response);
42:     }
43:
44:     public void doGet(HttpServletRequest request,             ⟳
HttpServletResponse response)
45:               throws IOException {
46:
47:        response.setContentType("text/html");
48:        ServletOutputStream  out = response.getOutputStream();
49:
50:        StringBuffer html = new StringBuffer();
51:
52:        html.append("");
53:        html.append("<html><title>CPoolServlet</title><body>");
54:
55:        html.append("<center><h2>CPoolServlet                  ⟳
Information</h2></center>");
56:        html.append("<p><center>Connection Pool is available    ⟳
under the pooler attribute.</center>");
57:
58:        html.append("</body></html>");
59:
```

Listing 45.2 *(continued)*

```
60:            out.println(html.toString());
61:      }
62:
63:      private void startBroker() throws Exception {
64:         try {
65:            broker = new DbConnectionBroker(
66:                     "com.sybase.jdbc2.jdbc.SybDriver",
67:                     "jdbc:sybase:Tds:localhost:2638",
68:                     "Test",
69:                     "Test",
70:                     5,
71:                     25,
72:                     "CPool.log",
73:                     1.0);
74:         }catch (Exception e) {
75:            throw e;
76:         }
77:      }
78:
79:      public void destroy() {
80:         broker.destroy();
81:      }
82: }
83:
```

Listing 45.2   *(continued)*

In this example, the servlet creates a connection broker object, in this case, a popular one from the Java Exchange. It places the attribute within the servlet context so that other components (servlets, JSPs) within the container can use it. This shows that there is an ability to create objects and make them available to the rest of the Web container. Why can't the container create these objects and make them available through the same JNDI lookups? It can. In fact, J2EE 1.3 containers are required to support resource pools, which are called *resource managers*.

Another interesting thing about the specification is that application developers are required to get their database connections through the javax.sql.DataSource connection factory. That means that to be compliant with the specification, developers ought to use this facility.

As an example, let's look at how you would do this using Tomcat. In this case, we are using an open-source connection pool factory provided by the Jakarta Commons project called DBCP (http://jakarta.apache.org/commons/dbcp.html). Assuming you have placed your JDBC driver and the connection pool JARs (if needed) in the right place (%CATALINA_HOME%/common/lib for Tomcat), the first step is to place a resource reference in your Web application's web.xml file—as demonstrated in Listing 45.3.

```
01: <resource-ref>
03:   <description>
05:     Reference to a factory for java.sql.Connection instances.  ⤺
The actual implementation is configured in the container.
07:   </description>
09:   <res-ref-name>
11:     jdbc/myDB
13:   </res-ref-name>
15:   <res-type>
17:     javax.sql.DataSource
19:   </res-type>
21:   <res-auth>
23:     Container
25:   </res-auth>
27: </resource-ref>
```

Listing 45.3 Excerpt from web.xml

As noted in the above declaration, you then need to configure the container to handle the actual implementation of the reference. In Tomcat, this is done in the server.xml file. Here is an example of what should be added to the file in order to create the resource pool.

Note this fits into the Context element, or in the DefaultContext element. More information on these can be read from the sample server.xml and other documents that the Jakarta project maintains on Tomcat. Listing 45.4 shows how to modify the server.xml in Tomcat to create the Connection Pool resource.

```
01: <Context ...>
03:   ...
04:
05: <Resource name="jdbc/myDB" auth="Container"
06:     type="javax.sql.DataSource"
07:   description="The PKO Portal DB"/>
08:   <ResourceParams name="jdbc/pkoDB">
09:       <parameter>
10:         <name>factory</name>
11: <value>org.apache.commons.dbcp.BasicDataSourceFactory</value>
12:       </parameter>
13:       <parameter>
14:         <name>driverClassName</name>
15:         <value>com.sybase.jdbc2.jdbc.SybDriver</value>
16:       </parameter>
17:       <parameter>
```

Listing 45.4 Excerpt from server.xml *(continued)*

```
18:              <name>maxActive</name>
19:              <value>3</value>
20:          </parameter>
21:          <parameter>
22:               <name>maxIdle</name>
23:           <value>3</value>
24:          </parameter>
25:          <parameter>
26:            <name>username</name>
27:            <value>user</value>
28:          </parameter>
29:          <parameter>
30:            <name>password</name>
31:            <value>pwd</value>
32:          </parameter>
33:          <parameter>
34:          <name>maxWait</name>
35:            <value>-1</value>
36:          </parameter>
37:          <parameter>
38:          <name>url</name>
39:            <value>jdbc:sybase:Tds:localhost:2638</value>
40:          </parameter>
41:    </ResourceParams>
```

Listing 45.4 *(continued)*

So, now the JDBC DataSource resource pool is available to the applications. The last step would be to actually use it. Listing 45.5 is an example of how to use the resource pool.

```
01: Context initCtx = new InitialContext();
03: Context envCtx = (Context) initCtx.lookup("java:comp/env");
05: DataSource ds = (DataSource) envCtx.lookup("jdbc/myDB");
07: Connection conn = ds.getConnection();
09: <<< Execute specific JDBC code here >>>
11: conn.close();
```

Listing 45.5 Using the resource pool

There are many different ways to create and manage resource pools. Like a lot of things in Java, better solutions evolve with time, and developers often are not aware of improvements offered in the platform. This is a common example where developers who have created their own mechanisms may not be aware of the improvements.

If you are working within a container, you should use the resource pooling capability provided by the container. Often it is invalid not to use the container resource pool, which can cause component developers to have problems with the portability of their code. Also, this allows for one convenient place for the container configuration to provide this service to all of its applications. It can be configured or changed without having to change every application that runs in the container.

The J2EE Connector Architecture is increasing in popularity for integrating back-end systems. This architecture provides for resource managers, which provide similar access to heterogeneous systems like Enteprise Resource Planning (ERP) and Human Resources Management Systems (HRMS) systems.

Item 46: JDO and Data Persistence

The foundation of any enterprise application is the data layer. This also determines how data will be persisted on your system. To me, deciding on a proper data persistence mechanism is like passing a very large kidney stone. Perhaps that is an overstatement, but it's an arduous process that requires an exhaustive understanding of your system and the technologies that will allow you to apply the best solution to your data storage/retrieval activities.

A proper persistence strategy typically consists of storing information in byte streams through serialization, hierarchically arranged data in XML files, Enterprise Java Beans, relational/object databases, and now Java Data Objects (JDO). The problem is that once you make a commitment to one technology, there's always a lot of second-guessing because of unforeseeable implementation hardships and performance issues.

Relational databases and EJBs can be effective tools for performing data persistence activities, but Java Data Objects offer a powerful new alternative that should be considered in allowing object-based access to your back-end data stores. JDO's strength lies in its ability to allow developers to use both Java and SQL constructs to manage data manipulation and access, and in its binary portability across data stores.

There are always design and implementation trade-offs in software development, especially when it comes to data persistence and retrieval. Although serialization is fairly simple to implement and does a decent job of preserving relationships between Java objects, it is nontransactional and can be a performance hog. JDBC is great for handling transactions, but it can require extensive field management and data mapping activities and can be tedious when you are implementing several SQL language constructs. JDO is fairly new and is not fully developed, but it promises to make developers more productive by allowing business logic manipulation through the use of Java interfaces and classes without having to explicitly understand SQL operations.

To gain a better appreciation of the strengths of JDO and how its transactional capabilities should be considered along with traditional methodologies, you need to understand data persistence in its most common form: serialization. Serialization is a simple technique used to transfer and store objects in byte streams and, most recently, in XML, but this is performed in a nontransactional manner. The code below demonstrates a simple manner that data can be serialized to the system disk space and read back. The `ObjectInputStream` class on line 122 deserializes data that was created previously using `ObjectOutputStream`.

```
001: package serialization;
002:
003: import java.util.*;
004: import java.text.*;
005: import java.util.Date;
006: import java.io.*;
007: import java.net.*;
008: import java.beans.*;
009: import java.util.logging.*;
010:
011: public class serializeBean {
012:
013: private String firstname;
014: private String lastname;
015: private String department[];
016: private String ssn;
017: private String comments;
018: private String filename;
019: private String filename2;
020:
021: //private String firstname2;
022: //private String lastname2;
023: //private String ssn2;
024: //private String comments2;
025:
026: private Hashtable errors;
027:
028: private static Logger logger =
Logger.getLogger(serializeBean.class.getName());
029:
030: public boolean validate() {
031:     boolean errorsFound=false;
032:
033:     logger.info("[validate:] lastname, firstname, ssn, comments=
" + lastname + ", " + firstname + ", " + ssn + ", " + comments);
034:
035:     if (firstname.equals("")) {
036:         errors.put("firstname","Please enter a valid Firstname");
037:         errorsFound=true;
038:     }
039:     if (lastname.equals("")) {
040:         errors.put("lastname","Please enter a valid Lastname");
041:          errorsFound=true;
042:     }
043:     if (ssn.equals("")) {
044:         errors.put("ssn","Please enter a valid Social Security #");
045:         errorsFound=true;
046:     }
047:     if (comments.equals("")) {
048:         errors.put("comments","Please enter a valid comment");
```

Listing 46.1   serializeBean.java

```
049:        errorsFound=true;
050:    }
051:
052:    return errorsFound;
053: }
054:
055: public String getErrorMsg(String s) {
056:     String errorMsg =(String)errors.get(s.trim());
057:   return (errorMsg == null) ? "":errorMsg;
058: }
059:
060: public serializeBean() {
061:
062:    try
063:    {
064:       URL url = null;
065:       Properties props = new Properties();
066:
067:       url =
this.getClass().getClassLoader().getResource
("serialization.properties");
068:     props.load( new FileInputStream(url.getFile()) );
069:     // Get properties
070:       filename = props.getProperty("filename");
071:       setFilename(filename);
072:       logger.info("[serializeBean:(constructor)] Filename is:
" + getFilename());
073:
074:       BufferedInputStream in = new BufferedInputStream(new
FileInputStream(filename));
075:       XMLDecoder decoder = new XMLDecoder(in);
076:       Object f = decoder.readObject(); // firstName
077:       Object l = decoder.readObject(); // lastName
078:       Object s = decoder.readObject(); // SSN
079:       Object c = decoder.readObject(); // comments
080:
081:       lastname = (String)l;
082:       firstname = (String)f;
083:       ssn = (String)s;
084:       comments = (String)c;
085:
086:       setLastname(lastname);
087:       setFirstname(firstname);
088:       setSsn(ssn);
089:       setComments(comments);
090:
091:       decoder.close();
092:
093:    }
094:    catch(Exception e) {
```

Listing 46.1   *(continued)*

```
095:
096:          System.out.println("ERROR: " + e.toString());
097:          System.out.println("Using default values.");
098:
099:          // use default values
100:          firstname="";
101:          lastname="";
102:          // department[];
103:          ssn="";
104:          comments="";
105:
106: }
```

Listing 46.1   *(continued)*

The serialization process described in lines 109 to 210 can be a problem with different versions of class libraries or Java Runtime Environments. The latest Merlin release has addressed this with the introduction of XML serialization. Since the data is saved in XML files, it is possible to serialize data, manually modify the serialized file by hand, and have it deserialized without losing a step. Previously, this would not have been possible because the data was saved in binary byte streams.

```
108:    /*
109:    try
110:    {
111:      URL url = null;
112:      Properties props = new Properties();
113:      url = this.getClass().getClassLoader().
114:          getResource("serialization.properties");
115:      props.load( new FileInputStream(url.getFile()) );
116:      // Get properties
117:      filename2 = props.getProperty("filename2");
118:      setFilename2(filename2);
119:      logger.info("Filename2 is: " + getFilename2());
120:      FileInputStream inputFile =
121:          new FileInputStream(getFilename2());
122:      ObjectInputStream inputStream =
123:          new ObjectInputStream(inputFile);
124:      // Read data
125:      lastname2 = (String)inputStream.readObject();
126:      firstname2 = (String)inputStream.readObject();
127:      ssn2 = (String)inputStream.readObject();
128:      comments2 = (String)inputStream.readObject();
129:
130:    inputStream.close();
131:
132:    }
133:    catch(Exception e) {
134:
135:      System.out.println("ERROR: " + e.toString());
```

Listing 46.1   *(continued)*

```
136:    System.out.println("Using default values.");
137:
138:    // use default values
139:    firstname2="";
140:    lastname2="";
141:    ssn2="";
142:    comments2="";
143:
144:    }
145:    */
146:    errors = new Hashtable();
147:    logger.info("lastname, firstname, ssn, comments= " +
148:      lastname + ", " + firstname + ", " + ssn + ", " + comments);
149: // logger.info("lastname2, firstname2, ssn2, comments2= " +
150: // lastname2 + ", " + firstname2 + ", " + ssn2 + ", " + comments2);
151:    }
152:  public void write()
153:  {
154:   try
155:   {
156:     logger.info("Filename is: " + getFilename());
157:
158:     System.out.println("Firstname= " + getFirstname());
159:     System.out.println("Lastname= " + getLastname());
160:     System.out.println("SSN= " + getSsn());
161:     System.out.println("Comments= " + getComments());
162:
```

Listing 46.1   *(continued)*

The code below demonstrates a new serialization mechanism that saves the states of internal methods in an XML format.

```
163:    // try XMLEncode
164:    BufferedOutputStream out =
165:     new BufferedOutputStream(new FileOutputStream(getFilename()));
166:    XMLEncoder encoder = new XMLEncoder(out);
167:    encoder.writeObject(getFirstname());
168:    encoder.writeObject(getLastname());
169:    encoder.writeObject(getSsn());
170:    encoder.writeObject(getComments());
171:    encoder.close();
172:
173:   }
174:   catch(IOException ioe) {
175:     System.err.println("IOERROR: " + ioe);
176:   }
177:   catch(Exception e) {
178:     System.err.println("ERROR: " + e);
179:   }
180:
```

Listing 46.1   *(continued)*

```
181:    /*
182:    try
183:    {
184:      logger.info("Filename is: " + getFilename2());
185:      // avoid XMLEncode
186:      FileOutputStream outputFile2 =
187:        new FileOutputStream(getFilename2());
188:      ObjectOutputStream outputStream2 =
189:        new ObjectOutputStream(outputFile2);
190:      outputStream2.writeObject(getFirstname());
191:      outputStream2.writeObject(getLastname());
192:      outputStream2.writeObject(getSsn());
193:      outputStream2.writeObject(getComments());
194:
195:      // close stream
196:      outputStream2.flush();
197:      outputStream2.close();
198:
199:    }
200:    catch(IOException ioe) {
201:      System.err.println("IOERROR: " + ioe);
202:    }
203:    catch(Exception e) {
204:      System.err.println("ERROR: " + e);
205:    }
206:    */
207:
208:      logger.info("[serializeBean:write] writing data.");
209:    }
```

Listing 46.1 *(continued)*

If you've used Remote Method Invocation in your software implementations, you've come across serialization. With RMI implementations, objects are compressed into byte streams when they are marshaled across a network. Performance becomes an issue during the deserialization of objects because it involves the conversion of byte array elements into object and data types. This process involves the use of reflection to discover properties of an object.

Some shortcomings with serialization are that once an object is written to, additional writes are ignored because the object reference is maintained, unless the reset() method is invoked. Certainly, performance issues have always been associated with serialization because of disk read (reflection)/write operations, but depending on your situation, serialization can be a perfectly appropriate persistence solution in your enterprise deployments. However, if your application requires concurrency in database access and queries, then Java Data Objects can be a solution for you.

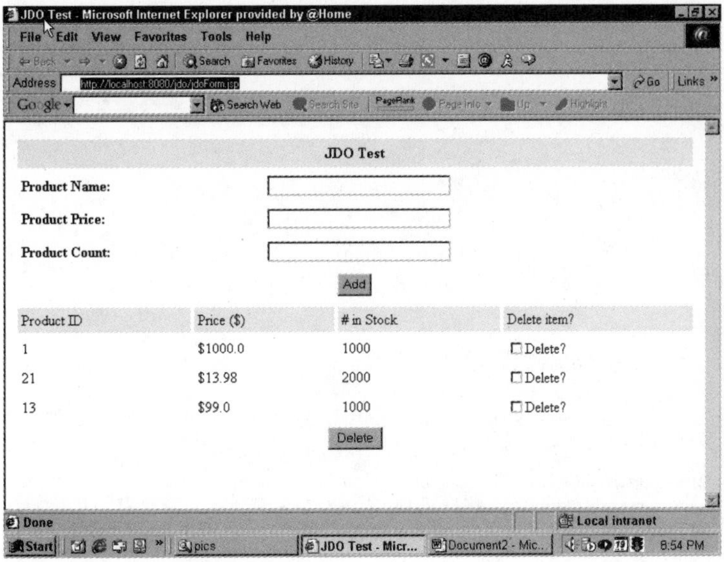

Figure 46.1   JDO Test form.

Now that you have a better understanding of serialization, I think you'll have a better appreciation of JDO and the great promise it offers in abstracting away the inane details of the SQL language implementation in Java applications.

A simple inventory program, shown in Listing 46.2, was crafted with a recent open-source JDO offering from the Apache Software Foundation (ASF) called ObjectRelational Bridge (OJB). OJB is a fairly ambitious project by the good folks at the ASF, and although their JDO implementation is not fully compliant with the JDO Draft (JSR-012), ASF promises to move in that direction. OJB uses a `PersistentBroker` API as its persistence kernel and has its JDO implementation built on top of it and XML data mappings that bind to your database elements.

What makes OJB JDO worthy of examination is its ability for transparent persistence of database elements in the form of Java objects. JDO abstracts away the complexities of SQL transactions and allows developers to query instances of data stores with very fine granularity and without having to understand the intimate details about the database structure itself.

With OJB JDO, caches can be transactional, which means that each cache area can maintain a different transactional view of the data store instances. This is an important concept that separates it from the serialization process described above.

Mentioned earlier, the following code is a simple inventory Web application that inserts, deletes, and displays inventory items using the OJB JDO libraries. The `jdoForm` is a simple JavaServer Page that accepts user requests and interfaces with a back-end MySQL database.

```
001:
002: <%@page import="org.apache.ojb.tutorial4.*" %>
003: <%@page import="org.apache.ojb.jdo.PersistenceManagerImpl" %>
004: <%@page import=
005:   "org.apache.ojb.jdo.PersistenceManagerFactoryImpl" %>
006: <%@page import="javax.jdo.PersistenceManager" %>
007: <%@page import="javax.jdo.Transaction" %>
008:
009: <%@page import="org.odmg.*" %>
010:
011: <%@page import="javax.jdo.Query" %>
012: <%@page import="java.util.Collection" %>
013:
014: <%@page import="javax.jdo.PersistenceManager" %>
015: <%@page import="javax.jdo.PersistenceManagerFactory" %>
016: <%@page import="java.io.BufferedReader" %>
017: <%@page import="java.io.InputStreamReader" %>
018: <%@page import="java.util.Vector" %>
019: <jsp:useBean id="pm"
020:   class="org.javapitfalls.item46.jdoPersistenceMgr"
021:   scope="application"/>
022: <jsp:useBean id="validate"
023:   class="org.javapitfalls.item46.jdoBean" scope="request">
024: <jsp:setProperty name="validate" property="*"/>
025: </jsp:useBean>
026: <head>
027:   <title>JDO Test</title>
028: </head>
029:
030: <%
031: String addItem=request.getParameter("Add");
032: String deleteItem=request.getParameter("Delete");
033:
034: if (addItem != null)
035: {
036:   String pName = request.getParameter("productName");
037:   String pPrice = request.getParameter("productPrice");
038:   String pCount = request.getParameter("productCount");
039:
040:   if (!validate.validate()) {
041:
042:     Product newProduct = new Product();
043:
044:     newProduct.setName(pName);
045:     newProduct.setPrice(Double.parseDouble(pPrice));
046:     newProduct.setStock(Integer.parseInt(pCount));
047:
```

Listing 46.2 jdoForm.jsp

The Transaction interface on line 49 provides the operations necessary to perform database transactions—specifically, accessing, creating, and modifying persistent objects and their fields. Prior to performing any database operations, a thread must explicitly create a transaction object or associate itself with an existing transaction object, and that transaction must be open (through a call to begin). All operations that follow the thread are performed under the transaction of the thread.

The operational states of a transaction are either open or closed. An open transaction means that the application has called begin() but has not invoked commit() or abort(). Once an application calls the commit() or abort() methods, the transaction is considered closed. The isOpen() method can be used to determine the state of a transaction. As objects are accessed by an application, read locks are implicitly used to allow proper access to data and write locks are used when objects are modified to ensure that only one transaction is modifying data at one time.

The makePersistent(...) operation on line 52 is executed on an open transaction so that the transient object can be made available for the commit method to make it durable. If the transaction is made available and the operation aborts, then the makePersistent operation is nullified and the target object is marked as transient.

```
048:     // now perform persistence operations
049:     Transaction tx = null;
050:     // open transaction
051:     PersistenceManager pmInstance = pm.getManagerInstance();
052:     pmInstance.makePersistent(newProduct);
053:     tx = pmInstance.currentTransaction();
054:     tx.begin();
055:
056:     // commit transaction
057:     tx.commit();
058:
059:     System.out.println("successful submission...");
060:
061: } else {
062:
063:     System.out.println("Validation error.");
064:
065: }
066: }
067: else if (deleteItem != null)
068: {
069:   String[] deleteArray = request.getParameterValues("deleteItems");
070:
071:   if ((deleteArray != null) && (deleteArray.length > 0))
072:   {
073:     for (int i=0; i < deleteArray.length; i++)
074:     {
075:       System.out.println("deleting: " + deleteArray[i]);
076:
```

Listing 46.2 *(continued)*

```
077:        Product test = new Product();
078:        test.setId(Integer.parseInt(deleteArray[i]));
079:
080:        PersistenceManager pmInstance = pm.getManagerInstance();
081:
082:        try
083:        {
084:          Product toBeDeleted =
(Product)pmInstance.getObjectById(test, false);
085:          Transaction tx = null;
086:          tx = pmInstance.currentTransaction();
087:          tx.begin();
088:          pmInstance.deletePersistent(toBeDeleted);
089:          tx.commit();
090:        }
091:        catch (Throwable t)
092:        {
093:          // rollback in case of errors
094:          pmInstance.currentTransaction().rollback();
095:          t.printStackTrace();
096:        }
097:  }
098: }
099: }
100:
101: %>
102:
103: <html>
104: <body>
105:
106: <form action="jdoForm.jsp" method=post>
107: <center>
108:
109: <table border="0" cellpadding="4" cellspacing="4" width="100%">
110:  <tr valign="top" bgcolor="#eeeeee">
111:    <td colspan="3">
112:    <table cellspacing="0" border="0" width="100%">
113:     <tr>
114:      <td align="center" valign="top">
115:       <table cellspacing="0" cellpadding="1" border="0"
width="100%" align="center">
116:        <tr>
117:         <td valign="top" align="center">
118:          <b>JDO Test</b>
119:         </td>
120:        </tr>
121:       </table>
122:      </td>
123:     </tr>
```

Listing 46.2   *(continued)*

```
124:    </table>
125:    </td>
126:  </tr>
127:  <tr bgcolor="" >
128:    <td align="left"><b>Product Name:</b> <b></b>  
129:    <font size=2 color=red>
130:    <%=validate.getErrorMsg("productName")%></font></td>
131:    <td align="left">
132:     <input type="text" name="productName"
133:      value="<%=validate.getProductName()%>" size="30"></td>
134:  </tr>
135:  <tr bgcolor="" >
136:    <td align="left"> <b>Product Price:</b> <b></b>  
137:    <font size=2 color=red>
138:    <%=validate.getErrorMsg("productPrice")%></font></td>
139:    <td align="left">
140:     <input type="text" name="productPrice"
141:      value="<%=validate.getProductPrice()%>" size="30"></td>
142:  </tr>
143:  <tr bgcolor="" >
144:    <td align="left"><b>Product Count:</b> <b></b>  
145:    <font size=2 color=red>
146:    <%=validate.getErrorMsg("productCount")%></font></td>
147:    <td align="left">
148:     <input type="text" name="productCount"
149:      value="<%=validate.getProductCount()%>" size="30"></td>
150:  </tr>
151:  <tr bgcolor="" >
152:    <td align="center" colspan="2">
153:     <input type="Submit" name="Add" value="Add">
154:    </td>
155:  </tr>
156:
157: </table>
158:
159: </center>
160:
161: <table border="0" cellpadding="4" cellspacing="4" width="100%">
162:   <tr bgcolor="#eeeeee"><td>Product ID</td><td>Price ($)</td><td>
163:   # in Stock</td><td>Delete item?</td></tr>
164: <%
```

Listing 46.2   *(continued)*

The following code performs the rendering of the inventory data to the user display. A query is performed using the product table mapping. If data items are found in the product table, a collection handle is obtained and iterated through in the JSP display. A screenshot is provided in Listing 46.1 for this application.

```
165: // List all items
166: Query query = pm.getManagerInstance().newQuery(Product.class);
167: try
168: {
169:     // ask the broker to retrieve the Extent collection
170:
171:     Collection allProducts = (Collection)query.execute();
172:     // now iterate over the result to print each product
173:     java.util.Iterator iter = allProducts.iterator();
174:     while (iter.hasNext())
175:     {
176:         Product a = (Product) iter.next();
177: %>
178:   <tr>
179:     <td><%= a.getId() %></td>
180:     <td>$<%= a.getPrice() %></td>
181:     <td><%= a.getStock() %></td>
182:     <td><input type="checkbox" name="deleteItems" value="<%=
183:             a.getId() %>">Delete?</td>
184:   </tr>
185: <%
186:     }
187: }
188: catch (Throwable t)
189: {
190:   t.printStackTrace();
191: }
192: %>
193:   <tr bgcolor="" >
194:    <td align="center" colspan="4">
195:     <input type="Submit" name="Delete" value="Delete">
196:   </td>
197:   </tr>
198:
199: </table>
200:
201: </form>
202:
203: </body>
204: </html>
205:
```

Listing 46.3   Inventory results

The jdoPersistenceMgr application which follows uses the JDO `PersistenceMan-ager` class on line 22 as its primary interface between the Web application jdoForm.jsp and the back-end MySQL database. The `PersistenceManager` provides both query and transaction management. It uses the resource adapter to access the data store, specifically the OJB libraries.

```
01: package org.javapitfalls.item46;
02:
03: import org.apache.ojb.tutorial4.*;
04:
05: import org.apache.ojb.jdo.PersistenceManagerImpl;
06: import org.apache.ojb.jdo.PersistenceManagerFactoryImpl;
07: import javax.jdo.PersistenceManager;
08: import javax.jdo.Transaction;
09:
10: import javax.jdo.Query;
11: import java.util.Collection;
12:
13: import javax.jdo.PersistenceManager;
14: import javax.jdo.PersistenceManagerFactory;
15: import java.io.BufferedReader;
16: import java.io.InputStreamReader;
17: import java.util.Vector;
18:
19: public class jdoPersistenceMgr implements java.io.Serializable {
20:
21:    PersistenceManagerFactory factory;
22:    PersistenceManager manager;
23:
24:    public jdoPersistenceMgr()
25:    {
26:      manager = null;
27:      try
28:      {
29:        factory = PersistenceManagerFactoryImpl.getInstance();
30:        manager = factory.getPersistenceManager();
31:
32:      }
33:      catch (Throwable t)
34:      {
35:        System.out.println("ERROR: " + t.getMessage());
36:        t.printStackTrace();
37:      }
38:    }
39:
40:    public PersistenceManager getManagerInstance()
41:    {
42:      return manager;
43:    }
44:
45: }
```

Listing 46.4   do.PersistenceManager.java

There are many discussions in the development community about JDO and the perception that it suffers from its association with Object Data Modeling Group (ODMG), which has not garnered widespread community support because of proprietary language extensions and nonstandard meta data support.

Personally, I feel that this misperception is badly placed and will be displaced once the development community implements new reference implementations by Sun and the ASF. JDO is still a young standard, but as products like OJB mature, developers will gain a better appreciation of JDO's ability to propagate consistent persistence behavior across implementations, its use of XML meta data representation for mapping data, and its ability to use mature Java Collection class libraries to manipulate data. These capabilities could make your persistence questions easier to tackle on your system's data layer.

JDO is relevant because it minimizes database transaction implementations by developers and it supports reuse, particularly with Java components. OJB JDO facilitates cache and object management through object models and avoids relational modeling and EJB/CMP intricacies that can be specific to an application.

Item 47: Where's the WSDL? Pitfalls of Using JAXR with UDDI

The Java API for XML Registries (JAXR) provides a Java API for accessing different kinds of registries. Built on the OASIS ebXML Registry Information Model (RIM), mappings between ebXML interfaces and JAXR interfaces are direct and seem intuitive. When JAXR is used with UDDI (Universal Description and Discovery Integration) registries, however, there is sometimes a bit of confusion. In our experience, Java developers that are new to JAXR face a learning curve and a few pitfalls that revolve around misunderstanding the relationships between JAXR objects and the UDDI data structures. This item shows examples of these pitfalls and provides guidance on how to avoid them.

To show these possible pitfalls, we will build a skeletal program that includes the basics of JAXR, shown in our Listing 47.1. In this listing, we have an empty make-Call() method on lines 64 to 69. After we explain our example setup in the listing, we will implement several versions of makeCall() to query the registry.

In using JAXR, you must first set up a connection to a registry server. Listing 47.1 shows the beginning of a program using JAXR to speak to a registry server. In this example, we are using the public Microsoft UDDI registry, passed in to the constructor of JAXRQueryExample. In lines 29 to 32, we are able to get a connection to the registry using the ConnectionFactory object from the javax.xml.registry package. From that connection, we are able to get the RegistryService object, which allows us to receive the BusinessQueryManager object on line 34.

```
001: package org.javapitfalls.item47;
002:
003: import javax.xml.registry.*;
004: import javax.xml.registry.infomodel.*;
005: import java.net.*;
006: import java.util.*;
```

Listing 47.1 The start of our UDDI query example

```
007:
008: public class JAXRQueryExample
009: {
010:    RegistryService        m_regserv     = null;
011:    BusinessQueryManager m_querymgr    = null;
012:    Connection             m_connection = null;
013:
014:    public JAXRQueryExample(String registryURL) throws JAXRException
015:    {
016:      ConnectionFactory factory     = null;
017:
018:      Properties props = new Properties();
019:      props.setProperty("javax.xml.registry.queryManagerURL",
020:                        registryURL);
021:
022:      try
023:      {
024:        /*
025:         * Create the connection, passing it the
026:         * properties -- in this case, just the URL
027:         */
028:
029:        factory = ConnectionFactory.newInstance();
030:        factory.setProperties(props);
031:
032:        m_connection = factory.createConnection();
033:        m_regserv     = m_connection.getRegistryService();
034:        m_querymgr    = m_regserv.getBusinessQueryManager();
035:      }
036:      catch ( JAXRException e )
037:      {
038:        cleanUp();
039:        //pass it on..
040:        throw e;
041:      }
042:    }
043:
044:    /**
045:     * Close the connection
046:     */
047:    public void cleanUp()
048:    {
049:      if ( m_connection != null )
050:      {
051:        try
052:        {
053:          m_connection.close();
054:        }
```

Listing 47.1   *(continued)*

```
055:        catch ( JAXRException je )
056:        {
057:        }
058:     }
059:  }
060:
061:  /**
062:   * Our main focus in this pitfall
063:   **/
064:  public void makeCall(String query) throws Exception
065:  {
066:    //We will use m_querymgr in this method
067:
068:    System.out.println("makeCall() Not implemented yet!");
069:  }
070:
071:  /** Simple convenience function, since strings from registry
072:   *  are in this format
073:   */
074:  public String convertToString(InternationalString intl)
075:  throws JAXRException
076:  {
077:    String stringVal = null;
078:    if ( intl != null )
079:    {
080:      stringVal = intl.getValue();
081:    }
082:    return(stringVal);
083:  }
084:
085:  public static void main(String[] args)
086:  {
087:    JAXRQueryExample jaxrex = null;
088:    try
089:    {
090:      String uddiReg = "http://uddi.microsoft.com/inquire";
091:      jaxrex = new JAXRQueryExample(uddiReg);
092:
093:      jaxrex.makeCall("truman");
094:
095:      System.out.println("-----------SECOND QUERY--------------");
096:      jaxrex.makeCall("sched");
097:    }
098:    catch ( Exception e )
099:    {
100:      e.printStackTrace();
101:    }
102:    finally
```

Listing 47.1   *(continued)*

```
103:      {
104:          jaxrex.cleanUp();
105:      }
106:    }
107:
108: }
109:
```

Listing 47.1 *(continued)*

On lines 64 to 69, we have an empty `makeCall()` method that will be our focus for the rest of this pitfall item. In that method, we will make extensive use of the `BusinessQueryManager` interface returned from the `RegistryService` object on line 33. Because this is where some of the confusion comes in, we have listed the available methods of the `javax.xml.registry.BusinessQueryManager` interface in Table 47.1.

Table 47.1 The BusinessQueryManager Interface

METHOD	DESCRIPTION

`BulkResponse`
`  findAssociations (Collection findQualifiers,`
`            String sourceObjectId,`
`            String targetObjectId,`
`            Collection assocTypes)`
	Finds `Association` objects that match parameters of this call.

`BulkResponse`
`  findCallerAssociations(Collection`
`            findQualifiers,`
`            Boolean confirmedByCaller,`
`            Boolean confirmedByOtherParty,`
`            Collection associationTypes)`
	Finds all `Association` objects owned by the caller that match all of the criteria specified by the parameters of this call.

`ClassificationScheme`
`  findClassificationSchemeByName(`
`            Collection findQualifiers,`
`            String namePattern`
`            )`
	Finds a `Classification-Scheme` by name based on the specified find qualifiers and name pattern.

`BulkResponse`
`  findClassificationSchemes(Collection`
`            findQualifiers,`
`            Collection namePatterns,`
`            Collection classifications,`
`            Collection externalLinks)`
	Finds all `Classification-Scheme` objects that match all of the criteria specified by the parameters of this call.

`Concept findConceptByPath(java.lang.String path)`	Finds a Concept object by the path specified.

(continued)

Table 47.1   *(continued)*

METHOD	DESCRIPTION

`BulkResponse`
`  findConcepts(Collection findQualifiers,`
`             Collection namePatterns,`
`             Collection classifications,`
`             Collection externalIdentifiers,`
`             Collection externalLinks)`
	Finds all `Concept` objects that match the parameters of this call.

`BulkResponse`
`  findOrganizations(Collection findQualifiers,`
`             Collection namePatterns,`
`             Collection classifications,`
`             Collection specifications,`
`             Collection externalIdentifiers,`
`             Collection externalLinks)`
	Finds all `Organization` objects that match the parameters of this call.

`BulkResponse`
`  findRegistryPackages(Collection findQualifiers,`
`             Collection namePatterns,`
`             Collection classifications,`
`             Collection externalLinks)`
	Finds all `RegistryPackage` objects that match the parameters of the call.

`BulkResponse`
`  findServiceBindings(Key serviceKey,`
`             Collection findQualifiers,`
`             Collection classifications,`
`             Collection specifications)`
	Finds all `ServiceBinding` objects that match the parameters of this call.

`BulkResponse`
`  findServices(Key orgKey,`
`             Collection findQualifiers,`
`             Collection namePatterns,`
`             Collection classifications,`
`             Collection specifications)`
	Finds all `Service` objects that match the parameters of this call.

As you can see from Table 47.1, the `BusinessQueryManager` interface queries the registry for information. In calling these methods, many searches can be constrained by collections of search qualifiers, patterns, classifications, external links, and specifications. Many of the methods return a `BulkResponse` object that contains a `Collection` of objects. Depending on the method call, the objects contained in the collection can be associations between registry instances (`Association`), taxonomies used to describe the classifications of registry objects (`ClassificationScheme`), taxonomy elements themselves (`Concept`) present in the registry, organizations in the registry (`Organization`), registry entries logically organized together (`RegistryPackage`), services that are available (`Service`), and bindings to interfaces of the service (`ServiceBinding`).

All of the objects in the collection contained by the `BulkResponse` objects are interfaces in the `javax.xml.registry.infomodel` package and are all subinterfaces to the `RegistryObject` class. Figure 47.1 shows the methods of the `RegistryObject` interface, as well as the classes that realize that interface. Because the `RegistryObject` interface contains a `getExternalLinks()` method, every class that implements this interface may have a named URI to content residing outside the registry—such as a Web Service Description Language (WSDL) document in a UDDI registry. As we show potential pitfalls in making JAXR searches, you will find that it is important to have an understanding of where objects in a registry reside.

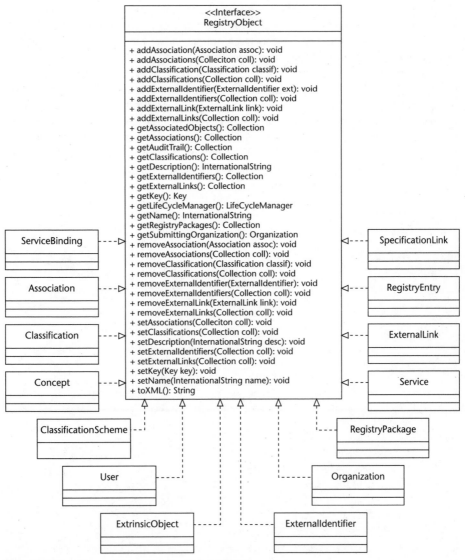

Figure 47.1   The `RegistryObject` **interface.**

Where's the WSDL?

We're about to embark on a quest for a Web service's WSDL found in a UDDI registry. For our example, we would like to constrain the search by searching for a string found in an organization name in the registry. From there, we would like to print out all available Web services—and more importantly, their WSDL—so that we can dynamically call their Web services. To do this, we will modify our original code from Listing 47.1 and will replace that code's empty makeCall() method. For convenience, we will list the following code listings starting with line 64—this will make it easier when you download the code for the examples from our Web site.

Listing 47.2 shows the makeCall() method where we are attempting to get the WSDL document from a search of the registry. Our search constraint, the query string, is set up to be a pattern on lines 74 and 75. At the same time, we qualify our search on line 74 by setting our responses to be sorted alphabetically by name. Our example then queries the BusinessQueryManager's findOrganizations() method with these parameters. Because a collection of Organization objects will be returned from the collection in the BulkResponse object, and because organizations contain services that can be retrieved by the organization's getServices() method, we will be able to get the services. Because the Service object inherits the getExternalLinks() method from RegistryObject, the programmer in this example assumes that we should be able to get the WSDL document with that method on the service. Just to make certain, the programmer calls that method from the service's ServiceBinding objects, which was returned from getServiceBindings() on the service on line 123.

```
064:    public void makeCall(String query) throws Exception
065:    {
066:      if ( m_querymgr == null )
067:      {
068:        throw new Exception("No query manager!!!!! Exiting
makeCall()");
069:      }
070:      else
071:      {
072:
073:        Collection findQualifiers = new ArrayList();
074:        findQualifiers.add(FindQualifier.SORT_BY_NAME_DESC);
075:        Collection namePatterns = new ArrayList();
076:        namePatterns.add("%" + query + "%");
077:
078:        BulkResponse response =
079:        m_querymgr.findOrganizations(findQualifiers,
080:                                    namePatterns,
081:                                    null, null, null, null);
082:
083:        Iterator orgIterator = response.getCollection().iterator();
084:
```

Listing 47.2   Our first attempt for WSDL, in makeCall( )

```
085:         System.out.println("Made an organizational query for '" +
086:                             query + "'...");
087:
088:       int orgcnt = 0;
089:       while ( orgIterator.hasNext() )
090:       {
091:         orgcnt ++;
092:         //Let's get every organization that matches the query!
093:         Organization org = (Organization) orgIterator.next();
094:         System.out.println(orgcnt + ") Organization Name: " +
095:                             convertToString(org.getName()));
096:         System.out.println("   Organization Desc: " +
097:                             convertToString(org.getDescription()));
098:
099:         //Now get the services provided by the organization
100:         Iterator svcIter = org.getServices().iterator();
101:         while ( svcIter.hasNext() )
102:         {
103:           Service svc = (Service)svcIter.next();
104:           System.out.println("   Service Name: " +
105:                               convertToString(svc.getName()));
106:
107:           //External links are associated with every registry
     object,
108:           //so maybe it's in the external link of service..
109:           Iterator extlinkit = svc.getExternalLinks().iterator();
110:           if ( !extlinkit.hasNext() )
111:           {
112:             System.out.println("   ? - " +
113:                     "No WSDL document at
     svc.getExternalLinks()..");
114:           }
115:           while ( extlinkit.hasNext() )
116:           {
117:             ExternalLink extlink = (ExternalLink)extlinkit.next();
118:             System.out.println("WSDL Document: " +
119:                                 extlink.getExternalURI());
120:           }
121:
122:           //Let's get the service binding object
123:           Iterator bindit = svc.getServiceBindings().iterator();
124:           while ( bindit.hasNext() )
125:           {
126:             ServiceBinding sb = (ServiceBinding)bindit.next();
127:             System.out.println("   Service Binding Name: " +
128:                                 convertToString(sb.getName()));
129:             System.out.println("   Service Binding Desc: " +
130:                                 convertToString(sb.getDescription()));
```

Listing 47.2   *(continued)*

```
131:               System.out.println("  Service Binding Access URI:\n" +
132:                       "   " + sb.getAccessURI());
133:
134:           //Maybe WSDL is on the external link here..
135:           Iterator extlinkit2 = sb.getExternalLinks().iterator();
136:           if ( !extlinkit2.hasNext() )
137:           {
138:              System.out.println("   ? - " +
139:                 "No WSDL document at \n" +
140:                 " svc.getServiceBindings().getExternalLinks()..");
141:           }
142:           while ( extlinkit2.hasNext() )
143:           {
144:              ExternalLink extlink =
(ExternalLink)extlinkit2.next();
145:              System.out.println("WSDL Document: " +
146:                              extlink.getExternalURI());
147:           }
148:
149:
150:          }
151:
152:
153:        }
154:
155:      }
156:    }
157:  }
```

Listing 47.2   *(continued)*

Our example in Listing 47.2 shows a search of the UDDI registry, and printing organization, service, and service binding information for the result of our search. Listing 47.3 shows the output of our program. There are two calls to makeCall(): a query including the string 'truman' and a query including the string 'sched'. Both queries return two results. As you can see by the bolded content in Listing 47.3, the programmer got it wrong.

```
01: Made an organizational query for 'truman'...
02: 1) Organization Name: TrumanTruck.com
03:    Organization Desc: Restoration of Truman Schermerhorn's Truck
04:    Service Name: TrumanTruck Page
05:    ? - No WSDL document at svc.getExternalLinks()..
06:    Service Binding Name: null
```

Listing 47.3   Output of our first attempt

```
07:     Service Binding Desc: hyperlink
08:     Service Binding Access URI:
09:      http://www.trumantruck.com
10:     ? - No WSDL document at
11:       svc.getServiceBindings().getExternalLinks()..
12: 2) Organization Name: Harry S. Truman Scholarship Foundation
13:     Organization Desc:
14:     Service Name: Web home page
15:     ? - No WSDL document at svc.getExternalLinks()..
16:     Service Binding Name: null
17:     Service Binding Desc: hyperlink
18:     Service Binding Access URI:
19:      http://www.truman.gov/welcome.htm
20:     ? - No WSDL document at
21:       svc.getServiceBindings().getExternalLinks()..
22: -----------SECOND QUERY--------------
23: Made an organizational query for 'sched'...
24: 1) Organization Name: LFC Scheduling
25:     Organization Desc:
26:     Service Name: Classroom Scheduling
27:     ? - No WSDL document at svc.getExternalLinks()..
28:     Service Binding Name: null
29:     Service Binding Desc:
30:     Service Binding Access URI:
31:      http://www.contest.eraserver.net/Scheduling/Scheduler.asmx
32:     ? - No WSDL document at
33:       svc.getServiceBindings().getExternalLinks()..
34: 2) Organization Name: Interactive Scheduler
35:     Organization Desc:
36:     Service Name: Interactive Schedule
37:     ? - No WSDL document at svc.getExternalLinks()..
38:     Service Binding Name: null
39:     Service Binding Desc:
40:     Service Binding Access URI:
41:
http://www.contest.eraserver.net/InteractiveScheduler/service1.asmx
42:     ? - No WSDL document at
43:       svc.getServiceBindings().getExternalLinks()..
44:
```

Listing 47.3 *(continued)*

The problem in that example demonstrates the programmer's misunderstanding of
where the WSDL document lives in the JAXR object hierarchy. This is a common problem with developers new to JAXR and UDDI. Luckily, Appendix D of the JAXR specification (found at http://java.sun.com/xml/jaxr/) shows the mappings of JAXR to
UDDI. In Figure 47.2, we have provided a graphical depiction of where the WSDL document is located. To get the WSDL document for a Web service, you need to somehow

traverse the structures to get to the registry object classified as a `"wsdlspec"`, and get that object's `ExternalLink`. Because our organizational query returns a collection of organizations, we have shown a logical "road map" from the `Organization` object. For the sake of eliminating confusion, we have left out potential paths to `ExternalLink` and `SpecificationLink` that are available from every object (since they all realize the `RegistryObject` interface).

> **TIP** If you are used to UDDI terminology, there are different terms for each of these interfaces. For example, a JAXR Organization is known in UDDI as a "businessEntity." A JAXR Service is known as a UDDI "businessService." A UDDI "bindingTemplate" is a JAXR ServiceBinding. There are many more of these mappings. For more information, download the JAXR specification at http://java.sun.com/jaxr/.

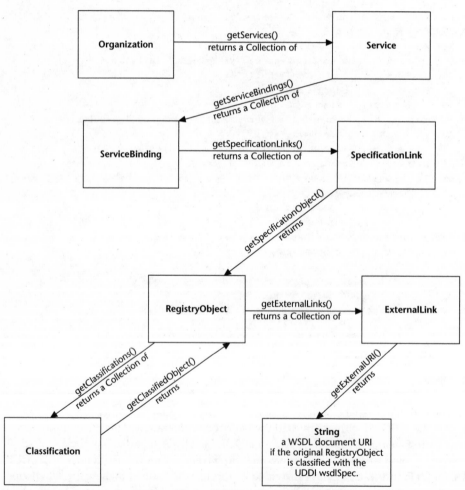

Figure 47.2 Navigating through JAXR objects to get WSDL .

Now that we have provided the "traversal road map" in Figure 47.2, we will demonstrate another potential programming pitfall. In Listing 47.4, the programmer traverses the objects as shown from the figure. On line 83, we get our collection of organizations from our `BulkResponse` object. On line 100, we get a collection of services from each organization. On line 109, we get a collection of service bindings from each service. On lines 120 and 121, we get a collection of specification links from each service binding. On line 127, we get a registry object from the specification link with the `getSpecificationObject()` method. Finally, on lines 128 to 134, we get the external link from the registry object, and we call the `getExternalURI()` method on the specification link.

```
064:    public void makeCall(String query) throws Exception
065:    {
066:      if ( m_querymgr == null )
067:      {
068:        throw new Exception("No query manager!!!!! Exiting
makeCall()");
069:      }
070:      else
071:      {
072:
073:        Collection findQualifiers = new ArrayList();
074:        findQualifiers.add(FindQualifier.SORT_BY_NAME_DESC);
075:        Collection namePatterns = new ArrayList();
076:        namePatterns.add("%" + query + "%");
077:
078:        BulkResponse response =
079:        m_querymgr.findOrganizations(findQualifiers,
080:                                     namePatterns,
081:                                     null, null, null, null);
082:
083:        Iterator orgIterator = response.getCollection().iterator();
084:
085:        System.out.println("Made an organizational query for '" +
086:                           query + "'...");
087:
088:        int orgcnt = 0;
089:        while ( orgIterator.hasNext() )
090:        {
091:          orgcnt ++;
092:          //Let's get every organization that matches the query!
093:          Organization org = (Organization) orgIterator.next();
094:          System.out.println(orgcnt + ") Organization Name: " +
095:                             convertToString(org.getName()));
096:          System.out.println("   Organization Desc: " +
097:                             convertToString(org.getDescription()));
098:
```

Listing 47.4   Our second attempt for WSDL, in makeCall() *(continued)*

```
099:          //Now get the services provided by the organization
100:          Iterator svcIter = org.getServices().iterator();
101:          while ( svcIter.hasNext() )
102:          {
103:            Service svc = (Service)svcIter.next();
104:            System.out.println("    Service Name: " +
105:                                convertToString(svc.getName()));
106:
107:
108:            //Let's get the service binding object
109:            Iterator bindit = svc.getServiceBindings().iterator();
110:            while ( bindit.hasNext() )
111:            {
112:              ServiceBinding sb = (ServiceBinding)bindit.next();
113:              System.out.println("    Service Binding Name: " +
114:                            convertToString(sb.getName()));
115:              System.out.println("    Service Binding Desc: " +
116:                            convertToString(sb.getDescription()));
117:              System.out.println("    Service Binding Access URI:\n" +
118:                           "       " + sb.getAccessURI());
119:
120:              Iterator speclinkit =
121:              sb.getSpecificationLinks().iterator();
122:              while ( speclinkit.hasNext() )
123:              {
124:                SpecificationLink slink =
125:                (SpecificationLink)speclinkit.next();
126:
127:              RegistryObject ro = slink.getSpecificationObject();
128:              Iterator extlinkit =                              ↩
ro.getExternalLinks().iterator();
129:              while ( extlinkit.hasNext() )
130:              {
131:                ExternalLink extlink =                          ↩
(ExternalLink)extlinkit.next();
132:                System.out.println("   WSDL: " +
133:                                  extlink.getExternalURI());
134:              }
135:              }
136:            }
137:          }
138:        }
139:      }
140:  }
```

Listing 47.4   *(continued)*

Unfortunately, the programmer was wrong again. As you can see in the output of the program in Listing 47.5, the first response from the 'truman' query returned no WSDL document. The second response from the 'truman' query returned an HTML document on line 17. Strangely, the first and second responses from the 'sched' query did return the WSDL document. What went wrong?

```
01:
02: Made an organizational query for 'truman'...
03: 1) Organization Name: TrumanTruck.com
04:    Organization Desc: Restoration of Truman Schermerhorn's Truck
05:    Service Name: TrumanTruck Page
06:    Service Binding Name: null
07:    Service Binding Desc: hyperlink
08:    Service Binding Access URI:
09:     http://www.trumantruck.com
10: 2) Organization Name: Harry S. Truman Scholarship Foundation
11:    Organization Desc:
12:    Service Name: Web home page
13:    Service Binding Name: null
14:    Service Binding Desc: hyperlink
15:    Service Binding Access URI:
16:     http://www.truman.gov/welcome.htm
17:    WSDL: http://www.uddi.org/specification.html
18: ----------SECOND QUERY--------------
19: Made an organizational query for 'sched'...
20: 1) Organization Name: LFC Scheduling
21:    Organization Desc:
22:    Service Name: Classroom Scheduling
23:    Service Binding Name: null
24:    Service Binding Desc:
25:    Service Binding Access URI:
26:     http://www.contest.eraserver.net/Scheduling/Scheduler.asmx
27:    WSDL:
http://www.contest.eraserver.net/Scheduling/Scheduler.asmx?wsdl
28: 2) Organization Name: Interactive Scheduler
29:    Organization Desc:
30:    Service Name: Interactive Schedule
31:    Service Binding Name: null
32:    Service Binding Desc:
33:    Service Binding Access URI:
34:
http://www.contest.eraserver.net/InteractiveScheduler/service1.asmx
35:    WSDL:
http://www.contest.eraserver.net/InteractiveScheduler/
InteractiveScheduler.wsdl
```

Listing 47.5   Output of our second attempt

The problem from our second attempt to find WSDL documents revolves around the concept of classifications. Because both registry objects for our first query were not classified as the UDDI "wsdlspec" type, they do not have WSDL documents. Unfortunately, this is a common programming mistake. If the programmer had assumed that these were both Web services registered with a WSDL URL, the program would have mixed results—the program may work for one query, but not for another. In the case of the false WSDL document output on line 17, if the program had tried to dynamically call the Web service using JAX-RPC, the program would have failed.

The answer to our dilemma lies in our call from the Classification object to the RegistryObject in Figure 47.2. If you call getClassifications() from the returned RegistryObject, and if the classification of that object is the "wsdlspec" classification, then you can call getClassifiedObject() to then get the WSDL-classified object, and then retrieve the external link. Listing 47.6 does just that in lines 123 to 150.

```
064: public void makeCall(String query) throws Exception
065: {
066:   if ( m_querymgr == null )
067:   {
068:     throw new Exception("No query manager!!!!! Exiting
makeCall()");
069:   }
070:   else
071:   {
072:
073:     Collection findQualifiers = new ArrayList();
074:     findQualifiers.add(FindQualifier.SORT_BY_NAME_DESC);
075:     Collection namePatterns = new ArrayList();
076:     namePatterns.add("%" + query + "%");
077:
078:     BulkResponse response =
079:     m_querymgr.findOrganizations(findQualifiers,
080:                                  namePatterns,
081:                                  null, null, null, null);
082:
083:     Iterator orgIterator = response.getCollection().iterator();
084:
085:     System.out.println("Made an organizational query for '" +
086:                        query + "'...");
087:
088:     int orgcnt = 0;
089:     while ( orgIterator.hasNext() )
090:     {
091:       String orgname  = null;
092:       String orgdesc  = null;
```

Listing 47.6 The solution to our dilemma

```
093:        String svcname  = null;
094:
095:        //Let's get every organization that matches the query!
096:        Organization org = (Organization) orgIterator.next();
097:
098:        orgname = convertToString(org.getName());
099:        orgdesc = convertToString(org.getDescription());
100:
101:        //Now get the services provided by the organization
102:        Iterator svcIter = org.getServices().iterator();
103:        while ( svcIter.hasNext() )
104:        {
105:          Service svc = (Service)svcIter.next();
106:          svcname = convertToString(svc.getName());
107:
108:          //Let's get the service binding object from service
109:          Iterator bindit = svc.getServiceBindings().iterator();
110:          while ( bindit.hasNext() )
111:          {
112:            ServiceBinding sb = (ServiceBinding)bindit.next();
113:
114:            Iterator speclinkit =
115:            sb.getSpecificationLinks().iterator();
116:            while ( speclinkit.hasNext() )
117:            {
118:              SpecificationLink slink =
119:              (SpecificationLink)speclinkit.next();
120:
121:              RegistryObject ro = slink.getSpecificationObject();
122:
123:              //Now, let's see the classification object..
124:              Iterator classit = ro.getClassifications().iterator();
125:              while ( classit.hasNext() )
126:              {
127:                Classification classif =
128:                (Classification)classit.next();
129:                if ( classif.getValue().equalsIgnoreCase("wsdlspec") )
130:                {
131:                  orgcnt++;
132:                  System.out.println(orgcnt +
133:                                  ") Organization Name: " + orgname);
134:                  System.out.println(
135:                           " Organization Desc: " + orgdesc);
136:                  System.out.println(
137:                           " Service Name: " + svcname);
138:
139:                  RegistryObject ro2 = classif.getClassifiedObject();
```

Listing 47.6   (continued)

```
140:
141:                    Iterator extlinkit =
142:                    ro2.getExternalLinks().iterator();
143:                    while ( extlinkit.hasNext() )
144:                    {
145:                       ExternalLink extlink =
146:                       (ExternalLink)extlinkit.next();
147:
148:                       System.out.println("   WSDL: " +
149:                                        extlink.getExternalURI());
150:                    }
151:
152:                }
153:              }
154:            }
155:          }
156:        }
157:      }
158:    }
159: }
```

Listing 47.6   *(continued)*

The result of our example is shown in Listing 47.7. In our output, our program only prints the listing of Web services that have WSDL documents.

```
01: Made an organizational query for 'trumantruck'...
02: -----------SECOND QUERY--------------
03: Made an organizational query for 'sched'...
04: 1) Organization Name: LFC Scheduling
05:    Organization Desc:
06:    Service Name: Classroom Scheduling
07:    WSDL:
http://www.contest.eraserver.net/Scheduling/Scheduler.asmx?wsdl
08: 2) Organization Name: Interactive Scheduler
09:    Organization Desc:
10:    Service Name: Interactive Schedule
11:    WSDL:
http://www.contest.eraserver.net/InteractiveScheduler/
InteractiveScheduler.wsdl
```

Listing 47.7   The output of our solution

It is important to note that we could get to the service much easier. If we knew the name of the service, for example, and we wanted to go directly to the `RegistryOb-ject` that has the "wsdlspec" classification, we could do a concept query. The `Reg-istryObject`, shown in Figure 47.2, on page 408, is always a `Concept` object when using UDDI registries (even though the `getSpecificationObject()` from the `SpecificationLink` interface returns the `RegistryObject` interface to be more flexible for other registries).

To demonstrate this, we will show another example of the `makeCall()` method in Listing 47.8. We will call the `findConcepts()` method on the `BusinessQueryMan-ager` object. To constrain the search, we will use the same `namePatterns` query pattern that we used in the previous examples, but we will add a classification constraint on lines 83 to 100. In doing so, the objects that are returned will be `Concept` objects that have WSDL documents and that match the query pattern passed in as a parameter.

```
064:    public void makeCall(String query) throws Exception
065:    {
066:        if ( m_querymgr == null )
067:        {
068:            throw new Exception("No query manager!!!!! Exiting
makeCall()");
069:        }
070:        else
071:        {
072:
073:            Collection findQualifiers = new ArrayList();
074:            findQualifiers.add(FindQualifier.SORT_BY_NAME_DESC);
075:            Collection namePatterns = new ArrayList();
076:            namePatterns.add("%" + query + "%");
077:
078:            /*
079:             * Find the classification scheme defined by
080:             *  the UDDI spec
081:             */
082:
083:            String schemeName = "uddi-org:types";
084:            ClassificationScheme uddiOrgTypes =
085:            m_querymgr.findClassificationSchemeByName(null,
086:                                                      schemeName);
087:            /*
088:             * Create a classification, specifying the scheme
089:             *  and the taxonomy name and value defined for
090:             *  WSDL documents by the UDDI spec
091:             */
092:            BusinessLifeCycleManager blm =
093:            m_regserv.getBusinessLifeCycleManager();
```

Listing 47.8   Good example of querying by concept *(continued)*

```
094:
095:        Classification wsdlSpecClass =
096:        blm.createClassification(uddiOrgTypes,
097:                             "wsdlSpec", "wsdlSpec");
098:
099:        Collection classifications = new ArrayList();
100:        classifications.add(wsdlSpecClass);
101:
102:        // Find concepts
103:        BulkResponse response =
104:        m_querymgr.findConcepts(null, namePatterns,
105:                             classifications, null, null);
106:
107:        System.out.println("Made an wsdlSpec concept query for \n'" +
108:                    "services matching '" +query + "'");
109:
110:        // Display information about the concepts found
111:        int itnum = 0;
112:        Iterator iter = response.getCollection().iterator();
113:        if ( !iter.hasNext())
114:        {
115:          System.out.println("   No matching items!");
116:        }
117:        while ( iter.hasNext() )
118:        {
119:          itnum++;
120:          Concept concept = (Concept) iter.next();
121:          System.out.println(itnum + ")    Name: " +
122:                        convertToString(concept.getName()));
123:          System.out.println("     Description: " +
124:                        convertToString(concept.getDescription()));
125:
126:          Iterator linkit = concept.getExternalLinks().iterator();
127:          if ( linkit.hasNext() )
128:          {
129:            ExternalLink link =
130:            (ExternalLink) linkit.next();
131:            System.out.println("    WSDL: '" +
132:                          link.getExternalURI() + "'");
133:          }
134:
135:        }
136:      }
137:    }
```

Listing 47.8   *(continued)*

The result of our program is shown in Listing 47.9. On our concept query for services with the string `'sched'` in them with WSDL documents, we had four results.

```
01: Made an wsdlSpec concept query for
02: 'services matching 'truman'
03:    No matching items!
04: -----------SECOND QUERY--------------
05: Made an wsdlSpec concept query for
06: 'services matching 'sched'
07: 1)    Name: Continental-com:Schedule-v1
08:       Description: Flight schedule
09:       WSDL:
'http://webservices.continental.com/schedule/schedule.asmx?WSDL'
10: 2)    Name: Interactive Scheduler
11:       Description: A Web Service that provides a method to schedule
                    meetings into someone else's calendar.
12:       WSDL:
'http://www.contest.eraserver.net/InteractiveScheduler/
InteractiveScheduler.wsdl'
13: 3)    Name: Lake Forest College-com:SchedulingInterface-v1
14:       Description: Scheduling Web Service for Institutions-
Scheduling Classes to appropriate rooms
15:       WSDL:
'http://www.contest.eraserver.net/Scheduling/Scheduler.asmx?wsdl'
16: 4)    Name: Metric-com:Aeroflot Flights Schedule
17:       Description: Web service deliver on-line flights schedule
information
18:       WSDL: 'http://webservices.aeroflot.ru/flightSearch.wsdl'
```

Listing 47.9   Output of querying by concept

In this pitfall, we demonstrated problems that developers encounter when using the JAXR API with UDDI registries. We showed two examples of potential pitfalls while traversing the data structures of the registry and provided solutions for these problems. Because of the difficulty that some programmers have with JAXR and UDDI, reading the JAXR specification is highly recommended.

Item 48: Performance Pitfalls in JAX-RPC Application Clients

The Java API for XML-based Remote Procedure Calls (JAX-RPC) allows us to continue to think like Java developers when we develop, deploy, and communicate with RPC-based Web services. Although JAX-RPC relies on underlying protocols (HTTP and SOAP), the API hides this complexity from the application developer. Using basic programming techniques that enterprise developers are accustomed to, you can create a Web service easily. Building a client that communicates with the Web service is also easy—proxy stubs for the Web service can be compiled prior to runtime, they can be dynamically generated at runtime, or the Dynamic Invocation Interface (DII) can be used to discover a Web service's API on-the-fly.

In this pitfall item, we use different techniques in building clients for a simple Web service. We run a timing experiment on each of the techniques and give recommendations for building clients using JAX-RPC. As a result of reading this pitfall item, you will understand the performance implications of using each technique—and hopefully use this to your advantage in your projects.

Example Web Service

For this pitfall item, we used Sun's Java Web Services Developer Pack (WSDP) and created a simple Web service called "SimpleTest." The Web service has one method called doStuff(), and the interface used to develop this Web service is shown in Listing 48.1.

```
001: package org.javapitfalls.item48;
002:
003: import java.rmi.Remote;
004: import java.rmi.RemoteException;
005:
006: public interface SimpleTestIF extends Remote
007: {
008:    public String doStuff(String s) throws RemoteException;
009: }
```

Listing 48.1   Interface to our simple Web service.

The Web Service Description Language (WSDL) that was automatically generated from the tools available with the developer's pack is shown in Listing 48.2. Because this was automatically generated and deployed with the developer tools that generated this from our Java interface, our implementation class, and deployment descriptors, we weren't forced to write it by hand. As JAX-RPC defines Web services as collections of remote interfaces and methods, WSDL defines Web services as a collection of ports and operations. The WSDL provided in Listing 48.2 is for your reference, as we develop our Web service clients later in the pitfall examples.

```
001: <?xml version="1.0" encoding="UTF-8" ?>
002: <definitions xmlns="http://schemas.xmlsoap.org/wsdl/"
003:      xmlns:tns="http://org.javapitfalls.item48/wsdl/SimpleTest"
```

Listing 48.2   WSDL for a simple Web service

```
005:        xmlns:xsd="http://www.w3.org/2001/XMLSchema"
004:        xmlns:soap="http://schemas.xmlsoap.org/wsdl/soap/"
006:        name="SimpleTest"
007:        targetNamespace="http://org.javapitfalls.item48/wsdl/SimpleTest">
008:      <types />
009:      <message name="SimpleTestIF_doStuff">
010:          <part name="String_1" type="xsd:string" />
011:      </message>
012:      <message name="SimpleTestIF_doStuffResponse">
013:          <part name="result" type="xsd:string" />
014:      </message>
015:      <portType name="SimpleTestIF">
016:          <operation name="doStuff" parameterOrder="String_1">
017:              <input message="tns:SimpleTestIF_doStuff" />
018:              <output message="tns:SimpleTestIF_doStuffResponse" />
019:          </operation>
020:      </portType>
021:      <binding name="SimpleTestIFBinding" type="tns:SimpleTestIF">
022:          <operation name="doStuff">
023:            <input>
024:              <soap:body
025:               encodingStyle="http://schemas.xmlsoap.org/soap/encoding/"
026:               use="encoded"
027:               namespace="http://org.javapitfalls.item48/wsdl/SimpleTest"
028:               />
029:            </input>
030:            <output>
031:              <soap:body
032:               encodingStyle="http://schemas.xmlsoap.org/soap/encoding/"
033:               use="encoded"
034:               namespace="http://org.javapitfalls.item48/wsdl/SimpleTest"
035:               />
036:            </output>
037:            <soap:operation soapAction="" />
038:          </operation>
039:          <soap:binding transport="http://schemas.xmlsoap.org/soap/http"
040:                        style="rpc" />
041:      </binding>
042:      <service name="SimpleTest">
043:       <port name="SimpleTestIFPort" binding="tns:SimpleTestIFBinding">
044:        <soap:address xmlns:wsdl="http://schemas.xmlsoap.org/wsdl/"
045:         location="http://localhost:8080/simpletest-jaxrpc/simpletest" />
046:       </port>
047:      </service>
048: </definitions>
```

Listing 48.2   *(continued)*

Next, we will get to the meat of this pitfall: writing different clients that will call the doStuff() method on the "SimpleTest" Web service. In the next sections, we show different approaches to building JAX-RPC clients.

A Simple Client That Uses Precompiled Stub Classes

The first, and easiest, way to call an RPC-style Web service is by using precompiled stubs. To create these stubs, the Java Web Services Developer Pack contains a tool called "wscompile." As a result, a client can communicate with the Web service interface using the java.xml.rpc.Stub interface. The wscompile tool is run against a configuration file listing details about the Web services (the URL of the WSDL, the package name, etc). When the wscompile tool runs successfully, it processes the WSDL for our Web service and generates proxy stubs so that our client can invoke methods on our SimpleTestIF interface at runtime.

Listing 48.3 shows a client that uses precompiled stubs. Lines 37 to 40 show the static createProxy() method that returns the stub that is cast to the SimpleTestIF interface in line 16. As a result, you do not have to know anything about SOAP or WSDL. Instead, you write code like you're using RMI. Note that in lines 27 and 28, we are printing out the invocation setup time. This will be used later in this pitfall item to compare pre-invocation times with our other techniques.

```
001: package org.javapitfalls.item48;
002:
003: import javax.xml.rpc.*;
004: import javax.xml.namespace.*;
005:
006: public class NoDynamicStuffClient
007: {
008:     public static void main(String[] args)
009:     {
010:         try
011:         {
012:             long initial, afterproxy, preInvokeTime, invokeTime;
013:
014:             initial = System.currentTimeMillis();
015:
016:             SimpleTestIF simpletest = (SimpleTestIF)createProxy();
017:
018:             afterproxy = System.currentTimeMillis();
019:             preInvokeTime = afterproxy - initial;
020:
021:             //Now, invoke our method
022:
023:             String response =
024:                 simpletest.doStuff("Hi there from NoDynamicStuffClient!");
025:             //Print out stats
026:
```

Listing 48.3 A simple client using precompiled stubs

```
027:                    System.out.println("Invocation setup took "
028:                        + preInvokeTime + " milliseconds.");
029:
030:         }
031:         catch ( Exception ex )
032:         {
033:             ex.printStackTrace();
034:         }
035:     }
036:
037:     private static Stub createProxy()
038:     {
039:         return(Stub)(new SimpleTest_Impl().getSimpleTestIFPort());
040:     }
041:}
```

Listing 48.3   *(continued)*

A Client That Uses Dynamic Proxies for Access

JAX-RPC includes the concept of using dynamic proxies—a second way for clients to access Web services. A *dynamic proxy class* is a class that implements a list of interfaces specified at runtime, and using this technique, does not require pregeneration of the proxy class. Listing 48.4 shows an example of building such a proxy. In line 30, we create a new instance of `ServiceFactory`. We then specify the service in lines 32 and 33 by passing the URL for our WSDL in the example, as well as the `javax.xml.name-space.QName`, which represents the value of a qualified name as specified in the XML Schema specification. By calling the `getPort()` method on our `javax.xml.rpc.Service` class on lines 35 to 37, we have generated a proxy class that is cast to our original interface class from Listing 48.1.

```
001: package org.javapitfalls.item48;
002:
003: import java.net.URL;
004: import javax.xml.rpc.Service;
005: import javax.xml.rpc.JAXRPCException;
006: import javax.xml.namespace.QName;
007: import javax.xml.rpc.ServiceFactory;
008:
009: public class DynamicProxyClient
010: {
011:
```

Listing 48.4   A simple client using dynamic proxies *(continued)*

```
012:    public static void main(String[] args)
013:    {
014:        try
015:        {
016:
017:            long initial, afterproxy, preInvokeTime, invokeTime;
018:
019:            initial = System.currentTimeMillis();
020:
021:            String UrlString =
022:              "http://localhost:8080/simpletest-
jaxrpc/simpletest?WSDL";
023:            String nameSpaceUri =
024:                "http://org.javapitfalls.item48/wsdl/SimpleTest";
025:            String serviceName = "SimpleTest";
026:            String portName = "SimpleTestIFPort";
027:
028:            URL WsdlUrl = new URL(UrlString);
029:
030:            ServiceFactory serviceFactory =
031:                ServiceFactory.newInstance();
032:            Service simpleService =
033:                serviceFactory.createService(WsdlUrl,
034:                    new QName(nameSpaceUri, serviceName));
035:            SimpleTestIF myProxy = (SimpleTestIF)
simpleService.getPort(
036:                            new QName(nameSpaceUri, portName),
037:                  org.javapitfalls.item48.SimpleTestIF.class);
038:
039:            afterproxy = System.currentTimeMillis();
040:            preInvokeTime = afterproxy - initial;
041:
042:            String response = myProxy.doStuff(
043:                        "Hello from Dynamic Proxy..");
044:
045:            //Print out stats
046:            System.out.println("Invocation setup took "
047:                        + preInvokeTime + " milliseconds.");
048:
049:        }
050:        catch ( Exception ex )
051:        {
052:            ex.printStackTrace();
053:        }
054:    }
055: }
```

Listing 48.4   *(continued)*

It is important to realize that this example requires a copy of the compiled Java interface class that we created (in order to cast it on line 35), but it does not require any precompilation steps. Where our precompilation process for our first example involved downloading the WSDL and creating the stubs before runtime, the dynamic proxy method does everything at runtime. This convenience will come at a cost. On line 46 of Listing 48.4, we print out our invocation setup time.

Two Clients Using the Dynamic Invocation Interface (DII)

A client can call a Web service using the Dynamic Invocation Interface (DII). The `javax.xml.rpc.Call` interface provides support for the dynamic invocation of an operation on a target service endpoint. In this section, we demonstrate two examples. In the first example, shown in Listing 48.5, we know where our Web service is, and we know the methods of our Web service. We will simply create our `Call` object and invoke the `doStuff()` method.

In lines 28 to 30 of Listing 48.5, we create our `Service` object. In line 35, we create the `Call` object by passing the port name (which is the qualified name for `"SimpleTestIF"` set up on line 32). In lines 36 to 55, we create our call by setting properties, setting our return types, and setting up our parameter information. Finally, on line 62, we perform the invocation.

```
001: package org.javapitfalls.item48;
002:
003: import javax.xml.rpc.*;
004: import javax.xml.namespace.*;
005:
006: public class DIIClient
007: {
008:
009:
010:     public static void main(String[] args)
011:     {
012:         String endpoint =
013:             "http://localhost:8080/simpletest-jaxrpc/simpletest";
014:         String servicenamespace =
015:             "http://org.javapitfalls.item48/wsdl/SimpleTest";
016:         String encodingStyleProperty =
017:             "javax.xml.rpc.encodingstyle.namespace.uri";
018:
019:         try
020:         {
021:
022:             long initial, afterproxy, preInvokeTime, invokeTime;
023:
```

Listing 48.5   A simple client using DII hard-coded calls *(continued)*

```
024:              initial = System.currentTimeMillis();
025:
026:          //Set up the service, giving it the service name
027:          //and the port (interface)
028:          ServiceFactory factory = ServiceFactory.newInstance();
029:          Service service = factory.createService(
030:                            new QName("SimpleTest")
031:                            );
032:          QName port = new QName("SimpleTestIF");
033:
034:          //Set up the call & the endpoint..
035:          Call call = service.createCall(port);
036:          call.setTargetEndpointAddress(endpoint);
037:
038:          //Set up the Call properties...
039:          call.setProperty(Call.SOAPACTION_USE_PROPERTY,
040:                          new Boolean(true)
041:                          );
042:          call.setProperty(Call.SOAPACTION_URI_PROPERTY, "");
043:          call.setProperty(encodingStyleProperty,
044:                 "http://schemas.xmlsoap.org/soap/encoding/");
045:
046:          QName qnametype =
047:              new QName("http://www.w3.org/2001/XMLSchema","string");
048:          call.setReturnType(qnametype);
049:
050:          //Set up the operation name & parameter...
051:          call.setOperationName(
052:                          new QName(servicenamespace, "doStuff"));
053:
054:         call.addParameter("String_1", qnametype, ParameterMode.IN);
055:         String[] params = { "Hello from DII Client!"};
056:
057:          afterproxy = System.currentTimeMillis();
058:          preInvokeTime = afterproxy - initial;
059:          System.out.println("Invocation setup took " +
060:                          preInvokeTime + " milliseconds.");
061:
062:          String response = (String)call.invoke(params);
063:      }
064:     catch ( Exception ex )
065:     {
066:          ex.printStackTrace();
067:      }
068:  }
069:}
```

Listing 48.5 *(continued)*

Our example in Listing 48.5 requires no precompilation or WSDL lookups. Because we knew the information in advance, we could hard-code it into our application. On line 59, we made sure to print out the milliseconds for invocation setup.

Our final client code example is another example of using DII. DII is quite powerful, because you can dynamically determine your interfaces at runtime, looking at the WSDL, and discover information about the operations that a Web service supports. Listing 48.6 is such an example. Like the last example, using DII is convenient because it requires no precompilation of code or local Java interfaces at compile time. Everything with DII occurs at runtime.

In this example, we ask the service for the first method, and we simply invoke the method. In our example, we know the method takes a string as a parameter. Because we pass the URL of the WSDL in lines 31 to 33 of Listing 48.6, our `Service` object will have the ability to download the WSDL and get call information for the Web service. In line 38, we ask the Web service for the names of available calls. On line 48, we request the first call available, which we know is the method we would like to invoke. Finally, we set up the parameter on line 52, and we invoke the method on line 63.

```
001: package org.javapitfalls.item48;
002:
003: import java.net.*;
004: import javax.xml.rpc.*;
005: import javax.xml.namespace.*;
006:
007: public class DIILookupClient
008: {
009:
010:
011:     public static void main(String[] args)
012:     {
013:         try
014:         {
015:             long initial, afterproxy, preInvokeTime, invokeTime;
016:
017:             initial = System.currentTimeMillis();
018:
019:             String UrlString =
020:               "http://localhost:8080/simpletest-jaxrpc/simpletest?WSDL";
021:             String nameSpaceUri =
022:                 "http://org.javapitfalls.item48/wsdl/SimpleTest";
023:             String serviceName = "SimpleTest";
024:             String portName = "SimpleTestIFPort";
025:             String qnamePort = "SimpleTestIF";
026:
027:             URL wsdlUrl = new URL(UrlString);
```

Listing 48.6 A simple client using DII with lookups *(continued)*

```
028:
029:          ServiceFactory serviceFactory =
030:               ServiceFactory.newInstance();
031:          Service simpleService =
032:               serviceFactory.createService(wsdlUrl,
033:                  new QName(nameSpaceUri,serviceName));
034:
035:          QName port = new QName(nameSpaceUri, portName);
036:
037:
038:          Call[] servicecalls = simpleService.getCalls(port);
039:          Call mycall = null;
040:
041:          /*
042:           * We will assume that we know to call the first method &
043:           * pass it a string..
044:           */
045:
046:          if ( servicecalls != null )
047:          {
048:              mycall = servicecalls[0];
049:              String operationName =
050:                  mycall.getOperationName().toString();
051:
052:              String[] params = { "Hello from DII Client!"};
053:
054:
055:              afterproxy = System.currentTimeMillis();
056:              preInvokeTime = afterproxy - initial;
057:
058:              System.out.println("Invocation setup took "
059:                          + preInvokeTime + " milliseconds.");
060:              System.out.println("About to call the "
061:                          + operationName + " operation..");
062:
063:              String response = (String)mycall.invoke(params);
064:              System.out.println("Received '"
065:                          + response + "' as a response..");
066:
067:
068:          }
069:          else
070:
071:              System.out.println("Problem with DII command..");
```

Listing 48.6 (continued)

```
072:              }
073:
074:          }
075:          catch ( Exception ex )
076:          {
077:              ex.printStackTrace();
077:          }
078:      }
079: }
```

Listing 48.6 *(continued)*

Everything in this example used the capabilities of DII, getting call information at runtime. Many more methods on the `javax.xml.rpc.Call` interface could be used, but for the purpose of simplicity, this example doesn't use them all. For more information about the JAX-RPC API and specification, go to Sun's JAX-RPC Web page at http://java.sun.com/xml/jaxrpc/.

Performance Results

For our experiment, we deployed our Web service and used the code from Listings 48.3, 48.4, 48.5, and 48.6. Our experiment was run with the Web service and the client running on a 1300-MHz Pentium IV PC with 1 GB RAM, using the Windows 2000 operating system. Each "run" was done by running each client, in random order, one after another. The client VM was Java HotSpot Client VM (build 1.4.0-b92, mixed mode), and the tools and Web services were running with the Java Web Services Developer's Pack, version 1.0_01. Table 48.1 shows the results.

As you can see, there is an obvious trade-off between flexibility at runtime and performance. The best performing clients (with respect to invocation setup) were those in Listings 48.3 and 48.5. Our hard-coded DII example in Listing 48.5 matched the performance of our precompiled stubs example. This makes sense, because no WSDL lookup was necessary in the hard-coded example.

The worst performance for call setup revolved around the clients where calls were determined at runtime, or where stubs were generated at runtime. The DII with call lookups example in Listing 48.6 and the dynamic proxy example in Listing 48.4 were approximately 2.5 times slower in performance for pre-invocation setup. Both of those clients downloaded the WSDL. The dynamic proxy example was slightly slower because of the generation of the stubs on the fly, but they were quite similar in speed.

Table 48.1   Table of Results: Pre-invocation Times

	LISTING 48.3 (PRECOMPILED STUBS)	LISTING 48.4 (DYNAMIC PROXY GENERATION)	LISTING 48.5 (DII HARD-CODED)	LISTING 48.6 (DII - WITH CALL LOOKUPS)
Run 1	590 ms	1683 ms	591 ms	1642 ms
Run 2	601 ms	1683 ms	581 ms	1653 ms
Run 3	591 ms	1672 ms	591 ms	1643 ms
Run 4	591 ms	1672 ms	581 ms	1633 ms
Run 5	591 ms	1783 ms	581 ms	1643 ms
Run 6	601 ms	1663 ms	591 ms	1653 ms
Run 7	591 ms	1692 ms	601 ms	1642 ms
Run 8	591 ms	1713 ms	601 ms	1663 ms
Run 9	591 ms	1672 ms	590 ms	1662 ms
Run 10	591 ms	1682 ms	641 ms	1662 ms
Run 11	641 ms	1662 ms	581 ms	1632 ms
Run 12	591 ms	1683 ms	581 ms	1642 ms
Run 13	591 ms	1722 ms	591 ms	1642 ms
Run 14	581 ms	1692 ms	631 ms	1642 ms
Run 15	591 ms	1682 ms	591 ms	1692 ms
Average Time	594.9333333 ms	1690.4 ms	594.9333333 ms	1649.733333 ms

Conclusion

Our simple example has shown that there is obviously a trade-off between the dynamic features of JAX-RPC and performance. Imagine if we needed to write a client application for working with multiple Web services, or a complex Web service with pages and pages of WSDL. The performance implications of doing everything dynamically—just because those techniques are available—would be awful. Just because you *can* do things dynamically doesn't necessarily mean you *should* do things dynamically with JAX-RPC. If there is a reason, do it. When in doubt, use precompiled stubs—your code will look prettier—and if your Web service's interface changes, you will simply need to recompile your client.

Item 49: Get Your Beans Off My Filesystem!

It is easy to overlook best practices for J2EE because some habits of using the Java 2 Standard Edition die hard. When designing Enterprise JavaBeans solutions, it is sometimes easy to forget what type of programming should *not* be done. We know, for example, that spawning threads within beans is a big no-no, because we understand that the EJB container handles all threading issues. Oftentimes, however, we overlook the pitfalls that await us when we use the *java.io* classes to access files in the filesystem.

To demonstrate this issue, we provide a very simple example of a session bean reading properties from the filesystem. In our example, a session bean is used to calculate the amount of tax that shoppers must pay when they proceed to check out. In doing so, the two-character abbreviation for the shoppers' state is passed to the bean, so the bean can calculate the approximate sales tax. Because sales tax varies from state to state, the bean reads from a local properties file with different sales tax percentages:

```
Salestax.AB=.04
Salestax.VA=.045
```

For brevity (and to do a simple demonstration of this pitfall), we are only listing two states. In our example, we assume that if a state is not in this properties file, the state has no sales tax. Listing 49.1 shows the code for our BadTaxCalculatorBean that reads the properties file. A client calling this session bean passes the purchase amount (double cost) and the two-letter state abbreviation (String state), and the tax on the purchase amount is returned. We load the properties file in our session bean's calculateTax() method, and we calculate the sales tax and return it as a double. In lines 18 to 31, we load the properties file using the java.io.FileInputStream class and calculate the tax:

```
001: package org.javapitfalls.item49;
002:
003: import java.rmi.RemoteException;
004: import javax.ejb.SessionBean;
005: import javax.ejb.SessionContext;
006: import java.util.Properties;
007: import java.io.*;
008: import javax.ejb.EJBException;
009:
010:
011: public class BadTaxCalculatorBean implements SessionBean
012: {
013:     public double calculateTax(double cost, String state)
014:     {
015:         Properties p = new Properties();
016:         double tax = 0;
```

Listing 49.1 Bean reading properties file for values *(continued)*

```
017:
018:        try
019:        {
020:            p.load(new FileInputStream("C://salestax.properties"));
021:            tax = Double.parseDouble(p.getProperty("Salestax." + state)) *
022:                cost;
023:
024:        }
025:        catch ( IOException e )
026:        {
027:            e.printStackTrace();
028:
029:            throw new EJBException("Can't open the properties file! "
030:                                    + e.toString());
031:        }
032:
033:        String taxString = p.getProperty("Salestax." + state);
034:
035:        if ( taxString != null && !taxString.equals("") )
036:        {
037:            tax = Double.parseDouble(taxString) * cost;
038:        }
039:
040:        return (tax);
041:    }
042:
043:    public void ejbCreate() {}
044:    public void ejbPostCreate() {}
045:    public void ejbRemove()
046:    public void ejbActivate()
047:    public void ejbPassivate()
048:    public void setSessionContext(SessionContext sc) {}
049: }
```

Listing 49.1 *(continued)*

What could go wrong in Listing 49.1? First of all, loading a properties file every time the `calculateTax()` method is called is bad practice. This is a given. More importantly, because the container is responsible for management of this session bean, who knows how many `BadTaxCalculator` beans may be actually instantiated during heavy loads on the server? When an EJB uses the `java.io` package to access files on the filesystem, bad things could happen, ranging from very poor performance to running out of file descriptors and bringing down the server.[5]

---

[5] Van Rooijen, Leander. "Programming Restrictions in EJB Development: Building Scalable and Robust Enterprise Applications." *Java Developers Journal.* Volume 7, Issue 7, July 2002.

For this reason, the EJB specification lists programming restrictions related to the java.io classes. In the "Runtime Environment" chapter of the specifications (EJB specifications 1.1, 2.0, and 2.1), the restriction is listed plainly: "An enterprise bean must not use the `java.io` package to access files and directories in the filesystem. The filesystem APIs are not well-suited for business components to access data. Business components should use a resource manager API, such as the JDBC API, to store data."[6] Simply put, because a filesystem is not transactional, and because there is no resource manager involved in `java.io` operations, you need to keep your beans off the filesystem! This presents us with a challenge: If a bean compiles and deploys into our EJB container without any problems, and it seems to work well when we test it, fatal errors may end up diagnosing the problem.

For our sales tax example, how should we rewrite it? If we store all the sales tax information in a database, this would eliminate the possible problems that we could encounter when using the `java.io` package. Unfortunately, using a database in this example may be overkill because sales tax usually doesn't change very often, and we could pay a performance penalty for hitting the database every time. In our bad example, we used properties files because they are convenient for configuring our Java applications. Luckily, we can do something similar—with our deployment descriptor.

To customize your beans at runtime, you can use the environment properties in your deployment descriptor. For data that doesn't change often, and for an alternative to using a database for storing information, environment properties work well. Listing 49.2 shows our deployment descriptor for our new bean, in a file called ejb-jar.xml. Each entry, designated by the XML tag `<env-entry>`, contains a `<description>` tag, a name designated by `<env-entry-name>`, a type designated by `<env-entry-type>`, and a value designated by `<env-entry-value>`. As you can see from our listing of this deployment descriptor, we converted the original properties file to this format.

```
001: <?xml version="1.0" encoding="UTF-8"?>
002: <ejb-jar>
003:  <description>GoodTaxCalculatorBean</description>
004:  <display-name>GoodTaxCalculatorBean</display-name>
005:  <enterprise-beans>
006:   <session>
007:    <ejb-name>GoodTaxCalculator</ejb-name>
008:    <home>org.javapitalls.item49.GoodTaxCalculatorHome</home>
009:    <remote>org.javapitfalls.item49.GoodTaxCalculator</remote>
010:    <ejb-class>
011:          org.javapitfalls.item49.GoodTaxCalculatorBean
012:    </ejb-class>
013:    <session-type>Stateless</session-type>
014:    <transaction-type>Bean</transaction-type>
015:    <env-entry>
016:       <description>Alabama Sales Tax</description>
```

Listing 49.2 Setting environment entries in ejb-jar.xml *(continued)*

---

[6] Enterprise JavaBeans Specification 2.1, Chapter 25; Enterprise JavaBeans Specification 2.0, Chapter 20; Enterprise JavaBeans Specifications 1.1, Chapter 18.

```
017:          <env-entry-name>Salestax.AB</env-entry-name>
018:          <env-entry-type>java.lang.String</env-entry-type>
019:          <env-entry-value>.04</env-entry-value>
020:       </env-entry>
021:       <env-entry>
022:         <description>Virginia Sales Tax</description>
023:         <env-entry-name>Salestax.VA</env-entry-name>
024:         <env-entry-type>java.lang.String</env-entry-type>
025:         <env-entry-value>.04</env-entry-value>
026:       </env-entry>
027:     </session>
028:   </enterprise-beans>
029: </ejb-jar>
```

Listing 49.2   *(continued)*

To access these properties, the bean must do a JNDI lookup. Listing 49.3 demonstrates this approach. On lines 18 and 19, the session bean gets the initial context and uses it to look up the environment entries. These entries are always found under JNDI in java:comp/env. Finally, the lookup for the sales tax for a certain state is done by looking up the value of the current state's sales tax on line 20.

```
001: package org.javapitfalls.item49;
002:
003: import java.rmi.RemoteException;
004: import javax.ejb.EJBException;
005: import javax.ejb.SessionBean;
006: import javax.ejb.SessionContext;
007: import javax.naming.*;
008:
009: public class GoodTaxCalculatorBean implements SessionBean
010: {
011:     public double calculateTax(double cost, String state)
012:     {
013:         double tax = 0;
014:
015:         try
016:         {
017:
018:             Context ctx = new InitialContext();
019:             Context env = (Context)ctx.lookup("java:comp/env");
020:             String taxString = (String)env.lookup("Salestax." + state);
021:
022:             if ( taxString != null && !taxString.equals("") )
023:             {
```

Listing 49.3   Using environment entries in our bean

```
024:                    tax = Double.parseDouble(taxString) * cost;
025:                }
026:
027:            }
028:            catch ( NamingException ne )
029:            {
030:                ne.printStackTrace();
031:                // Instead of throwing an EJBException, let's just assume
032:                // there is no tax!
033:            }
034:
035:            return(tax);
036:        }
037:
038:        public void ejbCreate() {}
039:        public void ejbPostCreate() {}
040:        public void ejbRemove() {}
041:        public void ejbActivate() {}
042:        public void ejbPassivate() {}
043:        public void setSessionContext(SessionContext sc) {}
044:
045: }
```

Listing 49.3 *(continued)*

In this pitfall, we discussed the potential problems our beans may encounter if they use the `java.io` package to access files and directories on the filesystem. We demonstrated a potentially flawed session bean that loaded a properties file with the `java.io.FileInputStream` class. We listed the programming restriction from the EJB specification and discussed what could go wrong. Finally, we modified our example and provided an alternative to beans loading properties files by using environmental entries in the deployment descriptor. As you are looking through your code base, you may want to look for this potential problem. If you see any code where beans are loading properties files, it will be an easy fix to switch to environment entries.

Item 50: When Transactions Go Awry, or Consistent State in Stateful Session EJBs

Many pitfalls are based on erroneous assumptions—assumptions that, at least on the surface, appear perfectly reasonable. As EJB developers become more educated, one of the first areas they branch out into is transactions. In one way or another, one of their EJBs becomes part of a transaction, and the developer feels confident that his or her code is stable and works correctly because, after all, when a transaction rolls back, the data is rolled back to a consistent state. Herein lies the pitfall; the developer *assumed* that the state of his or her EJB was rolled back when the transaction failed.

As you will recall, stateful session EJBs are those EJB components that maintain state between method calls. We can easily imagine such a bean in an example of a police call center. When you call the police operator, he or she remembers the context of your call. In such an example, each question to the call center represents a method invocation on the "call center" EJB. The assumption that EJB developers made was that when the transaction rolled back, the state of all the data within their EJB was restored to its pretransaction state. On the surface, it seems perfectly reasonable.

The problem with stateful session beans and transactions comes from the interaction of bean state and transaction state. The pitfall with session beans comes about as a result of assuming that the bean state is reset to correspond to the pretransaction state when a transaction fails.

Imagine a stateful session bean that represents a bank teller. A client speaks to the bank teller to make a withdrawal. The teller notes that a withdrawal has been requested (transaction start), attempts to perform the withdrawal (method during transaction), and then, depending on whether the teller's cash drawer has enough cash, either commits the transaction (hands cash to the client) or rolls back the transaction ("sorry, I don't have enough cash on hand"). A problem comes about if the client's passbook has already been updated to show the withdrawal. The client's passbook shows the withdrawal, but no cash was given (an inconsistency between the transaction state and the client state).

To solve the problem of inconsistent state within an EJB, we can implement the `SessionSynchronization` interface on our stateful session EJBs. The `Session-Synchronization` interface requires you to implement three methods: `beforeCom-pletion()`, `afterCompletion()`, and `afterBegin()`. Figure 50.1 shows the lifecycle of stateful session EJBs. Understanding the lifecycle will clarify exactly how we can use these methods to solve our state problem.

NOTE Note that the session synchronization interface is designed to be used with container-managed transactions. Obviously, if you are managing your own transaction state, you would know where transaction boundaries exist and you could store and reset the EJB state yourself.

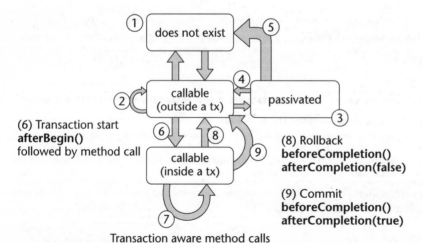

Transaction aware method calls

Figure 50.1   Stateful session EJB lifecycle.

Examining how a bean moves through its various states during its lifecycle will help us understand how transactions affect bean state and how we can solve the transaction state problem.

1. Initially, an EJB is in the *does not exist* state. In the *does not exist* state, a stateful bean has not been called for (often referred to as *pooled*) but is potentially ready for quick creation and use. Various application servers handle this state in different ways. Many, including BEA WebLogic Server, precreate beans so that they are ready for immediate use.

2. A bean moves into the *callable* state when a client calls the home interface `create()` method. In the *callable (outside a transaction)* state, a bean has been created and is ready for use. Beans in the callable state are method ready and stay in the method state until they are destroyed, or *passivated*.

3. Beans move to the *passivated* state because they have been inactive for a long period of time. Passivated beans are normally stored in some sort of high-speed backing store outside RAM to conserve system memory.

4. A bean can move from the *passivated* state back to callable as a result of a client calling a method on the bean. Under normal circumstances, *passivated* beans are restored without any developer work or interaction. However, the EJB specification provides methods for notifying a bean that it has been *passivated* and then restored.

5. If a bean is inactive long enough, it may be destroyed by the bean container. Further method calls on such a bean will result in a client exception. Many application servers will reset the state of such an object and return it to a ready-for-use object pool.

6. A bean moves to the *callable (inside a transaction)* state the first time a method is called after a transaction is started. The session synchronization interface method `afterBegin()` is called at this point, but before the method call is evoked, to signal the bean that a transaction has been started. We will use `afterBegin()` to signal we should store our state for reset later.

7. After a transaction has been started, all bean method calls become part of that transaction until either a commit or a rollback occurs. As long as the transaction is active, we remain in this state.

8. If a transaction is rolled back, the bean moves to the *callable (outside a transaction)* state. The `beforeCompletion()` method is called, followed by `afterCompletion(false)` being called. The bean could then revert its state to a known point before the transaction began.

9. When a transaction is committed, the bean moves from back to the *callable (outside a transaction)* state. However, unlike item 8 above, the transaction was committed and the `afterCompletion(true)` method is called. Since the session state is consistent with the transaction state, no action need be taken.

We can solve the transaction/bean state problem by a combination of the `Session-Synchronization` interface and careful store and reset logic within our application. The `SessionSynchronization` interface requires that we implement three specific methods:

- `public void afterBegin()`. Represented by transition 6 in the EJB lifecycle diagram. Here is where we would implement any logic to store current state. In the EJB lifecyle, `afterBegin()` is called after a transaction has begun but before any methods that would be part of the transaction. Transaction context can be obtained and manipulated within the `afterBegin()` method.

- `public void beforeCompletion()`. Represented by transitions 8 and 9 in the EJB lifecycle diagram. `beforeCompletion()` is called when a transaction is committed but before the actual commit operation takes place. Any work done within `beforeCompletion()` is within the context of the transaction.

- `public void afterCompletion(boolean committed)`. Represented by transaction 8 (failed) and 9 (committed) in the EJB lifecycle diagram. `after-Completion()` is called after the transaction has been committed or rolled back. The `committed` flag can be used to determine if the transaction was successfully committed. Here is where we would implement any required logic to store or update bean state. An important note: `afterCompletion()` is *not* called inside the context of a transaction.

NOTE A complete description of Stateless Session EJB is beyond the scope of this text. Only the implementation of stateless session EJBs is presented in this section. For complete coverage of EJB development, see *Mastering Enterprise JavaBeans, Second Edition* by Ed Roman (Wiley, 2002) or *Developing Java Enterprise Applications* by Stephen Asbury and Scott R. Weiner (Wiley, 2001).

In Listing 50.1 we can take advantage of transaction boundaries by specifying the session synchronization interface, as shown on line 7, and implementing the required methods. To solve our problem, we must save our current state, have all methods operate within transaction boundaries, and then be able to determine if our transaction succeeded or failed and restore state appropriately.

The `afterBegin()` method, shown on lines 28 to 32, called before the first method invocation inside a transaction, allows us to save our current state. All methods, which are transaction-aware, are then within transaction boundaries. Line 34 shows the before completion method, which is unused in our example but could be used for final cleanup, to reset transaction state (to rollback only for example). Once the transaction has been committed, we need to either reset from our prior state (transaction failed) or simply continue on (transaction succeeded). Lines 39 to 52 show the implementation of the `afterCompletion()` method and allow us to correctly reset our bean state when a transaction either commits or fails. The `boolean committed` flag tells us whether the transaction committed (we can discard our previous state) or failed (we need to restore our state).

```
01: package org.javapitfalls.item50;
02:
03: import javax.ejb.*;
04: import java.util.*;
05:
06: public class TellerBean implements SessionBean,
07:                                 SessionSynchronization
08: {
09:
10:     private SessionContext sc;
11:     private double balance;
12:     private double priorBalance;
13:
14:     public TellerBean() { balance = 0.0;}
15:     public void setSessionContext(SessionContext sc)
16:     {
17:       this.sc=sc;
18:     }
19:
20:     public void ejbCreate() { }
21:
22:     public void ejbRemove() { }
23:
24:     public void ejbPassivate() { }
25:
26:     public void ejbActivate() { }
27:
28:     public void afterBegin()
29:     {
30:       System.out.println("TellerBean::afterBegin");
31:       priorBalance = balance;
32:     }
33:
34:     public void beforeCompletion()
35:     {
36:       System.out.println("TellerBean::beforeCompletion");
37:     }
38:
39:     public void afterCompletion(boolean committed)
40:     {
```

Listing 50.1   TellerBean.java, using session synchronization *(continued)*

```
41:        System.out.println("TellerBean::afterCompletion ("
42:        + committed + ")");
43:        if (committed)
44:        {
45:          priorBalance=balance; // prior and current state match
46:        }
47:        else
48:        {
49:          balance=priorBalance; // restore state
50:        }
51:
52:      }
53:
54:      public double getBalance()
55:      {
56:        System.out.println("getBalance" + balance);
57:        return balance;
58:      }
59:
60:      public double Withdraw(double amount )
61:      {
62:        System.out.println("Withdraw" + amount);
63:        balance = balance - amount;
64:        return balance;
65:      }
66:
67:      public double Deposit(double amount )
68:      {
69:        System.out.println("Deposit" + amount);
70:        balance = balance + amount;
71:        return balance;
72:      }
73: }
```

Listing 50.1 *(continued)*

The Memento Pattern

Our previous scenario showed an example where we only needed to restore a simple set of variables. However, often in real life, we need to restore a complex set of data where setting and restoring variables can be a tedious and error-prone operation. To solve the restore problem, we can use a variant of the value object pattern known as the *Memento pattern.*

The Memento pattern is a rather simple pattern whose purpose is to store the state of an object. When using a memento, an originator, such as an EJB or other object that requires state, creates an instance of a memento and passes it to a caretaker, which manages the object's state on behalf of the originator. Typically, mementos hide the contents of the object from all but the originator of that object. In our case, the originator and caretaker are the same class; however, in a more complex system, we could easily envision an object monitor managing mementoes for us. When the originator needs to restore state, the caretaker provides the memento back to the originator, and the object can then restore.

The Memento pattern is actually a rather simple one to implement in Java. Using inner classes, as shown on lines 04 to 16 of Listing 50.2, we create a memento that contains two methods, a constructor and a restore method, which allows us to reset state using the contents of the moment.

In Listing 50.2, we use the memento by creating two instances representing current state and prior state, as shown in lines 19 to 21.

The value of the memento pattern is most clear when we need to contain a large amount of state. The actual object's state is contained wholly within the memento and not within the object itself. We access the object state throughout a set of state variables, currentState and priorState. Current state is used whenever we perform normal object operations such as getting and setting data. We store object state for later use into the priorState object whenever necessary. In the example, a simple method that changes the object's state, shown on lines 24 to 28, saves the current object's state contents in the priorState memento using the setFrom method. Likewise, line 31 shows how we might restore our state as required.

Our memento example is a rather simple one using predefined variables to contain an object's state. It's easy to imagine a more generic memento implementation that uses reflection to examine an object's content and save and restore state automatically without requiring object-specific code.

```
01: class MementoExample {
02:   Memento currentState = null;
03:   Memento priorState = null;
04:   private class Memento {
05:     int imaInt;
06:     double imaDouble;
07:     Memento(int i, double d) {
08:       imaInt = i;
09:       imaDouble = d;
10:     }
11:     void setFrom(Memento source) {
12:       imaInt=source.imaInt;
13:       imaDouble=source.imaDouble;
14:     }
15:
```

Listing 50.2 MementoExample.java *(continued)*

```
16:   }
17:
18:   public MementoExample() {
19:    currentState = new Memento(1,20.0);
20:    priorState = new Memento(0,0.0);
21:    priorState.setFrom(currentState);
22:    }
23:
24:   public void changeState(int i, double d) {
25:     priorState.setFrom(currentState);
26:     currentState.imaInt = i;
27:     currentState.imaDouble = d;
28:   }
29:
30:   public void restoreState() {
31:     currentState.setFrom(priorState);
32:   }
33:
34:   public void printState() {
35:    System.out.println("State:");
36:    System.out.println("    imaInt = " +
37:        currentState.imaInt);
38:    System.out.println("    imaDouble = " +
39:        currentState.imaDouble);
40:   }
41:   public static void main(String[] arg) {
42:    MementoExample mt = new MementoExample();
43:    System.out.println("Original state to 1,20.0");
44:    mt.printState();
45:    System.out.println("Changing state to 3, 7");
46:    mt.changeState(3,7.00);
47:    mt.printState();
48:    System.out.println("Restoring state");
49:    mt.restoreState();
50:    mt.printState();
51:
52:    }
53:
54: } // end MementoExample
```

Listing 50.2 *(continued)*

The StateTellerBean interface, shown in Listing 50.3, is a remote interface that extends the EJBObject class so that all the methods in it will be exposed to remote clients.

```
01: package org.javapitfalls.item50;
02:
03: import javax.ejb.EJBObject;
04: import java.rmi.RemoteException;
05:
06: public interface StateTellerBean extends EJBObject {
07:
08:    public double getBalance() throws RemoteException;
09:
10:    public double Withdraw(double amount ) throws RemoteException;
11:
13:    public double Deposit(double amount ) throws RemoteException;
14:
15: }
```

Listing 50.3   StateTellerBean.java

The `StateTellerBeanHome` interface, shown in Listing 50.4, extends the `EJBHome` class so that remote clients can access the application. Our application does not use this, but it is provided so that other applications can use it if they want to.

```
01: package org.javapitfalls.item50;
02:
03: import java.rmi.RemoteException;
04: import javax.ejb.CreateException;
05: import javax.ejb.EJBHome;
06:
07: public interface StateTellerBeanHome extends EJBHome {
08:
09:    StateTellerBean create() throws RemoteException, CreateException;
10:
11: }
12:
```

Listing 50.4   StateTellerBeanHome.java

Listed below is the output if the Memento pattern application is run. Notice the transitions between states and the restoration of the original values. This is the result of the Memento pattern implementation.

```
01: prompt> java org.javapitfalls.item50.MementoExample
02:
03:
04: Original state 1,20.0
05: State:
06:     imaInt = 1
07:     imaDouble = 20.0
08: Changing state 3, 7
09: State:
10:     imaInt = 3
11:     imaDouble = 7.0
12: Restoring state
13: State
14:     imaInt = 1
15:     imaDouble = 20.0
16:
```

As shown in the rather simple Memento application, the memento operation remembers the context of your call, which allows an application to roll back the state of all the data within an EJB.

Index

SYMBOLS AND NUMERICS

@ (at sign), 264
{ } braces, 262
[ ] brackets, 94
. (dot), 94
4 KB buffer size, 21
16-bit unicode characters, 18

A

abort() method, 393
`AbstractCollection` class, 162
abstracting details, bad example of, 39–40
`AbstractList` class, 162
`AbstractSelectableChannel` class, 18
`AbstractSet` class, 162
Abstract Windowing Toolkit (AWT), 122, 352
acceptChanges() method, 33
accept() method, 33, 152
AccessControl, 39–40
`AccessException` class, 41–42
`Action` event handler, 167
actionPerformed() method, 177–178
addMode() method, 173, 194
addOperation() method, 173
addType() method, 173
afterBegin() method, 434–436
afterCompletion() method, 434–435
allocateDirect() method, 26
`AllTests.java` example, 100
Another Neat Tool (ANT)
  BugRat tracking tool and, 92
  Checkstyle tool and, 94

command-line build operations, 94
CruiseControl and, 98
database creation, destruction and population, 96–98
Help targets, 91
JavaNCSS utility and, 93
JDepend utility and, 93
overview, 88–89
running JUnit tests using, 90
Apache Software Foundation (ASF), 391
applets, problems with, 227–231
application programming interfaces (APIs)
  collision of, 53–57
  Java Regular Expressions, 266
applications
  Java Web Start, 231–232
  servlet-based, 223
  XSLTransformFilter, 249
`ArrayList` class, 162
ASF (Apache Software Foundation), 391
assertions
  `AssertionExample.java`, 61
  enabling, 64–65
  errors, 60, 62–63
  how to use, 59
  invariants, 60
  postconditions, 60, 63–64
  preconditions, 60
  unreachable conditions, 63
at sign (@), 264
attachment() method, 31
attach() method, 31
`authenticateHelper` class, 239

LOVE, PHILLY: BOOK ONE

HIJACKED

a novel

SONIA
ESPERANZA

Cover Design by: Murphy Rae

Edited by: Melinda Utendorf, My Brother's Editor

Interior Formatting by: Books & Moods

For my mama.

Thank you for loving yourself enough to say, "this is enough."

Playlist

Best Part of Me — Ed Sheeran (feat. YEBBA)
Easy — Camila Cabello
Everything Has Changed — Taylor Swift
King of My Heart — Taylor Swift
Latch — Disclosure (feat. Sam Smith)
Liar — Camila Cabello
Lover — Taylor Swift
Now That I Found You — Carly Rae Jepsen
Pearl — Katy Perry
Real Love — Carly Rae Jepsen
Rojo — J Balvin
Secondhand Smoke — Kelsea Ballerini
Selfish — PnB Rock
Still Learning — Halsey

Trigger Warnings

Domestic Violence (Moderate Detail)
Drinking while Driving (Intermediate Detail)
Violence (Heavy Detail)

"And all at once, you are the one I have been waiting for."

-Taylor Swift

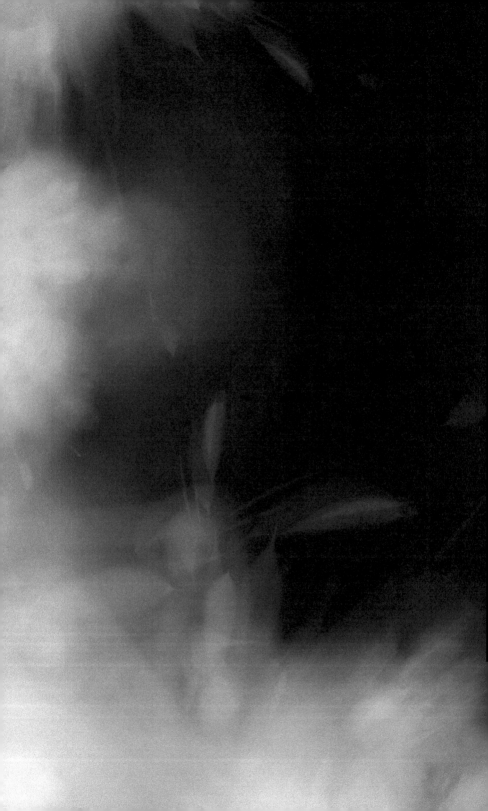

CHAPTER ONE

Annie

I don't know who I am.

The thought appeared suddenly, unwelcome, and not for the first time.

At this point in my life, I've lost count of how often those simple, but complicated six words came to mind. Hell, I lost count how many times those words assaulted my head today.

In my defense, I knew who I was as much as anyone else did. The important things, I guess you could say, the things that were written on paper.

Annie Miller. Twenty-two years of age as of a month ago, born on April thirteenth to Michelle Miller and he who didn't deserve to be named. I was a small thing then and I was a small thing now, standing a little bit under five and a half feet tall. I inherited my golden blonde hair and dark blue eyes from my mom.

That was all I knew. The basic things, the things anyone could find out with a quick internet search. But as important as those things were for being able to identify me, in the grand scheme of life, those things didn't really matter. Because who we were as people wasn't something you could find on a piece of paper, it was locked inside your chest, embedded into your soul and only those who loved you had the knowledge of who you truly were as a person.

The harsh truth that I faced each day was that I didn't have any of those people in my life.

I didn't have *any* people in my life. I barely had myself.

It had been like this for ten years. Ten years since my world as I knew it burned to the ground, taking everything I held close to my chest with its destruction.

I lost my mom. My childhood, my innocence. I lost Annie Miller as I knew her.

But unlike everything else that day, I still remained, even if it was a version of myself that felt foreign. After the tears dried and the anger settled deep inside every inch of my body, I rose on two unsteady feet, wiped the ashes from my skin and I vowed that I would get justice. A promise to myself. A promise to my mother. A promise to the world.

I could feel how close I was to righting the wrongs of my childhood. Closer as I'd ever been. Readier than I would ever be. And I refused to let something as trivial as the realization that at twenty-two years old I had yet to discover who I was, get in my way.

One plan. Five steps. Ten years of working tirelessly. A list that no longer felt physical, but a vital part of me, maybe the only part of me. The five steps stepped in for my brain, my heart, and my lungs doing what it had to, to keep me alive. It felt like that most of the time, anyway.

1. ~~Learn how to fight.~~
2. Graduate college.
3. Buy a plane ticket to Mexico.
4. Get revenge.
5. Start over.

In a few hours, after I walked across the stage and held my diploma in my hands, I will have scratched out three of my five goals. All I would have to do is rid the world of one less lowlife and not only would I be on the first international flight out of Philadelphia, far from the memories that haunted me every time I closed my eyes but finally, *finally* justice would be served.

"Hey, kid, you're gonna be late." I ignored the familiar voice that belonged to the city's most notorious STD-sharer.

Sliding off protective earmuffs and wrapping them around my wrist, I pressed the button to bring the target sheet toward me. Two dozen holes filled the sheet, and it elated me to see every shot met the head or chest area of the silhouette figure. I ripped the paper down and turned around, not surprised to find Matt, the owner of Philly Range, propped up against the bar in the recreational room, his stare aimed at me.

"You screw people my age, Matt. I sure hope you don't call them 'kid,' too."

He narrowed his eyes at me but I ignored his pointed look, well accustomed to him. Matthew Panini was harmless. If it didn't interest his dick, he couldn't give two shits about it. He was six years older than me and the closest thing to a friend I had, if swapping snarky comments made two people friends.

I met Matt three years ago, a couple of weeks into my sophomore year of college. I ambushed him one late morning as he opened the doors to his family business and scared the shit out of him.

Once he recovered from jumping out of his skin and squealing like a kitten being stepped on, he zoned in on my body. Of what he could see of it which wasn't much. I wore the same thing now that I wore back then. A pair of jeans, some graphic t-shirt of a band I couldn't tell you a song from, and a pair of Vans. That didn't deter Matt. He posted up against the door, a glint in his eyes, and his lips tilted in a smirk.

"What can I do for you, lady?" he purred, actually purred.

If I was a weaker woman, I'd have fallen under his allure. But guys weren't on my radar. No matter how beautiful their face appeared or how smoothly they talked. They weren't revenge and therefore they did nothing for me.

Matt fell under both of those categories. With his disheveled dark hair, sparkling brown eyes full of promise, and his unblemished tan skin, he was a picture-perfect example of what a woman in her early twenties was searching for in a man. But I wanted something entirely different from him.

"I want a job," I told him, steel in my voice because I already knew his answer.

The nonchalant Matt vanished, trading in for a more solemn version. He kicked off of the wall, turning away and writing me off instantly. "No."

"Oh. I'm old enough for you to fuck, just not old enough to work for you."

Philly Range wasn't the only shooting range in the city, although it ranked the best. It had what all others lacked: a young business owner. A couple months ago, Matt's dad, Victor, stepped away for reasons that the public was still dubious to. If anyone were to let a nineteen-year-old work for them, I was betting on Matthew Panini.

"Jesus Christ," he breathed out, rubbing his forehead in exasperation. "No one under twenty-one is allowed. You're definitely not twenty-one."

"I want a job," I repeated myself. "Cash under the table. I'll do whatever you need done."

He rejected me again, and that was that. Until I showed up the next day and the next, wearing him down each time until his resolve crumbled.

On the fourteenth day, he submitted. "Fine. I need someone to clean guns, anyway. Ten dollars an hour under the table and an NDA signed by you about this place. Whatever happens inside these walls, stays. I don't know if you're new to the city, kid, but it ain't safe."

I didn't know what safe felt like anymore, but I didn't tell him that. The shooting range wasn't my only option for work. A pretty, young girl in one of the best cities on the east coast, I could've worked anywhere. But I desperately needed to learn how to protect myself with something more potent than my hands. Earning money for a plan much farther in the future and learning how to shoot killed two birds with one stone.

Moving to the city from New Hazle, the town I was born and raised in, to the city to attend university, there wasn't much to me. I couldn't afford a gym membership in high school because I had to save every penny in case I didn't get a full-ride academic scholarship to the University of Philadelphia. Food wasn't much of an option, either. Belonging to a foster family earned me a spot on the free lunch program at school, which was where I got most of my nutrition, although it barely had any taste to it. A cup of ramen noodles for dinner every night saved me money, but it didn't give my body what it needed. The moment I received my acceptance letter and scholarship to the University of Philadelphia, that's when I started working on step one of my plan.

Learning how to defend yourself sounded easy. A class a few nights a week. I'm sure they offered somewhat cheap online classes for it. My body being smaller and weaker than I originally thought, it took time for me to become healthy, let alone kicking-ass worthy. Once I moved to the city, I took advantage of the free gym on campus and I joined the all-women self-defense class they offered for incoming freshmen. The class taught me everything I needed to know, but the knowledge felt meaningless when my body seemed so damn weak.

It took me months to add meat on my bones, far longer than I predicted. I struggled to eat all of the right things, cut back on cardio and focus my attention on weightlifting. With the exception of classes, studying, and a part-time job, I essentially lived in the gym my first year. I recorded every bit of progress I made, only to obsess over what could be done the following day. It took until the end of the spring semester nearing before I could be proud of my reflection in the mirror.

During the summer, I splurged on a self-defense class from one of the popular gyms. The three-week course, from start to finish, made me stronger. Not only physically, but mentally.

Sometimes it felt as if I hadn't aged a day. That little girl, ten years old, her world frozen, felt more reachable than the twenty-year-old. My body grew as did my mind but not my heart. My heart kept wishing, praying that this reality was a dream and I would wake up soon. I never did.

After my second self-defense class, something shifted. I felt strong for the first time in my life. I felt free. I no longer felt like a victim but a survivor. A survivor who, in due time, would raise hell on a man who was worse than the Devil.

That deep sense of freedom and independency stuck with me. When the next semester started, I signed up for a free archery class and it didn't take long for the instructor to show me how to wield a knife.

Enter Matt. He needed me to clean guns, and I needed to learn how to shoot. He didn't know that I couldn't or even that I wanted to, and I didn't offer that information up.

Learning how to work a gun went as smooth as my body training did. Painful and at a turtle's pace. There were only so many tutorials on the internet you could watch before you had to just do it. My first couple of weeks of working at Philly Range, I people watched. I watched people shoot, feigning interest in the rec room, the open room just beyond the firing lanes. I studied every shooter who passed through as long as I could without bringing attention to myself.

I didn't have to look far for an opening. Every afternoon at three o'clock, the range closed for lunch. For days, I crept out of my office and edged closer to the firing lanes. The first week, I left my gun in the office. The next week, I brought it with me but still didn't use it. A couple more weeks passed, and I knew I couldn't learn or watch anymore. I had to try. And so, I did.

With my feet spread apart, I held the gun in both of my hands at eye-level, my arm fully extended. I translated every piece of knowledge I'd learned in the past couple of weeks into my body. My shaky fingers barely touched the trigger as I took one last deep inhale and shot for the first time.

I failed miserably at being a decent shot the first time. I did succeed in giving myself a swollen eye and a strained wrist. The next time didn't improve. Or the next day after that. Every day that I worked, I went out there and practiced. If you wanted something bad enough and dedicated yourself to it, failure didn't exist.

Weeks passed by and I had finally stopped flinching every time I pressed the trigger when Matt busted me. "If I would have known you couldn't shoot to save your life, I would have hired you that very first day."

"Ha ha ha," I deadpanned.

"You know," he said, his amusement clear as day. "I could be of help."

"You could help? Or you could get off while you rub up against me?"

He grinned wickedly. "Annie," he said, pressing his two hands across his heart. "You have my word that I won't try anything with you." I shot him a doubtful look. "You have a gun in your hand. And even without that, I like my dick and since I met you, I've come to realize, unlike the rest of the 215, you are not a fan."

In the end, I accepted his help that came with no strings attached or touching. Fast forward three years later and I could outshoot him anytime, anywhere.

"Are you sure you don't want me to come?" he asked, following me into my office. "I promise to be on my best behavior."

"I'm sure. Plus, it might be dangerous for you. Eighty percent of the graduating class has been one of your one-night stands."

"Ha ha ha," he deadpanned.

I locked my gun away and grabbed my backpack, swinging it over my shoulders. "Good luck, graduate. I'll be rooting for you from here."

I rolled my eyes at him before kicking him out of my office. I wanted to roll my eyes at this entire day. I just wanted to get my diploma and get out.

I survived four years at one of the top academic colleges on the east coast. Surely, my prize didn't involve spending hours in a humid room with thousands of people whose names I didn't know and faces I didn't recognize.

Trucking through the city, not paying attention to the bustle around me, I walked the two miles it took to get from Center City to campus.

The University of Philadelphia seemed just as beautiful as it appeared in the brochure. If anything, the brochure didn't do the real thing justice. Being one of the youngest colleges in the country, it had a contemporary look to it. Breathtaking windows that allowed every room on campus access to natural light. Recycled steel exterior that gave the buildings a fresh glow each day. The school itself spanned almost eight thousand acres. Four years and counting and I knew for certain, I hadn't seen half of it. I traveled from my dorm room to my classes, which somehow managed to only be located in two of the eight halls, the gym, and the library.

The same gym that would soon be filled up with teachers, family members, and the graduating class. Not to mention every news reporter and journalist since the school was turning one hundred years old.

Walking into the gym, nothing met me but peaceful silence. I knew all too well that the people in your life left a mark on you long after they were gone. But places did, too. I could easily picture eighteen-year-old me enter the doors I stood in front of today, determination in her eyes to change her life. I didn't make any friends while I was here. I most definitely didn't date. But I took full advantage of this opportunity that I had earned. I worked hard and I didn't give up. In a few hours, I'd be holding the reward in my hand.

"There is my valedictorian." The familiar voice and the individual it belonged to caused my skin to crawl. I looked away from the doors of the gym, turning around to face the dean. It took real courage to not roll my eyes at him as he stood way too close, his feet spread apart and hands on his hips, looking down at me pouting.

"Yes, Mr. Jensen?" I asked, already over this conversation. His gaze snapped down to my lips and I had to fight the urge to clench my fists at my side.

"Do you have your speech ready?"

I nodded.

"Can I hear it?"

"No."

"Why ever not?" he asked with a smile that under weaker control, would have made me wince.

"I don't want to ruin the surprise." I scoured the auditorium, filled with chairs for the graduates and their families, looking for an excuse, any excuse, to escape the dean. He was one of the youngest deans in this college's history and I didn't know if he knew a lot about the college or academics in general; what I did know was that he took every chance he had at leering at women, in particular, college girls, i.e., me.

No excuse magically appeared, probably because the one person who wanted to show up for me, I had just told to stay home. I had to get out of this on my own.

"I left my notecards in the back," I said, and his eyes finally shifted from my lips to look me in the eye. He had the nerve to smirk. Disgusting asshole. He stepped aside, motioning for me to pass him. He didn't do it to be a gentleman. He did it in the hopes I would brush my body against his (not a chance in Hell) and to stare at my ass as I walked away from him (if I could do something about it, I would).

Once backstage, I unpacked my dress and changed into it, my graduation gown long enough to hide the fact that I wore a dress at all. The white graduation gown looked as hideous as I suspected.

Over the top of the atrocious gown, I lined up my honor cords until they evened out. I didn't put on my cap as I faced myself in the mirror in the dressing room usually designated for the theater club. A pair of deep blue eyes stared back at me, a determined glint to them.

Graduation marked an end to a chapter in my life. When I woke up tomorrow, not in my dorm room but in an unfamiliar hotel room, a page would be flipped and I'd be filling the pages on a new chapter. Every single person who walked the stage with me today had big plans. Internships and graduate school and jobs lined up.

I wanted none of those things. I wanted something far closer to my heart than a dream job. I wanted revenge.

Today, I graduated and in a few days' time, if everything went according to plan, this world would be ridden of one less evil person and I'd be on a plane to Mexico. Annie Miller would be as good as gone. I would no longer have to wonder who she was. Olive James would be born and I would be somebody new, somebody that my mom could be proud of.

"Annie." A girl I had never seen before popped her head around the corner. "You're up."

"Thanks," I replied before her head disappeared, grateful for the reminder. Graduation, now. Murdering Daddy Dearest, later.

CHAPTER TWO

Annie

"**W**here the fuck are you going dressed like that?"

I squeezed my eyes shut, not wanting to deal with this right now. The door clicked behind me and I waited. Maybe if I ignored him, he would go away. Not that that tactic ever worked before.

For the past three days, I managed to dodge Matt, his curious eyes, and what I knew to be his twenty-one questions. I opened my eyes slowly in the hopes that he wouldn't be standing in front of me and I was instantly disappointed. He placed his hands on his hips and closed the distance between us, his nearly seven-foot frame towering over me. "Well?"

I glared at him. "What did I tell you about commenting on my body?"

He huffed out a humorless laugh. "You said not to objectify your body, which I haven't. Why the fuck are you dressed like that, Annie?" His normal playfulness gone, replaced with suspicious eyes.

Moments like this I wished, like the rest of the people I've crossed paths with in the past ten years, Matt had stayed on the sidelines of my life. On the outside looking in. He's gotten too comfortable with me. I've *let* him get too comfortable.

I equally hated and loved how he much seemed to care about me. At times over the past couple of years, having Matt in my life hollowed out some of the loneliness I felt. He felt like the first sight of daylight after a three-month Alaska darkness. But with his friendship, came questions. Questions I couldn't and wouldn't answer.

I looked down at myself, at the clothes I wore. I still wore jeans. Tight black ones instead of my normal faded boyfriend jeans. A black long sleeve that exposed my midriff and shoulders. Turning away from Matt's looming, I grabbed my jean jacket from the back of my desk chair. Shrugging into it, I purposely took my time on rolling the sleeves on each arm.

I hoped Matt would say something or leave but he did neither.

I spun around and held my hands up in the air, showcasing the newest addition to my outfit. "Better?" I asked, a fake smile glued to my lips.

Matt shook his head and fell into the chair he brought into my office just for himself. "Where have you been?"

"I've been here. You've been busy."

His eyes fell away from my face, sticking to the bare skin at my midriff, looking like he wanted to ask that damn question again. I wouldn't tell him the truth, no matter if he asked a million times.

Instead, he asked another question. A question he'd been asking me since the beginning of my last semester. "Have you thought about it? Moving in with me?"

I sighed, preparing to lie to him. Again. *I don't have to make a decision right now, Matt. The school is not evicting me until the summer semester starts. I haven't made up my mind yet.* "Won't I put a crimp in your style?"

In response, I didn't get the sly tilt of his lips I've grown accustomed to. Instead, he glared at me, his brown eyes darkening.

I shrugged nonchalantly. "Hey, I had to ask."

I didn't tell him I left campus last weekend with my diploma, my backpack, and the lone suitcase I owned and booked a hotel room at the cheapest hotel in the city I could find. I didn't tell him anything about my future because after tomorrow he wouldn't be a part of it.

The thought of Matt no longer ceasing to exist in my world tugged at my chest but I shook it off and started throwing things in my backpack. In the grand scheme of things, Matt wasn't important. Hell, I wasn't important. The only thing that was important was the worn-out piece of paper sitting in my back pocket holding the knowledge of what I had to do.

Tomorrow, I would come in here for the last time. In twenty-four hours, I would be packing this same bag including the gun I owned but had never before carried with me. I would have to wave to Matt with a promise to see him the next day, the day that would never come.

When I chanced a look at him, his head was thrown back against the top of the chair, his fingers intertwined, covering his closed eyes.

Throwing my backpack over my shoulder, I walked over to him and poked him in the middle of his forehead.

His fingers fell away from his face but his frown went nowhere. "Why do I get the feeling you're hiding something," he mumbled petulantly.

I forced a small smile to my lips. "It's good to be a little mysterious. You might've gotten sick of me otherwise."

I didn't give him the chance to pry more. And I didn't give myself a chance to feed him another lie. I fled from the range, feeling like I could breathe again once the sun kissed my skin and the bustle of the city consumed me, reminding me what it felt like to be invisible once more. I walked a couple of blocks until I could no longer see Philly Range before I found a bus stop. I grabbed fifteen dollars from my pocket and waited. Every day for the past week, with school no longer a part of my routine, I caught this bus after my shift at the shooting range.

I stood up when the familiar red, white, and blue bus, New Hazle scrolling across the LED sign, stopped short in front of me. I paid my fee and held on to the strapped handles until I found an empty seat near the back.

I was going home. Home, where I spent the only good twelve years of my life. Home, that turned into a nightmare. Home to my mother.

If I closed my eyes, I could still picture her face. Her blonde waves that felt so smooth when she let me brush her hair. Impossibly dark blue eyes that always shined with amusement on my behalf. Perfect pale pink lips that would attack me with kisses all over my face first thing in the morning.

Michelle Miller was the perfect mom.

I had no complaints of a bad childhood for the most part. If I wasn't at school, I was attached to my mom's hip. I used to park my butt at the kitchen table while she cooked or cleaned. Every Friday night I would sit on the toilet in the bathroom or plop on her bed, next to her vanity, my hands holding my face as I studied her every move before she went to meet some friends and left me with our next door neighbor for a few hours. Even as I grew up, our relationship hadn't skipped a beat. If anything, I wanted to be more like her. Pretty like her. Kind like her. Smart like her.

The only gloom that settled over my childhood was Cameron Wade.

The only thing less certain than my identity was that of my father's. I couldn't remember a time growing up when he felt like a father. If I were ever captured in a picture, I would be in the same shot as my mom and Cameron would be the distant figure just outside of the picture, using this occasion to place a beer bottle to his lips.

I couldn't remember a time when he even told me he loved me. I didn't remember him holding me when I was a toddler nor kissing my bruises as I grew into a tiny human. He was there, but at the same time, he wasn't.

As I grew up and befriended other kids at school and they talked about all of the fun stuff their dad did with them, I realized my dad wasn't normal. And by the time I grew brave enough to ask my mom about him, about why is the way he is, I had long since been acquainted with the brown bottle of peroxide and the soft feel of cotton balls as I relieved her skin of the marks he left on her in a fit of rage.

I could still hear her words in my head, in that delicate voice of hers. "He's not a perfect man, but he once was."

I felt my stomach recoil then at her words, and now just thinking of them. I only knew him to be one sort of man. The worst kind of man, the Devil dressed in men's clothing.

I often wondered why they bothered to have a child. I had neither mom nor dad to confirm that I was, in fact, an unplanned mistake, but I knew that I was. I had to be. He was never home, always out with his work colleagues, and if he was at home, he always made my mom send me to my room so he could spend time alone with her. It surprised me that I never much minded his absence in my life but I knew it was my mom's doing. She loved me enough for both of them.

For the first twelve years of my life, I never questioned love, she gave it to me so freely.

It wasn't until he made the occasional appearance before she tucked me in at night that I realized my home wasn't as happy as I originally thought.

I knew because my mom's usually radiant smile slipped from her face. The happy, loving side of her vanished, transforming into a version of her that felt wrong. I turned invisible as soon as he called or stepped through the door. Her sole attention focused on him or ensuring the house was spotless, not stopping until her hands stained red.

The days following his appearances improved and worsened at the same time. I got my mom back but she wasn't the same. Her smile didn't reach her eyes and when I tried everything to force a laugh out of her, it sounded off-key like she hadn't laughed in so long it felt foreign to her.

The physical signs, I noticed a little more each day. She limped from the kitchen to the sink. Bright red spots appeared on her skin, usually around her neck. I'd only notice when she didn't bother with her makeup. Anytime I asked about it, she shrugged her shoulders and blame it on her clumsiness.

I never questioned it. Not until I saw it with my eyes.

Not until the one night she tucked me in bed early, telling me that Daddy was bringing home very important people over for dinner. Upstairs, already tucked in, stubbornly not falling asleep waiting for her to come give me my goodnight kiss, I heard her pleading whimpers. I snuck out of bed, hearing the word "stop" flow from her lips like the lone word was a song stuck on repeat. Stopping on the middle of the stairs, it happened. I couldn't tear my eyes away when I witnessed his brutal hands on her. Her watery eyes met mine from across the room and my heart broke for the very first time.

Every day after that night, for years, I begged her to leave, just the two of us. Her answer remained the same. Smiling down at me and running her long fingers through my hair, she kissed my forehead and promised, "Your mama's got this, baby girl." And like the innocent child I was, I believed her. And when she finally decided to leave, he wouldn't let us.

I dabbed at the wetness on my cheeks with the sleeve of my jean jacket before pressing the button for my stop. New Hazle greeted me as soon as I stepped off the bus. I traded in tall buildings and bustling traffic for lifeless trees and a ghost town.

I walked down the familiar street leading me to Locust Cemetery. I bowed my head, avoiding any and all surveillance systems. As far as anyone knew, the last time I stepped foot in New Hazle was four years ago, right before I started college.

I walked the familiar path until I reached her headstone.

Michelle Miller. Loving Mother and Friend. 1977–2007.

I kneeled down and ran my fingers across the hard marble, ridding it of all of the spiderwebs. "Hey, Mama," I whispered. "It's your little girl."

I ground my teeth together in hopes of keeping the tears at bay. "I don't know if you would be proud of this version of your daughter. I wonder what you would think of her. Half of the time, I don't even know what to think of her."

A shaky sigh escaped me as I leaned back, letting my ass fall to the splintering needles of grass. Resting my head on top of my knees, I shut my eyes, my hands falling to the dirty ground clutching a fist of the earth. "I have to do this, Mom. Not just for you, but for me. And I hope, if we ever meet again, that you'll be able to forgive me."

I stood abruptly, pressing a kiss to two of my fingers before placing them directly on her name and I ran.

I pushed my legs faster and faster, my feet thudding against the cracked sidewalks, vicious with every step. I ran, not seeing which direction my feet carried me. I didn't stop when my heartbeat sounded in my eardrums or when sweat dripped from my forehead down the crevice of my nose and onto my parted lips. I didn't stop until my legs grew shaky and my breakfast threatened to reappear.

I slowed to a jog before settling into a walk. I glance up and found myself exactly where I needed to be. Hank's Bar and Grill, one of the only bars in this town and Cameron Wade's home away from home.

Without pause, I yanked open the old, heavy wooden door, ordered a glass of water and took it with me to a booth in the back.

The inside of the bar reeked of smoke, booze, and scum, and my father hadn't even shown up yet. The bar itself wasn't in bad shape. Its dark vibe and slow, melodic music filtering through the room complemented the dark wood of the walls, floor, and bar. It wasn't the owner's fault that this place attracted the worst kind of humans.

The door swung open and my eyes snapped toward the movement, my heart stuck in my throat. Afraid it would be him walking through the door, afraid it wouldn't.

This wasn't the first time this happened. It happened every time I was here. They wouldn't let me in here when I was a minor but as soon as I turned eighteen, I frequented this place on a weekly basis. During my four years of college, I used it as my excuse to study, laying out notebooks and textbooks without ever seeing them at all. The real reason I was here was to watch, to study, to memorize Cameron Wade's habits.

He walked in, dragging his feet across the few steps from the door to the one side of the bar, his back facing me. He slurred his drink order at the bartender who shook his head in pity but obliged anyway. He gulped one drink after another for the first hour. He seemed to wake once the alcohol pumped its way through his veins. His booming voice carried across the room to reach me. "One more fucking day in that hellhole and I'm free."

No one paid attention to him. No one other than me.

I sat there and watched him drink beer after beer. Laugh at his own crass jokes. His eyes roaming the room for any attractive woman stupid enough to give him a second of attention.

Rage burned through my veins like fire. How dare he laugh so easily when I couldn't remember the sound of my mother's laugh? Talk so simply when it was hard for me to remember the sound of her voice? Breathe in a way she no longer could? Live however he wanted when he single-handedly ruined my life. I clenched and unclenched my fists for so long, somehow resisting the urge to claw his eyes out in front of a room of a dozen people.

"Hope you enjoy that beer," I hissed under my breath, "it's one of the last ones you'll ever have."

At a quarter to ten o'clock, Cameron closed his tab and paid for his drink and the woman's next to him, who he spent the last two hours trying to convince her to allow him to take her home.

Cameron was a creature of habit. In the four years I had been watching him, his life felt like a loop. Every day was a song stuck on replay.

He still lived in that same old house in New Hazle on Mercer Road, a few blocks from the bar. He still worked as a paper pusher for Mackenzie Enterprise. And he still spent all of his money on beer and women.

I had his days and nights memorized.

The lights in the house switched on at about eight-thirty in the morning. Only the downstairs. Which told me one thing: he passed out on the couch before he ever made it into one of the two bedrooms upstairs.

Fifteen minutes later, he stumbled out of the front door into his beat-up Buick and traveled the twenty or so minutes into the city to be at work by nine-thirty. If he arrived there early, he reclined his seat back and took a little power nap in the parking garage.

At nine twenty-nine, he shuffled onto the elevator, taking him up to the fourteenth floor where he spent eight hours behind a stifling desk piled high with papers. At exactly four thirty-five, he'd be on the elevator in the parking garage, hell-bent on being the first person out of the building, trying to beat the evening traffic. He'd fail. He made it back into New Hazle in no less than an hour and spent two hours in that same chair he sat in now. Guzzling beer after beer, shooting predatory looks at women both his age and mine.

Disgusting.

He always left the bar with someone but he never took them home and I never followed him. I always just waited for him, blending with the trees and darkness across the street until he finally made it home, always alone. Maybe the place where you murdered the woman who loved you ten years ago really killed the mood.

I didn't follow him when he stumbled out of the bar, his arm wrapped around a woman. I needed this night to myself because tomorrow, I would make my move.

The last decade I spent learning how to use my body as a weapon would all be worth it to see Cameron Wade within an inch of his life, pleading for me to have mercy on him, and denying him that freedom. It would all be worth it. After all these years, my mom could finally be at peace, knowing he would never be able to lay his hands on another woman, knowing that I sent him on a one-way trip to the deepest part of Hell.

She would receive justice in the name of her daughter.

CHAPTER THREE

Hector

"**D**on't you think I've suffered enough, Pops?" He dropped the barbell in the hook, the heavy clang echoing in my ears. Looking down at my son, sweat covering every inch of his face, I wondered how his vision hadn't blurred. From the moisture gathered at his eyebrows dripping toward his eyelids, it looked like he dumped a bottle of cold water on his face.

I raised an eyebrow in disbelief. "You haven't even finished fifty reps yet."

He sighed, his arms reaching for the hooked bar to resume lifting. I towered over him, resting my hands against the machine, on alert in case he couldn't handle it which from where I stood didn't seem all that unlikely.

He snuck in sometime between my breakfast and my first workout. I had grown well accustomed to his early morning, or as he would say, late night, arrivals home. At seventeen years old, Samuel had the sex-drive of a porn star who wasn't in it for the money.

I couldn't fault him for it though seeing as how I celebrated my sixteenth birthday mere weeks before he was born. He wasn't foolish or careless about sex. The one thing I drilled into his head since I found the magazine stash and trash can full of soiled tissues in his room.

I sat him down, nerdy brace-faced then, nothing like the smooth talker babyface he was now, and I laid down the law of women.

Respect the woman at all times.

Both of you should voice your consent. I promise it will not kill the mood.

Condom. One or ten. Your choice.

This isn't your show. It's hers. Remember that.

Take care of her after.

Samuel and I didn't have the most traditional father-son relationship.

I'd often compared our relationship to food. The ingredients, the spices, the seasonings, all made up communication. You could measure them all out, mix them just right, but if you missed a pinch of something, the entire meal had to be scrapped. Samuel was all I had for the past fifteen years of his life and vice versa. It was just the two of us. Well, for a few more days anyway.

If I couldn't find him in his room, at school, or at basketball practice, he was at his apartment. Was his own apartment smack dab in the middle of the city considered normal for a seventeen-year-old?

Probably not. But Samuel wasn't exactly normal.

I didn't allow anyone at my house. The only people, other than the two of us, who've made it past the gates were family. My father, who only showed up on Samuel's birthday, and Nolan, my best friend and right-hand man.

The Rivera name was a well-known name. It intimidated some. It frightened some. It pissed some off. It didn't matter if I was the best kind of man. Or if I raised my son to be. Our last name was still the same and with that came a target on our backs. I couldn't risk the safety of my family, especially raising Samuel through the years. And I took no pride in risking others' safety.

From a young age, I taught him how to fight, knowing his last name alone was cause enough for someone to try their luck. I started with simple self-defense moves before I moved on to boxing. Samuel craved knowledge and loved being the best at everything. It didn't take him long to conquer karate before moving on to Jitsu. At the beginning of his senior year last fall, I succumbed to allowing private shooting lessons at Philly Range.

It didn't matter if he could bench press two hundred pounds over one hundred reps. He had the intelligence to see any threat and take them down in under a minute, regardless if his only weapon was his body.

"This fine ass woman at Philly Range last night. Older, much older. Your kind of old, but this woman was a knockout. So, me being me, I had to shoot my shot."

I glared down at him. "You did not have sex with a woman my age."

He extended his arm, weights and all, and smirked at me, flashing his straight white teeth and the dimples he inherited from me. "Of course not."

I couldn't stop the sigh of relief that escaped me even if I tried. "You're going to kill me."

He resumed lifting until he hit fifty reps. He slammed the barbell against the hook with finality and sat up. He wore no shirt, just a pair of basketball shorts. The same as me and yet somehow his abs were perfect. Not too much to where he looked like he worked in the gym every second of his life and not too little where you could see his body fat.

I worked out two, sometimes, three times a day. I could lift what Samuel could handle with one hand and somehow his body still was in impeccable shape. He wiped the sweat from his face with a towel and walked toward me, snatching the water bottle out of my hands. He drained the entire thing in a few gulps. He handed the empty bottle back to me and his fingers twisted over the towel hanging loosely from his shoulder.

"I see the look on your face, Pops."

I frowned, confused. Samuel shook his head, patting my shoulder gently.

"You look good. Not as good as me, but still good."

I gritted my teeth like every time he started with one of his smart ass rants.

"Sex cures everything. You should try it sometime."

I felt a growl climbing up my throat but I crammed it down because it only made him gloat. Instead, I quickly grabbed for the towel across his shoulder, twisted it up and slapped it across his chest.

He grabbed his chest in mock hurt and I threw the damp towel in his face. He caught it effortlessly. "You know some women like being whipped. I know a few if you're interested."

I didn't even bother to acknowledge he said anything. I left our home gym in favor for the kitchen.

Ever since Samuel and I made a collective decision about college, if and where he would be attending, he had been relentless about my love life. Or lack of it.

In the seventeen years of his life, he never saw me with a woman. Because I hadn't been with a woman long enough to bring her into his life. The last woman I fully gave myself to was his mom. She was my first and my only. The girl who I thought I loved, who I thought loved me. But at sixteen, you barely know who you are or what you want and it turned out that we both were unsure of that answer.

I couldn't regret her. I couldn't even hate her for wanting to leave me. She gave me the biggest blessing of my life. The reason I wanted to wake up each morning. She gave me my son. And I spent each day thanking God she gave me that much.

I still kept in contact with her. I knew she lived in Los Angeles, remarried to some hotshot lawyer and a mother to two more kids. I'd been waiting for Samuel to ask about her, to want to get in contact with her. Anything. But he was mute on the subject of the woman who brought him into this world. If he didn't keep a lone photograph of me and his mother on the day we brought him home from the hospital on the desk in his room, I would have thought he didn't think about her at all. Every time I brought her up, he seemed less like himself and more like me.

Guarded. Aloof. Not wanting to have this conversation, ever.

"I'm going to shower. Think about what I said," Samuel said, walking backward and smirking at me all the way from the kitchen until he reached his bedroom. Before he turned around, I flipped him off. His booming laugh bounced off of the walls as I cracked a couple of eggs open and transferred them into a glass.

My cell phone buzzed in my pocket. Digging it out, Nolan's name flashed across the screen. I accepted the call and put the phone up to my ear. "Yeah?"

I gulped the eggs in two swallows, waiting a few minutes in silence before I knew Nolan would start talking. "Boss," he stammered, his breathing ragged. I said nothing in return, well accustomed to Nolan seeing as how he became a permanent fixture in my life in elementary school.

"Matt Panini."

I barely held back a groan. What the fuck could he want?

The young kid and I had a bit of a standoff a few years ago, ending me with a flesh wound and him with a dead father.

Victor Panini's family business didn't rake in enough money as the greedy bastard liked, so he decided to start his own business. Making nightly trips to Bottoms Up, a strip club in the city that I co-owned, luring young women out of the club with promises that they'd never have to take off their clothes for money again if they worked with him. What he didn't include in the fine print of his promises was that they'd never have to strip willingly, but forcingly. He set up Philadelphia, *my city*, to start his vile business of sex trafficking.

Girls were disappearing faster than I could blink. There were missing reports coming in at every precinct in the city. Mothers crying, brothers and fathers raising hell. They looked to me for answers when the police, as they often did, failed them.

I would have never caught on if Katya, a young girl who worked at Bottoms Up, didn't see Victor every night talk to the youngest dancer only for that same girl to never show up again. I asked Katya if she would help me take him down and she instantly agreed. I had everyone's schedule switched around so Katya would be picked by Victor.

Like clockwork, he strolled in just when the performances started and as soon as Katya climbed off of the stage, he made his move. With my pistol tucked into my waistband, I followed them. He took her to Elite, a club by membership only. He didn't take her through the front door where two bodyguards stood. He led her to the back of the bar, to the basement door. I followed as stealthily as I could.

Victor paused at the top of the stairs, looking over at Katya. "Welcome, sweet girl. Your life is about to change forever."

She smiled timidly at him and before I could even react, he caressed the side of her face before grabbing a handful of her hair and throwing her down the steps with all of his strength. He walked down the stairs, taking each step at his leisure. I slunk out of the darkness and looked down at the dim cellar. I couldn't see much, but what I did see twisted my stomach and broke my heart at the same time. Girls naked, shivering lying on the cold cement floor. Some were chained up like animals. Bruises on every inch of their skin. Sniffles and sobs filled the room.

With each step Victor took, I took one as well. Katya's unconscious body sprawled across the bottom step. He paused, looking down at her. He shook his head and muttered one lone word, "Bitches."

He stepped on her as if she was an added stair instead of a human being. I pulled my gun out of my waistband before sitting on a step as I watched him take in his work. I didn't look at any of the girls but those who were lucid, I could feel their eyes on me.

"There's only one bitch in this room." My voice echoed through the basement. Victor turned around at the sound of my voice, his eyes wide with alarm.

"Rivera," he breathed shakily. I smiled at the fear I could hear through his voice and the look of it I saw in his eyes.

I hated Victor Panini with a passion. He was one of the biggest influencers in and around Philadelphia and instead of helping kids out of the bad neighborhoods and lifestyles they grew up in, he did his best to keep them there. He let kids learn how to shoot at fifteen years old as long as they swore their allegiance to him. He had people as old as me still under his thumb. If you were with Panini, you were with him for life. He was responsible for so many deaths but the news outlets always blamed it on the drugs, on neighborhood violence, on the parents.

I'd been killing since the day I turned eighteen. It was my job to protect this city. I didn't like it. I didn't enjoy it. It came with my last name, passed down. If there was a legal way to see justice served, I always went that route. If the justice system failed, I didn't.

But that was before Victor Panini targeted women. Young girls. No amount of justice could be served for the things he did to them, things I couldn't and didn't want to imagine.

"I hate you," I told him. He reached for the gun that he wouldn't find since I taught Katya how to strip him of one. "You are the poster boy for what a scumbag looks like and I will sleep better tonight knowing your kind of evil can't hurt anyone else."

I raised my gun, aimed directly in the middle of his forehead, not sparing him one more breath, and shot it. I tucked my gun back inside my jeans at the sight of his lifeless eyes and slipped my phone out, dialing Nolan.

"I need women's clothes and first aid kits." Together, Nolan and I worked side by side as we cleaned up the girls' cuts and bruises. Let them call family if they had any or shipped them off to a nearby hotel for the night. I told them they still had a job at Bottoms Up if they wanted it. After that, I worked with Katya who was a bad ass trooper, to set up a free therapy group at a church in New Hazle, just outside of the city.

Matt Panini was a different story entirely. He was a good kid, nothing like his father. His mother essentially raised him on her own so he remained innocent, oblivious to his father's ways. The day after, before the police recovered his body from the basement at Elite, I paid Matt and his mom Karla a visit.

I wasn't sure what their reaction would be to finding out I killed the man in their life but I knew I had to let them know before the media got a whiff of Victor's death. Karla burst out in tears and thanked me. She was finally free. It turned out young girls weren't the only ones Victor liked to use and abuse. Matt remained quiet throughout the whole process. Listening to each word I said and absorbing it. He offered to walk me out and I accepted. Next thing I knew, I woke up in the hospital with a flesh wound the size of a banana beneath my ribs.

I survived, just barely and I never heard from Matt again. I didn't pay him a visit. I didn't seek revenge on him. He lost his father. If someone killed my father, a stab wound wouldn't be enough for me. Nolan handled Samuel's lessons to Philly Range and Matt and I called a silent truce. Until now.

"What does he want, Nolan?"

"He needs a favor from you. His exact words were, 'If you do this for me, I'll owe you my life.'"

I sighed heavily, slamming my now empty glass on the bar. So much for spending the last few days I had with my son peacefully. "Text me the details," I told Nolan before hanging up. A beep sounded a second later and I stared down at a picture of a younger woman and a simple request from Matt. **Protect her.**

I wanted to know what she needed protection from. Or who. I'd learned long ago not to enter a rescue mission blind but for some reason unknown to me, I slipped my phone into my pocket with a silent promise to look into her later.

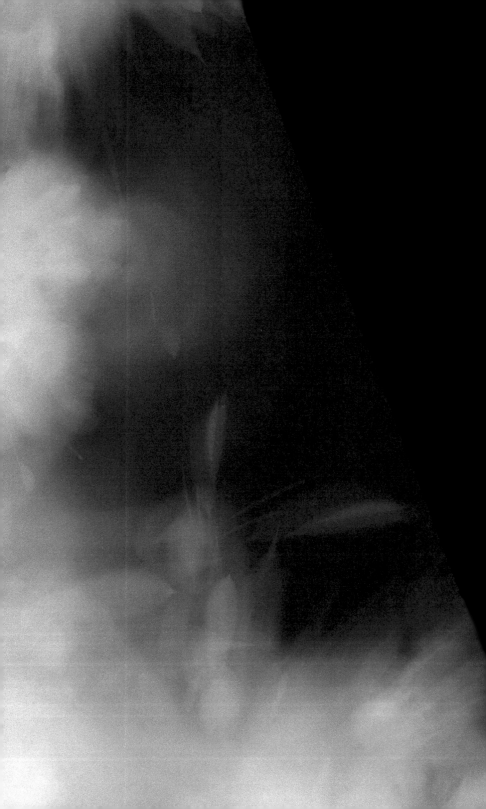

CHAPTER FOUR

Annie

Tonight marked the seventh straight night I spent sitting in this exact booth at Hank's. Nothing but Cameron Wade and my glass of water to keep my attention.

Tonight felt different. It felt like the last page of a chapter with the next chapter peeking through the thin layer of the pages.

I wouldn't be heading back to my hotel room once Cameron got cut off by the bartender tonight. I'd follow him into a home I hadn't stepped foot in for ten years. I'd step back into my childhood with no assurance of how the night would pan out, only with the knowledge that my life would be altered forever.

Once the sun rose with the promise of a new day, I hoped for a dead Cameron Wade and me making it past security onto my booked flight to Mexico tomorrow morning. The place where I would ditch Annie Miller in favor of Olive James, a girl with no past and an unwritten future.

Underneath my calm, cool, and collected exterior, my heartbeat thumped so fast and hard against my chest, the sound an abrasive echo against my eardrums. I could feel the heaviness of the knives that I had tucked in my black pair of Vans and I could feel the sleek coolness of the gun tucked into the waistband of my jeans.

Tonight, I would take a life.

Tonight, I would become a killer.

Murder had been on my mind for a very long time. While kids my age were getting ready for dates and proms, I spent my every waking moment dreaming of the day I would make him pay.

When Cameron Wade decided to kill my mom, he was whisked away by the police for questioning and I was thrown into the system. I spent the first few weeks without my mother a shell of a kid. I couldn't wrap my head around my new reality. I was thrust into a group home while my social worker stalled on trying to find me a new home in case I would have to testify.

As it turned out, I did have to testify. His statement to the police painted my mother as the villain. She hurt *him*. She violated *him*. She tried to kill *him*.

That day my social worker visited me at the girls' home and told me that it would be entirely up to me if I testified or not, I took it for what it was: a lie. I didn't have a choice. My mom couldn't speak up for herself. She couldn't defend herself. So, that left me.

I told them the truth. I pointed them to the bruises on her skin, the unhealed welts on her back. I told them what I knew of the day. How she planned to leave him. How he wouldn't let us.

Immediately after my testimony, I spent my last night in the group home before they found a family willing to take me in.

They were decent people but I knew they weren't foster parents because they love kids or wanted to make a difference. They were in it for the government aide and the income tax money. I knew from the beginning they weren't going to be a family to me.

I was on my own. I took care of myself and stayed out of their and the other kids' way and I survived. It wasn't ideal for a thirteen-year-old girl but I had given up on normalcy the moment my mom died.

One of my first few nights with the Thatchers, I sat at the table with a newspaper looking for someone who would hire a teenager when the six o'clock news came on and I heard his name attached with two words. Only then, did I really allow myself to fall apart.

Cameron Wade: not guilty.

The state of Pennsylvania found Cameron Wade to be the victim.

Not Cameron Wade, the abuser, the killer, the pathetic excuse for a man.

Cameron Wade, the victim.

He didn't hurt my mother night after night until finally he went too far.

No, he was a victim of robbery. A woman he offered shelter to turned on him, draining his bank account but not before she tried to kill him.

Him. The media. Everyone painted my mother as a villain. And I was her mini-me, the daughter Cameron Wade never even bothered looking for.

My mother wasn't the villain in Cameron Wade's life but I sure as hell planned to be.

I stayed put in New Hazle, only applying to schools near and around Philadelphia. I trained my body and my mind to be the strongest and the wisest. And it was all for this moment.

When you want something for such a long time, when it's finally within your grasp, you're mad at your hands for being shaky when you finally go to grab it. That's exactly how I was feeling.

I should have my head held high. My body should've been as solid as a rock. My breaths should've been coming out even. My hands should've been steady. But what my mind wanted and what my body was doing were two completely different things.

The door swung open and I sat up straighter, knowing it could be him. It wasn't.

Two older men walked in. Both of them were tall, at least over six-foot. One guy's skin was the palest I'd ever seen while the others was a rich brown color. I couldn't make out their facial features from where I sat but I could tell both of them were stunningly beautiful. The entire bar turned quiet at their entrance. The darker of the two rapped his knuckles against the bar and ordered a drink. Demanded a drink. The white man remained silent, his eyes glued to the bartop.

The door opened again and my father walked in, the two handsome newcomers immediately forgotten. I watched him as he slapped the backs of people sitting at booths before making his way to the bar, plopping down on his normal stool and ordering a bottle of beer and a shot of whiskey.

The once quiet bar turned loud at his arrival. He griped about the workweek. Drank. Played a couple rounds of pool with some fellow lowlifes. Drank. Flirted with every woman he could find willing. Drank. After four long, excruciating hours, the bartender cut him off right before the bar closed for the night.

During the workweek, he never stayed past eleven. But tonight, a night when he didn't have work the next morning, I guessed was different. I chose this night to kill him, just for that reason. By the time anyone noticed him missing, I would be in a different country with a different name.

I sucked in a deep breath of air when Cameron staggered to his feet and threw a handful of twenties on top of the bar and all but spun out of the bar. I waited as long as I possibly could without seeming suspicious and followed after him, grabbing my backpack and leaving a tip on the table. When I made it outside into the thick, humid air, Cameron's car was gone. I ran the couple of blocks between the bar and his house.

I slowed to a walk as my childhood home came into view. I could see myself running off of the school bus, flinging that heavy wooden door open, but staring at it now, it felt unfamiliar in a way a stranger's house would.

I found Cameron stumbling out of his car, his steps sluggish until he reached the short sidewalk leading up to the front door and face-planted into the cement sidewalk. His body lay there motionless on the ground for so long, I began to think he lost consciousness. I didn't move from my spot, hidden in the darkness of the night and dead trees across the street.

When he finally mustered enough energy to pick himself up off of the ground, he staggered up the sidewalk, tripping on every step of the porch until he slammed himself up against the door.

I've always kept my distance from him. Always across the room at Hank's or across the lot in the parking garage or hidden in the darkness outside of his house. Up until now, I watched. Not tonight. Tonight, he and I were going to be officially reacquainted.

Stepping out of the secluded darkness, I followed him inside, seeing he only made it past the door before falling again. I quietly shut the door behind me and squeezed my eyes shut, affording myself one last moment of just Annie, stuck in between who I was and who I would be once this night ended.

I tried not to think about the last time I was in this house. I tried not to think about the last words my mama said to me in this house. The past decade of my life had all been leading up to this moment and it was finally here.

I couldn't mess it up.

When I opened my eyes again, I stood there in shock, and equally if not more, in disturbance. It felt like I was standing in the middle of a memory, not real life.

I stood inside my childhood home, a place I left ten years ago without a second glance, where not a single thing had changed. The same old ratty brown sofa sat in the middle of the floor, perfectly aligned with the black entertainment stand.

Keeping one eye on the slobbering man on the floor, I looked past the open living room into the kitchen and there it was. The apple wallpaper. My mom was obsessed with decorating her kitchen with apples. Dishtowels. Potholders. Said wallpaper. Fake apples. Her kitchen and me, the things that made her the happiest.

I shook off the memory as best as I could, and looked down at the pathetic excuse of a man. No longer in a drunken slumber but in a state of shock as he stared up at me, eyes wide. His lips moved but they made no sound.

His little girl returned home at last.

My lips tilted, sending his eyes into a panic, looking from me to the door behind me. How ironic, that when he held my mom within an inch of her life, her eyes, the same deep blue as mine, pleading with him to just let her go and here I stood before him with those same eyes ten years later, planning on doing the same thing to him. I didn't hold back my smirk any longer when he held his body up on unsteady elbows, his movements turning frantic.

"Cat got your tongue, Father?"

"A-A-Annie."

I frowned down at him, a trace of a smile still shaping my lips as I walked the length of his body on the floor, stopping just short of his propped up elbow and kicking it until his body collapsed, his other elbow not strong enough to keep holding him up. He groaned as his back hit the wooden floor.

I walked the length of his body and I could feel his eyes follow my every move. I wondered what he saw in mine. Did he see how badly I wanted to kill him? How long I spent leading up to this moment? How the hate I had for him filled up more space in my body than the blood that pumped through me?

"Time to go to sleep," I murmured as my feet aligned perfectly with his head. I tipped his head to the side with the toe of my Vans, my foot following his face, resting gently on the side of his cheek, knowing the city grime would leave a pretty print on his face. He held his breath, his chest as still as the tense air between us. I lifted my foot from his face and heard the deep inhale of relief he took before I slammed my foot down on his temple as hard as I could. He wanted to scream; his mouth opened wide to do so but before the noise could escape him, he blacked out.

Once I was sure his body was lifeless for the time being, I set up shop. I tossed my backpack onto the couch and drug his body into the space between the couch and the TV stand before transferring him onto the bare coffee table. I zip-tied his wrists and ankles to each leg of the coffee table and I waited.

I wasn't sure how long he was out, but after the third time of taking my gun apart and putting it back together, he finally regained consciousness.

The first few blinks, he laid still, staring blankly at the ceiling.

I didn't say a word. I didn't announce my presence. I waited. I waited until the memories of the night caught up to him, until his blinking increased and he started to realize that this wasn't his normal drunken daze.

He groaned loudly, twisting his head against the table, his eyes squeezing shut in pain. He lifted his hands up to rub at his temple only for the ties to halt any mobility.

His eyes snapped open and found me on the couch almost instantly. I wiggled my fingers in way of greeting.

He sat up. Or tried to. The zip-ties along his puny wrists and ankles made it impossible. "Wh-what do you want?"

I didn't answer him. I blatantly ignored him as I pretended to look around the house. After a couple of minutes, his body started to thrash from side to side on the table, struggling to get free.

Taking a ponytail band from my wrist, I gathered up my hair into a loose bun before looking to the man in front of me. "Wh-what are you doing here?" he sputtered, tears leaking from the corner of his eyes when I gave in and gave him the attention he had always craved so much of.

His tears did not make me sad. They sure as hell didn't make me feel guilty. They made me nauseous. He should've considered himself lucky that I was giving him time to adjust to this new reality. My mom didn't have the chance to beg for her life. He did, not that it would make a difference.

I hitched a shoulder nonchalantly. "This is my house as much as it is yours."

His lips trembled. His mouth opening and then closing like his motions were stuck on a loop. "Ann-Ann-Annie, I'm so sor—"

Before he even got that word out, my gun was in my hand, dangerously close to touching the clammy skin at his temple. "Finish that sentence and you're dead."

He wisely shut his mouth, but I didn't lower my gun. My heart pounded against my chest, warmth flooded my body, but my arms were strong and steady. I could do this. *I was going to do this.*

"Most fathers support their daughter's dreams," I informed him, cocking my head to the side so I could see him clearly. "My dreams, I have to tell you, are a bit different. My dream for the past ten years has always been you. Finding you. And then killing you."

He choked on a sob and I fought hard to not roll my eyes at his theatrics.

"You cannot be this upset. You killed *her* in cold blood. *You killed my mother in cold blood.* What did you think would happen? That I would run away and leave my past behind me? That I would not seek justice?"

He rolled his head to the side, away from me. That wasn't going to work. Reaching down into my shoe, I gripped one of my hunting knives. Teetering on the edge of the couch, I raised the knife to my eye-level and slammed it down as hard as I could into his thigh.

"Fuuuuuck," he screamed out.

"You haven't seen me since I was a little girl," I said once he faced me again. "It's rude not to pay attention to me."

His lips kept on quivering, but he didn't make a sound. I reached over and pulled the knife out of his leg, wiping the blood off on the arm of the couch. After placing it back where it belonged, I grabbed a Sharpie I found in the kitchen and leaned forward. Taking pieces of his greasy hair, I swept it off to the side, exposing his temple. The Sharpie made a perfect x.

"That's the spot," I murmured, grazing the muzzle against his marked skin. "Now all I need are the words." I released one hand from the gun and tapped a single finger against my own temple. "What were your famous words that day? Ah, don't tell me." I pinned him with a glare of such hatred he flinched, his head knocking into the table. "You think you can leave me? I own you. You're nobody without me. And I'm going to make sure of it."

My heart thrashed against my chest and I bit the inside of my cheek so hard I tasted blood, trying like hell to keep the emotion out of my voice and hidden from my face. I inched the gun until the coolness of the gun felt the thump of his hard skin. My finger on the trigger. All I had to do was pull my index finger back once and he was as good as gone. Everything I worked for would finally become worth it.

Closing my eyes and taking one last deep breath, I placed my hand back on the gun and readjusted the steel in my hand. This was it. He was going straight to Hell for what he did and I was going to be the one who sent him there.

Before I got the chance to press my finger against the trigger, someone's hand covered mine on the gun and I felt my arm go limp as the rest of my body turned rigid. I swung my eyes from the man I was destined to kill to a man I had never seen before.

One word played over and over in my head as I took in the stranger: fuck.

My heart and mind flew into panic mode but my eyes didn't get the memo. I drunk in the sight of him like he was the last thing I would ever see. Seeing as how he caught me trying to kill someone, it might very well be.

He was older. I didn't know how much older. He fit the bill for tall, dark, and handsome like he was the model for it. Dark brown hair, cut on the sides and a few inches longer on the top. Piercing brown eyes that matched his skin tone like the two were twins. His full lips were parted, giving me a sneak peek of straight white teeth and a pink tongue. I wasn't sure how long I stood there, staring at him, but as the seconds, that felt like long excruciating years, went by, his hand grew firmer on the gun that no longer pointed at Cameron but the man himself.

"Who are you," he asked, no, demanded. His voice a mixture of rough and quiet. I'd never, not once in my life, been affected by a man's presence, but the sound of his voice paired with those intense brown eyes focused solely on me sent shivers racing down my arms, only concealed by the light blonde hair there.

"Who are you," I countered, embarrassed by how high my voice climbed.

His eyes locked with mine and a smile slowly took up his face, revealing two identical dimples in the center of his cheeks. Between his eyes and that smile, I already figured out, that this man was going to be a problem if his hand over my fully loaded gun wasn't the first sign. The way his eyes glinted in amusement bothered me because I knew, immediately, he had cast me aside. To him, I wasn't a threat. I was cute.

I wasn't either at the moment. What I was, simply, was panicked. I wasn't a killer. I couldn't kill my father and *him*. This was a one-time thing only. It was a coupon; after one use, it expired.

"I don't want to hurt you, girl. I just want to know who you are and what you think you're doing."

"What does it look like I'm doing?" I grumbled, my annoyance at his obvious condescendence outweighing my panic.

Chuckling, low and soft from his chest, he said, "I can't let you kill him."

Frowning, I tried to take control of the gun and get some space between me and Mr. Tall Dark and Handsome. Much to my avail, I got nowhere. Not when I used a small portion of my strength and not when I used all of it. He had me pinned, his hand on the gun overpowering mine and consequently, my entire body. I curled my finger over the trigger once more and glared up into his eyes. "Girl," he growled, "don't even think about it."

"He deserves to die," I grit out behind clenched teeth.

"I know, bonita. But it won't be you who will be doing the killing."

My teeth ground at the Spanish endearment directed toward me. I wasn't beautiful or pretty. Or at least I didn't want to be, not in this moment when this man hit pause on the night that I've been dreaming about.

And then it hit me, what he was saying. He wasn't going to let me kill him; he was going to do it himself. I should've felt relief, elation, happiness. But all I felt was sick. No, this was the destination of my journey. Everything I've ever done since I found myself motherless was for this exact moment. Like hell he was going to take it away from me. "I don't know why you're here but *I* am going to be the one to end him."

"It's cute how you think you're the one in control here."

My nostrils flared and my eyes closed into slits as I looked into his eyes. He didn't seem intimidated by my anger. Probably because he had about a half a foot and at least one hundred pounds on me. But I was the one with a gun.

I dug in my heels and stood up straight, my eyes parallel with his collarbone. I still had a good grip on the gun even with his hand still covering the cool steel in a vicious hold. I looked up at him. He was already looking down at me, his eyes squinting, suspicious of me, of my next move. As he should be.

"Come down here for a second," I whispered before looking at *my* victim whose lips were moving in a rushed prayer. "I want to tell you something privately."

He scowled, not moving an inch, staring into my eyes like they told him everything my lips wouldn't. It took every ounce of strength in my body not to falter. Not to look away from his intense gaze, to not fidget under his scrutiny. Finally, after moments of our silent standoff, he leaned down and I didn't waste any time.

I kissed him.

My top lip caught between the two of his. It surprised me how soft his lips were. It surprised me that the touch of his lips against mine shot sparks throughout my body.

His lips were frozen against mine. But I surged on, stepping closer. My stomach pressed against his, the gun still in between us. I pressed on his lips harder and his lips parted in surprise. I took advantage and feasted on his mouth.

It didn't occur to me that I had no idea what the hell I was doing. If it was good for him. I just knew I couldn't overthink this. I had to feel, and hope I would weaken him enough his grip of the gun would slip and I could do what I came here to do.

His free hand gripped the back of my head, bringing my face closer, this time a gasp escaped me and then his tongue forced its way in my mouth. The second his tongue touched mine, a strangled sound escaped my mouth. He licked and pressed his tongue hard against mine. He swirled his tongue with mine. And then he sucked my tongue into his mouth and a feeling I'd never experienced happened just below my hips.

He took his tongue away, but his lips went nowhere. He kissed me, long and slow. His big lips overpowering my smaller ones. His tongue snuck out and licked at my bottom lip a second before his teeth bit down on it. My entire body shuddered and my hips thrust in his direction involuntarily.

In response, I got a growl and a tongue back inside my mouth. I fought his this time. This was my show. I initiated this kiss. I was going to be the one in control. My hands gripped his shirt as I kissed him with a fierceness I didn't know I possessed. When I felt like I couldn't breathe, I pulled back, taking his bottom lip along for the ride. My eyes popped open, his lip still captured by my teeth. His eyes were already open, staring at me with such heat, I swear that one look alone could have warmed my entire body. I pulled on his lip harder and his hand on my head trailed from my shoulders down to my back until his large palm rested right over my ass. He squeezed the cheek and an unfamiliar wet warmth gathered between my legs. I gasped, feeling that hand everywhere, letting go of his lip and watching it pop into place, now swollen and red.

I looked down between us and cursed. How did he end up with the gun? I swallowed roughly before I chanced a look back up at him. He wasn't grinning. He wasn't looking at me in pity or like I was cute for trying to disarm him. His eyes had a glint in them. And I wasn't sure if it was a glint of surprise or respect. Maybe a bit of both.

"What's your name?" he asked, his voice husky.

"What's your name?" I whispered, not trusting my voice.

"Hector," he answered simply.

I took a deep breath. "Annie. I'm Annie."

He looked at me skeptically. "Are you sure your name isn't Olive?"

I frowned. That wasn't who I am. It was who I was going to be. As soon as I made it out of the country. "No. And how do you know about th—?"

His hand slipped from my body and held up a fake ID. My fake ID. "I've been doing this a long time. I know how to go undetected. You didn't hear a thing because you were so focused on him."

I couldn't reply. I felt so stupid. Stupid enough that heat flooded my cheeks and I broke our intense eye contact, staring at the floor. From my peripheral, I saw my fake ID land on the couch and then I felt his fingers under my chin, forcing my gaze back to him.

"I'll tell you what I'm going to do. I'm going to take you to my place and then I am going to come back and blow this lowlife's head off. Sound good?"

"No, it doesn't fucking sound good," I hissed, my face heating for an entirely different reason. "He is mine to kill."

He sighed, his whole chest heaving once. "Don't be difficult, bonita. I don't want to hurt you."

The respect in his eyes I found minutes before vanished. Maybe he saw me as a capable girl. Maybe even a strong one. But he was *the man*. It was his job to kill, to protect, to get his hands dirty. I had no problem protecting myself for the past decade but I didn't tell him that. He saw me as weak. Nothing would change his mind.

"Fine," I relented with a whisper.

"Fine," he repeated, his voice sounding incredulous.

I looked up at him, into his suspicious as ever eyes, and nodded. "Fine." I turned from him, bending down to tie my shoe that didn't need tying, fishing for my last weapon. Returning to my full height, I turned around to face him, my hand already swiping the knife in front of me. The sharp edge grazed his right eyebrow but that's as far as I got before his fingers wrapped around my throat. "I didn't want to hurt you, Annie. But I'm not letting you do this."

I wanted to curse him out. In both his preferred language and mine. I wanted to scream the words but his hands were tight around my throat, my vision growing hazy as I fought for my next breath. I scratched at his hands with my nails but he just stared at me as he slowly choked me into unconsciousness.

The last thing I heard before my world went dark was a promise. "Te veo pronto, bonita."

I'll see you in a bit, beautiful.

CHAPTER FIVE
Hector

I gathered her in my arms to catch her from falling the moment her body gave up its fight. For the first time since I walked in and saw this woman, her hands steadier holding the gun than my hands had ever been in the fifteen plus years I've wielded one, I let out a singular shaky breath.

My eyes swung from the unconscious fireball of a woman in my arms to my best friend hidden in the darkness across the room. His eyes displayed the shock I felt. Like he had no idea what the fuck just happened. Well, I didn't either.

He stepped out, shook off the surprise of tonight's unfolding, and met my frozen body. "Which one do you want me to take care of?"

Inadvertently, my grip on Annie tightened and I forced my hand to relax against her skin. Nolan's eyes flicked to the movement before looking past me to the coffee table where Cameron Wade thrashed against the coffee table, the zip-ties cutting off his circulation, his usual pale skin turning a sickly purple color.

I didn't have to guess why anyone would want him dead. He was a drunk, a sleezeball, and a nuisance to everyone he came into contact with. He was the most uninteresting human I've ever been in a room with. He drank, he fucked, and he made sure the whole world knew. That's it. He didn't have a family, a woman, or a business. His love could be found inside a glass bottle, and unbeknownst to me, it made him happy. I had no complaints against the man who, every night, spent his money racking up his tab, keeping one of my last businesses in New Hazle thriving.

I frowned as I fought the urge to look down at the woman I clutched to my chest. The woman hell-bent on killing Cameron Wade. The woman who so clearly had been wronged by this man and decided to take justice for herself. The woman who didn't flinch when she saw my face or when I told her my name. The woman who didn't bow down to me. The woman who made me bleed. I could feel the slice she got of my eyebrow, the gash burning from the exposure of air, the wetness slowly dribbling down the side of my face.

I bit my lip, unsure if I was making the biggest mistake of my life. "Stay with him. I'll be back." I tossed her body over my shoulder, easily lifting her, at most, one hundred and twenty pounds. Before I pulled open the front door, I looked over my shoulder to find Nolan sitting in the same spot Annie accompanied moments ago, his hands holding a book, his feet propped up on the coffee table, or rather digging into

Cameron's struggling body. A smirk made its way to my lips. "Gather her things, Nolan. No one needs to know she was ever here."

For an answer, I received a short nod and a flipped page. I tucked Annie into the back seat of my car before hustling around to the driver's side. I hopped in, turning the music off as soon as the engine clicked over. I didn't think Annie would regain consciousness on the short drive to my house but the fearlessness I caught a glimpse of in those deep blue eyes of hers was enough warning that the moment she woke up, there would be hell to pay.

Most of my days, I spent in the city. The only two places in New Hazle that you could find me was at my house or at Hank's. And no one knew where my house was. I could never live in the city. Too many people. Too much noise. Not for me. I loved my silence and I loved my solitude.

I shouldn't be taking Annie back to my house. I knew I should keep her in this car until she wakes and either let her kill me or take her where she wants to go. I shouldn't care about the look I saw pass over her face when I placed my hands over hers on the gun like I saved and destroyed her all at once.

Stopping at a red light, I looked back at her. Her face was squished against the leather seat, her hair shielding her face from me. A deep sigh escaped me as I turned back around, following the back roads to my secluded home.

The moment I passed the gates, Samuel came to mind. I didn't know how the fuck I was going to explain an unconscious woman half my age. Or bringing her into the house that only he and the other two men in my life knew about. He left for a summer program abroad in the afternoon tomorrow. There was a fifty-fifty chance he would spend the night at home and get some rest or spend his last night in the city, getting his chance at one last American girl. For the first time in my life, I hoped for the latter.

I pulled up, relieved to see his Camaro nowhere in sight. Throwing Annie over my shoulder once more, I carried her into the house and upstairs into my bedroom. I switched the light on, only dim enough to see our surroundings.

I let her body slip from mine as I transferred her onto the bed. I pulled back the covers, tucking her body underneath the blanket before I took a step back. I shoved my hands in my pockets as I studied her face.

She was beautiful. An oval face, a straight feminine nose, and rosy cheeks. Long wavy blonde hair. She looked like she belonged on the cover of Vogue, not unconscious on my bed. Those eyes that I found underneath that pretty face, the ones I found myself getting lost in, almost to the point where she almost did overpower the gun from me.

My eyes slid down to her lips. Pale, pink, and plump. The swollenness from our kiss long gone but I could still feel them on my skin. Remember the taste on my lips. Her fight for control. Her weakness when my tongue touched hers, the way her hands flew from the gun to grab the lapels of my jacket. She didn't even notice. All of her focus transferred onto me, on the way I set her on fire and exposed her weakness.

I shouldn't have kissed her back. She was closer to my son's age than mine. She had her whole life ahead of her. Not to mention, I didn't think the little gash through my eyebrow would be the last time she'd make me bleed.

I stepped forward, knowing I shouldn't. I grabbed tendrils of her hair, spreading it across the pillow her head rested upon.

I couldn't see her eyes now but I didn't have to. As steady as her hand held the gun, as unmoving as her finger curled around the trigger, her eyes told a different story. Those pleading deep blues burned in my memory, reminding me of another set of pleading eyes.

I knew that look all too well because that was how I looked at my father the night of my eighteenth birthday when he took me out for my first kill. The week before my only worry was Samuel teething and then my father revealed to me that when I turned eighteen, I wouldn't just become a man, I'd become the successor to the Rivera name. A name that involved money, drugs, and blood.

My eyes pleaded with him the same way Annie's did. All I got was a rough hand around my shoulder and a demand.

You always remember your first kill. It's the one that changes your life, the one that ruins you forever.

I hesitated. I refused. I couldn't do it.

My father came prepared, though, already underestimating me. He had one of his men bring over a chair and a video of the man I was supposed to kill. The man in front of me with tears running down his face, promises spilling from his lips.

I looked from the man in front of me to the man on the television screen. They had the same features, but didn't resemble the same man. The man on the screen was sadistic and cruel. Digging beer bottle after beer bottle into a woman's skin, slurring vile, demeaning things against her tear-streaked face.

I begged my father and his men to cut the video. I screamed

and growled for them to stop. But they kept playing the video. The woman's whimpers turned into hyperventilated sobs until she couldn't hold in her pain any longer. Her screams felt vivid like they weren't being played from a speaker, but from right next to me. It felt as if she screamed directly in my ear, begging me to save her from this monster.

They didn't stop the video, not when I grabbed the gun, not when I placed my finger over the trigger, not when I put a bullet in the middle of the man's brain. They didn't stop the video until it was over. The video that still seemed to play on a loop in my head over fifteen years later.

I blinked past the memory, refocusing on the present. On the woman whose life would've changed forever, if Matt hadn't contacted me.

"¿Quién es, bonita?" I whispered, my eyes roaming every inch of her face. *Translation: Who are you, beautiful?*

Sighing, I snatched my hand from her hair, grabbed the remote from the nightstand and left her sleeping. I locked the doors and hopped back in my car, returning to Cameron Wade's house.

My phone rang as I cut the engine. I answered, not knowing what the hell I was going to say to him. Matt didn't give me a chance to speak. "Did you find her?"

I slammed the car door shut. "Yes."

A relieved sigh escaped him like he couldn't help it. "Bring her to my house. I owe you, Hector."

I remained quiet as my feet led me to the almost condemned porch. There was no way I was handing her over to him. Not unless she made that choice. If he had been in her life long enough to be worried about her, there had to be a reason she kept her secret from him. "I think I'll keep her for a bit."

"The fuck you will," he boomed through the speaker.

I gritted my teeth. "You told me to save her, keep her out of trouble and I have. You owe me your life now. Those were the terms, Panini. Now, I have my own terms."

He cursed under his breath but otherwise remained silent. "You tried killing me once, Matt. I haven't forgotten. When it comes to Annie, stay out of my way or your mama's going to have to bury you next."

I hung up, not waiting for his response. I shoved open the front door and saw Nolan in the same place I left him. I knew he heard my arrival but still, he finished the page he was reading before removing his feet from Cameron and closing his book.

"I scrubbed everything down so any handprints she left behind are as good as gone. Her backpack only had an extra pair of clothes and a few dollars. I gathered up her two knives and gun and put it in a plastic bag." He paused, looking at me curiously. "I wouldn't return those to her unless you're sure she won't try to kill you again."

My lips tilted up against my will. "I'll keep that in mind, Nolan. I'll take it from here. You can go."

I waited until he left before I turned my attention back to Cameron. He had stopped struggling, every piece of visible skin turning a ghastly gray color. At this point, death might have been his wish, not his fear.

I walked over and bent down to his purple wrists and loosened the tie around them. Then the same with his feet. I knew Nolan wouldn't. Nolan, as nervous as women made him, he recognized their heart and respected their decisions. A woman didn't tie a man up and plan to shoot him for no good reason. I hoped Cameron would make this easy on me and confess what he did to Annie.

I sat on the couch, my ass hanging off the edge as I looked at the drool and tears running together down his neck. I slapped his face and waited. No response. I sighed, sticking my hands in the couch cushions. Surely, a drunk like him had a bottle nearby. My hands closed around the glass, unmistakably a beer bottle. I pulled it out. A lite beer, piss warm, and half full. It would do. I twisted the cap off, flicked it behind me, and poured the contents over Cameron's face.

He lurched against his restraints, gasping. "Fuck," he groaned.

I sat back against the couch, throwing a foot over my knee. His head slid in my direction and his eyes widened. "Whatever she told you, I didn't do it."

"Who's she?"

"Katya," he whispered her name.

I frowned. What the fuck did Katya have to do with this? "I haven't been back to the club since she kicked me out."

Interesting. I almost asked why she kicked him out but I didn't care about any of that right now. The only thing that concerned me in this moment was a beautiful woman with dark blue eyes, a wicked mouth, and a mind set on murder.

"I want to know about Annie," I said lowly, my eyes boring into his.

He flinched at the mention of her name. "I don't know an Annie," he whispered more to himself than me. His hands curled into fists and his eyes glazed over every inch of this room that wasn't me. A strong reaction for someone you didn't know.

"You're going to die, Cameron." I stood up, throwing Annie's backpack over my shoulder. I leaned down and released Cameron from his restraints. Before he even thought about escaping me, I delivered an uppercut to his jaw, catching his lifeless body before it hit the ground. "But she's right. You're not mine to kill."

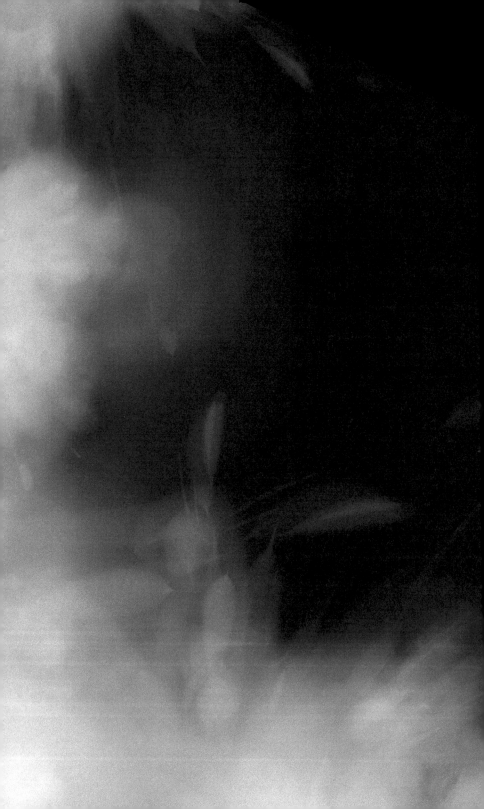

CHAPTER SIX

Annie

I was in heaven. I had to be. There was no other explanation. The mattress I found myself lying on top of was something out of a daydream. A cloud of cushion underneath my body, a sheet of delicateness sliding against my cheeks. No springs from the flimsy box spring digging into my ribs. My arms and legs didn't dangle over a familiar edge. The blanket wrapped around my every limb felt smooth against my skin rather than the scratchy surface I was used to.

I stretched my arms above my head, my body distorting into an unknown shape as I worked out all of the kinks. I opened my eyes and frowned. Where was I?

The unfamiliar room was huge. The ceiling was about ten feet from my face. I sat up, letting the gray blanket fall from my body as I studied the room. Spacious and empty. Other than the king-size bed I found myself in, there were two small tables at each head of the bed and what had to be an eighty-inch LED TV mounted to the wall adjacent from where I sat.

I closed my eyes, rubbing my temples as pain edged at the corners. I frowned and made my way out of the bed. The end table next to me held a plate of pancakes, sausage, a glass of orange juice, a bottle of ibuprofen, and a note. I skipped everything and snatched up the note.

> *Annie,*
>
> *Here's breakfast and something to help with the pain. I would appreciate it if you didn't try and burn my house down. I have something to do in the morning but I'll be back in the afternoon. I'm looking forward to talking to you.*
>
> *Hector*

Memories came rushing in of how I spent my night. Or rather, how I was supposed to spend my night. I was supposed to declare victory in my ten-year plan of revenge. I was supposed to succeed. I was supposed to be on my way out of the country to start over. Cameron Wade and Annie Miller were supposed to be dead. And I was sure only one of us got the pleasure.

Fucker. I wasn't going to burn his house down. The moment I could get my hands on him, I was going to burn him alive.

I stomped over to the bedroom door and pulled it open. Or I tried to, but it didn't budge. Not even an inch when I put all of my strength behind my pull. It was useless. The door was locked. I crossed the room again and grabbed the butter knife next to my untouched breakfast, rushing back to the door and trying to pick the lock to no avail. After a good thirty minutes, and a string of curses and huffs of frustration, I gave up on my lock picketing, assuming he had more security in place than just an old-fashioned lock.

Hours passed, and I paced the room, from one side to the other, tracing my way around the bed, along the walls. After I counted the minutes for two straight hours, I finally succumbed and took the pills for my still throbbing head.

Begrudgingly, I cut up the pair of pancakes, still warm after being out for who knows how long. I ate the food. But I ate it angrily. Like an animal who hated its owner but ate the good stuff they fed him anyway. I grunted and I growled. I paced and paced. I pulled at my hair and flopped on the bed.

There were large windows in the room but after several shoulder tackle attempts, I realized that those were on lockdown, too. After the sun rose to its highest point, I grew anxious. I had no clue who this man was or what he wanted from me. Most importantly, why he stopped me from killing my lowlife of a father. I intended to find out…if I didn't kill him first.

Just when I was considering trying to kick the bedroom door down, it opened and there he stood. The man from last night. The beautiful one. The dangerous one. The one that destroyed ten years of preparation in a matter of minutes.

I didn't speak and I didn't jump into action like I swore I was going to the moment he appeared. I just stared at him, taking him in. He wore different clothes from the night before. A black pair of basketball shorts and a plain white t-shirt covered his body. His feet were bare if you didn't count the plain white ankle socks. He looked like he came back from either playing a game of basketball or watching it from another room. He wasn't exactly dressed for "having things to do."

That's what I decided to focus on. Even though my stomach landed two front flips when I saw the intensity those deep brown eyes had to offer me, I looked him up and down, feeling my lips curve in a sneer. "Those don't seem like the type of clothes that kept you from locking me in this room all day."

He grunted, his lips upturning. "I see you're already in a good mood. Did you sleep well?"

I folded my arms across my chest, my hips jutting out on their own accord, and glared at him. His eyes left mine for the barest second, shooting down to my hips before they returned. I glared harder.

He stepped into the room, not bothering to shut the door behind him, each slow, cautious step bringing him closer and closer to me. I refused to cower away from him. He might have been a cat, but I'd be damned if I ever became his mouse. His feet didn't stop moving until our chests grazed. "We should talk."

His breath floated across the skin at my temple and I barely caught the shiver it caused in time to conceal it. I tilted my head up, looking him in the eye. "So, talk," I bit out.

He stepped to the side, sitting down on the edge of the bed. I turned my body, my eyes never leaving him. "I want to know why you want to kill Cameron Wade."

He folded his hands in his lap, his eyes searching mine. Such a simple answer but my lips pressed together, reluctant to give him any sort of truth. I certainly couldn't tell him my truth. Not that any of it mattered. Nothing did. He took the only thing I wanted away from me. "Why did you want him dead?" I countered, squaring my shoulders.

He shrugged. "He's a bit handsy with the women down at the strip club. He crossed a line for the last time."

My stomach, all of a sudden, dropped as if someone delivered the perfect round kick. He was still hurting women. I wasn't naïve enough to think my mom was the exception to his behavior or that he felt remorse for what he did to her and spent the years respecting women. But hearing it out loud, I could no longer deny the truth. My mom wasn't the only one. There were more. Countless more.

I turned away from Hector, digging my fingers into my denim-clad thighs.

It was a good thing Cameron already took his last breath. The rage swelling up in my gut felt as dangerous as a loaded gun and, like always, he was my target.

"I have a proposition for you."

I spun back around to face my kidnapper. His eyes froze on my curled fists and I forced myself to unclench them, soothing them across my thighs. I had no idea what he was thinking. I had no idea why I was still here. He got what he wanted and I didn't. End of story.

Ignoring the knot in my stomach, I took a step closer to him. Closer until I could feel the heat radiating from his body. I tucked my body in between his spread thighs, our bodies a breath away from kissing. He tilted his head back, still looking at me with those intense brown eyes. His lips pulled up in a smirk, his eyes almost sparkling.

I lifted my hands until they came to rest on top of his wide shoulders. I curled my fingers around his impressive muscles in a soft grip. His breath hitched and the soft sound made me want to sport a smirk of my own. I refrained, just barely. I bent down until our breaths mixed. If either of us moved the barest inch, we would be kissing. Again.

I couldn't let that happen. He won the first round; I was winning this one. I slid my hands up from his shoulders, along his neck, until my fingertips grazed the softness of his hair. I pulled on the barely-there strands, tilting his head back and then, his bottom lip did graze mine, just the barest brush of skin. "You know," I whispered with faux confidence. "Most people consider it a crime to choke a woman into unconsciousness and then kidnap her."

His brown eyes shined with amusement. "It's also illegal to tie a man up in his own house and kill him."

I did smirk then. "I suppose so."

He chuckled. And then my hands weren't the only ones in play. His hands came up to my hips and tugged my body closer. No space separated us now. Our foreheads crashed together. My hips brushed against his stomach.

I tried to control my breathing, but it seemed nearly impossible. His body was so close to mine. The memory of kissing him at the forefront of my mind, yet so far away. I almost convinced myself I needed his lips one more time just to prove I remembered how it felt. "Anyone ever tell you that you are tempting?" I blurted out, immediately regretting it.

I could feel the rumble of his laugh against my hips and I hated that I noticed how beautiful it sounded. Like he didn't do it too often, so it was always a moment when he let one slip. I grabbed his hands, peeling them from my hips before placing them on the bed on either side of him. He obeyed my silent command, allowing me to push his back against the mattress. He tilted his head to the side, asking me without words what the hell I was up to. I didn't plan on answering that question.

I didn't follow him.

I made a run for it.

I didn't get far. He caught me way before I even made it within reaching distance of the door. His hands, once again, claimed my hips and before I could even sputter a protest, I found myself slung over his shoulder. He made his, *our*, way back to the bed, sitting down in the same spot, taking me with him.

He slid my body down from his shoulders until we were about as eye level as we could get with our height difference. He wrapped my legs around his waist, making me sit atop his thighs.

I was back under his control and I hated it. I hated myself for not being more careful last night. I hated him for ruining my plans. I hated this whole goddamn situation.

"As I was saying," he said, not a speck of aggravation or irritation in his voice. "I have a proposition for you."

I remained quiet. Nothing he could offer me would be worth anything. He took the only thing I ever wanted away from me. I stared at him, unflinching.

After several minutes of my silence, his eyebrows scrunched up. "You don't even want to hear what I have to offer?"

"The only thing you have that I want is a plane ticket with my name on it since you made me miss my flight by locking me up in this room all day," I bit out.

His frown intensified. "What are you talking about?"

My own frown took place. Did he seriously not get it? "The murder plan. The fake ID. Have you never watched an episode of *Criminal Minds*?" I didn't pause to find out. "Murder and flee, the golden rule."

"You don't think you would have been caught by the time you fled?"

"Why would I? I wasn't planning on leaving any trace behind. And I hadn't seen him in over ten years. There was no connection."

He seemed to think about my answer. "So, that's all you want in life? To kill him and start over."

A weight as heavy as a rock from the Grand Canyon settled on my chest. Yes. That's all that I wanted but coming from his lips, it sounded pathetic. He didn't say it mockingly. I could tell from the way he looked at me. He wasn't judging me; he wasn't belittling me. He simply wanted to know.

I decided to go with the truth. "That's as far as I planned."

He nodded slightly and I tore my eyes from his. I didn't want him to see, for my sake, how he stripped everything from me.

"Look at me," he said, after a few moments of the only sound being our tangled breaths, his voice soft but demanding.

When I grew brave enough for his eyes again, his hands found my face and cradled it in his palms. I was too surprised by his suddenness to flinch or wrestle out of his hold. His palms felt rough but oddly comforting against my skin. "I didn't kill him."

That time, I did flinch. I tried to back up to get away from him but his hands gripped my head, holding me in place. "What do you mean you didn't kill him?"

"Just that. He's yours to kill, bonita."

"You. Didn't. Kill. Him." I whispered each word slowly as if they were their own sentence, trying my hardest to make his words sink in. "Why?"

My body rose as he sucked in a deep breath. "I was going to. I'm not going to lie, I was going to. But there's a history with the two of you. He just pissed me off. So, I'm giving him to you."

I pressed my lips together to keep me from gaping at him. My heart felt like it had been crushed and revived all within seconds. I wasn't sure if I was disappointed or in awe that he didn't kill him. "Where is he?"

"He's somewhere," he said slowly. "Where he will remain until you're ready for him."

I sat up straighter on his lap. "I'm ready for him now."

Hector shook his head, his words coming out soft. "No, you're not."

I huffed a humorless laugh. "You've known me for two seconds. *I'm ready.*"

"You think you're ready?"

I nodded.

"Tell me your one-year plan after you kill him."

"What does that matter?"

"In order to carry the weight of taking a life, yours has to be worth living, so, tell me. Annie is freed from the chains she thinks are binding her, what's her first move?"

SONIA ESPERANZA

A growl slipped out of my mouth. "I don't have to answer to you."

"You don't," he agreed, plucking me off of his body and setting me down on the bed beside him, eliminating his touch. "But until you figure out your future, I'm not letting you bury your past."

I stared after him as he walked across the room with ease like he didn't have a care in the world. Just as he crossed the threshold of the room, he paused but didn't look back. "Dinner will be ready in an hour. Hope you like Mexican food."

I watched him disappear down the hallway and noticed he left the door open. I didn't chase after him. I didn't step foot out of the room I had been dying to escape all day. Instead, I sunk deeper into the bed, something uncomfortable curling up in my stomach.

CHAPTER SEVEN

Annie

Hands folded under my head, knees tucked deep into my chest, eyes open but unblinking, I let my mind consume me, something that was as natural to me as breathing.

It had been so long, year after year, seeming to span an entire lifetime, since I had someone in my life. I had to be so many things for myself: my best friend, my caretaker, and my family all wrapped up in one. I never connected with other kids that shared a roof with me or those I attended school with.

Once I booked it out of New Hazle and moved onto campus, I let myself have hope. I would no longer be the only one without a family. For the first time in a while, I'd be on a level playing field. Reality slapped me in the face almost instantly when I got assigned a roommate who moved in and moved out in less than twenty-four hours. As it turned out, my nightmares weren't her jam. Funny thing is, they weren't mine either but changing rooms didn't really work for me.

The day my mom died, I was left all alone. No one to share my meals with, no one to watch daytime soap operas with, no one to give me makeup tips. She was a mom and best friend all wrapped in one. When I lost her, I lost everything. Other than when I needed to be vocal for school or work, I was the definition of silent. Just me and my rapidly spinning thoughts thinking ahead to the next hour, the next month, hell, sometimes even the next decade.

I didn't know how long I lay there, body curled so tight, trying not to fret about my life being derailed in the matter of a single day. I tried not to think about how Cameron Wade would have been lifeless by now if only I wasn't so caught up in my emotions. I could have been in Mexico by now, with a clean slate, instead of I don't even know where, with a man whose eyes studied me a little too closely.

Letting out a long sigh, I sat up, surprised to notice the sun had long since set and the smell of something good, something food, filtered through the open bedroom door.

Living on nothing but packaged noodles and instant meals, my stomach never failed to embarrass me when I caught the smell of food that wasn't prepackaged. My stomach growled or groaned, maybe a mixture of the two. My mouth watered. And somehow, my feet led me out of the four walls that had confined me for the past twenty-four hours.

The moment I crossed the threshold of my prison cell, my eyes bounced from side to side, up and down as I took in the interior of the house I found myself in. I stood on the second floor, surprised to see that there was nothing to it. Other than the bedroom behind me and a corridor the same size, the second floor was bare. An old-style banister, golden with an intricate design spanned across the room perfect for a king to spread his arms and stare at those beneath him.

I traced my fingertips across the golden steel until I reached the stairs. Pausing at the top, I gripped the handrail and looked down over the banister, confirming my suspicions. From this very spot, the whole first floor layout was visible. The bottom of the stairs ended where the dining area began, leading into the kitchen. Beyond the obvious space were hallways on both ends, rooms lining the walls. The interior of the house was beautiful, all golden hues and warm tones.

The smell of food grew stronger and I could hear soft Latin music playing in one of the rooms, presumably the kitchen. I knew that's where I would find him.

I didn't know much about my kidnapper, if you could even call him that. I knew his first name and I knew he wanted to kill Cameron, so obviously he had some sense to him. A feeling in my gut told me he wouldn't hurt me. Still, I wasn't keen to be here, to be under his thumb. To not have set a flame to my past life, starting a new one for myself.

Sighing, I took one stair at a time, unsure of what would happen next. I wanted to stay defiant. I wanted to prove to him that I was more than ready to bloody my hands. I was more than ready to do the thing almost half of my life had been leading up to. But he held all of the cards. I was in his home, having no idea where I was or how I could get the hell out of here and he had Cameron in his possession. There was not a damn thing I could do but listen to what he had to say and agree to it.

I grunted as I reached the bottom of the stairs, not the tiniest bit happy to be stuck at anyone's mercy.

My footsteps were quiet as I rounded the kitchen to see two pans on the stove, steam rising from each of them, tortillas in Hector's hand as he heated them on a burner, and his head tilted on his shoulder as he held his cell phone in between the space. "Ha ha," he deadpanned to whoever he was talking to. "You're not planning on leaving the airport, are you? Because I will ki—"

The other person must have cut him off because he didn't get to finish his sentence but he did grit his teeth and slap a heated tortilla on a plate on the burner with a little bit too much force.

I rounded the table and pulled out a chair as quietly as I could, soaking up the few seconds of Hector's gaze not being focused on me. Since the moment we met, I had pointed a gun at him, kissed him, cut him, and straddled him. I was almost afraid of what would happen next.

"It's never too late," he replied, his voice thick with emotion. At the hint of concern, the love so loud in his soft voice, turned my body hot, my uncomfortableness making my entire body clammy. I was eavesdropping, but it didn't feel like it until he said those few couple of words. I feigned a cough just so he knew he wasn't alone.

His head whipped in my direction and I sat up straighter, immediately cursing myself for it. Those intense brown eyes focused in on me and I wanted to look away but I couldn't. He held me hostage and those eyes felt no different. A few minutes of our eyes pinned to each other, the pain I felt from digging my fingernails into my thighs became too much at the same time Hector realized someone was still on the phone. His eyes left me as did his body. I collapsed against the wooden chair, letting out the breath I didn't realize I was holding in.

"Yes, sorry," he said, turning back around. "I was distracted. What were you saying?" A pause, and then, "Alright. Alright, ass. Call me when you land, yeah? I don't care what time it is."

When he hung up the phone, he placed it on the counter and switched off all the burners on the stove before turning around to face me again. "You do eat meat," he said gruffly, but it sounded like a question.

I answered in the form of a nod. I watched him as he grabbed two plates from the cabinet, stopping at the fridge before focusing on me once more. "What do you want to drink?"

"Wh—" I started to say, but my voice didn't cooperate with me. I cleared my throat, rubbing at the sore skin there and tried again. "What are you having?"

A look similar to guilt flashed across his eyes before he moved them back to the fridge. He held up a bottle of Corona so I could see it. "I'll have one of those, too," I whispered, unsure if my voice would give away again.

He set the drinks down on the table before returning to the kitchen. He poured the meat he cooked into two separate bowls and fetched some side bowls in two trips. Once he laid out all of the food before us, he sat down, claiming a seat close to me, not the one beside me, but the one next to it, leaving space for me not to feel confined but close enough that we could still talk comfortably. He didn't look at me again and he didn't offer me any words, either. He loaded up his plate like a starved man. Remembering that he wasn't eating alone, with an overloaded taco halfway to his mouth, he stopped to look over at me to see I hadn't moved an inch.

And I realized a little bit too late that I was staring at him. He dropped the food back on his plate and looked at me. I averted my eyes, feeling my cheeks heat. "Annie." My name was a soft growl on his lips. When I looked back up at him, his jaw clenched as he rested his elbows on the table, his hands clasped together, and leaned slightly forward. His eyes, hard and intense, solely focused on me. "I'm not going to hurt you," he said, his voice softening to a whisper.

I looked away from him, disgusted with myself. I thought I was stronger than this. I thought I could protect myself enough to never be put in this position. I did everything in my power to make sure I didn't end up like my mother, under a man's thumb. And I didn't know what it was about the man sitting next to me, but I knew he wouldn't hurt me, not unless I hurt him, and maybe not even then. But it still stung like a motherfucker to know he was the one in control. I tried to swallow my pride, but it felt like a dozen bullets lodged in my airway, making it impossible.

His eyes still had me pinned and I wished I could shake this feeling of despair off. "The only reason you're in pain right now," he gritted out between clenched teeth when I didn't make a move to acknowledge his words or to eat the food he made, "is because you fought me."

I broke our eye contact, looking to the side, taking in more of the detail of the interior of this house but not really registering anything, just wanting to escape his attention. Once I felt his eyes no longer on me, I grabbed one of the tortillas and added some meat and veggies before wrapping it up. Just before I took a bite, I realized that Hector was only the second person to ever cook a meal for me. Him and my mom.

I chanced a look his way. His brown eyes softly shut as he tipped the beer bottle to his lips. *It's been a long time since someone cooked for me.* I wanted to speak those words aloud but he and I weren't friends. We weren't quite enemies. We were strangers. As soon as he handed over my father, I would never see him again.

This was all temporary. Him. This house. His rules. I had to do what he wanted in order to get what I wanted. I wasn't a woman under a man's thumb. I was a survivor, just like I had always been.

I survived a dead mother, a piece of shit father, and getting tossed into a strange home. I survived, no, I thrived at an elite college with no support system.

What was this one man in comparison to a life of struggle and sorrow?

I would survive him. I had to.

I let my mouth close around the taco and just barely held back a groan. It was so fucking good. After eating the entire thing, in less than four bites, I popped open the tab from my beer and took a long pull. Barely even noticing Hector anymore, too consumed with the delicious food he prepared, I loaded up my second taco. I looked around the table for salsa. A red chunky sauce that looked like exactly what I wanted popped out at me. I didn't bother with a spoon. I tilted the little bowl until the salsa spread across my taco like ketchup on a hot dog. Bringing the taco to my lips, I heard Hector's voice call out my name, but it was already too late. I took a big bite and as soon as the first bite hit my tongue, I dropped the taco, already searching for his face. His eyes grew huge and he looked ready to launch out his chair.

I was fine one second and then the furthest thing from fine the next. I felt heat. Burning heat. My tongue felt the heat of a thousand fires. My cheeks felt like acid had been tossed in their vicinity. I looked at him again, sure my eyes were just as wide as his had been if not bigger. Hands flying up to my cheeks, the usual cold skin was scalding hot like I had been baking under the sun. Hector exploded from his seat, running into the kitchen, opening the fridge, retrieving something and rushing back to me. He pulled my chair out and angled it so we faced each other. I looked down at what he brought: a half-gallon of milk. He hastily uncapped the liquid and cupped my jaw to stop me from moving and pressed the jug against my lips.

The coolness of the milk against my tongue canceled the fire burning in my mouth. Chasing the spicy taste away, I chugged the half-gallon. I've never chugged anything in my life and if I had to predict my first time, it would never have been like this.

I could feel the milk that my desperate mouth missed dribbling down my chin, onto my clothes but I couldn't find it in me to care. I felt a hard cloth dabbing at my mouth. I slid my eyes down to see Hector's hand holding my face, dabbing at my wet chin. I couldn't find it in me to be embarrassed.

It took a while and almost the entire half-gallon of milk, but the burning heat finally receded and Hector took away the jug that quite literally saved my life.

"Good?" he asked and although he sounded concerned, I couldn't help but notice the smirk that was playing on his lips.

I wanted to threaten him with bodily harm if he let the laugh that was so clearly building up through his chest out but I let it go and instead gave him a steady nod. He lifted the napkin that he was still holding close to my face and wiped what was left off of my lips. His growing smile slipped from his face as his eyes left mine and stuck to something lower. When he pulled the napkin away, I didn't miss the way he let his fingertip graze over the soft skin of my lips, just barely dragging the skin down. When my lip popped back into place, he looked away, but not before I caught the grimace on his face.

When he cleaned up the mess I made, I asked, in the only way I could, "What the hell was that?"

"Salsa," he said, shrugging as if I didn't already know that. "But not the kind you find at the grocery store. It's homemade."

"You made it," I asked him, pushing my plate away.

He nodded, mid-bite. While he returned to his chair and resumed eating like it was a sport, I peeked over the table to see what he was eating. It was different from what he made me. I recognized it as a Mexican taco immediately.

After taking four years of Spanish in high school, I decided to take it in college as well. I knew even before I moved to the city, I'd be exchanging Annie Miller in one day for Olive James. Where do you go when you run? As far away as you can get. Running to Mexico from Pennsylvania seemed like the best option. I tested out of Elementary Spanish I and II and took Intermediate Spanish my freshman year. The first day of class, I walked in and on every desk, a concoction I'd never seen before was laid out on each desk. The teacher, an older woman with golden olive skin and black bouncy curls, walked in the room. "It's true," she had said. "You've been lied to all of your lives. You haven't had a taco until you've had a true Mexican taco."

"Do you want a bite?"

I jerked back against my chair when I heard his voice. I closed my eyes and took a deep breath before I found his eyes once more. I didn't utter a word but I knew my eyes betrayed my curiosity.

He smiled. He smiled like he couldn't help it. "Try it," he said, holding his taco toward me. "If you like it, I'll fix you up one."

I took the taco from his hand and ripped off a good chunk before returning it to him. Hesitant, because obviously, this man's taste buds were much stronger than mine, I took a bite the size a baby would. A light chuckle came out of Hector, causing me to take a much bigger bite. I chewed the meat and tortilla and who knew what else. The minute my tongue registered the taste, I let my eyes close and just enjoy it. It was damn good.

When I finished chewing, I opened my eyes and Hector already had a taco ready for me in his hands. I scarfed it down and the next one he made for me, too. When all of his meat was gone, I leaned back in my chair, eyes closed, sipping on my bottle of beer, feeling my stomach bloated and the skin at my waist pressing against the buttons of my jeans. "That was amazing," I said, but mostly it came out as a breath. "Best meal of my life, hands down." I peeked my eyes open to see Hector leaning back against his own chair, his bottle pressed against his lips, and staring at me. I tilted my head to the side as if I was considering him. "Maybe you're not an absolutely horrible person, after all."

I didn't give him time to reply or time for me to see if he would shoot me another smile, I stood up, collected our dishes, rinsed them off in the sink, found my way back upstairs and almost immediately passed out on the biggest bed I'd ever slept on in my life.

I tug on the end of her shirt. It's the only part of it I can reach. She's in the kitchen, wiping the tables, counters, sink. Over and over again. Almost as if she can't get them clean enough.

"Mama," I whine, tugging once more. "You promised makeup time. I want to be pretty."

She looks down at me as if she just registered my presence. Her frown smooths out and a soft smile plays on her lips. "Annie, baby. Mama is busy right now. Why don't you go up to your room for a bit and play?"

"You promised," I say, moving my hands down to my hips. "You said Tuesday is our night together. You said we can do whatever I want. Just the two of us."

"I know, sweetheart. But your dad is coming home and bringing people over who are very important. We have to be on our best behavior."

She gives me a look that tells me she will not hear any of my pleads or my whining or I'll be in trouble. I give up and go back to my room. I stay there when I hear my dad come in. I stay there when different, unfamiliar voices float up the stairs. The moment I hear the strangers say goodbye and the click of the door shut, I wait for my mama. She always comes for me. Maybe she'll still have time to put blush on my cheeks and gloss across my lips. I wait and I wait. And then the sun disappears from my window. I walk down the stairs, trying to be as quiet as possible, knowing where every creak in the wooden floor is so I don't make a sound.

When I reach the middle of the stairs, I hear a sharp whisper. My dad's sharp whisper. His angry whisper. "You fucking embarrass me," he seethes, the belt he wears to keep his pants up, in his hands and striking something. Something I can't see. My hands cover my mouth. He's really, really angry. Angrier than I'd ever seen him. "All I ask you to do is clean. And you can't even do that. Toys all over the place. Dust making my nose fucking twitch. Useless. That's what you are, Michelle, useless."

My eyes widen in horror. Mama. Where's Mama? I see his leg lift and with it my mama's head comes into view, on the floor beside the couch. Her shirt is off, her back entirely red and swollen.

My eyes grow big. A scream is lodged in my throat but I stuff it down. I'll just make it worse. Seconds that feel like years pass and I hold my breath, knowing I am only going to make it worse. My entire face hurts, aches from keeping the screams, the cries, the sobs from surfacing.

I can't take it anymore.

I have to let it out.

I scream. I scream. I scream as if my life depends on it.

CHAPTER EIGHT

Hector

This was a bad idea. The worst idea I've ever fucking had. I knew it last night when I carried her over my shoulders and into my home. I knew it today when I opened the bedroom door and those murderous blues locked on me. And yet if given the chance to go back to last night, I wouldn't change a damn thing.

She could look me in the eye, curled fists at her sides and determination in her voice and tell me she was ready to take a life until her voice ran dry but I would never believe her. Not because I wouldn't listen or because I believed she was incapable of murder.

My hands touched enough of her body between last night and tonight to know her body wasn't only healthy but strong. The slice on my eyebrow alone advised me not to underestimate her.

The strength in her body, the calmness in her movements may have fooled her but the look in her eye, the breath she let out when my hands gripped the gun revealed the truth. The truth that maybe even she hadn't discovered yet.

I didn't have anyone to take away a choice that never felt like a choice. Annie did. She could hate me. She could bring havoc to my life. She could do whatever the hell she wanted to me if it meant saving herself.

I dropped onto the couch, a heavy sigh escaping me. I closed my eyes and rested my head against the soft material. In the darkness of my house and underneath my eyelids, her face never slipped from my mind.

Her eyes haunted me. Her mouth taunted me.

I was so fucking screwed.

Opening my eyes, I sat up, blindly reaching for the remote and the game controller. Once the TV turned on, I muted the sound and started a basketball tournament ruling out sleep for the night.

The ball barely tipped off when I heard her screams. I flung the controller out of my hand and booked it up the stairs two at a time. I burst through the doorway to the sight of her body thrashing against the bed. Her eyes clenched together, tears leaking out of the corners as I made it to her bedside and reached for her blindly.

"Annie." I tried to shake her shoulder enough to rouse her. I backed away once her body calmed, unsure of how she would react to me.

The cut on my eyebrow I was fond of. Long after I handed over Cameron and she moved on with her life, I knew every time I looked in the mirror, I would remember her. But I did not want any other scars from this woman and the way she handled a knife, I knew if she wanted to hurt me, she could.

Her body remained still and her screams turned into whimpers, the wetness gathering from her eyes soaking her cheeks. "Annie," I said hesitantly, giving her another shake.

Nothing. Her head began to shake and the word 'no' cascaded from her lips in a pleading chant. I reached for her face, my hands cupping her cheeks. I thumbed away the tears, whispering her name as softly as I could.

Her head stilled underneath my hands and the tears finally stopped. I breathed out a sigh of relief, letting my hands linger on the softness of her cheeks, my fingers brushing away the damp hair collecting at the top of her head and temples.

I pulled my hands from her skin and watched her chest rise in unsteady breaths. I remained an arm's length away until her tremors completely quieted. I covered her with the blanket she must have kicked off and left her sleeping.

I barely made it to the doorway when her screams started up again. It wasn't just a scream. Unlike the screams before, she yelled. "Stop it. Please, just stop it. No. No. Stop."

I no longer cared of bodily harm. I rushed back to her side and gripped my hands around her arms and shook her. "Annie. Wake up. Please, Annie."

The moment her eyes fluttered open, I yanked her into my arms, setting her shaking body on top of my thighs, my larger frame swallowing her. Her eyes opened just to close. I didn't look at her and I didn't relinquish my hold at all. It wasn't until her body grew tense that I knew she regained consciousness and with that, clarity. Our eyes connected and she flinched, scurrying away from me as fast as she could. I easily let her go, trying not to take her reaction to heart.

I twisted my body, reaching for the lamp on the bedside table. A warm glow settled over the room in my next blink and our eyes locked, neither of us looking away. I watched as her eyes calmed, followed by the rest of her body. Without her ragged breathing, the room fell into a tense silence.

She tore her eyes away from me, pulling her knees into her chest and burying her face against her thighs.

I took her moment of hiding to get myself in check. I have heard screams pour out of a woman before. It became a part of my job as a Rivera man. I took pride in helping women when needed. I didn't think I could've handled the family business without doing something good to outweigh the bad.

The screams were the worst part. I could never get them out of my head. The number of women I've heard scream because a man thought he could handle them however he wanted made me sick to my stomach. But I remembered each scream, each face.

Yet, the sound of Annie's screams did something to me. Something that made my hands shake with rage, my body coil with hatred.

I knew I should tear my gaze from her. I should ask her if she was okay even though I knew what her answer would be. I should leave this room and let her handle her own shit, not sit idly by and watch what I could guess was a nightly routine. No one had nightmares at random. Not the kind of nightmares that bring a strong woman to tears, anyway.

"Are you okay?" I asked her softly. She didn't give me an answer or even acknowledge I had said anything at all but I waited her out, in case she did.

She lifted her head after a few minutes that felt like hours to me, my hands itching to reach out to try and ease her pain. She looked me straight in the eye and lied to me. "Yes."

I knew she was lying because her eyes brimming with tears drooped with exhaustion.

"Are you sure," I pressed on.

"I said, yes," she bit out.

I nodded, knowing I shouldn't push her anymore. "Do you need anything?"

She shook her head before slipping back under the covers, pulling the material up to her chin. I sat there and stared at her until her eyes closed. Even then, I didn't move. I took in every inch of her face. From her tight jaw to her flushed cheeks. I wanted to kill the person who made that beautiful face twist in despair. I wanted to torture the person who made that delicate voice scream in agony.

I didn't have conclusive evidence, but it didn't take a genius to put two and two together. The plan to kill a man almost twice her age and the nightmares. He hurt her. In what way, I wasn't sure and I honestly didn't give a fuck. All I knew was that he was going to wish I killed him last night.

I stood up from the bed, turned off the lamp, and started to head downstairs. I paused in the doorway, wanting to turn back but knowing I shouldn't. Before I could take one more step, her small voice drifted across the room. A lone word I equally hated and loved in that moment. "Stay."

I turned back into the room, not muttering a word. I walked over toward the bathroom, tapped my knuckles against the wall until a drawer slid out. I picked up the blanket and joined her on the bed. I sat on the edge of the bed over the blanket she covered her body with. I unfolded the blanket before tossing it over my frame. It was to ease her mind. I had no plans of sleeping tonight. I shifted the pillows behind my head so I was half lying down and half sitting. I folded my hands across my stomach and closed my eyes, not offering her any words.

Because she didn't need me. We both knew that. She didn't want my words. She didn't even really want me. I offered her my presence and my protection, not asking anything in return.

I felt her eyes on me. The want, the need to get lost in those blue eyes had my cheek twitching, but I refrained.

"Who was on the phone earlier?" Out of all the things she could have whispered to me, that was one I hadn't expected.

I felt the bed shift but I didn't dare open my eyes. "My son."

"How old is he?"

"Eighteen."

"How old were you when he was born?"

"Sixteen."

"Where's his mom?"

"Gone," I bit out. She didn't ask another question but I still felt her eyes on me. Her breathing evened out and I started to count the minutes until I could leave this room and do what I did best.

"This proposition of yours?" Her voice thickened with sleep.

"Yes. What about it?"

"I want to hear about it. First thing tomorrow morning, I want to talk."

I nodded, knowing her eyes would be peeled open until she got a reply out of me. I opened my eyes to see her body facing me, her hands folded underneath her cheek. She seemed even more beautiful asleep. Her eyes weren't waging a war in their depths. Her lips parted slightly, looking so tender it almost tore a groan from me. They weren't pressed in the thin line I'd quickly grown used to. She looked like a normal woman. Breathtakingly beautiful with no worries and no pain. But I knew that wasn't the truth. Someone hurt her and I knew exactly where that someone was.

I drove the back roads of New Hazle until Hank's came into view. I parked in the back, opening the door leading into the basement. My shoes thudded against the stairs, filling the otherwise quiet space. I spotted Nolan sitting on a lone metal chair in the center of the room, his nose stuck in a book. Beyond him, Cameron Wade's body strung in the air. His hands and ankles trading in Annie's zip ties for my metal chains.

Nolan shut his book, standing once I made my way into the room. "Boss."

I didn't take my eyes off of Cameron's unconscious form. "Find everything out you can about him." I shrugged out of my jacket, placing it over Nolan's abandoned chair. "In one hour, I need you back here with blood bags and morphine. Call Lily, she'll get you what you need."

Nolan grunted his agreement. Tearing my eyes away from

Cameron, I looked to my best friend, the only one who could rein me in. "I don't know what you'll be walking into when you come back." I sighed, looking away. "He can't die. Not by my hands. Understood?"

I briefly saw Nolan nod his head before leaving me alone with Cameron. He hurt her. Physically or mentally, I couldn't be sure. Either way, he would be regretting it tonight.

Sauntering up to him, I arched my arm back before extending it, delivering a hard blow to his jaw. His head snapped up, a scream of agony tearing from his throat. He closed his eyes, groaning once the disorientation left him and I took its place.

"All of this because of some whore." He spit blood on the floor between us.

I knew he wasn't talking about Annie. He thought all of this was because Katya kicked him out of the club, a fact I hadn't even been privy to. The girls at the club were the farthest thing from my mind.

The image of how I left Annie sleeping snuck into my head. If you took one look at her, you'd make a million assumptions. And all of them would be wrong. Thinking of the way she used her mouth, her body to overpower the gun from me. If I was being honest, she almost succeeded. The cut on my eyebrow was proof enough that she was the kind of woman who didn't give up easily.

She wasn't a killer, but she wanted to kill this man. And that, along with the eerie screams and panicked look after her nightmare, gave me more reasons than I needed to torture this son of a bitch.

Working with one of the best doctors on the east coast worked in my favor. I joked with Lily that I was halfway to earning my medical degree, though she never found it funny. Over the past couple of years of knowing her, I've watched Lily do her thing. Lily was about three things: her family, her fiancé, and being a doctor. Her goal was to save lives, it's the reason we crossed paths at all, whereas mine edged into the gray category of that. I knew how to take someone to the edge of death before reaching for their hand at the last second.

I stared at Cameron. "It's so much more than that."

I closed the distance between us and wrapped my fingers around his throat. His eyes widened in fear, his jerky movements causing his body to swing on the chains.

Unleashing his throat once his eyes rolled into the back of his head, I stepped back, bending down to grab two identical hunting knives out of my shoes. I gripped the handles before driving them into each of his thighs.

His head snapped up, the scream ripping from him. I took a step back, tugging at my ringing ears. Blood slipped down his bony legs, dripping onto the concrete floor. Sauntering back up to him, I drove my fist into his face over and over again. I didn't stop when I felt his skin crack open or when I felt my own skin break at the knuckles. I didn't stop until the incessant flinching stopped, darkness taking over him once more. Grabbing the last two knives tucked on me, I slammed them into each of his forearms, backing away before he could assault my eardrums again.

His scream mellowed out into a plea. His eyes fluttered shut, but he remained conscious. "Please. Stop. Please, just stop." His pleas fell upon deaf ears. His screams did nothing to me while the woman who slept in my bed, her screams transformed into a song in my head, stuck on repeat, making the rage inside of me turn hot.

I turned my focus back onto the knives sticking out from his thighs. Latching onto the handles, I dragged the knives down, cutting his skin open. His screams filled the room once more but I didn't hear any of it. I repeated the motion in his arm, careful of his veins. I got lost in the pain I inflicted on him, lost in the feeling that I was doing right by her.

"Boss." Nolan's voice snapped me out of my dangerous haze. His voice, unusually loud, held a warning. I stepped back, nodding once. Cameron, once more, passed out. I took each of the knives from underneath his skin and threw them to the cement floor. Nolan pushed a chair toward me as well as a medical tray equipped with everything I would need to put Cameron's limbs back together again.

Well accustomed to this routine, Nolan easily moved around me, setting up fluids, a blood transplant, and a liquid antibiotic to limit the chance of infection.

"I've never seen you like that." Nolan's hesitant whisper broke through the sound of my heartbeat thudding against my ears.

I looked over to see him stitching Cameron's skin back together. "He hurt her."

Nolan bit his lip, concentrating on his sutures. "They all hurt someone, don't they?"

I looked away from him, unable to explain myself. Unable to explain what was different about Annie. I couldn't explain it to him. Hell, I couldn't even explain it to myself.

Hours passed as we worked side by side to clean up my mess. We transferred Cameron from his chains to a bed in the corner of the basement. I left Nolan in charge once I was sure Cameron's life wasn't in jeopardy, demanding he call me if anything changed.

I walked up the stairs leading to the bar, swerving right, into my office where a shower and fresh pair of clothes awaited me. Turning the hot water to scalding, I stepped under the pressure, washing away all of the blood and grime from my skin. I scrubbed underneath my fingernails until it hurt.

By the time I showered and dressed, it was well past the afternoon. I exited the bar from the back and hopped into my car. Pulling out on the road, I let a finger trail over the cut on my eyebrow. I didn't have plans of going home anytime soon, but when I did, I knew there was going to be hell to pay delivered by a five-foot fireball of a woman.

I ran around town before venturing into the city, checking in on all of my businesses.

The sun set deeper and deeper until it disappeared completely and I knew I couldn't put it off any longer. I whipped my car back in the direction of New Hazle. Any trust Annie gave me yesterday was as good as gone. Not when I disappeared after promising her my time.

I parked my car in front of the house, my feet dragging up to the door. With any luck, she would be asleep.

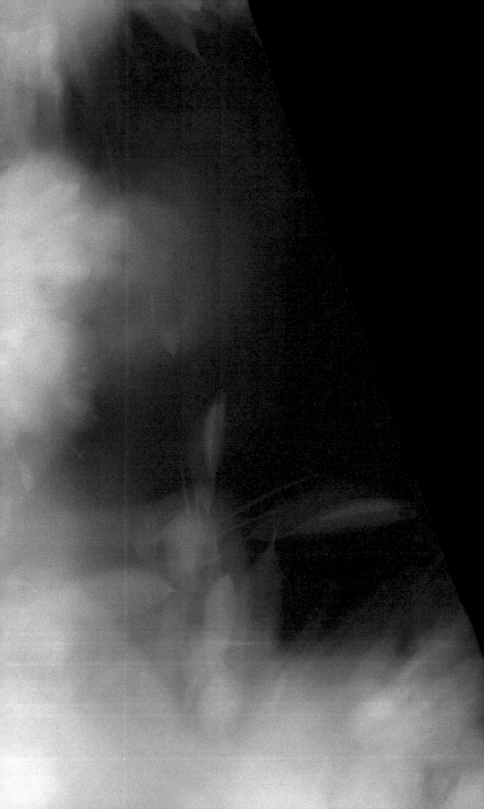

CHAPTER NINE

Annie

The first thing I did the next morning was thank the universe that the nightmares, *the memories*, did not make a reappearance after I fell asleep again. I sat up in bed and looked over to where Hector laid next to me the night before. His presence felt like a dream in contrast to the weight of what haunted me when I closed my eyes at night.

He was long gone, leaving no trace that last night had happened at all. But it did. He saved me from my own personal ring of hell with a promise of hearing this proposition of his today.

Tossing the covers from my body, steel determination set in my bones. My kidnapper and I were going to talk today, and as much as it killed me, agreeing to his terms, I knew it's what I had to do to see my ten-year revenge plan get back on track.

I noticed, unlike the day before, that the door to the bedroom was left open. I rushed into the bathroom to take a shower. I only had one outfit with me, but it was in my backpack and I had no idea what Hector would have done with that. Once I was done in the shower, I stood in the bedroom in nothing but a towel and felt up the wall. The bedroom, which I hadn't cared to notice before, was the definition of minimalistic. There were no dressers, no closets, just empty space. But seeing Hector retrieve the blanket from a secret wall opening last night convinced me that the room was filled with secret compartments. The best I could find was a plain white t-shirt two times my size and I had no choice but to throw my jeans back on, which wasn't ideal but whatever.

Even though last night was the best I ate in years, my stomach growled at me before I even made it out of the bedroom. I strained my ears for any sign of life but it was a ghost town. Finding eggs in the fridge, I scrambled a couple over the stove, doused them with ketchup, and scarfed them down in record time before searching for the man who invaded my life a mere forty-eight hours ago.

The house was massive. He could've been in any of the rooms downstairs and I wouldn't know it. Down one of the hallways, toward the back of the house, sat three rooms on each wall, diagonally from each other. The hallway at the front of the house only fit one room, so deciding to start there seemed like the best idea.

I cracked open the door into what had to be a bedroom. I assumed it belonged to Hector's son. The space was clean and dark. Dark ebony wood filled the room, everything from the desk to the entertainment center to the bed frame. I didn't step into his room, not wanting to invade some kid's room that I didn't even know. Before I shut the door, a lone photo frame sitting on the desk caught my eye.

I found Hector. A younger version of him. I knew it wasn't any of my business and I shouldn't have been even a little curious, but I pushed the door open and walked toward the desk and picked up the frame.

It was a family photo. Hector, I could tell by those intense eyes and the matching dimples in his cheeks, his son, and who I assumed to be the mother of his son. True to his words, he looked no more than a teenager. His smile took up his entire face as he stared at the woman next to him holding their son. Her smile mirrored Hector's. Her fair skin glowed underneath the sun, highlighting just how beautiful she was. She had brown eyes and sleek, shiny dark brown hair. They seemed so happy, in that moment.

He told me just yesterday that she was gone. The clip of his tone told me that the subject of her was off limits but I found myself wondering what happened to her.

After I placed the photo frame back onto the desk, I shook my head, trying my best to stop thinking about Hector, this beautiful woman by his side, and their son.

None of them were important. No matter how nice he was to me, how protective, no matter how deep he seemed to look at me, I had to take what I wanted and get out of here.

The original plan was still in effect. This, me being in this oversized house with this man, was just a detour.

I left the room and continued exploring the massive first floor. On the opposite side, where most of the rooms were, there was an office and a home gym. There was an empty room, the only thing inside was a bed, a couch, and a TV hanging on the wall. The last room was locked, a security code pad to the right of the door. When I tapped it, it asked for a handprint instead of a passcode. I doubted it would work but I placed my hand against the screen anyway. It beeped twice and then very loudly, almost admonishing, it announced, "Access denied."

I didn't know what could be in that room. It had to be something good to be secured. I retraced my steps back into the kitchen, still no sign of Hector.

Because I was in the habit of disappointing, I walked to the front door and I tried to open it. Another fail. I was stuck here. Again. I paced every inch of the downstairs so long that I cursed Hector in his preferred language and mine. I even threw in some of the French ones that I knew. Giving up on him showing up anytime soon, I trudged back upstairs and crawled underneath the covers again. I turned on the TV, finding a marathon of *Criminal Minds* playing on one of the channels. I watched a few episodes before sleep pulled me under.

When I awoke for the second time, there was still no sign of Hector. Which just pissed me off more. He said today we would talk. He would propose what he was going to propose. And I would determine how long it would take me to win my victim back, take care of him, and get the hell out of this country.

I ate lunch and then dinner.

He still didn't show up.

I went through an entire season of *Criminal Minds* and the featured serial killers taught me some tricks I would never have thought of on my own. They might come in handy when the owner of this house finally decided to return home.

Once the darkness started filtering in through the bedroom through the windows, I couldn't sleep. Every time I closed my eyes, I was afraid of what memories my mind would be burned with this time. That and I was pissed off. Too pissed off to sleep. I wanted to punch something. Or rather, someone. Giving up on sleep, I settled for the punching bag in Hector's home gym downstairs that I spotted earlier in the day.

Still dressed in my lone pair of faded blue jeans and another one of Hector's oversized t-shirts, I headed downstairs. I lived my life in jeans, even in the gym, especially at the shooting range. If I were to switch my jeans out for a pair of leggings, sweatpants, or hell, a dress, it would make me too comfortable. The tightness around my waist and the slightly rough interior that wrapped around my legs reminded me that I couldn't get lazy. I couldn't let my guard down. I had to be aware of every moment, every second. I wasn't safe and the clothes I wore every day never let me forget it.

The home gym was as big as a house. A normal-sized house, not the mansion I found myself stuck in. The space was big enough for someone to have a decent-sized concert in. The room itself rivaled the best gyms in the city. He had all types of machines. There were treadmills and stair masters. But mostly he had machines for arms and leg strength. No less than twenty different ones. I skipped all of that for the black punching bag that hung from the ceiling in the center of the room, a black wrestling mat on the floor beneath it.

I ran my fingers along the smooth leather to get accustomed to the texture of it. I swung it in my hands, before delivering a soft punch and kick to it. The last thing I needed right now was to go full force and have a bag of sand put me on my ass. Once we got acquainted, I beat the living hell out of it. Punches, kicks, arm tackles, shoulder tackles. I went at it. I went at it for so long I wasn't even sure how long I had been in there. All I knew was that my heart thrashed against my chest and I was in jeopardy of becoming dehydrated. After steadying the swinging bag, and wiping it down with a wet cloth, I made my way into the kitchen.

If the home gym was the size of a normal house, I didn't know what the kitchen would be the size of. Hector was a good cook if last night's dinner was anything to go by. It made sense seeing as how his kitchen was so beautiful. Brown accents covered the room from the paint on the walls to the marble countertops and the floor paneling. The only things that brightened the room were the appliances. A matching white stove and refrigerator. I grabbed a glass from one of the cupboards and poured myself a glass of ice water.

I drank and I drank until my breathing returned to normal. I placed my cup on the counter, ready to pass out now that I worked my body so hard. The sound of a car door slamming halted my footsteps. I waited until I heard footsteps just outside of the house. I grabbed a steak knife from the block of knives on the counter by the stove and made my way into the living room.

I leaned against the wall that separated the kitchen from the living room, my fingers twisting around the handle of the knife and I waited.

There were no locks on these doors, I realized. And if there were, they didn't work. This entire place was operated by a heavy security system. He stepped through, automatically turning around and closing the door behind him. I stood tall with my feet shoulder-length apart, closed one of my eyes, aimed and let my knife sail through the air. It stuck inside the door, mere inches from his face. If he turned his head in the slightest, his skin would feel the coolness of the knife. His head hadn't moved but I could tell he was looking at the knife.

I heard the deep steadying breath he took before he turned around to face me. "Welcome home," I said, the irritation I felt like fire in my veins, sneaking out.

"You have to stop trying to kill me like this," he said, sauntering up to me, leaving the knife lodged in the door.

Stopping right in front of me, our chests almost touching, his body rigid as I hoped mine was. But I played it cool, leaning up against the wall. Our height difference forced me to look up at him and I almost lost my cool facade because the corner of his mouth tilted, impossibly close to smirking and his eyes glinted in the glow of the kitchen light. There was not one single trace of anger written on his face.

He was not supposed to find this amusing. He was not supposed to find me cute. I literally almost splattered his brains across his living room walls. His smile widened at my troubled expression. Two of his brown fingers appeared and gently tugged my chin. "You may have better aim than me, bonita."

His fingers and body left me in an instant as he brushed past me, heading into the kitchen. I stood there in complete exasperation. Really? That's it. No anger, no yelling. Nothing. What did I have to do to get this man pissed off? As pissed off as he's made me?

"Correct me if I'm wrong," I said, following him. I watched as he picked up my glass, sniffed it before filling it back up with water and ice. Before he lifted the glass to his lips, he quirked one eyebrow up at me. "We had a deal. This proposition of yours. As lovely as your *presence*," I snarled the word, "is, I'd rather be anywhere but in it."

He snorted. "You're such a sweet talker. I think I might die if I don't hear more."

A tiny growl climbed up my throat and escaped through my lips. "This is my life we're talking about."

He finished off his glass of water with his eyes closed. He slammed the glass on the counter and his eyes were on me in an instant. No amusement shown in them now. They were dark brown, almost black and I wanted to hide from them, to not be under their scrutiny. But I didn't dare move an inch.

His lips parted and I braced myself for his anger but it never came. He pushed himself off the counter and walked away. Because I was a complete dumbass, I followed him. Upstairs and into the bedroom. He headed straight into the bathroom with me hot on his heels. I crossed my arms over my chest and leaned my hip against the doorway. "Let me have it."

He hadn't looked at me since we were downstairs and I didn't think he had any intention of casting those browns on me anytime soon. "Let you have what, Annie?"

"Your words. Your anger. I let you have mine."

"I say what I really want to say. You won't miss next time." His voice fell quiet but it carried over the small distance between us.

I glowered over at him, not that he noticed. He was too busy whipping his shirt off and tossing it to the floor. "What are you doing right now?" I asked as he moved to unbutton his jeans.

He looked at me for the first time since I followed him upstairs but didn't answer. He slid the jeans down his thick thighs and it took every ounce of my control not to let my gaze follow his hands. He turned from me and started running the water for a shower. Was he really going to shower with me in the room? "If I promise no more knives, will you tell me?"

He looked at me. No, he studied me. His gaze held mine for so long that my skin started to warm and itch all at the same time. "You shouldn't have to die to kill someone." His face and body disappeared inside the shower before I could even think about his words. I turned around, sauntered into the bedroom, and threw myself on the bed, not even bothering to close the door to the bathroom. It seemed Hector wasn't one for modesty.

You shouldn't have to die to kill someone. What the hell did that even mean? And why did he care? He didn't know me. He was not going to know me. Why couldn't he just deliver my father to me and then I would be on my merry way.

I didn't know how long I lay there, but I knew the moment that he entered the room. I removed my forearm from my eyes to see Hector in all his naked glory. He had his back to me but what I did see, I liked. His strong shoulders, ones just a couple of days ago I knew I was on the back of. His long, wide back. His ass, a perfect handful. His strong thighs and his muscular legs. He was a sight, that's for sure. He pressed into the wall and out came drawers of what he needed. Socks, boxers, and a pair of pants. He decided to forgo a shirt.

The bed dipped and there he was staring down at me, his eyes boring into mine. "If I were to let you go, right now," he whispered.

His voice sent chills down my arms and spine and his words put me on edge. "Would you give up on this murder plan of yours? Or would you never stop until you knew he was six feet under?"

When he looked at me like that, I found I couldn't lie. "I don't know how to stop."

He nodded once, accepting my truth. "Come downstairs with me and we'll talk."

He didn't wait for an answer and I found myself following him. Again.

I sat at the table with a Corona he offered me and I sipped on the bottle as I watched him move around the kitchen effortlessly. He grabbed a pack of meat out of the fridge, dumped it into a pan and started pouring some sort of seasoning on top of it as it fried. I could admit to myself that it was beautiful to see him like this. I had a feeling that not many people have been introduced to this side of him. "Did your son make it to where he was going?"

His head whipped in my direction and his eyes found mine, a look of surprise in them. "Yeah. He's studying the summer abroad before he starts college."

"That sounds cool," I said slowly. "Is he going to college here?"

"No, California. He wanted to study here because it's closer to home but the school in California had the best program." I nodded and he turned his eyes back to the stove. "Are you hungry?" he asked, digging through a cupboard of food.

"I could eat," I said with a shrug. Thirty minutes later, we were both sitting down with a plate of seasoned meat and orange rice mixed with corn. It looked amazing and smelled even better. "I hope you don't hold me hostage much longer. I'm going to get so fat."

He chuckled softly before he dug into his food. We ate silently, until, much like the night before I slumped back in my chair, hands over my stomach, stuffed like a cow.

He laughed at the sight of me before he stood to clean up our mess and returned with a fresh beer and a small bowl of butter pecan caramel ice cream. "You're trying to kill me," I announced even as I sat up already reaching for a spoon.

Those dimples popped out as he sat down next to me and handed me a spoon. "Really," he hummed around a spoonful of ice cream, before pulling the spoon out and grabbing for some more. "I thought that was the other way around."

"Ha ha ha," I deadpanned.

The ice cream was delicious and somehow the bowl ended up closer to me and Hector put his spoon down and picked up his beer. "I was with *him* earlier."

I didn't have to ask who he was referring to, the way he snarled the word pretty much said it all. I knew I wanted this, demanded this. But now that we were talking, my heart thumped hard against my chest and I'd somehow forgotten how to breathe.

"He's alive. And that's how he's going to remain until you're ready for him."

"I am ready for him now," I said, setting the ice cream to the side. "I didn't just wake up one day and decide to kill him, Hector. I've been planning this for almost half of my life."

"I've seen you with a knife, bonita. And I have a feeling you're even better with a gun." I couldn't help the smirk that tugged at my lips because he wasn't wrong. "Physically, I believe you're ready. Mentally? Emotionally? I have my doubts." I glared at him but otherwise remained silent. "I meant what I said earlier. You shouldn't have to die to kill someone. And that's your plan right now. You want to kill him and then you want to run away, start over, be someone new. But killing isn't an eviction notice. It's not a bad break up. It's not a failure in a career. Before you take anyone's life, you have to be secure in your own."

I don't know who I am. Those words popped up again but I didn't dare voice them. "So you want me to kill him and stay," I asked, almost incredulous.

"It doesn't matter what I want. It's what you want. I killed my first person when I was younger than you. I was forced into it. Then, I killed again and again. But the one thing that kept me from laying down, from giving up was that I knew who I was and what I wanted my future to look like.

"I had a son. A son who was born into a bloodline that he didn't ask for. Same as me. But I vowed I would be different. I would give him the choices that I didn't have. And so that's how I'm here today. I didn't run *because* of him. Every killer needs an anchor to their humanity. My son was mine. You have to find yours and before you call me a sexist, an anchor could be anything. A career, a friend, hell, a dog if you want. When you're in survival mode, you need something to live for. You have to want something more than you want his death, is what I'm trying to say."

I heard every single one of his words and I knew he was right. But the only thing I knew for sure that I wanted more than Cameron

Wade's death was to have my mom back, but life didn't work that way. "What is it that you want from me? How do I pass this test?"

He studied me closely, his hands folded together underneath his chin. "Six months."

I started to protest before he could even say anything else but before I could utter a word, he reached over and put a finger over my lips, effectively silencing me.

"Do what you want for six months. Live your life for six months. Don't think about him. Don't think about anybody but yourself. Be Annie for six months and I'll hand him over."

I don't know how. I wanted to scream the words at him. I wanted to plead with him. But I kept it in. "Am I allowed to leave the house?"

He nodded. "You'll be escorted everywhere you go. Either by me or someone I trust. But whatever you want to do for the next six months, I'll make it happen."

I didn't want to agree. I didn't want to be *Annie,* whoever the hell she was. But I did want Cameron Wade's blood on my hands and as far as I could tell, this was the only way. I nodded. "Fine," I murmured, and his finger fell away. "Six months."

"Six months," he repeated.

"Six months from the night you kidnapped me."

"Six months starting tomorrow."

I scowled at him, but we both knew he held all of the cards here. "Fine," I huffed and I hauled my ass upstairs to bed, exhausted from a full belly and my workout earlier in the night.

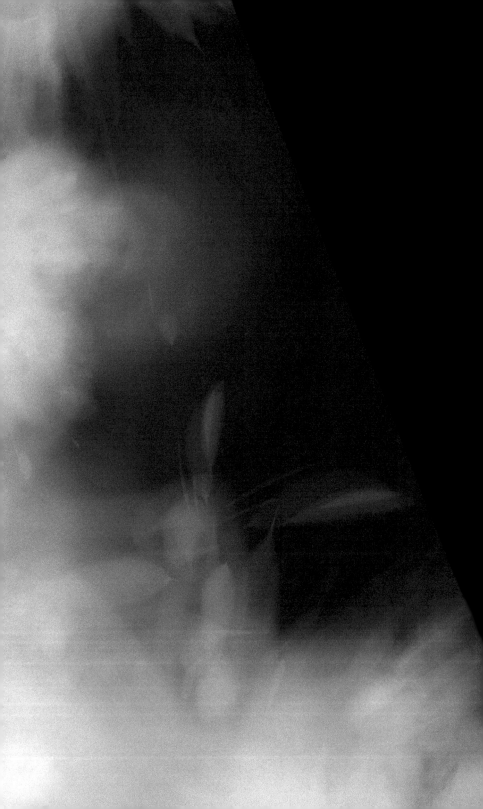

CHAPTER TEN

Annie

The first six days of our six-month agreement were
uneventful.

They passed by the same as the few days before. I'd
wake up, have breakfast with Hector before he left for the day. I'd
spend my day in the gym or watching marathons on the TV upstairs.
Then, Hector would come home, cook us dinner and I'd follow him
upstairs and lie in bed while he showered.

I didn't know if it was because I actually felt safe with him or if
because he was the first person who held me after a restless night.
He didn't bang on the wall and yell at me to shut up when I couldn't
hold in the screams any longer. He didn't find somewhere else to sleep

when I tossed and turned and sweat through the sheets. He didn't look at me like I was a freakshow for being a grown-ass adult who let the memories get the best of her.

What he did do was hold me. Swept my clammy hair from my face. Whispered against my skin that everything was going to be alright.

And so an unspoken agreement transpired between us. He slept in bed with me every night. I didn't ask him to but I didn't kick him out, either. I'd only suffered from one other nightmare since that first night, but I knew a strong man sleeping next to me hadn't cured them. They'd return and hopefully, I could live with the weakness I showed him when they did. He still slept at the edge of the bed, taking out that extra blanket each night.

Every morning, Hector would be long gone before I woke up, leaving me to notice an unrumpled side of the bed and the sound of clinking weights that filtered upstairs. By the time I made it downstairs each day, I'd find him in the kitchen drinking eggs out of a glass and making enough breakfast for the two of us.

We didn't talk much. He gave me his terms and he was waiting for me to accept them, with so much patience that it drove me crazy. Maybe it was petty of me, maybe the only person I was hurting was myself, but I didn't want to be the one to admit defeat. I wanted him to get sick of me, taking up space in his house and eating all of his food. Granted it didn't seem as if my plan was succeeding because as soon as he asked me the golden question each morning after he fed the both of us, he fled the house and didn't return until dinner time.

Being alone felt as natural to me as breathing so I didn't mind it much but it did feel like I was standing still. I had nothing to look forward to. I had no plan. I had no job and no school and no matter what I did, I wouldn't get reins on Cameron Wade's life for another five months and twenty-three days.

Hector's voice cut through my thoughts, the tiniest smirk on his face. He must have caught me glaring daggers at him again and probably stabbing my food and calling it by his name, too. "What's on the agenda for today?" And there it was. For the past six days, he would ask me this very question. I would answer it with a glare and then he would leave. The same thing every day since I agreed to his terms. But today was different.

Today, my answer changed because I quite literally couldn't be confined to this house for the next six months. There were only so many seasons of *Criminal Minds* a girl could watch before she went stir crazy. I huffed. "I've run out of clothes."

A frown formed on his face as he popped an entire egg white into his mouth. "The washer and dryer—"

I cut him off. "I know where they are. I need more than the two outfits I have here." During his earlier morning workout, I made some phone calls. The first to the hotel I had booked. They were still charging me for the room every day and I had a lot of money saved, but I had never been wasteful of money, especially since I knew how it felt to have little to none at all. And I supposed it wasn't true that I had no plan because I did, it was still the original plan, just set back by a man who thought he knew what was best for me after five seconds of knowing me. "Before." I narrowed my eyes at him, which just caused that annoying smirk of his to grow. "I booked a hotel last week. I called the receptionist to cancel my room today. I just have to be there by noon to pick up my stuff."

He nodded, still stuffing his face. The man could eat. Every night he would cook something different, food I had never even heard of let alone tasted, mostly with a Hispanic touch to it. I was so consumed in the taste testing myself, I never paid attention to his eating habits but I knew he consumed a lot. Each morning, he had at least four egg whites and he did that annoying thing that athletes sometimes do, drinking the yolks.

His eyes were focused solely on me, silently asking me if there was anything else on the agenda for today. There was.

The second phone call I made earlier was to Matt. When he picked up the phone, laying on that thick Yankee accent, I couldn't help it, I snorted and asked him the utmost important question. "Are you running a gun business or a phone porn operation?"

I expected him to laugh or grunt, his usual response to me. "Annie," he whispered.

"Yes, Matthew."

A shaky sigh escaped him before he laid it on me. "Where the hell have you been? Where are you now? Are you safe?"

I waited for him to calm down, it only took ten minutes or so until he finally allowed me to get a word in. I ignored all of his questions because if I wasn't okay, I wouldn't be calling. "Do I still have a job?"

"You're my best friend. Of course, you still have a job. Now get your ass back here."

"First of all—"

"Yeah, yeah, yeah," he mumbled. "We're not friends. We're barely coworkers. And if I tell you what to do one more time, you're going to sever my most cherished body parts."

Matt covered all of his bases, leaving me nothing to say; I hung up. Now, I told Hector, "And, I also talked to my old employer. Apparently, he misses me, so you can drop me off there after the hotel."

"Just today or every day?" he asked after a gulp of some kind of mysterious green smoothie.

"A few times a week." I shrugged my shoulders and admitted, "I love it there."

Since the moment I found myself in a power struggle with this man, his eyes followed my every move. At first, I assumed he didn't trust me. I did point a gun at him and deliver a nice nick to his eyebrow. But it had been over a week and his eyes never left me, with the exception of at night when he climbed into bed next to me without offering me a spare glance. Any time the two of us occupied the same room, his eyes sought me out. His didn't look at me warily, trying to guess my next move. His gaze lingered on me, his eyes studying me in a way I couldn't understand.

He looked at me from behind his drink, a spark of curiosity in those brown eyes so prominent I'd have to be blind to miss it. I never offered up any information; this was a first.

I hated that those lit up eyes made my heart do a funny little hiccup against my chest. "Where did you work?"

"Philly Range." I pushed my empty plate to the side, grabbing my still warm cup of coffee. I narrowed my eyes at him over my mug. "Speaking of, where is my gun that you confiscated?"

He didn't even try to conceal the smirk spreading across his lips. "I think I'll keep your weapons for now." I glared at him, only causing his smirk to grow. "We're going to the hotel and then, you're going to work?" I nodded, deciding to let the subject of my confiscated weapons go. For now. "Anything else for today?"

"Nope," I said before standing up, collecting all of our dishes. The two of us had fallen into a routine over the past week. He cooked and I helped him clean up. We weren't living in the 1950s and I was the farthest thing from a Stepford wife. After protesting the first few times I offered my help upon deaf ears, he hadn't said anything else about it. I think he was just happy that I quit trying to physically harm him.

He grabbed the keys to a car I knew I'd been in but never seen. My eyesight had been limited to these walls and the little bit of sunlight the windows provided and I couldn't control the way my heart sped up in anticipation to get back into the world. To be consumed by the bustle of the city, to hear the honking of the cars, to see pedestrians flipping off anyone and everyone.

I followed Hector to the front door with tentative steps.

He opened the door as I grabbed his wrist with my hand. He turned around to look at me, his eyes shooting down to my fingers wrapping around his wrist. I dropped my hand like his touch burned and took a small step back. "You haven't made tacos since that first night," I blurted out, immediately regretting it.

He pressed his lips together and I hated my eyes for being traitors to the movement. A second later, the smile he had been fighting won the battle. "Are you asking me to make you dinner?"

I huffed with annoyance, closing the space between us and placed my hands on his hard as rock shoulder blades and all but pushed him out of the door. "You make dinner every night, anyway," I muttered, not amused.

"Tacos, it is," he said as he swiveled around me to shut the door and set the very mysterious alarms. Without waiting for me, he sauntered over to his car, an all black Range Rover. He walked to the passenger side and opened the door, waiting for me.

I didn't follow. I stood right where he left me, frozen in place. Because he lived in a fucking mansion. I pretty much guessed so but actually seeing the house from the outside, my jaw dropped open in awe. The exterior was painted a simple, clean white color with a balcony that wrapped around the entire second floor of the house. White gates stood high on each side of the house that led to some kind of beautiful land. The only thing I could see from behind the fence were tall southern magnolia trees, spread out on each side of the house.

It took Hector clearing his throat to bring me back down to Earth. I looked from him back to the sight of this beautiful house I found myself a tenant in. After several more moments of taking it all in, I spun around on my heel and made my way to Hector whose hands were in his pockets as he leaned against the door he opened for me, his eyes steady on me. I narrowed my eyes at him. "I knew it was a mansion but damn."

He chuckled, standing taller as I passed him before he shut the door behind me.

He pulled out the cobblestone drive where we were met with a tall, iron gate. He pressed a button on the dashboard and the gates opened. Holy security. Once the gates closed behind us and a back road met us, I realized I still had no idea where we were. We could have been in Canada and I wouldn't have known it. "Where are we?"

"New Hazle." He looked over at me briefly. "Where did you think we were?"

I shrugged my shoulders, not answering. My eyes studied every fork in the road as Hector drove, trying to recall exactly where in New Hazle we were in but it all looked unfamiliar.

Soft Latin music played over the speakers and Hector drummed his fingers against the steering wheel to it. I found myself consumed by the altering scenery. A two-lane, curvy back road with huge, overbearing trees filling up the view on each side. Once several miles passed and Hector swung a couple of right turns, the first glimpse of the city came into view. I sat up in my seat, soaking in the tall buildings and the hectic sounds I could hear over the music.

It didn't hit me until this moment how much I missed the city. It felt like I could breathe again. This is what I was used to; this is what my eyes have been desperate for. Without thinking, I pushed the power lock for the windows, not stopping until the outside breeze smacked me in the face, whipping my hair in all directions.

I closed my eyes, enjoying this moment. A dreamy sigh escaped me as I relaxed farther into the seat. I opened my eyes when I no longer felt air hit my cheeks. The window rolled back up. I snapped my head in Hector's direction, already glaring.

His face didn't give anything away but he did tell me, "The air works just fine."

"I'm not hot. I just wanted to feel the wind on my face."

He didn't even give it, or me, a second of thought. "No windows," he said curtly, not leaving me any room to argue. I huffed loudly and turned away from him, resting my elbows on the door rest. As he drove farther into the city, the urge to defy him became stronger and stronger with each teeth-grinding second. We stopped at a red light just as Center City came into view. I looked over at him to see his thumbs flying over his phone, sending a text. Turning back around, I pushed the button for the window. A tiny growl escaped me as I hit the button repeatedly, knowing damn well it wouldn't work.

"Really," I gritted out, looking over at him. "The kiddy locks?"

He tucked his phone back into his jacket pocket and pinned me with a look. "You'll forgive me if I don't believe you when you say that you'll listen." He tapped the tiny white scar on his forehead, directly above the edge of his eyebrow.

I pursed my lips together before tearing my gaze away from him and watched as the city passed by us until the car stopped in front of the hotel I directed him to.

I didn't feel bad about cutting him.

That night, he stood in the way of the only thing I cared about. Since then, he had pulled me out of my nightmare hell and has not once talked to me with disrespect. The man had essentially kidnapped me but treated me like an A-list guest in his home.

I opened the door with such force because being so close to him, all of a sudden, felt suffocating. Maybe I did feel a little bad.

Before I hopped out of my seat, I sought out his eyes and asked, "You're not coming in?" He shook his head once, already pulling his phone out. "And I'm allowed to get out," I said slowly, waiting for the catch.

Almost as if he couldn't help it, he laughed. "Yes."

I looked at him skeptically but for once his eyes were focused on something other than me. I took each step tentatively, making it inside without him grabbing me and whisking me away back to his mansion. Before I pulled the doors to the hotel lobby open, I looked back, curiosity winning over me. Hector held his phone pressed against his ear, his lips moving, a look I've never seen on his face.

I quickly turned around, chiding myself for looking back in the first place. Walking into the lobby, I headed straight to the elevators. I stepped out on the fourth floor and dug my hotel key card out of my pocket. When I walked into the room, everything was exactly how I left it. The duffle bag sat in the center of the unrumpled bed. Though I had no reason to suspect anything, I opened up the bag, relieved to see that all of my clothes remained and my two copies of the *Count of Monte Cristo* still buried between the layers. I zipped the bag back up and reached into the side pocket.

The crumpled piece of paper was exactly where I left it. My ten-year plan list. Now, my ten-year plus six months list. A fire lit in my chest, as it always did when I thought about killing Cameron Wade.

I thought I would feel less about him after spending a week surrounded by Hector. Where Cameron was my mother's nightmares, Hector pulled me from mine. Cameron used his hands to demean my mother, Hector used his to protect me. While Cameron called my mom every degrading name in the book, Hector stuck with "bonita." *Beautiful.* The two men were polar opposites. And knowing that men like Hector existed, that not all men were monsters, I thought the hate I carried for Cameron would simmer but it didn't.

I folded the piece of paper back up and abandoned my things in favor of the small desk in the room. Grinding my teeth, I put pen to paper.

1. ~~Learn how to fight.~~
2. ~~Graduate college.~~
3. ~~Buy a plane ticket to Mexico.~~
4. Survive Hector.
5. Get revenge.
6. Start over.

I studied the revised list. This single sheet of paper that kept me going for ten long years. Six months was nothing. I would give Hector this six months. I would survive the next six months with him. I would go back to my old schedule. I would work my normal four days a week at Philly Range. I would make my body stronger than it was before. I would make my aim more precise. I would be more ready than I ever was before in six months' time.

Hector wanted me to find Annie, the real Annie, the future Annie. But I was the same Annie at twelve as I was now, as I would be in ten years from now. I was a survivor; it's all I knew how to be.

I placed the slip of paper in the pocket of my jeans before grabbing all of my belongings and heading down to the lobby. I paid off my bill before making my way back to Hector. He didn't make a move to open my door or offer help with my bag. Not that I needed him to but it didn't quite fit the man I've quickly grown accustomed to. I opened the back door of his car and set my bag on the seat before hopping back into the passenger seat. "Thanks for the help," I huffed.

Hector didn't utter a word before he threw the car in drive, barely affording me enough time to buckle up. He weaved his way through the city traffic, making it to Philly Range in less than ten minutes. He pulled the car into an empty parking spot right in front which I found odd because there was never any parking available. I wouldn't be surprised if this wasn't just a case of luck, but Hector asking for something and receiving it before he could even snap his fingers.

"How long do you want to stay today," he asked quietly.

I looked over at him to see his eyes glued to the front door of the range, his fingertips tapping impatiently against the steering wheel. "A few hours. I can call when I'm ready to be whisked away," I told him with a sweet, fake smile.

He ignored my snipe. "Call me an hour ahead of when you want to leave. I have some business on the other side of the city I need to attend to."

Three things happened, almost simultaneously, since we left the isolation of his house. He kiddy locked me. He didn't help me with my suitcase. And his mood, that with me, at least, always seemed to be on the teasing or concerned side, turned grave. Like he was disappointed in something. Something that I gathered to be himself. Hector, I was learning, was a man with manners, a gentleman. In the deep pit of my gut, I knew him not opening and closing doors for me, asking me if I needed help or just him beside me was eating him up on the inside.

I opened the door but paused, looking back at him. "Walk me to the door?" I asked him softly.

He turned his gaze on me, his eyes studying my face, moving over every inch, darting between my eyes and my lips. I couldn't help the barely there tilt to my lip and he noticed. "Get out," he growled, a chuckle escaping him and just before I shut the door I let out the laugh I had been holding in, too.

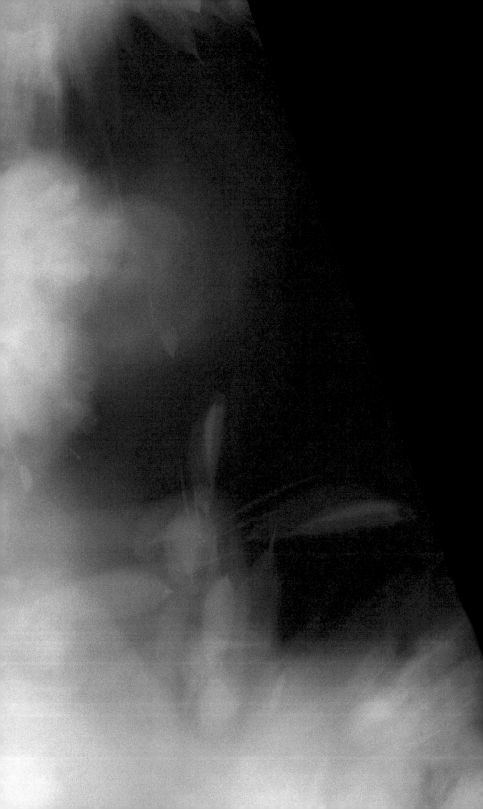

CHAPTER ELEVEN
Hector

My eyes followed her retreat. I couldn't help but let the gloom that had settled over me since we pulled into the city slip from my skin. She threw her head back and I could hear the laugh that tore out of her as she swayed her way into Philly Range. In the past week of knowing her, I've been faced with the many sides of her. The most familiar being the pissed off version. The skin above my eye and the chip in my front door could attest to that.

But this was the first time I'd ever seen a laugh spill from her lips with no trace of carefulness. I had a feeling that laugh was as free as Annie had gotten in a long time.

I didn't know a lot about her, only what I learned in the past week. She loved that sugary cereal Samuel used to eat as a kid. She never turned away food. Even if she had to covertly unbutton her jeans; even if I thought something might be too spicy for her. She watched crime shows each night to unwind. She never complained about anything. Stuck inside the house for days, albeit her choice, she not once muttered a word about being confined. Something I realized from the very first night, and grasped each moment I spent with her, she was strong as hell. Not her physical strength, but through her perseverance.

We didn't talk about Cameron. We didn't talk about the six-month sentence I forced on her. We talked enough that our space filled with harmony and not awkwardness.

She agreed to six months and her acceptance was the last thing she uttered about it. She didn't complain. She didn't try to back out of our deal. She didn't even hate me. Though, my face did become the target of her glares when she got lost in her head, I welcomed them. Pathetic as it may be, I knew one name circulated her thoughts. Mine. I was glad because she not only invaded my house, my life, my everything, but for the life of me, I could not get her out of my head. It didn't matter how close or far from her I was, I wanted to, no, I *craved*, to know every single thing out of her. I wanted to go to the school of Annie. I wanted to earn my degree and go back and get my doctorate's.

She didn't offer up anything about herself. And she always hid those eyes from me, like she knew I could read her perfectly from one look alone.

The only time she let her guard down was when she taunted me.

A trace of a smile remained on my lips as my eyes followed Annie as she walked into Philly Range. I focused on her wavy blonde hair swaying across her back, willing my eyes to focus on her retreating head. I lost the battle, my eyes lowering to the sway of her hips in her dark wash jeans.

I wish I could put a stop to this attraction I felt toward her. I didn't make this arrangement with her in the hopes that she would kiss me again. This arrangement benefitted one person. Her. If everything went according to plan, in the next couple of months, hell, it might not even take the full six months, she would have found something, or several things, that made her happy. And she would realize that Cameron unknowingly stole an essential piece of her, and she needed to reclaim it once and for all.

Cameron was still going to die. Like she told me that day I offered up my proposition, this wasn't something she woke up one morning and decided to do. She had been planning this for ten years. According to the state of Pennsylvania, Annie turned twenty-two a month ago. It didn't take a genius to figure out that whatever Cameron did to ruin her life, his actions followed her into adulthood. It was okay if she forgot about him because I never would.

Once she disappeared inside of the range, I threw my head back against the seat, pinching the bridge of my nose. Only two hundred and seventy-five more days of this self-imposed hell.

Pulling my phone out of my pocket, I dialed Matt.

"Yeah," he answered distractedly.

"Annie's back."

The line went quiet for a moment. "I know. She called me earlier."

"Don't forget my warning, Panini."

"Yeah. I got it, Rivera," he bit out.

I should've hung up. I should've just left it that. But she had a control over me I wasn't sure I ever wanted to shake. "One more thing. Let it be known she's under the protection of the Rivera family."

Despite his obvious contempt for me, he sucked in an audible breath. "Are you sure?"

Not a lot of people found themselves under the protection of my family name. Similar to a tattoo, once you received it, it lasted forever. Nothing in this world could hurt you. Unless you betrayed me. Then, there was nothing in this world that could protect you. "If I wasn't, I wouldn't have said it," I said, more to myself than to him.

"I got it. Anything else?"

"Nope. I'll have the funds deposited into your account by midnight for your cooperation." I didn't give him a chance to protest or thank me. I hung up.

Throwing the car in reverse, I lost myself in city traffic. I didn't have business on the other side of town. I had business in New Hazle.

Cameron Wade was proving more difficult than I thought.

Over the past fifteen years of my life, I honed my craft of torture, and if necessary, murder. I dealt with shitty people who deserved shitty deaths, and that was that. I called it a day. I never had to make sure someone didn't die. But I promised Annie I wouldn't kill Cameron and I meant it.

Stopping at a red light, I texted Nolan.

Where are you?
Hank's bound.

That made two of us. I didn't bother texting back; I'd see him soon enough. The thirty minutes wading through traffic didn't take my mind off of Annie. I imagined her at work. I wondered about her relationship with Matt. For him to call me, of all people, to protect her, he had to have been desperate.

He was closer to her age. He never killed anyone. Never even attempted until I confessed my crime against his father. He owned a thriving business. I wondered if she taunted him the way she taunted me.

Groaning, I changed the radio station, the soft Latin melodies no longer soothing me and my spiraling thoughts. I hit the seek button until I gave up, slamming the heel of my hand on the power button, surrounding myself in silence.

The silence didn't help any, it only invited more questions that I would never know the answers to. I pulled in the parking lot of Hank's, noticing Nolan's car already parked. I parked in between his and another car. A car I recognized by the decal on the rear windshield, the number 15 in Boston colors.

Fuck.

I looked down at my phone to see one missed call from Lily and a message from Nolan, dating ten minutes ago.

You're in trouble. Please hurry. I have no clue as to what to say to this woman but she keeps screaming.

Everything inside of me screamed to start my car up and drive the ten miles back home. I hadn't planned to deal with Lily today.

They say when your kid leaves the house, your life is supposed to feel like you're on a permanent vacation. If that's true, this was the worst fucking vacation known to mankind.

If only Annie didn't look up at me, determination set in those deep blues, powerful words coming out in a shaky whisper. "He's mine to kill."

I made a promise to her. A promise I didn't intend to break. But I also made a promise to myself, to protect her and I didn't plan on breaking that one either.

I slammed the car door shut and walked through the main entrance of the bar. The bar was closed, only Manny, the bartender and my co-owner of the bar, visible busy cleaning out glasses from behind the bar, a Reggaeton beat playing through the speakers.

He tilted his head up in greeting and I did the same. "Pour me a whiskey neat, will you?"

He nodded. "You don't usually do whiskey, Hector." He wasn't wrong. I was a simple man who loved nothing more than a bottle of Corona at dinner. Being a father to Samuel so young and raising him by myself for most of his life forced me to grow up fast. Drinking and partying were never really an option for me.

I afforded myself with whiskey when I found myself on edge. With a woman who tried killing me sleeping next to me each night and another woman who tried killing me waiting for me downstairs, I was as close to the edge as I could get.

I downed the fiery liquid in one gulp, slamming the glass on the counter. "Any trouble here lately?"

He shook his head, taking my cup and placing it in the steel basin behind the bar. "It's been quiet. Busy but quiet. This annoying drunk hasn't shown up in over a week. Maybe Allah answered my prayers."

I smiled at him. Not his god or anyone else's, just me. "Thanks for the drink, man. Call me if you need anything."

He tipped his head once more. "Good luck. The beautiful ass woman who walked in here ten minutes ago looked like she was on a rampage and this was her first stop."

I chuckled. That sounded like Lily. I walked away from him without another word. I opened the basement door, closing it behind me. I didn't hear her or Nolan's voice. I crept down each step, trying to escape Lily's notice. If I could watch her, catch a glimpse of her body language, see how hot the fire in her eyes was, maybe I could do some damage control.

Reaching the bottom step, I saw Nolan tucked against the wall, his hands folded in front of his waist, his eyes closed. Lily bent over the mattress, her hands hovering over Cameron's still body.

As if sensing me, she whipped around and pinned me with a glare, her finger pointed at me accusingly. Before I could even ask what was wrong, she gained on me.

One delicate brown finger nudged my sternum and she angled her head to look at me. "Hector Rivera."

I took a deep breath and waited for the lecture bound to come. "What is this," she asked, flinging her hand backward, motioning to Cameron. I didn't look.

I pursed my lips together, saying anything would be worse than saying nothing it all. This wasn't my first rodeo with Lily.

"I will tell you what this is. This is a body that should be in the hospital. You hit an artery, Hector! A fucking artery and you thought some blood and antibiotics would fix him. When Nolan came in, the man's skin was green."

I lost her when she said artery, my eyes flicking to Cameron's body. Please don't tell me. Please don't fucking tell me I killed him. She would never look at me the same. She wouldn't kill me. This would kill her. *I would kill her.*

I pushed away from Lily's finger, rushing to his bedside. The puffs against his oxygen mask almost had me sinking to the floor in relief. I turned around to see Lily's hips jutted out, her hands curled into fists resting upon them. She held my eyes for so long, neither of us uttering a word, our eyes doing all of the talking.

Her body relaxed as she sighed. "Walk me out, Hector."

She headed toward the stairs, not giving me a chance to oblige. "Nolan." His head popped up. "I'll be back. Watch him." He answered in the form of the nod and I took the stairs two at a time to catch up with Lily.

I followed her outside and she popped the trunk. Two recyclable bags full of medicine greeted us. "What's this?" I asked quietly.

"What did he do, Hector?" she whispered. Her voice held no disgust for what I did to him.

I didn't answer immediately. Over the years, Lily has seen a lot from me. This was different. As much as I hated to admit it, even to myself, this was personal. "I don't know," I finally admitted, resting my head against the top of the trunk.

"This is what you do to someone whose crimes you don't know?" She looked at me, her eyes widened in horror. "Hector, I've seen what you do to rapists and women abusers. That man inside..." Her voice trailed off, dismay ringing in her voice.

"You didn't hear it, Lily. It's been a week and I can still hear it. The sound of her screams is something I'll never be able to get out of my head."

My eyes snapped open when I felt the warmth of her skin wrapping around my wrist. I sought out her eyes and I could see a hint of a smile in them, a bigger one stretching across her lips. "So, this is for a woman?"

I felt my own lips tug in a smile. "Isn't it always?"

CHAPTER TWELVE

Annie

The minute I stepped into Philly Range, I felt a familiar calm wash over me. While Hector unknowingly made it his favorite hobby to rattle me, Philly Range was my meditation, my peace. And it had been a long two weeks without it.

No one went out of their way to greet me. As I walked through the building, from the shooting range itself, to the cozy room artists sketched their ideas for new guns, to the rec room where people socialized after a shooting session, I received a few nods from the regulars. It felt like I hadn't been gone at all. I didn't bother seeking out Matt. The longer I could hold off his inquisitive eyes and his demand for answers, the better.

I headed straight to my sanctuary and within moments, I lost myself in guns. Lost in my calm. I didn't have knowledge of how much time had passed; I only counted the number of guns I tore apart, cleaned, and put back together. I counted number twenty-eight when a sharp knock on the door brought me back to the real world.

Matt leaned against the door frame, a cocky smile plastered on his face.

I held my breath as I soaked him in. It felt like an eternity since the last time the two of us stood in this room. I always joked with him that we weren't really friends but the way my lips curved up without a second thought at his presence, I knew I'd been lying to the both of us for a long time.

"Hey," I said softly and then frowned. I didn't do soft. Matt's expression mirrored mine.

"Are you actually being nice to me right now?" One of his hands, previously stuffed in his pockets, shot to his chest, clutching his shirt in mock surprise.

"Ha ha ha," I deadpanned, hitching a shoulder up. "I did ghost your ass. Pretty sure that breaks at least five friendship rules."

How the hell would I know? I'd never had a friend before. I thought I would never see him again. I thought he'd be out of my life forever. I also thought I'd be in Mexico having everyone call me Olive James and putting my rusty Spanish to use.

A shit-eating grin shaped his lips, his brown eyes sparkling. "Oh, so you're admitting we're friends now."

I bit my lip to stop a smile from blooming on my face. "Don't make me regret it."

He mock saluted me. "I ordered some pizza from Buzzi's. Take a break and explain to me where the hell you've been."

Ignoring his demand, I put the gun I was working on back together and placed it back where it belonged. "I left a note."

I didn't have to look up at him to see his disbelief; I heard it across the room when he scoffed.

I grabbed my favorite gun in the room since Hector still held my gun captive. A sleek, black railed pistol and loaded it up with bullets. "Anyone in the shooting range right now?"

"It's all yours, Annie," he mumbled as I passed him, heading straight for the range room.

I knew I hadn't heard the last from Matt. I knew the note I left pissed him off. But it was better than leaving nothing at all. At least, I thought so.

I grabbed a pair of earmuffs from the rack and a few extra packages of bullets. I could hold a gun in my hand all day and not fully realize just how powerful it was. Not until I stood in position. Shoulders straight, arms level, two steady hands holding the butt of the gun, my eyes studying my target.

In that moment, every single time, it felt like I was something else. Something more. I wasn't an orphan. I wasn't a girl with a ten-year revenge plan. I was in a bubble of adrenaline, doing something I knew for a fact I was good at. In that moment, with my finger brushing against the trigger before curling around the steel and sending a single bullet blasting through the air, I knew exactly who I was. I was just Annie and I didn't have to define her.

When I ran out of bullets, I brought the paper target forward, satisfied to see that every round went in the head or chest of the figure on the paper. After I returned to my office, I picked up where I left off, getting lost in the machinery. After the overflowing bin of guns that needed to be cleaned disappeared leaving only a few left, I chanced a glance outside through the lone small window in the room, perplexed to see the sun setting. I picked up my phone, wincing at the time. I did not intend to stay that late. I stared at the phone in my hand, unsure of how to get a hold of Hector. I didn't even have his phone number. Except I did. Looking through my contacts his was located at the top, right before Jessica's, a woman who could have been my friend if I could have afforded one.

I shook the thought of her away and tapped on the call button next to his name and held the phone to my ear. It didn't even ring once before his gravelly voice filled my ear. "I'm already waiting for you outside."

He didn't give me a chance to reply. He just hung up. I stood there for a moment, unable to move my feet to take me outside, to take me to him. My heart thumped hard against my chest and it wasn't the only part of my body in overdrive. I shook my body out, taking a deep breath, and went to him. His car sat in his earlier spot. I climbed up in the passenger seat and looked at him. "I hope you weren't sitting out here all this time," I said, almost guiltily. I did tell him I was only going to stay there for a few hours, not the entire damn day.

He avoided my words. "Do you have anywhere else you would like to go today?"

I shook my head. "No, but I am starving."

"Do you want to wait for dinner or do you want me to stop and get you something to eat to hold you over?" I looked over at him just as he pulled on the highway. Everything about him was hard. His voice, his muscles, his hands. But for as hard as he appeared, he was so soft. I've not had a lot of experience with guys. My dad being my first and worst experience in that department. And the boys I interacted with in college weren't much better. I wasn't used to someone, let alone a man, care about my well-being, care about me. Hell, I wasn't used to anyone sticking their neck out for me. I definitely wasn't used to someone taking care of me.

I didn't let him know that, before he stole his way into my life, I survived on a cup of ramen a day. "I can wait."

He looked at me, brows furrowed. "Are you sure?"

I nodded and we were silent for the long drive back to his mansion. At least I was, I fell asleep before we even made it out of the city.

I woke when I felt my body moving. I blinked a few times to clear my vision and saw an ass. A literal ass. Hector's ass. I was upside down, being carried up the well-lit driveway of his mansion. Hector had me thrown over his shoulder, his arm settling across the back of my thigh, holding me in place. The feel of his skin on my body, even through the material of my jeans, created a mix of fluttering and heat deep in my stomach.

"I'm being carried," I said aloud.

I felt his body vibrate with a laugh. "So observant, bonita."

"I can walk."

"We're already inside," he said, and a second later, he flipped the switch by the door and flooded us with the dim lights in the living room. He brought me to the couch and deposited me there. His touch, his warmth disappeared in a second and I had to fight the urge not to pout. "Your stomach was making more noise than the music in the car. I'll get started on dinner."

I watched him go. I would like to say that I laid there on the couch with my eyes closed. Or that I went upstairs to unpack the rest of my things that Hector set by my feet. But I didn't do any of those things. I kicked off my shoes, climbed to my knees and sat on the couch, my arms resting on the back of it, and I watched him. I watched him move around the kitchen like he belonged there. It reminded me of myself at the shooting range. It was second nature. I watched him until he started heating tortillas on the stove. I rearranged my legs, preparing to join him in setting the table when his gaze snapped in my direction. I froze as he held me captive with those brown eyes until one of them slowly shut, sending me a wink causing my heart to stop altogether.

He turned around, going back to the tortillas while I fought to regain my composure. I stood slowly before making my way into the kitchen, dancing around him to help lay the dishes of food across the table. I grabbed a bottle of Corona for him without asking and a carton of tea for myself. He didn't look at me as I walked from the kitchen into the dining area. His concentration focused on pulling cilantro leaves apart.

"How did today go?"

I looked over at him before snapping my eyes back to the table and the silverware in my hands. I needed to stop looking at him. "It was good. I definitely didn't mean to stay that late."

"When did you learn to first shoot?" he asked as we both sat down and loaded our plates. Somehow, he knew I wanted a Mexican taco, not that American bullshit.

My eyebrows pressed together. "Why?"

He shrugged nonchalantly. "I'm just curious."

I was quiet while I polished off my first taco. "At home," I said, leaving out the "foster" part. "I lived with two older boys. Two older boys who were big nerds. They had every violent video game you could get your hands on. I guess that was my first time shooting a gun, even though it was through a TV screen. Truth is, I didn't touch my first gun until the first semester of my sophomore year of college. That's when I started working at Philly Range. Matt didn't want to hire me, even when I told him that it didn't have to be on the records. But I was persistent. I showed up every day and I guess I wore him down over time. I clean the guns and he pays me and I get access to the shooting range. I've been there ever since."

"Matt Panini?" Hector's inquisitive eyes were glued to me.

I nodded, covering my mouth.

"He taught you to shoot?"

I laughed abruptly, shaking my head. "No. If Matt teaches you how to shoot a gun, it's only because he wants to get in your pants or vice versa."

He grunted. "Sounds like him."

"Do you know him?"

Hector nodded. "I've known the Panini family a long time. My son knows him more than I do. I've only met him a couple of times."

"He's not horrible." That earned me a chuckle from behind his bottle of beer. "So, I taught myself. It didn't go great the first time or the second, or well, you get the idea. Black eyes and strained hands for weeks, maybe months, if I'm being honest. But by the time the spring semester came around, I was a natural."

Each of us polished off a couple more tacos before his next question came. "What did you study at college?"

My entire body froze, a steely guard rising and taking over. "What is this? Twenty questions?"

He flinched at the harshness in my voice and his once relaxed lips turned into pressed lines. I instantly felt horrible but I couldn't take it back and even if I could, I knew I wouldn't. He couldn't know that side of me.

If he knew about the bachelor's degree I held in Social Work and my experience in the field, I wasn't sure if there would have been a six-month deal on the table. I wasn't sure if he would've given me a choice and it's too late in the deal to risk it.

I knew he thought that he was doing me a favor with this agreement. To find my anchor to keep living, to not let the fact that I took a life drown me. But the truth was that everything I have done, every decision that I have made since the day my mom died, was to avenge her. My entire being was for her, even if she wasn't here to see it.

He got up and for the first time, he left the dishes where they lay, silently walking up the stairs. It was quiet for a few minutes until I heard the water running for a shower and the bathroom door slamming shut. I let out the deep breath I'd been holding, sinking into my chair. I rested my head over the back of the chair and closed my eyes, listening to Hector's shower running. A Latin beat jerked my head up. Hector's phone lit up with a picture of a guy, a few years younger than me who was the clear resemblance of his father. This had to be Hector's son.

Against my better judgment, I picked up the phone and answered.

"Hey, Dad." He sounded happy like he was having the time of his life.

"Not your dad."

His side of the line was quiet for a long moment before he finally said, "That voice is too sexy to belong to my dad. So, who do I have the honor of speaking with?"

I almost laughed. He was smooth, that's for sure. "Annie. Your dad's in the shower."

When he spoke, I could just picture him smirking. "And you're not in there with him?"

Heat spread from my chest to the top of my ears and I was glad no one was around to see it. "I am afraid not."

He chuckled. "Well, will you just let him know I called? I'll catch him some other ti—"

"No," I interrupted before he could hang up. "He won't like that he missed your call."

"Ahh, you got him all figured out, huh?"

I grunted. "Not really," I said, getting up from the table and trudging up the stairs.

He kept talking. "Please enlighten me on how you and my father met. As far as I've known, he hasn't been in a female's company since I was a toddler."

My eyebrows raised on their own at that tidbit of information. "It's kind of a weird story," I admitted to him. When I walked into the room, the bathroom door was still closed but I could no longer hear water running. I opened the door at the same time Hector pulled it open and I would have fallen if he didn't catch me. His hands grabbed at my arms as mine clutched his chest. His naked chest.

I squeezed my eyes shut and stood still. After a moment, Hector's hands loosened their grip on me and rubbed my arms softly. I made the mistake of opening my eyes and all of my resolve crumbled. The bad decision of flicking my eyes below instead of looking up at the naked man who still stood too close to me.

His dick was out and proud, curving up and almost resting against his stomach. It was a lighter shade of brown than the rest of his body. If I thought his wink from earlier stopped my heart, the sight of him, *the sight of all of him*, was enough to give me a premature heart attack.

"Annie." His voice cut through my thoughts and I snapped my eyes up to his face, knowing my face was flushed. "What are you doing in here?"

"Oh," I said, looking around for his phone. I found it a few feet from the door. "Hey, are you still there?"

"Yes, I am. And I'm not 'Hey,' I'm Samuel. What just happened?"

I ignored him and tried my best to mentally bully the blush from my face. I glanced at Hector. "It's Samuel." He took the phone from me wordlessly, walking past me and into the bedroom. My body didn't follow him but my eyes did. I watched him throw on a pair of boxers and a pair of shorts. I didn't hear a word he said to his son and soon, he was out of the room, heading downstairs and I didn't dare follow him.

I laid my palm over my chest, willing my heart to calm the fuck down. I walked into the bedroom, sitting on the edge of the bed and closed my eyes once more.

So, I'd seen Hector in all of his naked glory. That wasn't a big deal.

Except that his eyes made me nervous enough. And now he knew that I knew what the most delicate part of him looked like.

Not delicate at all.

I threw my body against the mattress, groaning. If only I could burn the image of him from my head.

I crawled up the bed, turning on the TV and climbing underneath the sheets. I couldn't focus on the episode of *Criminal Minds* playing, my traitorous eyes flicking toward the doorway too many times to count, wondering what he was doing.

For the remainder of the night, I stayed put. I didn't go downstairs to clean up the mess from dinner. I didn't go and retrieve my luggage from where it still sat by the couch in the living room. I was too much of a coward to face Hector.

Long after the episodes of *Criminal Minds* ended and the infomercials started, I laid on the bed, with the TV on mute, staring at the doorway, convinced he would walk through at any moment. I strained my ears to listen for him, but I couldn't detect a thing. Was he working out his frustrations in the gym? Was he cleaning up from our dinner? Did he leave? Or worse, had he decided to sleep down there?

Ever since that night he woke me up from my nightmare and I asked him to stay, he slept beside me. Always at the edge of the bed, making sure no part of him touched me. He always slept on top of the blanket I covered myself with, always getting the flannel one from the closet. I watched him every night until I fell asleep. I watched the steady rise and fall of his chest until it lulled me into sleep.

I didn't want tonight to be any different. I wanted to fall asleep to the sound of his steadying breaths, to the sight of his warm skin and his nervous cheek twitch because I had my eyes on him. The entire time I curled up on the bed, his flinch from earlier in the night replayed in my head like a bad dream.

The clock on the wall struck two o'clock when I noticed a shadow of his figure enter the room. I sucked in a breath when he moved closer to the bed. His hair was astray, sticking up in every possible way as if he spent the last few hours with his hands tugging at it. He dug out his blanket and resumed his normal spot.

Once he was settled in, I whispered, "Thought you were going to stay down there all night."

He grunted, offering me nothing more. I guess I deserved that. I turned to my side, as I always did and looked at him. "I don't think I can handle your eyes on me tonight, Annie."

His words were a hit to the heart but I didn't listen to him. My eyes were glued to his face. To his closed eyes, his clenched jaw, and his slightly flared nostrils. "The scariest things happen in the dark, Hector."

I had to swallow past the massive lump in my throat to get the next couple of words out. "I met you two weeks ago and you're the person who knows me best." Better than I fucking knew myself. "I've been alone for a long time, so long I forget how to act around other people. Case in point, snapping at the one person who is only trying to help." Albeit, I didn't ask for that help, but I kept that tidbit to myself.

His head fell to the side and his eyes opened and I didn't back down by looking away. This man knew me from only what I've dared to show him. Which other than him catching me trying to kill a man hadn't been much.

His eyes softened and his head snapped back into place. His jaw loosened and he lay there like it was a normal night between the two of us. In that moment, I wanted to tell him my truth. I wanted to tell him just what kind of man Cameron Wade was. I wanted to tell him about my mom. I wanted to tell him everything.

I opened my mouth, unsure of what would spill from it when his voice flooded my ears wrapping me up in a warm blanket.

"Samuel was born in the dark." My breath caught in my throat at the sound of his soft admission. "He wasn't planned, obviously. I was only sixteen and his mother was fifteen at the time. We had been dating for a little over a year. The summer before high school. She was a good girl and I was the bad guy she thought she wanted."

I couldn't help but notice how his voice turned hollow, but more than that, I couldn't imagine Hector being a bad guy. I knew he killed, he told me as much. He wanted to kill my father and I suspected he had a good reason for it. "Define bad guy."

He tilted his head to the side, thinking. "I had a dangerous last name. Every girl, Summer included, wanted to show up to parties on my arm. Kids and grown-ass men were afraid of me. Sure, I did some stupid things like arena fights on weekends. But really, my family was dangerous and that extended to me.

"My dad, for all of his faults, was a romantic. He married my mom as soon as they turned eighteen. He worshipped the ground she walked on until the dangerousness of our life caught up to them. My mom was caught in the crosshairs of a drive-by shooting when I was thirteen. After he buried her, he never so much as looked at another woman again. He warned me about Summer. He pulled me aside one night after I had come home late from some kind of high school dance and he asked me, 'Is she a queen?' My fifteen-year-old self snorted at that which earned me a slap in the back of my head."

The fond smile that curved on his lips made my heart ache. He lost his mom, too. "And then he went on and told me, 'Your mama was a queen. There are a lot of women, son, a lot of women who will be interested in your reputation, in your lifestyle, in the money you make. But a woman who is a queen will only be interested in three things: your heart, your health, and your happiness. Once you find that woman, that's when you become a king.'"

I thought about his dad's outlook on love and though it riled my feminist feathers a little bit, I realized his theory was gender-neutral. A woman was just as capable of power and wealth as a man was. But it wasn't about the material things when it came to love. You had to peel off the layers of a person to know them, to love them.

"He asked me if Summer was a queen that night. I told him I was going to bed. A couple of months later, she came to me crying and pregnant. She was scared of how her parents would react, but I wasn't. There were no secrets in my family. I took her back to my house, held her until she fell asleep and then I told my dad. He gripped me by the shoulders and asked me that same question. It was the first time I told him yes. Because I was a sixteen-year-old kid who thought he knew everything and would rather die than to admit that I was unsure. Unsure about her and unsure about becoming a teenage father, unsure about everything. We got married before Samuel was born, with my dad's signature and fifty thousand dollars sent to Summer's parents and their signature, too.

"Summer moved into my dad's house and a few months later Samuel happened. He wasn't just born, he happened. It was an event. It was the night before Valentine's Day and with Philadelphia's sick humor, they were calling for a blizzard. Summer woke me up at two-thirty in the morning with her water broken and my son coming. I loaded her into the car, woke up my dad who drove us to the hospital. Except Samuel was impatient and he couldn't wait until we got to the hospital." He chuckled, a soft smile spreading over his face as, I assumed, he thought of his son. "I read a lot of baby books. I knew I had my dad to help me but he wasn't going to raise Samuel; the responsibility fell to me. But nothing prepared me for having to deliver my own child in the back of a Lexus in the midst of a blizzard."

I couldn't help it, I let out a soft laugh. Hector dropped his head to the side to look at me. His eyes, for the first time, weren't studying me, weren't intense. His eyes were alive, living in this moment between the two of us recounting a moment in his life that shaped him.

"He turned out all right," I mused. I wasn't sure how long Summer had been out of their lives but if I had to guess it would have been a long time. He didn't say her name like it hurt him. Her name was just another word on his lips. I wasn't positive that he had raised Samuel on his own, but the way he talked about him just now, and the way he never missed one of his calls, told me all I needed to know about their relationship. They were close, as close as I had been with my mom when she was alive.

"He did," Hector conceded, a faint smile lingering on his face.

I fell into a peaceful sleep to that smile.

CHAPTER THIRTEEN
Hector

The sound of my alarm blared next to my ear. I cursed, grabbing it from the nightstand and silencing it. I blinked my eyes as the time came into view. Seven. I looked over to see Annie still knocked out, curled into a ball facing me, one of her hands outstretched, her fingertips barely missing the skin of my forearm.

I always woke before her. Even before Annie, I never needed an alarm clock. I guess waking up with Samuel for over a decade gifted me with a diurnal clock. Since the night she asked me to lay with her, I set this alarm just in case my body didn't rise before I needed to.

And I needed to. All trace of me had to be gone by the time those blues opened. For the both of us.

Each morning, I would lay here and look at her. Her face so beautiful, so delicate. Her lips parted, just barely, that small pink tongue of hers sneaking through. Her eyes fluttered close, the skin between her eyebrows smooth, unaware that she'd been frowning all day. Each day, from across the table, I wanted so badly to reach over and smooth the creases when she got lost in her head.

This was Annie, unfiltered. This was Annie before she woke up to a world that had been cruel to her and she'd never forgiven. I craved her thoughts. I starved for any knowledge of her that she would willingly give up. But this right here, watching her at peace, sated me enough to get through the day.

And the thought of that scared the fuck out of me. She was quickly becoming an obsession for me, a drug that I knew would go out of stock and never return. I ripped my gaze away from her, heading downstairs for my morning workout.

I stretched my limbs before jumping into cardio. I started with a slow walk before building myself up to a light run. My phone rang in my pocket, flashing Samuel's name. I slid my thumb across the screen, accepting the call before placing it against the treadmill and putting it on speaker.

"Why is Uncle Nolan ignoring my phone calls?" he asked bluntly before I had the chance to greet him.

I pressed the button to quicken my pace. I pushed my legs harder and harder against the belt. "Because I told him to."

He scoffed and I shook my head. "What if I have to call him to confide in him?"

"About what?" I asked dumbly, knowing exactly where my son was headed.

"About the fact that my father, who I've never seen with a woman once in my life, has suddenly got one answering his phone, talking about, 'he's in the shower.'"

I couldn't help it, a laugh rumbled through me. "You sound like a forlorn teenager, not a man."

"Dios mío," he grumbled, switching languages. "El momento en que me vaya, se consigue una mujer. Yo quería tener asiento en, primera fila, papá. Te he estado presionando para que salgas por años." *Translation: The moment I leave, he gets himself a woman. I wanted the front row seat, Dad. I've been pushing you to date for years.*

I changed speeds again. "It's not like that, mijo."

"Ya te gustaría." *Translation: You wish it were.* I reached forward, pressing the button to the highest speed and adjusting my legs to the change in velocity.

"La esperanza es lo más peligroso que puedes tener, especialmente cuando eres de la familia Rivera." *Translation: Hope is the most dangerous thing you can have, especially when you're a Rivera.*

He sighed from the other side of the world at a lesson I drilled into his head since before he could speak. You couldn't hope for the best, you had to fight for it. I didn't put it past him to fly all of the way home from his trip abroad to scope out the situation. To ease his burning curiosity, I offered up some semblance of the truth. "Le impidió cometer un error. Le ofrecí una salida de la ruta en que ella estaba. Sólo el tiempo lo dirá si la toma." *Translation: I stopped her from making a mistake. I offered her a way off of the path she was heading. Only time will tell if she takes it.*

Samuel was quiet and I prayed he would drop it. I didn't need him asking about her every time we talked. I had a hard time enough trying to get her out of my head, I didn't need my son nudging me in a direction I knew I shouldn't even consider a possibility.

"Is she hot?" Samuel asked suddenly and I knew a smirk glossed over his face.

"Don't you have a class to attend?"

Samuel's laugh filled the room. "Sure, Dad. I'll let you get back to your woman."

"She's not my wom—" The line clicked; he hung up.

I slowed to a walk, knowing I'd have to spend an extra hour with weights if I did any more cardio. Fifteen minutes and I hit the stop button on the treadmill, grabbing a towel and wiping the sweat off of my face and neck before heading into the kitchen. I stalled at the bottom of the stairs, straining my ears to any movement upstairs.

Nothing. I looked at my watch to see it was only eight-thirty. She'd still be asleep for another half hour. I walked into the kitchen, grabbing a glass of milk before taking out a pair of skillets. The plantains I bought earlier this week should be ripe by now.

I was known to many people as many things. A father. A man of power. A protector. If it was up to me, I'd be known for my food. Samuel and Nolan had been well accustomed to my cooking. They were the ones who taste-tested everything until I was happy with a new dish.

I was born here in the United States, Philadelphia born and raised, but that didn't take away from my Mexican heritage. My mom made sure of it, teaching me how to cook her favorite dishes as soon as I grew tall enough to peek over the countertops without a stepladder.

She always made sure I knew where I came from. We vacationed to Mexico, where her mom grew up, a few times a year. Since she died, I still made it a mission of mine to escape the city in exchange for the calmness of the home my father owned at my mother's request in Oaxaca a few times a year. She forbid my dad from speaking English around me until I turned four, determined it would remain my mother tongue no matter where we lived. She was proud of her heritage, proud of where she came from and she wanted the same for me.

I thought of her each time I stepped into a kitchen. Each time I opened the fridge or turned on the stove. She left me long ago but I could feel her in every step I took. I grabbed a pair of plantains, setting them down on the brown marble countertop. I smiled as I looked down, seeing my mama's face underneath the countertop. No one ever noticed it but in every kitchen I owned, I snuck a picture of her into the room. Here at the house, I hired an artist who excelled in blending their art into everyday objects. The marbles, a different variety of brown, scattered to the shape of her face. From her jet black hair to the holes in her cheeks where her dimples always shown, to the brown eyes I inherited from her. She was a beautiful woman who loved me like no one else ever did.

I pulled off the peels, cutting the plantain into diagonal slices, placing them into a bowl. I poured canola oil into one pan and butter into the next. I cracked three eggs into a glass and two more into the smaller pan.

I grabbed a fork, mixing the eggs in my glass. Light footsteps padded down the stairs and I tried to keep my eyes trained on the bubbling oil but I had no control when Annie was in sight. I lifted my head, seeking her out. She walked toward the kitchen in her normal pair of jeans and an oversized white sweater, her hair wet from her morning shower. The skin of her shoulder peeked out as well as the beige strap of her bra.

I tore my eyes away as she walked past me, heading for the fridge, not uttering a single word. She poured a glass of orange juice before sitting down at the bar across from me. "What kind of eggs do you want?" I asked her as I poured the plantains into the skillet of oil.

She sat up on the stool, folding her knees under her and leaned over to watch me. A smile tugged at my lips. Her eyes were just as traitorous as mine. "Scrambled." I nodded, taking a spatula and skipping the eggs in the pan. "But I'm more interested in that."

I looked up to find her teeth sinking into her bottom lip, looking at the now brown plantains. "Fried bananas?" she asked curiously.

"Close. Maduros."

I watched her closely, blindly flipping the plantains. Her teeth released her lip and a small smile let loose on her lips the second I rolled my tongue to say the word. She squirmed in her seat and I had to muffle my laugh behind a gulp of milk.

"Like I know what that means," she muttered. Maybe I hadn't been successful enough in hiding my amusement.

"Fried plantains, bonita. They're sweet. You'll like them."

She hummed behind her orange juice. "Do they go good with eggs?"

I hitched a shoulder. "They're good with anything. It would be better with ham, but I didn't get any at the store."

She was quiet for a moment, watching me cook while I stole

glances her way. I didn't even try to be discrete; I knew she felt it every time my eyes flicked in her direction. After a few minutes, I piled her eggs onto a plate and the maduros on another one. Pouring a dusting of powdered sugar over the fried plantains, I carried both plates to the table and sat down, waiting for Annie to follow.

While she ate her eggs in small bites, I swallowed the three I put in a glass earlier. I divided the maduros up, placing them on two smaller plates, pushing one toward Annie. "Try it, bonita."

She picked a piece up with delicate fingers. My eyes didn't leave her once as she took a small bite of it, her eyes automatically closing, a sound too close to a moan for my liking escaping her lips. She opened her eyes, the color of her irises a darker blue than I'd ever noticed before.

My heart thrashed against my chest. My thoughts spiraling in one direction. If I had that tiny body of hers pinned underneath me, would those blues turn just as dark? Fuck, could I make them shine even darker?

I shoveled a few of the maduros in my mouth, leaving some of mine for her, knowing she'd want them. "I'm gonna take a quick shower before I drive you into the city," I announced, not making eye contact with her. I picked up our plates, all except the one she was eating from, and headed for the kitchen, trying to hide any proof that she affected me.

Her hand shot out, latching onto my wrist. I looked down at her in question. Her other hand covered her mouth. I waited as she swallowed her food, angling my wrist, hoping she'd get the hint to drop it. She didn't. "I don't have work today."

"Okay. Do you need me to take you anywhere else?"

"No, but can you spot me?"

I looked at her dumbly because she didn't just ask that of me. I knew she didn't. "What?"

She narrowed her eyes at me. "You just said you're going in the gym. Can you spot me while I lift or do you have somewhere else you need to be?"

I didn't need to be anywhere for the next couple of hours. But I sure as fuck did not want to work out with her. I wasn't a goddamn saint.

"Yeah. Whenever you're ready."

I ripped my wrist from her and headed into the kitchen. I turned the water on and grabbed the dish soap from the cupboard. Annie slid next to me a few moments later, slipping her plate and our empty cups into the sink, before grabbing the dishtowel I had slung over my shoulders and began drying the dishes and moving around me to put them away.

We worked together perfectly in comfortable silence. Once everything was cleaned and put away, she grabbed two bottles from the cupboard and filled them with ice. "Do you want water or something else?"

"I'll take water." She handed me the chilled water and I had no choice but to follow her into the gym. She hopped on the treadmill and I headed for the bench press. I slug two fifty-pound weights on each side of the bar. I hadn't lifted that little in years, but then again, I never let myself get distracted in the gym. All of that went out of the window knowing Annie occupied the room. I laid down against the cool leather, the bare skin of my back welcoming the chill. As soon as I gripped the bar steadily, I closed my eyes and started to lift.

The only way I could focus in a room that had Annie in it was to eliminate my sight. I lifted rep after rep, counting up to two hundred before losing count. The weight stilled at the top and my eyes flashed open. Annie's hands curled around the weight, halting me from completing a rep. "My turn."

She backed up and I placed the bar back home. "How much weight do you want?" I asked, standing and wiping off the bench.

She scrunched her nose up and I fought the urge to kiss it back to its normal state. "I haven't lifted in a few weeks. Maybe just forty pounds for now." I nodded, taking the weights off and adding a twenty-pound weight on each side. I motioned forward for her to get in position. She sat on the bench and I took her place behind the bar.

She grabbed the ends of her sweater and ripped it off, leaving her in only her bra and jeans. She fucking wanted me dead. A knife didn't work, the first or the second time she wielded one against me. So, she succumbed to this: murder by sexual tension.

She laid down as if everything was normal. As if she didn't expose her creamy, smooth skin to me. As if the swell of her breasts didn't cause my mouth to water and my dick to salute her. I blinked down at her, not making any move to help her lift the bar.

Her eyes flicked from my face down to my bare chest, her eyebrows raising as if to say, "Fair game." As soon as this gym session came to an end, not only would I be throwing a shirt over my head but I would be getting the fuck out of here. A few day's trip to Mexico might be just what I needed. Nolan could more than handle all of my business meetings, escorting Annie to and from work, keeping an eye on Cameron, and taking care of any situations that should arise in my absence.

I helped her guide the bar down to her chest and I kept my hands hovering over the bar for her first few reps. I kept my eyes glued to her face, to the puffs of air escaping her lips on each exhale.

"You okay, bonita?"

"Mmhmm," she managed through gritted teeth.

I moved my hands and her eyes shot to me in alarm. I reached for her elbow, moving it a few inches wider. I did the same with the other. "That better?"

She nodded. She started counting her reps and I started counting the seconds until I could get the hell away from her. She quit a while later, reaching a hundred reps. She wiped down the bench as my eyes stuck on the sweater discarded on the floor. Any minute she would bend down and retrieve it and I would be able to breathe again.

Except she didn't. She laid her hand on my arm until I raised my gaze to meet hers. My eyes didn't miss an inch of her body. The top of her jeans resting just below her belly button. The skin at her waist playing hide and seek. Her toned stomach called to my fidgeting fingers. All I wanted to do was to reach out, trace her smooth skin until goosebumps broke out. Her breasts, rising and falling with each breath she took was a picture I'd never have to see again to forget. Her soft pink lips, delicate nose, and eyes that took my breath away could kill a man.

"I'm sorry," she said softly.

She should be sorry. Wait. I frowned at her, knowing damn well she wasn't sorry for giving me a taste of my own topless medicine. "What for?"

"For shutting down on you last night. I could have handled it better."

With her soft admission, I forgot about her lack of shirt. I forgot that this six months wasn't about anyone but her. I forgot that we had an expiration date. I lifted my hand to her face, tucking a strand of hair behind her ear. "It's okay, bonita. I can handle you."

All of the softness disappeared from her face as she slapped my hand away and all but growled at me. "Just barely, Hector. Just barely."

I chuckled, walking away from her, knowing damn well she was right.

CHAPTER FOURTEEN

Annie

The sound of the front door slamming had me flopping back on the bench, a pressure on my chest immediately inflating. I shut my eyes, allowing the coolness of the bench to soothe the heat I felt vibrating through my body.

Hector's eyes on me made me feel a lot of things. At first, uneasiness. I wasn't used to someone looking at me so much, so intently. But every day since the night we met, I'd grown accustomed to his focus. Despite my mind blaring off warnings faster than a machine gun, I wanted his eyes on me. I craved the way his gaze brought my skin to life.

And for the two weeks I've been living with him, he trotted around the house shirtless. Sometimes, in just a towel. The man had no modesty or respect for how the image of all of him did to a girl. So, today, I decided to return the favor.

After my shower, I picked out my best bra and sweater and came downstairs to handle business. And it backfired. Big time. The look in his eyes made it almost impossible not to reach up, take his face in my hands, bringing him down to my level, and kiss him until we were both left breathless.

I didn't do that, though I really, *really* wanted to.

I laid there on the mat, knowing Hector I-didn't-even-know-his-last-name already broke me. I wasn't the same Annie I was when he dragged my unconscious body in this house two weeks ago. It almost frightened me to think about the Annie he would turn me into by the end of our time together.

I leaped up, a resolve setting in my bones. It didn't matter who I would become in a little bit over five months. It didn't even matter what happened between the two of us, if we succumbed to the attraction at the end of this agreement or not. The only thing that mattered was Cameron being six feet under by the power of my two hands. With that thought, adrenaline spiked through my veins. I walked up to the punching bag, wrapped my hands in tape and I gave it my all. I delivered hits and jabs to the punching bag, getting lost in the feeling of the power it gave me.

I tried to wait for him but it was well past eight o'clock, the normal time he'd come home when he didn't have to pick me up from work. My stomach ached from not eating since this morning, the sounds it was making were downright embarrassing. I gave up and searched in the kitchen for something to eat. I grabbed the gallon of milk and a bag of cereal Hector bought for me when the door clicked open. Hector came bursting into the kitchen with bags in his hands.

"What are you doing?" he asked before I could offer my help.

"I was just about to eat."

He shook his head firmly, spotting the contents of my dinner. "No. I brought some food. I would've been home earlier but my meeting ran late. Come eat with me."

I helped him with the couple of paper bags, taking the to-go containers out and placing them on the table. He shook his head. "We'll eat in the living room tonight."

I raised an eyebrow. I hadn't seen him in that room once. He split his time at home between the kitchen and the gym, other than at night when he laid next to me while I slept. I had a sinking feeling that he never fell asleep at night; he only waited long enough for me to.

I followed him into the living room and he turned on the overhead chandelier, brightening the room.

I almost dropped the containers in my hand when I noticed a man sitting on the edge of the couch.

"Annie," Hector said, taking the food away from me.

The man stood and smiled sheepishly at me. He was gorgeous. A few inches shorter than Hector and a lot leaner. His hair was jet black, disheveled on top of his head and his skin was a pale ivory color. I looked into his light green eyes and he flinched, his eyes escaping mine before I could blink.

"This is Nolan. He's family. I figured it was time for you two to meet. In case I'm tied up with work, he's the only one I trust you to get in a car with."

I nodded dumbly and looked at Nolan again. He still stood facing me but his eyes were on the floor and I could see his hands turning into fists underneath the pockets of his black denim jeans.

"Come, bonita. I have something new for you to try."

I stepped past Nolan and claimed the spot next to Hector. "It's playoff season," he explained. "If you want to wait, I can heat this up at halftime and eat with you at the table if you prefer."

Fuck. How was this man single? "I can eat in here but what am I eating?"

He handed me a fork, a spoon, and a takeout container that fit perfectly in my lap. I opened the container slowly, almost afraid of what I would find.

This was the first night Hector hadn't cooked dinner himself. He cooked everything in seasoning with his heritage in mind. Some things he cooked I'd never even heard of and some I did. All of the dishes he's made me so far have assaulted my taste buds in the most delicious way.

Hector nudged me with his elbow and I looked over at him.

He wore a crooked grin. "It's not Deal or No Deal. It's just food."

I rolled my eyes and finally lifted the lid. Of course, it looked amazing. "What is it?" I asked again, already unwrapping the silverware.

"Cilantro lime chicken and rice."

My mouth watered and only half of the reason could be blamed on the smell of the chicken and my empty stomach. The way the man spoke, even just a word, a simple roll of the tongue was enough to leave me fidgeting in my seat.

"It smells incredible," I murmured, capturing my first bite with my fork.

Hector's eyes flickered above my head. "While you're in there, grab me a beer." He paused looking to me and I nodded my head for one, too. "Two, actually." His gaze returned to me. "Take a bite."

I chewed on my lip and held his eyes. He must have read the question regarding Nolan in my eyes because his hand came down over my thigh and squeezed. "Later," he whispered.

I nodded and tasted my first bite of chicken. My head fell back against the couch at the first taste. Damn it. It was amazing. I savored it before going back for more.

"Good?" Hector wondered.

I nodded, needing my mouth for other things at the moment. I got lost in my dinner, forgetting Hector in the moment. When my fork met nothing but Styrofoam, I looked around me. Hector and Nolan sat in identical positions on either side of me. Both of them sat on the edge of the couch, legs playing seesaw with the carpet beneath their feet. Hector's hands were folded in between his legs while Nolan's held his chin, both of their eyes glued to the TV.

"What is happening?" I wondered aloud, positive I would be ignored.

Hector's head snapped in my direction. He took the container from me and set it on the coffee table. "Basketball playoffs. Do you want some churros?"

I should've said no. The button of my jeans pleaded with me to say no. "Yes."

He handed me a smaller container and the bottle of beer I'd barely touched. "You don't have to stay down here if you don't want to. I'll be up when this is over," he whispered, leaning in way too close to steal one of my churros.

My heart thudded at his closeness and I shrugged to avoid allowing my voice to embarrass me.

For the first time all night, Nolan spoke up. "You still got your money on Boston?"

I raised an eyebrow at Hector and turned my attention to the TV. Two teams. One in white and green jerseys and the other in red and blue. The score box at the bottom of the screen showed Boston down by fourteen points.

"Yeah. I talked to Lily earlier and she was a blushing mess. The only time Knight plays like shit is when something is wrong with her."

Nolan grunted and I slid my eyes in his direction. His voice was soft and strong at the same time and it perfectly suited him. I wondered how he and Hector met. Hector referred to him as family but based on looks alone, I knew Nolan wasn't the biological kind.

Nolan's head turned slowly, as if he felt my eyes on him. His green eyes were guarded but he offered me the smallest tilt of his lips before returning his attention back to the game.

I placed my empty container and beer on the coffee table before trying to grasp the concept of the game. I watched possession after possession of ten men running back and forth across the court. Boston closed the scoring gap with just a few minutes left. I fell asleep to a Boston player with the number fifteen across his back shooting a pair of free throws.

I jolted awake when I felt movement. I blinked my eyes open, trying to make something out of the darkness. As if he felt me stir, Hector's arms, already surrounding me, tightened. "I got you, bonita," he whispered. A moment later, he carefully set me down on the bed, quickly covering me with my usual blanket.

My eyes followed him across the room until he settled in beside me. I turned my body, tucking my knees into my chest. He didn't look at me; he never did. With his eyes closed, he rested one arm over his stomach and the other one across his face, in hopes I didn't see his cheek twitching from the focus of my stare. It never did.

"Nolan's cute. I'm thinking he should have kidnapped me instead," I lied. There was something about this man, something about a part of him I knew and a part of him I had yet to discover that he was the only person who could stop me. He was hard as he was soft. Strict as much as he was lenient. He knew exactly what I needed in any given moment.

He barked out a laugh. "Nolan would have given you anything you wanted the moment you sicced those blues on him."

I didn't miss the glow of his teeth in the darkness or the dimples popping up as his cheeks stretched with a smile.

"I definitely should have gone with him, then." I let my own little laugh escape. "Was he there, that night?"

I didn't see him. But I didn't see Hector until his body came into contact with mine.

Hector's arm moved with his head as he nodded. "Yes. He's almost always with me. He's my brother, my best friend, and my business partner all wrapped in one."

"He's your brother," I asked him softly.

He took a deep breath, his chest rising and falling. "In every way that counts. My mom wanted an army of kids."

I curled my knees tighter against my chest, fisted the pillow underneath my head and soaked up every word he offered to me in the darkness. "If life went according to plan, if she was still alive and healthy, I'm sure she'd still be popping out siblings of mine. That's what she did. She loved. She was fearless about love. She loved her husband, her family, herself. She was in love with the idea of love and its healing powers. She always used to tell me, 'Love is the channel of everything, mijo. It works for anyone. If you don't have love, you have nothing. If you don't give love, you give nothing. Blood may be pumping through your veins but it's love that keeps you alive.'"

I instantly liked his mom simply for the way Hector's entire demeanor changed when he talked about her. Long gone was the brooding man with the frown lines and pressed lips. This man reverted to a pre-teenage boy who only cared about one woman and that was his mama.

"She never got to meet Samuel," I whispered, almost afraid to ask the question.

He didn't open his eyes but his hands tightened across his stomach and a grimace stretched across his face. I reached for him but his whisper stalled me. "No. He came two years after she died. I know Samuel was the result of careless teenagers but I'd love to think she sent him to me. He's exactly like her."

I couldn't help the smile that stretched across my lips. "The biggest blessings of my life. I wouldn't be the man I am without either of them."

Tears sprung to my eyes and I bit my lip, trying to keep them at bay. I knew all too well about one person shaping your life.

"Nolan was her second son," Hector said after a long moment of silence stretched between us. I felt a single tear roll down my cheeks but I didn't dare acknowledge it. "We met in kindergarten. He had shitty parents who only cared about their next dollar and their next fix. My mom and him, they were perfect for each other. My mom wanted more kids and Nolan needed a family. The moment she noticed the bruises on his skin, she took Nolan and marched over to his house. She threw money at his parents and packed his things. For years, his parents siphoned money out of my mother. She would pay them and they would forget about Nolan for a month, unless they ran out of drugs. Then, they'd bargain for more, threatening to go to the cops and tell them she kidnapped him if she didn't agree. She never told my dad about it. Not until Nolan turned ten and called my mom 'mom' for the first time. Only then did she go to my father, asking to pay them off to sign the papers so Nolan could become her second son."

Hector chuckled and his white teeth glinted in the darkness. "He naturally told her no."

I gasped, immediately covering my mouth. Hector's eyes slowly opened and his head fell to the side, pinning me with a smile in those brown eyes. "It was just how they operated. She asked him for something and instead he somehow always gave her more. My father was the outlier in our household. The only time he allowed vulnerability to seep through was with my mom. Since the moment she brought Nolan home the first time, he was building a case against his parents. The next morning, the two were arrested for a pile of charges, enough to put them away for life. They were offered a deal, sign over adoption pages and they'd get off on ten years of probation. They wisely took the deal and Nolan became a Rivera."

His eyes fell shut and so did mine. A throbbing of pain at the memory of my own mother assaulted every inch of my body. From my head to my toes. I curled my fists against the sheets, grasping for control over my emotions. "Does it," I whispered. "Does it devastate you to see people take their parents or children for granted when every moment of every day, you wish you could have just one more moment with them? One more smile. One more kiss. One more 'I love you.' One more anything."

I felt his fingers hover over my forehead but I couldn't open my eyes, afraid to see what would be swirling in those irises, afraid he could see what was in mine. "All of the time, bonita. All of the time."

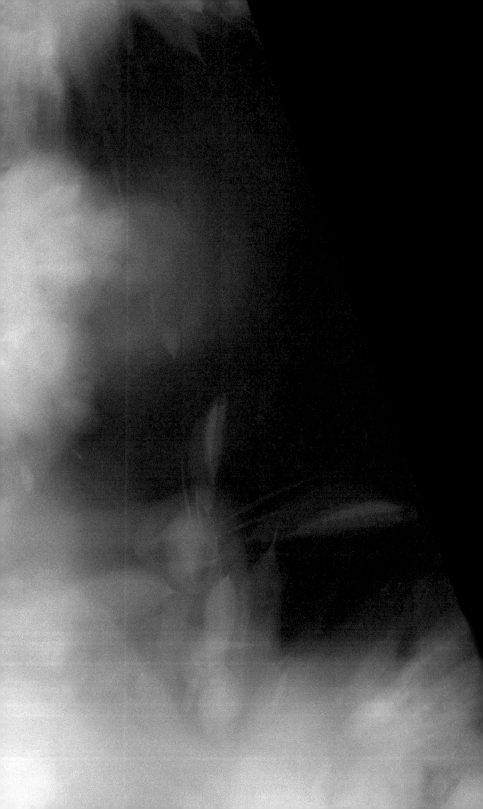

CHAPTER FIFTEEN

Annie

My favorite memories of my childhood always took place with me on my mom's bed, my eyes glued to her while she sat at her vanity getting ready for the day.

Usually first thing in the morning before I went to school. But the fondest memories, the ones that made my cheeks ache from smiling and my chest tighten like her death was a fresh wound, were the nights she went out with her friends. She only went out a few times a month, sometimes less. Usually when Cameron was out of town for a conference.

I'd watch as she effortlessly crafted her makeup to either match what she wore or where she was heading. A black smoky eye went perfect with a tiny black dress. A natural look best with a flowy blouse and tight jeans.

Many lessons happened right there. Me, laying on my stomach, my hands holding my head up, eating up every second of her time. Her, in nothing but a towel, as she took an already beautiful face and made it even more flawless. Her eyes, every so often, would flick to the mirror catching a glimpse of me in the background.

I think the thing I loved most about my mother is that she didn't treat me like a child. She held no power over me. I never felt like she owned me. She talked to me like a best friend and loved me as if I was an essential part of her being. "What do you think is the most beautiful thing about you?" she asked once, a few nights after my tenth birthday.

I scrunched my nose up. "I look like you. So everything."

She burst out laughing, immediately cursing afterward because she messed up her eyeliner. She was still smiling when she spoke again. "That's not what I meant, Annie. When you look in the mirror, what do you see that you love?"

I sighed from my spot on the bed.

"Do you want me to tell you my answer?"

I nodded, my eyes focused on her reflection in the mirror.

She turned around slowly, lifted the towel from her body, exposing the skin above her hips. Pale white scars lined her skin. "This is the proof that I created something beautiful. When I'm having a bad day, I look down at my stomach and my hips and I remember what it felt like when you were growing inside of my belly and I thank God because today may have been bad, but I get to snuggle into the arms of my tiny daughter and that's more happiness than sunshine, or rainbows, or fairy tales could ever give me."

My lips turned up in a grin. "You love me that much?"

She released her grip on the towel and pushed off of her wooden chair, walking over to me. She bent down, her blue eyes clashing with mine. She caressed my face with the back of her finger before grabbing my chin and giving it a gentle tug. "That's only a fraction of how much I love you."

I leaned forward, giving her a sloppy kiss on her cheek. "You brat," she playfully scolded. "Now I have to reapply foundation."

I shrugged, settling back into the bed.

"Now, answer my question."

I flopped around on my back and closed my eyes. "When I look into the mirror, the thing I find most beautiful about myself are my eyes." She didn't say anything but I knew she was waiting for an explanation. "Everyone has a pair of eyes. Different colors. Same color but different shades. Some with flecks in them. Some that change depending on the sun. No two pair of eyes are the same. Other than you, I've never seen anyone with eyes as dark as mine."

I opened my eyes to see her looming over me. "You're a little poet, love bug."

I snorted. "Not likely. Miss Weathers hates my guts."

"That's because you don't do your homework and lie about your dog eating it when we don't even have a dog." She pinned me with a disappointed look. "Take your homework over to Millie's, okay? And hand it in tomorrow."

I begrudgingly got up but I sure didn't do my homework. I played with Millie's dog and the next morning, in English class, I had an honest excuse.

My favorite time of day after my mother died was split between two times. The moment I woke in the morning and the moment I laid my head on the pillow at night. Morning because I had the next sixteen or so hours to be the best version of myself I could possibly be. Night because one day had passed, one day bringing me closer to receiving justice for my mother.

My favorite time of the day changed once more in the past couple of weeks. My favorite time of day I spent in the dark, lying a hair's breadth's away from Hector as he told me about his life, about himself. I feigned for any word he was willing to give me. I soaked up his memories like he was the sun. Some mornings I woke up and dreaded the day because they stood between me and my next fix. And always, always I hated the moment I fell asleep while he still whispered a piece of his memories.

Our nights hadn't been the same since he told me the story of Samuel's birth and how Nolan became his family. We ate dinner and cleaned up as our normal, but neither of us tried to escape each other like an unhappy married couple. I showered while he squeezed in his phone call with Samuel and his nightly workout. He would come up to shower as I finished up an episode of *Criminal Minds*.

He'd come in with just a towel wrapped dangerously low on his hips. I had questions for him and myself. Did he think I was a saint? Did he not know how beautiful I found him and how sexy I found his body? Did he have any modesty at all? The question I had for myself every single night as I watched him dress was, why the fuck couldn't I look away?

Once he was fully clothed, t-shirt and all, he'd lie on the edge of the bed and I would ignore the TV. I found his face, his warm smiles, his memories far more entertaining than anything I could find on the six hundred channels on the TV. He told me more stories between him and Nolan. He told me all about Samuel, moments from when he was a child to him to how much of a sarcastic fool he'd grown into.

After the second night of his confessions, I wouldn't even let him start telling me a story before I made my demands of him. One night I asked him to tell me something funny and he told me the story of him catching Samuel jerking off for the first time. How his son's face turned tomato red and how Hector didn't apologize and leave the room but hassled his then fifteen-year-old son.

I barely saw him at all today, both of us putting in long shifts. Matt needed me to come in earlier than normal and stay later. Something about a city inspection. Hector didn't end up picking me up until closer to nine. We heated up leftovers from last night and he came upstairs and straight into the shower, skipping his precious nightly work out.

He pulled his shirt over his head and collapsed onto the bed. He landed on his side, nowhere near close to touching me but chills ran down my arms at the sight of him. Flat on his stomach, his knee bent a few inches from my stomach, his arms folded under his head in utter exhaustion. His hair was a dark mess on top of his head and my hands ached, wanting nothing more than to reach out and glide through the damp strands.

I wanted his body.

I think I had from the very second that I smashed my lips to his.

Each day with him made the feeling stronger. Not blinking once as he dressed. Sneaking peeks into the gym as he lifted weights. Across the kitchen, tracking his every move as he cooked. Wanting him had become very close to admitting to myself that I needed him.

I needed him to pin me with those dark, brown eyes, caressing every inch of my body with that heated gaze. I needed him to touch me. Light touches on my back as we walked. Tucking a strand of my hair behind my ear. Laying a warm hand over my thigh. I needed him to drive me wild. Crazy to the point that my heart thudded against my chest, chills ran across my skin, and the pressure between my hips was almost unbearable.

But the thing I needed most from Hector had nothing to do with my eyes on his body, but his soft admissions in the dark.

Maybe it was selfish of me. Maybe I should've let him sleep, rest his tired eyes. I still had near a hundred and fifty nights just like this one. But I couldn't convince myself to keep my mouth shut, even when I bit my tongue to the point of pain. "Tell me something that surprised you," I whispered.

His eyes fluttered open but the rest of his body didn't move an inch. His eyes, a liquid brown, held me captive. I forgot to breathe. I forgot everything. Everything but the soft look in his eyes. The skin at the corner of his eyes crinkled and I had to tear my gaze away, afraid to miss the upturn of his lips. A soft smile stretched his lips, a flash of his pink tongue peeking through.

"You'll like this one," he hummed, sitting up. He fetched his blanket before lying down again. He stretched one hand behind his head and the other on top of his stomach. He tapped a couple of fingers on top of his abs and started to chuckle softly.

I sunk farther into the mattress, ready for his words. "A woman once tried to kill me."

My mouth dropped open. He paused, looking over at me, his smile widening tenfold.

I managed to close my mouth. "You mean I wasn't the first?"

He held my gaze for so long that my eyes burned with the need to blink. He seemed to get lost in his own thoughts because he snapped his head back and closed his eyes. Only then did he speak again. "A few years ago, I was attacked and ended up in the hospital." His words were vague, his tone cautious. I frowned but otherwise remained quiet.

"It was just a flesh wound. I should have been in and out of there. And I would have been if it weren't for Liliana Carter." A smile broke out on his lips at the mention of her name, a fond, maybe even prideful smile. "She knew exactly who I was. She walked in, shutting the door first and then the blinds. I underestimated her." He looked at me again, smirking and I couldn't help my own small smile. "I should have learned, huh?"

I lifted my shoulders in a shrug. "She didn't say a word as she brought a needle out of her lab coat. She looked up at me and said, 'You don't know me but I know you.' There was steel in her voice, demanding my attention. Demanding that if I didn't give her what she wanted, I might not be leaving the hospital alive. She flicked the liquid a few times like she was a professional killer in disguise of a doctor. It was kind of badass to see. She told me to raise the prices of drugs."

I looked at him in shock. He was a drug pusher? Noticing my reaction, he closed his eyes. "I'm not a good man, Annie. You know this. Anyway, she told me to stop making the drugs cheap because it targeted kids of color. She argued that if I raised the prices, the minorities wouldn't be able to afford to touch it. The white kids would pay as much as I sold it for, though. And through them, it was the only way to get a discussion going on about a change of how we treated drugs, both selling and using in this country."

Liliana Carter was a smart woman, and a badass activist by the sound of it.

"I asked her if she really had it in her to kill me. If she was prepared to live with that weight on her shoulders for the rest of her life." He threw me a pointed look which I ignored. "Her eyes were sad when she told me, 'I'd rather take one life in exchange for thousands, even if that life was my own.'"

Damn. That was my only thought. Damn. "So, I'm guessing you conceded."

He grinned wolfishly. "I'm still breathing, aren't I?"

"Is that the last you saw of her?" I whispered, fighting my tired eyes. Hector reached over and turned the lamp off, plunging us in darkness.

"No. The last time I saw her was a few days ago. She and I work closely together."

"On America's drug problem?"

"That and she's my unofficial med school teacher." I raised my eyebrows up at that. "She's one of the best surgeons on the East Coast, her and her soon-to-be brother-in-law. She's won every award in her short career that you could think of. Breakthrough research, her name is attached to it. Groundbreaking surgeries, she's the lead surgeon behind it. I'm a fan of hers. I'm obsessed with her mind."

"Is it like being friends with Lebron James?"

A light chuckle floated to my ears, but my heavy eyes refused to open and see his smile. "You know who that is?"

"I searched the best professional basketball player after watching the game with you last time. His name popped up."

"Being friends with Lily..." His voice trailed off as darkness pulled me under.

Annie. Annie. Annie. ANNIE.

I woke to the sound of my name and urgent hands wrapped around my arms. I blinked back my vision until I could see clearly. Worried brown eyes darted across my face. "Hector?" I asked, but my voice came out in a breathy gasp. His hand cupped the back of my neck and I cringed, registering how hot my body felt, sweat making my hair stick to my face.

Some nights were like this. These nightmares wrecked my body but showed mercy to my brain. I didn't remember the memory, but I felt it. I'd wake up, hands shaking, sweat coating every inch of skin, and my throat soar from the screams that never woke me up.

He pulled me up into a sitting position. He didn't say a word. He didn't ask me if I was alright. He didn't try to pry into what I had been dreaming about. He simply held me, one hand firm on my nape, the other hand tracing soft circles on my back.

The only sound in the room was my breathing, ragged and heavy. My hair clung to my forehead. My heart powered into overdrive and my hands shook. Even though, I didn't remember it, I knew a memory haunted my closed eyes.

Weeks ago, I told Hector the scariest things happen in the dark. Since then, he had told me some of his darkest moments and some of his best. He told me his truth each night. I leaned into his touch, afraid of how he would look at me once I told him mine.

I rested my head on his chest and his arms automatically wrapped around me. I took a deep breath before I bared it all. Every piece of me. It was his now.

"Cameron Wade is my father." I felt his entire body freeze beneath me but I didn't falter. "He wasn't much of a father as far as I can remember, but my childhood was nothing short of amazing. My mom made sure of that. She was the light of my life, sunshine in human form. Her name was Michelle. She was more of a best friend than a mom.

"Sure, she helped me with my homework and fed me but more often than not, she did my hair and read me books. She taught me how to do my makeup and there were days where we would just lay in her bed, open the curtains and watch cars as they drove by and just talk. She loved me unconditionally. If you were to see the two of us in a room together, there was a good chance you'd be blinded by our identical smiles. She was a happy, beautiful person. And that's how I remember her. But she changed into a different person when *he* was around. His presence drained the life out of her. That nightmare I had that first night…" I paused, tilting my head to look up at him only to see his eyes clenched shut. "It was actually a memory. The first memory I had of him hurting her. I was just eight years old at the time. He had invited some people over from work and I was forced to stay in my room until they left. When she didn't come to rescue me like she always did, I crept downstairs. He was saying nasty mean things and he had a belt in his hand. He was lashing her back and I tried not to scream only because I didn't want to make him angrier. But I couldn't help it. He stormed out of the house after he ordered her to shut me up and I spent the next two days icing my mom's back, but some scars don't heal no matter what you do."

His arms tightened around me and I let them. "Bonita," he whispered, his voice contradicting the strength of his arms.

"Shhh," I told him, my own voice barely holding up. "That was the first of many incidents. I tried to talk her into leaving for years after that. But she liked to pretend that the bad times didn't exist and I wasn't allowed out of my room when he was home and drunk. She tried sheltering me from seeing it, seeing her like that. But I would lay there in my bed and I would hear the sounds of him hitting her, of her feeble whimpers, and the really bad nights where she couldn't hold it in anymore and howled in pain. Little did I know, she was discreetly stealing money from him ever since that first time. She opened a savings account and just after I turned twelve, she had enough saved to where we could move and start over, just the two of us.

"He came home early that day and she told me to hide as best as I could so she could talk to him. He was livid. He called her all sorts of names and he yelled louder than I'd ever heard. Before I knew what was happening, I heard the blast of a gun going off. I held my breath and I waited. I told myself that she killed him and she was going to come and find me at any moment."

I squeezed my eyes shut, tightening my fist into Hector's shirt as the memory of the worst day of my life assaulted me. "She never came because she was the one who was shot. She was the one who died."

Hector's arms loosened around me. His hands slid from my stomach up to my hair. He secured my head against his shoulder and laid the two of us back down. When my head hit the pillow, he placed the softest kiss at the edge of my temple. So tender it made me want to open my eyes to catch a glimpse of what swirled in those eyes but I refrained, afraid of how he would look at me after my confession.

So, I kept talking as his fingers sifted through my hair, effectively calming my erratic heartbeat. "I didn't move from my hiding spot and Cameron never came looking for me. He probably figured she would have sent me someplace safe until she could get away. I stayed in that spot, afraid to breathe, until the cops showed up and whisked him off to jail. The moment the sirens faded, I ran out of the house, to my babysitter's house. The next morning, she took me to child services. I was secretly put in the system and landed with a foster family until I turned eighteen. He went to court and painted my mother as a criminal. He got away with murder. Since the day I found that out, before I even got the chance to be who I was going to be, I knew that I was going to be the one to kill him."

I ignored my cheeks soaked with tears. I opened my eyes to see Hector's face twisted in a look I knew all too well. Heartbreak. His eyes scrunched together, his long lashes disappearing in their depths. His jaw clenched so tightly, I was afraid he'd break something. His skin color took on a florid color, replacing the shade of brown I loved.

I lifted my arms up and cupped his cheeks in the palm of my hands until he opened his eyes. His normally intense and soul searching eyes were murderous. Angry beyond belief. If I wasn't certain that he wouldn't hurt me, I would have flinched. But I held my ground. "I'm sorry I've tried to hurt you." My fingers danced across his face, my knuckles brushing the tiny scar above his eyebrow. "This is all new to me. The last person who mattered to me was my mother. Since she left, I've had no one. Not even myself."

His eyes softened at my admission, but he didn't say anything. He plucked me from his lap, scooting my body across the bed before tucking me under the blanket. His hands swept underneath my hair, allowing it to fan out across the sheets. He returned to his spot at the edge of the bed and I turned on my side to face him, reaching across the space between us for his hand. He let me have it.

We laid there in silence for a long moment. At some point, both of our hands relaxed but neither of us made a move to let go of each other. His thumb swept over my skin and that small touch of his eased all of my worries.

I should have known better. I should have known he wouldn't look at me any different. I should have known he would allow me to tell him my truth without being penalized for it. I sunk deeper into the bed, my breaths becoming steady until I felt like a fully deflated balloon.

Just before the darkness pulled me under, I swore I heard him say, "He will pay for every day he caused you pain."

I wanted to tell him that there weren't enough ways for that many days but I was already too far gone.

CHAPTER SIXTEEN
Hector

No trace of Annie's confession lingered.

The moon disappeared, flooding the room with light each passing second. Our soft breaths didn't skip a beat. The room didn't suddenly burst into flames. The ground I stood on didn't shake.

But I felt the impact of her words everywhere. Echoes in my mind. Fire in my veins. A tremble in my hands.

It didn't feel right. That time pressed on. That the world kept moving.

My world stopped at two o'clock in the morning at the sound of Annie's scream. Screams that sounded like she was being burned alive and held down under water at the same time. My heart hurt and with each word she whispered against my chest, it cracked a little bit more. No words she said later had their desired effect on me. Not even a touch from the one person I craved it from most could ease the anger welling up inside of me.

The only thing that kept me in this room, the only thing that didn't have me in my car, racing to get to that piece of shit and obliterating him worse than I already had, was the voice in the back of my mind warning me of breaking the promise I made to Annie. I knew in five months' time, if I didn't hand over a healthy Cameron Wade, she'd never forgive me.

And that was the one thing I'd never risk.

So, I stayed in the room with her, my eyes affixed on her sweet face and my hand still wrapped lightly around hers. I stayed because I had to. Because she grounded me. Because I was addicted to the feeling being around her gave me.

The sound of my alarm resonated through the room and I quieted it as quickly as possible. I chanced one last look at Annie before I forced myself to get up and acknowledge the day.

I soaked up her creamy skin, her blonde waves framing her small face. Her small nose and pleading lips. I looked down at our interlocked hands. Her white to my brown. Her small to my big. Her elegance to my jagged. I couldn't ignore the tightness in my chest at the sight of us.

I wanted nothing more to protect her, to chase away her fears and hold her hand as she flew to her dreams. Not that she would ever let me.

I ripped my hands from hers and trudged downstairs. Ignoring the kitchen, I headed straight for the gym. I turned on the stereo, settling

on one of Samuel's playlist titled: **Beast Mode: Hip Hop Workout.**
I rarely listened to music that didn't come from a Latinx artist but
there was something about hip hop, 90s preferably, that fueled the
adrenaline when you needed to release some energy. I didn't recognize
the song that came on but I felt the hard bass in my veins and that was
enough for me.

I skipped stretches, sauntering over to the punching bag before
pummeling it. I threw my entire body into every punch, jab, and kick
with the hopes to release some of the rage bubbling up inside. It didn't
work. If anything, the sudden adrenaline made my anger more palpable.

What kind of fucking man puts his hands on the mother of his
child? What type of despicable human do you have to be to take
someone's mother from them? What kind of human does it take to
not take one look at Annie and not fall to your knees at her mercy?

I punched the bag so hard, letting go, losing control. "Fuck," I
yelled into the empty room, not caring to stop the bag when it swung
back in my direction and knocked me on my ass.

Over the years, rescuing women became the best part of being a
Rivera. Doing something good. Aiding women as they left the abusive
assholes behind. Watching them rise from the ashes, more beautiful
and stronger than ever.

Annie was different from the start. She had a plan to save herself.
A plan I hijacked. Part of me wanted to call the whole thing off. Drive
her down to Hank's, drop her off, and tell her I would be back to clean
up her mess. Then, I'd buy her that plane ticket I owe her and send her
off to the next phase in her life. Her next chapter. The one without me.

I groaned and rolled over on to my stomach, lying my cheek

against the cool mat. I knew the right thing to do. Set her free to allow her to live the rest of her life as she planned before we crossed paths. Set her free before I fell too far.

But for the first time in my life, I was a selfish bastard because I knew I wouldn't do it. I didn't want to let her go yet. I wanted the six months I proposed and she agreed to. I wanted every second of our agreement accounted for. I didn't want to say goodbye until the very last moment. I didn't want to say goodbye at all.

I propped myself into a sitting position and dug my phone out of my shorts knowing only one person could understand.

I tucked the phone between my shoulder, closing my eyes and resting my arm on the top of my bent knees while the phone rang. "Are my eyes deceiving me? Is this really my son calling me?"

I couldn't help but shake my head at my father's antics. "I thought Samuel got his theatrics from Mom but maybe I need to reevaluate the blame."

He didn't reply immediately. I knew he wouldn't at the mention of my mother. Through my teenage years, after her death, he talked about her. Her name on his lips became a permanent fixture. He could barely hold a conversation without talking about her.

His wife. Hector's mama. His light. His life. His queen. Maria Jazmín Rivera.

He never shied away from the loss of her. He felt her in between every bone in his body, with each breath he inhaled. My mother was his religion and even if he couldn't see her, he'd sink to his knees every day to worship her name.

Grief affected him, even twenty years later, like a fresh wound. So,

I waited him out. "How is Samuel? I haven't heard from him for a few days."

"I haven't talked to him this morning. But when I talked to him yesterday, he seemed to be living it up. Making his way through all of the Italian girls."

He snorted. "Ahh, I can't wait for the day he meets his queen. The fall to his knees is going to be a glorious sight."

"I'll bring the popcorn."

His booming laughter eased some of the tension in my body. "Tell me the reason you're calling, Hector."

I swallowed past the lump in my throat. I loved him but there had always been a divide between us since the time I was a teenager. Because of the last name we shared. Because he cut my childhood short, not caring to see if I wanted to claim the reins on the family business. And then after I took over. He believed I have and still am diminishing our last name. Because I wouldn't sell the hardcore drugs he did when he was in charge. Because I cared more about my city and the people in it than I cared about being the most powerful man to step foot in it. I fell backward, welcoming the thud of my body colliding with the cool mat. "I think I found her."

He didn't say anything for a long moment but the sigh that escaped him spoke volumes. "It's wrong but it doesn't feel like it." I didn't shut up. I kept going, flaying my skin open with the truth. "It feels momentous, Dad. There's this pressure in my chest every time I look at her. I need to let her go, allow her to live her life but I—" I shook my head, irritation settling deep within me. "I can't imagine waking each morning, opening my eyes, and not seeing her face."

"Damn, boy." That's all I got. Two words.

"Yeah," I mumbled, picking at the hem of my shorts.

"Finding her is the easy part, son. It's the every day that's hard. It's paying attention. It's listening to her. It's stepping away from yourself, your need to protect her, and putting her first. Your mama raised you how to treat a woman, Hector. I know you know how. You just didn't wait to find *your* woman and that was the problem." He didn't have to say her name for me to realize who he was talking about. "Love her with reckless abandon. Give her your all. With every touch you place on her body, make sure she knows that she's the one."

"No one said anything about love," I grumbled, feeling more my son's age than mine in the moment.

"You're a Rivera, no?"

I answered his rhetorical question with a semblance of a grunted yes.

"You didn't have to say anything. We give it our all or we don't bother."

I hung up shortly after, the anger I felt dimmed a little but not much. I still wanted to tear Cameron Wade's body apart, inch by inch until I could build a jigsaw puzzle out of him. But he wasn't the only person my anger settled on.

I had to look in the mirror for that.

The night I met Annie and the way I treated her put a sour taste in my mouth. I didn't respect her. I saw her as another one of the many women I had helped start anew over the years. I thought she was going to be like all of the rest. I'd set her up with a temporary place to stay, take care of the asshole in her life, line her up a spot at a job in the city or in New Hazle and I'd be on my merry way as she set the restart button on her life.

That was before she kissed me, before she went down swinging. She wasn't a little kitten I had to save from a fire. She was a lion, baring her sharp teeth to protect what was hers. And Cameron was hers. Hers for the killing.

Who the hell was I to think I knew what was best for her? Then or now?

I huffed, turning the playlist back on and settling into the bench press. I loaded up each side of the bar with two hundred pounds on each end. Four hundred pounds without a spotter was pushing it. I could lift up to five hundred with one but I'd only ever went as far as three-fifty without one.

A DMX song started blaring through the speakers and the grittiness in his voice clashing with the harsh production had me lying against the bench and my fingers gripping the bar. Fuck it. At this point the crushing weight on my chest would be a warm welcome.

After twenty-five reps, I could feel the burn of my muscles stretching from my arms into my shoulders, following all the way to my core. My back clung to my shirt in a soaked sweat. I completed one more rep before sitting up and tearing my shirt over my head, using it to wipe the perspiration from my face. I positioned back into place and started lifting.

I had long lost count of the reps. The music ringing through the room sounded muffled against the sound of my racing heart and the pulse sounding in my eardrums. Only the clearing of the throat that could only belong to one person brought my body into focus.

Placing the bar back into place with a loud clang, I looked over to see Annie. She stood in the doorway, her hip jutted out against the woodwork, her arms across her chest, her deep blue eyes narrowed into slits, looking straight at me.

I made no move to get up. I let those eyes focus on me, feeling my skin heat under her gaze. "You're angry," she said, not asking.

I heaved a sigh, wishing I could shake out of this feeling. I tore my gaze away from her and grunted, not sure what I could say to her. The words "Not with you. Never with you," were on the tip of my tongue but I pressed my lips into a thin line to avoid them escaping.

From the corner of my eye, I saw her kick off the wall, unfold her arms before stuffing them in the pocket of her jeans. Now, I wasn't the only one pissed off this morning. "Remember your part of the deal," she said, coldness seeping through her usually soft voice, speaking to me in a way she hadn't in weeks.

I immediately regretted getting out of bed this morning. I regretted putting my body through torture I would have to pay for come later, not because my body would feel like I was bulldozed by a truck but because, I knew if I stayed, I would have talked to her, let her ease me instead of taking out my anger on my body and allowing her to see the cold look I knew still settled in my eyes.

I sat up, snapping my head in her direction, a frown taking over my face. "You're seething. I can feel it. I'm just reminding you that I've been doing, *I am doing*, everything you asked, so don't cross me." How did we go from her holding my hand while she slept back to her threatening me? "You've been angry for ten minutes. I've been sitting on it for ten years."

I gulped past the lump in my throat. God, I was a fucking asshole. Taking away her pain and her anger because the truth about Cameron and why she made it her mission to kill him caused my blood to boil. "Annie," I whispered, standing and walking toward her, but she held her hand up to stop me. A scathing slap from her palm would have hurt less.

"Don't. Kill. Him," she gritted out between clenched teeth before spinning on her heel and leaving me in her wake.

I sunk onto the bench once more, running my hands through my damp hair. I sat there, thinking about her words for too long. *You've been angry for ten minutes. I've been sitting on it for ten years.*

I couldn't imagine what it felt like to be Annie, at any point in the past ten years. She was a child when her mom died, feet away from her, even longer since she saw her mom hurt by the hands of her killer. When my mom died, I was sad. But I didn't have to wait long to avenge her death. Before we even laid my mother to rest, my dad tortured the life out of the person who took her away from us. I couldn't imagine not having my dad, growing up alone, and working tirelessly on my mind and my body to prepare myself to take a life.

I shouldn't have been angry about Annie's truth. I should've been kneeling at her feet in awe of the strength she possessed.

I tossed my head back, brushing my hair out of my eyes, regret filling my lungs. I walked out of the gym, not sparing a second glance toward the kitchen where I knew she would be. I headed directly upstairs and into the shower.

Twenty minutes later, I dressed and headed downstairs. Annie sat at the kitchen table, her eyebrows arching once catching sight of me. I ignored her, wordlessly making my way into the kitchen. I didn't dress in my normal plain crew neck t-shirt and jeans, instead trading it in for a pair of deep blue slacks, a crisp white dress shirt and a pale yellow tie. It didn't escape my attention that the colors I wore reflected the woman sitting a few steps away from me.

I had to apologize for my behavior. And I knew I had to wait until tonight to do it because she was due at work today. "Do you want eggs or do you want me to make you something else?" I asked from behind the fridge.

"Neither. I already ate."

I glanced from behind the refrigerator door to see her pulling a jean jacket on. Today, she wore tight black jeans, a slit on each knee exposing a few inches of her skin, and a plain white shirt with the sleeves cuffed. "What do you mean you already ate?"

"Just that. You were working out all morning, Hector. Have you even looked at the time? I'm late for work."

I pulled out my phone and blinked at the time. It was a few minutes after twelve. "Shit. I'm sorry. Do you want me to stop on the way and get you something?" I put away the eggs and reached in the dish bowl for my car keys.

"I'm good but can we go? You can stop if you're hungry. Matt's cool with me being late; he'll just make me work later than usual."

I followed her out to the car, not answering her question but a million questions swirling in my own head. We were quiet through the drive in the city. "Annie?" I asked, once we were only a few blocks away from the shooting range.

"Hmm," she murmured, tearing her gaze from the window.

"Why'd you never tell Matt?"

She bit her lip. "What makes you think he doesn't know?"

I knew he didn't know. He's the reason we met. I didn't say that, unsure if I'd ever speak those words. "I got the feeling, last night, that I'm the first person you ever told."

She nodded her head slowly. "That makes sense because you were."

She didn't offer up anything else and we spent the rest of the ride in silence, some of the tension leaking out of the car after her admission. "I'll call you when I'm ready," she said, opening her door.

"Okay. If I'm not able to make it, Nolan will pick you up."

"How about you just pick me up," she said, narrowing her eyes at me for the second time today. I was not fond of her eyes pinning me that way.

"I will if I can. I have meetings all day," I said. I had a night to plan. For her, to get back in her good graces. To try and get her to hold my hand again while she slept. God, I sounded like a lovesick teenager.

I could hear her teeth grinding together but I'd make up for that later, too. Once the door slammed shut, I switched gears from park to reverse. I looked toward the entranceway of Philly's Range, frowning when I found Annie nowhere in sight.

"Hector." The sound of her voice startled me and I whipped my head to where she sat, her arms crossed over her chest, glaring at me. I barely held back my groan of frustration. "Promise me."

"Promise you what?"

"Two things, actually."

I nodded, waiting for her to continue.

"Promise me that you'll pick me up and promise me that you won't touch him today."

She didn't have to say his name for me to know who she was talking about. My next stop was Hank's. I planned on heading straight for the basement, a beautiful woman's colors, a suit of armor on my body as I headed into battle, beating the piece of shit who tore her world apart ten years ago. I'd never kill him, as much as I wanted to, because she was right all of those nights ago. He was hers to kill.

I knew I needed to give her my word but I really wanted to make that bastard bleed today. I rested my head against my seat, running my fingers through my hair. The sound of her seatbelt clicking back into place brought my eyes back to her. "What are you doing?"

"Promise me or I'm going to be stuck up your ass all day."

I groaned, watching her cross her legs, making herself comfortable. I closed my eyes while I relented, used to the feeling of surrender when it came to her. "I promise you I'll be the one to pick you up and I won't touch him."

I didn't open my eyes to see her reaction. I didn't even open my eyes when I heard her seatbelt unclick once more. I did open my eyes when I felt her nails scrape against my scalp as her fingers slid through my hair. She gasped when our eyes clashed, a sound shooting straight down to my groin. I sat there frozen, wanting to close the distance between us to feel those lips in a way I'd only had the pleasure once. I wanted to trace every inch of her lips with my tongue, so I would never forget how they felt. I looked from her wide blue eyes down to her parted lips. The things I would sacrifice for her to close the distance.

Her other hand closed around my tie in a tight fist, yanking me closer. Not close enough. My eyes swung back to meet hers. "Such a good boy," she cooed at me, her lips breaking out into a shit-eating grin.

Gritting my teeth to keep from smiling, I snatched her hand from my head and placed it in her lap, glaring at her the entire time. She slid back to the passenger side and opened the door. She threw her head back, the laugh she'd been holding back escaping her as she hopped out of the car, not looking back the entire way she swung her cute little ass into work.

As soon as Annie disappeared from my line of vision, I pulled out my phone connecting it to Bluetooth before making my way back to New Hazle. I dialed Nolan's number at a red light along the way.

"Boss."

"What's on the agenda today and what can be cancelled or replaced by with you?"

He emitted a small grunt. "Annie," he guessed correctly.

I could still feel her fingers wrapped around the fine strands of my hair, her mouth impossibly close to mine. "Yeah," I admitted blatantly.

"Four meetings today with stockbrokers but I can take care of them all."

"Are you sure you can handle everything?" I wanted to take his word for it, but I knew my best friend like the back of my hand. His social anxiety would catch up to him after a day filled with meetings and I didn't want to deal with the aftereffects of him being a moody asshole while he recovered. "You can cancel two of them and I'll make sure my schedule is cleared tomorrow."

"I got it, Hector," he uttered, his voice hardening.

"Okay, but don't expect me to rub your back and buy you fried ice cream."

A laugh boomed out of him. "Fuck you."

"Did you kill him?"

My eyes fell shut at the sound of her voice. "No, Annie. I didn't even see him."

She didn't offer me anything back, silence filling my ear for a long moment. "What are you doing, then?"

"Calling you to see if you're done with work yet."

"Yeah," she whispered, her voice softening. "I'm going to shoot around until you get here."

I hung up, grabbed my keys, and weaved through the light traffic to bring her back home. She was posted outside when I pulled up, immediately kicking off of the wall when she spotted me.

She climbed into the car, leaning over the middle console, eyeing me suspiciously. My lips twitched as I fought a smile. Satisfied with her inspection, she leaned back and buckled up before I pulled out of the parking space.

"You really shouldn't wait outside for me when you work this late," I said, knowing she'd probably get pissed at me.

She huffed, but to my surprise, her usual annoyance at my protectiveness lacked. "I know Jujutsu."

I looked over at her to see her expression serious. "You're not lying," I said dumbly.

She smiled at me, her tongue flashing out as she bit it softly. Oh, fuck me. "I can teach you if you want."

I coughed. "No, thank you." Close combat and Annie didn't seem like a good combination for me unless my endgame included some serious blue balls.

Annie's eyes were glued to the city lights until the trees replaced them. My mind drifted to what waited for us at home.

I pulled into the drive, anxiety coursing through me. My heart racing as fast as it did this morning as I lifted four hundred pounds.

Warmth around my wrist snapped me out of my head. I looked down to see Annie's pale fingers wrapped around my dark skin. "You're much more beautiful when you're not angry," she whispered, immediately looking away.

I clasped onto her wrist before she could break the connection. Her eyes darted back to me in the darkness. Her face illuminated by the outside lights set up around the house. I wanted to kiss her so bad. "I could say the same about you, bonita," I told her just as softly, as close as I could to admitting the truth. My truth. Her eyes opening every day became a blessing and a curse. A blessing because I'd get to soak up as much of her time as she'd allow. A curse because I couldn't put the peace that illuminated her face while she slept when her eyes were open. Life hardened her too much and no amount of love I could ever offer her could be enough.

I let go of her and we came together in front of my car, walking side by side to the house. "I hope you plan on cooking because I think my stomach's starting to eat itself."

I placed my hand on her lower back, spreading my fingers to feel the most of her. "You're in luck," I whispered into her ear and grinned when her neck flushed red and goosebumps rose on her perfect skin. "I made your favorite."

She grabbed my hand from her back and shoved it in my direction. "Then, open the door. What are you waiting for?"

I chuckled and did as I was told.

She hung up her jacket while I headed for the kitchen. "What do you want to drink?" I called over my shoulder.

I grabbed a beer for me and waited for her response, but it never came. She stood frozen at the head of the table, looking at the meal I prepared. "What is all of this?" she breathed, stepping forward and picking up one of the flowers that I scattered across the table.

Morning glories. A perfect resemblance to her in botany form. The deep blue of the petal a perfect match for eyes. The yellow sprouting from the stem an uncanny match to the color of her hair. I closed the fridge, ambling my way to her.

Her words froze me mid-step. "My mother used to grow these as much as she could. She'd set one on my nightstand every morning before I woke up. They always died by nightfall but I never knew because she replaced them."

"Annie," I croaked out, feeling the pain behind her shaky voice pressing against my breastbone. Her glossed eyes darted to mine. "I'll get rid of them," I rushed, closing the distance between us and reaching for the one she held.

"Hector, wait." She lowered into her normal seat and started to collect each flower. I stood behind my chair, hands gripping around the wood. I watched as she positioned the flowers until they shaped into a 'M.' "One time she forgot to replace them and I woke up to an old brittle thing instead of the fresh flower I'd grown accustomed to. I ran downstairs crying, wailing this poor flower in my hand. She picked me up and placed me on the counter, helping me dry my tears before explaining to me how flowers worked. 'Beautiful things die' she had told me 'and there was nothing anyone could do about it.'

"She reached behind me where my new morning glory sat in water. She tucked my hair behind my ear and followed it with the flower. 'I love this flower because it's beautiful like you. It makes you happy each morning.' She bumped my nose with her knuckle. 'And you make me happy each morning.'"

She finally looked up from the flower to me. "My life hasn't always been scarred, Hector. I was happy for a lot of it."

I nodded, remembering my own short time with my mother. Her stomach growling snapped us both out of the silent conversation our eyes held. "Do you want me to grab you a beer or something else?"

"Just a water," she answered distractedly, uncovering the plates on the table. She looked up at me, smiling. I winked before turning around and pouring her a glass of ice water. Instead of sitting in my normal spot, I walked to her side of the table and pulled out the chair next to her.

I cracked open my beer as she scarfed down her first two tacos. "Do you have room for more?"

She wiped her face with a napkin before looking at me with a quirked eyebrow. "I made salsa for you." Her eyebrows shot up. "I've never made it before without thinking about a weaker taste bud."

She jabbed me in the stomach with her fist. "I tasted a little bit but I'm afraid it might be too strong still. You want to try it on a chip first?"

She nodded. I unwrapped one of the final plates she abandoned once she found all of the toppings she loved. A chip sauce with cream cheese, the toned-down salsa, and mixed shredded cheese on top. I moved it between us and grabbed the plate of tortilla chips I baked. She grabbed a chip before scooping up some cheese and salsa.

She moaned around her mouthful. I grabbed a tortilla and started making her a third taco, this time adding the salsa on top. She took it wordlessly while I pulled at my beer and watched her devour the food I spent the day preparing.

She leaned back after one more taco, her hands resting on her bloated stomach. Her eyes closed. "You're making me so fat. I'm going to need new jeans."

She peeked one eye open, catching me staring. She didn't sit up and I didn't look away. I reached up, my fingertip tracing the smooth skin along her cheekbone. "I'm sorry," I whispered. "I'm sorry for taking your pain and making it about me."

"It's okay. If our roles were reversed, if someone dismantled your life, I'm not sure I would be able to hold myself back, regardless of the consequences."

Someone did dismantle my life. I was looking straight at her. And I didn't want to take action against her. I wanted her to do it over and over again. I wanted her to ruin my life every day until I forgot how I lived each day without her.

"Do you have room for dessert?"

She closed her eyes once more, letting out a dramatic sigh. "What is it," she cried out softly.

I stood from my chair and fetched two bowls of vanilla ice cream from the freezer. I heated up the bowl of my homemade caramel. Bringing all of it to her, I sat next to her again, our knees brushing. She held her hand out for a spoon and I obliged.

"What is this?" She peeked into the bowl of hot caramel.

"Dulce de leche," I supplied, electing the Spanish term in favor for the one she would know. I hid my smirk behind my hand as I watched her cross and uncross her legs, before shoving a spoonful of vanilla ice cream into her mouth.

I drizzled the caramel across the remainder of her ice cream before doing the same to my own. It had been a long time since I made a batch of caramel and as soon as it hit my taste buds, I melted against the seat, my legs spreading farther apart, knocking against Annie's knee.

Her hands gripped my thigh and my eyes jolted open to find her head thrown back in ecstasy. Now, it was my turn to readjust my thighs. "That is so good, Hector. Damn."

Once she recovered from that first taste, she dove back in, not stopping until no trace of caramel or ice cream remained. She turned to me. "That is my new favorite."

I smiled. "You say that every night."

"You know what to do in the kitchen." Her eyes filled with praise but my eyes snuck away, trailing down to her lips, a dab of caramel sitting on the corner.

Two months ago, she sat in that same exact chair with milk dribbling down her chin and the urge to kiss her had been so strong. That feeling returned ten fold. I wanted to kiss her back then. Now, I wanted to devour her until I forgot both of our names.

I reached over, wiping the sauce away, not allowing my touch to linger. "Do you want to get a shower?"

She nodded. "We can clean up first."

I shook my head. "No, you go ahead. I'm tired. We'll clean up in the morning."

She stood up, relenting. She turned toward me to get out. She bent down and I tilt my head back to look up at her. Her hands came over my shoulders. I felt all of her body weight leaning on me and my hands twitched to grab at her waist. I tucked them underneath my thighs to avoid temptation.

She closed the distance between us, closing those soft lips over the skin between my eyebrows. "Thank you for tonight," she whispered against my skin. And this time, the goosebumps pebbling weren't on her skin.

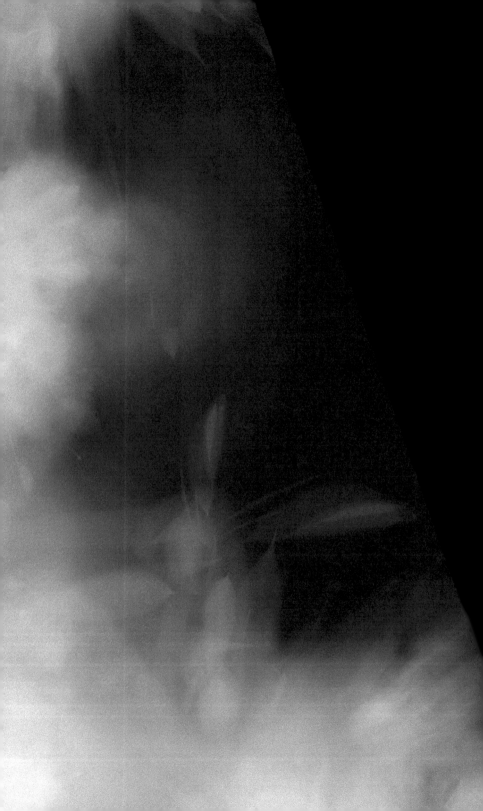

CHAPTER SEVENTEEN

Annie

Things changed between the two of us. If I was being honest with myself, they had been changing for quite some time.

I no longer viewed Hector as my enemy or kidnapper. He was my friend, my best friend. The one I could tell all of my deepest secrets to in the dark and he wouldn't hold them against me once daylight arrived. The one I trusted enough to smile around. The one who put my mind and my heart at ease. The one I missed the moment I stepped behind a door separating us.

A week passed since his apology dinner and each night when we laid down for the night, we swapped mother stories. I learned about Maria Jazmín Rivera and I relayed every single one of my memories of Michelle Anne Miller.

He lost his mother at thirteen, getting one more year with his mom than I had with mine. Our childhoods mirrored each other's so perfectly. While my dad didn't have anything to do with me, all Hector's dad showed him was tough love. Both of us were raised by our beautiful, graceful angels we liked to call Mom.

I grew obsessed with him. I counted down the hours until our lives permitted us to come back together. And when we were together, he was the subject I needed to have a perfect score in. I wanted all the extra credit of Hector I could sign up for. I basked at the sight of each smile I managed to wrestle out of him, my insides doing victory dances whenever those lips tilted up.

His smile was the best sight I'd ever seen, putting the Liberty Bell I passed by for the four years straight I attended college to shame. Any words tumbled from his lips became my new favorite words.

Annie, a growl when I mercilessly teased him.

Bonita, a whisper when I took a piece of me and handed it over to him as keepsake.

I turned off the TV when I heard the click of the bathroom door. Hector walked in, not looking at me. I swore the only reason he didn't find my eyes after his shower was because of the want he saw in them.

The towel wrapped around his waist was my exclusive form of torture, giving me just enough to have my imagination run wild. His hardened stomach forming a V, a trail of dark hair disappearing into the towel. His wide shoulders and hard chest coated with little drops of water he missed. He dropped the towel, giving me a stellar view of two perfect globes of ass. Delicious ass. Better than cinnamon rolls, at least that's what I told myself when I couldn't tear my gaze away from the sight.

I climbed on the bed when he turned around, in the middle of pulling his boxers up his muscular thighs. "You see something you like, bonita?"

I smirked, folding my body under the blanket and turning on my side. "It takes two to tango, right?" I blinked behind my lashes.

He threw on a pair of shorts and a t-shirt faster than I could blink. The memory of the two of us in the gym assaulting his memory. I laughed, settling deeper into bed. He threw his towel in the hamper and grabbed his blanket before settling in next to me.

A request of another memory of his time with his mom was on the tip of my tongue when he beat me to it. "I've always wondered something."

"Hmm," I hummed.

"What's with the jeans?"

I rubbed my legs together underneath the blanket, reveling in the feel of the material. I grabbed a fist around the collar of one of Hector's shirts I had on. "My mom's dream was to be a mom. She could've been anything. She was smart and she was always the prettiest woman in the room. But all she wanted was to become a mother, and she always wanted a daughter. Someone she could dress up in cute clothes, do each other's makeup, paint our nails together. She was the textbook definition of a girly-girl. From ages one to twelve, I didn't own a pair of jeans. She coordinated my outfits every day, always either in dresses or cute sweaters and leggings.

"We were the picture perfect mother-daughter combo. After she died, after I realized what I was going to do." His hand reached over, curling around the ends of my hair but I didn't call him out on it. "I bought my first pair of jeans from the thrift store. They were tight. I felt them with each step I took. With dresses and sweaters, it's comfortable. I wasn't comfortable. I was on edge, running toward the future as fast as I could."

I shrugged. "I guess it stuck. I wear jeans because it reminds me not to get comfortable. It reminds me that I have to be on edge. I feel the denim digging into my skin from the waist all the way down to the hem."

He didn't say anything for a while in a silence I had grown familiar with. Each time I shared a piece of me, he seemed to think about it, process it, and maybe even tuck it away somewhere like he'd have to call back on it in the future. I couldn't read him, see what thoughts swirled inside of that head of his, not when he hid those brown eyes from me.

We spent the night in silence. Him thinking about my jeans and me falling asleep to the beauty of him. Just before I fell asleep, his finger tugged at my hair and my eyes fluttered open. "Thank you," he whispered.

"For what," I whispered back.

He seemed to think, to search for the perfect words. "For letting me see the real Annie. She's so much more beautiful without her weapons."

I swallowed past the lump in my throat and closed my eyes, but I didn't fall asleep for a very long time.

***

His words echoed in my head all through the night and they were the first thing I heard when I opened my eyes. *For letting me see the real Annie. She's so much more beautiful without her weapons.*

I stopped, the very next morning, and took a pause on life. I didn't rush to go downstairs to eat breakfast with him. I didn't anticipate a day of work, a shooting session at lunch time. I didn't think about tonight, if Hector would sit next to me again, or what we would confess to each other once we were both tucked in for the night.

I turned the water on, allowing it to heat up before stripping out of my clothes, and standing before the massive mirror Hector had above the basin.

I didn't flinch at the sight of my reflection. My skin no longer felt prickly like it belonged to someone else. Leaning up against the framework of the sink, looking into the depths of my eyes, a blank canvas didn't appear. The words that have assaulted me for years resurfaced, but this time they weren't admonishing. No, this time, for the first time, they seemed hopeful.

I don't know who I am but it's not the end of the world that I don't.
I don't know who I am but it doesn't make me uncomfortable anymore.
I don't know who I am... but I'm learning.

Turning away from the mirror, I jumped into the shower, the pressure from the shower head pelting my skin, effectively soaking my face allowing me to believe that the water was the reason for my soaked cheeks.

After I dressed for the day, I ventured downstairs. I peeked into the gym, thinking I'd find Hector lifting. But the room was empty. I walked into the kitchen and he wasn't in there, either. I pulled out my phone to call him when I noticed a chain of text messages from him.

I have something to take care of this morning.
Nolan will take you to work today.
Go easy on him, please.
Have a good day, bonita.
There is a plate of pancakes on a hot plate in the
microwave in case you're not in the mood for cereal.

The warm feeling in the pit of my stomach crawled through my body until a smile blossomed on my lips. I didn't bother fighting it.

I turned, heading straight for my pancakes when I caught sight of Nolan sitting at the bar, sipping a cup of coffee. My phone slipped from my hands, a shrill scream escaping my lips. "Shit. Fuck. Shit. Fuck." I didn't even know what I was saying, my erratic heart cutting a circuit somewhere in my brain.

"Are those the only words you know?" he asked quietly before averting his gaze from my gaping.

"Nolan." I said his name, pressing a hand over my chest.

He peeked up from his lashes and nodded at me. "Annie." His voice held a soft note to it, like my name settled him.

I retrieved my phone from the floor, trying to get to my pancakes once more. "How many times have you been in the same room as me and I haven't noticed?"

I grabbed my plate before sitting beside him at the bar. "A handful of times, I suppose," he admitted from behind his coffee mug.

"Why don't you ever do something? Clear your throat. Scuff your shoes. Something."

He hitched one shoulder up in a shrug. "I'm used to being alone, I suppose. And if I'm not in a room by myself, the people in the room are usually too self-absorbed to notice anyone but themselves."

I held up a fork, offering a some of my food. Nolan shook his head. "You know something about being alone?" he asked warily, vulnerability leaking out of his voice that I felt like a crack in my chest.

I nodded, chewing Hector's fluffy goodness. "There were a few years in my life when I had no one. I was utterly alone and I felt it in each step I took like loneliness was a tangible thing. Once I moved out of New Hazle into the city for school, things shifted. I met Matt, who somehow saw past my bitchy comments and decided I was worth talking to. And now, I have Hector."

I didn't know how long I had him for. I tried not to think about that. At all.

Nolan scrunched his nose at the mention of Matt's name. "Do you have an issue with Matt?"

He squared his shoulders defensively. I would be asking Matt about that later. "He's tolerable."

I snorted. "That he is."

I considered the man in front of me. The one who liked to stay hidden. The one who never sought out company. "Do you feel alone?"

I averted my eyes, hoping that would make him comfortable to talk to me. His whisper came not even a second later. "Sometimes. I have a family I adore. People in my inner circle I care about. But my mind always keeps them at an arm's length. I could be in a crowd of a million people and I'd still feel like I'm stranded on a deserted island."

I wanted to reach out to him but if he flinched from my touch, I wasn't sure my heart could take it. "I've felt like that before."

I snuck a look at him to see his lips tilted, a dimple poking out on his left cheek. It was adorable. It brought out a boyish look to his features I decided right then and there I loved. "But not anymore," he mused, his smile growing.

My nose scrunched up. "Do you have something to say, Nolan?"

He shook his head and looked down at his phone. "Are you ready?"

I let his musings go, probably because he wanted an answer I wasn't ready to give.

❄

The only time I called Hector was to tell him when my shift ended. He and I never texted before, the only texts I received from him was the chain from this morning. He didn't seem like a person who texted. And if the unread messages from Matt and the two almost-friends who still texted me every so often from my internship at the shelter said anything, I wasn't much of one either. So, it made no sense that in the six hours since Nolan dropped me off at work, I pulled open a blank message labeled to him and stared at the blank screen.

I would write a message before promptly deleting it, letting my phone turn black before repeating the process all over again. Even the meticulous process of cleaning guns couldn't keep my mind off of him.

After deleting the first thirty drafts, I couldn't take it anymore. I wanted to hear his voice, even if I got sent to his voicemail that would be enough to hold me over until he picked me up. He was a drug and I'd become way too addicted to him.

It didn't even ring once before his sigh rang through my ear. "I'm in the middle of a meeting right now. I'll have Nolan pick you up." He didn't say my name. He didn't call me beautiful. But his voice was tender, instantly warming my skin.

I frowned. "How long are you going to be?"

"Probably about an hour but I can just have Nolan come and get you."

I thought about them two. About how they seemed to switch from partners to brothers so effortlessly. That worked for everything but me. The two weren't interchangeable. No one could replace Hector in my eyes. "I'll wait for you."

He groaned over the line.

I chuckled. "I'll just grab something to eat nearby. Just come whenever you can." I hung up before he could argue with me. It was a tactic I learned from him whenever he talked on the phone. He'd give his command and hang up. It was a thrilling feeling.

I grabbed my jacket and closed my office door, slipping out of the range without gaining anyone's attention. I noticed, over the past couple of weeks, on my trip to C&C, a locally owned coffee shop and bakery combo, during my lunch break, a new buzz-worthy food truck opened. I kept waiting for the line to diminish but it had been weeks and the line, if anything, expanded.

I walked to it now, time on my hands. I shoved my hands in the pockets of my jean jacket and let my eyes roam the city. Though I've lived in the heart of the city for four years, I'd never been able to appreciate it before now. I had a one-track mind, focusing on the next thing. A shift at the shooting range. An arm session in the gym. A due paper. I was the farthest thing from a city college girl.

I walked to the end of the line spanning two blocks, my eyes wandering. I caught glimpses of couples on the street kissing, a group of girls with barely anything on, shaking their asses, clearly a little bit tipsy, a guitarist playing on the corner, his guitar case open accepting tips, young guys with their chests painted a deep green and white shouting, "Go Eagles!" My lips curved up in a smile, caught up in other people's moments when a harsh voice sounded beside me. "Yo, little girl, move your pretty little ass, I'm hungry."

I whipped my head back to reveal a man standing too close, looming over me, impatience written across his face. I narrowed my eyes at him, but he wasn't fazed, a slimy smirk spreading across his face. I turned back around and did exactly what he said. I stepped up, placed an order of two sandwiches. One loaded with peppers, cheese, and onions for Hector and one with just onions and cheese for me.

Once I paid and took my sandwiches, I stepped to the side of the truck, leaning up against it, waiting for the guy who thought he could comment on my body and I wouldn't have something to say about it. I never took my eyes off of him as he ordered a sandwich, already forgetting about me. Thankfully, he walked my way.

"Yo," I called out to him, my voice dripping with sarcasm. "Move your pretty little ass, you're blocking my view."

His head whipped around to the sound of my voice and he slunk toward me, his asshole energy potent in the air. He bit off a big piece of his already unwrapped sandwich, the grease dribbling from his chin.

Gross.

The closer he got to me, the more arrogance I could smell rolling off of him. He didn't stop until his body brushed up against mine and I had to fight the urge to shudder. "I know just the thing to hush that mouth up," he said, his eyes darting to my lips.

I tilted my head to the side. "You know what's more powerful than my lips?" I whispered, standing on the tips of my toes, my mouth parallel with the shell of his ear.

"My hands." I grabbed him by the balls and twisted with all of my arm strength. His eyes went wide, glossing over with tears, forgetting his precious sandwich. With my other hand, I covered his mouth before he could scream. His knees connected with the concrete beneath my feet.

"My feet." I ground the heel of my Vans into his groin until he laid flat on his back, my feet pinning him to the ground. I kicked him away when I noticed a trail of tears sliding down his cheeks. He rocked back and forth, groaning and cursing under his breath.

I stepped over his writhing body, just barely holding back an eye roll. "A piece of advice: there's as much power in being a woman as there is in being a man. Think about that the next time you want to catcall one."

With my head held high, I walked back to the shooting range to wait for Hector.

That familiar black car pulled into his normal parking spot moments later and I kicked off the building, the one thing my eyes starved for behind those tinted windows. I reached for the door, as a crunch sounded beneath my feet. I looked down seeing a crumpled piece of paper. Reaching down, I lifted the paper and unfolded it.

It was a flier, a picture of a black woman outlining the piece of paper. The woman tilted her head back, gripping a microphone so tightly the veins in her hands bubbled. Her high cheekbones, hard jaw, and a long, narrow nose contrasted against her rich brown skin to create the image of a breathtakingly gorgeous woman. A hoop nose ring glinted on her face bringing the only light to the photo. The woman's eyebrows scrunched together, worry lines spreading across her forehead. If pain could be something physical, it would be the look on her face.

My eyes studied the piece of paper, something foreign taking up inside of my chest. My hands gripped the flier, my heart thudded hard against my chest. Something about this woman called to me. I couldn't understand it but I knew I had to.

My eyes roamed the rest of the flier seeing the name of a café located a few blocks away from the range. At the bottom, the woman's name was written, identifying her as special guest, Aliyah Rae. The date was set for Friday, tomorrow night. I folded the paper and stuffed it in my pocket.

Opening the door, I immediately sought out Hector. My heart skipped a beat, seeing him. He sat behind the steering wheel, his legs spread, both of his hands tapping on the top of the steering wheel to the beat of the Spanish music playing quietly in the background. He was too goddamn sexy for his own good. Climbing up into my seat, ignoring how the sight of him made me forget about how most men were complete animals, I said, "I got you a sandwich. Every pepper they had in stock is on it."

His lips tilted up into a smile as he pulled the car from the curb.

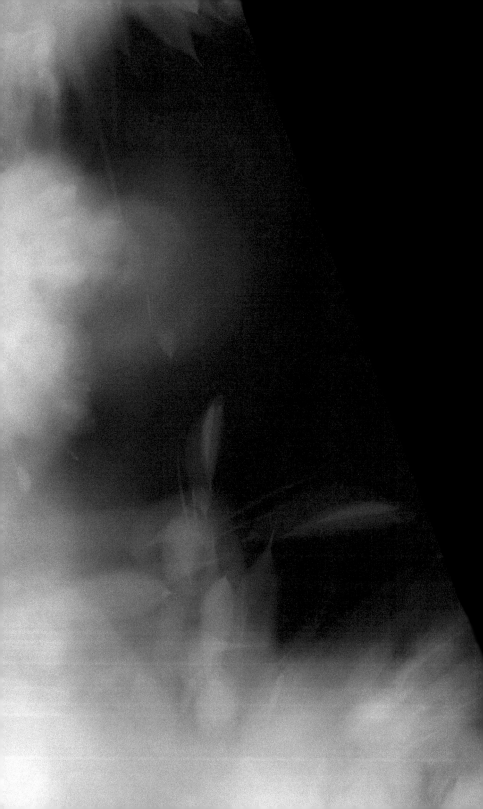

CHAPTER EIGHTEEN

Annie

O pening my eyes the next morning, a different face greeted me. Replacing the familiar brown eyes that had become my favorite sight, this face belonged to an unfamiliar person.

Aliyah Rae. The woman from the flier.

All through the night I tossed and turned, the image of this woman flashing through my mind. The flier, I had since memorized, informed me of only her name and that she wrote and performed poetry.

I needed to know this woman, her story. I couldn't explain it but I felt as though her haunted face was calling out to me. The image of her becoming clearer and clearer until I memorized every inch of her face. Sitting up in bed, I plucked the crumpled piece of paper from my pocket, unfolding it once more, my fingers trailing over the front.

I sprang from the bed, my decision made. I was going out tonight. And for the first time, it wasn't for work or school. A night out in the city, just me for me. The idea seemed foreign but not uncomfortable. My heart raced with excitement, the feeling ranging somewhere between an insufferable weight on my chest and someone clipping my wings.

This felt big in a way I couldn't quite describe. It was the same feeling I got on the day my mom woke me up, kissing my cheeks all over and telling me we were leaving New Hazle behind. More importantly, we were leaving Cameron Wade behind. The same feeling on the day I knew I'd have my chance at killing him, the same feeling a day later when I woke up in Hector's bed.

Just like my mom's death and Hector invading my life, I didn't think I'd be the same Annie I was the day before. That woman with a beautiful face in spite of the pain that twisted her features had words. Words I was desperate to hear.

I grabbed my basket of dirty clothes and headed down to the laundry room. I called Matt once I transferred a load into the washer. "What's wrong?"

I frowned, rarely ever hearing worry settle into his voice. Not unless he was ranting about his mother signing him up for an online dating website. "Why would something be wrong?" He grunted, offering me nothing else. "Someone's moody."

Another grunt. I opened my mouth to ask him if he was having sex withdrawals when his whisper sounded in my ear. "Why didn't you tell me, Annie?"

My heart stopped, the fear of my plan of murder keeping my blood flowing. I didn't want to be seen as someone capable of murder. I didn't want to be seen as evil. Not by Matt, not by anyone. Hector, and maybe Nolan by association, was the only person I could trust with that part of me. Because he's killed. Because when he learned the truth, he held me tighter instead of shoving me away.

"Tell you what?" I asked, afraid of the answer.

"That you were in trouble. I could have helped you. I could have saved you."

I wanted to tell him I didn't want or need help. And I sure as hell, didn't need anyone saving me.

"Instead, you chose Hector Rivera out of all people. You have no idea what kind of man he is."

Rivera. I finally had a last name. I temporarily forgot about Matt, thinking about how it suited him. I wanted to hear it coming from his lips, his tongue rolling on the r's, producing my favorite sound in the world.

I zoned back in to hear Matt droning on. "You should come live with me. Pack your bags, tell me where you are, and I'll come pick you up."

Annoyance consumed me. He and Hector were polar opposites, day and night.

Matt was daylight, always happy and strutting through life carefree. Nothing bothered him. If it didn't happen today, it would happen tomorrow. He wanted to save me. He wanted to own me. I was an accessory he could put on his arm and show off to all of his friends. The sad truth was he didn't even know me. Not even a version of me.

Hector knew all of me. He was nightfall, a tightness in my chest as I looked at him, knowing the next day the confessions I made in the dark would only make his eyes grow fonder when the sun rose. He didn't want to save me; he wanted me to save myself. I was something to be cherished and respected. And that flooded my chest with warmth more than a million grins ever could.

"Matt."

He hummed. He was drunk, half-asleep by the sound of his voice. I didn't think he'd remember this phone call by the time he sobered up but I had to say the words.

"You have to give up on this idea that there's going to be an us."

I shut my eyes, letting my face fall to the glass window of the washer, the water soothing me. I knew if I'd ever become an us with anybody, it would be with the man I would never deserve. The one who forced me to look in the mirror and urged me to love what I saw reflecting back at me. The one who made my heart sing with one flash of those brown eyes. Whose touch lit my body up like the fourth of July. Who became a part of my identity with each passing day, that I forgot what it was like to not soak him up every day.

I hung up the phone and turned around in desperate need of coffee. I screamed when I caught a glimpse of Hector posted on the wall, said cup of coffee in his hand.

He lifted an eyebrow in amusement before kicking into his full height and ambling toward me slowly, as if he were approaching a wild animal. I didn't take my eyes off of him, not until I could smell the sweat on him from his morning workout.

His free hand reached up, tucking a strand of loose hair behind my ear. The slightest brush of his fingertip on the shell of my ear spread a wave of goosebumps from my shoulders to my ankles. I curled my toes against the soft plush of the carpet.

"Are you okay, bonita?"

I pressed my lips together, not trusting my voice when the effect of his touch still lingered, and nodded. I just squealed at his sudden appearance. I wasn't about to let him know his touch held the same effect.

The look in his eye told me he didn't believe me. He was a smart man. "We're going to be late," he said, before turning away from me.

"I'm staying home today." I still had to text Matt since that's the reason I called him in the first place.

He handed me my cup of coffee and I relished in the warmth it spread through my fingertips.

He frowned. "You don't have work today?"

"I called Matt and told him I wouldn't be there."

"Are you planning on staying here?"

I nodded my head as I followed him into the kitchen.

"Do you want me to stay with you? I could have Nolan—"

I shook my head, behind the mug, maybe too quickly because his jaw clenched. "No, you go and do whatever it is that you do." I paused, avoiding his eyes. "I do have to go somewhere tonight."

"Where?" he grunted, suspicion lining his features.

"A café. There's sort of a show I want to go to." He smiled. A big, toothy smile. One I didn't even have to fight for. I pressed my hand against his chest, relishing in how it started beating faster almost instantly. I batted my eyes up at him. "Will you be my date?"

Nothing had changed from that first day he drove me into the city. He still wouldn't be seen with me in public. Whenever I did bring it up, he reverted back to the broody version of himself. And as much as I found the frown lines in his forehead goddamn adorable, I much preferred his soft smiles and his teasing tone.

His teeth snuck out and captured his bottom lip and I fought the urge to break our eye contact. But I must have been smiling because he scoffed, folding his hand over mine and tearing it away from his chest. He turned on his heel, heading toward the door. "Breakfast is on the table. I'll be back in time to drop you off," he called over his shoulder.

I spent the rest of the day in solitude, nothing to keep me company but the vanilla ice cream and caramel Hector had me hooked on and the *Criminal Minds* marathon running on TV.

I hopped in the shower, my nerves turning jittery as the night approached. I was actually doing this. Getting out of the shower, I walked into the bedroom, pressing on the wall closest to where I slept, revealing a closet.

The closet was easily the size of my dorm room at college. A simple white bench with dark gray cushions lined the wall. Shelves for hanging up clothes overlooking the seating area. There was a single mirror on each end of the room. Hector showed me this space that was only for me months ago. Every day before today, I'd go in, avoid the mirrors and pick out clean clothes to wear.

I didn't fill the room. I barely filled a foot of the room. It remained as empty as it was when he originally showed me the room with the exception of the clothes I brought with me, my two copies of *The Count of Monte Cristo*, and my suitcase and backpack. I fit my outfits in three drawers, although I probably could have fit them all in one.

Nine outfits in plastic bags hung on the clothing rack.

Nine outfits for the nine birthdays of my mom's I've missed.

She was a beauty queen. Her dress code consisted of heels and dresses or cute silky tops and slim fitting jeans. It genuinely surprised me she didn't have a modeling career. Where I was a size six, okay, maybe it was closer to an eight since I've been here with Hector who cooked the best of everything, my mother had been a size zero. Tall and skinny, a beautiful face that made the silly selfies we took in the bathroom mirror seem like professional photos.

Her birthday was the only day of the year, every year, that I let myself go. I spent the day doing the things I knew would make her happy. I went shopping, buying an outfit she would wear. I went to a salon and got a matching manicure and pedicure. I had my eyebrows done. It was the one day I channeled my inner-mama. I knew, if she was alive, she would have been dragging me out to do these things, not just on special occasions but probably every weekend. We would have told each other secrets. We would have talked about boys.

I wondered if she would like Hector. If she would like him for me. She was my best friend but she was also a mother. Maybe she would hate him. Maybe she wouldn't approve of the gap between us. But maybe she would see things in him that she never saw in Cameron. A man who really saw me, who wanted to protect me, who cared about me.

I groaned, shaking both of them from my thoughts. This night had me jittery enough. I didn't need to think about questions I would never know the answers to.

I grabbed the outfit I bought last year. A deep red floral print cami-romper. I pulled it over my legs and stomach, not glancing in the mirror until the straps settled over my shoulders. The silk rubbed against my skin, an acute contrast to my normal jeans. The hem of the shorts ended a little bit above mid-thigh. I could bend over and not flash anyone, but just barely. My neck was completely exposed, a deep V plunging down to reach the top of my navel. A thin strip of fabric across my breastbone helped my breasts stay tucked away. I threw on a pair of white Vans, avoiding all mirrors, scared I'd chicken out.

I flew down the stairs the moment I heard Hector arrive, just barely throwing on my jean jacket. He hadn't even made it out of the darkened living room when he caught sight of me. He froze mid-step and I did, too, holding on to the banister to keep my balance as he perused the length of my body.

He didn't say anything.

He didn't come forward.

But I could see his eyes caressing every inch of my body.

I wrapped my hands around the lapels of my jacket, thankful they hid my breasts. We'd both be in trouble if the layer wrapping around my upper body was exposed.

After an excruciatingly long moment, he cleared his throat. "Don't you have a strict dress code of only wearing jeans?" he asked, his voice scratchy.

I bit back my smile, stepping off the last stair and sauntering up to him. I shrugged like it was no big deal. "Are you ready?" I asked, laying my hand in between his pecs.

He plucked my hand from his chest, placing it by my side before giving me a tight nod. I followed him outside, pausing as he locked the house up. "Me juró que dejaría de intentar matarme. Pinche mentirosa," he muttered under his breath. *Translation: She swore to me she'd stop trying to kill me. Fucking liar.* I ducked my head, hiding my smile at his words.

We didn't say a word to each other as he drove into the city. The Latin station played through the speakers and Hector tapped the steering wheel, but his fingers couldn't catch the beat to save his life.

As for me, I tried my hardest not to fidget in my seat. I felt bare. I felt naked. It wasn't so much that more of my skin was unconcealed than not. It had more to do with the fabric. It felt fun and flirty. No hardness, no faux protection.

"How long is this thing?" Hector grumbled from his side of the car.

I looked over at him. He stared straight ahead even though I knew he felt my eyes on him. "It starts at eight and it's a two-hour show." I paused. "Is that past your bedtime, old man?"

He glowered straight ahead but the corners of his mouth twitched, giving him away.

He pulled in the first parking spot he could. The city starting to wake up as the dusk settled in. I leaned forward, adrenaline coursing through me. "Can I see your phone?"

I pulled my phone out of my pocket and handed it over. "I put Nolan's phone number in there. If something happens, call him. He'll be the closest to you."

I narrowed my eyes at him. "Is Nolan going to be in there?"

"No. This is something you need to do alone, right?"

I swallowed past the lump in my throat. "Yes." My voice nothing more than a gust of breath.

"Give it your all, bonita." He leaned toward me, grabbing my chin in between his two fingers before planting a kiss on the center of my cheek. My eyes fell shut, torn between wanting to escape this car and asking him to never deny me his lips again. "I'll be back to pick you up in two hours."

He let me go and I grabbed the handle, looking back at him. He smiled at me and tipped his head in encouragement, cementing the fact that I didn't deserve him.

After I hopped out of the car and watched Hector drive away, I stood in line at the entrance of McNutt's Cafe. A couple of minutes later, I paid the admittance fee and headed straight to the bar and ordered a beer, hoping it would quiet the anxiety thrumming through my veins.

The stage was located on the opposite end of the café from the entry doors. A bar ran across almost the entire length of the room on each side of the stage. Little round tables filtered through the center of the room. Most of the tables were filled with duos and groups of people, so I found a seat at the bar closer to the stage. I leaned back against the bar, bottle pressed against my lips and waited.

At exactly eight o'clock, the lights dimmed and the busy chatter turned into last minute whispering. A spotlight focused on the center of a stage where only a microphone and a bar stool sat. The bartender who got me my drink rushed to the stage, announcing the first act.

The woman who walked on stage introduced herself as Maya Reynolds, adjusting the microphone to fit her barely five-foot frame. She was a curvy girl with ivory skin, faded pink hair and bright green eyes. In contrast, she looked nothing like the woman on the flier that had drawn me here.

Kissing
I see it everywhere
In the streets
On the big screen
I see my mother kiss my dad when she passes him in the kitchen
I see it in the malls
I see it in my favorite spot,
On the elevator.
Up, up, up the feeling when you kiss someone.
It makes your hands shake,
And your heart race,
It sets fire in your veins,
Brings a curve to your lips
When people see you kiss.

She paused for a long moment, pulling in a deep breath.

When people see me kiss,
It's a different story.
It makes their hands shake
With fury
What kind of example are two girls kissing setting for their children?
It makes their heart race
With hate
Because how dare I kiss someone who also has ovaries
It sets fire in their veins
With unease

Because I can kiss my girlfriend whenever I want as long as they don't have to see it

It brings a curve to their lips

Full of distaste

Because the sight of two girls in love is not natural.

Kissing.

It's just *kissing.*

My heart had stopped beating from the moment Maya started speaking. Her voice was loud and strong and passionate. I never thought passion could be something physical, something I could see with my own two eyes. In under a minute, a poet by the name of Maya Reynolds proved me wrong. The way she spoke the words. Her tone fierce and her face confident. Before I could blink, I was certain of one thing, I was in love.

She read a few more poems that had to deal with being an out lesbian. Every word she spoke brought chills across my arms and bare legs. Her set finished just after thirty minutes and the bartender returned to the stage to announce that the floor was free for the next half hour.

I drained my first beer and ordered another one, barely taking my eyes off of the stage. The people who jumped at the open mic opportunity were all different and what they shared on stage just as equal in difference. There were women, men, and non-binary poets from all different ethnicities, and their poetry reflected that. Some talked about being invisible. Some talked about anger and passion. Some talked about love and heartbreak. And some just talked about how good they were at giving head.

When the clock struck nine o'clock, a wave of silence fell over everyone. The bartender did not return to the stage to announce the main event poet. No, the woman that had drawn me here in the first place, walked on the stage slowly, until she was under the bright light. She didn't seem fazed by everyone's attention on her. Her face was somber, her eyes unreadable. She hadn't said a word yet and I found myself teetering on the bar stool, feeling a wave of awe settle over me.

Thirty seconds.

Nine months.

That's how long it takes for you to be born.

A pair of scissors and a steady hand is all it takes for you to be free.

It's not the same for me.

I am old enough to buy alcohol,

Enlist in the army,

Buy a car.

But it feels as if I'm just two seconds old.

That cord wrapping around my neck when I turn on the TV

And I see it.

I see white people painting their faces black

I see cops killing innocent men because their skin is black

I see racial slurs at basketball players when the sport is dominated by men who are black

I see people who look like me being treated as

Entertainment

Slaves

A Statistic.

I claw at that cord that's wrapped around my neck.
I'm screaming for it to become loose.
I'm crying for it to become loose.
I'm dying for it to become loose.
Before my chance at life is over and
I lose.

I was a believer in having your life changed in a matter of seconds. It happened to me before. Once when I lost my mother and once when Hector hijacked his way into my life. And now, it was happening again. With Maya and Aliyah's words, with poetry.

Long after Aliyah left the stage, I sat there on the bench, my eyes glued to the center stage, my heart hurting, my mind inspired, and my jaw still dropped in awe. I was mesmerized. It wasn't until the bartender nudged me that I tore my eyes away and shut my mouth. "You want another one," he asked, motioning to my almost full bottle.

I shook my head and paid my bill and somehow made my feet move me outside and then toward Hector's car. For the first time, I didn't seek him out as I got in and buckled up. I collapsed against my seat, closing my eyes, completely spent.

I didn't know what I expected from tonight but it wasn't this. I felt like my mind was swept of all knowledge and the only thing I now knew was the prose of poetry. About the written word transferring to spoken word in such a powerful way, it's almost as if I dreamt it. I didn't feel real in this moment. It was too beautiful to be real. It was too inspiring to be real. It was too real to be real.

It was a few minutes before I felt the car move, almost hesitantly.

"Did you have a good time?" Hector asked softly when we made it outside of the city. I didn't respond. I couldn't. I hadn't felt like this before. Like I found something that was so vital to me as a human that I didn't know how I lived without it before.

"Let's not talk," I said, my voice hard and unrecognizable even to my own ears. He didn't say another word and I was grateful.

I blinked my eyes open, turning my head to face the window. Flashes of green greeted me, calming my wild heart. I couldn't stop the tears welling up in my eyes. And I didn't fight them as they fell past my eyelids, staining my cheeks.

Tonight changed me. Something altered inside of me that, if I'm being honest, had been settling in over the past two months.

It had been the morning I woke up in a strange bed thinking it was heaven. It was when I ate a pound of *hot* hot sauce and he made it all better. It was how his anger became all-consuming when I told him who Cameron Wade was to me. It was how he made a deal with me so I could have a life after taking one.

I twisted my head, seeking him out. He was beautiful, growing sweeter on my eyes every time my eyes landed on him. His eyes focused on the road, an elbow propped up on the door, his fist holding his head upright. His other hand didn't strum against the steering wheel to the beat of the music. Probably because there was no music. He must have turned it off and I hadn't even noticed.

I reached out for him, trailing my fingers across his forearm. The dust of dark hair rose against his skin. He shot me a questioning glance, grabbing the steering wheel with his other hand. I peeled his hand from the steering wheel, bringing it down between us.

I stared at our hands. His big to my small. His brown to my white. Yet, somehow, in spite of how it looked, it felt so right. It was him who separated my fingers with his and curled his palm around mine.

I was a planner, and by default, a thinker. It hit me tonight as Aliyah was sharing her story through prose that somewhere along the way, I had stopped feeling a long time ago. Tonight changed that. If I was being honest, *he* changed that.

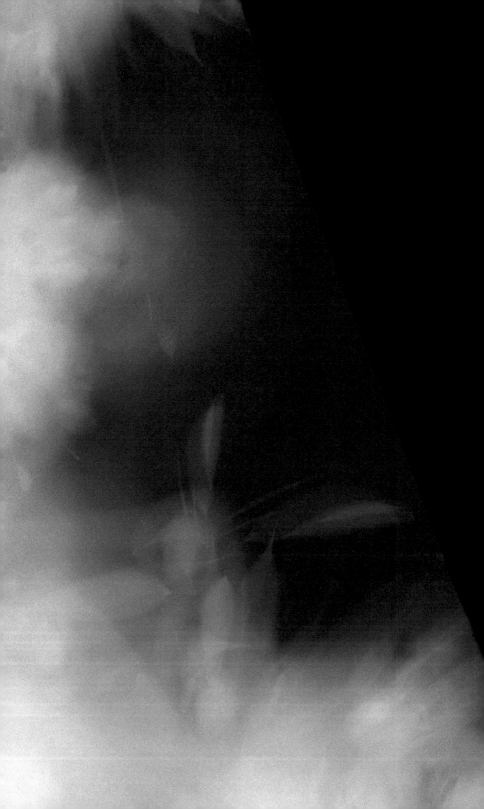

CHAPTER NINETEEN

Annie

I held Hector's hand the entire way home. Once we were out of his car, I recaptured his hand and followed him into the house and into the room we shared. We laid down in silence. I had a confession to make to him. Several. But not tonight. Tonight, I wanted to look at him. To study his face until I had every blemish and crevice memorized.

He didn't offer up any confessions of his own, knowing exactly what I needed in the moment. I fell asleep in his soft grip, the smallest of smiles curving his lips, and the knowledge that this man who had seemed like the biggest curse of my life a few months ago was masked as the biggest blessing of my life.

When I woke the next morning, my hand gripped where his hand should've been but I only grasped the sheet beneath my body

He always woke up before me. There were days I was grateful for it. Sometimes after one of our long talks, I needed to be alone. To face that fact that I confided him in a way I'd never imagined I could to another person.

But this morning was different. I wanted to look at him like I did each night in the light of day. I wanted to see his cheek twitching because he felt my gaze on him. I wanted his hand to still be cradling mine. I wanted him.

I threw the blankets off of me and trudged downstairs to find him. I followed the sounds of a soft Latin melody and the sizzling of grease. He stood over the stove, a spatula in one hand, his glass of eggs in his other.

I stopped in my tracks when our eyes clashed. His eyes focused on me, a question swirling in them. This wasn't the same Hector that I woke up to the day before. His face and body were still the same. He wore his usual getup of basketball shorts and a naked chest. But the way he looked today, felt different.

"Annie," he whispered, his eyebrow raising with concern.

The sound of my name on his lips tore a small gasp out of me. "Do you have a pen and paper?"

His eyebrows scrunched together but he turned around searching for the items I asked for. He slid them across the bar to me and I put pen to paper, scribbling furiously as words assaulted my brain.

I've heard people say
a girl with a gun is a powerful thing.
So why, when I held one in my hands,

did your kiss still bring me to my knees?

I read what I wrote once. And then once more. I read it again until I memorized the four lines. My head snapped up to Hector who studied me from across the small space.

"Are you okay, bonita?"

I nodded because I didn't want to lie to him. The truth is I was the farthest thing from okay. Poetry invaded my life in the same way that Hector did. One I fell in love with instantly and the other, it wasn't instant and it wasn't easy, but I was still halfway there.

We ate in silence and the drive into the city passed the same way. He didn't press me and I didn't offer anything up. The moment the car parked I was grabbing the handle and lurching out of the car, barely hearing his yell. "Call me if you need anything."

I walked into Philly Range with my head down and quickly slipped into my office. I sat down and got started on the cleaning of guns.

I didn't get lost in the mechanics of tearing the gun apart and putting it back together again. I couldn't get lost because I already was. Lost in a man. Lost in a man who supported me, who encouraged me. Who wanted nothing more out of me than for me to be who I am.

A knock at the door snapped me out of my thoughts. Matt stood there, his hands shoved in the pockets of his hoodie, a sheepish look on his face.

I set the gun down and hitched an eyebrow in his direction. "You know where I've been." It wasn't a question. How else could he have known about Hector when I hadn't once spoken his name inside of these walls? As much as I hated Hector's rule of being seen in public with him, I respected it.

He shuffled inside and sat down on the edge of the desk. "He saved you, right? You were in trouble and he saved you."

A couple of months ago, I would have argued that he didn't save me. He stopped me. He stalled me. But the Annie I was slowly discovering didn't want to argue because she agreed. "Something like that."

"What would have happened if he didn't save you? What would have happened if I saved you?"

"I would be settling into my new life in Mexico."

He flinched at my words but I couldn't find it in me to feel bad. He wanted the truth and he got it.

"Matt, there's a reason I never let you in on any of my secrets. You were never going to be a part of my escape plan. That's why I resisted our friendship for so long. The plan was always to leave you behind. I would miss you. I would think about you often. But you were always going to be a part of my past. Hector is different. Hector is everything. I can't imagine a future without him and I can't remember how I ever lived without him."

Matt sighed and stood tall, reaching his hand out for me. I accepted it warily, unsure of how he would accept my words. He pulled me into a hug and I let him. There was a time before Hector where Matt was all I had.

I could let him have this moment. I didn't wrap my arms around him; I just stood there as he took what he needed from me. He pulled back after a long moment and held me at a close distance. "We would have been great together," he murmured. I didn't say anything. It didn't help either of us to bruise his ego any more than I already had.

I stepped back, hoping he'd relinquish his hold on me. His hands gripped tighter around my biceps and before I knew it, his lips smashed against mine. I opened my mouth to protest and his tongue dipped inside of my mouth. I used my feet to kick his shin as hard as I could. He cursed, tearing his mouth away from mine. The disgust from his forceful kiss soaked every inch of my body. I no longer cared about his feelings. I only cared about mine.

I took advantage of his lessened height as he rubbed his shin and drew my hand back before landing an uppercut to his jaw. I didn't pull my punch, too much anger coursing through me. He fell backward as he howled in pain. His skin cracked at the contact, blood dripping on the floor.

"Annie, what the fuck?"

I leaned down until our eyes met. "That's the difference between you and him, Matt. You take what you want, fuck the consequences. He takes what I give him, nothing more and nothing less."

At my words, reality washed over him and regret flashed across his face. He opened his mouth to say something but he grimaced in pain. I hopped up and fished for my phone, calling for an ambulance.

I returned back to Matt's side and held his hand until the EMTs showed up. I wanted to tell him that I was sorry but I couldn't find it in me to voice the words. Friends or not, what he did was a dick move.

I backed away as soon as the paramedics swarmed in the room and started to assess him. I looked in the doorway just as a flash of white skin and raven black hair came running in, wild eyes searching for something, searching for me.

"Nolan?" I questioned.

He ran up to me and placed his hands on me warily. His eyes

traced over my head, down to my arms, looking for any sign of harm. "I'm okay," I promised him.

His eyes left me, narrowing in Matt's direction, somehow putting the puzzle pieces together. I grabbed his hand to distract him. "Do you know anything about bank accounts?"

As soon as he nodded, I started to steer us out of my office. "Good. I need one and we could have lunch while we're out." My eyes flicked to the EMTs transferring Matt's body onto a stretcher. "Unless I need to make a statement once the cops arrive."

"The cops aren't coming, Annie."

"Isn't that what usually happens?" I didn't know. It's not like I went around assaulting people.

Nolan quirked a shoulder up. "Usually."

CHAPTER TWENTY

Hector

"Are you planning on eating dinner in here, bonita?"

I had been standing in this spot for the past ten minutes staring at Annie. Her silence from this morning had transferred into the evening. She's barely said ten words to me all day and we'd been home for over an hour. On her way in, she brushed past me, heading straight into my study. I didn't use this room for anything. Mostly, I used it to file receipts and other documentation from my various businesses. But Annie found my computer, the various blank notebooks and pens, and made herself comfortable.

Her head snapped up, her cheeks flushing a deep shade of pink.

I tilted my head suspiciously. She dropped the pencil she'd been writing with on top of the desk, slamming the cover to her notebook

I had to bite my lip to hold back the hundreds of questions I wanted to ask. She would come to me in her own time. I knew she would.

"Is it ready?"

I hummed my answer, my eyes glued on that notebook, her hands still curled around the closed notebook. My eyes only left the bundle of paper when she stood, moving around the desk. She ducked her head, avoiding my eyes, brushing past me. I turned to walk in step with her. I reached out, my fingers grabbing her neck softly, my fingers splayed across her warm skin. She froze at my touch. "Are you okay?" I whispered.

She tilted her head back and I let go of her neck, trailing my hands down her back. "I'm okay, Hector," she assured me just as quietly. She turned against me, resting her palm in the center of my chest. Before I knew what was happening, she curled up against me, wrapping her arms around my back.

I tensed for a few seconds until my mind caught up with the rest of my body and enveloped the woman in my arms. I palmed her head against my chest, running my hands over her hair in deep, slow strokes.

"A while ago, you thanked me." She spoke into my chest, her voice muffled. "You thanked me for letting you know me." She cleared her throat, bunching my shirt up in two fistfuls. "The thing is, when we met, I didn't know who I was. So, it's really me who should be thanking you."

I tugged on her hair until those eyes raised to meet mine. Her hands loosened against my back. "Thank you, Hector. Thank you for seeing me when I was too afraid to look in a mirror. No matter what your intentions were when we first met, you changed my life."

I dropped my forehead to hers. "I didn't do anything."

Her hands snuck up and cradled my face. I wanted to kiss her so fucking bad. Her lips were right there. All I'd have to do is lean in, barely an inch, and the lips I felt like I'd been craving my whole life would be mine again. "I know you're dying to ask me about what's happened last night and then this morning and I want to tell you." Her thumb swept across my cheeks. "But I don't think I'm ready yet."

I nodded, moving both of our heads in the process. Taking a deep breath, I opened my eyes, placing my hands over hers and lifting them from my face. I closed the space between us, ghosting my lips across her cheek. "Tell me when you're ready. I'm not going anywhere."

She nodded, curling back into me as we walked into the kitchen.

We started eating the moment we sat down. Annie stuffing her face like she hadn't eaten anything all day. Neither of us made it through one serving before my phone went off, flashing Nolan's name.

I walked into the living room before picking it up, turning on the TV to the basketball pre-show. "Yes?"

"Matt's in the hospital."

I frowned. Since when did I give a fuck what happened to Matt Panini? "Nolan, there better be a good reason behind this phone call," I grumbled.

"His jaw is fractured. It was touch and go for a while but the doctors said a wiring wasn't necessary for him to recover."

"Why do I care, Nolan? He probably deserved it."

Nolan's voice dropped to a whisper as he dropped a bombshell on me. "He tried to kiss Annie."

"What?" I roared.

"I was waiting for her to come out of the range for her lunch when I saw the ambulances pull up in front and rush into the building. I ran in, afraid she was hurt. Once I realized she was fine, we left and the paramedics escorted him to the hospital."

My blood boiled at the thought of him touching her. I collapsed onto the couch, shoving my hands into my hair. "Did she kiss him back?" I whispered.

"No, Hector. She pushed him off and then decked him. And Hector, she didn't pull her punches." Nolan chuckled, admiration evident in his voice.

"Is he still there now?"

"Room 204."

I ended the call, sliding into my sneakers and grabbing my keys from the kitchen. Annie was long gone, tucked back into the study. I left without telling her and raced down to New Hazle Medical.

I didn't know exactly what I planned to do. Annie took care of the situation and herself. There wasn't really anything for me to do. But I warned him. I fucking warned him not to get between me and Annie.

I arrived, taking the elevators to the second floor. I hopped off of the elevator, my eyes seeking out his room. "Can I help you?" A woman stepped into my path, a bright smile lighting up her face.

"I need room 204."

She narrowed her eyes up at me and I didn't know why but I wanted to knock my knuckles against her nose. She was the most adorable thing I'd ever seen. A short woman with short brown hair and delicate features. "Are you family?"

"Would I be here if I wasn't?"

Her lips puckered. "You didn't answer my question."

"You didn't answer mine."

"Lacey." Lily's voice snapped our banter, both of our eyes turning to my favorite doctor.

She shot daggers at me as she wrapped her hands protectively around the woman's shoulders. I received the message clearly as if she'd spoken the words aloud. *Don't fuck with her.*

"Mr. Collins is calling for you again." Lacey sighed halfheartedly. "And you, go ahead back. It's the last room on the left. I have to get going before I miss tip-off."

Lily walked past me, hissing a warning at me. "Behave."

We all went our separate ways. I walked down the long corridor, sliding the glass door open before closing it behind me. I drew the shades, enclosing us in the dim light of the hospital room.

Matt's eyes flicked open as if he felt my anger palpitating through the room. I could barely see his face, gauze wrapped around his jaw. His uncovered eyes said everything his mouth couldn't. Hatred spilled through his irises. "What the hell do you want?"

"How's the jaw?"

He glowered at me. I took a seat next to his bedside, leaning back and folding one leg over the other. "I'll survive," he gurgled.

Annie never talked about him. I think the last time his name was even uttered in my presence was when she announced she'd be returning to work. I wanted to kiss her so badly, sometimes it hurt to even steal a glance at her lips. I'd never force myself on her. I'd learned from the night I met her, if Annie wanted something, there wasn't any stopping her until she got it. "Why'd you do it?"

He reached up, rearranging the gauze around his jaw. "I'm in love with her." He shook his head, closing his eyes as if the pain of realizing his feelings weren't reciprocated from her hurt worse than his jaw.

"How could you be in love with her? You don't even know her."

A humorless laugh escaped him. "Funny. She said the same thing." His eyes snapped open just to close into slits. "But you know her. I've been begging her to let me in for two years and in three months, you've managed everything I couldn't."

He needed to get this off his chest and though I wanted to pound his face until he was unrecognizable, I stayed rooted in the chair. "And the fuck of it all is that you wouldn't even be in the picture if I hadn't put you there."

I grunted. I didn't like to think about the possibility of never crossing paths with Annie. The idea felt so farfetched.

"She loves you."

Three words and my world stopped. "What did you just say?"

"I don't even know if she realizes it. I'll walk into her office and she'll be lost in a memory of you. A smile, a fucking smile so big, if I didn't see it with my own eyes I wouldn't believe it as she stared into space. She used to sometimes stay and hangout with me after her shifts. Until you. Everything she used to be is tied to you. There was Annie before you. And now there's just the version of her after."

"Which version do you like better?"

He huffed. "I'm a selfish bastard. I want her. I might always want her. But she's happy with you so don't fuck it up."

I snickered. "That a seal of approval?"

"Get the fuck out of here, Hector. Go home to your woman."

Gladly. I rose from my seat and planned to race back home to the woman who made my life better. I turned back before I closed the glass doors. "Matt?"

"Hmmm," he hummed, the painkillers kicking in.

"Don't lay your hands on her again."

He raised two fingers in the air before promptly passing out.

Three words bounced in my head, warmth spreading against my breastbone, almost painfully.

She.

Loves.

You.

The second I opened the door and kicked my shoes off, I went in search of her. The door to the study was cracked open, a soft glow from the lamp basking the room. I creaked open the door to find Annie, her hand stretched across the desk, her sleeping face resting on top of her bicep, a pencil still curled in between her fingers.

Soft Annie had made her return and the image brought a smile to my face. One that made me feel absolutely obnoxious and certainly not my age. "Annie," I tried, closing the distance. She didn't budge. I walked around the desk, preparing to carry her up to bed when a few lines scrawled next to her cheek on her open notebook snagged my attention.

His hard body. My soft curves.

His intense brown eyes. My weak resolve.

Oh, how I miss those lips on mine.

My eyes fell shut as I gathered her in my arms, guiding us both upstairs.

"Hector," she mumbled sleepily.

"Yes, bonita." I laid her down on the bed, bringing the covers over her. I tried to entangle her arms from but she refused to let go. I grabbed her fingers and tried to pry them apart but her grip only tightened.

"I think you're beautiful."

I chuckled, unable to resist kissing her forehead. "Go to sleep, beautiful."

CHAPTER TWENTY-ONE

Annie

A million people will look at you in the span of your lifetime. While you're traveling, through work, anywhere, really. Your face has been the object of someone else's eyes, some strangers and some not.

But if there was one thing knowing Hector has taught me since the night we met, it was the knowledge that most people look at you, but only a couple people actually see you.

No one has seen me in the way that Hector has.

No one has ever cared to.

And I saw him. I saw him even when he wasn't near. Even with my eyes closed. Even when I didn't want to.

The only other person who made me feel seen was Nolan. Ever since that day he burst into the range, and we spent my lunch hour signing up for a bank account and eating subs, I'd started to notice him. He'd follow from a distance, under Hector's orders I was sure. That didn't fly with me.

The first day our eyes locked, his guilty emeralds clashing with my accusatory blues, he slunk out of the shadows, falling in step with me. I slid my arm through his, and once we reached my favorite spot for lunch, I ordered for the both of us.

After we fought over who was going to foot the bill (he won), I made him make a promise to me, maybe holding over his head the fact that his best friend would do anything I asked of him. "Within reason," he relented.

"You can hide from the world, Nolan, but please don't hide from me."

He placed his hands on top of my shoulders, his light green eyes darkening. "What would Hector do if I kept you for myself?"

I pushed him away. "I don't think you want to find out."

Every day since then, I shared my lunch hour with him.

"Did he tell you about me?" Nolan whispered from underneath his blacked fitted Phillies hat.

He took control of our lunch date today, driving me to the outskirts of New Hazle to a low-key restaurant. It was the perfect spot for this humid summer day. The inside consisted of a bar where you ordered your takeout or a hostess escorted you to the dining area, a spacious patio that felt like home. Some people sat at glass tables, an umbrella protecting them from the sun. Some sat on a fortress of blankets and pillows. It had as much of a summer feeling you could get in urban Pennsylvania.

Nolan chose a set of wide stairs for us to eat our shared pizza on. "He told me a little bit."

"I was every parent's worst nightmare. They waited nine months, brimming with excitement to meet this beautiful thing that they created. And instead, they got me."

I frowned. "Nolan. You're gorgeous."

He pulled the lapels of his jacket up, hiding his face from me. I pulled at his arm. "Why are you telling me this?"

He righted his jacket back into place, turning toward me and gathering my hands in his. "As you know, Maria adopted me at a very young age and the one thing she ingrained in my head was to be selfish."

I blinked back my surprise. That didn't sound like the woman Hector spoke of. Nolan laughed, catching my wary look.

"She was the perfect mom because she knew what each of us needed. I was too soft and Hector wasn't. Hector was strong and secure and I wasn't. She taught me to be selfish. No matter how much Hector felt like a brother and Maria treated me as if I came from her womb, I clung to the fact that I would never be normal. I would always be known as the outcast. I would always be known by the kid whose parents didn't love him. Every day, until the day she was ripped away from us, she pounded selfishness into my head. And it wasn't until after she was gone that I knew what she was trying to tell me all of that time. I had to love myself enough to live. I had to be my own anchor. I realized if I couldn't do that, it would only be a matter of time before I drowned."

"Nolan."

He shook his head. "I'm telling you all of this because I like you. I don't just like you because you've got my brother wrapped around your fingers." My lips tilted at that comment. "I like you because you treat me like I'm normal. I like you because you look at me like there is something there to love."

I let my head fall against his shoulder. How did I ever think, when Hector pitched a six-month deal, that I would just survive it? I wasn't surviving it. I was living it, picking up people to love as I went.

"You're a bad ass woman, Annie. So, I hope you don't get too pissed off at me trying to protect you."

"Protect me from what," I whispered.

"Life." I think it was too late. For the both of us.

"Hey, guys." A peppy voice had our heads snapping up. A girl around my age beamed down at us, thrusting out a piece of paper toward me. I took it from her. "There's a poetry reading tonight at McNutt's. I'm sorry if this is rude but I swore I saw you there last time."

I nodded my head. "Yeah, the one with Aliyah."

"You should come. This one's supporting a great cause."

She turned on her heel, walking back into the restaurant. Once she disappeared from my line of vision, I finally looked down at the paper.

My heart stopped beating at the sight of another woman. If I thought I was entranced by Aliyah's face, then this woman's face completely consumed me.

The photograph perfectly captured this woman's happiness. Her black tight curls fanned against her face as if the shot was taken while she spun around in the middle of the street. She smiled so widely. Her brown eyes glinted underneath the sun, a curious tint to them.

All of her bright, sparkling features almost distracted me from the protrusive scar marring one side of her face, like someone took a knife from her lower eyelid down to the tip of her chin. Her name was in big, bold letters: Eliza Reyes. The bottom of the page listed the date and time as well as a disclaimer of all proceeds being donated to Philadelphia's only women's shelter that helped women escape and move on from their abusive pasts.

I curled my hands around the paper, unable to take my eyes off of the woman's face. Though they looked nothing alike, this woman reminded me of my mother. The woman's scars were visible while my mom's hid underneath her clothes but they somehow felt connected. Like they had the same story, shared the same memories.

This is what I have been waiting for. My second poetry reading.

I looked down at the flier again. Excitement coursed through me knowing I'd get to hear her story through prose. But my heart thudded with fear knowing this woman's story would hit a little too close to home.

"Nolan."

I tilted my head toward him, finding him studying me. "Yes?"

"I need a favor."

The rest of the day at the range passed at a snail's pace. I couldn't relax, a swarm of emotions sitting heavy on my gut. I was excited to go to a live poetry event. I was curious about Eliza Reyes, the story behind her beautiful face. But I was scared shitless about what she would say. Even more of the impact her words would leave on me.

But I was certain of one thing. I needed Hector. I needed him to go with me. I needed to feel his warmth next to me in case my world shattered. And even if it didn't, I still wanted him there.

I wanted to share with him this new part of me I discovered. It was time I finally came clean to him. The moment the clock struck five, I rushed out of the range and into Hector's idling car.

I didn't say a word to him the entire drive but he didn't pry, well accustomed to my growing silence for the past two weeks. I followed him into the house, stalling by the doorway to see where he headed. He went straight upstairs as I was rooted in the same spot. It wasn't until I heard the shower running that I shook out of my anxiousness and followed him.

I trudged upstairs, past the bedroom, and stormed into the bathroom. "Annie," he called out, even though his eyes were still shut, water running down his face. Enough nerves plagued me; I didn't dare follow the trail of water with my eyes.

"There's another poetry reading tonight. I'd like to go." Before he could say anything, I sucked in a deep breath and let it out. "With you."

He immediately shut off the water, opened the glass doors and reached for his towel hanging on its rack. From his silence, I already knew what his answer would be.

He walked into the bedroom, leaving me no option other than to follow him. "When we made this deal," I said, my voice steely. "You said whatever I'd want, you'd make it happen. This is what I want."

He pulled a pair of boxers up over his hips, ready to follow them with a pair of sweatpants but I snatched them from his hands before he had the chance. His gaze snapped up to me, his nostrils flaring. "I know I've never spoken this out loud but I know you're not dense enough to know that I'm not the type of man that you can be seen with in public. My answer is no," he said, easily ripping his pants from my grip.

He put the pants on in one swift motion and brushed past me, heading downstairs. I followed him. "Okay, so you don't want me to be seen with you in public, there are ways around that."

He groaned, slapping a palm over his face. "Annie," he groaned, his voice holding a warning I easily ignored.

I was never much one to back off when he used that voice. He should have known that by now. He walked into the kitchen, turned on the speaker and blasted the volume, effectively silencing me.

A growl slipped passed my lips but I didn't linger. I jumped in the shower and got myself ready, timing the process perfectly so I had time to bitch out Hector before Nolan was due to arrive. I wore a sage green silky button-up top tucked into a pair of high-waisted blue jeans with my normal white Vans. I pulled half of my hair up in a bun and let the rest flow down my back in waves. I went downstairs just as Nolan texted me that he was outside.

The music was turned down to its normal level and Hector was making two plates. "I'm not eating," I announced.

He turned around, looking at me, his apology written across his face. His eyes telling me that as much as he wanted nothing more than to make me happy, there was a line in the sand and this was it.

"I'll drive you and heat this up when I get back," he told me, already grabbing plate covers.

I shook my head. "Nolan is going to drive me."

His head snapped up, his hurt eyes clashing with my determined ones. Maybe it was wrong of me but I couldn't help it. I needed him in a way I swore I wouldn't ever need anyone. "You are the one who asked for this. You demanded I needed this time. Time to find my anchor to keep me grounded to my humanity. I was fine with who I was before, but you thought it was a great idea." I closed the space between us not stopping until our heaving chests bounced off of each other. I stabbed at his chest with a single finger. "For me to explore who I was. This is your fault." He closed a hand over my finger and I jerked away from him. "You are going to get glasses, a scarf, a hat, I don't care what," I said, taking the folded flier out of my jean pocket and slapping it against his chest, my other hand taking his and putting it over the space so I could let go without the paper falling to the floor. "You are going to change your clothes, jump in that fancy car of yours and meet me in the city in a café. And you are going to sit next to me, stand behind me, be close enough to me that I can feel your presence, and you are going to be there for me, damn it."

I turned on my heel and walked out of the front door into Nolan's sleek black two-door car. Once I was buckled in, I let out a sigh and Nolan started to drive. I managed to calm down by the time we made it into the city but I didn't feel any lighter.

I wondered if he would show up. I wondered if the one person I let myself be vulnerable with wouldn't be there when I really needed him. I knew one thing for certain, whether he showed up or not, tonight would change our relationship forever.

Nolan dropped me off, promising to pick me up in two hours unless Hector directed him otherwise. We both knew he wasn't going too far. His warning of his overbearing protectiveness from earlier resonate in the air between us.

I let him lie to me and slipped out of his car. I paid the admission fee and roamed inside, searching for an empty table, hoping like hell he would show up.

I ordered a beer and sipped on it, watching the lights dim and one of the workers set up the stage. I tried not to look around the room, not pay attention to the revolving groups of people coming through the doors.

I tried not to be hopeful. I tried not to be desperate for this man to show up for me. But the truth was that I was hopeful; I was desperate. I wanted to know for once that someone cared enough about me to pull through. To be there for me despite the consequences and the fears.

The lights in the cafe dimmed and I reluctantly tore my eyes away from the entryway and focused on the stage where a bartender was busy doing a mic check.

"Hello everyone and welcome to McNutt's Cafe. We're happy to bring you another poetry night in the city." In true Philadelphia fashion, a scattered group of people cheered almost indecently and raised their glasses. "We have two special guests tonight. Carly Evans will open the show for us and then we'll open the floor up to you all before the beautiful and incredibly talented Eliza Reyes takes the stage."

He bowed and promptly rushed off of the stage. A blonde woman took his place and the light chatter filling the room fell quiet. The woman walked slowly to the center of the stage, her head bowed, eyes glued to the floor. Her long blonde hair covered her face, but the leggings and loose silk shirt she wore hugged her skin to perfection.

Only when she reached the stool did she look up, revealing hazel eyes and a face so angelic I thought I was dreaming. A round face framed by two rosy pink cheeks, full lips, and eyes that made you want to become her new best friend.

A sudden heat pressed against my back, a pair of hands wrapping around the top of the chair. I turned my head to see my favorite pair of rough hands that held me so gently.

I shut my eyes, trying to stop the inevitable smile from blooming. I didn't last long. When it came to Hector, my resolve flew straight out of the window.

I'd never had a dream for myself. Everything I've done has been in honor of my mother. I've never dared to want anything for myself. Hector was the exception to the rule. The rarity in my life. Because there wasn't anything more in the world than I wanted this man to show up for me when I needed him and even when I didn't.

I tilted my head back and there he was.

My roommate. My best friend. My man.

Okay, maybe he wasn't my man but a girl could dream.

"Sit," I demanded, motioning to the empty chair next to me. He listened without hesitation and I had no choice but to let my smile break free. I caught sight of Hector's crisp white button-down shirt tucked into a pair of navy blue slacks paired with a pair of burnt copper boots I'd never seen him wear before. He had on an all black fitted 76ers hat that almost covered his eyes. I surmised this was his attempt at going undercover.

If I thought he looked sexy in nothing but a pair of sweatpants, I had no word to describe how sexy I found him now.

The sound of a throat clearing made me tear my gaze away from him and look to the stage. I straightened in my seat as she introduced herself and I noticed Hector did the same. Carly started off with a poem about how society viewed plus-sized individuals before she transitioned into a story about how she started to hate herself because society taught her to before finally, she shared her final poem with us. A poem about acceptance, about not giving a fuck about what people who don't know you think of you, about accepting your own definition of beautiful and no one else's.

Just like the poetry I devoured any chance I could, the poetry I found myself writing more and more of, and all of the poetry I listened from my last time in this café, my chest ached from the beauty of prose, from the awe I felt connecting with a complete stranger from across the room.

Once she thanked the crowd and walked off stage, I turned to Hector, unsure of what he'd think. I hadn't even confessed to him the truth behind the past two weeks of my behavior. I hadn't told him that

I've fallen in love with poetry, fallen in love, maybe for the first time, with life.

"What did you think?" I whispered.

His eyes were glued to my face, caressing me without a single touch. He didn't react, his soft eyes boring into mine. Just as I went to ask him again, he whispered one word so softly it felt like a brush of breath. "Beautiful."

Someone stood from a few tables from us and made their way to the stage. "Be gentle on me. This is my first time." Screams of encouragement sounded from all over the room. I was just thankful for the reprieve from Hector. From eyes that could bring me to my knees and lips I wanted so desperately to taste again.

His hands were a different story. Something I wanted on me all of the time. I found his underneath the table, intertwining my fingers through his. His rough skin gliding against mine felt like home. I looked down to where our hands set, on top of his thick thigh and I had to fight a dreamy sigh off.

Over the next hour, I listened to newbies and old-timers share their poetry and I felt invincible. Nothing could touch me here. Not with Hector's hand in mine and my heart opening for each person who was brave enough to grace that stage.

I was happy in a way I didn't think I ever had been before. Happy in a way I could have never imagined for myself. Not ten years ago, not even three months ago.

When the lights flickered back on, the break between the open mic and the special guest on stage, I looked over at Hector to catch him looking at me. I tipped my beer up at him in offering and a second later his hands wrapped around mine on the neck and I tried to fight off a full body shiver and lost. Even when he brought the bottle to his lips, he still didn't tear his eyes away.

I lost that battle, too. I straightened from my chair with a promise to be right back and went to the bar and placed an order for food. Meanwhile I let my body sag against the countertop. The bartender looked at me in question but I just shook my head. How could I explain that a man who I had once thought ruined my life was actually the best thing that had ever happened to me?

When the bartender handed me a tray with two plates of appetizers, two glasses of water, and another bottle of beer, I made my way back to the table. As soon as Hector saw me, he stood, reaching out to help me but I brushed past him and set the food on the table. He glowered at me and in return, I shot him a grin.

When we both sat down, I moved the plate of chicken wings closer to me and the jalapeño cheese balls closer to him. He raised his eyebrows at me and I shrugged. "The only spicy thing they had."

He smiled and in response, I shoved a chicken wing in my mouth. We ate in silence until Hector had one last cheese ball twirling between two of his fingers. I looked at him curiously and a sly smile spread across his face. "Want a taste, bonita?"

My eyes dropped to stare at his curved lips and the pink tongue that darted out to lick his bottom one. *Yes.*

"No," I said, shaking my head. He popped the ball into his mouth and I watched as he chewed slowly, running the tip of his finger across his bottom lip, erasing the nonexistent crumbs. I didn't know being jealous of food could ever be a thing but apparently it was.

The lights dimmed a moment later and Hector was no longer the reason for the fluttery but painful butterflies floating around in the pit of my stomach. I took one more long pull of our shared beer before standing up. I didn't look over to see Hector's reaction but I did inhale deeply before letting a shaky breath out. Then, I turned to him, leaned down, and pushed his thighs apart. He didn't resist; he let me have my way with him, use his body as I saw fit. I plopped down on top of his thighs, my hands sneaking out to grasp his shirt. His hands shot out, gripping me at the hips. His body turned rigid as I settled deeper into his chest. He settled underneath me after a few minutes, his hands securely around me loosening into a gentle hold. I let my head fall against his chest just as Eliza Reyes walked on stage.

She walked confidently, similar to that of a runway model. I couldn't see much of her since she hadn't stepped into the light yet but I could tell she had a figure a lot of girls would kill for. She wore tight jeans and a tank top that showed off her boobs. She stopped walking just as the tips of her shoes came into the spotlight. She raised her hand, microphone in hand, and let her voice take over.

She
She is someone's mother
She is someone's sister
She is someone's daughter

When a man lays his hands on a woman,
labels are attached to their names.

He's the bright star on the swim team.

He's the hopeful politician.
He is the one who just *made a mistake.*

It's different for women.

She is someone to someone else.
She is not just *someone.*
She is someone
to someone else.

Every word she spoke, I clung to Hector's shirt, my fingers curling against him. I couldn't think. I couldn't breathe. All I could do was feel. If I trusted my feet enough, I would stand and walk far, far away this very moment.

She took a deep breath through the microphone before stepping into the light. My entire body drew into a tight ball at the sight of her. The deep scar that ran along her face wasn't her only scar. With the lack of a modest shirt, I could see multiple scars running along her arms and the scariest looking one that formed an edged horizontal line like someone had slit her throat.

Eliza's face transformed. Instead of dark, jagged skin, I saw pale skin that matched mine and scars of lashes on her back. I didn't see a face of a stranger; I saw the one that I was the splitting image for. I remembered everything. Her scars. Her pain. Her screams. Her pleads.

Movement pulled me out of the memories assaulting me. Hector's hands slid from my waist to the center of my back, drawing slow, soft circles against my spine. His breath coasting across my cheek as he whispered, "Breathe, bonita, I got you."

Slowly, I relaxed, his touch and his touch only, grounding me. Eliza's face returned to me, replacing my mom's, to see a woman who had been through hell and escaped it and was now standing before me, brave enough to share her scars with a room full of strangers and potentially people like me. People who shared her experiences who needed to hear the truth about living in a nightmare and moving on from it.

She ignored the stool and the mic stand and worked the stage like it came naturally to her. She didn't sit once and her steps were never hesitant or faltering. Not only through prose did she tell us she was as strong as strong could get but she showed us with each foot she put in front of the other. The foreshadowing was enough to break my heart. Throughout her poems, her voice flowed smoothly from one emotion to another. Her voice became loud when she was feeling frustrated and angry before turning into a soft whisper when she was feeling hopeful. She walked to the edge of the stage and she sat down for the first time. I found myself leaning away from Hector, scared that I would miss a single word she said.

They tell us how to act.
They tell us what to wear.
They tell us a lot of things
and we're just supposed to do it without question.

But let me tell you something.

I am not a toy.
I am not something you can throw across the room

once you have grown tired of it.
I am a woman with a beating heart and
I'd rather die than to allow a man to break me.

The light to the stage shut off, plunging the room into darkness. All was quiet for a second before all of the lights turned on to reveal Eliza already making her way backstage. I unclenched my hands from Hector's shirt and I clapped. He followed suit and the rest of the room joined us. Before Eliza disappeared from our view, she turned back and smiled, offering us a little wave. Her smile was so big, you would've never guessed she just finished pouring her heart out on that stage.

It reminded me of my mother's smile, of her happiness when it was just the two of us. When I was younger, I never understood how she could be happy, knowing how the blows and the verbal matches were just a few hours away. Tonight, I realized that just because you were broken, beaten, and scarred, didn't mean you had to be unhappy. I thought back to what Hector told me about how everyone needed an anchor in life, something to hold on to when you felt like giving it all up. I was that something for my mom.

I couldn't stop the tears from pouring down my cheeks. I cried for Eliza and for my mom. I cried for everyone who has had to suffer at the cruel hands of someone who promised they loved you as they bruised your skin.

Hector tightened his arms around me in silent support as the café reverted back into its normalness. People ordered coffee and snacks and soft melodies played on the speakers throughout the room.

Without wiping the tears from my cheeks, I turned to face him. He lifted his eyes to me, his expression somber. He frowned when he caught notice of my small smile. It wasn't the usual smile I gave him. It wasn't sarcastic or teasing. It was a smile I hadn't worn since my mom was alive. It was a smile that wasn't formed with my lips but my heart.

I flicked the tip of his hat. "You clean up nicely," I told him quietly.

He chuckled and I squirmed in his lap, effectively turning his laugh into a low groan. I tilted the lip of his hat until I could clearly see his face. His brown eyes were light in a way he only reserved for me.

I didn't think. I didn't do anything but what I wanted in the moment. I erased the distance until our breaths mingled and then, I was kissing him. Again.

It wasn't like the kiss we shared the night we met. That kiss was between two strangers. It was sloppy. It was fierce. It was both of us fighting for control.

This kiss was the complete opposite.

This kiss was soft. This kiss was hesitant. This kiss was so fucking hopeful.

His hands danced their way from my back, up my sides until his palms cradled my face. I moved my own hands, wrapping them around his neck, my fingers raking through the soft hair at the back of his neck.

Our kiss turned feverish. I couldn't get enough of him and by the feel of his hands gripping my cheeks like they were his lifeline, I knew he had to be feeling the same. When I had no choice but to come up for air, I leaned back to look at him. His hands loosened on my face but went nowhere. "Thank you for coming," I whispered against his lips.

He didn't say anything in return, instead using our moment of silence to bring my face back to his and slip his tongue past my parted lips. I eagerly met him stroke for stroke, my entire body melting against him.

When I started to make noises not suitable for public, he pulled back, taking my bottom lip for the ride. I squeezed my thighs together which I knew he felt because he smirked at me, before bringing my face back to his, dropping quick pecks to my lips.

He pulled his hat back down, hiding his eyes, and said, "Let's go home."

I nodded in agreement but couldn't get my legs to cooperate, not when my heart hiccupped at the mention of "let's" and "go" and "home." He started to stand, me still in his arms and perched on his lap.

"Okay, okay, okay," I said, giving in and standing on my own two feet. Hector led me outside, his hand wrapped around mine. I immediately sought out that familiar black car of his but didn't see it in sight. When I looked up at him, he winked before hitting a button on his key ring. A white Lexus beeped, its lights flashing. I tore my eyes away from the beauty back to Hector, my mouth gaped open. "Why are we not riding around in this all of the time?"

"Because it's for emergencies," he responded immediately.

"This was an emergency," I mused, smirking.

He ignored me, tugging me toward the passenger side and holding my door open for me. Once I was inside, I kept my eyes on him as he walked around to the driver's side. A poetry reading wasn't an emergency. Me needing him to be there for me, whether I spoke the words aloud or not, was. I tried to keep the smile off of my face as he ditched the hat and ran his fingers through his hair and started to drive us home but it was so fucking hard.

At some point, I reached over for his hand and he let me have it and before I knew it sleep drug me under. I woke up to the sound of my door opening and Hector reaching for me. "I can carry you," he whispered, already moving his hands under my legs and around my back.

I swatted at him. "I can walk."

Once we got inside, we both headed straight upstairs and I all but fell on the bed. I was fighting to keep my eyes opened as Hector stripped out of his clothes and threw on a pair of sweatpants and a t-shirt. Tonight of all nights, I cursed my little episode in our first and only time in the gym together.

He climbed on the bed, covering himself with his blanket.

When I left this house with Nolan a few hours earlier, I knew Hector and I would never be the same two people. We were no longer individuals. We were a unit. We were an us. As much as I didn't plan on this and as much as he might think that I'll want to leave when our six months is up, I knew I wouldn't be this version of myself. I started to love myself because he made me feel safe enough to do so. I wasn't planning on saying goodbye to him. Ever.

I lifted the blanket from my body, rising to my knees and crawling across the bed. I scooted myself into his space, his flannel blanket barely covering the both of us. My legs snuck in between both of his and I forewent a pillow, using his chest as a replacement. His arms wrapped around me and in a matter of seconds, my breathing evened out and I was a goner.

CHAPTER TWENTY-TWO
Hector

I woke with a start, pain stabbing my stomach like someone was twisting the skin as hard as they could. I opened my eyes to find that to be exactly the case.

I slipped my hands from around Annie's back to pull her away from me, grabbing her tight fists clinging from my skin and holding them. My shirt was soaked from the sweat that dripped from her hair onto her skin. Her body shook and her breath escaped her lips in short, anxious puffs.

I untangled her fists from my skin, laying her on her back. Sweeping the damp strands of hair from her face, I tried to call her name. Angling my face so when her eyes did flutter open, she had a clear version of who she was with and that she was safe.

"Annie, wake up," I whispered, my fingers still combing through her hair.

Her body shivered, worry lines appearing on her forehead as she tried to open her eyes. Eyes that looked sad from a memory that assaulted her consciousness, but warmed the moment they clashed with mine.

"Hey," she whispered, her soft voice breaking.

"Do you want to talk about it?"

She shook her head, reaching her hands up to run across my cheeks, her fingers tickling the thick layer of scruff across my jaw. Her grip on me turned firm in an instant, dragging my head down until our lips touched.

I guessed this was a thing we did now. Kissing.

I melted against the softness of her lips. I pressed my hands, turned into fists, against the mattress to maintain some semblance of control. Her lips closed around my top lip before retreating and capturing my bottom one. The tenderness she kissed me with spread shivers down my spine. It wasn't just my body I had signed over to her, however unwilling it went, she had my heart, too.

I sighed against her mouth and she used my moment of weakness to slip that little pink tongue into my mouth. The moment her hot tongue pressed against mine, I groaned. Her lips spread into a smile against mine, no doubt feeling the evidence of how deeply she affected me, digging into her stomach.

I pulled back, needing her eyes in the moment. Her big blue eyes stared back at me, the happiness I felt inside apparent on her face. I dropped my face, my lips resting on her exposed collarbone.

I pecked at her skin because I couldn't help myself. She gave permission to kiss her. And I planned on kissing her. Soft kisses. Slow kisses. Deep kisses. Hard kisses. Soul crushing kisses. Any kind of kiss that involved her lips was what my future held. Even if I could only kiss her for ninety-four more days, I would take it.

"You." A kiss to her collarbone.

"Kill." A kiss to the dainty curve of her chin.

"Me." A kiss to the edge of her smiling lips.

A laugh bubbled between her lips, tickling mine. She grabbed a hold of my face again, until I met her eyes. "I swear, I'm not trying."

I gulped past a sudden lump in my throat, a request dangling on the tip of my tongue, one I refused to voice, desperation be damned. *Please don't ever stop killing me. I want you to make me weak until my last breath. Hurt me and be the one to put me back together again.*

I laid back down on my back, bringing her with me until her head rested on my chest, her arms wrapping around my torso. I avoided her eyes, scared she'd see the truth in them. The truth she could never know.

"I want to talk to you about something." I didn't reply, using my fingers to urge her to go on.

My reprieve was short lived as her hands slid from around me to lift her face on my chest, bringing our faces impossibly close together. "A few weeks ago, the night you were late picking me up, a flier fell at my feet just before I opened the car door."

Ah, she was finally telling me about poetry. I smiled, tucking a strand of hair behind her ear.

"This may sound like total bullshit, but it called to me. I guess like a guitar would to a musician. It was a flier for a poetry reading and my gut told me I had to go. So I went. Two hours and a dozen people who shared their stories through prose completely altered me. Inspired me to write my own."

The words she wrote about me. A smile played on my lips remembering the last line she wrote. *Oh, how I miss those lips on mine.*

"I don't know how good I am at it right now but I know I want to be better."

"You love it."

Her lips curved into an uninhibited smile, flashing her white teeth and pink tongue. "I do. I've been waiting for a second show. Today, while I was having lunch with Nolan, a girl came over to us and handed me another flier."

I quirked an eyebrow up at her. "Since when have you and Nolan been eating lunch together?"

My best friend was a fucking dead man. The moment I got my hands on him, I was going to strangle him. My mother would disapprove, but she would forgive me. I'd beg for it.

Here I was, trying my fucking hardest to keep Annie's identity a secret. Protect her name, shield her face from any association with my name while he paraded her around the city, placing a target on all of our backs.

Her hands reached out, her fingers dancing across my skin, smoothing out my frown. "Nolan and I, we understand each other in a way you can't." My frown grew tenfold, unsettled that anyone could understand her better than I could. "Our childhoods shaped us differently. He needs someone to understand him, Hector. And I do."

I nodded. "I just wish you didn't have to do it publicly," I grumbled.

She patted my cheek softly, silently telling me to get over it. I never would. A connection to the Rivera family could protect her but like my mom, even our protection was limited.

I closed my eyes, feigning tiredness. I couldn't look at her anymore. Now that she gave us the green light, I wanted to drive full speed. But I couldn't do that, not when life warned me to pay closer attention to the other drivers surrounding me. There was more of a chance they'd hurt me before I hurt myself.

She settled against my chest again, her hand trailing to palm my cheek. "Thank you."

"For what," I murmured, my eyes wide open now that hers were hidden.

"For seeing me."

I swore the moment her breathing evened out, I would scoop her body off of me and hunt down my best friend and try my best not to inflict too much damage on him, now that killing him was no longer an option since he meant something to the woman in my arms, but her arms felt too good to leave.

I woke up to the feel of Annie's hands resting directly over my heart. Sometime in the night, they must have slipped underneath my shirt. The direct contact had my dick stirring to life. I threw my eyes shut, fighting off a groan.

I'd give myself one minute. One more minute to lie next to her, bask in the feel of her, before I had to get up.

One minute turned into ten. Ten turned into an hour. The only thing that forced me out of bed was an incoming call from Samuel. I untangled our bodies before answering and heading downstairs.

"Hey, Dad. How was your date last night?"

I frowned. How the fuck did he know about that? I asked him as much.

His laughter boomed, making me wince. "I was fucking with you, Dad. But fuck, she really got you out on a date."

"I thought you talked to Nolan," I grumbled.

His laughter still hadn't subsided. "Like he would tell me anything. His loyalty to you is unmatched."

I snorted, opening the fridge and grabbing milk and eggs. "Maybe that loyalty is slipping."

Samuel's laughter died. "What's going on? Do I need to come home?"

It was my turn to laugh. "No. Annie and him, they're close."

Samuel's playfulness returned at once. "He's got it bad. You got it bad. When do I get to meet this perfect woman?"

I ignored him, not liking the inevitable answer to his question. She'd be long gone before he came home from school over Christmas break. "How is Europe?"

"It's good. I'm learning the language of love."

I snickered. "The actual language or the one you learn at night after you pick up a woman?"

"I think it's a fairly equal balance," he said thoughtfully and it took great effort not to roll my eyes at him. "I only have a couple more weeks here. I wish I was coming back home but we're flying out two days before my first day of classes, so I won't be able to swing it. Maybe I can call Annie on a video chat, let her know there's another Rivera at her mercy."

"Samuel."

He hummed like the smart ass he was. I hung up without another word.

I was cracking three eggs into a glass when, a pair of small hands slid around me, lacing together in the middle of my rib cage. I tossed my head over my shoulder to find Annie, a sleepy smile on her face. I just got rid of the effect she left on my body and here she was, lighting my body up with a single touch.

She pressed a kiss against my spine and I hurried and gulped a raw egg, the coolness as it glided down my throat relieving some of the tension in my tight body.

"Morning," I grunted, holding the glass in my hand a little too tightly.

"Good morning," she whispered against my back.

"What are you doing up so early?"

She let go of me to grab a glass of orange juice. When she turned back around, her lips pressed together in a pout. "My heater left me."

I tugged her hair. "Do you want me to make breakfast since you're already up?"

She shook her head behind her glass. "No. I'm going to get a workout in. My pants are not loving how much I've been eating."

I grinned wolfishly. My cooking fed her well, her bones had long been filled out by fat. She rolled her eyes at me. "I'm not helping you lift again. Not after the last time."

She threw her head back and laughed. She sauntered up to where I leaned on the counter, swirling my last egg in a cup. Her fingers reached out, her fingers brushing the hem of my t-shirt, before her fingers danced underneath my skin, my abs contracting at her teasing touch. "I regret that decision now."

"Why," I asked, unsure of what we were talking about. Her hands flattened so her palms pressed against my skin. She leaned on me, closing the space between us.

"I kind of miss seeing this."

"Are you asking me to ditch the shirt, bonita?"

Her cheeks stained pink. I reached behind my back with one hand and lifted my shirt over my head. Her face fell forward, her forehead landing directly on my sternum. Her nails reached out, lightly scratching at my skin. "You'll really do anything I ask of you."

I let my hand trail the length of her hair. "Whatever you want, it's yours," I repeated the sentiment I once assured her with when I proposed these six months to her. The words taking on a whole new meaning in such a short amount of time.

She slapped her palms against my chest before backing away, grabbing my shirt from the floor and tossing it over her shoulder. "Great." She paused, turning around as she hit the first stair. I hadn't taken my eyes off her. "I work until seven and we'll go out on a date."

I nodded until I picked up on the last word. "Date?" I asked, quirking up an eyebrow.

"Yes. I know our meeting was unconventional. But dates, they're still a thing. We are going to have one, preferably tonight."

"No." In a different world, I would have dated the fuck out of her. She'd probably have two rings on her hand at this point if we were different people. But I was who I was and there wasn't anything I could do to change that. Not even for her.

"No," she mused, relaxed as could be.

"No. No dates. The only reason I came last night was because I know you needed it."

She turned around fully, crossing her arms across her chest. "If I'm not mistaken, you kissed me back last night. You let me sleep on you. I felt you when I sat in your lap. I woke up in the middle of the night to find your hands all over me. What do you mean 'no'?"

I sighed, knowing our bubble of bliss was about to pop. "This six month deal we have isn't an ulterior motive, Annie. It's not so I could be close to you or convince you to stay. It's about you. I don't matter in this. I wanted you to live a life for yourself that you could keep, that could make you happy. When six months is up, you're gone and I'm going to be here. Getting closer, going on dates, is just going to mess with your head about what you want your future to look like. I'll tell you one thing for certain; your future doesn't have me in it."

There was nothing more than I wanted more than to date Annie. To show her a life so good, she wouldn't even dream about leaving but I didn't want to erase another woman's identity. I didn't want to fall in love a second time just to erase another woman's touch from my memory and my life from hers. I wanted a love like my parents. A love you would kill for. A love you would die for. But I've come to terms with the possibility that that kind of love wasn't in the cards for me.

She flinched and I wanted to take the words back, take the truth back, but it was too late. "Okay," she conceded after a long stare down. "No dates."

I tried not to let her flippancy, her easy agreement get to me, but the moment her feet disappeared from view, I gripped the countertops for support. But nothing could ease the sharpness drawing tight in my chest.

We were quiet on the way to work. She didn't come in to the gym to work out like she planned. She didn't even let me prepare her breakfast, instead choosing the sugary cereal bullshit. I was ready to drag us both back to bed and press restart on this day.

Things took a turn for the worst when my phone chimed with a text from her two hours after I dropped her off.

Matt needs some help booking clients. The new guy called off. I won't be done until eight tonight.

After I attended my last meeting, I headed home, wanting to sleep to forget all about this shitty day. After twenty minutes of tossing and turning and smelling her lavender shampoo in every crevice of the bed, I headed down to the gym to lift.

My phone chimed. I looked down at the screen to find Annie calling. I looked at my watch, confused. She still had another two hours. "Are you ready now?" I asked without saying hello, grabbing my keys, already heading for my car.

"Nolan picked me up actually," she admitted quietly.

I groaned, loud and long, realization catching up to me. I should've been pissed but I could only smile at her antics. This was classic Annie.

I'd tell her how something was going to be, she'd easily agree, and the next thing I know, I have a brand new scar marking my body. "What do you have up your sleeve, bonita?"

"Nothing. Except I'm here waiting for you and I really hope you don't stand me up on our first official date."

"Didn't we have this conversation earlier?"

"We did," she agreed. "I just didn't much care for the outcome."

I dropped my keys on the table, backtracking upstairs.

"You can go, Nolan. Hector's on his way."

I always thought that everyone deserved a choice. The right to say no or yes as they pleased. But with Annie, my choice has been stripped away. Making her happy wasn't an option; it was a duty.

"Annie," I said on a sigh.

"Old Style Theater. GPS it," were her only instructions before she ended the phone call.

No one hung up on me. No one got the last word with me. Always the fucking exception.

I hurried up, threw myself in the shower before dressing in a pair of dark wash jeans and a black hoodie. I traveled to the side of the house where I usually parked the Lexus. My teeth grinding as I rounded the corner to find it missing.

I trudged back to my car, already dialing Nolan. He didn't answer the first time. Or the second time. After trying a third time, I said fuck it, and climbed in my car. I made it to the end of my driveway before his car came flying my way.

I killed the engine, hopping out. Nolan did the same, throwing his keys over to me. "Take mine."

"We're going to have words," I promised him. He ducked his head, avoiding my eyes.

"I'll wait here until you two get back," he muttered, pulling at his fitted hat.

"Does she have the Lex?"

He nodded. I slammed a hand over his shoulder. "Get in the car. You'll talk while I drive."

He sulked around toward the passenger side like a scolded teenager.

I sped out of the driveway, not slowing down until I hit the evening traffic. "What's going on with you and Annie?" I asked the question softly, knowing he had his limits before he would shut down. And Annie probably pressed all of them today.

He threw a panicked look my way, his usual pale skin glowing with heat. "Nothing. Nothing in *that* way."

I reached over and patted his shoulder, silencing his outburst. "I know, Nolan. I know there is nothing between the two of you. You're friends," I said, but it came out more of a question.

"She understands me." His confession sounded a lot like her. "She understands me in a way no one ever has. She sees me in a crowded room. She sees me in the dark. It's oddly comforting to know that a million people could be in a room and she wouldn't even sort out ten before her eyes found me. I'm undetectable to everyone but her."

I smiled softly, racing my way to a woman who didn't only manage to sneak into my heart but snuck into my best friend's heart, too. "Unless you're in the same room. Then, all bets are off." My smile only grew at his words.

It wasn't until I saw the drive-in theater pop into view before I remembered the real reason I was pissed at him. "You shouldn't be parading her around the city, Nolan. It's dangerous."

I parked his car just outside of the venue.

"Why?"

I bit my tongue, my mother's dying wish stopping the words from tumbling out. "It's dangerous. I'm never short-handed of enemies. The kind of people who find out who we love and target us that way."

I turned to him. "Annie's not going to stick around forever."

"Why the fuck not?" he shouted, a deep frown settling into his forehead.

I rubbed his shoulder to calm him down. "She's only here because I made a deal with her. I should have told you, and I'm sorry. In three months, I'm handing over Cameron and she's leaving."

Nolan rubbed at his chest with his palms. "I could kill Cameron," he whispered. "Then, she'd have no choice but to stay."

"Nolan, no. She would only run farther away. I don't know if she'll stay in Philadelphia or not. I don't know what she'll do in three months' time. Wherever she goes, you can follow her if that's what you want. If that's what she wants."

"And what about you?"

"I don't matter in this."

He tilted his head, looking at me in confusion.

I just shook my head. "I have to get in there before she kills me. We'll talk later about this."

We both got out. I handed him the keys as we met in front of the hood of his car. He pulled my hand and wrapped his arms around my back in a tight hug. "I'm sorry if I put her in danger. That wasn't my intention. Hopefully, she'll forgive me."

Before I could rebut his guilt, he slid into the driver's seat and tore out of the parking spot, his black car disappearing in the city lights.

My mother's dream car was the closest car to the exit, the hatchback popped open, a head of blonde hair staring up at the drive-in screen. I didn't even realize drive-ins were still a thing. I rounded the car, choosing to lean up against it rather than to make my presence known.

I knew, at some point, she must have returned to the house to steal my car and change clothes. She wore tight, distressed jeans, her creamy skin teasing me. A simple black sweater with cuffed sleeves covered her top. My eyes perused her skin, noticing the goosebumps covering her wrists, the light dusting of almost invisible blonde hair rising against her skin.

Her eyes didn't flicker my way once but she felt my presence. "Annie," I barked.

Her eyes didn't leave the screen as a new trailer for an upcoming movie flashed on the screen. Instead, she waved her hands in my direction, dismissing me. "Shh. The movie is about to start."

I stood there, towering over her but her stubbornness and my weak resolve won in the end. I lifted the blanket she had tucked beside her and sat down, my large frame barely fitting. I shook out the blanket, spreading it across to cover our thighs. I kept my eyes on her while she kept her eyes on that forsaken screen.

Just when I was ready to grab the tip if her chin and force her eyes to mine, her head fell against my shoulder, her hand sneaking out to find mine and lacing our fingers together. The movie started but I couldn't even be bothered to spare anything outside of the car a glance.

If my eyes could focus on one thing for the rest of my life, it would be her, no qualms about it. In the dark, surrounded by people, she was the only thing I cared about.

By the end of the first movie, I had moved her onto my lap, my arms wrapped around her shoulders as I placed soft, whispering kisses against her neck.

She was irresistible to man who didn't much want to resist.

CHAPTER TWENTY-THREE

Annie

My mom would have been forty years old today.

Every year since she died, her birthday had been something I dreaded. In the beginning years, this day brought out a mixture of anger and sadness in me. So damn angry that she was gone and that she didn't take me with her. So damn sad that I had to live in a world where my favorite person didn't exist.

When I was sixteen, things changed. I was in my second year of high school and working as many hours as I could at a local diner. I read *The Count of Monte Cristo* for the first time in my Honors English class and it gave me the courage to say what I wanted aloud, even if it was a whisper in the shower where no one else could hear. It became real then. He was going to pay for what he did to my mother, did to me.

The anger didn't disappear but I focused more on my mother. Who she was. The things she liked. So, her birthday wasn't tainted by him or what he did to her all of those years, or the fact that she wasn't aging.

Her birthday became a tradition. A way to remember her in a way I knew she'd like. In a way, if she was still alive, we would spend the day anyway.

So, I took some of the money I had saved since I started working and I spent the day like I knew she would.

"First thing you need to make yourself feel beautiful is spending the day with your favorite person." Her words hurt because she was gone and I no longer had a favorite person.

Her voice rang in my ear, a memory surfacing of me asking her what her perfect day looked like. *"Nothing will make you feel lighter than getting your hair done. A cute new outfit will make you feel brand new. And lastly, although my favorite, is a killer pair of heels. All a woman needs is a killer pair of heels and the ability to confidently walk in them to make this world bow down to her."*

Six years ago, I started a tradition as a way to never let go of the first person who ever loved me. Every year, I got my split ends trimmed and my highlights touched up. I traded in jeans and t-shirts for something she would wear, usually something cute and flirty and way too revealing for my liking. I never wore the heels but I did own six pairs that made me feel amazing the total of thirty seconds it took to try them on.

This morning after Hector drove me into this city and I put in a few hours at the shooting range, I began my mother's day. Getting lost in the hustle and bustle of the city, my first stop was at McNutt's

Cafe where I ordered an iced coffee and a quick sandwich. I ate it at the bar meanwhile I stared at the now empty stage wondering when the next poetry reading would be and living through the memories of the last one.

I could not get Eliza Reyes out of my head. She couldn't have been up on that stage longer than an hour and somehow, she managed to change me. She made me see that there was beauty in weakness as well as in strength. Before her words, I didn't know how my mom felt, being a victim of domestic abuse. When it didn't happen to you, it was easy to judge. It was easy to say, "well if I was her, I would have just left." It's easy to see a woman being hurt by the hands of a man and question her. What did she see in him? How could she love him? Why was she still with him? I'm ashamed to think that as a kid and having to see what he did to her and having to take care of her *after*, that I wondered the same question. There wasn't a day after that first night of taking my kid mask off and realizing what was going on that I didn't beg for the two of us to run away. When I was eight and even during the last year when I was twelve, I didn't understand why she wouldn't leave, why she wouldn't give us a chance at having a better life.

I didn't understand my mom even now. I couldn't. When I was younger, I was so mad that my tiny feet couldn't fit into her shoes and now I was glad that I've never had to.

But it felt like I knew her better after listening to someone talk about their experience that felt so close to her experience. I realized now that her abuse didn't define her life. She was so many things before she was a victim. She was a mother. She was a friend. She was a woman. She was a human.

That's how she would want to be remembered by me. She would want me to remember the way she used to braid my hair after my nightly showers and rub my back when I didn't feel good. She would want me to remember the look on her face as she kissed my face and left me with our neighbor when she went out for drinks with her friends. She would want me to remember all the things that made a woman beautiful. And she would want me to remember her heart, how big and impossibly full it was. She would never want me to remember her as a victim. And so I wouldn't.

My next stop of the day was the salon. There were a few people ahead of me and I flipped through the few stylist magazines they had lying out. I had never wanted to do anything crazy with my hair; it was almost always up in a ponytail anyway.

A smile blossomed on my face and I quickly grabbed a magazine to cover it.

Shit.

Hector. I groaned internally. This was not a good time to be popping up in my head.

Hector, who always made it a mission to make my ponytail holders disappear. Apparently, the man liked my hair. The only thing I particularly liked about it was at night when we were lying down, he would let my hair down and run his fingers through the strands until I fell asleep.

I set the magazine down, dug my phone out of the pocket of my jeans and bent over so no one could see the smile I knew for sure would come with texting the man in my life.

Me: I have a question.

Him: I have an answer. One you probably won't like.

I barely controlled the laugh that climbed up my throat. He had a point.

Me: What should I do with my hair?

He didn't reply right away. In fact, he didn't reply for a few minutes. So, I tried again.

Me: I was thinking bangs. Maybe a bob cut. Oooh, what about going all pink?

He didn't text back. He called me.

"Yes," I yell-whispered. I was not a fan of taking calls in public places especially inside of a business.

"Where are you?" he grunted, sounding distracted.

"At the salon," I said, stepping out of the busy area of the shop.

"What are you doing?"

"Getting my hair done," I deadpanned. What else would I be doing at the salon?

He was quiet for a moment before I heard him inhale a deep breath and then let it go. "Would you like some company?"

My body froze as my heart kicked into overdrive. He was offering his time with me out in public. A very small part of me wanted to decline. This wasn't about him or us or what the future held. It was about my mother. But I supposed it was time my two loves met.

"Yes," I said a little too breathlessly because what the fuck?

Loves.

Love.

Hector. Is that what we were doing? Love? How the hell was I supposed to know? I knew I cared about him. I knew that if I had to, I would kill for him. I would protect him against anything or anyone. In a few short months, I went from trying to kill him to waxing poetry about him every day.

I couldn't deny it any longer. It was true. I was a goner.

"Annie," he barked in my ear.

"Yes?" I asked, cringing at how high my voice had just climbed.

"Are you okay?"

I didn't trust my voice right now so I hummed my yes.

"What salon are you at?"

After I told him the address, we hung up. A hairstylist called my name and I went to tuck my phone back into my jeans but it went off before I got the chance. I looked down and saw that Hector texted me back.

If it was up to me, I wouldn't change a thing about you, bonita.

Gag me was the first thing that came to mind but the butterflies in my stomach told a different story as they worked on perfecting their gymnastics routine.

When the stylist asked me what I wanted to be done today, I gritted my teeth to prevent smiling like I was high on drugs as I told her just a trim and my highlights touched up. My mom was right when she said that getting your hair done changed a woman's world. It did make you feel brand new.

Thirty minutes later, with a much lighter head and a treatment of shampoo and conditioner that made my hair feel like I could walk on to a photoshoot for a commercial, I turned toward the door, catching sight of Hector immediately.

I was happy to see him, even though it had only been a few hours. Irritation settled in as I took him in. He wore that fitted hat again, pulling it down, masking his face. Not seeing those brown eyes felt like a hate crime against me.

I sauntered over to him. As soon as I reached him, I glided my hand in his and my heart did a little happy dance when he let me get away with it.

"I see you took my advice," he said as we walked out of the salon.

I grunted in response. It was either that or grin so hard that my cheeks hurt. "Do you have anywhere else to go?" he asked, escorting me to the passenger seat of the Lexus.

I turned around before I got in. "I have a few places to go actually, so if you're busy, you don't have to—"

I was silenced by his hand grabbing me around the waist and nudging me in the car. "I'll take you wherever you want," he said before he shut my door and walked over to the driver's side.

Before he could join me in the car, I crossed my legs tight hoping to relieve some of the want I had for him. Once he was in and buckled, he reached for my hand and placed my palm on top of his thigh, his hand covering my own. Well, there went that thought.

"Where to?" he asked as he pulled out of his parking spot.

"How do you always have a parking spot? In the city? It doesn't matter if it's late at night or in the middle of lunch hour."

He shot me a wicked grin, answering without words; he had his ways.

"There's this cute shopping center up by The Bellevue I want to go to." I looked over at him to see his eyebrows raised in confusion. "What?" I asked defensively.

He squeezed my hand, effectively calming my ass down. "You don't spend money," he said, shrugging. "And I know any place that's by The Bell is going to cost you a pretty penny."

"I spend money," I insisted half-heartedly.

He snorted. *He actually snorted.* "Fruity cereal does not count, bonita."

I was quiet for a moment, wondering if I should tell him why today was different. In my silence, his thumb reached out to run soft circles on the top of my hand.

I already gave him my heart, what the hell was a little more?

"It's my mom's birthday," I told him in a rush. His thumb froze on my skin and before I could even let out a deep breath, his thumb was back in motion. It might have been my imagination but I could've sworn his touch grew softer.

"She would have been forty today. And over the past couple of years, I started this tradition on her birthday. I spend the day doing things that she would have loved doing. Hair cuts and outfits and high heels." My heart hurt speaking the words aloud and I think Hector knew that because he flipped my hand over and laced our fingers together before giving my hand a reassuring squeeze.

We were both quiet as he drove deeper into the city. But I felt his hand in mine heavy almost feeling like he was holding my entire body in his. "The outfit you wore to the first poetry reading. Is that one you got on her birthday?"

I looked over to see his lips turned up in a smile. "Yes," I said slowly, remembering his reaction to that outfit.

"Do you think you're like her at all?" he asked as he pulled into a parking garage.

I wanted to say no. She and I, we were complete opposites. She liked shiny things; I didn't. She cared about things like fashion and looking beautiful. I cared about justice and women and poetry. I cared about her. About people like her who haven't lost the battle yet.

"I actually do," I told Hector as we exited the car and started walking to the shopping center I had in mind. "Maybe she wasn't good at protecting herself but she would be at the forefront of the battle for me and in a way, I guess for the past ten years or so, I have been preparing to do the same for her."

Hector reclaimed my hand before giving it a squeeze.

He followed me from boutique to boutique, as patient as I had ever seen him and he had come into one too many close calls with the edge of my knife. I tried on skirts and dresses and rompers and anything else remotely cute. I showed Hector every single outfit which he offered no opinion on except for a single question almost every other outfit. "Are you planning to wear that outside of the house?" To which, I replied with an eye roll.

We made our way through the entire shopping center with only one store left. I was sifting through the racks with Hector following close behind. I jumped when I felt his hand at my hip. He leaned down, his chest coming into contact with my body and I shivered.

"Have you ever thought about combining your styles?"

I looked up at him over my shoulder. "What do you mean?"

"You and your mom's," he explained, turning around and starting to look through the racks of clothing. I bit my lip to fight the smile. Just like I had moments ago, he outstretched his hand once he found something he approved of with the intention of handing it to me. When I didn't reach for it, he spared a glance at my amused expression before huffing and throwing the clothes over his own arm.

Twenty minutes later, he all but stuffed me and the clothes he picked out into a dressing room. All of his picks were a combination of what I tried on earlier today with some of my regular denim added into the mix. He picked out flowy tops with jean shorts. Some jean overalls and even some jean skirts.

When I tried on the first outfit, I fell in love. A black tight fitting midriff-baring tank and a pair of black jean short overalls. My almost nonexistent boobs looked amazing as did my legs, but most importantly the fabric. The fabric that I was used to made the outfit feel completely normal when it wasn't something I would normally wear. I sat down on the tiny seat in the tiny room and fought the urge to cry.

I knew it wasn't normal. I knew that someone knowing you,

understanding you shouldn't make you cry. But at the same time, there was a time not too long ago that I came to terms with that no one would know Annie. Hell, just a few months ago, I didn't even know her.

A light knock sounded at the door. "You okay in there, bonita?" His voice was as soft as his knock. Fuck. I stood and walked over to the mirror and dabbed at my eyes, willing the tears to go away.

I opened the door instead of answering. His eyes searched mine and then dipped lower. I might have pushed my chest out a tiny bit. His eyes snapped up and his jaw clenched. "Do you like it?" I asked, batting my eyelashes.

His only response was a grunt. I tried on a few more of his selections and after the third one where I caught him readjusting his jeans, he said, "I trust your opinion."

Tucked safely back into the dressing room, I let out a soft chuckle. The last outfit was the one. The jean shorts were a soft sage green color and the belt was wrapped in a bow in the front and the white flowy tank-top with a plunging neckline it was paired with was simple but elegant. I felt more naked than I did clothed. But it wasn't uncomfortable, just different.

I didn't show it to Hector. I was sure he would see it at a later time. I dressed back into my original clothes and we made our way to check out. He offered to carry the outfit and I let him. When it was our turn to pay, I grabbed my paper thin wallet out of my pocket to supply the cash I brought with me but when I looked up Hector had already paid the bill and was staring down at me in amusement, my bag of clothes tossed over this arm.

I took it, huffing. "I could have paid for my own stuff."

"I know," he said, opening the doors for me. "So could I. And I did."

I felt my nostrils flare but any aggravation I had dissipated when he took my hand. When we tucked back into the Lexus, he asked me if I needed to go anywhere else.

I looked into his brown eyes and felt my chest caving in. My breaths didn't come as easily. My hands shook so bad I detangled my hand from his. I needed to be anywhere else but with him.

I lied to Hector for the first time in a very long time. "Matt needs me back at the range for a few hours."

His jaw tightened and his eyes averted from mine, knowing damn well his eyes were the truth and my lips were the lie. But I couldn't feel regretful over it. The day with him had been so easy, so natural, so comfortable. But it had been hard. Hard not to lean into him. Hard not to rip that hat off and kiss him senseless. Hard not to tell him that I loved him.

When I walked into Philly Range, Matt stood in the lobby, his head tilted in confusion at my return. Without a word or second glance, I walked past him and straight into my office. I shut the door, grabbed one of the guns that needed cleaning and took it to my desk. I all but fell into my chair and I started to work. Or I tried to but my hands wouldn't cooperate. My hands shook so bad, it was a miracle that I could hold the gun in them at all.

A moment later, Matt opened the door and looked from me to the gun in my hands. "Drop the gun if there's no chance of you shooting me today," he said calmly like he was negotiating with a criminal.

I dropped the gun on the desk and he walked across the room to sit across from me. "What's wrong?"

I stood up and started to pace the room. I felt out of control and I didn't like it. I needed something. I needed a one-on-one session with a punching bag. I had so much pent up energy and words that just wanted to be free, I felt like a bomb, each second a loud tick before I couldn't take it anymore and just exploded.

Right now seemed like that time.

Even though I never told Matt about Hector, not even when I visited him in the hospital the day after I punched him. "It's his fault," I boomed, clenching my fists at my sides. "I never wanted him. I wanted one thing and he took that one thing away from me and now I want him. Only him. All of the time and I have no fucking clue how he feels. And I hate him. I hate him so fucking much for making me love him."

I huffed out a breath and then the only sound in the room was my chest heaving. It felt good to say the words out loud. To share them with anyone even if it wasn't the person I was dying to tell. It felt like someone had been standing on my chest for months and finally, they took their feet off of me. I could breathe again.

Matt whispered, "He loves you."

I whipped around to face him. "What did you just say?"

He looked from me to my empty chair and he leaned back into his seat and folded his arms across his stomach waiting me out.

I was desperate for his words and I didn't pretend otherwise. I plopped my ass back in that chair and looked at him expectantly. "You know who he is to the public, right?"

I leaned forward, propping my elbows on the desk. "That's the one thing he doesn't talk about. All he tells me is that he is a dangerous man and I know he kills."

"He is dangerous and he does kill. The Rivera name is powerful but with each new leader, they turn less into a crime organization and more into a martyr for this city. In the past couple of years, he has raised the prices of drugs so kids of color won't have easy access to them. He built a private tuition-free primary school for kids with autism. In the past five years, he has killed close to one hundred women beaters and rapists."

Matt smirked but I could barely see him through my blurry vision. I thought I knew what kind of man Hector was, but I was wrong. He was so much *more*. "Basically, he's the real police. He's the one who promises justice and actually follows through." Matt respected him, maybe even admired him.

I knew Hector was a mixture of good and bad, of Heaven and Hell. He was a blurred line. And I loved every inch of him.

"He got married young and no one knows what happened to her, just that she disappeared and left their son behind. That was over ten years ago, Annie. And he's never even looked at another woman. No one until you."

And boy, does he look at me.

"The day you came back to work, about an hour before you showed up, he called me. He asked me if I knew you and then he told me that you were under the Rivera protection. Not a harm would come to you now or after what situation you have going on with him ends." He looked at me like that should mean something to me. From what it sounded like, he protected the entire city. "The only other two people on that list are his son and Nolan."

His son and his childhood best friend. And now me.

His family.

I was already gathering up my things to go home, to go to him.

"He would burn this city alive for you, Annie," Matt said. His face wasn't its usual cocky, smirking swagger, it was serious.

I rushed outside without calling Nolan or Hector or having any idea where home actually was. But it turned out, I didn't need it. Hector was still parked where he left me, his head leaned back against the seat's headrest with his eyes closed. I walked to the driver's side and pulled open the door. His eyes snapped open but I didn't wait for him to say something.

I fell into his lap and crashed my lips against his. He caught me. His hands slipped around my waist and gripped my hips closing any gap between us. I blindly reached for his hat and knocked it away before my fingers sunk into his hair. Our kiss was as frantic as my heartbeat. I couldn't get enough of him. I would never be able to get enough of him.

I kissed him to tell him that I was sorry for running, for lying.

I kissed him because I wanted to. Because I needed to.

I kissed him because he was the first man I'd ever loved.

When we came up for air, I let my forehead rest against his as we fought hard to get our breathing back under control.

"Take me home," I whispered and he did.

CHAPTER TWENTY-FOUR

Annie

In college, you learn a lot of things. It's kind of what the entire four years are about. But there are a lot of things that you learn outside of academics. You learn through experience or through entertainment. And in my case, poetry.

Eliza Reyes at a poetry reading and through her two books of poems I had absolutely devoured in the past couple of weeks taught me something. Something that seemed so simple but I had never come to fully realize before.

A woman doesn't need a sword to be a warrior. A woman doesn't need to have the strongest muscles or the best reflexes. A woman doesn't need to know how to wield a knife or aim a gun. A woman is strong in her passion and in her fight. There's strength in softness and

It wasn't a conscious decision but when I had an hour of gap time after a shift at the range, it wasn't food that was calling my name. It was something else entirely.

The Center, the only women's shelter located in the city, offered refuge to women escaping pasts of domestic violence and sexual assault. I stopped just outside of the old Victorian building. It competed with major businesses and corporations as being the tallest building in this part of the city but it had no competition of being the prettiest. It felt like it belonged in a small town rather than a vibrant city.

My heart pounded against my chest as I forced my legs to move up the few stairs leading up to the front door. It wasn't the first time I'd been here, but it had been awhile. The door had an old-style brass knocker and my shaky fingers wrapped around it, slamming against the door three times before stepping away, my head knowing too well how it feels to get hit with the heaviness of that wooden frame.

It took a few minutes, a few minutes I willed my feet to stay planted on the ground and not run as far away as I possibly could. Out of all the workers I knew from when I interned here between my sophomore and junior year of college, the person that opened the door with a booming smile was Eliza Reyes herself.

My mouth gaped open as she stood there with a smile on her face and the door half-opened. This woman who I didn't even personally know who absolutely touched my soul was standing in front of me smiling like my world wasn't just thrown off balance.

"Annie, right?" she asked.

I nodded, still staring, still in awe. She reached out to grab my arm and dragged me inside. I was thankful for it because I would have probably stayed glued to the same spot for hours.

"Yes," I confirmed slowly and suddenly suspicious. How did she know me? I was pretty loud when she was on stage at McNutt's Cafe, but I didn't think I was so loud that she would pick me out of the crowd.

"You don't remember me, do you?" she questioned, still having a hold of my arm and pulling me through the house. I followed her upstairs and into one of the empty offices.

She was hard to forget when I had just seen her weeks ago but it didn't sound like she was talking about weeks ago. "Should I?" I went with, confused as hell.

"Yeah," she said, finally letting go of me and moving behind the desk and sitting in a chair. She worked here, I realized. I racked my brain searching for a memory of mine that she was in but I came up empty.

"You worked here three years ago," she stated. "I sought out help three years ago."

I blinked back my surprise. Was she here when I interned? This shelter held a lot of women and some went faster than they came; it was impossible to recognize every single face in the span of the three months I spent here.

"If I'm being perfectly honest, back then, I didn't come here believing that anyone could say or do anything that would help me. I fell in love with an angry man. A man who told me he loved me and told me he would protect me always. His promises lasted as long as the honeymoon stage did. A few months, if that. I didn't make his favorite thing for dinner, he backhanded me. I didn't iron his clothes, he filled up the iron with scalding hot water and poured it over me while I was sleeping."

Her words were honest, so honest I felt like her words were a knife lodged into my heart and with each syllable, she twisted the knife. "The thing about abusers is that after they hurt you, they take care of you. And for a reason unknown to me, you believe them. You believe them when they tell you they're sorry. You believe them when they say that it will never happen again. You believe them when they tell you that they love you. And you stay and you let it happen again and again."

At some point, while she poured her truth out to me, my eyes fell shut, my body sagging against the chair. "But you said something, Annie, you said something that changed my life."

My head snapped up and I saw she was fighting back tears with her hands stretched across the desk. I slid my hands in hers and squeezed. "It was just a couple of weeks before your internship ended. You held your first group meeting and you told us the story of your mom, of what happened to her. You stood up in front of a group of strangers and shared your biggest lost. You lost your mom to domestic violence and you weren't bitter. You weren't mad at your mom, you were devastated for her and for yourself. The last thing you said that night was, 'Love yourself enough to get out and if you don't love yourself enough to do that, think about those who do love you. Whether it's your child, your sister, your mom, or the lady at the supermarket who says hi to you every time you buy groceries. Your life matters and the only person who has the power to say enough is enough is you.'"

I nodded, tears running down my face as I remembered that night. I hoped I would get through to one woman. That was enough for me. I knew I couldn't save every single one of them; not everyone wanted to be saved, but I was just hoping for one.

That one sat across from me today.

"I left right after you did. I went back to him. We hit the reset button. The only way he put his hands on me was to show me how much he loved me. Three months passed and it started all over again, this time with a vengeance. It wasn't just his hands this time. He was a welder and I was his favorite piece of metal. And then, I found out I was pregnant." I barely held back a gasp as my hands grew tighter in hers. "I didn't want her to be Annie 2.0. I didn't want her to grow up and watch her mother be degraded and destroyed. I waited until he left for work and I left with nothing but the clothes on my back and I came here. That was over two years ago and the girls here, they did help me. They helped me find a job and then a house. Even after I left, they helped me submit my application to community college. They stood with me throughout it all. I look back at the woman I was then and I can't recognize her and every morning when I wake up to the sound of my little girl crying for breakfast, I thank God I can't."

I was speechless. So utterly speechless. So in awe of this woman.

"Thank you for sharing your story, Annie. I'm afraid of who I would be today if you didn't."

"Shut up," I told her because I didn't know what else to say. She withdrew her hands from mine, reached into her desk and supplied us with tissues. After we wiped our eyes and blew our noses, I said, "Your poetry reading was amazing. I was there."

She smiled knowingly. "I know." She batted her eyes at me while looking me up and down.

"What?" I demanded.

Just then, the two workers I knew from years ago busted in the door. Jessica and Rachel. "Annie," they both exclaimed in unison and I found myself lifted out of my chair and in a three-way hug. When we pulled away, Jessica took my face in her hands and had a good look at me. Rachel looked past us and grimaced at Eliza. "We couldn't wait any longer."

"How did you know I was here?" I looked between the three of them. "I get the feeling you were expecting me."

"We were also at Eliza's poetry reading. Two tables behind you. Watching you kissing an older man senseless."

Jessica screeched so loud I had to cover my ears with my hands. Rachel peeled my hands away and all three of them were looking at me expectantly. "The Annie I knew a few years ago would rather light her eyes on fire than to ever be involved with a man."

I shrugged my shoulders. How could I explain Hector? There weren't words in the dictionary or anywhere else that could describe the man he was and more importantly, the man he was to me. "I always thought I had my life mapped out. I had a checklist and every day, I was living to mark one of those boxes off. I've come to learn that life is unexpected and the unexpected changes you. He hijacked my plans and made me love him without even trying."

I looked at each of them and they all wore different expressions. Jessica sported a sappy smile. Rachel held a prideful glee in her eye and Eliza had tears welling underneath her eyelids once more. "You deserve it," she whispered.

I stood up and checked the time. "I would love to stay but I have to get to work."

"Do you still work at the shooting range?" Jessica asked.

"Yeah."

"So, you don't have any time to volunteer here?"

I perked up at that, looking between the three of them. "Do you have a spot available?"

Rachel nodded. "As long as you can provide me with a copy of that Social Work BA and your clearances come back clean, we want to have you. Right now, we have a lot of young women. Teenagers and women in their early twenties. We would love a badass woman around here. They have been pleading for months for a self-defense class."

That I could do. I would have to cut back my hours at the shooting range but if I could go back to honoring my mother's memory in a way she'd be proud of, I'd drop everything.

"Yes," I said without hesitation. "I'm in."

I had no idea what the night held.

An hour ago, Hector barged into the house and ordered me into the shower, requesting me to wear the outfit I bought on my mother's birthday.

The past week had been hectic. Philly Range had a state inspection due at the end of the month so it would be another two weeks before I could cut down on any hours. Matt said I owed it to him, for not seeing what a fine specimen of a man he was. I ignored him but still worked my eight hours despite already working my way into the day to day routine at the shelter. I scheduled an appointment at a clinic to take a drug test. I dug my diploma and license out of my backpack and handed it over to Jessica to make me official. I went in a few hours a day to tour the building, re-learn safety clearances, and sign papers.

Today, I worked at the range for eight hours and spent an additional two hours at the shelter. I worked side by side with Eliza who I was still a little too star struck by. It was like meeting Wonder Woman and her telling you, you inspired her to be the strongest woman known to mankind. It didn't feel real. She introduced me to a few of the women in the shelter. Some snuffed their nose up at me but some of them really opened up to me.

It was a good day but I felt drained emotionally. All of the feelings I shoved down, all of the memories I've done a stellar job of forgetting, rose up like demons haunting me. It felt good to talk to some of the women and their children. My heart soared any time they sought me out, but I felt my mom in each look, in every conversation. She was with me. I could feel her but I'd never be able to see her. Two years ago when I interned here, the feeling almost drowned me. And if I was being honest, even now, my head barely bobbed above the water.

But this was Hector. Hector who always gave me what I wanted. So, it didn't matter if I could barely keep my eyes open or if my bones hurt from exhaustion, I would get dressed and I'd let him take me wherever he wanted.

Dressing in the green shorts, white tank, and the black leather jacket I picked up on a shopping spree with Nolan this week, I headed downstairs. I found Hector at the kitchen table, his eyes closed as he hummed along to the soft music playing from the kitchen.

"I'm ready."

His eyes snapped open, immediately seeking me out before

traveling down my body. He looked at me long enough the goosebumps on my arms turned into shivers. "We're going out tonight."

I raised my eyebrows at his admission. "We're going out? In public? Willingly?"

A noise escaped him, sounding like a mixture between a grunt and a chuckle. I followed him to the car, a warmth settling underneath my skin that had nothing to do with the humid Philadelphia air I stepped into.

Spending five minutes with Hector felt like winning a lottery ticket. Roping him into dates was the best part of my day. To have him take me out for a change, grumbling and all, felt like all of my wishes had been granted.

I tucked my hands underneath my thighs so I wouldn't mess with the blindfold Hector placed over my eyes before he started to drive. Just as I started to wonder where he could be taking me, I felt a warmth settle over my thigh.

His hand gripped my bare leg in a reassuring hold. I sat up straighter, feeling his hand *everywhere*. "Relax, bonita," he whispered when the car stopped. "You're safe with me."

I knew that. No one would fuck with me with him by my side. Unless it was the man himself with his warm brown eyes and his soft but electrifying touch. Unless it was my traitorous heart that skipped a beat by just looking his way.

"Unless you decided that you were sick of sharing your bed and food with me and you're taking me someplace to kill me," I said, more to distract myself than anything else.

Hector barked out a laugh and for the hundredth time, I cursed this blindfold. After his laughter ceased, he squeezed my leg. Yes, most definitely trying to kill me. "Should I remind you, bonita," he said and I could just picture his lips tilting up into a smirk, "of how many times you have tried to kill me?"

I knew exactly how many times and if he wasn't careful, the last time wouldn't be the last. I told him so and his laughter, once again, filled the car and my heart.

I didn't know how much time had passed, but when Hector stopped and the ignition cut off, I knew we were here. "Can I take this thing off yet?" I asked impatiently as I let my hands out from underneath my thighs.

His hand moved from my thigh and I barely held back a protest. I heard his car door open and close but I wasn't too eager to make an ass out of myself by attempting to get out of the car without his help. I felt the hot summer air on my bare arms and legs when he opened the door. Then, Hector's hands were on me again and if I had any talented vocal cords, I would have started singing his praises. His intertwined one of my hands with his and his other hand grabbed me by the waist, helping me lower on to a sidewalk. I could hear people talking among themselves, but it was too quiet for us to be in the city.

"Where are we?" I asked him not for the first time. He ignored me as he guided me down the street. He paused and a second later, we walked into somewhere. I only knew that because the heat I felt from the beating sun changed into a cool breeze. Then the smell hit me. Food. Not just any food, Mexican food. I could smell peppers and onions and so many of the spices I have grown accustomed to Hector cooking with.

344

"Where are we?" I asked again. Hector answered me this time but with no words. He untied the blindfold and I blinked a few times as my vision returned to me. We were in a restaurant. As I took in the sight in front of me, one word came to mind. Romantic. That's how it felt. The room had a dark, sensual glow to it. The walls were a light brown while the tables and booths were a deep, darker shade of brown. Candlelight on each table and along all of the walls lit up the room but it wasn't bright. More of a glow than anything. It was beautiful.

A young woman rushed out onto the floor from a wall that I swore was just a plain wall but must have been a door. "I'm so sorry," she said, smiling once seeing us standing just inside the door. When she looked from me to the man beside me, her body straightened and the smile on her face disappeared in an instant. "Mr. Rivera," she said, half-bowing to him.

I couldn't control my reaction. My eyebrows drew together and a laugh bubbled up inside of my throat and I couldn't catch it in time. This girl was bowing at his presence like he was a king. He was a king of my heart but he didn't know that and even if he did, hell would have to freeze over before I greeted him like that. The girl looked at me frantically like my outburst was going to get us both in trouble. I tilted my head to look up at him. His jaw was clenched and he wouldn't meet my eyes but the edge of his lips were tilted, barely containing his own amusement. I reached back and hit him in the stomach. He caught my hand and tucked it into his.

"We'll be in the back. Send a waiter." He urged me forward without a second glance at the girl who scurried back to where she came from. He led me past the tables where couples and families were eating, each one of them acknowledging him with a nod.

I felt like I was a newborn and I was opening my eyes for the very first time after being secluded in darkness for nine months. I knew Hector. I knew the dangerous man. I knew the vigilante side of him from what Matt had told me just days ago. This version of him I did not know. He didn't smile. His face warned you of fucking with him and the way he spoke was clipped. I didn't say a word as we walked through the dining room. Hector stopped us when we reached a table that was out of view of the other guests; we could see them but they couldn't see us.

He pulled out my chair for me before he took his right next to me. I rested my elbows on the table, placing my face in my hands, and stared at him. It took him a while but when he locked eyes with me, the slowest, sexiest smirk I'd ever seen took over his face.

For the second time in less than ten minutes, laughter spurted out of me. "Who was that back there?" I asked, placing my hand over my aching stomach.

He shrugged. "Dominique."

"Not the girl. You." He only frowned. "That wasn't my Hector back there," I told him quietly.

"Your Hector," he mused, scooting his chair closer and grabbing a tendril of my hair before wrapping it around his fingers and tugging me close so our faces were almost touching. In that moment, I forgot how to breathe. "He's yours for a reason, bonita. No one else gets him. Only you."

A throat clearing made me jump and breathe again. A waiter stood a safe distance away and greeted Hector the same way Dominique had.

This time I only rolled my eyes. "What can I get for you, sir? Ma'am?"

As Hector told the waiter to go grab me a menu, I shut my eyes. This was my fault. I was the one who had the great idea of roping him into public dates. Tonight was so different because he was the one who planned this. The idea of us was just that: an idea. It was in my head for so long. Yes, we went on dates. Yes, he always showed up when I needed him. Yes, I was always wrapped in him at night. Yes, I pictured him naked at least a million times a day. But the idea that we were something more always seemed like it was all in my head. We didn't talk about it. The kissing, the hand-holding, the I miss you's every evening when he picked me up from work. We never talked about it. We weren't talking about it now but it felt like it.

"Where are we?" I asked him, yet again.

"A restaurant."

"Why?"

"Because we haven't had a date night in over a week."

I perked up at his response. It had been over a week. "You noticed that," I whispered.

He bit his lip before he answered. "Yes. When it comes to you, I notice everything."

"I thought you couldn't be seen with me in public."

"That's why I brought you here."

"Where is here?" I was starting to sound like a broken record. He didn't answer me until the waiter returned with a menu for me. I took it after thanking him. The front of the menu read, "Welcome to Maria's."

That was his mom's name. My gaze snapped up to Hector. "This—this is yours?"

He hummed a yes. I flipped open the menu and every item featured on the menu was something I had eaten over the past couple of months. "What do you want, bonita?" he asked me softly when I shut the menu and simply stared at him.

You. I didn't say that and I hid my eyes so he couldn't see the real answer in my eyes. I turned in my seat to where the waiter stood. I motioned him forward. "I want everything."

He chuckled nervously and looked to Hector which would have pissed me off if Hector didn't just show me a part of him I didn't know about. He nodded his head. "Have Joseph cook a sample of each dish but bring out a taco platter. And bring us two a pitchers, water and a Corona." He looked to me, a silent question in his eyes. I nodded my approval and then, we were alone again.

I looked around the restaurant again. "This really is yours," I said in awe. "How long?"

"This was my mama's dream. As soon as me and Nolan were eighteen, this was her plan. I've told you she's the one who taught me how to cook. I learned how to make her signature meals before I learned how to kiss a girl. My papa always argued with her that I didn't need to waste time in the kitchen. She would roll her eyes at him and remind him that he, too had to learn how to cook before she agreed to marry him. She always said, 'A woman's place is wherever she damn well wants it to be. I love to cook for my family but when I don't, someone else is going to pick up the slack.'"

I loved his mom. I felt like I knew her even though I'd never get the chance to meet her and my heart hurt for him, for losing his mom so early. I reached across the table for his hand. "Moms are the best."

He sat back in his chair, lost in his own thoughts. "Are you sad that Samuel didn't have a mother figure growing up?"

His eyebrows drew together. "Yes. I had my dad who never showed me anything but discipline and tough love but my mother, she allowed and encouraged me to be soft. Too soft if you were to ask my father. She taught me how to treat women and to be a gentleman. I learned from my dad how to use my body as a weapon and from my mama, I learned how to use my heart. Samuel doesn't remember his mom. He was only three when she left. I did my best with him and I think he turned out okay."

From what I knew about Samuel, I was sure Hector did more than okay. I asked him the one question I had been dying to for a while now. "What happened to her?"

He sighed and looked away from me. "I told you what happened to her, Annie. She couldn't handle being in my life."

There was a hardness to his tone, almost daring me to follow her lead. I didn't know her but I did know that she and I weren't the same and neither was our relationship with the man sitting across from me, a broody look I hadn't seen in a long time taking over his face. I leaned forward and rubbed the pad of my thumb across the creases in his forehead until he gave me his eyes.

"I'm not her," I whispered and his face immediately softened. "I knew what kind of man you were the moment we met. I'm still here." And not because I have to be, but that part I kept to myself. He lifted our hands to his mouth, placing a tender kiss on the edge of my palm.

Our dinner arrived moments later but I still needed my answers. "Where is she, Hector?"

"I thought we were done discussing this."

"You were. I wasn't. Where is she?"

"Gone," he said like I knew he would.

"Hector Rivera," I grumbled.

He groaned but relented. "She's dead. At least her old life is. I bought her a new alias and set her up with a monthly account. Last I knew, she was living in Tennessee, settled down with an investment banker and was working on her white picket house fence dream."

"You're still giving her money?" I asked incredulously. He nodded, stuffing food in his face. I suspected he didn't particularly want to have this conversation. "For what reason?"

"She's the mother of my child, Annie," he said, his voice holding a warning in it. A warning I decided to ignore.

"Exactly! The mother who hasn't seen her son in fifteen years. If anything, she should be paying you."

He waved me off. "That was the deal. I promised to compensate her in case Samuel ever wanted to get in contact with her."

"You paid her, are continuing to pay her, so she will be nice to her son if ever he should call," I said slowly, hoping it would make more sense to my own ears.

"It's for my son, Annie. I don't care if you don't like it. It's what I had to do to make sure my son was going to be okay if it turned out that I wasn't what he wanted, either."

I looked at him and for the first time, I could see the man behind the walls he had built up. The man who struggled to be *enough* for every person in his life. He wanted to be the type of man his mom was proud of. He wanted to be the son his father wanted. He wanted to be the perfect husband and a good dad.

I didn't know who moved first but before I could even blink, I was sitting atop his thighs, my arms thrown around his neck and his head sought comfort against my chest. I didn't care that we were out in public. I didn't care that we just had our first real fight since I got over trying to kill him. He was a man who needed love, who was begging for it and even though I wasn't sure what would happen in three months' time, I was all too eager to give him my touch, my heart, my everything.

CHAPTER TWENTY-FIVE

Hector

I never touched drugs. Not as a teenager and not once through my adult life.

Part of it had to do with Nolan. How his parents completely disregarded the fact that they had a son. How they acted while they were going through withdrawals. Many times, Nolan would disappear from school before my mom officially adopted him and they'd use him to syphon money out of my mom.

Part of it was because I became a father at an early age. And a single father only a couple of years later. I couldn't do anything in fear of someone swooping away my reason to live. I did everything by the book.

It wasn't until the age of thirty-four, three months ago, that I got my first taste of a soul consuming drug. Except she wasn't something you could buy. She was something that gave herself willingly to me and me only.

Annie Miller was my drug. She was my weakness. Outside of my son, she was the best goddamn thing that's ever happened to me.

Every time she was in my sight, I couldn't stop thinking about kissing her. Touching her. Making her smile. Hell, even her frown did things to me.

But just like a drug when I couldn't feel her, the doubts crept into my head. I hadn't been in love with a woman in a very long time. Not since Samuel's mom. I knew because of the life that was forced upon me, I would never get a real shot at love. Women loved their men bad; what they didn't love was the lifestyle that came with it. I learned that lesson when I was still in my teenage years. I accepted it. I accepted that the family business and raising my son to not be a complete dickhead were the only things that could be important to me as a man. Annie, or any other woman, weren't in the cards. At least long term.

Annie couldn't be long term. She'd been living on fumes since that piece of shit father of hers killed her mom. She saw one thing, blind to everything else. I didn't get a choice over my life. I was born a Rivera, my destiny was sealed before my parents even knew what my name would be. I knew what it was like to not have a choice. Just like I have with Samuel, I gave Annie a choice. A choice to be something more than the dirty deeds you thought were your destiny.

She fought me at first, but over the past couple of weeks, I have watched her become her own person. The poetry that she reads and watches make her happy and I've watched from the crack in the door as she wrote her own, bent over the desk in my study, pencil to paper, writing so intensely I was surprised she didn't rip the paper. She may have found her passion, but there were small changes that I noticed that absolutely fucking thrilled me. She laughed more than she frowned. Just weeks ago, she wouldn't so much as grunt a laugh if I had Kevin Hart play a live show in the living room, and now I was growing obsessed with the way she would throw her head back and laugh at something. Her weight changed, too. When I first met her, she was all bones. She was strong, she trained herself to be, but there was nothing to her. She informed me she was on a ramen diet for years preparing for her next life. Watching her become healthy, especially given how much I've noticed she loves food has been the greatest thing for me to see.

She didn't share the same opinion. "Hector," she groaned this morning, padding down the stairs while I made us breakfast.

"Hmm?" I asked around a swig of coffee.

"I'm fat," she declared, that frown of hers making an appearance.

I didn't bother dignifying that statement with a response. She walked over to me, not stopping until our arms brushed, hot stove be damned.

"Did you hear me?" she pressed.

I looked down at her. "I heard you," I told her. Our eyes locked and her pupils grew wider and wider until she threw her hands up in the air, frustrated with my lack of response or something else entirely, I wasn't sure.

"My jeans don't fit anymore. My shirts are too tight. I need to go shopping."

I brought our plates to the table and we sat down. She was already digging in before I could grab a fork. I kept my laughter at bay, not wanting to face her wrath. "We'll go shopping. Do you work today?"

She sighed in exhaustion. "Yeah. I'm off tomorrow. We can go then."

We spent the next half hour eating in comfortable silence until she grabbed both of our plates, taking them into the kitchen. She announced she was going to get a shower and I nodded, awaiting my morning call from Samuel who would be going on break.

I felt Annie's hands in my hair as soon as Samuel's name flashed across the phone. I answered it at the same time Annie tugged the hair at the nape of my neck, tilting my face up. Her lips found mine in a second as Samuel launched into a story from the night before. She kissed me softly, slowly like that was going to drive me less crazy than our deep, desperate kisses. She was wrong. She pulled back and smiled down at me. That fucking smile. As the thought of watching her walk up the stairs popped in my head, she leaned back down, showering me with quick pecks on the lips. She lightly smacked the side of my face after she delivered me with one last kiss.

I stopped her from killing me when we first met, and here she was, making it her mission to kill me.

After her shower and a very long, very detailed description of the women my son shared the night with last night, we were on our way to the city. "You really need to stop kissing me," I said just before the city came into view.

I felt her gaze on me immediately but I was too preoccupied veering onto the ramp to spare her a glance. "I would," she said solemnly. "If I knew you didn't like it so much."

When I chanced a glance at her, a smirk bloomed upon her lips. I shook my head at her, trying like hell to fight my own grin.

Hours later, in between meetings in the city, Annie crept back into my mind. My mind kept going back to that poetry reading. To the woman with the brightest smile and the ugliest scar. To the women's shelter who aided women who have been domestically abused. To Annie's reaction. She tried to remain calm, but I had a feeling that that night was the scariest thing Annie has done in years. When she had Cameron tied up in his living room, she was eerily calm. She wasn't even scared when I showed up and ruined her plans. But that night she spent in a café on my lap, she showed me a weakness. The tiniest of flinches. The clearing of her throat when I knew she was fighting her emotions from showing. The way her arms would tighten around my neck when the poet's words were just a little bit too graphic.

The women's shelter was on the way to my next meeting. I had more money than I knew what to do with. It killed me to know that there were women out there like Annie's mom and even kids who had to see and go through what Annie had to from a very young age.

I knocked at the door and a white woman with dark brown hair cut short answered the door, her ready smile slipping at the sight of me. "Can I help you, sir?" Her voice sounded alarmed. I guess I shouldn't have been surprised since these women were hurt by men. That pissed me off. Not all of us were despicable human beings.

I smiled politely at her, unfolding the paper in my hands.

She looked down. "Ah, Eliza. She's one of our counselors. Do you need to see her?"

I shook my head. "No. I wanted to see about making a donation to the facility."

Her smile brightened. "Oh, well then. Come in my office and we can talk." I followed her up the stairs into a room, where she closed the door. When we both sat and I placed the check I had already filled out on her desk, she leaned back in her chair and folded her arms across her stomach. "Do you have someone who has dealt with domestic abuse?"

I frowned without meaning to. "More of a secondhand smoke type of thing."

"Ah," she said, her voice soft, full of understanding. "The kids. Hurt my heart. Here we do lots of things with the kids, if you're interested in hearing."

I nodded and she proceeded.

"With the women, the mothers, we do our best to try and be a shoulder for them to lean and cry on. Their days are mostly filled with therapy sessions, group sessions with the other women, finding a hobby, or job searching. With the kids, it's difficult. Some of the kids are so young that they won't remember seeing their dad do horrible things to their mom, so for them, we just focus on making them the happiest. With toys and playtime, we pretty much succeed. The middle age kids, ranging from five to twelve years old, it's tricky. They remember and they remember vividly. Therapy sessions are vital to their recovery. They are at such a vulnerable point in their life. We try to get them into sports or reading or learning. It's escapism for a little while. With the older kids, the teenagers, it's both harder and easier. Teenagers are stubborn creatures, so there's a chance of about twenty percent that they'll love therapy sessions. With the young men, we have an entire game room downstairs with every game console known to mankind. That keeps them pretty occupied. For the girls, we just had a new volunteer come in and has been an actual blessing. She teaches them self-defense." She looked down at her watch. "Actually, the first class happens in about twenty minutes."

She heaved a big breath, taking a sip of water. "A lot of good things happen here and I'm grateful for your donation. Most of what happens here is positive. Of course, we wish there wasn't a reason women needed to take refuge but we try to make it positive for them while they're here."

"From what I could tell, they're in good hands."

She smiled at me, dimples in both of her cheeks. "Okay, tour time and then I have to ditch you because I need to oversee that new defense class."

I rose from my seat and followed her back downstairs. She showed me every room I saw when I walked in. Pointed out all of the areas, the kitchen, and the offices.

"Ooh," she said, grabbing my arm, clearly excited. "Our volunteer is here right now. I'll give you a look into the class." She didn't let go of my arm as she pulled me down the hall. The room was wide, with mats laid all over the floor, mirrors covering one entire wall. There were about two dozen women in the room. They were all facing the mirror, legs spread shoulder length apart, punching the air. Their form was perfect.

"Okay ladies," the trainer who I couldn't see said. "I want to see you partner up. Focus on your swings and on blocking. If anyone somehow gets a black eye, both parties are banned from class."

That voice was a caress to my heart. This woman. This fucking woman. The women parted, letting me see her. Her eyes widened when she saw me. She walked toward me, her eyebrows drawn together in confusion.

"Hector." My name was a breath on her lips.

"Hey, bonita," I murmured softly.

She smiled, sliding up to my side, wrapping her arms around my back. "What are you doing here?"

"I could ask you the same question."

She lifted one shoulder in a shrug, not answering me. Our eyes connected and we were silent, unconcerned about the twenty or so people that were in the room. Her fingers tightened against my t-shirt.

"Hey, Annie." A girl came into view, breaking our spell. Annie jerked away from me, her eyes focused on the girl in question. She was a white girl, no older than fourteen years old, determination set in her eyes. "I was wondering if you could show me that move again. How to get out of a hold. It's the one thing I can't seem to do."

Annie didn't smile, she just nodded and followed the girl, not even bothering to say goodbye. I watched after her. The girl took at least twenty attempts of breaking out of Annie's hold, Annie whispering a comment after each failed try. She tried again, this time succeeding and sending Annie to the floor, flat on her back. Annie smiled then and the look on the teen's face was pure bliss.

Her eyes found mine from her spot on the ground, a soft laugh escaping her.

From the moment I encountered Annie, I knew I wanted her hardness to fade. I wanted to see her open, see her soft. It hit me in that moment when she was teaching a girl no older than fifteen or sixteen how to escape from a hold, I realized there was softness in being hard. When her eyes connected with mine, I felt my heart stop completely like it had escaped my body and was placed directly in her hands to do with whatever she wanted.

Six months didn't matter.

Cameron didn't matter.

Hell, I didn't even matter.

She was the only one who mattered.

CHAPTER TWENTY-SIX

Annie

Hector stuck around until I finished with the class and talked with almost every woman to see how they were feeling. He was leaning up against the passenger door of his car, one foot across the other, hands stuffed in his pockets, his eyes glued to the door I just walked out of.

He kicked off the car when he caught sight of me. What I wanted to do was run down the stairs and sidewalk and jump into him with a hope that he would never let me go. I settled for strolling toward him, a small smile I couldn't help but reveal to him. He opened the door for me without a word and I slid in. He pulled out of the parking spot and before pulling out into traffic, his hand grabbed mine and pulled it and me toward him. I exchanged the passenger seat for the one in the middle, not a single part of my body not feeling the heat of him.

We didn't talk the entire ride home. The only sound were my unsteady breaths caused by being this close to him and his soft humming along to the radio.

The closer we got to the house, the harder my heart beat, the louder my thoughts seemed to ring inside of my head. I snuck looks at him from my spot against his shoulder. Sometimes he would catch me, either with his eyes or giving himself away with the tilt of his lips. The last traffic light before we left the city hit red and I felt his gaze on me. I lifted my head to see his focus entirely on me.

"Kiss me, bonita," he whispered, his breath fanning across my cheeks.

He didn't have to tell me twice. I wanted to ravage him, to show him how desperate I was for him. How needy I was. How needy he made me. But he was looking at me in a way he always did and in a way he had never before. He looked at me like he saw me and he was looking at me like he could never get enough of seeing me. My hand that wasn't in his reached up to grab the collar of his shirt, pulling him toward me. His lips parted on an almost inaudible gasp and I took that has my opening. I kissed his top lip, then his bottom, then both of them. His hand tightened in mine which did not help the ache in my lower belly. Our kisses were soft, softer than they had ever been. My lips on his mine, this time, felt different from all of the other times. This was me giving him more. More than my touch, more than my mind. This time, my heart was in it, too.

Blaring horns snapped me out of my Hector bubble. I started to pull away but he yanked me back to him, sinking his teeth into my bottom lip. I opened my eyes to see him close.

"Las cosas que me haces," he whispered. *Translation: The things you do to me.*

I placed one last ghost of a kiss to his lips before resuming my place against his shoulder. When he started to drive again, I let the smile I had been fighting loose. He did something to me, too. Tonight, I was hoping he would do a lot more.

When we got home, Hector started on dinner while I went into his office and started pouring all of the things out on paper that I was too afraid to admit to the man on the other side of the door. The words rushed out of me. My hands were barely capable of writing them down fast enough. I barely registered Hector when he came into the room. It wasn't until his knuckles lifted my chin that I set my pencil aside.

"Come eat." I didn't even have a chance to look at what I had written before I followed him out to eat. He had already had the table set. I sat down while he got us drinks. "What will it be tonight?" he asked over his shoulder.

I had many answers to that question. Answers that I wasn't sure he was ready for. Answers that I needed liquid courage for. "I'll take a beer," I said flippantly, even though I was feeling anything but.

We ate in comfortable silence until he pushed his plate away, leaned back in his seat, and touched his beer to his lips, and waited for me to talk. So, we weren't going to wait to talk until we were in bed. I rolled my lips to keep from smiling. He was falling straight into my plan without even knowing it.

I took my last bite of rice on my plate and he never took his eyes off of me. I stood and he lifted an eyebrow in question. I walked around the table toward him, his head following my every move. I took the beer out of his hands and allowed myself to take a long pull until I drained the entire thing. I set it down behind me on the table and he had already figured me out because his hands were spread, waiting to wrap around me when I plopped on his lap. I did just that.

I took his chin between my two fingers to distract myself. "Do you remember when you asked me what I studied in school and I..." I paused, trying to swallow past the lump in my throat. His hands gripped my hips in a reassuring squeeze. "Anyway, the answer to that question is social services. I have a bachelor's degree in social services. I'm not sure if I would have ever used it." I chanced a look up at him and his eyes that felt like home felt like a caress the way he was looking at me. "If my plans weren't thrown off balance." That was close as to saying "because of him" as I could voice at the moment. "I actually was an intern at the women's shelter the summer before my junior year and I loved it there. Eliza, the poet we saw together, donated all proceedings from her poetry night to the shelter and so, one day I just swung by. Eliza is one of three workers over there. We talked for a long time and Jessica and Rachel are the two people I knew from my internship. They asked me if I had time to volunteer a couple of hours a day. I jumped at the opportunity and now I'm there for a few hours after my shifts at the shooting range."

We both were quiet for a moment. He reached up and removed my hands from his chin and wrapped them in his. He leaned down and pressed a soft kiss to my temple, my nose, the corner of my lips. For the first time since I met him, I didn't fight him to be in control. I let him devour me when his lips turned hard against mine. We were both out of breath a few minutes later but I was needier for him than

I had ever been.

I let my head fall, my forehead falling against his shoulder. "I'm gonna go shower," I whispered, pressing a kiss to his collarbone.

"Go ahead, bonita. I'm going to call Samuel and talk to him. I'll meet you up there."

The only reason I didn't run up the stairs was because I didn't want him knowledgeable of my plan. The plan that consisted of me and him naked under the sheets. Just thinking that had heat washing through my entire body.

Once in the bedroom, I only grabbed one of Hector's t-shirts before locking myself in the bathroom. I didn't take one step into the bathroom; instead, I sagged against the door, my heart beating a million miles a minute.

"I love him," I whispered into the empty room. Only silence met me. I pushed off the door and began stripping off my clothes. With each piece that dropped, I grew braver in admitting my truth. By the time I faced the mirror above the vanity with no clothing left to shred, I smiled so hard that I had to grip my hurting cheeks. "I love him," I said to my reflection. "I love him more than I thought I could love anything else."

I turned on my heel and started running my shower water before facing the mirror again. I took out my ponytail, still obsessing about the man downstairs.

I loved his body that was so goddamn breathtaking. So hard, yet so soft when he was holding me. I loved his mind, his beautiful, intelligent, thoughtful mind. More than anything, I loved his heart. I loved his heart for protecting Nolan when they were just kids. I loved his heart for being such a great father to Samuel. I loved his heart for seeing me, seeing something in me that I couldn't even begin to explain. I loved his heart for whisking me away, and not saving me, but urging me to save myself.

Nerves hit me then. I didn't know how to do this. How did I please a man who had an entire twelve years on me? He had enough money, power, and looks combined that he could get any woman he wanted. I was inexperienced in life and in the bedroom. I squeezed my eyes shut and tried to get control of my nerves. That wasn't who I was and that wasn't who he was either. He didn't want just anyone and I wasn't just anyone.

"Annie Miller," I said to my reflection fiercely. "You are great at throwing knives, shooting a gun, and fighting hand to hand. You are going to be great at this, too." My pep talk was cut short when the mirror fogged up.

I took the quickest shower of my life, afraid I would lose my nerve. After brushing the knots out of my hair, I pulled it up into a loose bun on the top of my head, threw his shirt over my head, and unlocked the door and went to face the music.

Hector was already upstairs, lying in his usual spot, his hands folded over his stomach, eyes glued to the TV. When some steam entered the room behind me, his eyes snapped to mine. But they didn't stay there for long. His eyes trailed over my body, having never seen so much of it uncovered.

His eyes eventually found mine again. "Annie," he groaned loudly, one of his palms snapping up and covering most of his face.

I couldn't help the small laugh that escaped my lips. I walked over to him, somehow forgetting my vulnerability at his reaction. I sat on the edge of the bed, my hand covering his own on his face and tried to peel it away. He was stronger than me so it shouldn't have budged, but he let it go and I saw those brown eyes, fire igniting behind them.

"You're killing me," he whispered against our connected hands.

Leaning down, ever so slowly, so he could stop me if he wanted to, I covered his lips with my own. His hand squeezed in mine. Our kisses started soft and sweet, but the more my body descended onto him, the harder his mouth pushed against mine. I gasped when his teeth bit into my lip and Hector wasted no time tangling his tongue with mine.

He dominated my tongue.

He dominated me.

His hand left mine, both of his hands wrapping around the back of my neck, crushing my face to his. I moaned into his mouth and his grip got tighter, his tongue wilder. Placing my hands on each side of his head onto the pillow, I readjusted my body so I was straddling him.

His eyes flew open, his t-shirt the only fabric separating our bodies. His brown eyes flickered from my face to my exposed legs, his hands bunching up the sheets beneath us. I inched the shirt up, revealing more of myself to him. He squirmed from underneath me.

"What are you doing to me, bonita?" he whispered, his voice coming out scratchy.

"Making you mine," I told him truthfully, taking his lips again. This kiss was a kiss we had never shared before. We were past desperate, past hungry.

His hands traded the soft fabric of the sheets for the smooth skin of my thighs. His hands wrapped around my skin, dangerously close to where I needed him. His hands moved from my thighs, grazing my ass until his hands spread across my back sending goosebumps down my spine. "Take this off for me, bonita."

I leaned up, his hands following my body. My hands found the hem of my shirt and before I could even grow anxious about revealing my body to another person for the first time, I whipped off the shirt, threw it somewhere behind me, and plastered myself to his fully clothed body.

"Uh-uh," he whispered against my skin before placing a kiss at my temple. "You've never hidden from me. Don't start now."

His words weren't a demand and they weren't quite a request. They were a question. He was asking me to trust him in a way I have since the moment he came into my life.

After a deep breath, I placed my hands on his strong chest and raised my body, baring my body for his eyes.

His gaze was a caress, a touch I felt that started from my eyes down to my breasts. A slow perusal that didn't stop until his eyes landed to where my legs wrapped around him. Then, his gaze wasn't the only form of his touch.

His fingers trailed over every naked inch of me. The tips of his fingers caressing my shoulders all the way down to my fingertips, then jumping onto my bare stomach, traveling up and then completely stopping when he reached the underside of my breasts. I thrust them into his palms, giving him silent permission, and his hands cupped them before his thumb swiped over the nipple, making the tip harden to the point of pain. I tried to clench my thighs to relieve some pressure but they were on each side of Hector's hips so I just clenched against his stomach which had him groaning deep in his throat. When I relaxed after a few seconds, two of his fingers wrapped around my nipple and pinched the bud. I yelped, clenching against his stomach again. My eyes flew open, looking down at him.

His hands trailed from my breasts until he gripped my hips softly, his eyes never leaving mine until finally, he smirked.

In one swift movement, I was on my back and his hands spread my legs, fitting himself in the crevice of my hips. His mouth landed on my neck, leaving a trail of long, slow kisses until those lips landed over my nipple. I bucked underneath him at the sensation. One of his hands let go of my legs, trailing up to squeeze the underside of my boob as his tongue swirled around my nipple, laving at it until I felt the heat of his tongue down below my hips.

I felt a pressure that I never felt before. I tried to squeeze my legs but he had me pinned in a way where I could receive no traction. I groaned in frustration.

I could feel his smile against my breast. "It's not too late to try to kill you," I said, my voice coming out shaky. His other hand slid from my leg to my sex, separating my folds and running one single finger through my slit. Oh, fuck. I didn't know if that felt better or worse.

"Hector," I whimpered, throwing my head back against the pillows. I was pleading for something; I just couldn't be sure of what.

"Mmhmm," he hummed with my breast in his mouth. "Say my name, bebita."

I melted into his touch. Anything he wanted to do to me in this moment, I wouldn't have put up much of a fight. I writhed. I clawed at him, his hair, his neck, his back. His fingers started rubbing circles against my clit, my legs involuntarily spreading wider. He pulled back and looked down at me, those brown eyes the softest I'd ever seen them.

"Are you sure, Annie?"

As much as I needed his fingers to start moving again, I knew he needed my assurance more. "If there is one thing I'm sure about, it's you."

He looked at me for one long moment before I felt his finger tease my opening before he slipped it in. My body tensed at the intrusion. There wasn't any pain but the feeling of having something in me felt foreign and uncomfortable. With his free hand, he brushed the hair that had fallen out of the ponytail from my face.

"Try to relax, okay?"

I nodded and I tried, his fingers caressing my cheek making it easier on me.

I felt it when I finally calmed down, when my legs fell against the mattress and I wasn't squeezing my abdomen to the point of pain. He must have felt it too because he pulled his finger out completely just to slip it back in. He was slow the second time, allowing me time to adjust to the feeling. He did it over and over again until I could no longer remember the slight discomfort. He worked his finger in and out and his name became a breathless chant on my lips.

"Hector. Hector. Hector."

He added a second finger until my body grew frantic and I was just short of humping his hand. I was too in the moment to be embarrassed about my reaction to him. My thighs started to shake and my stomach started to clench.

"Let me have it," Hector whispered against my neck. "Let me have you."

I let the shaking take over and before I could blink, I was breaking apart, soaking his hand.

With his free hand, he brushed the few strands of hair from my face. It was tender, so gentle I had the urge to cry. I tilted my head, placing a feather-light kiss at the edge of his palm. He grabbed my abandoned t-shirt and wiped his fingers off, coming back to wrap me in his arms but I wasn't done with him. My hands traveled down to where he still was fully dressed.

"Off," I demanded.

He chuckled in my ear. "We don't have to do that tonight," he said, his hands in my hair.

I looked up at him, hoping he'd see the love I felt for him. "I want to. I want you. Now."

"You're a bossy little thing, you know that?"

I smiled up at him. "And you're the one who gives me everything I want." I pinned him with a challenging glare, silently asking him if this was anything different. His shirt and pants were off in less than five seconds.

When he was wrapping himself up in a condom, I felt the need to tell him what he probably already knew. "This is my first time."

He looked at me like he thought I was adorable. "I know," he said, suddenly serious. "I'm going to take care of you, bonita. But you're going to have to tell me what hurts or makes you uncomfortable. Tell me to stop at any point. Your wish is my command, okay, Annie?"

I nodded. He pulled my body to the edge of the bed, moving his cock against my lips, coating himself with my leftover wetness. He kneeled on the floor, his hips parallel with the top of the bed. His hands were on my thighs, keeping them wide. His tip nudged at my opening and my core was already clenching. He pushed in slowly and I grabbed the sheets, the tightness from his fingers returning tenfold.

He stopped once his tip was seated in me. One of his hands traveled up to my stomach and started to rub smooth circles above my navel, willing me to relax. We looked at each other, both of our expressions soft when he slid in another inch. A gasp escaped me and I wiggled when he stopped again, trying to adjust myself to him. Inch by inch, he surprise-attacked me until our pelvises met. He stayed still for a long time before pulling all of the way out, hitting every one of my nerve endings. He pushed back in without pausing. His strokes were deep and slow. I wrapped my legs around his back and the movement brought us tighter together.

He picked up the pace, keeping his strokes just as deep but sliding in and out faster. I broke out in a sweat, feeling the heat of us connecting all the way up to my temples. I couldn't help but to call out his name.

He disconnected our bodies and pushed me into the middle of the bed as he climbed on the bed after me. He pressed my right leg wide open and my left leg, he balanced over his shoulder. My view from down here was downright sinister. I bit my lip before Hector leaned down and took my lip away from me, kissing me hard as he pushed back into me.

I met him, thrust for thrust. It was sloppy. It was frantic. It was desperate. And I loved every fucking second of it. His thumb reached down to rub small circles on my clit and before I could even prepare,

I exploded on his cock, my walls tightening around him. He collapsed onto me, his hands digging in my hair as he sporadically thrust into me. I wrapped both of my legs around his waist and he cursed.

His face nudged into my neck and I held him as impossibly close to my body as I could. He grunted into my neck as he found his own release.

I kept my arms wrapped around him, knowing we'd both have to get up any second to clean ourselves up. His hands snuck under my back, hugging me to him. This man has infected me. First, he was in my mind. Then, he wormed his way into my heart. And finally, *finally*, he has conquered my body.

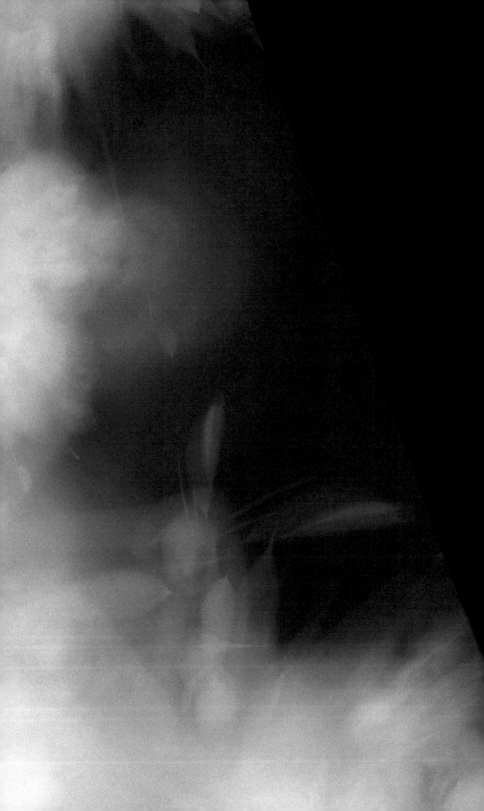

CHAPTER TWENTY-SEVEN

Annie

When I woke up the next morning, I felt cold. There were no arms wrapped around my body. There wasn't a set of brown eyes looking down at me and laughing at me when my body distorted while I stretched. There wasn't a soft voice asking me if I wanted him to cook me breakfast.

I sat up, holding the sheets up against my still naked body. The house was still and as quiet as it was months ago when I woke up in this bed for the first time. There was no sign of Hector laughing while he talked to his son. The bathroom door was open and the shower wasn't running. The clinking of the weights in the gym was vacant. The silence meant one thing, a fear just below him rejecting me: shit got too real for him and he left. He left me.

I let the sheet fall from my body and contemplated not moving from this spot all day. Maybe if I didn't get out of bed, then none of this would be real. I wouldn't go downstairs to an empty house and a locked system. That was a fairy tale and I had never believed in them. I was never one to cower and hide and so even if my chest hurt from his absence, I would get up and deal with it.

My entire body was sore, getting up turned out to be harder than I expected. When I eventually convinced my body to cooperate with me, I found a note on the nightstand. I huffed humorously. If this wasn't déjà vu from the first time I woke in this bed to an empty house, I wasn't sure what was.

There was a glass of orange juice and two ibuprofens next to the note. I picked up the note quickly, just to get it over with.

If you need anything, call Nolan.

I laughed, though I found no humor in the situation. No "I hope my dick didn't break you." No "I'll be back later." No, "Call me when you wake up." No nothing.

Just to spite him, I ignored the juice and pills, padding downstairs and making myself a heaping bowl of cereal. I stabbed the cereal as if it was the man himself. I traveled into the gym and threw myself into cardio and weights which probably wasn't the best idea when my body was already hurting. After an hour, I nearly had to drag my body up the stairs and into bed. I fell asleep instantly.

When I woke up, the house was still nothing but empty silence. Despite my wanting to wallow in bed all day, I decided it was best to get out of the house for a bit. I called Nolan.

"Annie."

"If you're not busy, I'd like to go to the store."

He was silent for a few seconds, probably checking his calendar for the day. "I'm free for another two hours. I'll be there in thirty minutes."

I quickly dressed in the first pair of jeans and shirt that I found. I tried the front door, unsure if I would have access to it, even now. It opened up right away. Nolan showed up a few minutes later and I locked the house with my handprint, sure to leave my phone on the stand beside the door.

Before he could get out of the car, I was already sliding in the passenger seat. "I just need to grab a few things for dinner."

He nodded, driving us to the closest grocery store. When we got there, I handed him a list and asked him if he could go inside instead. He was about to get out when I swiped his phone from his jacket pocket.

"I will be quick," he assured me.

I smiled tightly at him. As soon as I saw his body disappear past the sliding doors, I opened his phone, opening his contact list and hitting the call button when I came across "Boss."

Hector picked up on the second ring. "Yeah?"

I wanted to say so many things. I wanted to yell at him, curse him with every colorful word I knew both in English and Spanish. But I remained silent, a million words on the tip of my tongue, but just staying there.

"Hello," he asked, impatience in his tone. He waited a few seconds, his breathing ragged, before sighing and hanging up.

I loved him. I wanted to curse him, yell at him, hit him. And it's only because I loved him. It's only because I loved him that I was staying. That I wasn't packing my bags up and running as far away from him as possible.

As soon as the thought crossed my mind, I froze, the phone slipping from my hands, bouncing off my thighs before landing on the floor between my feet as the realization hit me.

I didn't care about Cameron anymore.

I didn't care about his life. Whether he was dead already, would die in a few weeks, or would keep living his pathetic, miserable life until he crossed the wrong person or his liver failed him. I didn't care. My work with the women's shelter, my newfound love of poetry, and living my life the way she would have wanted me to was honoring my mother much more than taking care of the monster who took her away.

Hector was the reason I was staying. Because he saved me. He saved me from one of the biggest mistakes of my life. He saved me from a life of running and regret. He saved me from me. I may have found this version of me all by myself, but he was the one who led me here.

I didn't even know I was crying until a sob tore out of my throat. I slipped an arm out of my t-shirt and wiped my cheeks furiously with my sleeve. Hurriedly, I picked up the phone, needing to call one more person before Nolan returned.

Samuel answered on the first ring. "Uncle Nolan. Do you need some advice on how to explore a woman?"

I snorted. "Are you an expert on it or something?" I asked, laughing despite my splintering heart.

"Annie," he said, his voice surprised. "I was not expecting you."

He coughed and if I didn't know any better, I would say he was embarrassed.

I looked over and saw Nolan heading this way. Shit. "I have to talk to you. But Nolan is about to catch me on his phone so I'm texting you my phone number. Call me when you get a chance later."

I didn't give him a chance to reply before I hung up. I texted his phone my number and I quickly deleted the message and the two calls I made. I flung the phone in the drink holder just as Nolan opened the back door and started to unload groceries.

After I got home and put all my groceries away that I had no intention of using except the one thing I left out, I sat down at the kitchen bar and waited for Samuel to call me. I was about a third into my half-gallon container of cookie dough ice cream when my phone rang. I answered even though it came across my screen as an unknown number.

When the line clicked over, Samuel asked me bluntly, "What idiotic thing did my father do now?"

A laugh burst out of me. I took a deep breath before admitting, "He ghosted me."

Samuel didn't say anything back for a few minutes. "Tell me everything, from the very beginning."

"Okay. It all started with how we met." I told him everything. About how he stopped me from killing Cameron and making me promise my next six months of my life would be about me and not my revenge. I told him about forcing him on dates and I finished on the way we met on the shelter, and the way he looked at me like he might just be in love with me.

"Okay," he said. "I don't need any more information on that. Has he told you about my mom? What he does for a living?"

"Yes," I told him on a sigh. "I've gotten the story behind your mother and he told me a little bit about what he does."

"What did he tell you about my mother?"

"She couldn't handle his lifestyle."

He huffed a humorless laugh. "My mother is a gold digger."

I didn't think I had it in me but I laughed around a spoonful of ice cream. Otherwise, I remained quiet. "She messed him up bad. I don't know how he felt about her but he was prepared to love and care for her and protect her for a lifetime. She took what she wanted from him and she left. There hasn't been any woman since he shipped her to wherever the hell she is these days. Not until you."

I leaned back against the chair and squeezed my eyes shut. "The past few months, he's been different. He seems lighter, happier. He grunts less and laughs more. You've made him happy."

He's made me the happiest, I didn't dare admit aloud.

"I don't know how much he loved her. She's not his or my favorite subject to talk about but she broke him in a way I don't think he's ever gotten over. He has it in his mind that since she couldn't love the darkness in him, no one would. That's why he won't let himself be seen in public with you. He wants you to find your happiness and leave him. It's what he's used to."

"I love him," I whispered, my heart splintering at the truth. "But love only matters when it's equal."

We were both quiet for a while, my fingers furiously wiping the tears running down my face. "I have a few days off before I start school next week. I'll swing by and talk some sense into him."

"And what if that doesn't work?" I asked hesitantly, afraid of the answer.

"You leave his sorry ass," Samuel told me bluntly.

Long after we hung up, I sat there at the table thinking about everything. Everything Samuel said on the phone to everything that has happened between the two of us since he dragged me here. There was nothing more I wanted than to be with him, but if he taught me anything at all during our time together, it was that I deserved to live life for me, no one else. Not even him.

He didn't show up that night. Or the next night. Or the night after that. It was seven days later when he showed up, while I was in bed upstairs watching a *Criminal Minds* marathon.

He stood there, leaning up against the doorframe, his hands in his pockets, looking at the carpet beneath his feet, not offering me one single word. After what seemed like an hour of me pretending he wasn't there, he walked into the room and sat on the edge of the bed, his head hung low.

His hair stood up in each direction and he was sporting a thicker beard than what he usually wore. He looked miserable, but I found myself unable to feel bad for him. This was on him. He left. He ran. Not me.

I turned the TV off, grabbing a blanket, needing to not be around him right now. "If you didn't want to have sex with me," I said, my voice hard. "All you had to do was say so." I padded down the stairs and into the living room. It did not escape my notice that he didn't call after me, didn't try to stop me. He just let me go.

CHAPTER TWENTY-EIGHT

Hector

I forced myself to not go after her. I dug my heels in, clenched my hands around the mattress. I stared off into the dark hallway to where she disappeared. Things had to change. If she was going to be with me for two more months, the six-month deadline, I had to go back to my original plan. I had to go back to my life before, business and Nolan would be in charge of driving her into the city each morning and bringing her home each evening. And in sixty days, we would sit down and I'd hand Cameron over or I would get the pleasure of killing him myself. Either way, Annie was going to leave and it would be just me once more.

I counted two hours out exactly before I went downstairs after her. I just needed one more night. One more night to hold her in my arms.

One more night to be close to her. One more night to witness her growing softness. I found her curled up on the sofa with my blanket, covering her from chin to feet. Hauling her up in my arms, I carried her upstairs and placed her on the bed, underneath the covers, following her. Her knees uncoiled from under her chest and wrapped around my body, her hands reaching for me. I took a deep, shaky breath as I let her fold herself into me.

I reveled in the way her body fit in with mine. Our ages, our size, our lives all different but our limbs still tangled like they were made for each other. I closed my eyes tightly, knowing tonight would be the last night I could hold her like this. It wasn't fair to her. She signed up for six months of finding herself, not six months of me. And that six months was winding down. I didn't need to give her a reason to think she'd had to stay. I'd already given her too much.

"I love you, Annie," I confessed. And then I whispered my absolute truth, despite my own breaking heart, "I love you too much to keep you."

I removed her arms and legs from me and placed her at arm's length and I watched her. I watched her sleep until the sun rose. I watched her soft breaths and her nose twitch and a few frowns that marred her face when she tossed and turned throughout the night. Just as the sun made its ascent over the room, I made my way downstairs.

My mind was set. I'd shake off some of this self-loathing in the gym until she woke up and killed me with her anger and hurt. But my feet didn't take me to the gym. They took me to the kitchen.

I didn't regret making love to her. I never wanted to stop loving her. And that was the problem. I was a man of my word and when she agreed to these six months, I promised her that I didn't matter. This entire plan was for her. For what she really would choose if the choice was given to her.

This wasn't about me. It didn't matter if she was the best part of my day. It didn't matter if I wanted her way past the six-month mark. It sure as hell didn't matter that for only the second time in my life, I fell in love.

I took my time in the kitchen making her breakfast, replaying every moment we shared since the first night. It played in my head like a movie. A movie that didn't have an ending yet. A movie that might never have an ending. A happy one, anyhow.

I filled her plate with plantains, ham, and scrambled eggs and grabbed a glass of OJ from the fridge. I took the stairs two at a time to find her fast asleep. I set her breakfast on the nightstand by her head and kneeled on the carpet next to her.

She was so goddamn beautiful. Inside and out. The prettiest woman I've laid my eyes on attached with a fiery heart. She was my dream come true and I was an idiot for even thinking about letting her go. But I had to.

I leaned my head down, my forehead resting on her stomach. A million what-ifs floating around in my head.

What if history repeated itself? I couldn't bear to see her hurt. And that's what would happen if she truly became mine. A target would be placed on her and every one of my enemies would be searching for blood. Maybe we'd get a few months, maybe we'd get a few years. We couldn't get a grow old together love. Not when I was a Rivera.

What if she couldn't handle my lifestyle? What if Annie grew to be like Summer, where she could no longer look past all the darkness in me? What if I was ruining her life with the mere thought that we could be something more?

Annie's stomach tensed underneath my eyes and I raised my head. Her eyes remained closed but her breathing hitched so I knew she had awakened. "Annie, I'm sorry." My mind raced with my tongue, trying to get the words out before her anger could fully resurface.

"Sorry for which part exactly," she ground out, still hiding her eyes from me.

"For abandoning you after..." I choked on the words. Her jaw clenched as did her fists by her side. I stumbled for something to say, to make her feel better but I could only find the truth. "I've been kissing you for weeks." Falling for you even longer. "When you let me have your body, it felt like everything changed. You were no longer Annie. I was no longer Hector. We were just us and I didn't know how to handle that."

I watched her throat bob and fucking finally, she uncovered those blues from me. Unshed tears covered my favorite sight in the world. I hated myself for putting that look on her face.

"You gave me the one thing you've never given anyone else."

"Hector." Her voice was a shaky whisper. "I have given you everything I never even thought to give to someone else."

My head fell against her stomach once more. God, how was she even real? How did I even get the privilege of knowing her for one second? How did I deserve to kiss her lips and wrap her body around me?

Her hand fell to my head, her delicate fingers running through my hair, sending shivers down my spine. "There's less than two months left."

I tried to lift my head, to find her eyes, but she applied pressure to my scalp and I didn't fight her hold. "I want out."

"That wasn't the deal." I had to clench my jaw to not fight her hold on me, to not fight the tears balling underneath my eyelids.

"Keep him." She dug harder in my hair and I wasn't even sure if she was conscious of her strength. "I've come to terms that he's not important. He never was. Him dying won't bring my mom back. There are other ways to honor her and her memory and her impact on my life than killing her murderer. So, I'm out. If you want me out, then, I'm out."

I opened my mouth to say what, I wasn't sure before clamping my lips together, struck speechless. This is what I wanted. I wanted her to make this choice since we struck our deal. I wanted her to realize there was more to life than revenge. She was free now. There was just one problem: I didn't want to open her cage; I didn't want her to fly away.

Our moment was broken apart by the slamming of the door downstairs. I ripped her hand away from me, reaching for the gun in the nightstand before the voice of the intruder floated up the stairs.

"Yo, Dad."

Samuel. What the hell was he doing home?

His footsteps grew louder and louder until he appeared in the doorway of my bedroom. My son, in the flesh. I rose on my two feet to greet him but he didn't spare me a second glance. He dove headfirst on to the bed, landing on his elbows and looking mischievously at Annie.

I felt a growl form in my chest, but both of them ignored me. "Hot

Mama, it's so nice to finally meet you."

That tore a small laugh out of Annie and Samuel started to dive in on his million questions. I tried to catch her eye but she refused to glance in my direction.

I didn't know what to think as I made my way to the gym. I knew I felt numb. Numb to the core because if Cameron wasn't holding her here, then she could leave. Then, she could be out of my life forever.

I was determined to distance myself from Annie two hours ago. Then, she hit me with a truth bomb that my plan worked after all and now she put the choice in my hands. If I let her stay, I'd become who I've always hated. I wouldn't be giving her the choice. If she stayed, it was forever. Whether she liked it or not. If she stayed, a target would be put on her back. If she stayed, it made me one hell of a selfish son of a bitch. If she left, she kept her choices, her freedom, her life. My heart.

I spent a good part of the day pounding my fists and legs into the bag of rocks two rooms away from my son and a woman who could have been the love of my life if we both were two different people.

The two of them do not leave each other's sight the entire day. Samuel's overnight bags were still where he dropped them by the front door. It wasn't until I announced that dinner was done that they joined me in the kitchen. I made tacos because one, he complained to me every day about the lack of Mexican food overseas and because I knew it was Annie's favorite. I sat in my normal seat, waiting for Annie to sit beside me but she headed straight for the bench, across from me, forcing Samuel next to me. I watched her throughout the entire dinner as Samuel filled her in on everything he did for the past couple of months abroad. He was just getting into his sexcapades when Annie stood up.

"I'm heading to bed now before I'm scarred for life."

I stood, ready to follow her, but she pinned me with a look.

"I stole your son all day, stay."

I sat my ass back down and watched her disappear upstairs.

I felt Samuel's eyes on me but I refused to acknowledge him. But like father like son, he was not one to be ignored. "You're a fucking dumbass if you let her go."

I whipped my head around to look at him. I looked at him closely, intently. My son was a sarcastic little shit; he'd never taken life too seriously. He always got good grades and he was always safe and prepared for anything but he wasn't as serious as I was. Hell, I didn't think he was half as serious as I was. But he was blunt. When he talked, he didn't bullshit. He told you exactly what he thought, unafraid of hurting your feelings. He didn't hold back. Looking into his eyes, I knew this was one of those moments that he wasn't going to hold back. "You don't understand. She doesn't deserve this life."

He scoffed, dismissing me with a wave of his hand as he got up and rinsed off his plate in the sink, his back turned to me. "You can come up with one excuse or a thousand, as many as you like, really. But none of those matter, only the truth." He turned around, his hands landing on top of the bar. "You're scared. Of her. Of what a life with her would be like. You say she doesn't deserve this life but look at the way you met. And it's not like this is going to be your life forever. In four years time, I'm coming back from LA and I'm taking over. You're going to retire and stay here or move to Mexico or travel or whatever it is that you want to do."

"Sam—" I tried, but he cut me off.

"I'm taking over, Dad. I should've already taken over by now but you wanted it to be my choice. It's my choice now. I'm majoring in computer science and business to help the Rivera name. It's going to be my choice in four years."

I ground my teeth together, not wanting to have this fight again with him. Also, knowing I'd rather talk about anything else but the woman upstairs in my bed. "You're scared of her. Of what she makes you feel. Of what will happen when she wises up and leaves your sorry ass. She's not Mom."

I snapped my angry gaze to him, hating him in that second for bringing her up. "She's not," he pressed on, ignoring me completely. "And it's unfair that you're still letting her affect your life now."

I didn't say anything back. For the second time that day, I was at a loss for words. Samuel disappeared into his bedroom and I sat there in the kitchen feeling like my body was split into two. When I made my way upstairs, Annie was on the edge of the bed on her side under the comforter and she laid my blanket out on my side, her message clear: don't fucking touch me. I didn't bother lying down on the bed. I grabbed a chair from the corner of the room and sat on it, looking at her while she slept, hopeful that this wasn't the last time I would get the privilege. But you know what they say about hope, it hurts like a bitch when it's destroyed.

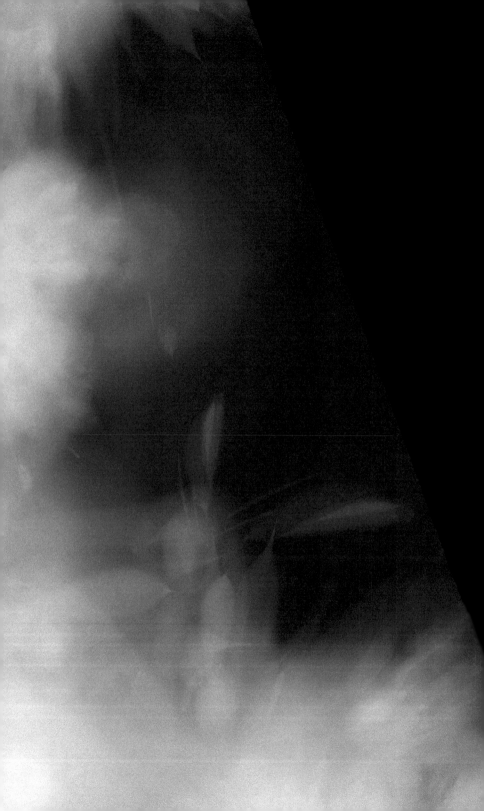

CHAPTER TWENTY-NINE

Annie

I slept horribly, well accustomed to a body holding me through the night. I looked to where Hector should be, unsurprised to find the space empty, the blanket I laid out last night exactly where I left it.

I wasn't too eager to face the day. To not kiss Hector good morning. To sit in a car with him while he dropped me off in the city in tense silence. To try not to look at his face, knowing it was one of the last times I would get the privilege.

It was insane to think that Hector had come in my life four months ago and I thought I could survive him. Survive the six months of derailment he forced upon me. But leaving him, leaving this house, leaving our built routine, leaving my favorite pair of brown eyes didn't feel like surviving. It felt like I lost everything. I've felt that before but I could get revenge on behalf of my mother; there wasn't any revenge I could seek for my broken heart.

Samuel was my last shred of hope. If there was anyone Hector would listen to, it would be his son. I knew they talked last night but I wasn't brave enough to face the things Hector might, or worse, wouldn't say.

I flipped the covers off of me and headed to the bathroom when I just barely held back a scream. Hector was sleeping on a chair in the corner of the room. His head hung low, his chin resting against his clavicle like it was against his choice to fall asleep, but his eyes failed him. I collapsed on the edge of the bed willing my heartbeat to slow down. I couldn't take my eyes off of him. His brown skin that I knew was soft and hard at the same time. His hands that held me like they were made just for that reason. The way those lips curved up into the most delicious smile whenever I teased him.

A sigh escaped me and I tensed, afraid it would wake him but he didn't budge. Five more minutes, I silently promised, five more minutes and then I had to get out of this room.

My promise was broken when ten minutes passed and I still couldn't convince myself away from him. I couldn't tear my eyes from his face. I couldn't stop thinking about how he was once a stranger that stood in the way of what I wanted and now the only thing I wanted was him.

It wasn't until he jerked in the chair that I forced myself to run out of the room. There was another Rivera man downstairs, one that would actually tell me the truth.

When I walked into the kitchen, Samuel was already at the table, a textbook, notebook, and pen lying out in front of him. "What are you working on?"

His head raised and he shot me a slow, seductive smile to which I rolled my eyes. "I'm taking women's studies," he said, waggling his brows.

Oh, brother. I coughed out a laugh. "You know your dad isn't going to be too pleased when you become a father your freshman year of college."

Samuel chuckled. "Not me, Annie. I *date* smart chicks. They always make sure I wrap it up even if I forget." The way he said the word "date" told me everything I didn't want to know.

We fell into a comfortable silence, him continuing with his reading and note taking and me with a bowl of cereal and coffee. The sound of soft footsteps descending the stairs caused the hair on my arms to stand. I locked eyes with Samuel, the burning question written all over my face: is he going to let me go or is he going to keep me?

Samuel looked from the stairs where his father had just emerged back to me. He shook his head, his eyes becoming sad in an instant.

In that moment, I experienced heartbreak in a way I never had before. The way you could love someone so much and still have to walk away from them because love was only love when it was unselfish. I had to be unselfish. I couldn't stand, go over to him, and demand he love me back. Demand he ask me to stay. Demand to never let me go. That's what I wanted. But it wasn't what he wanted and to accept that, it broke my heart more than he ever could.

Your heart is the most important part of your body. I figured when it was breaking, it would make a noise. A sound as loud as fireworks exploding, a creak of a branch being stepped on in the quiet woods, anything. But nothing happened, nothing but deafening silence as your world stalled and started back up again.

Hector came up beside me, careful not to touch me, and poured himself a cup of coffee. I was thankful and pissed at the same time at him for denying me one last touch. I excused myself upstairs using the excuse of a shower and waited until I heard the clinking of weights before I snuck downstairs again. Samuel was in the same place, tapping the butt of his pen against his temple.

I sat down beside him. "You'll take me then," I whispered. "When you leave?"

He didn't look up at me, just kept frowning at his textbook, but he did nod.

"One more thing."

He inclined his head, silently letting me know he was listening.

"Keep him busy until then." A sob rose its way up and I had to cover my mouth to halt the noise.

Back upstairs, I turned on the shower and only when I stepped under the water did I let my tears cascade down my face. I stayed in the shower until I had no tears left. Then, I got myself ready for the day because I was Annie Miller and my world was so much more than a man even if it was the only one I'd ever loved.

I went back downstairs to find the kitchen empty. The sounds of weights still going. I contemplated just calling Nolan for a ride, but decided against it. Roping Hector into things was a big part of our relationship and I didn't plan to stop until our goodbye was over.

When I walked into the room, Hector was spotting his son who was doing bench presses. He was always so serious all of the time. Even now, spending the day with his son, his mouth formed into a straight line, his emotions locked up tighter than a princess in an abandoned castle. If I didn't know how much Samuel meant to him, I would think today was just another day for him.

Samuel was counting out his reps and when he unsteadily breathed out one hundred, he let the barbell of weights slam back on the machine. He moved to get up, his chest heaving erratically, but Hector moved fast, pressing Samuel's body back into the bench.

"You're weak. Go again."

Samuel groaned, but Hector didn't budge, not until Samuel's hands found the barbell again. "Does it really matter if I can do five hundred reps of lifting three-hundred pounds in the long run?" Samuel asked as he continued to lift.

"Sometimes being the smartest person in the room isn't enough, mijo. Sometimes you have to be the strongest, too."

I had a feeling he was no longer talking about Samuel and more about himself. About me and about us. I wanted to call bullshit on him, but Samuel beat me to it.

"Mamadas," Samuel huffed, not skipping a beat in movement, switching over languages. "No me quites tu frustración porque no puedes ser hombrey mantener a la mujer que amas." *Translation: Don't take your frustrations out on me because you can't be man enough to keep the woman you love.*

I pressed my lips tightly together as I put Samuel's words together. Damn, this kid was fearless. I knew I needed to announce my presence, but I couldn't. My feet were glued to the spot and my mouth felt like sandpaper.

Hector ignored Samuel. "Someone ambushes you, then what?"

"Blow their fucking brains out," Samuel said as if that was the only answer.

I tried to suppress my laugh but failed. Two heads snapped in my direction. Samuel shot me a sinister smirk and Hector's jaw was wound so tight I was afraid it might snap. I didn't cower or hide or apologize for my intrusion. "Speaking of guns, I need a ride to work."

Hector nodded and immediately started to clean up the gym. Samuel tilted a curious eyebrow at me.

"I, for sure, thought he would have locked you up in this mansion, allowing you no outside contact."

I frowned. "That's not who he is."

Samuel grunted and smiled at my real meaning. That's not who he was, at least not with me. "That's not who I am either. I would have burned this place down a long time ago."

A sound emitted from Hector and if I hadn't heard it thousands of times within the last three months, I would have never taken it for what it actually was: an amused laugh. "But to answer your question, yes, I do work. I have two jobs."

"For what reason?" he asked, bewildered.

"Because I love them," I told him honestly.

Samuel walked over to me, grabbed my arm and escorted me from the room. "I can't believe you work for Matt."

I laughed. "Yes. You know, you might be his doppelganger."

He visibly shuddered. "Yeah. No. Has he never hit on you?"

I scrunched my nose up at him and he took that as answer enough.

A laugh boomed out of him, his shoulders shaking. "I could see you giving him a run for his money. Is that where you have to go today? I wouldn't mind pestering him."

I only nodded, grabbing my shoes and slipping my feet in them.

"Dad, I'll take Annie. You can stay here and be broody."

Hector walked into the room, heading straight toward us. He grabbed his keys from the dish and smacked Samuel on the back of the head. "Keep dreaming, mijo. You can barely lift five hundred pounds without wheezing. I don't trust you to take care of Annie."

He was calling me Annie. I remember the first time he called me beautiful in his mother tongue, how it raised my hackles and now here I was dying to hear it just one last time. I ignored the searing pain in my chest.

"I can take care of myself," I said, meaning to sound strong and sure but my voice came out strained and soft.

Samuel walked away when Hector turned around to look at me. I wasn't expecting him to look at me the way he was looking at me. Like nothing changed, like I was still the best part of his day.

"Yeah, I know," he said, his voice just above a whisper.

Then he, too, walked away from me.

***

The next couple of days followed in suit. Samuel kept his promise to me. While all three of us were in the house, Samuel ate up Hector's time. The only time Hector and I were even in the same room was when we were eating dinner or the two of them drove me to work and picked me up. On the days that I didn't have to work all of my jobs, I'm cooped up in Hector's study, alternating between crying and writing. Turns out, I was exceptional at both. I skipped dinner the past two nights, unable to fake it. Unable to fake that I was happy. Unable to fake that my heart wasn't being stepped on when Hector and Samuel made plans. I had no plans with Hector, and I never would. I wondered if Samuel would keep in contact. Or Nolan. Would it be like I never existed in Hector's life? Was he okay with that? Would he be happy with that?

Hector came up into the room for his shower, not uttering a word to me as he passed my sprawled-out body on the bed. As soon as the water turned on, I clutched the only thing, other than my heart, that I was leaving behind. I had written him an entire notebook of poems. Within the hundred or so pages, I poured my heart out to him. I wasn't sure if he would ever read them or if he would just toss them into the fire watching the pages turn to smoke. I just knew I needed him to know that he changed my life. He saved my life and I wouldn't be able to thank him enough for these past three months.

The bed dipped and through blurry eyes, I saw Samuel. He reached out, brushing my tears away. "Are you sure you want to do this?"

He was leaving tomorrow. *I was leaving tomorrow.*

I sat up, wiping the rest of my tears away and slapping my cheeks to snap me out of it. I pulled open the closet and I grabbed one suitcase and Samuel grabbed the other. We walked downstairs and placed both in his room with the rest of his luggage.

"I don't want to do this, but I'm not the one with the choice here," I whispered to Samuel before we entered Hector's study. I set the book on top of his desk. On the front cover was the only picture of us I had, from the night he took me out for the first time. I forced him into a picture once I promised him it would be for my eyes only. Underneath read the title: *YOU, ME, & HER.*

"If I'm being honest, I don't know if this is the right thing or not. He changed my life, Samuel. He saved me, but he won't let me save him. He wanted me to figure out who I was going to be after I killed *him,* and I did. I want to help women like my mother stand on their own two feet. I want to help children who had to witness the stuff I had to witness as a kid."

I let my fingers trail over the book of my heart once more before shutting the light off and hugging Samuel. "I want to love your father," I whispered into his neck. "But I can't do that if he doesn't want me to. So, I'm going to help women and maybe, that'll be enough to not focus on the fact that I let the love of my fucking life go without a fight."

His arms tightened around me in a way that I wished his father's would, instead of me being sand in his hands, falling effortlessly away from him.

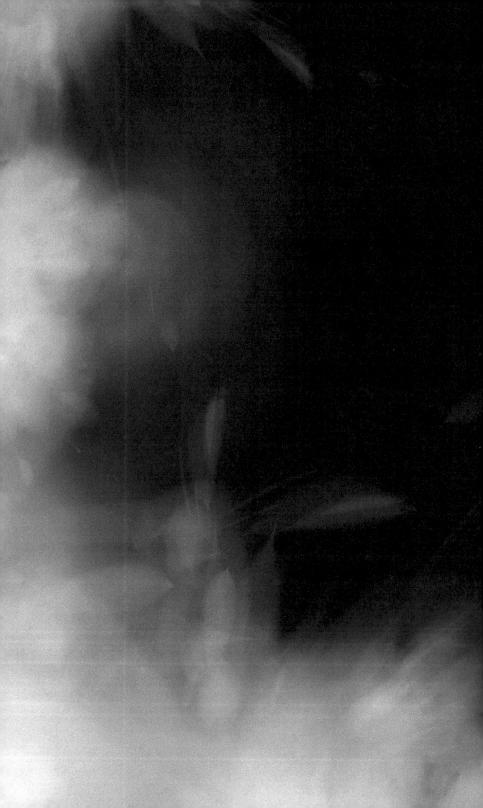

CHAPTER THIRTY

Annie

"**W**here is it that you're taking me?" I asked Samuel as he drove right past the hotel I told him to drop me off at.

He looked over at me, a rare frown on his face. "You're not living at a hotel, Annie."

"No," I said slowly. "I'm staying at a hotel until I can put a security deposit down on an apartment."

We were already outside of New Hazle and deep into the city. "Why, when I have an apartment that you can have?"

"And it has the Rivera name attached to it," I questioned.

He shrugged from the driver's side. "Yeah. So?"

So, I'm not a Rivera and I never will be, I thought but didn't say. "Will you accept rent?"

"Nope," he said, pulling over and parking his car.

"Then I can't accept," I insisted. He ignored me, getting out of the car and collecting my bags from the trunk.

"Samuel," I hissed when he walked past me and headed toward a white building and retrieved a key from his pocket. "I can't accept this," I tried again.

After he set my suitcases inside of the door, he grabbed my hands and then pulled me inside, too, before closing the door.

"You have three months left in your agreement with him. Honor the rest of the time and stay here."

"Why would I do that?"

"Because if my dad doesn't come for you before your time is up, he's not the man that I thought he was and frankly, he's not the man you've spent the previous months with either."

"I'm not holding out hope," I lied, and based on the look Samuel shot me, he knew it, too.

"It's just a studio apartment, but it's one of the bigger ones you'll ever see." I looked around at the empty space because that's literally all it was. It had white walls and a hardwood finish on the floors and countertops. The only thing in the entire room was a king-size bed, sheets bunched up in the middle. Samuel scratched his head and looked at me almost bashfully. "You might want to get rid of the bed and maybe bleach the countertops and the walls."

I stared at him for a long moment until I realized his meaning. "This is your sexcapade apartment?"

He grinned, no longer shy, and shrugged his shoulders. "I don't bring anyone to the house for safety reasons and the girls I tend to bring here are good girls. They tend to not want their parents to hear them screaming my name."

I laughed. "Bleach the entire apartment. Got it."

"Well, I don't want to miss my flight but call me if you need anything, okay?"

I nodded.

"He will come for you, Annie," he said, leaning down to plant a kiss on my forehead. "And when he does, make him work for it."

He turned to go, but I reached out for him. "I'm not going to wait for him forever, Samuel. I deserve more from life, he's the one who taught me that. Three months and I'm gone."

He nodded tightly, squeezed my hand and I was all alone. I was well attuned to the feeling but for the first time in my life, it felt different. I wasn't just passing time, waiting for the right moment to go in for the kill. There was no revenge and there were no plans. It was just me, finally letting go of one of the longest chapters of my life. It was me being brave enough to flip the page and see what the next chapter would bring.

Before even thinking about unpacking my suitcases, I looked up different furniture stores in the city in search of a new, sterile bed. The first store I went into had the softest bed and I was sold immediately when they said they would get rid of my current bed and deliver my new one in no less than four hours. I took the city bus down to the grocery store and bought enough food to last a few days, i.e. different flavors of cereal and ice cream so I could eat my feelings, and the cleaning products I needed. And maybe I happened to pick up a few poetry books from the limited selection they had.

When the sun set and dusk turned into darkness, I could no longer avoid the bed I had been excited about buying hours ago. Because I would be sleeping alone. There was no my side or his side. It was just one. All mine. Only mine.

I climbed in under the white comforter I purchased from a boutique down the street accompanied by a pint of caramel chocolate ice cream. Only then did I stop and think about him.

I wondered how he felt when he realized I was gone. I wondered if he searched every crevice of that mansion of his, hoping to find me. I wondered if he found the book of poems I left for him. I wondered what he would do with them when he did.

It hurt to not be with him.

It hurt to think about him.

It hurt to love him.

But regardless of the hurt, I wouldn't change a moment between us. He showed me a world I was blind to. He forced me to take a deep look at myself, of who I could be if I let go of my past. I wasn't really sure if I believed in God or even fate, but it felt like Hector was a godsend, a gift personalized for me to change the course of my life. And he did, he hijacked the hell out of my life.

***

I gave up on sleep before midnight struck. No matter which way I laid or whether the blankets covered my body, my eyes wouldn't close.

I tossed the blankets off of me and switched on the lights. It had been only a few months since I lived in the heart of the city, but I could barely remember what it felt like.

The horns of cars. The loud drunkenness of pedestrians. The city lights. It was beautiful in its own chaotic way. But Hector spoiled me. He made me love a soft Latin beat and strong and gentle hands holding me in a way I knew I was both cherished and safe.

I turned on my phone, tapping on the music app, and let Latin R&B fill the small space of the new apartment. Sitting in the middle of the floor, I started to unpack my bags. Since the space was a studio, I didn't have a closet. Most of my clothes had to sit folded on the counter space until the mobile hanging rack I ordered was delivered.

I went about folding each piece of clothing as the soft Spanish sounds eased some of the tension in my body. I had no idea what they were talking about, my skills too rusty to follow along completely. If I had to guess, every word was about heartbreak because it was the only thing right now I could connect to.

My hands gripped around a card. I frowned, retrieving it from the bag. It was an ID card. The one I had made months ago. The one that belonged to Olive James.

I clutched the ID to my chest and fell back against the wooden floor, not even flinching when the coolness hit my bare skin.

I should have been Olive James. I should have been her for four months. Annie Miller should be dead.

A breath of air escaped me. I didn't want Annie to die. The thought of the last few months not happening sounded nothing short of a nightmare.

I was realizing that just like anything else, knowing who you are took effort. You weren't just born and knew exactly who you were going to be. Like anything else, you had to open yourself up like a book, study the pages, commit them to your memory for a chance at knowing yourself. It took my twenty-two years, having my world blown to pieces, almost making the biggest mistake of my life, and falling in love for me to realize that.

❦

It had been just a week since I left Hector's and Samuel brought me here. In those few days, I had started to fill up the studio until I felt like if someone who knew me (the list was very limited) were to walk in the front door they would know that this was my home.

My bed rested on the wall that separated the kitchen from the rest of the space by a few stairs. Directly across from the bed, in between two tall windows overlooking the city, I had one of the workers from the appliance store mount the TV so I could watch it while I was in bed. In front of each window sat identical reading nooks. I set up two small rugs on each side of my bed that I was embarrassed to admit I might have fallen asleep on a time or two. On one of the two empty walls, I placed my matching white desk and bookshelf. On the opposite wall, I broke down and bought a small dresser and a clothing rack.

Even if a part of me didn't feel complete and even though I was sad more hours of the day than not, I was happy with my little apartment.

A double soft tap came sounded at the door and I whipped my head in its direction, my heart picking up like I was in the midst of running a marathon.

"It's not him," I whispered to myself, knowing exactly who was at the door.

I took a deep breath before opening the door. I was greeted by two pairs of beaming smiles. Rachel and Jessica stood outside, Rachel offering me a small smile and Jessica's attention already focused on the space behind me. She all but shoved the housewarming basket she brought into my hands before pushing me aside and taking in the sight of my very own first apartment.

Rachel simply shrugged as if that explained Jessica's behavior and it kind of did.

"Oh. My. God. It's so pretty," Jess said, her eyes taking in every inch of the small space.

Rachel laughed beside me. "It's definitely you," she murmured, stepping past me but not before squeezing my shoulder.

I averted my eyes and tried my best to swallow the lump in my throat. Four months ago, I didn't even know who I was past what to put on some government forms and now I could make an entire apartment, albeit a small one, match who I was.

"You have Eliza's new book," Jessica screeched, said book in her hands.

"Yes," I said, walking toward her and taking it from her tight grip.

Did she not know that books must be held with infinite gentleness? After all, it was a work of art. You wouldn't just clutch a painting that way, now would you? I smoothed my hand over Eliza's portrait on the front cover. It was the same image I was first struck by, before even realizing who she was. Now that I knew her story and not just what she shared in her poems, the picture of her was even more breathtaking as was the title. *I Am a Woman.*

I found a copy of it in my locker at the shelter last week and that night when I got home, I snuggled up in my bed with my eyes glued to her words. I read it in two hours. I cried for two hours. The woman was talented and I absolutely ate up everything she had to offer. Over the past couple of days, we would leave notes for each other since she worked the night shift and I was usually gone before she came in. Usually, it was just me gushing over her and her being bashful about how great she really was.

"Is it autographed?" Jessica asked.

I shook my head. "No. I'm just happy that I got it before it even releases. It's so good."

"Do you want her to sign it? I'm sure she will if you ask her," Jessica said.

"I'm scared to talk to her. She is literally a superhero."

Rachel bumped my shoulder, a question in her eyes. I knew, from years ago when I first met them, that neither of them had dealt with domestic violence or sexual assault or had to witness someone close to them go through it.

"We all speak our own language and only those who walk a similar path can pick up on the linguistics. I haven't been through what she had to experience, but my mom did and I was a shadow that couldn't get the image out of my head. I still can't. Her sharing her story so openly and so beautifully, let me see my mom in a different light, like a fogged window becoming clear for the first time. So, yes, to me she's Wonder Woman and I'm sure I'm not the only one who thinks so."

Rachel squeezed my bicep. "You inspired her three years ago with a story of your own and now she is the one inspiring you," Jessica whispered shakily, tears already filling her eyes.

"Don't start that shit," I said, pointing a finger at her. "I've officially declared this apartment a no-cry zone."

Jessica sniffled her laugh. Rachel tipped up the bottle of wine she had in answer and we followed her into the kitchen.

"Do you have a corkscrew because I don't."

Rachel whipped one out of her purse. "I figured you didn't."

I brought three glasses from the cupboard and placed them in front of each of us. Rachel poured us some and like any respectable women, we all kicked off our shoes, climbed in my bed, and talked. Rachel talked about her husband. Jessica talked about a woman she had been on three dates with and was ready to get naked with. Then all eyes turned to me.

I wasn't one to share. Usually, I had nothing to share. But they met Hector and when it came to him, I didn't think; I just acted. "Hector and I," I whispered, trying to swallow past the lump in my throat. I took a swig of wine for the courage to say the words aloud. "Whatever we were, we aren't anymore."

My words were met with two identical frowns. "What do you mean?" This came from Jessica whose head was tilted in confusion.

"Why do you think I'm here, in this apartment? We're done."

Rachel huffed a laugh. "Go look out your window, Annie."

It was my turn to be confused. "What? Why?"

"Because if you two are really done, I don't think Hector got the memo."

I moved faster than any of us could blink. My wine sloshed over my glass and onto the floor but I didn't have it in me to care. I ran to the window, my knees sinking into the softness of my reading chair and there he was. That black Range Rover was parked across the street with the man I loved inside. It looked like he was sleeping but I knew he would never fall asleep in the middle of the city. It was too much of a risk for his safety.

I kept my eyes open until they hurt from not blinking. I didn't want to close my eyes. I didn't want to reopen them and have the sight of him all be a dream. When I couldn't take it anymore, I closed my eyes and took a long, deep breath before opening them again. He was there in the same exact position. I exhaled a sigh of relief.

And then the questions started to kick in. What was he doing here? Why was he here? Why the hell hadn't I noticed him there? How long had he been camping outside of my apartment?

I turned back around in my chair and melted into it, looking at my two favorite women. "I love him. And I told his son that I wouldn't wait for him forever but I lied. I would wait for him for my entire life and maybe the next one, too."

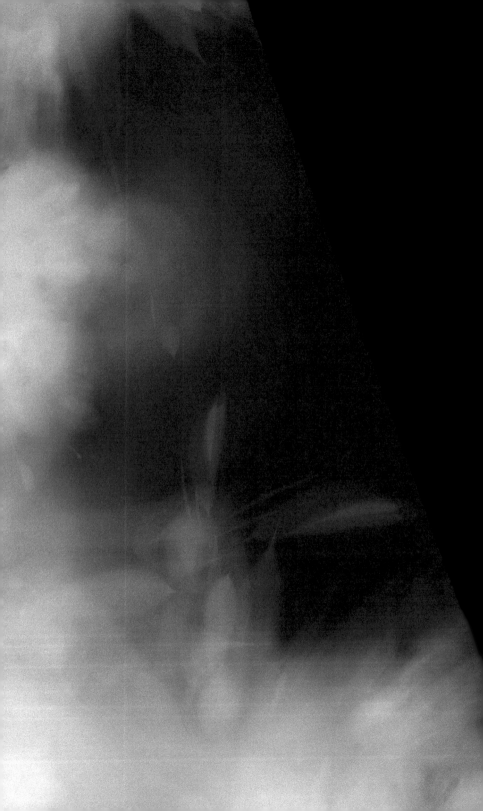

CHAPTER THIRTY-ONE

Hector

Opening my eyes was not an option. Well, it was if I wanted to face the truth. The truth of saying goodbye to my son for the second time this year, unsure if he'd be back for Christmas or not until next summer. The truth of saying goodbye to Annie. Because I had to. As much as I wanted to look into those deep blue eyes for the rest of my days, I knew she deserved better. She deserved more. Between her and my son, I knew, by the end of the day, I was going to be left heartless.

I let my head flop to the side, opening my eyes, hoping to get one last glimpse of her beauty. Except she wasn't there. I sat up straight in bed, straining my ears for the sound of her feet padding against the treadmill or her crunching that stupid kid cereal she was obsessed with.

Nothing. I whipped the covers off of me and took the stairs by two. More silence met me down there. I walked by the kitchen, making my way into Samuel's room to find him gone. Back in the kitchen, I found a note next to the still-warm coffee pot.

Headed out early. I'll text you when I make it to the campus. -S.

One was gone. I wasn't too worried about him. He didn't have a choice but to see me again. Where was she? Where was Annie? I guess I could've called out her name, but the knowledge of her being gone could be felt deep in my bones.

I took the stairs again in search for her things. I opened her designated dresser drawers and looked for her suitcase and backpack in the closet where she'd stuffed it. Gone and gone. I searched my nightstand and hers. No note, no nothing.

My hands gripped my hair as if that would help. It did a little, easing the pain from my chest to my scalp. I couldn't even remember the last time we talked. When Samuel busted in the door, he stole her. And the following days after, he stole me. Come to think of it, I hadn't been alone with her since before his arrival. Since before she told me she didn't care if Cameron lived or died. When she told me that she would stay or go, whichever I decided. Did she see the answer in my eyes then?

I sat up straight, remembering. The study. She spent more time in that study over the last couple of weeks than she did in bed. Rushing down the stairs, I slammed the door open and was relieved to see something, foreign to my eyes, in the center of the desk. Grabbing it, I saw it was a journal. But not one you bought at the store; this is one you made with your own two hands. This one people put hours and hours of work into. The cover had both sketches and patches of fabric, jean fabric, a small photo of us that night at Maria's tucked into it. My lips tilted upward, despite the feeling like my chest was being put into overdrive. I let my hands trail over the fabric and I let my eyes close, knowing she did this. For who, me or her, I was uncertain. I finally let myself read the words on the cover. *YOU, ME, & HER: Poems by Annie Miller.*

Without the book leaving my hands, I sat in the chair behind the desk. I let my fingers trace her name, over and over again, until I memorized the pattern. Then my anger took over. I didn't want her poems. I didn't want to read her poems. She should have been here. She should have read me her words her damn self. Clenching my jaw, I flung the book of poems back onto the desk and stormed out of the room.

I headed straight into the gym, foregoing stretching, I jumped right onto the treadmill, choosing the highest speed and the steepest incline. She left. She was gone, out of my life forever.

Good for her.

Good for me.

Good for everyone.

I pushed my legs harder and faster until my feet were as far up on the track as they could go. Sweat poured off of my skin but I ignored it, letting it fall where it wanted to go.

When my limbs didn't want to cooperate with me anymore, I

turned off the machine and headed back upstairs for a shower. My hands were shaking, whether from the uneasiness settling in the pit of my stomach or from the adrenaline, I wasn't sure but I was betting on the former.

I showered with my eyes shut, reaching for a towel when I was done. When I opened my eyes, I realized I grabbed the wrong towel. It was Annie's towel, the one she used to dry her hair. "Fuck," my heart, body, and mouth hissed.

I dressed as quickly as possible and was out of the house as soon as I could manage it. The memories of her in that house so loud, I could barely concentrate. The way her eyes would follow me as I dressed for the day or undressed at night. Her stupid cereal sitting in the cupboard right next to the coffee filters and grounds. The kitchen table where I broke down her resolve and she told me her truths. The front door where she almost sliced my ear open after I disappeared on her the first time. I had to get out of the house before I turned into a deranged man, throwing things like they had any control in her staying or going. No, that was me. That was all on me.

This is what I asked for. This is what I wanted. For her. She was better off without me, without my life holding her back, or masking her in darkness.

The car wasn't any better. I missed her eyes on me. I ached for her fingers to reach over and fold themselves in mine. I missed the small smiles she afforded me, and I missed her glare. I missed her frown and her pouty lips. I missed everything. I didn't have anything to do, seeing as I had canceled all meetings or delegated anything of importance to Nolan since Samuel was in town. But now he was gone and so was she.

Before I even knew it, I was driving toward Hank's. As soon as I saw it come into view, I knew why. Cameron. She didn't care about him anymore. She didn't care if I killed him, locked him up in the cellar for the rest of his miserable life, or if I let him go. He wasn't worth a simple thought of hers any longer. I parked my car behind the building, knowing if someone said the wrong thing to me today, I'd make a mess and then I'd have to clean it up.

I sat in this exact spot months ago, after driving a blonde-haired, blue-eyed beauty queen to my house and locking her away for the night. I planned on killing him then, and I'd planned on doing the same thing today. But just like that night months ago, something was stopping me and I wasn't sure what it was.

If I went in there now and killed him, it wouldn't be for her, it would be *because* of her. The only thing I wanted other than seeing her one last time was her to get her justice. This man took a life, took a life precious to her, and twisted the perception of it, making it seem like it was her fault she was killed. My anger would last for a total of ten minutes, but he deserved worse than me pounding his skull into the concrete. He deserved far, far worse.

I pulled out my phone, hitting the number one. My emergency number.

"Please don't tell me you got yourself shot."

I chuckled at the groan in her voice. "No bullet holes, I promise." She breathed a sigh of relief. "But I do have to ask for a favor."

"Is it illegal?"

"Not your part."

She grunted. "I'm afraid to ask."

"That brother of yours," I said, slowly. The girl was protective over him. "He's still got the same phone number?"

She was quiet for a moment, and then she grumbled a reluctant, "Yes. Should I even ask?"

"Probably not."

"Is this dangerous for him, for my brother?"

I thought about that. No. If my plan worked and if Ezra was as good as a lawyer as his sister was a doctor, then Cameron would rust inside a jail cell. If my plan didn't work, he'd remain rotting in Hank's cellar. "No."

"Alright," she conceded after sucking in a deep breath. "I'll let him know to expect your call. If anything happens to my brother..." she warned, her voice the coldest I've heard it, and she did threaten to kill me once or twice since our first meeting.

"Yeah, yeah, yeah," I said begrudgingly. "Bodily harm."

After I hung up with Lily, I pulled out of the parking lot. I drove the thirty minutes back to the house and locked myself in my study, my shaking hands gripping her book of poems.

I let my fingers trail over the cover, over the letters in her name. For minutes upon minutes, hours upon hours, I told myself I was going to flip open the cover and see what was waiting for me there. I fell asleep before I grew the courage. I woke up in the middle of the night, reaching out. Reaching for something that wouldn't be there.

Placing the book still gripped in my hands on the desk, I left it behind, grabbing a beer from the fridge and letting myself out of the back door. The one place no memory of Annie would assault me. I never got around to showing her the back yard which was almost another world entirely. Maybe it was because I knew she wasn't here to stay or maybe because I needed just one part of this place that wasn't tainted by her.

The back yard was so much more than just a back yard. It took up most of the acres on this land, with its house-sized pool, half a dozen exotic trees, and a deck that was almost as big as the entire floor plan inside. It was beautiful. Beautiful and unique and rare. And I was a little bit in love with it. I had one housekeeper come and take care of it discreetly because I never indulged in it. It made my life seem lighter than it was. It was a falsity. It was a farce.

I wish she was a falsity. I wish I had dreamed her up. I wish I wasn't in love with her. The lies eased my mind even though I knew they were lies. I'd never give up a second I had with her, damn the eternal pain.

For an entire week, I slept outside, in a canopy that I'm surprised didn't snap from my almost two-hundred-pound frame. Each day, I was in the house for an hour, at most. Enough to grab a beer and stare at that book from the girl who was off somewhere, my heart in her clasp.

I lasted ten days. Ten days until I couldn't take it anymore. I missed her so much. So damn much. I needed her words. I needed her mind and her heart.

Storming into the study, I slammed the door shut behind me, and all but collapsed in the chair. My hands were shaking and my breaths were coming out in harsh, fast puffs.

One poem a day, I decided. I could ration her words. The book had to be at least two hundred pages. If I only read one page a day, I'd have something new from her for a long time. Long enough time for me to forget her, or realistically, to patch up the hole in my chest so it no longer bled.

I flipped the book open until I got to the very last page, the very last poem. I took one last deep breath before I let my eyes look at her words. It was a poem called "Love."

I read the lines once. Twice. Three times. A hundred times. I couldn't believe my eyes.

She loved me. I planned on breaking my own heart, that was no big deal, I just didn't realize that hers was also in the conversation.

I flipped the book closed, squeezed my eyes shut together. After a moment, I opened the book up and flipped to the first page, devouring every single word she left for me.

CHAPTER THIRTY-TWO

Annie

"What do you mean, he's sitting outside of your apartment?" Samuel asked from the other side of the phone.

Ditching my bowl of cereal in the kitchen, I walked to the two windows of my apartment. A week had passed since my first ever girl's night and the realization that Hector was still in love with me. He still was in my life, silent but still present.

I peeped around the curtains to see him sipping on a cup of coffee. I had become well accustomed to him being parked across the street. Every morning, he was there with a cup of coffee in his hand and he wouldn't leave that spot until I left the apartment for the day. And when I got home each night, he would show up momentarily. He, I thought, was learning my schedule just as much as I was learning his.

In a week, I had seen a glimpse of him every morning when I woke up and every night before I fell asleep. I didn't see those brown eyes, so although I was happy he hadn't completely forgotten about me, I felt like I was being robbed, nonetheless.

"Exactly what I said," I told Samuel, my eyes glued on his father from a distance. "He's here in the morning. He's here at night. But he just sits in that damn car. He never looks. He doesn't ever approach me. I don't know what he's doing."

I had thought about just going over to his car and demanding what the hell he thought he was doing. But I knew this was something that he would have to figure out for himself. It wasn't loving me that scared him. Those brown eyes told me way before his own lips did that I had his heart. This was his own struggle. It really wasn't about me at all. This was about him handing his heart over when he's done it before and paid a steep price for it.

So, I let him be. I watched him when he wasn't watching me and that had to be enough for now.

"Talk to him, Samuel. Don't be a dick, either. He needs you."

Samuel chuckled at my serious tone and I couldn't fight a smile. The Rivera men had the kind of effect on me. "Your wish is my command, Mama."

I rolled my eyes even though I knew he couldn't see me. "Would you stop calling me that?"

"You think I'm bad, now?" I could just picture the devilish grin he was sporting. "Wait until the wedding."

"Goodbye, Samuel," I sing-songed, ignoring him.

When I walked into the shelter hours later, Jessica greeted me.

"Anything yet?" she asked, her eyes as hopeful as a Disney princess.

I shook my head. "Radio silence."

She pursed her lips up in disappointment and I swatted her ass. "We have work to do. No time for sulking."

I started to walk away, toward Rachel's office where I usually locked my stuff in while I was here but Jessica grabbed my arm. "I actually have something to talk to you about."

I turned around to look at her. Her wide eyes and beaming smile gave me pause. What did she have up her sleeve? I squinted my eyes up at her suspiciously.

She grabbed my arm again and pulled me down the corridor. We passed her office and then Rachel's and then Eliza's. There was a fourth door that was unmarked. The door was shut and there was no light behind it.

"What is this?" I heard myself wonder aloud.

Her hand wrapped around the doorknob and she looked at me one more time before twisting the doorknob. At the last second, before the door moved, she shot me a wink over her shoulder. And then, she all but pushed me into the darkened room. The lights came on in an instant and balloons, confetti, and Rachel and Eliza filled the room, excitement in the air. I looked from three smiling faces to the banner hanging from the ceiling. It read: *Welcome to the Team.*

My eyes bounced between the three of them, smiles lining each of their faces. "What is happening?"

"You're hired," Jessica said, clapping.

"What do you mean, I'm hired? I didn't even apply. I'm just a volunteer."

It was Eliza who pinned me with a look. A look that held me captive. "A volunteer helps people, Annie Miller. You save them." Her eyes shone with tears as she mouthed so only I could see, "You saved me."

I bit my lip to stop myself from crying. Rachel stepped forward, a pile of papers in her hands. "You have a degree in Social Work. You've worked with us and these women twice now. There's no reason you shouldn't make a career out of it. All you have to do is sign these papers and you're officially a part of our team."

"I don't know what to say," I whispered aloud as I took the papers from Rachel.

"Say, yes, dummy."

I shot Jessica a dirty look but she wasn't the least bit fazed.

I smiled. "Yes. Yes. Yes. A million times, yes."

After all of us ate pizza and ice cream, I followed Rachel into her office to sign papers. "Your schedule might be a little bit crazy. I work mornings, Jessica works afternoon, and Eliza covers the night shift. I'd like for your normal hours to overlap Jessica and Eliza's shift. I was thinking two to ten. That way it covers your self-defense classes, it's eight hours a day so you'll be able to get forty hours a week in, and I'd like Eliza to have the help to make sure everyone is settled for lights out at ten."

"That's perfect because I don't want to give up my job at the range."

She nodded, taking the papers away from me.

"It's okay for you to walk home that late?"

I shrugged. "I can take care of myself and if I can't, I always have a little friend who will."

She knew I was talking about my gun because she laughed. I had convinced her to come to the range and learn how to shoot. As soon as she walked in, Matt snatched her up before I could get out of my office. He was a disgrace to his own business.

"She's happily married," I had announced when I saw him pulling her hair back so she could put on her safety goggles. "And who knows what diseases you're carrying in your pants."

Chuckles and snickers surrounded me as he backed away from my friend and glared at me. "You make me regret the day I let you work here," he said to me.

"You love me and you know it," I said to his retreating back. He flipped me off.

"Speaking of protective friends, I had a safe installed in your office, just as a safety precaution. I don't want any of the women getting their hands on that."

I saluted her, understanding her caution.

On my way home, I stopped at Maria's for dinner. I worked and lived in the city and Hector's restaurant was located at the center of New Hazle so I had a long bus ride ahead of me and I was somewhat grateful for it. I didn't want to pass his occupied car, knowing he still hadn't made up his mind about us yet. Or even worse, maybe today would be the day he did make his mind up and neither he or his car would be there. It had been two weeks of his silent presence and each day I grew more anxious, more nervous, more afraid.

The same girl that was working the night Hector brought me was standing ready near the hostess stand, a smile ready on her face. She greeted the couple in front of me and escorted them to a table. She was back in record time, that same smile pasted on her face.

"Hi. Welcome to Mar—" Her words died off when she looked from the menus in her hands to my face. A genuine smile appeared. "Annie, right?"

I nodded. "Is it just you tonight?"

The knowledge that there should be someone with me here tugged at my chest. "Yes. And I don't need a table. I just want to take it to go."

She held out her hand and for some odd reason, I took it. I followed her around the bar and past the kitchen doors. "Mr. Rivera has a lot of rules and one of them is no takeout."

I didn't look at her like she was crazy. I didn't look surprised because I wasn't. It had Hector written all over it. He was good at everything, but if you asked him what the most important things to him were, he would say food and family. That's where he put his heart and soul into. "Okay. I'll just take a table, then."

I wasn't sure if she hadn't heard me with all the clinking of pans and the upbeat Spanish music filtering through the kitchen, but she still had a hold of my arm and didn't let go.

"Hey, Joseph," she shouted over the music to a man who seemed to be floating around the kitchen. He paused and waved his hand at a kid who was drying dishes and the music lowered instantly.

"What is it, Dominique?"

"This is, uhh, Annie. She needs to put in an order for takeout."

With my one free hand, I covered my face, embarrassment washing over me. I felt the gaze of at least twenty employees on me and I wished the floor would open up and swallow me hole. "Dominique, I could have just gotten a table. It's not that big of a deal," I muttered.

I looked from her to Joseph, gearing up to apologize but he was looking at me expectantly, a pen and pad in his hand. "I'm ready whenever you are."

I sputtered out my order of an entire platter of tacos because I didn't see myself coming back any time soon.

"I'll have it done in twenty. Have a seat by the bar and one of us will bring it out to you, okay?"

I nodded and followed Dominique back the way we came. "You didn't have to do that, you know," I told her as I sat at the bar. Her eyes bounced from me back to her empty hostess stand.

"He likes his rules. And at the top of the list is, 'what Annie wants, she gets.' There are no rules when it comes to you." She didn't stick around to hear the air I had to suck in and the shaky breath that escaped me a second later.

There are no rules when it comes to you. I mulled over Dominique's words as I waited for my food. They followed me on the long bus ride back into the city until I was dropped off a few blocks from my apartment.

Her words stuck with me because they were true. There had never been any rules where I was concerned. He might have kidnapped me, but he always gave me a choice. He always let me do whatever I wanted, be whoever I needed to be. He gave me the green light to find the girl I had been ignoring since my mother's death. He breathed life back into a soul that had been dying. He was the sole reason that I now know who I am. And I wouldn't be who I am if I didn't fight for my happiness.

I didn't seek out my apartment when I reached my block. My eyes searched the street until that black car that held so many memories between the two of us came into view. Without a second thought, I trudged my way to the passenger side. I froze at the sight of him this up close. His eyes were closed, his hands folded over his stomach. He was the kind of beautiful that had nothing to do with appearance, but a connection that I felt every time I laid my eyes on him.

I closed my own eyes and didn't open them until I heard a click. My eyes snapped open at the sound of the door unlocking. My heart beating a mile a minute, I raised my gaze to the man inside who was now sitting up straight, my favorite pair of eyes focused on me. But they were different, they weren't warm or teasing or loving. They were what I felt from the heels of my feet to the top of my head: sad.

Somehow, my hand found the door handle and I pulled it open and hopped in the car silently, too afraid to even breathe, now deathly afraid of what he would say or what he wouldn't. I unwrapped my takeout.

"Are you hungry?" I whispered but those three words felt like I was screaming.

Hector grunted. The simple sound, the familiar sound was almost enough to break my demeanor. I chanced a look over at him but he was looking at me so deeply, so intently, it felt like I was a glass of water and he was the most dehydrated man in the world.

"Are you going to say something or are you just going to stare at me while I eat? I haven't eaten all day, so if you're going to eat, I would act soon before I devour all of this." There was no way I could eat every single taco I ordered. There was enough to last me all week. But I had no control over my mouth, now that we were face to face. So, I stuffed it.

As soon as the meat hit my taste buds, his whisper filled up the space between us. "Love. So easy to say, so hard to understand. Silent, but loud. Felt, but not seen."

My heart stopped as I registered his soft words, realizing he was reciting the last poem I left him.

Love.

So easy to say, so hard to understand.

Silent, but loud.

Felt, but not seen.

Or so I thought.

Until he took my hand.

Until he gave me his smile.

Until he held me at night.

Until he pushed my boundaries.

Until he broke rules.

Until he invaded my body.

Until he owned my heart.

Until he conquered my soul.

Love can be seen.

And for me, it's in a set of deep brown eyes that let me know I am seen.

He read the entire poem aloud, word for word, from his memory. There was no way I could stop the tears that escaped by the time he whispered the last word.

It had been enough that he cared about me making a mistake I would regret.

It had been enough that he was the first man who had put butterflies in my stomach.

It had been enough that I fell in love with him.

It had been enough to share my body with him.

But to recite words that I wrote for him, word for word, almost a month after I left him was one thing I had never expected. I thought he would read them. I thought he would like them. Never in my wildest dreams, did I imagine that he would treat them like a bible, reading the same lines over and over until he could reel them off.

I set my food to the side, my hunger forgotten. "Hector," I shakily whispered.

"Bonita," he whispered back, his voice just as weak.

I swallowed past the lump in my throat, past the fear. "Te quiero, Hector. Mi corazón es tuyo y no quiero de vuelta. Está incompleto sin ti." *Translation: I love you, Hector. My heart is yours and I don't want it back. It's incomplete without you, anyway.*

His eyes widened in surprise but he didn't comment on my use of his mother tongue but his eyes softened and his shoulder dropped against the seat. "I see you. I love you. If you will still have me, I'm yours."

I didn't know which one of us moved first, but his hands grabbed at my hips and my hands raced their way to find the skin at the back of his neck. Electricity filtered between our limbs. I felt the racing of our hearts as our chests slammed together. "It's been hell without you, Hector Rivera. I will kill you if you do that to me again."

He planted the softest kiss in the middle of my forehead as his fingers wove through my hair. "Threatening my life already, bonita?"

I knocked my knuckles against his chin as I looked into his eyes. "You love it," I whispered.

His answer was the softest press of his lips against mine.

I relished in the feel of his lips. Every press felt like opening up a tailor-made gift. This is what I wanted. This is what made me happy.

Sitting on top of his lap, want crashed through me. I wanted to crash my lips against him. I wanted to remember the taste of his mouth, of his skin. I wanted to shed each of us of our clothes. I wanted him inside of my body. I wanted to not know where I ended and he began. But I didn't feed into the lust because I was thankful for the love.

Samuel told me to give him hell. A big part of me wanted to give him hell. But I couldn't put up a fight. I knew his soul. I knew what kind of man he was.

I parted my lips and he took advantage of them, pressing soft pecks on my skin. I pressed my hands against his chest and looked him in the eye, forcing the words out. "How do I know that you won't do that to me again? How do I know that I'll never wake up one morning and you'll just be gone?"

"Oh, bonita," he whispered, his hands rising and taking my cheeks in his palm. His thumbs swiped softly against my cheeks. "You don't. I have to prove it."

"And you're willing to do that?" Please say yes. Life is too cruel to love someone and not be with them.

"I'm willing to do anything for you, Annie."

I framed his face and looked into his soft eyes. "Come in."

He tilted his head and my hands to the side. "Is that a good idea?"

I shrugged. "It's what I want."

He lifted me from his lap, grabbed the food, and opened his car door. I guess my wish really was his command. I shuffled out of the car and he held his hand out for me to take. It took some serious resistance to not start dancing in the middle of the street. Once I unlocked the apartment, I flipped on two of the lamps, kicked off my shoes, grabbed a tall glass of water and hopped in bed. Hector was still standing just inside of the door, bag of food still in his hand. I patted the space beside me.

"Come eat with me."

He took a step, discarding his shoes where I toed mine off. "Come lay with me."

Just as he knelt down on the edge of the bed, I whispered, "Come stay with me."

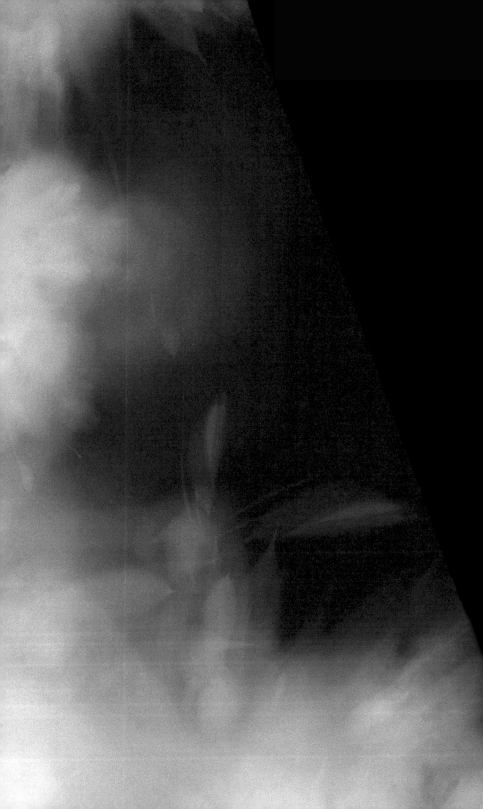

CHAPTER THIRTY-THREE

Annie

I was afraid to go to sleep. Afraid that this was all a dream. Afraid that if I closed my eyes, when I opened them again, Hector would be gone.

I stayed up, wrapped in his arms, way past two o'clock in the morning because I was so afraid. But Hector's warmth was better than any blanket and his voice reciting his favorite poems I'd written him verbatim lulled me into the best sleep I've had in weeks.

I woke up with his name on my lips. "Hector."

"I'm right here, bonita." To prove his words, two arms snaked around me, dragging me into his body.

He held me as I held him, and I never wanted to let go. "What took you so long?" I whispered.

He unwrapped himself from me and climbed out of bed. I sat up straighter, my mind running a mile a minute. "Technically, I would have taken longer but you hijacked my plans."

Despite my heart racing, a smile formed on my lips. "I know the feeling."

Hector grabbed a manila folder on the table that wasn't there when we climbed into bed. He walked back over to me and kneeled on the floor next to me, handing the folder over to me.

I opened it and Cameron's face met me. It didn't take me long to realize these were my mother's case details. How he even had access to these was beyond me.

Hector lifted his hand, nudging my chin with his knuckles until I met his gaze. "I tried, Annie. Me and my lawyer, we searched every option but it's not plausible. I'm so sorry. If there was anything I'd want to give you, it would be justice for your mom."

I melted into his touch. "Thank you for trying, sweet man, but your love is the only thing I want from you. It's enough for me."

I brushed the papers aside and pulled the love of my life underneath the sheets and showed him how much I meant those words.

I woke up in a dream. Or at least that's what it felt like.

Warmth radiated through my entire body. My legs were tangled up in a stronger pair. Two possessive hands pressed against my lower back. My hands were feeling up Hector Rivera under his t-shirt.

"You're not going to make it to work on time if you keep that up," he murmured, his voice groggy with sleep.

I was caught in between wanting to squeal that this wasn't a dream or cry because he was real and he was here.

Peeling my eyes open, I saw a pair of smoldering, brown eyes zoned in on my face. I snuck my hands out of his shirt and reached for his face. His disheveled face. It looked like he hadn't taken a razor to his face once in the past month. "Are you real?" I whispered, my fingers moving delicately over the stubble.

"As real as you want me to be," he whispered back to me, his teeth darting out to nip the edge of my palm.

I tried to hold back my I'm-so-fucking-in-love smile but failed. I wanted to always feel like this with him. I wanted to wake up tangled up with him every morning. I wanted us to share every single meal together. He was the sun and I wanted to be anywhere and everywhere he decided to shine on. I bit my lip, still unsure of where we stood.

He untucked my bottom lip and caressed it with the edge of his fingertips. "What is it, bonita?"

I took a deep breath, dread, hope, and the uncertainty of our future pressing down on my chest. "What happens now? Now that we no longer have an expiration date?"

He let out a ragged sigh and let his eyes fall shut, his fingers and his body separating from mine in an instant.

My own body sagged against the bed, the fear of losing him again shaking every single bone in my body.

"That's up to you, bonita."

My eyes snapped open but he remained quiet, still distant. "What do you mean?" I demanded.

He didn't say anything for a long moment. It's almost like he didn't know that my heart was hanging on by its last thread. His brown eyes finally found mine and they melted me on the spot.

"Are you sure this is what you want? This" —he pointed at himself— "wasn't even on your radar four months ago. You deserve so much more." He didn't say the words but I heard his meaning in his silence. I deserved much more than him.

It took everything in me to not reach for him, to not fold into his arms and threaten bodily harm if he ever tried to leave me. Instead, I looked into eyes that had become my favorite thing and I spoke from the heart. "I deserve what I want and what I want is you."

"Then, you have me. You have me for as long as you want me, Annie."

"And what if I want you forever," I mused, reaching for him and bringing him closer until I was wrapped in his warmth once more.

He swiped my hair from my face and tucked the strands behind my ear. "I can't promise you forever but I can promise to be yours until my last breath."

"I'll hold you to that promise, mi amor."

A grin split over his face. "You knew what I have been saying all of this time?"

I shrugged. "I took four years in high school and then a few classes in college. I figured it would come in handy with social work. Or you know, my move to Mexico."

He lifted his eyebrows in a question.

"That was the plan. Kill Cameron, bury Annie as I knew her, and start over in Mexico."

"Mexico, of all places."

"Yup," I confirmed, smiling. "I was going to cash in on revenge and move to Mexico. Instead, I fell in love and that love saved my life."

Hector crashed his lips down on mine, all of the softness from this morning and last night nowhere to be found. His hands pushed me down until I was lying flat on my back, his lips bruising against mine. When I couldn't hold back a moan, his tongue slipped inside my mouth and I instantly dissolved.

I didn't know my name. I didn't know where I was. All I knew was him. His hands. His tongue. His body. My hands reached out blindly, not knowing what to do but knowing I needed more. I managed to pull him into me until his weight pressed down on me.

A spark shot down my groin and I didn't even try to hold back my moan. "Hector," came my ragged plea when he came up for air.

He moved in between my hips, wrapping my legs around his waist. I reached for his shirt. "Off," I demanded gruffly. He trailed his fingertips up my jean-clad legs and I clenched my legs around his body.

"The way you react to me, bonita." Hector shook his head, dazed. "You are my dream."

His fingers gripped the top of my thighs, right where I needed him the most.

"I'm," I breathed out. His fingers undid the button of my jeans and the sound of my zipper being pulled sent my body into havoc. "Yours."

In one swift movement, my jeans and panties were ripped away and tossed over his shoulder. He locked eyes with me, that smoldering look from earlier back with a vengeance. "Out of all the Spanish endearments I know, I stuck to bonita because it means something precious, something beautiful. If I'm being honest, all I wanted to call you was one I'd hoped you always would be: *Mía.*"

Mine.

I loved the sound of that. He pressed a soft kiss against my lips before pulling away. Then, he slid down the bed and wrapped his arms around my bare ass, pulling me toward his face. He never took his eyes off me. Not when he blew on my bare sex. Not when he swiped his tongue through my folds. Not when his expert tongue hit my sweet spot.

He worked me until my hair plastered to my forehead and neck with sweat, my body was writhing against the bed, and his name was an endless chant spilling from my lips. The moment he added his fingers into the mix, I was a goner.

I lay there, limp, all energy sucked from my body and he still didn't stop. He cleaned me up with his tongue to the point of pain. I shoved his head away. He chuckled against my bare thigh before placing a kiss against my skin.

He crawled up my body until I felt his erection where his mouth had just been. I whimpered, an all too familiar heat racing down. "We don't have time for that, bonita. You have to be at work in less than an hour."

I whimpered again, this time for a completely different reason. He pressed a soft kiss against my lips and I hugged him to my body. I didn't want to let go. Not now. Not in five minutes or an hour. I would have lived a satisfied life if I could just hold him like this until my last breath.

"Get ready and I'll take care of breakfast." He untangled himself from me and I moved enough to watch him walk into the kitchen and start making me breakfast.

"Since we're doing this forever thing," I said, propping my elbows up on the bed. He looked at me, a beaming smile plastered on his face. "I think we should follow a set of rules."

"Okay," he said, cracking an egg. "What are these rules?"

"Well, just one for now." He grunted. "Hector Rivera must always cook while shirtless."

Hector laughed and my heart wasn't intact anymore, it was floating in the air between us. Is this what it would feel like every day for the rest of our lives? This feeling of loving someone so much and them loving you back the same.

"Done. For every rule you have, I also get one."

"Fair enough," I conceded, working my way out of bed. I didn't bother getting dressed as I walked toward him. He was cutting up vegetables as I used him as a leaning post. "What's your rule?"

"That you be happy every day for the rest of your life."

I blew out a breath. "That's a big rule compared to mine."

He nodded. "That's because it's more my priority than a rule. I want to make you happy every day for the rest of your life."

"Thank you for hijacking my life, Hector Rivera. I can't imagine it without you," I whispered against his skin. He turned to face me and tilted my face up so he could kiss me.

His phone ringing was the only thing that managed to make me snap out of my Hector haze and get ready for the day. He picked up the phone and planted a final kiss on my temple before he shooed me into the bathroom. Just as I closed the door, I heard Hector say, "Hey,

Dad. Remember that question you always used to ask me? I have the answer now." His eyes found mine between the crack of the bathroom door. "I found her."

※

"When are you coming home, bonita?" Hector asked not for the first time. I hadn't been back to my home of the past three months since I left it with Samuel. Over the past few weeks, Hector had become a permanent fixture in my little apartment. There hadn't been a night that I didn't fall asleep wrapped up in him.

But something was holding me back from giving up my own space and moving back into his. My hesitation didn't make any sense to him. I knew that because it didn't make any sense to me, either. I loved him. I was obsessed with spending time with him. If our lives allowed it, I would have him attached to my hip.

But for the first time, I could answer the most important question in life. I could look in a mirror without flinching. I could talk for hours about all of the things I loved. I finally found the answer to who Annie Miller is, and I wasn't ready to give up that independence quite yet.

"I still have one month of our agreement left," I said teasingly because I didn't know what else to say.

A growl came from the doorway of the bathroom. I didn't bother looking at him. I tightened my hair tie and took one last look at myself in the mirror. Wearing the outfit that Hector bought on my mom's birthday, I was beyond excited for the day. I had no idea what he had planned. All I knew is that he asked me to schedule a day where I was off from Philly Range and the women's shelter.

I finally turned to him. "I think you should move here, instead."

He grunted. "That's not going to happen."

Curling my fists against my hips, I demanded, "And why the hell not?"

He sighed and reached for me but I stood my ground. He kicked off the doorway and sauntered over. I didn't back down or cower, just held those brown eyes captive. When he was within reaching distance, he hooked his finger on the shorts of my overalls and pulled me to him. I braced my hand against his chest and looked up at him. "I don't want to live in the city." I was already gearing up my rebuttal but his other hand reached up, placing a single finger against my lips. "Neither do you. You toss and turn all night because of the noise. And it's not safe here. The house in New Hazle is."

I knew he was right. "I don't want to go back," I admitted quietly, looking away.

He tugged at my chin, forcing my eyes back to his. "Why?"

I tried to create some distance between us but he kept a firm hold on me. "I feel independent, Hector. For the first time in my life, I'm not using anything as a crutch. Not my mother's death. Not my revenge plan. And not you. I feel like that's going to change if we go back to the way things were." He frowned but remained stoic. "I miss your house. I miss watching you cook from the living room. I miss working out together. I miss writing in your study. I miss your bed. But it's all yours."

He hid those eyes from me, his nostrils flaring as he took a deep breath. When he opened his eyes again, he said, "Okay."

I blinked once and then twice. And a third time just as a precaution.

That's it? No fighting or throwing me over his shoulder, damn what I want? "Just okay?"

"Yes. We won't go back, but this is Samuel's apartment so we'll have to go house hunting, okay?"

I smiled, standing up on my toes to kiss his lips. "I love you," I whispered against his skin.

His hands wrapped around my lower back, squeezing my body to his. "I love you, too, bonita. Now come, we have a busy day."

I backed away just enough to catch his gaze. "Tell me what we're doing."

He placed a quick kiss on my nose before telling me, "No."

I frowned but followed him, anyway. Once we were loaded in the Range Rover, Hector took my hand as he drove toward New Hazle.

I pinned him with a look once he was driving down the familiar path to his house. "It's not what you think it is."

"Then tell me where we're going."

He tried to hide his smirk but I still caught it. "See, Annie." There was that name again in that playful tone of his I loved so much. "When a man loves a woman." He paused, looking over to catch me rolling my eyes. "Before he gets down on one knee." My entire world stopped, my heart still and a lump the size of Alaska lodged in my throat, I waited for his next words. "And asks her to spend the rest of her life with him, he usually has to get a blessing from her parents."

I waited for him to say more but he didn't. He simply put the car in park. I tore my eyes from him to see where we were.

New Hazle Cemetery. "Please tell me you fucking didn't," I whispered, my emotions getting the best of me.

"Annie," he tried, softly reaching out for me. "I have things to say. Please hear me out."

All I could manage was a sharp nod. "I want to meet the woman who raised you, who sculpted the love of my life."

I looked at him through blurry vision. "Hector," I whimpered.

He gripped both of my hands. "Introduce us, love."

I nodded and watched Hector climb out of the car. I wiped at my face furiously as he walked over to help me get out.

"We don't have to do this if you don't want to. I just thought—"

I shut him up with a salty kiss. He thought this is what I wanted and he was right. It wasn't his fault I couldn't stop crying. I led him through the graveyard to where I knew my mother rested. Fresh flowers were laying against her headstone. I looked at Hector in question.

"I would do the same thing if she was alive," he admitted softly.

I read her headstone.

Michelle Miller. Loving Mother and Friend. 1977-2007.

I felt Hector's presence behind me, his light touch grounding me. "Hi, Mama. I'm sorry I didn't make it on your birthday. Someone was holding me hostage."

I felt Hector's sharp poke against my ribs and I laughed. I no longer wondered if my mom would approve of Hector or the two of us together. There was no doubt that she would love him and how grateful she would be that I had met a man who put stars in my eyes, butterflies in my stomach, and respect in his touch.

"I met someone, and I'd like you to meet him."

Hector stepped from behind me and crouched down by my feet. I sifted my hands through his hair as he bowed his head toward my mother's headstone. After a few minutes of him paying his respects and me in the presence, no matter how silent hers was, of the two people I loved the most, Hector stood and faced me.

"Hector," I whispered.

He wiped my tears away and he tucked the loose strands of my hair behind my ear. "Yes, bonita?"

I wrapped my fingers around his hands still holding my face. "Will you marry me?"

I was met with a grin brighter than the sun.

EPILOGUE

Annie

Seven Months Later

The sound of sizzling woke me up. That and the smell of bacon. My stomach growled but my body ached. "Do I get breakfast in bed?" I called.

No reply. I knew he was there. No one else would be in my apartment cooking before the sun even rose. "Hector," I called.

Still nothing. I positioned myself up on my elbows and craned my head but I still couldn't see him. "Pretty sure you broke my vagina," I yelled into the void of our apartment.

A snicker broke out from him as he walked down the stairs toward me. "Good morning, love," he said, giving me my morning kiss followed by a glass of OJ.

"Hi." I smiled. I was not a morning person. But I was a Hector's voice person. And I was a Hector's face person. Really, I was just a Hector person.

"You did schedule off from work today, right?"

I nodded behind my coffee.

"Good. We have a lot of work we have to do today."

I looked from him to the clock on our nightstand. "Please tell me you did not wake me up at four o'clock in the morning."

He smiled guiltily. "I made you breakfast and I have a surprise for you, so you have to get up and get ready so we can leave."

Over the next hour, I folded into his demands, groggily, but I did it. By the time we made it out of the apartment, I managed to be somewhat awake.

I looked down at my outfit. I was told to dress in something that could get ruined. I wore one of Hector's t-shirts and a pair of fleece sweatpants.

"Where are we going?" I asked him, even though I knew he wouldn't tell me.

As he drove on, I realized we were heading to his house. I still hadn't been back, and he never brought it up again. We leased an apartment month to month because Hector wanted to "explore our options."

I didn't say a word, not until we reached the gates. "What the fuck happened?" I blurted, staring at nothing. The house that once was my prison for a few short days and then my home for three months was gone, turned into a pile of debris on the ground.

He parked the car just short of the destruction and turned to me, papers in his hand. I took them from him and scanned them. "The deed to this property is now in your name, Annie Rivera."

I couldn't help my smile at the new last name that I was still getting used to. We didn't have a wedding; we didn't even have a ceremony. We simply walked into the courthouse and promised each other forever.

"A house is just a house to me. I don't care what it looks like or what's inside. My home is where you are. Where you go, I follow. So, I have only one request."

I looked up at him, at the man I loved, wondering how the hell I got so lucky.

"Envision our future and I'll help you start building," he promised.

I leaned into him, looking at the ground before us. I didn't see the rubble underneath our feet as destruction anymore; I saw them as a new beginning. My hands curved under the tiniest swell of my stomach, knowing he had already made good on his promise.

"Who knows? Perhaps your love will make me forget all
I wish not to remember."
— Alexandre Dumas, *The Count of Monte Cristo*

THE END

Acknowledgements

I wrote my first full length novel when I was fifteen years old. I had no idea about anything except that I wrote a book and people seemed to love it. So, I sent a partial of my manuscript to someone, I don't even know who, and of course, as anyone can predict, it got rejected. And that was that.

I stuck to writing poetry and I kept it to myself. As I grew older, I was that girl who got excited over writing essays and I was the girl who took too long on the open-ended questions in AP Euro. I loved to write and even if I wasn't writing what I wanted to, I still found a way to do it.

I love writing and I love thinking about life and its journey. I love the way every single decision you make alters the course of your life. Every single person you meet plays a role. So, I want to thank every single person I've ever come across, whether we've had a good experience or a bad one. You've inspired me in some way and I may never get to tell all of you how or why so I'm saying it here now.

Specifically, I want to thank some special women in my life.

I want to thank my mother, for who this book is dedicated to. Thank you for being the strongest woman I know each day and loving me unconditionally.

I want to thank my best friend, Jay, who not only introduced me to the romance genre but encouraged me to write my own. You were meant to be a permanent fixture in my life, I honestly believe that.

A huge thank you to Jess, Fatima, and Anna for blindly supporting me and being so excited for my writing. I lost count of how many times your positive messages have made me cry.

I want to thank both of my editors who were the first people I trusted with Hijacked. The way you were so supportive and gentle with me made me so grateful and both of you were just a complete thrill to work with.

I want to thank my favorite English teacher in high school who wrote in my senior yearbook that she had faith I would write a book someday and she couldn't' wait to read it. Those words stuck with me in my darkest days and now those words have become a reality.

Lastly, I want to thank anyone who buys this book, who reads it, or talks about it at all. I hope I reach some of your hearts. I hope I bring a little light into your life. Thank you for taking a chance on me.

xoxo, Sonia

Author Bio

Sonia Esperanza lives in a small town in Pennsylvania where she tries to find the balance between real life and the fictional characters in her head who seem to never shut up. She's also probably listening to Taylor Swift.